Falklands
Air War

Falklands
Air War

Chris Hobson
with Andrew Noble

Midland Publishing

*This book is dedicated to all of the
British and Argentine soldiers, sailors and
airmen who served in the South Atlantic.*

Falklands Air War
© Christopher Michael Hobson, 2002
ISBN 1 85780 126 1

Edited by Bob Munro

First published in 2002 by
Midland Publishing
4 Watling Drive, Hinckley, LE10 3EY, England.
Tel: 01455 254 490 Fax: 01455 254 495

Midland Publishing is an imprint of
Ian Allan Publishing Ltd.

Worldwide distribution (except North America):
Midland Counties Publications
4 Watling Drive, Hinckley, LE10 3EY, England
Tel: 01455 233 747 Fax: 01455 233 737
E-mail: midlandbooks@compuserve.com

North America trade distribution:
Specialty Press Publishers & Wholesalers Inc.
39966 Grand Avenue
North Branch, MN 55056, USA
Tel: 651 277 1400 Fax: 651 277 1203
Toll free telephone: 800 895 4585
www.specialtypress.com

Design concept and editorial layout
© Midland Publishing and
Stephen Thompson Associates.

Printed by Ian Allan Printing Ltd
Riverdene Business Park, Molesey Road
Hersham, Surrey, KT12 4RG, England.

Half-title page illustration:
*The seafront in Stanley has long had a memori-
al to those lost in the Battle of the Falklands on
8th December 1914. Today it has been joined by
the Liberation Monument which bears a simple
and apt inscription: 'In Memory Of Those Who
Liberated Us 14 June 1982'.* FIGO

Title page illustration:
*The Royal Navy's Sea Harrier force was to
become synonymous with the UK's military
campaign to wrest the Falkland Islands from
Argentine control in 1982. Without their
contribution, the campaign would have been
doomed to failure.* MoD

Contents

Foreword

by Chief of the Air Staff
Air Chief Marshal Sir Peter Squire GCB DFC AFC ADC DSc RAF

Twenty years have now passed since the British Government ordered military action to regain the sovereignty of the Falkland Islands. At the height of the Cold War, this very British endeavour seemed, at the time, something of an aberration, albeit in a worthy cause. My squadron had recently completed its annual deployment to North Norway to exercise our commitment as a NATO Regional Reinforcement Unit at a time when the Northern Flank seemed particularly vulnerable. The notion that within weeks we would be deployed on an aircraft carrier more than 7,000 miles south of our NATO Forward Operating Base did not seem credible. But deploy we did, as part of the United Kingdom Task Force, to demonstrate resolve in the face of aggression towards one of our remaining Dependencies. But perhaps there was also a wider setting, for a failure of deterrence in another direction would have had consequences far greater for us all.

Since the fall of the Berlin Wall and the demise of the Soviet Union as a military power block, we have become used to Joint Operations being mounted on a tri-Service basis to resolve politico-military issues in an increasingly unstable world. But in 1982, Joint Operations were not well understood and perhaps not particularly welcomed, with each Service keen to shine in the battle for prestige and resources. If, on the one hand, the Falklands conflict was an aberration in its day, then, on the other, we learned hugely from it in terms of Joint Operations; and those lessons have been invaluable to our development of a Joint Rapid Reaction Force, a concept that has proved its value in the Gulf, the Balkans, West Africa and now Afghanistan.

Chris Hobson's book focuses, as its title suggests, on the air component of the Falklands conflict. In the last ten years, we have become used to the concept of air operations being mounted to shape the battlespace. But in 1982 the lack of forward mounting bases seemed likely to deny air a meaningful role and yet, through innovation and a sense of purpose, air power contributed across a full spectrum of roles – offensive and defensive counter air, strategic and tactical reconnaissance, close air support and air interdiction, air resupply

and tactical air transport. The success of the Sea Harrier/Sidewinder combination is well known but, had the Vulcan not successfully reached and bombed the runway at Stanley, would the Argentine Air Force have withdrawn large elements of its fighter force to defend Buenos Aires, thus exposing its fighter-bomber force without top cover? The rapid fitment of air-to-air refuelling equipment to the Nimrod gave the RAF a capability to mount maritime reconnaissance missions south to the Total Exclusion Zone. Strategic reach through tanking the Hercules Force south from Ascension Island permitted the aerial resupply of the Maritime Task Force with urgently needed spares and weapons as well as the mail on which so many relied for their morale.

Chris Hobson's detailed account also highlights the human contribution to the air war and brings to life the part that individual endeavour has always played in conflict. It is the contribution of the men and women in the air power loop that make it so flexible and provide the free thinking and innovative approach that our chosen medium demands. Technology is immensely important as a catalyst for military capability but it is the practitioners, both on the ground and in the air, who refine and fuse the information, and ultimately arrive at the decisions and deeds that make the difference.

February 2002

Introduction

To say that the Falklands conflict was unexpected is an understatement. The tiny and remote Falkland Islands had been in British hands since 1833 but by the early 1980s they were a forgotten anachronism. If one had asked the average man or woman in the street in the UK to pinpoint the Falklands on a world map and explain how they came to belong to the UK, very few would have been able to provide an answer. The Falklands were of little economic or cultural value to the UK at the time, but the very fact that they were inhabited by people who had emigrated from the UK at some time in the past made them important to the UK. The background to the dispute was long and confused and there were flaws in the claims of both the UK and Argentina to the ownership of the islands; and moral ascendancy could be, and was, claimed by both sides with some justification.

In the months before the invasion there had been signals of Argentine intentions that were reported by the British attaché in Buenos Aires and by the Captain of HMS *Endurance*, but these had mostly been ignored in the UK until the last moment. There is no doubt that the Argentine invasion of the Falklands and South Georgia came as an unpleasant surprise to the UK government. The same level of surprise appeared to be felt in Buenos Aires when the UK quickly put together a powerful Task Force to regain the islands.

For the UK the Falklands conflict came at a bad time, militarily speaking, although had it been delayed by a year or two the situation would have been even worse. Because there was no longer the need for long-range reinforcement of garrisons in the Far East and the Middle East, the UK was concentrating its military strategy and effort towards supporting its role as part of the NATO alliance. This meant that the UK could reduce the size of its armed forces and concentrate on relatively short-range actions within the NATO theatre of operations. Although plans for emergency Out of Area operations (i.e. not within the NATO geographical area of Europe and the North Atlantic) were in existence, the pruning of major elements of the UK armed forces during the 1970s and early 1980s meant that the means to put those plans into action were being lost. It is therefore all the more impressive that the UK armed forces could respond so rapidly and so effectively to mount a large expeditionary force to fight nearly 4,000 miles from the nearest friendly base and some 8,000 miles from the UK.

Prior to the Falklands conflict the UK had very little recent experience of major combat operations. Small-scale campaigns such as those in Aden and Oman and the period of Confrontation with Indonesia provided only limited experience, and were very specific to those parts of the world. The British Army had gained considerable experience in urban counter-terrorist operations during its time in Northern Ireland but this would be of little relevance to a conventional land war. The RAF transport force had been involved in a number of emergency long-range emergency airlift operations in the 1970s (Anguilla, East Pakistan, Malta, Nepal, Bangladesh and Cyprus) but much of its strategic transport fleet had been sold off in 1976. One has to go back to Operation 'Vantage' in Kuwait in 1961 and to the UK's response to the Brunei Revolt in 1962 to find a major operational overseas deployment involving UK armed forces, although the capability had been tested in various exercises since that time.

The Falklands conflict taught (or perhaps retaught) many valuable tactical lessons. For the Royal Navy the vulnerability of its ships to air attack came as something of a shock, even though attrition was actually lower than had been expected. Although the Sea Harrier FRS1 performed very well, the lack of airborne early warning (AEW) reduced its effectiveness by a large factor.

The experience of the short but brutal conflict resulted in a considerable number of modifications to UK weapon systems, equipment and tactics. The improvements to the UK armed forces in the mid- to late 1980s as a result of the Falklands experience bore fruit in the 1990s during the coalition campaigns against Iraq, Bosnia and Serbia. In retrospect, perhaps the Falklands conflict could be seen as a wake-up call to the UK. Having run down its armed forces to a dangerously low level the conflict led to a reversal of the downward trend and resulted in a stronger, more capable force with which to meet the challenges of the post-Cold War world.

Writing about recent history is fraught with dangers. Under the UK government's 30-year rule much of the official history of the Falklands conflict is still classified and therefore not yet available. Information that is readily available, both official and unofficial, is sometimes contradictory or incomplete. I am also aware of the sensitivity of writing about recent past events and have tried not to moralise or criticise nor dwell on the horrors of war to any great extent.

This work is a joint effort as my friend and colleague Andrew Noble wrote Chapter One on the political background to the conflict and the diplomatic manoeuvring that took place prior to the British landings on 21st May 1982. As a politics graduate who maintains a keen interest in world political affairs, he is far better placed to write about the wider issues of the Falklands conflict and its background than I am.

In researching the Falklands conflict we have used a large number of references that are listed in the bibliography, but particular mention must be made of the British Aviation Research Group's book *Falklands: The Air War*, a seminal work and a model of research that has rarely been surpassed. We have also been most fortunate in being able to enlist the assistance of a number of our military colleagues who were involved in Operation 'Corporate'. We would like to thank in particular Commander Colin Haley, Commander Simon Chelton, Wing Commander Paul Lyall and Wing Commander Nigel Arnold for their generous help and loan of material. Their experiences, often painfully gained, have added immeasurably to this work. The authors would also like to thank the Falkland Islands Government Office in London; and Air Chief Marshal Sir Peter Squire GCB DFC AFC ADC DSc RAF, the current Chief of the Air Staff of the Royal Air Force and the commanding officer of 1 Squadron during Operation 'Corporate'. His generosity in agreeing to write the foreword to this book is greatly appreciated.

Chris Hobson
February 2002

List of Abbreviations
and Glossary

AAA	Anti-Aircraft Artillery		FADGE	Falkland Air Defence Ground Environment	OEU	Operational Evaluation Unit
AAC	Army Air Corps				PNG	Passive Night-vision Goggles
A&AEE	Aeroplane and Armaments Experimental Establishment		FCO	Foreign and Commonwealth Office	QGM	Queen's Gallantry Medal
					QRA	Quick Reaction Alert
AAR	Air-to-Air Refuelling		FIGAS	Falkland Islands Government Air Service	RAF	Royal Air Force
AAWO	Anti-Air Warfare Officer				REBRO	Relay-Broadcasting
AESS	Air Engineering and Survival School		FINRAE	Ferranti Inertial Rapid Alignment Equipment	RFA	Royal Fleet Auxiliary
					RM	Royal Marines
AEW	Airborne Early Warning		FIPZ	Falkland Islands Protection Zone	RN	Royal Navy
AFC	Air Force Cross				RNAS	Royal Naval Air Station
AMG	Aircraft Maintenance Group		Flt	Flight	RNAY	Royal Naval Aircraft Yard
AOA	Amphibious Operating Area		Flt Lt	Flight Lieutenant	RWR	Radar Warning Receiver
AOC	Air Officer Commanding		FOB	Forward Operating Base	SAM	Surface-to-Air Missile
ARA	Armada Republica Argentina		FSAIU	Flight Safety and Accident Investigation Unit	SAR	Search and Rescue
ASEAN	Association of South East Asian Nations				SARBE	Search and Rescue Beacon Equipment
			GPMG	General-Purpose Machine Gun		
ASW	Anti-Submarine Warfare		HDS	Helicopter Delivery Service	SAS	Special Air Service
BAe	British Aerospace		HE	High Explosive	SBS	Special Boat Service
BAM	Base Aerea Militar		HIFR	Helicopter In-Flight Refuelling	SHORAD	Short-Range Air Defence
BAN	Base Aeronaval		HMS	Her Majesty's Ship	SOBS	Seccion Operativa de Busqueda y Salvamento
BAS	British Antarctic Survey		HDU	Hose Drum Unit		
CAB601	Batallon de Aviacion de Combate 601		HUD	Head-Up Display	Sqn	Squadron
			ICRC	International Committee of the Red Cross	Sqn Ldr	Squadron Leader
CANA	Comando Aviacion Naval Argentina				STUFT	Ships Taken Up From Trade
			IFF	Identification, Friend or Foe	TACAN	Tactical Air Navigator
CAP	Combat Air Patrol		INS	Inertial Navigation System	TEZ	Total Exclusion Zone
CBAS	Commando Brigade Air Squadron		LADE	Lineas Aereas Del Estado	TRALA	Tug, Repair and Logistic Area
			LGB	Laser-Guided Bomb	UN	United Nations
CBU	Cluster Bomb Unit		LSL	Landing Ship Logistic	USAF	United States Air Force
CIWS	Close-In Weapon System		Lt	Lieutenant	USAFE	United States Air Force Europe
DFC	Distinguished Flying Cross		Lt Cdr	Lieutenant Commander	VERTREP	Vertical Replenishment
DSC	Distinguished Service Cross		LTW	Lyneham Transport Wing	VLF	Very Low Frequency
DSM	Distinguished Service Medal		MAMS	Mobile Air Movements Squadron	VOR	Very High Frequency Omnidirectional Range
DSO	Distinguished Service Order					
EAN	Estacion Aeronaval		MEZ	Maritime Exclusion Zone	V/STOL	Vertical/Short Take-Off and Landing
EEC	European Economic Commission		MOD	Ministry of Defence		
			MV	Motor Vessel	VT	Variable Time
EOD	Explosive Ordnance Disposal		NGS	Naval Gunfire Support	VTOL	Vertical Take-Off and Landing
ETS	Engineering Training School		OAS	Organisation of American States	Wg Cdr	Wing Commander
FAC	Forward Air Controller					

Part One

Political and Military Events
Prior to the Argentine Invasion

*Edinburgh 8,274 miles… Elgin 8,364 miles…
Hawaii 7,996 miles… Murmansk 17,900km. Back in
1982, the first reaction of many British people to
news of the Argentine invasion was, 'Where are the
Falkland Islands?' Today, the Falkland Islanders
themselves know where the islands are in relation to
various towns and cities around the world. FIGO*

Chapter One

History of the Falkland Islands
and Background to the War

The Falkland Islands, consisting of two main islands and 200 smaller ones, are an archipelago at the southern tip of the South American continent. The islands cover about 4,700 square miles, a little smaller than Northern Ireland, and prior to the conflict of 1982 relied predominantly on sheep breeding and the fishing industry to support a population of about 1,800 people.

According to Argentine historians, the first Europeans to see the islands were Spanish and Portuguese seamen in 1522. These included Esteban Gómez of the Magellan expedition. Even this modest claim, however, is disputed, with the *Encyclopaedia Britannica* stating that the first sighting of the islands was actually 70 years later by the English navigator John Davis. The first undisputed sighting of the islands was in 1600, by the Dutchman Sebald de Weerdt. No one officially set foot on the islands until 1690, when an English sea captain named John Strong led a British expedition ashore. The landing party claimed the islands for England, naming the sound between the two main islands after Viscount Falkland, a British naval official, the name later being applied to the group of islands as a whole.

The first permanent settlement was created on East Falkland island in 1764, by the French navigator Louis-Antoine de Bougainville. This was subsequently manned by Frenchmen from St Malo (hence 'Iles Malouines' from which the Argentine name 'Islas Malvinas' is derived). The following year the British settled on West Falkland island. The origins of the legal dispute of ownership occurred in 1767 when the Spanish bought the French settlement of Port Louis on East Falkland. As far as Spain was concerned, this implied official recognition by France of Spain's rights to the land. A Spanish flotilla arrived in 1770 with the purpose of 'asking' the British to leave, to which the British officer in charge of the garrison, a Captain Hunt (a name eerily reminiscent of the islands' governor during the conflict of 1982), replied:

'I have received your letters by the officer, acquainting me that these islands and coasts thereof belong to the King of Spain, your Master. In return I am to acquaint you that the said islands belong to His Britannic Majesty, My Master, by right of discovery as well as settlement and that the subjects of no other power whatever can have any right to be settled in the said islands without leave from His Britannic Majesty or taking oaths of allegiance and submitting themselves to His Majesty's Government as subjects of the Crown of Great Britain.'

Such defiance was short lived as the Spanish returned with a superior force and encouraged the British garrison to leave on 14th July 1770. It is this incident from which Argentina derives its claim as the 'agreement' between Britain and Spain of 1770, which precluded British sovereignty of the islands. It made little impact on the demographics of the islands, however, the British outpost on West Falkland being restored shortly after the confrontation following British belligerence in the region.

However, the link with Britain was tenuous, even 208 years before the Falklands conflict, as the British questioned the economic viability of the island settlement. In 1774 the British withdrew from the islands for economic reasons, while Spain maintained its settlement on East Falkland (which it renamed Soledad Island) until 1811, when it too was withdrawn. In 1816, Argentina declared itself independent from Spain, and four years later the Argentine government first proclaimed its sovereignty over the Falklands.

The first recorded Argentine settlement in the islands occurred in the 1820s when a garrison and settlers were dispatched there for menial work. In another foretaste of future developments, the United States of America, another new country finding its colonial feet, entered the already complicated legal and political fray. In 1831, the American warship USS *Lexington* attacked the Argentine settlement on East Falkland in reprisal for the detention of three American ships that had been hunting seals in the area. Two years later, afraid that the Americans might seize the islands, the British returned to the Falklands, forcefully deposing the Argentine governor.

For the remainder of the 19th century the British consolidated their presence, creating a community of some 1,800 people on the islands, which was largely self-supporting. This was formally recognised in 1892 when colonial status was granted to the Falklands. The next significant development in Falklands history and an important stage in shaping Argentine views on the matter, was the Roca-Runciman treaty of 1933. This was a bilateral trade agreement between the UK and Argentina that provoked a negative reaction within some quarters of Argentine society and resulted in widespread anti-British feeling.

Another increasingly important factor in Argentine nationalism and the desire for territorial gain was the instability of the country's political system. Since 1930, politics in Argentina has been largely dominated by military rule resulting in high levels of political violence and unrest. The first coup d'état overthrew President Hipolito Yrigoyen but the military government lasted for only two years before civilian rule was restored. In 1943 a second coup overthrew the government of Ramon Castillo of which the future nationalist leader Juan Peron was a member. Peron became President in the 1940s and enjoyed popular support, but by now the relationship between government and military had become an habitual one. In 1951, loyalty tests were adopted and spying was common in the ranks of the armed forces to monitor disaffection, introducing an atmosphere that would persist throughout the Falklands crisis.

Between 1958 and 1976 there were a further 30 attempted coups and rebellions, leaving Argentina mired in corruption, terrorism, political agitation and a need for sudden political dividends to prevent political dissatisfaction that could lead to further upheavals.

Self-determination and post-imperialism were the dominant themes of the United Nations in the 1960s and the ongoing Falklands dispute represented both. In 1964-65, the islands' position was debated by a UN committee on decolonisation. Argentina utilised a number of arguments to justify its claims to the islands including the Treaty of Tordesillas of 1494 (by which Spain and Portugal divided the Americas between themselves); the islands' proximity to South America; and the need to end colonial rule.

On the other side of the argument, and one which serves to the present day, the UK based its claim on 'open, continuous, effective possession, occupation and administration' of the islands since 1833 and its determination to grant the people of the Falkland Islands self-determination as recognised in the UN Charter.

In 1965, the UN General Assembly passed Resolution 2065, which urged Argentina and the UK to 'proceed without delay with negotiations with a view to finding a peaceful solution to the problem'. In his memoirs, Lord Peter Carrington noted that the Labour government of Harold Wilson was quite prepared to cede sovereignty to Argentina, but that the wishes of the Falkland Islanders were, and remained, the only obstacle.

Despite these apparently intractable differences, some progress was made. A package was developed between the respective foreign ministries in 1966 for future negotiations and in 1971 the UK signed a Communications Agreement with Argentina to formalise air and sea links between the islands and the South American continent. Two problems persisted, however. Firstly, the threat of force was never far away. For example, in 1971 a group of armed Peronist youths embarked on Operation 'Condor' by hijacking a Douglas DC-3 over Patagonia and flying to Port Stanley with the aim of arresting two British officials. Though Royal Marines intervened and returned the individuals to Argentina, the incident was embarrassing and London realised that the Falklands were defenceless against a surprise attack. The response

was to increase the strength of the marine garrison to 40 soldiers.

Economic considerations were also a severe hindrance to British plans to assist in a greater level of autonomy for the islanders. Unfortunately for the new Communications Agreement, funding approval from the Overseas Development Ministry for the sea link was not forthcoming; a decision seen by the Argentines as yet another delaying tactic. Moreover, Whitehall's internal wrangling over resources led Buenos Aires to perceive that British interest in the future of the Falklands was waning. The combination of Argentine scepticism and the return in 1973 of exiled nationalist President Juan Peron, a figure of almost mythological status to many Argentines, resulted in a more extreme form of Argentine nationalism. Once again pressuring the UN for a solution, Argentina caused to pass through the General Assembly a resolution calling on the two sides to accelerate negotiations on sovereignty.

However, it seemed that each time the British government appeared to gently push the islands towards mainland control, a combination of factors frustrated any genuine movement. For example, in 1974 Argentina's state oil company, Yaciementos Petroliferos, agreed to supply a large proportion of the islands' fuel needs at Argentine prices, which were low. But within a few months, Buenos Aires again pressed to make every Falkland Islander a citizen of Argentina, a situation unacceptable to the UK. The negotiations were therefore drifting with little sign of an early resolution.

In early 1976, the Labour peer Lord Shackleton arrived in the Falklands with a survey team charged with examining the future possibilities for economic development of the islands; a vital issue as the economy had started to decline and people were leaving in increasing numbers. An invitation was submitted to Argentina to participate in discussions about economic co-operation, but not about sovereignty. Argentina refused to take part in the survey. Any agreement with the British over the Falklands was seen as a tacit acceptance of the UK's influence there. Shortly after the Shackleton survey was announced, Argentina's representative to the UN outlined his government's position:

'We are prepared to continue our efforts but the limits of our patience and tolerance should not be underestimated if we should have to face an obstinate and unjustified refusal to negotiate by the other party.'

This thinly veiled threat of the use of force became a reality when an Argentine destroyer fired shots at the British scientific research vessel MV *Shackleton* (coincidental with the visit by Lord Shackleton to the islands) in February 1976. The incident took place some 80 miles south of the Falklands, in what Argentina viewed as its own territorial waters. British intelligence regarded

Port Howard, situated on the Falkland Sound coast of West Falkland, is typical of the small settlements dotted around the Falkland Islands. The blue skies and sunshine belie the fact that this is a tough and rugged land. FIGO

The letting of a contract for an Argentine company to salvage scrap metal on South Georgia, including material from these abandoned vessels in Grytviken harbour, is seen as the spark that led to the Argentine invasion of the Falkland Islands. MoD

this as 'part of a policy of continued pin-pricks' designed to force the issue. It can also be regarded as an early indication of the hawkish sentiments within the Argentine Navy.

Within a month a military coup had toppled the democratic regime in Argentina and General J R Videla became President. This development further alienated the Falkland Islanders as well as the British Parliament, and several left-wing MPs now joined the right in their condemnation of the administration in Buenos Aires. The Shackleton Report concluded that greater economic investment by the UK was needed. The report also concluded that the concept of 'lease-back' should be pursued whereby the British government 'rented' the islands from the Argentine government. The 'lease-back' idea was fiercely rejected by the Falkland Islanders, and the failure to act on Lord Shackleton's proposals simply increased the sense of frustration in Argentina. Use of force was by now a serious proposal in Buenos Aires.

The Argentine Navy had developed an invasion plan for the Falklands (Plan 'Goa', named after a successful Indian seizure of a Portuguese enclave in 1961), and in late 1976 it carried out a more limited territorial seizure, to test the UK's reaction. The target was the island of Thule in the British South Sandwich Islands, 1,000 miles southeast of the Falklands and of little other than scientific value. British intelligence believed that the landing of technicians on Thule was an act designed to demonstrate Argentina's sovereignty over these British islands and to gain bargaining leverage. It was a tactic they would use again in South Georgia, encouraged by the British inaction over the Thule incident (it was not even announced in Parliament until 1978).

Towards the end of 1977 the Argentine Navy cut off the supply of fuel to Port Stan-

ley, although this time the British government quickly responded by secretly diverting two frigates and a nuclear-powered submarine to the Falklands area in preparation for further action that thankfully never occurred.

In 1979 Margaret Thatcher came to power and further obstacles were placed in the way of negotiations. Although 'lease-back' was reluctantly being accepted within the Foreign and Commonwealth Office (FCO) as the only realistic option, Prime Minister Thatcher was unhappy with the concept as the British way of life could not be guaranteed for the islanders. She was also wary of any further discussions with an increasingly totalitarian regime in Buenos Aires. Argentine claims of sovereignty were cited as the sole reason for little progress in negotiations.

Nonetheless, Foreign Secretary Lord Carrington and Minister of State Nicholas Ridley believed that serious negotiations with the Argentines should be resumed in order to negate the threat of unilateral military action. In the Falklands winter of 1979, Nicholas Ridley visited the islands and delivered essentially the same message as his predecessor, Ted Rowlands, that serious sovereignty negotiations with Argentina were in order.

Towards the end of 1981, Secretary of State for Defence John Nott produced the annual statement on defence estimates and a report entitled 'The Way Forward'. It ruled out the creation of any major intervention force to operate outside Europe as the majority of the UK's forces were now committed primarily to NATO operations. The report also advocated swingeing defence cuts, of which the Royal Navy would bear 57 per cent. On 22nd December 1981, General Leopoldo Galtieri, head of the Argentine Army, succeeded Roberto Viola as President of Argentina. While

Galtieri made no mention of the Falklands in his inaugural address, he was generally viewed as a hard-liner on this issue. A speech he had made on Army Day in May 1981 outlined his views:

'Nobody can or will be able to say that we have not been extremely calm and patient in our handling of international problems, which in no way stem from an appetite for territory on our part. However, after a century and a half they [the problems] are becoming more and more intolerable.'

In addition to the increasing signs of declining British interest in the Falklands and the approaching 150th anniversary of the UK's sovereignty over the islands, Galtieri was holding what he perceived to be another important bargaining chip: the American card. High-level talks between President Ronald Reagan's advisers and Argentina's military leaders, including Galtieri, had proceeded well, with the result that President Reagan was willing to end the Carter administration's arms embargo that had been imposed as a result of Argentina's poor human rights record. Instead the United States would enlist the aid of the junta to help fight Communist insurgency in Central America, specifically Nicaragua. Galtieri was given the impression that he was an important element in Reagan's crusade against Communism, and this new relationship influenced subsequent foreign policy decisions.

As far as the Falklands dispute was concerned, the US State Department underestimated the UK's position over the islands. Neither they, nor the Argentines could believe that the UK would be prepared to send its fleet half way around the world to recover land that was obviously more important to Argentina than it was to the UK. Therefore American backing of the British line would simply alienate a valuable South American ally.

Buenos Aires was also aware of divisions among the White House staff. Europeanists and NATO supporters such as Secretary of State Alexander Haig and Undersecretary Larry Eagleburger were at odds with 'Latinists' such as Assistant Secretary for Latin American Affairs Thomas Enders and UN Ambassador Jeane Kirkpatrick. Unfortunately for Argentina, it would be Alexander Haig who would direct US foreign policy throughout the crisis. In 1981, he laid out his foreign policy goals as being: the restoration of Western and American economic and military strength; the reinvigoration of alliances and friendships; and in particular the support of regional alliance structures such as the EEC, ASEAN and OAS. Although this could be interpreted as maintaining the status quo, Haig also sought to establish relationships with developing world countries to encourage peaceful change. Finally, containment of and communication with the Soviet Union were a priority and any conflict that presented opportunities to the Eastern Bloc was to be avoided.

With the prospect of war between two of its allies still only a source of near amusement in Washington and confusion as to who directed policy, at the very least Argentina expected the US to remain neutral in any conflict and perhaps even exert pressure on the UK not to overreact. In addition, Argentine Foreign Minister Niconar Costa Mendez and the Argentine government in general also believed that they would enjoy continued UN support against the UK from Third World nations championing decolonisation.

The first result of this renewed confidence was a bolstering of Argentina's demands in the weeks preceding talks planned for early 1982 in New York. Costa Mendez requested a swift resolution of the sovereignty issue, suggesting that a commission be set up to meet once a month during the course of the ensuing year. In outlining the Argentine government's position, reference was made to consideration for the 'interests' and not the 'wishes' of the Falkland Islanders, thereby shifting the emphasis away from the importance of the Falklands population's role in the negotiations. Lord Carrington at the time detected nothing unusual in this approach and believed relations between the two countries might even be improving. This was a viewpoint echoed by junior FCO minister Richard Luce, who believed the creation of an administrative body might delay tough decisions further.

The signs of impending military action were there, however. The Argentine newspaper *La Prensa* wrote a series of articles outlining Argentina's firm resolve on the issue, presuming US and European support, and warning that a military attempt to resolve the dispute was a real possibility. The British took this message seriously, Prime Minister Thatcher requesting that contingency plans be drawn up in the event of action. British intelligence, however, interpreted Argentine claims of active US

support in any war as mere bluster. They therefore discounted this particular element in the newspaper articles, and also underestimated the resolve of the junta to take unilateral action. This is not entirely without justification as US intelligence, which the British regarded as being more sensitive to Latin American developments, was also disregarding Argentine rhetoric.

According to Alexander Haig, in retrospect, the United States, like the UK, had failed to see the significance of the 150th anniversary of British rule in the Falklands on Argentine public opinion. Thomas O Enders, for example, the US Assistant Secretary of State for Inter-American Affairs, had visited Buenos Aires but had reported only non-committal responses and no negativity towards the British.

When negotiations resumed at the end of February 1982, the two sides (the British led by Richard Luce and the Argentines by Enrique Ros, the Argentine ambassador to the UN) proposed a commission that would hold regular meetings presided over by ministers and attended by two Falkland Islands councillors at all times. The key aspect of the plan, however, was the one-year life span of the committee; a timeframe within which Argentina had established its deadline. The two sides drew different conclusions from this development. Argentina believed the negotiations had an urgency to them and a rigid framework; Richard Luce, in keeping with the UK's policy since the 1960s, felt they had bought themselves an extra three to six months' delay.

However, as would become a key feature of the conflict, the Argentine government, riven as it was by crises and rivalry, was not speaking with one voice on the issue. Costa Mendez, hoping to capitalise on latent nationalism, issued his own, more aggressive message, attacking British

intransigence and suggesting that the use of force was still a possibility. The domestic political situation in Argentina was deteriorating as austerity measures were introduced and the middle class became more and more disenchanted with anti-Communist rhetoric. The loss of the Beagle Isles to Chile in 1977 (by legal means) convinced Costa Mendez that the Falklands could be won without a fight, but also that they would have to be claimed soon to prevent revolution or another coup.

Costa Mendez backed down three days later, but his rhetoric set alarm bells ringing in Whitehall. However, the lack of any serious defence measures sent signals to Argentina that the UK's only course of action would be political negotiation, whereas British intelligence still believed that the extent of Argentina's possible aggression would simply be a naval blockade and economic sanctions. Meanwhile the British Treasury was determined to maintain budgetary constraints, rendering the diversion of ships to the Falklands impossible, and planned to withdraw the South Atlantic patrol and scientific survey ship, HMS *Endurance*, despite the concerns of a wary Lord Carrington.

An attempt to repeat the success of the Thule expedition was made on 19th March 1982, when Constantino Davidoff, an Argentine scrap-metal merchant, landed on the British island of South Georgia. He had been contracted to remove scrap metal from an abandoned whaling station, but he set up camp and hoisted the Argentine flag and there was a suspicion that some of his 'workers' were actually Argentine marines. To the dismay of the junta, *Endurance* was dispatched to South Georgia from Stanley with a detachment of Royal Marines on board. Argentine citizens were about to be evicted from an island over which they claimed sovereignty. The

Prior to the actual invasion, various aircraft types in Argentine service, such as the Fokker F-28, provided an air link between the islands and the mainland. MoD

junta hoped for public outrage in Argentina, but feared that renewed British interest in the islands would scupper a 'quiet' invasion. It was too soon for military confrontation: *Endurance* was still in the South Atlantic and a British fleet could still be sent south to the islands.

The unwillingness of the junta to back down following this miscalculation and the momentum inspired by a national mood that they had fostered, propelled the junta inexorably towards war. Alexander Haig described the leaders at the time as being driven by 'the most basic emotions toward fateful decisions'. Publicly the response in Argentina was one of startled indignation. The Argentine government officially denied any knowledge of the events on South Georgia, but on 21st March *Endurance* was ordered not to intervene for fear of provocation. Margaret Thatcher has maintained that this was necessitated by geography, as it would take at least three weeks for any reinforcements to arrive to assist *Endurance* in deterring any attack due to the distance involved.

By 28th March, Prime Minister Thatcher was becoming increasingly concerned about the situation and contacted Lord Carrington at Chequers to seek his reassurances. Regular contact with the United States eased British fears and Lord Carrington still believed that the most likely course of events would be a naval blockade by the Argentines. The UK sought American support and Alexander Haig entered the fray personally for the first time when he received a letter from Lord Carrington requesting that he contact the Argentines to seek an explanation of their presence on South Georgia.

The next day, Thatcher and Carrington discussed possible responses while on their way to a conference in Brussels. They decided to dispatch two submarines to the area. The Treasury, under the stewardship of Leon Brittan, remained reluctant to find additional financial resources for any contingency that exceeded these modest steps. A decision to deploy seven surface ships was deferred, as that act would no doubt be seen as provocative; an indication of both continued underestimation and financial restrictions. As the British government hesitated, Argentine naval exercises took place in the South Atlantic. However, British military intelligence was to report no unusual activity in South American waters for another day.

On 31st March the first reports of a possible invasion began to reach British intelligence, with 2nd April projected as the actual date of the invasion. John Nott called an emergency meeting consisting of the Prime Minister, Humphrey Atkins and Richard Luce of the FCO and Sir Henry Leach, Chief of Naval Staff. Prime Minister Thatcher was given two viewpoints, John Nott believing that diplomatic activity to halt the invasion was imperative as the islands could not be retaken if invaded and Admiral Leach stating boldly that a Task Force could be assembled within 48 hours and could defeat Argentine forces.

At 1830 hours that evening, President Reagan spoke with General Galtieri and offered to mediate, but this offer was declined. Asked directly whether he intended to use force, Galtieri responded that with no British negotiation for 150 years he was entitled to use whatever resources necessary unless the UK ceded sovereignty that very night. President Reagan responded to Galtieri's ultimatum, stating that the new relationship being fostered between their two countries would be wrecked if the action went ahead. As history now relates, the action did go ahead as planned.

Following the invasion, urgent diplomatic moves took place at the UN, where British Ambassador Anthony Parsons immediately alerted the Security Council, seeking to address the General Assembly and draft a Resolution condemning the invasion. Resolution 502, as it became, called for an immediate cessation of hostilities, the withdrawal of Argentine forces from the islands and a negotiated settlement. From the very outset, the UK's primary diplomatic goal was to retain the sympathies of the UN while avoiding that organisation becoming too deeply involved and thus impeding the UK's efforts. Margaret Thatcher saw her role as defending the UK's honour and upholding international law, and she feared that the UN would seek compromise and ultimately impose a settlement upon the UK. She was also aware that the United States wished to preserve the government of Galtieri because of its value in the fight against Communism. President Carter had excluded Argentina from any normal relations with the United States after the coup and civil war in 1979, but President Reagan had been more conciliatory, leading to a slight reduction in human-rights abuses in Argentina.

Washington took a cautious route throughout the entire crisis, ruling out stringent sanctions against Argentina from the outset. Thatcher later believed that this apparent even-handedness by the United States ultimately served the UK's interests as it allayed the fears of many nations at the UN. There was a commonly held belief at the FCO that the UN was not best disposed towards the UK's position. The FCO foresaw problems on the diplomatic front including a possible backlash against British expatriates in Argentina, a lack of support from the EEC, the risk of the Soviet Union becoming involved in the crisis and the UK being viewed as a colonial power. The anti-colonial mood of many members of the UN was very strong at this time, as was the South American position.

The British government had clear ideas as to what role it wished Washington to play. These included the withdrawal of the American ambassador, Harry W Shlaudeman, from Argentina, unequivocal condemnation of the invasion, the raising of the matter with the OAS and an embargo of arms shipments. The US response was more pragmatic and more limited. Washington aimed to maintain diplomatic links in order to facilitate communication and remain neutral as a friend to both countries. The United States was aware that the OAS would support Argentina as a matter of principle and that an arms sales ban was in place anyway because of Argentina's poor human rights record. The UK's aims were therefore directed more toward public displays of support rather than actual practical steps.

Alexander Haig reflects that, initially at least, neither the State Department nor the White House took the crisis seriously, seeing the dispute as almost comical. However, Haig viewed the ramifications of the invasion in much the same way as Thatcher. Haig was also mindful of how many other disputed territories there were in South America. He believed that the Argentines thought they could get away with their actions because they misunderstood the British, were 'militarised, authoritarian, xenophobic' and because they believed that the UK was weak and the United States corrupt. The West had spent 40 years preventing the Soviet Union from believing this and so could not allow others to do the same. Haig also had no doubt about the UK's legal right, or that she would eventually win a military fight; a view certainly not shared by other White House staff, many of whom in the National Security Council believed simply that the conflict was over oil resources.

The British public sought retribution but without a costly war, and was indignant at the lack of foresight in predicting the invasion. Lawrence Freedman argues that the Thatcher government would have fallen if the islands had been lost. In a particularly bruising session at Westminster on the morning following the invasion, Lord Carrington saw that his only option was to resign, but delayed his decision until 5th April, following further attacks in the press. He was followed by Humphrey Atkins and Richard Luce of the FCO. John Nott found himself being blamed in the Commons for unpreparedness due to the defence reductions announced in the defence review of

1981, and he too offered his resignation. This was refused by the Prime Minister, eager to retain some consistency in her cabinet, at least for the duration of the coming conflict.

Resolution 502 was passed in the UN on 3rd April, while in London, a war cabinet was quickly formed consisting of: Margaret Thatcher (Prime Minister), Francis Pym (Foreign Secretary), John Nott (Defence Secretary), Willie Whitelaw (Deputy Prime Minister), Cecil Parkinson (Media), Sir Terence Lewin (Chief of Defence Staff) and Michael Havers (Attorney-General). On the advice of former Prime Minister Harold Macmillan, Thatcher kept the Treasury (and the Chancellor, Geoffrey Howe) out of the proceedings, given their previous reluctance to pay for an adequate defence of the Falklands. At the war cabinet's third meeting it was decided to send a task force, a decision which Thatcher believed surprised many in the Commons.

Among the first countries to offer diplomatic support was France, acutely aware of her own overseas possessions and their vulnerability. Diplomatic overtures began in earnest on 6th April, with initial soundings decidedly mixed. Within the broad framework of diplomacy, the United States was counted as a supporter of the UK, as were France, West Germany, the Commonwealth (with the exception of India) and Chile. Each country had its own agenda: loyalty to the UK, their own colonial concerns and hostility to the Argentine government. Public opinion also played a factor, especially among those unprepared to support a military struggle for the Falklands. Italy, Spain and the Republic of Ireland

were three such countries, bound by cultural and trade ties to Argentina or antipathy to the British cause. They all supported Resolution 502, but were eager to maintain that this was in no way an acceptance of British sovereignty.

A commonly held belief was that military action was unnecessary. Even Haig thought that an economic embargo would probably have exhausted Argentina within weeks. Latin American governments gave ambiguous responses, clearly uneasy with British and Argentine imperialism alike. Predictably, the Soviet Union opposed the British position, a point not lost on either Thatcher or Haig, fearful that any sign of Western weakness would be of benefit to Moscow.

The first diplomatic move following the departure of the Task Force on 5th April was the arrival of Alexander Haig in London. He brought with him a three-point plan, which proposed a withdrawal of British and Argentine forces and the formation of an 'interim administration' in the Falklands. This was initially rejected by Thatcher as it failed to recognise the UK's legal claim of sovereignty, neglected the wishes of the Falkland Islanders and failed to guarantee their safety during the handover period. Upon his arrival Haig was informed that he was seen as an ally of the UK, there to give assistance, not as a mediator, a role that was largely played out for the benefit of the media. Despite this, the concept of some sort of interim government to allow time to discuss sovereignty was accepted in principle by London.

The following day, Haig took the same plan to Argentina. Upon his return to Lon-

don the plan had been expanded to seven points to accommodate more specific Argentine interests. These included an agreement by the UK and Argentina to withdraw forces, with all military units being returned to 'normal duties'. This point was unacceptable to the British government given the greater time it would take for the UK to deploy a deterrent force to the South Atlantic in comparison with that for Argentina. The creation of a commission made up of British, Argentine and American officials, replacing the role of former Governor Rex Hunt, and Argentine representation on the Falklands Council, was also unacceptable to London. In all subsequent negotiations the Argentines pointedly avoided including the wishes of the islanders in any settlement. The lifting of sanctions on Argentina and immediate negotiations for increased trade links were acceptable to the British, but a timetable for sovereignty negotiations that would cease at the end of the year was something that London could not accept, as it implied tacit approval for reoccupation and made no reference to a neutral third party such as the United States.

As well as clear difficulties with this plan, Thatcher also suspected that Galtieri and Costa Mendez were deciding policy on the spur of the moment and that their word could not be trusted. Haig, in his memoirs of the conflict, described the situation as

A view of Ross Road in Stanley, capital of the Falkland Islands, with Christchurch Cathedral dominating the skyline. Much military traffic would pass along Ross Road in 1982. FIGO

Government House, on the outskirts of Stanley, was the official residence of Governor Rex Hunt prior to the conflict. Governor Hunt was responsible for day-to-day management of the Falkland Islands. FIGO

crowds of 300,000 patriots and envisaged joint Anglo-Argentine ceremonies transferring sovereignty of the islands, contrary to all the evidence and rhetoric from the UK. Hopes were expressed that Peru would come in on the side of Argentina, fuelling pan-Latin nationalism. In the midst of this heady atmosphere, Haig attempted to convey the reality of the situation, informing Galtieri that the majority of the liberal Western states supported the UK, but by this time Galtieri and his junta had effectively stopped listening.

Haig's final meeting with Galtieri on 16th April took place after a number of US diplomats had requested visas to travel to Uruguay, fearful of a hostage situation developing. This comparison with the situation in Iran saddened Galtieri and, according to Haig, triggered a brief moment of reticence, but Haig reflects that by then the Argentines had deluded themselves into believing that the UK would back down, that Argentine politics was overrun with machismo and that Galtieri was no longer in control of the situation. According to Haig, Costa Mendez appeared to have a different agenda from Galtieri, for even as Haig boarded the aircraft to return to Washington, he was offered a new draft that completely reversed all of Galtieri's concessions. This would later be adopted as official Argentine government policy but Haig described it at the time as a 'formula for war'.

Haig returned to Washington on 20th April, where he met Francis Pym who told him of the decision to retake South Georgia by force. Haig, ever the diplomat and still adhering to his own strict code of diplomatic conduct, felt compelled to inform Argentina of this development, but in fact refrained from doing so when asked not to by Margaret Thatcher.

The difficulties encountered by British Special Forces in their attempt to retake South Georgia caused some brief last-minute jitters in British diplomatic resolve. Francis Pym returned from Washington on 24th April, convinced that the UK should reconsider the American proposals, an opinion he had expressed to Haig. However, this position was again rejected by Margaret Thatcher who was heartened the next day by the news that there had been a successful attack on South Georgia. The way was now clear to regain the Falklands by military force. All now depended on the performance of the British armed forces.

one that General Galtieri did not create. It was 'a Navy operation, conceived and urged upon the junta by that service'. The Air Force, knowing it would do the majority of the fighting, was 'unenthusiastic', as was the Army to a lesser degree. Haig suggested that Galtieri had blocked an invasion on three previous occasions and that it was likely that the Air Force and Army were not informed about the invasion until shortly before it took place. It was his opinion that the Navy had always resented Army influence, especially with its Spanish aristocratic traditions, and their rivalry was an important element in the background to subsequent events.

Galtieri could not act alone as he lacked the authority under the rules of the junta. Had he been able to act, he might have dissuaded others from their course of action. The military build-up continued, however, with the British 200-mile exclusion zone coming into effect on 12th April. The next day, to the great annoyance of Margaret Thatcher, the United States publicly stated that it was restricting use of the NATO facilities on Ascension Island, vital to the UK as a staging base. The island was a British territory and this statement portrayed the United States as neutral in the situation, something Thatcher was eager to avoid. In fact the United States continued to allow the base to be used and Thatcher was reasonably secure in the knowledge that Haig had made promises to the effect that, in the event of war, the UK would be supported.

Alexander Haig travelled to Buenos Aires for a second time on 15th April for five days of negotiations. The proposals he took with him included the additional conditions that the wishes of the Falkland Islanders be taken into account, that a British adminis-

tration continue in the interim but that an Argentine official act as a liaison with the islands' executive. Immediately upon his arrival, however, Haig was faced with counter proposals. The junta's revised plan included an agreement for Argentine forces to withdraw and some British administration to remain, a UN-style force to have a presence on the islands and an official Argentine representation to be present there. These changes, as well as being a cause of frustration for Haig, also made it clear that the government in Argentina was not speaking with one voice and that both Galtieri and Costa Mendez were simply reacting to outside forces, with every statement on the issue needing to be cleared by various levels of the armed forces.

Worryingly, there was talk in Argentina of seeking assistance from the Soviet Union. Emilio Aragones, the Cuban ambassador to Argentina, claimed that the Soviet Union might offer military backing to resist the British Task Force. Galtieri even hinted that the Soviets had offered to sink HMS *Invincible* and give Argentina the credit for it. In an attempt to maintain American interest, Galtieri stated that if he withdrew Argentine armed forces from the islands, his own position would be untenable within a week and that Soviet-backed forces within Argentina would be in the ascendant. The veracity of these threats must be doubted, however, due to the junta's vehement anti-Communist policies, but they were probably designed to prick the Cold War instincts of Haig and his colleagues.

Haig was also aware of the very high level of belligerence in Argentine society, not just from the military but with pressure from the Peronist political parties adding to the rhetoric and bombast. Galtieri addressed

Chapter Two

Military Assessment
and Preparations for War

Following the invasion of the Falkland Islands and South Georgia, the British government had to decide whether or not it could mount an expeditionary force to try to regain its possessions by force, or whether it had to rely purely on diplomatic means. The decision to act militarily while also pursuing a diplomatic solution was swiftly made. However, at first sight the military situation looked far from promising for the UK. The first and most obvious problem was the distance of the Falklands from the UK, resulting in a major logistical challenge to any form of military response. Nearly 8,000 miles away from the UK's shores, but only 350 miles from mainland Argentina, the geography of the Falkland Islands seemed to favour the invaders right from the start; and no doubt this factor had played a major role in the Argentine junta's decision making.

The nearest possible base that any expeditionary force could use was Ascension Island, a small British protectorate about halfway between the UK and the Falklands. Although the use of Ascension Island was to prove invaluable throughout the conflict, the logistics of maintaining a naval task force and thousands of troops for several weeks would stretch the UK's resources to the very limit.

It was not simply the geography of the conflict that proved a challenge, for the Falklands crisis arose at a time of great change for the British armed forces. Recent defence reviews had recommended the reduction of the UK's military presence overseas throughout the 1960s and 1970s as a result of the move towards independence for the UK's former colonial possessions and protectorates. The withdrawal from the Far East, the Middle East and the Mediterranean resulted in a huge reduction in the size of the UK's armed forces. For example, by 1982 the RAF's strategic transport fleet had shrunk from the five squadrons available in 1975 to just one squadron of VC10s. Similarly the Royal Navy's active fighting force of aircraft carriers, cruisers, destroyers and frigates had been reduced from 92 ships to 68 in the same period. In fact, as a result of swingeing cuts announced in the 1981 defence review, both aircraft carriers

in service with the Royal Navy in 1982 were earmarked for sale, HMS *Hermes* to India and HMS *Invincible* to Australia.

The reduction in the UK's interests overseas was accompanied by a concentration of effort on its role in NATO, with its armed forces reshaped to fight a short-range, short-duration war against the Soviet Union in Europe as part of a larger alliance. Consequently, capabilities like those of the long-range Vulcan bomber were being replaced in the early 1980s by the shorter-range Tornado. The technology in such weapon systems was considerably more advanced, but they were not designed to fulfil roles now deemed to be unnecessary.

Perhaps because of the UK's focus on NATO operations, little was known about the military capabilities of its new opponent in the Falklands conflict. In fact Argentina had some of the best-equipped and best-trained armed forces in South America. Unlike most South American nations, Argentina's armed forces were of a significant size as the country is huge with a long border to defend. The armed forces were also in a better state of readiness and had more operational experience than most in the region, as conflict with Chile was never far from the surface and guerrillas within Argentina had been active in recent years. According to *The Military Balance* of 1981–82, the annual publication of the Inter-

national Institute for Strategic Studies, the strength of the Argentine armed forces in autumn 1981 was as follows:

Argentine Navy

Like its near neighbour, Brazil, the Argentine Navy (Armada Argentina) possessed an aircraft carrier, albeit an old one with limited capability. In fact the *25 de Mayo* was the Royal Navy's old HMS *Venerable* of Second World War vintage, which had been bought first by the Dutch Navy in 1948 before being modernised and sold on to Argentina in 1968. The Argentine Navy's other major surface vessel was the ex-US Navy Brooklyn class cruiser, the *General Belgrano*, which, although even older than the *25 de Mayo*, could outgun any Royal Navy ship afloat at the time.

Having been on friendly terms, both culturally and economically, with the UK for so long, Argentina had bought a variety of British armaments over the years. Thus the Argentine Navy was equipped with two new Type 42 destroyers ordered from the UK in the late 1970s. These were highly

As a consequence of swingeing defence cuts implemented in the 1970s and early 1980s, the RAF's strategic transport force comprised just 13 VC10 C1s in a single squadron when the Argentine invasion commenced. B Munro

Armed with two 20mm Hispano DCA-804 cannon, four 7.62mm M2-30 machine guns, and two underwing and one centreline hardpoints for a variety of ordnance, the Pucara was a potent light attach threat. FMA

capable air defence destroyers similar in most respects to the Type 42s of the Royal Navy and were the most modern ships in the Argentine Navy. The two Type 42s served alongside three modern French Type A69 frigates bought in 1978 after their sale to South Africa fell through, although these were so small that they could be more correctly classed as corvettes. However, apart from these vessels the Argentine Navy consisted largely of elderly ships including seven ex-US Navy destroyers of Second World War vintage, although some of these had been refitted to carry the deadly Exocet anti-ship missile. Also in use were two ex-US Navy Guppy class submarines, both of Second World War vintage, as well as a pair of more modern German-built Salta class submarines that were delivered in 1974.

Argentine Naval Aviation Command (Comando Aviacion Naval Argentina; CANA) had a squadron of 11 McDonnell Douglas A-4Q Skyhawks that could operate from the *25 de Mayo* or from land bases. CANA also operated seven Aermacchi MB-326GB and ten of the newer MB-339A light attack/training aircraft as well as a number of helicopters and maritime surveillance and ASW aircraft. Of more importance were the 14 Dassault-Breguet Super Etendard strike fighters armed with Exocet anti-ship missiles on order from France.

Argentine Air Force

The Military Balance of 1981–82 identifies the Argentine Air Force (Fuerza Aerea Argentina) as possessing some 201 offensive combat aircraft in March 1982, this figure consisting of 68 McDonnell Douglas A-4B/C Skyhawks, 21 Dassault-Breguet Mirage IIIEA interceptors, 26 IAI Dagger As (an-Israeli-built fighter-bomber variant of the Mirage 5), nine English Electric Canberra B62 bombers, 32 Morane Saulnier Paris light attack aircraft and 45 of the indigenous FMA IA-58A Pucara counter-insurgency aircraft. In the anti-shipping role the Skyhawks and the Daggers could pose

a serious threat, although the Daggers were not equipped for in-flight refuelling and had a very basic avionics fit. The Canberras were elderly but effective and had an impressive high-altitude capability; while the Mirage III was a very capable high-speed interceptor, although it too lacked the ability to refuel in flight.

Although it had been exhibited at Farnborough in 1978, the Pucara was not well known to British analysts at the time; but, as it was designed for the counter-insurgency role, it obviously had a useful air-to-ground capability that could prove troublesome to British land forces. The Argentine Air Force also had a number of transport aircraft (including nine C-130E/H Hercules) and helicopters of various types. Two of the Hercules were the KC-130H tanker variant that became worth their weight in gold during the Falklands conflict.

Argentine Army

The Argentine Army (Ejercito) had its own combat aviation battalion (Batallon de Aviacion de Combate 601; CAB601) to provide air mobility over such a large country. According to *The Military Balance* of 1981–82, CAB601 possessed about 70 helicopters of many different types, the most useful of which were about 20 ex-US Army Vietnam-era examples of the ubiquitous Bell UH-1H and three examples of the more modern and larger Aerospatiale SA.330L Puma. These helicopters were supplemented by a pair of Boeing-Vertol CH-47C Chinooks acquired for heavy-lift duties, while nine Italian-built Agusta A-109A Hirundos were operated as gunships in the light attack/reconnaissance role.

British Forces

Although the British armed forces were much larger and equipped with more modern weaponry than those of Argentina, in many ways they were not equipped for the sort of war they were now being called upon to fight. The distance of the Falklands from a main operating base precluded the

use of much of the RAF's supporting firepower, so as far as air power was concerned the UK had to rely on aircraft that could be carried on board the Task Force ships and on those that could reach the Falklands from Ascension Island.

The Royal Navy's two aircraft carriers could only take a maximum of about 25 BAe Sea Harrier FRS1s and as there were only 32 in existence in March 1982, it was clear that Royal Air Force BAe Harrier GR3s would have to be deployed as attrition replacements and to reinforce the Sea Harriers in the air-to-air and air-to-ground roles. The only combat aircraft capable of reaching the Falklands from Ascension Island was the ageing Avro Vulcan B2 bomber, which was in the process of being phased out of service, with many having already been scrapped. However, a small number of Vulcans were rapidly prepared for long-distance bombing missions and their crews trained for the role.

The main limitation for Vulcan raids was the lack of tanker capacity. The RAF had a total of 23 Handley Page Victor K2 tankers available and about 16 Victor sorties were required to get a single Vulcan from Ascension Island to the Falklands and back. The Victors were also needed to enable the deployment of aircraft from the UK to Ascension Island and later to refuel Hercules and Nimrods operating over the South Atlantic. Long-range maritime patrol and surveillance could be performed by Nimrods and Victors but the shortage of AEW, air defence and offensive aircraft posed major problems for the Task Force. The delivery of essential equipment and personnel fell to the RAF Hercules fleet that was also heavily engaged on the airlift to Ascension Island. Several Hercules were modified to extend their range so that they could reach the Task Force even when it was operating close to the Falklands.

Another limitation was that of helicopters, which were vital to the movement of troops and supplies throughout the campaign. Although the UK had a large number of helicopters in military service, including a newly formed squadron of Boeing-Vertol Chinook HC1s, there was a limit to how many could be accommodated on the Task Force ships. Even by using a number of converted merchant ships as aircraft transports, there was not going to be enough helicopters available for all the many requirements during the ensuing conflict. This problem became much more acute with the loss of the SS *Atlantic Conveyor* and its cargo of Chinooks and Wessex.

Most of the Royal Navy's ships were undoubtedly superior to those of the Argentine Navy but the long-range guns of the *General Belgrano*, the aircraft of the *25 de Mayo* and Argentina's submarines all posed a major threat that had to be taken seriously. The Royal Navy's major deficiency was the lack of AEW to give advanced warning of air attack. The Royal Navy's ships were less well armoured than their predecessors of the Second World War and consequently were more easily damaged when hit by bombs or missiles.

The Task Force that eventually deployed to the South Atlantic consisted of 63 Royal Navy and Royal Fleet Auxiliary (RFA) ships together with a large number of supporting merchant ships. Numerically the Task Force was much larger than the Argentine Navy, which only possessed about 20 major warships in total. Also, the average age of the Royal Navy aircraft carriers, destroyers, frigates and submarines in 1982 was ten years, whereas the average age of equivalent Argentine warships was 27 years.

It transpired that the figures in *The Military Balance*, which were probably very similar to those used by British intelligence at the outbreak of the Falklands conflict, were slightly inaccurate, at least insofar as aircraft were concerned. The total number of combat aircraft theoretically available to the Argentine Air Force was actually slightly higher, at 208, with the corrected figures being 52 Skyhawks (a reduction of 16 aircraft), 17 Mirage IIIs (a reduction of 4), 37 Daggers (an increase of 11), 10 Canberras (an increase of 1), 32 Morane Saulnier Paris' and about 60 Pucaras (an increase of about 15). The Argentine Navy had just 10 A-4Q Skyhawks left in service. However, in addition to the data recorded in *The Military Balance*, the Argentine Navy had received five of its order for 14 Super Etendard strike fighters. In addition, the Argentine Army's CAB601 actually had nine Pumas in service (an increase of six).

Whatever the figures on paper, the number of aircraft actually available for operations was significantly reduced by a low serviceability rate and a shortage of spare parts resulting in the cannibalising of airframes. The Argentine Air Force later claimed that it never had more than 82 combat aircraft operationally available during the conflict. It seems likely that the combined total of Argentine mainland and Falklands-based Air Force and Navy com-

bat aircraft of all types theoretically available for use over the Falklands was actually around 230 with rarely more than about 50 per cent being available at any one time, and that this figure dropped throughout the conflict due to attrition.

However, in the air at least, on 1st May, when the shooting started, the odds were still heavily in favour of Argentina, with the number of mainland-based jet combat aircraft available (A-4s, Mirage IIIs, Daggers, Canberras and Super Etendards but not including the MB-326GB, MB-339A and Paris light attack aircraft) totalling 131 compared to just 20 Sea Harrier FRS1s, giving a ratio of 6.55:1. By 21st May this ratio had been reduced to 3.8:1 thanks to attrition and the arrival of more Sea Harriers and the RAF's Harrier GR3s; the figures were now 119 Argentine aircraft (various types) versus 31 Harriers/Sea Harriers. Poor serviceability and the effects of battle damage to Argentine aircraft must have reduced this ratio still further.

The poor state of readiness of many Argentine aircraft was partly due to ageing equipment and inadequate spares holdings, but may also have been a result of the high percentage of conscripted personnel in the Argentine armed forces who did not have the same level of experience or training as permanent servicemen. The Army had 90,000 conscripts in its total strength of 130,000 (69 per cent), the Navy 18,000 conscripts in its total of 36,000 (50 per cent) and the Air Force 10,000 conscripts in its strength of 19,000 (53 per cent). To what extent this heavy reliance on conscription was a factor in the performance of the Argentine armed forces is difficult to establish with certainty, but it is known that many of the soldiers who were sent to defend the Falklands had only been serving for a few months. Compared to the UK's all-volunteer armed forces, the Argentine armed forces appeared to be less well trained, less well equipped and less well led.

The other major problem facing the Argentine Air Force was similar to that facing the British forces: geography! The nearest Argentine airfields to the Falklands were Rio Grande on Tierra del Fuego (381 nautical miles from Stanley), Rio Gallegos (420 nautical miles away), San Julian (about 395 nautical miles away) and Comodoro Rivadavia (525 nautical miles away). The only tanker aircraft possessed by the Argentine armed forces were two KC-130H Hercules and many Argentine combat aircraft (Daggers, Mirage IIIs and Canberras) did not have an in-flight refuelling capability. This meant that for most of the time, Argentine aircraft would be operating close to their limits of range and endurance, leaving very little time for combat once the Falklands had been reached. In an attempt to solve this problem, thought was given to using Stanley airport, but its short runway (just 4,100ft in length) would not permit safe operational use by the Argentine Skyhawks, Mirage IIIs, Daggers and Super Etendards.

As far as air power is concerned, despite the seeming disparity of forces and the problems caused by geography, on paper at least, the two proponents suffered from severe limitations that dictated their tactics and rate of operations and left them more evenly matched. Argentina might have seemed to be in a strong position and its combat aircraft may have outnumbered those of the UK by a handsome margin, but the British forces had some crucial advantages: more modern hardware (Sea Harrier FRS1, AIM-9L Sidewinder, Seawolf); better training; better electronic warfare capability; closer operating bases (the two aircraft carriers sometimes sailed to within 100 miles of the Falklands) and better overall leadership.

It was immediately obvious to British analysts that the major threat to the Task Force was going to be the five Super Etendards and their Exocet missiles, and that the conventional bombs carried by the

The Argentine Air Force would come to rely heavily on 17 examples of the delta-winged Mirage IIIEA single-seat interceptor during the Falklands conflict. Argentine Air Force

Skyhawks, Daggers and Canberras also posed a significant threat. The question was: could the British forces shoot down enough Argentine aircraft to allow an amphibious landing to take place and give British troops the time necessary to defeat the Argentine Army on the Falklands? The answer to this question was still very much in doubt when air hostilities commenced on 1st May.

Preparations for War
Even before Argentine forces set foot on the Falklands the first British ships had set sail for the South Atlantic, and plans were being drawn up to form a Task Force to retake the islands by force. On 29th March RFA *Fort Austin* sailed from Gibraltar to rendezvous with HMS *Endurance*, which was monitoring events at South Georgia. On 1st April two Royal Navy submarines (HMS *Spartan* and HMS *Splendid*) set off for the Falklands, ready to enforce a maritime exclusion zone if called upon to do so.

On 2nd April, the day of the invasion, plans to put together and equip a large naval Task Force were quickly put into operation. Ship's companies were recalled from shore leave and various aircraft were embarked on vessels in harbour as thousands of tons of stores started to arrive at Portsmouth and Devonport to be loaded on board. The RAF dispatched four Hercules transports from RAF Lyneham to Gibraltar to start the massive airlift that would help sustain the Task Force throughout the forthcoming campaign.

A number of Royal Navy warships had been conducting an exercise to the west of Gibraltar for several days and ten of these ships formed the Advanced Group of the Task Force, sailing south later on 2nd April. Two more nuclear-powered submarines left for the South Atlantic on the 4th and the next day, less than 72 hours after the signal to go, the nucleus of the Carrier Battle Group left Portsmouth and Devonport. By

9th April, within one week of the invasion, no less than 36 Royal Navy, RFA and requisitioned merchant ships were en route to the South Atlantic.

The rapid dispatch of the Task Force meant that not every ship had received every item of stores or equipment that it would need. Consequently a huge reloading task was performed when the ships started to arrive at Ascension Island. Helicopters flew hundreds of sorties redistributing stores and troops between ships and delivered tons of extra equipment that had been delivered by air to Ascension Island while the ships were in transit. Further redistribution would be required just outside the Total Exclusion Zone (TEZ) as the Task Force began its final preparations for the amphibious landings. Despite the huge effort put into ensuring that each ship had the correct load there were some instances of loads being split and delays caused, but these were fairly minor.

A major feature of the Falklands crisis was the large number of merchant ships requisitioned or hired to supplement those of the RFA to support the Task Force. Ships Taken Up From Trade (STUFT) played a major role in the Falklands conflict and were crewed by civilians who often faced the same dangers as their Royal Navy counterparts.

The distance from the UK and the length of time spent in transit and at war meant that the warships of the Task Force required almost constant resupply and refuelling. In addition to ten RFA tankers and five stores ships, a total of 43 merchant ships were used to support the Task Force before the end of the conflict. These consisted of 15 tankers (eight of them from British Petroleum), eight troop transports (ferries or passenger liners), eight cargo vessels, five trawlers (converted for minesweeping) and eight other vessels including tugs and offshore repair ships. The first of these ships left the UK on 9th

May and STUFT vessels became an integral part of the Amphibious Group.

In addition to the major effort to set the Task Force on its way and ensure that it could be maintained throughout the campaign, much work was done to prepare equipment. The peculiar requirements of the Falklands campaign would necessitate the modification of much of the equipment that was about to be used. For example, many of the Vulcans, Nimrods and Hercules used during the conflict were rapidly fitted with in-flight refuelling probes to extend their operational range. In the case of the Vulcan, this addition resurrected a capability that had existed within the force some years earlier, but even this was not without difficulty. The British aviation industry worked miracles to ensure that these modifications were completed in record time.

Other examples of modification programmes included adapting the Harrier GR3s for operations from the deck of HMS *Hermes*; replacing the AIM-9G Sidewinder with the AIM-9L version on the Sea Harriers; equipping Nimrods with Sidewinder and Harpoon missiles; fitting the Victors and Vulcans with inertial navigation system equipment; fitting SNEB rocket pods to Gazelles and Harriers; stripping-out Sea King HAS2s for use in the transport role and modifying Vulcans and Harriers to carry Shrike anti-radar missiles. Additionally, a number of new weapons, notably the Sea Skua anti-ship missile, the Stingray torpedo and the RAF's Paveway laser-guided bomb, had not yet been fully introduced to operational service, so development work was accelerated to ensure these weapons were ready for use. Night-vision goggles for aircrew were also in the early stages of service in the RAF and Royal Navy, but their use in the Falklands proved their worth and led to further development.

Further information on the preparations for war can be found in the chronological section. It is true to say that although the British armed forces were considerably better equipped than those of Argentina, there were some unforeseen problems and some major deficiencies, many of which were addressed after the conflict. However, by 1st May, with the real shooting war ready to start, the Task Force was undoubtedly one of the best-equipped forces that the UK had ever fielded.

Sea Harrier FRS1 XZ499 of 800 Squadron taxies along the deck of Hermes. *The aircraft has empty wing pylons so this photograph may have been taken prior to the commencement of hostilities. Lieutenant Dave Smith shot down a Skyhawk on 8th June while flying this aircraft.* MoD

Part Two

Chronology of the Air War

*Times throughout (with the exception of
South Georgia where local times are used) are
Zulu time, which is Greenwich Mean Time
and some three hours ahead of local time on
the Falklands. So while dawn breaks at
0800 hours local on the Falklands, it is recorded
as being 1100Z in the text.*

*Aerial refuelling was essential for the longer-range Argentine missions but there were never enough tankers available.
This Grupo 5 A-4B Skyhawk was one of two aircraft shot down over Choiseul Sound by Flight Lieutenant Dave Morgan
on 8th June a few hours after the bombing of the LSLs in Port Pleasant.* Argentine Air Force

Chapter Three

The Invasion and
Events to 30th April 1982

The Landings on South Georgia

Prior to the invasion of the Falklands and the subsequent British response, the only British military presence in this remote part of the world was the Antarctic patrol ship HMS *Endurance* and a small party of Royal Marines based at Moody Brook Barracks near Stanley. *Endurance* was primarily engaged in scientific survey of the southern oceans and the coast of Antarctica. However, as the only Royal Navy vessel permanently based in the southern hemisphere, she was armed with two Oerlikon 20mm cannon and normally carried a small complement of Royal Marines. *Endurance* also carried two Westland Wasp HAS1 helicopters each of which could be armed with two AS-12 air-to-surface missiles and a gen-

eral-purpose machine gun (GPMG). One of the Wasps (XT418) had been badly damaged as it was landing at St Andrews Bay in South Georgia on 12 December 1981 and was replaced by XS539, which was embarked at Montevideo, having been flown out there in an RAF Hercules.

Endurance spent the Antarctic summer season supporting scientific research and monitoring the movement of large icebergs, which could be a hazard to shipping. The ship also spent part of the season visiting the Falklands, South Georgia, the South Sandwich Islands and the South Orkney Islands. *Endurance* also made occasional goodwill visits to naval bases in Argentina and Chile, where the crew was usually made most welcome.

19th March (Friday) – Uninvited Visitors

Under the command of Captain Nick Barker, *Endurance* arrived at Stanley on the 19th having just made one of her infrequent visits to South Georgia, 800 miles to the southeast of the Falklands. However, tension was already rising in the South Atlantic, as two incidents on the 19th indicated. A Gates Learjet 35A (T-23) photo-reconnaissance aircraft of the Argentine Air Force's

Endurance *was known throughout the Royal Navy as the 'Red Plum' due to her bright red hull, painted as an aid to identification in the Antarctic waters. Wessex HAS3 XP142 from* Antrim *is seen here transferring stores to the ship.* MoD

Endurance's Wasps wore bright red markings pre-war as an aid to location in the white and grey vastness of the Antarctic Ocean where they spent much of their time. The Wasps were hastily camouflaged soon after one of the helicopters was spotted on South Georgia by an Argentine Alouette III. MoD

Grupo 1 de Aerofotografico suddenly appeared over Stanley and landed unannounced at Stanley airport. The crew explained that they had experienced 'undercarriage problems', which was a curious reason for landing at such a remote location. Neither did this explanation fit with an incident the previous month when another Learjet 35A was substituted for an FMA Guarani II light transport aircraft that normally calibrated Stanley's VOR equipment. On that occasion the Learjet did not land because, the islanders were told at the time, the runway was too short! Whatever the real reason, Learjet T-23 soon took off and returned to the mainland on the 19th.

Meanwhile, events on South Georgia were taking on a much more sinister complexion. On the morning of the 19th four British Antarctic Survey (BAS) scientists discovered the Argentine naval transport vessel *Bahia Buen Suceso* berthed in Leith harbour, unloading men and equipment. Although some of the 50 men present were undoubtedly civilians who had been contracted to dismantle parts of the old whaling station for scrap, some also appeared to be military personnel, most likely marines. This event set in motion a series of confused diplomatic moves in London and Buenos Aires in the hope of averting serious disruption to the UK's friendly and longstanding relationship with Argentina.

21st March (Sunday)
Endurance left Stanley for South Georgia with a platoon of 21 Royal Marines commanded by Lieutenant Keith Mills. That same day the *Bahia Buen Suceso* left Leith harbour for the open sea, leaving a party of men behind at the whaling station. Through diplomatic channels the Argentine government was told that *Endurance* was on her way to South Georgia to remove the scrapmetal merchants who had landed on South Georgia in contravention of the legal formalities.

23rd March (Tuesday)
The BAS vessel *John Briscoe* sailed from Montevideo with a group of 40 Royal Marines who were due to replace the existing garrison at Stanley as part of the normal rotation of units. Rather than wait for *Endurance* to return from South Georgia, the BAS had been persuaded to transport the marines to the Falklands in their ship.

24th March (Wednesday)
As a result of a change in orders so as not to aggravate the situation, *Endurance* arrived in Cumberland East Bay, some 12 miles to the south of Leith, where she anchored off Grytviken in the early morning. Grytviken was another abandoned whaling station set in the tiny King Edward Cove. BAS personnel had been keeping a close watch on activity at Leith from a nearby vantage point, but with the arrival of *Endurance* the Royal Marines took over these surveillance duties and the Wasp helicopters inserted two-man observation posts during the daylight hours.

25th March (Thursday)
The *Bahia Paraiso*, a polar research vessel like *Endurance*, arrived off Leith during the afternoon of the 25th carrying an Argentine Army Puma (AE-504 of CAB601) in addition to her own Alouette III (0699/3-H-110 of 1 Escuadrilla de Helicopteros) and the usual contingent of marines. The Puma had been embarked on the *Bahia Paraiso* in connection with the ship's recent visit to the Orcadas Islands.

26th March (Friday)
A new observation post on Grass Island, closer to Leith, was established on the 26th in order to get a better view of Argentine activity. One of *Endurance's* Wasps flown by Lieutenant Commander Tony Ellerbeck airlifted the first observation team up to the new position.

The Argentine invasion fleet sailed for the Falklands on 26th March, thereby putting Operation 'Rosario' into motion. The fleet consisted of two main task forces. Task Force 40 was the amphibious element with two destroyers (*Hercules* and *Santisima Trinidad*), two frigates (*Drummond* and *Granville*), a submarine (*Santa Fe*) that carried a team of frogmen, a tank landing ship (*Cabo San Antonio*), a polar vessel (*Almirante Irizar*) and a fleet transport ship (*Isla de los Estados*). Task Force 20 provided cover for the amphibious group and consisted of the sole aircraft carrier (*25 de Mayo*), four destroyers (*Segui, Hipolito Bouchard, Piedra Buena* and *Comodoro Py*), a fleet tanker (*Punta Medanos*) and a patrol vessel (*Alferez Sobral*). The amphibious force carried a total of about 1,200 marines and soldiers. A smaller force, designated Task Force 60 and consisting of a polar vessel (*Bahia Paraiso*) and an escorting frigate (*Guerrico*), was tasked with the occupation of South Georgia. Storms in the South Atlantic slowed down the passage of the amphibious group of ships so the planned landings on East Falkland were delayed from the original target date of 30th March for two days.

27th March (Saturday)
On the 27th one of *Endurance's* Wasps landed a few miles from an observation post so that Captain Nick Barker, commander of the vessel, could see the activity in Leith for himself. While on the ground the helicopter and its occupants were overflown by the Alouette III from the *Bahia Paraiso*. The Wasp had been easy to spot as it was still wearing its special red Antarctic markings, designed to make the helicopter more visible against a background of snow and ice. Following this encounter, both Wasps were hurriedly camouflaged during the night of the 27th in an attempt to reduce their conspicuity.

28th March (Sunday)
On the 28th the Puma and the Alouette III assisted in putting ashore a small number of Argentine marines and the *Bahia Paraiso* left Leith harbour for the open sea with the intention of keeping *Endurance* under surveillance.

29th March (Monday)
Captain Barker decided to put to sea in an attempt to locate the *Bahia Paraiso*, which he did later in the day, despite poor visibility. The two ships shadowed each other closely some 15 miles offshore of South Georgia. Lieutenant Commander Ellerbeck in Wasp HAS1 XS527 was ordered to fly a strange mission in the hope of scaring the *Bahia Paraiso* away from the area. The Wasp took off from *Endurance* and flew over the horizon in response to mock radio calls, which it was hoped would be picked up by the Argentines. The radio conversation was intended to dupe the captain of the *Bahia Paraiso* into thinking that the Wasp was picking up an injured seaman from a British nuclear submarine, but the ruse failed and the Argentine ship stayed in the area as *Endurance* made her way back to Grytviken.

It was obvious by now that *Endurance* would be required to stay in the South Atlantic for longer than planned and would therefore need resupplying. Consequently, on 29th March the fleet replenishment ship RFA *Fort Austin* sailed from Gibraltar to reinforce and replenish *Endurance*.

At 2300Z an Argentine Air Force C-130 overflew Stanley; not in itself an unusual event as Hercules often flew over the Falklands en route to the Antarctic, but this overflight probably had more significance than previous such events. Earlier in the month a KC-130H (TC-69) had made an unexpected visit to Stanley airport, apparently due to a minor technical fault involving a damaged fuel line.

31st March (Wednesday)
On 31st March *Endurance* again put to sea from Grytviken to locate the *Bahia Paraiso*, which had been cruising up and down the coast of South Georgia for the previous five days. However, early in the afternoon Captain Barker was ordered to proceed to Stanley at best speed as evidence pointed to the possibility of an imminent invasion. The two Wasps recovered all of the men who had been manning the observation post near Leith while Lieutenant Mills and his 21 Royal Marines disembarked from *Endurance* and occupied Grytviken to protect the BAS personnel and establish a British military presence on the island. *Endurance* then slipped away under cover of darkness, unobserved by the *Bahia Paraiso*, and set course for Stanley.

1st April (Thursday)
The first British combat ships to be sent to the South Atlantic, the nuclear-powered submarines HMS *Spartan* and HMS *Splendid*, left Gibraltar and Faslane respectively for a rapid transit to the Falklands, where they arrived on the 12th. An initial planning conference was held in London by the First Sea Lord, Admiral Sir Henry Leach, with the intention of planning a task force in response to the expected Argentine invasion of the Falkland Islands. The first signals went out to the aircraft carriers HMS *Hermes* and HMS *Invincible* during the afternoon to warn them of the likelihood of an imminent operational deployment to the South Atlantic.

2nd April (Friday) – Invasion!
At 0015Z on 2nd April Argentine commandos landed near Stanley. The invasion had begun. By 1215Z the Argentine marines had secured Stanley, including the airfield, and were threatening the residence of the Falkland Islands Governor, Rex Hunt. In order to avoid unnecessary bloodshed among the civilian population, Rex Hunt ordered the Royal Marines to lay down their arms after they had put up a spirited resistance. During the invasion CANA Sikorsky S-61D-4 Sea Kings of 2 Escuadrilla de Helicopteros and the Westland Lynx HAS23s from the Type 42 destroyers flew Argentine marines from the deck of the polar ship *Almirante Irizar* to key points around Stanley and elsewhere.

Air power had played little part in the invasion although Argentine Air Force C-130s and Boeing 707s had flown reconnaissance missions in preparation for Operation 'Rosario'. However, once Stanley was secure the airlift of the occupation force could commence in earnest. On 1st April four C-130E/Hs, one KC-130H and five Fokker F-28-1000 Fellowships had been moved to Comodoro Rivadavia in preparation for 'Aries 82', the airlift of the Falkland Islands garrison to Stanley.

At 1130Z, even before Stanley was fully secured, the first C-130H (TC-68) touched down at Stanley airport, bringing in the initial elements of the Argentine Army's Regimiento de Infanteria 25, which was to form the nucleus of the garrison for the Falklands. Three more C-130s and an F-28 arrived on the 2nd, the last of these aircraft touching down at 1900Z carrying, among other things, a Westinghouse AN/TPS-43F radar that would be crucial to the defence of the Falklands. The captured Royal Marines were flown out to Comodoro Rivadavia in a C-130 while the Governor and his party were flown in the F-28.

As part of the Argentine garrisoning of the Falkland Islands four Grupo 3 de Ataque Pucaras flew to Stanley via Rio Gallegos on the 2nd. Although it seems that the original plan was to station no more than a handful of Pucaras at Stanley, the British response eventually led to a total of 25 being flown to the Falklands. By early April the Argentine Air Force had taken delivery of about 60 of these indigenously produced light attack aircraft. Although it was designed only for counter-insurgency duties, the Pucara was one of the few combat aircraft in Argentine service that could operate safely from Stanley airport's short runway.

In conjunction with the invasion of the Falklands, the situation on South Georgia was also about to flare up into open warfare. At 0930 local the *Bahia Paraiso* sailed slowly in a force 10 gale into Cumberland East Bay. It was probably the original intention to land Argentine marines at Grytviken at about the same time as the invasion of the Falklands but bad weather prevented this. After sending a radio message to the British troops saying that the ship would return the next morning, the *Bahia Paraiso* left to anchor in Stromness Bay. Word was sent to *Endurance*, which turned around and headed back towards South Georgia as she could be of no use in the Falklands once the invasion had taken place.

Meanwhile in the UK, news of the Argentine invasion rocked the nation. The British response was as swift as it was dramatic. A Task Force was to be organised with all possible speed for dispatch to the South Atlantic to recover the British territory that had been invaded by Argentina. The most up-to-date contingency plans for just such an eventuality had been drawn up as recently as September 1981. The plans had to take into account the 20-day transit time to the Falklands as well as the huge logistic effort required to keep even a small force supplied at such a distance.

The code name for the military response was Operation 'Corporate', perhaps reflecting the joint nature of the force being put together. Admiral Sir John Fieldhouse, Commander-in-Chief Fleet, was placed in overall command of the operation as commander of Task Force 317, which consisted of all surface ships, land and air forces, and Task Force 324, which consisted of submarine forces allocated to the operation. Operation 'Corporate' was very much a tri-service affair, although it is true to say that the Royal Navy had the lion's share of the resources and command positions assigned to the task forces. Air Marshal Sir John Curtiss, AOC 18 Group, was Admiral Fieldhouse's air commander and Major General Sir Jeremy Moore, Major General Royal Marines Commando Forces, was his Land Forces Deputy. Command headquarters was at Admiral Fieldhouse's headquarters at Northwood in Middlesex, which was also the headquarters of 18 Group. Major General Moore was later sent to command land forces assigned to the Task Force as Commander Land Forces, Falkland Islands and his place taken by Lieutenant General Sir Richard Trant.

Originally the land forces were to consist of just 3 Commando Brigade of the Royal Marines, commanded by Brigadier J H A Thompson. However, when the Argentines started reinforcing the Falklands with large numbers of troops, the 5th Infantry Brigade, commanded by Brigadier M J A Wilson, was also dispatched south. Commodore M C Clapp was appointed as Commodore Amphibious Warfare to control the all-important amphibious landings phase of the operation.

Fortunately there was already the makings of a naval task force readily available and at sea because of Exercise 'Springtrain', an annual major naval exercise that had commenced in the Gibraltar Exercise Area under the command of Rear Admiral John 'Sandy' Woodward on 26th March. On 2nd April ten of the participating ships were ordered to make for the South Atlantic immediately. This group became known as the Advanced Group and consisted of the destroyers HMS *Antrim*, HMS *Coventry*, HMS *Glamorgan*, HMS *Glasgow* and HMS *Sheffield*, the frigates HMS *Arrow*, HMS *Brilliant* and HMS *Plymouth* and the RFA tankers *Appleleaf* and *Tidespring*. Of the ten vessels *Antrim*, *Plymouth* and *Tidespring* (later joined by *Brilliant*) were later detached to form a small task group to recover South Georgia. 'Sandy' Woodward was appointed commander of the Task Groups in the South Atlantic, in effect becoming the in-theatre commander, and transferred from *Glamorgan* to *Hermes* on 15th April.

At home ports in the UK other ships received notification of deployment. The aircraft carrier *Hermes* had just returned to Portsmouth and her decks had to be hurriedly cleared of scaffolding intended for maintenance work in order to allow the eight Sea Harrier FRS1s of 800 Squadron to re-embark from RNAS Yeovilton later in the afternoon of the 2nd. Three more Sea Harriers arrived on board on 4th April and the last of 800 Squadron's 12 assigned aircraft landed on board the carrier shortly after it set sail on the 5th.

Many of the personnel of 801 Squadron had to be recalled from leave on the 2nd but all was ready and prepared for the full complement of eight Sea Harriers to embark on *Invincible* in Portsmouth harbour on the 4th, in time for the aircraft carrier to set sail the following day. The RAF's first contribution to Operation 'Corporate' was the dispatch of four Hercules C1 transport aircraft (XV189, XV196, XV304 and XV306) from Lyneham to Gibraltar on the 2nd.

3rd April (Saturday)

On the 3rd the focus of attention moved back to South Georgia. In the early hours of Saturday morning the Argentine frigate *Guerrico* arrived off Leith to join the *Bahia Paraiso*. Both ships then sailed for Grytviken and at 1400 hours the *Bahia Paraiso's* Alouette III flew off on a reconnaissance and the Puma started to airlift the first load of 20 marines to assault the British positions at Grytviken. The Alouette III was flown by Teniente de Navio Remo Busson with Teniente de Fregata Guillermo Guerra as observer and Sub Segundo Julio Gatti as crewman. The helicopter circled for about ten minutes, apparently not able to see the British troops who were well dug-in near the shoreline.

The *Bahia Paraiso* then entered Cumberland East Bay and the ship's captain radioed ashore with an offer of a cease-fire. Shortly afterwards the *Guerrico* sailed close to shore past King Edward Cove and almost simultaneously the Alouette III landed five marines close to Lieutenant Mills who was waiting on a jetty. Moments later the Puma arrived over King Edward Point and prepared to land a contingent of marines. As the helicopter settled into the hover just a few feet above the ground the Royal Marines opened fire from their concealed positions and scored dozens of hits on the helicopter. The pilot, Primer Teniente Juan Villagra, and his co-pilot, Primer Teniente Eduardo Leguizamon, skilfully managed to fly the damaged helicopter across to the far side of the cove where it crash-landed and rolled over. With two marines dead and all the other occupants of the helicopter wounded, the assault had started badly for the Argentines.

As the Alouette III returned to the *Bahia Paraiso* to collect more marines the *Guerrico* re-entered the cove, firing her 100mm and 40mm guns at the British positions. However, the frigate came under withering return fire from small arms and rocket launchers and was badly damaged. During the firefight the Alouette III made a total of 15 trips, landings marines at various points on the shoreline as well as evacuating the wounded from the crashed Puma. The Alouette III was hit by machine gun fire but sustained only minor damage.

Eventually, despite taking more casualties, the Argentine forces gained the upper hand as the *Guerrico* started to register accurate fire with her 100mm gun. Lieutenant Mills realised that his men had put up an excellent fight, but that to continue would be futile and would endanger the BAS civilians at Grytviken, so he surrendered after a firefight that had lasted over two and a half hours. Just one Royal Marine had been wounded.

As the brief battle for Grytviken was in its final stages, *Endurance* was rounding the southern tip of South Georgia. Captain Barker dispatched a Wasp HAS1 (XS527 flown by Lieutenant Commander Tony Ellerbeck and Lieutenant David Wells), which flew up the coast and landed in the hills just behind Grytviken, from where the crew observed the two Argentine ships in the bay below.

Having arrived at about the time of the surrender, the Wasp crew returned to *Endurance* to report. The captain was restrained from taking further action as the ship's value as a reconnaissance asset was too great to risk losing at this point. *Endurance* sailed north on 5th April and rendezvoused with *Fort Austin* on the 12th for replenishment before joining up with *Antrim*, *Plymouth* and *Tidespring* on the 14th. These three vessels had been detached from the Advanced Group of the Task Force to retake South Georgia under the operation code name 'Paraquat'.

In the Falklands itself the final phase of 'Aries 82', the initial deployment by air of the Argentine garrison, took place on the 3rd. Once again, C-130s and F-28s flew in supplies, ammunition and personnel from bases on the mainland. However, the airlift into the Falklands resumed a short while later with greater intensity when it was realised that the UK was going to attempt to regain the islands, and forces on the Falklands were considerably reinforced.

Also on the 3rd the first of two CANA Grumman S-2E Trackers from the Escuadrilla Antisubmarina was detached to Stanley from the *25 de Mayo* to fly reconnaissance and survey flights around the Falklands for the new military governor. These aircraft were used to look for potential new bases for Argentine aircraft, and one such site found was the existing small landing strip at Pebble Island. Both aircraft returned to Espora air base on 13th April.

An RAF VC10 C1 (XV106) of 10 Squadron flew to Montevideo in Uruguay to collect Governor Rex Hunt and the Royal Marines who had been captured on the Falklands. The aircraft departed Montevideo the next day and arrived at RAF Brize Norton, via a stopover at Ascension Island, on the morning of the 5th.

4th April (Sunday) – The UK Prepares

As the Argentine occupying forces continued to consolidate their positions in the Falkland Islands and South Georgia, frenetic activity was taking place back in the UK as the main group of the Task Force prepared to depart. At 0940Z the peace of Palm Sunday morning in Portsmouth was shattered when eight Sea Harriers arrived to land vertically onto the deck of *Invincible*. Three more Sea Harriers arrived from Yeovilton to embark on *Hermes*. The two

squadrons were brought up to their war strength by the transfer of aircraft from the Yeovilton training squadron (899) and by the use of trials aircraft.

In addition to the Sea Harriers, both aircraft carriers had a full complement of helicopters. Nine Sea King HC4 utility helicopters of 846 Squadron had embarked on *Hermes* from Yeovilton on the 3rd along with nine Sea King HAS5s of the ship's resident ASW unit, 826 Squadron, which flew from their base at RNAS Culdrose the same day. *Invincible* was better placed in that the nine Sea Kings HAS5s of 820 Squadron were already embarked on board the ship at Portsmouth before the warning order came through on 2nd April, but two additional helicopters were flown on board that day. The aircraft carrier had just returned from taking part in Exercise 'Alloy Express' off Norway, so its crew was well experienced in operating in the cold weather conditions they would face in the South Atlantic.

It was not only in ships that aircraft were being embarked for the South Atlantic. A major factor in the mounting of Operation 'Corporate' was the use of Ascension Island as a staging post for the Fleet and for aircraft transiting south. Situated some 4,260 miles from the UK and 3,915 miles from the Falklands, the island was the most suitable location available for use as a staging base. Although a British possession, the Americans had built a 10,000ft runway in 1942 to enable the base to be used as a staging post for aircraft being ferried to North Africa and the Mediterranean. Under a leasing agreement with the UK the US continued to operate the airfield as a staging post for Military Airlift Command transport aircraft and to support a communications and satellite-

tracking station located on the island.

Ascension Island became the major forward operating base for Operation 'Corporate' ships and aircraft en route to and from the South Atlantic. Although over 2,000 miles from Argentina, the facilities on the island were nevertheless potentially vulnerable to surprise attack by naval or air forces and therefore had to be defended. Consequently, Harrier GR3s equipped with Sidewinder air-to-air missiles provided air defence until relieved by Phantom FGR2s and an air surveillance radar was set up to provide radar cover. An RAF Regiment squadron protected the airfield and provided additional air defence with its Rapier missiles. A Royal Navy warship was assigned guardship duties around Ascension Island and Nimrods flew daily patrols to monitor shipping movements within 400 miles of the island.

Ascension Island was also a vitally important communications centre, storage depot, and maintenance base for aircraft. Almost all the ships of the Task Force stopped at Ascension Island for the transfer of stores, for replenishment and for training. A huge amount of matériel was flown into Wideawake airfield on Ascension Island on a daily basis. In addition to the allocation of matériel arriving by air, much of the equipment already on board the hastily loaded ships of the Task Force had to be transferred to other ships to ensure that each vessel had what it needed for the campaign.

The requirements soon outstripped the meagre facilities at Wideawake airfield, which was used to only two or three flights a week, and facilities had to be rapidly upgraded, including accommodation for aircraft and personnel and the supply of

Short Belfast G-BFYU entered service with Heavylift Cargo Airlines just two months before the invasion of the Falklands and flew eight sorties to Ascension Island during the conflict, three of them carrying helicopters. These huge aircraft had been prematurely retired from RAF service in 1976 following a stringent round of defence budget cuts. C M Hobson

vital aviation fuel. Aircraft movements at Wideawake eventually peaked at about 400 a day as the Task Force ships staged through. Helicopters were going to be vital to meet this massive logistics challenge. Two Westland Wessex HU5s (XT468 and XT765) from 845 Squadron were stripped down for air transportation and a Short Belfast (G-BEPE) belonging to Heavylift Cargo Airlines arrived at Yeovilton on the 3rd to load the helicopters for the journey to Ascension Island. The Belfast had, until 1976, been one of the RAF's strategic air transports and was the only RAF aircraft of its day with an outsize load-carrying capability. It was ironic that the MoD should now have to lease back these huge aircraft to transport helicopters to Ascension.

Piloted by Captain Keith Sissons, the well-known B-17 Flying Fortress display pilot, the Belfast took off from Yeovilton on the 4th with the two Wessex on board and arrived at Ascension Island on the 5th after stopping for the night at Dakar in Senegal. The two Wessex were destined for deployment aboard *Fort Austin*, which was being prepared for a rendezvous with *Endurance*.

As the aircraft carriers and various other ships were being readied for departure, two nuclear-powered submarines, HMS *Conqueror* and HMS *Courageous*, slipped quietly out of Faslane and headed for the

South Atlantic. One of these boats was destined to make history just four weeks later.

5th April (Monday)
On 5th April the main element of the Carrier Battle Group of the Task Force set sail for the South Atlantic from Portsmouth and Devonport. At 1015Z the carrier *Invincible* left Portsmouth harbour to a rousing send-off by thousands of spectators who lined the harbour walls and shoreline. She was followed 30 minutes later by *Hermes* and then by RFA *Pearleaf*, a support tanker that was to accompany the aircraft carriers. Crowds at Devonport saw the departure of the frigates HMS *Alacrity* and HMS *Antelope* that were to escort the aircraft carriers, along with the Fleet tanker RFA *Olmeda*.

As *Hermes* sailed down the English Channel, 800 Squadron's twelfth and final Sea Harrier FRS1 (XZ455), still in 899 Squadron colours, was flown on board by Flight Lieutenant Bertie Penfold. Having transferred eight aircraft and 11 pilots to the two carrier-based squadrons, 899 Squadron, the Sea Harrier FRS1 training squadron, virtually ceased to exist at Yeovilton. The pilots on board *Hermes* included the squadron's own commanding officer, Lieutenant Commander N W Thomas, who was attached to 800 Squadron.

The two aircraft carriers embarked a total of 49 aircraft for Operation 'Corporate'. *Hermes* had 12 Sea Harrier FRS1s of 800 Squadron, nine Sea King HAS5s of 826 Squadron and nine Sea King HC4s of 846 Squadron, while *Invincible* had eight Sea Harrier FRS1s of 801 Squadron and 11 Sea King HAS5s of 820 Squadron. Once *Invincible* had set sail, two of her Sea Harriers flew off and dropped a number of 1,000lb retard bombs within the sea range located off the Isle of Wight. This was the first time that this type of bomb had been dropped live by the Sea Harrier.

10 Squadron dispatched its first VC10 flight to Ascension Island on the 5th when XV109 took off from Brize Norton with a load of freight and returned the next day. As Belfast G-BEPE arrived at Wideawake airfield on Ascension Island on the 5th, another Heavylift Belfast (G-BFYU) took off from Yeovilton carrying Wessex HU5s XT464 and XT473, which were to be embarked on *Tidespring* for Operation 'Paraquat', the recovery of South Georgia. The Belfast arrived at Ascension Island on the 6th, and the Wessex were reassembled

and flown on board *Tidespring* on the 11th. Neither of the helicopters would make the return journey back to the UK.

Another helicopter that would not make a return journey to its point of origin was a Bell 212 of the Argentine Air Force's Grupo 7 de COIN, the first Argentine helicopter to be based on the Falklands. This helicopter was flown into Stanley on the 5th in a C-130 and was to be used in the SAR role. The Seccion Operativa de Busqueda y Salvamento (SOBS) was formed on this day to control SAR forces in the Falklands and along the coast of Argentina. In addition to helicopters the Argentines also used a number of fixed-wing aircraft for SAR patrols from the mainland, including three civil-registered Mitsubishi Mu-2 light transports that were impressed into service as part of Escuadron Fenix.

The RAF deployed its first aircraft detachment as part of Operation 'Corporate' on the 5th. Two Nimrod MR1s (XV244 and XV258) from 42 Squadron left RAF St Mawgan for Lajes in the Azores and completed the flight to Ascension Island on the 6th in preparation for their first operational mission the next day.

6th April (Tuesday)
The first major element of the Amphibious Group of the British Task Force left the UK on the 6th. RFA *Sir Percivale* had departed Marchwood on the 5th but three other LSLs, RFA *Sir Galahad*, RFA *Sir Geraint* and RFA *Sir Lancelot*, set sail on the 6th. Each of the four LSLs carried three helicopters of 3 Commando Brigade Air Squadron (3 CBAS), all Westland Gazelle AH1s except for three Westland Scout AH1s that were embarked on *Sir Lancelot*. The two other LSLs would eventually join the Amphibious Group but *Sir Tristram* was in Belize and *Sir Bedivere* was in Vancouver and would take several weeks to arrive off the Falklands.

HMS *Fearless*, one of the Royal Navy's two assault ships and the Task Force's designated Amphibious Headquarters Ship, also sailed on the 6th and also carried three Scouts of 3 CBAS, bringing the total number of Royal Marine helicopters embarked to 15. As *Fearless* passed Portland the ship also embarked three Sea King HC4s of 846 Squadron, which brought on board the headquarters staffs of 3 Commando Brigade and the Commodore Amphibious Warfare.

The Argentine AN/TPS-43F radar that was brought to Stanley on 6th April enabled the Argentines to avoid many of the Sea Harrier CAPs and to estimate the location of the British Task Force at sea. MoD

Three of the RAF's new 18 Squadron Chinook HC1s (ZA670, ZA679 and ZA716) flew from RAF Odiham to Culdrose on the 6th to assist in the last-minute loading of Task Force ships at Devonport. Another Chinook (ZA706) joined the other three on the 7th.

Within hours of leaving Portsmouth on the 5th, *Invincible* developed a problem with one of her starboard engine gearbox couplings. A new coupling was flown out to the aircraft carrier by one of the Chinooks (ZA679) on the 6th and it was fitted between the 8th and the 15th, with the ship sailing at reduced speed on just two of its four Olympus gas turbines.

Three Westland Lynx HAS2s (XZ242, XZ247 and XZ730) were embarked on *Fort Austin* at Ascension Island on the 6th. The helicopters had been transported to Ascension from Yeovilton on the 4th inside RAF Hercules and all three were later distributed to other ships of the Task Force. The two 845 Squadron Wessex HU5s that arrived at Ascension Island on the 5th also embarked on board *Fort Austin* during the next two days.

By the 6th the Argentine AN/TPS-43F radar had been set up on Sapper Hill, just southwest of Stanley and started to provide radar coverage out to a radius of 240 miles. This radar and its skilful operators would become a major thorn in the side of the Task Force as it provided excellent information on aircraft movements around the islands. However, like most radars of this vintage, it did not offer good coverage of low-level targets. About four days after it became operational the radar antenna was blown over in a strong wind, which led to the radar being moved to a more sheltered spot on the outskirts of Stanley itself, where it was also largely immune to bombing due to the proximity of civilian buildings.

7th April (Wednesday) – Argentina Reinforces the Falklands

On 7th April the UK declared a 200-mile Maritime Exclusion Zone (MEZ) around the Falkland Islands, to come into effect from 0400 hours on 12th April. Any Argentine ship that entered this zone would be liable to attack. Meanwhile the reinforcement of the Argentine garrison on the Falkland Islands continued. On 6th April two Pumas and an Agusta A-109A Hirundo from CAB601 had flown from their base at Campo de Mayo to the naval airfield at Comodoro Rivadavia, and from there they embarked on board the *Bahia Paraiso*, which had returned from South Georgia. The ship sailed for the Falklands and the three helicopters took off from the vessel early the next morning and flew the remainder of the way to Stanley where they set up home at the former Royal Marine barracks at Moody Brook.

As well as the CAB601 helicopters, another helicopter arrived at Stanley on the 7th in the shape of an Argentine Air Force CH-47C Chinook (H-93) from Grupo 7 de COIN's Escuadron Helicopteros, which flew a three-hour non-stop flight from Rio Gallegos to arrive at Stanley in a howling gale. The Chinook joined the Bell 212 of the SOBS unit under the command of Mayor O Posse Ortiz de Rosas.

The Nimrod detachment at Wideawake flew its the first operational sortie on 7th April when a Nimrod MR1 (XV258), captained by Flight Lieutenant J G Turnbull, flew a 6 hour 45 minutes sortie, the first of an eventual 111 Nimrod sorties to be flown from Ascension. Over the next week the 42 Squadron detachment flew six more long-range sorties before being replaced by two Kinloss Wing Nimrod MR2s. The longest sortie flown by a 42 Squadron Nimrod was a 9 hour 50 minute flight on 11th April.

8th April (Thursday)

On 8th April another flight by a Heavylift Belfast (G-BFYU) brought a brand-new Sea King HC4 (ZA312) to Ascension Island. The helicopter was fresh from temporary storage at Culdrose and was assigned to 846 Squadron, but its initial task was to assist in the movement of supplies to and from the ships that would soon start to arrive at Ascension Island. Known as Helicopter Delivery Service, or simply HDS in naval parlance, the movement of supplies was critical to the operation at Ascension Island, especially as much matériel also had to be moved between ships to ensure that each ship had the correct stores and sufficient supplies. This had not always been possible to ensure in the hurried departure from the UK. The Sea King was reassembled and commenced its two-week spell of HDS duties on 11th April. It was joined by a pair of Wessex HU5s (XT451 and XT460) of 845 Squadron, which arrived in another Belfast (G-BEPE) on the 9th. These two helicopters would spend almost a month at Ascension Island performing HDS duties for the Fleet.

As the aircraft carriers proceeded south the air squadrons started their intensive programme of training and a planning meeting took place between the staffs of *Hermes*, the flagship, and *Invincible* to plan the way forward. During the 8th an 820 Squadron Sea King dropped a live depth charge, while 801 Squadron Sea Harriers fired the unit's first 2-inch rockets at a splash target towed by *Invincible*.

9th April (Friday)

By 9th April the original section of four Pucaras that had flown to Stanley on the 2nd had been increased to 12 aircraft and the operating unit titled Escuadron Aeromovil Pucara under the command of Mayor Miguel Navarro. Also on the 9th another CAB601 Puma and an Agusta A-109A arrived at Stanley, having been ferried part of the way to the islands by ship.

The three airfields that came to be used by the Argentine forces on the Falklands received new names. Stanley became BAM (Base Aerea Militar) Malvinas, while Goose Green became BAM Condor and the strip at Pebble Island became EAN (Estacion Aeronaval) Calderon.

Fort Austin set sail from Ascension Island on the 9th for her rendezvous to replenish *Endurance*. In addition to carrying three Lynx and two Wessex helicopters the ship

A Wessex HU5 undergoes maintenance at Wideawake airfield on Ascension Island. Nine Wessex spent a cumulative total of 146 days at Ascension performing logistics task for the Task Force ships as they staged through the island base. MoD

was also carrying about 120 troops of a combined SAS/SBS force, some of whom were to play a major role in the retaking of South Georgia. Meanwhile Lieutenant Commander Nigel 'Sharkey' Ward, the commanding officer of 801 Squadron, tossed a 1,000lb VT fused bomb as part of his squadron's training programme.

10th April (Saturday)

Two more CAB601 helicopters arrived at Stanley on the 10th, including the first of nine Bell UH-1H Iroquois (AE-409) that would be deployed to the Falklands. The first group of Hueys left Campo de Mayo on the 7th and flew in stages to Espora. On the 9th AE-409 was flown to San Antonio West and from there to the *Bahia Paraiso* for the overnight trip to the Falklands. During its first day on the Falklands AE-409 flew more than six hours on urgent logistics tasks. The other Argentine Army helicopter to arrive in the Falklands on the 10th was the third and final A-109A. By this date the Argentine garrison had four Pumas, three A-109As, and single examples of the UH-1H, Chinook and Bell 212, with a second CH-47C arriving the next day and a second Bell 212 on the 13th.

Meanwhile the British Task Force was continuing its intense preparation and training schedule as it sailed south. On the 10th a Sea Harrier of 801 Squadron flown by Lieutenant Alan Curtis fired a live AIM-9G Sidewinder missile, which scored a direct hit on a LEPUS flare. Supplies of the more advanced AIM-9L version of the Sidewinder were en route to Ascension Island where they would be loaded onto the aircraft carriers. The AIM-9L had an all-aspect capability which meant that the missile could, in theory, be fired head-on rather than from the target's six o'clock position. As it transpired, most air-to-air combat engagements with Argentine aircraft resulted in the Sea Harriers approaching their targets from behind.

Also on this date a programme was commenced to repaint all the Sea Harriers and helicopters in order to remove all areas of white paint as well as superfluous titling and badges, leaving only the aircraft serial and code in black or dark blue. The undersides of the Sea Harriers were painted in Extra Dark Sea Grey to reduce their visibility from below.

The three ships that had been detached from the Advanced Group for the recovery of South Georgia (*Antrim*, *Plymouth* and *Tidespring*) arrived at Ascension Island on the 10th and spent the next two days taking on stores before proceeding south. These were the first of more than 60 ships of the Task Force to stage through this vitally important base. Some of the vessels visited Ascension Island on more than one occasion during the conflict.

11th April (Sunday) – The Air Bridge

With the growing awareness that a strong British Task Force was on its way to the Falklands and the imminent imposition of the MEZ by the British Government, the problem of resupply and reinforcement of Argentine forces soon became acute. Any shipping making for the Falklands would soon be liable to attack by the Royal Navy's submarines. Such was the fear of submarine attack that the cargo ship *Cuidad de Cordoba*, which was about to leave the port of Puerto Deseado for Stanley, was unloaded and her cargo, assessed as the equivalent of 100 sorties by C-130, taken by road to Comodoro Rivadavia.

Eight more CAB601 UH-1Hs arrived at Comodoro Rivadavia from Espora on the 11th, ready to embark on a ship and be transported to the Falklands. However, it was deemed too risky to send the helicopters by sea so they were partially disassembled for carriage in C-130s to Stanley airport, an operation that did not commence until the 18th.

On the 11th the Argentines instigated the Punte Aereo (air bridge) from the mainland to the Falklands as a direct result of the British imposition of the MEZ around the Falklands. The bulk of supplies, men and equipment was to have been taken to the Falklands by sea but the risk from British submarines now forced a change of plan. Argentine military and civil transport aircraft started to ferry troops and equipment to Stanley at an ever-increasing rate. Aircraft taking part in the air bridge included Air Force C-130s, Fokker F-27s and F-28s, Navy Lockheed Electras and F-28s, LADE F-27s, and civilian-registered Boeing 737s and BAC 1-11s.

Other events were taking place on the Argentine mainland in preparation for war. Twelve A-4C Skyhawks from Grupo 4 de Caza flew from their base at El Plumerillo, Mendoza to the small civilian airport at San Julian in Santa Cruz province, one of the closest Argentine airfields to the Falklands. This rough and ready airfield presented many problems for the Argentine Air Force units that operated from the airfield. It required aluminium planking to extend the limited ramp space and also had to have its communications facilities upgraded. By the end of April the temporary base was ready and the A-4Cs were flying regular combat training missions from San Julian.

The remaining seagoing element of the Advanced Group (*Arrow*, *Brilliant*, *Coventry*, *Glamorgan*, *Glasgow* and *Sheffield*) arrived at Ascension Island on the 11th. After replenishment, five of the ships continued their journey south three days later; the destroyer *Glamorgan* was sent north to meet and reinforce the Carrier Battle Group.

12th April (Monday)

At 0400 hours the British MEZ came into force around the Falkland Islands. This move had two immediate effects. Firstly, it restated the UK's claim to sovereignty over the Falkland Islands; and secondly, it severely restricted the movement of Argentine troops, equipment and supplies by sea to the islands as, theoretically at least, any Argentine vessel found within 200 miles of the Falklands could now be torpedoed and sunk. Meanwhile, on the islands themselves, Argentine Army troops were being deployed to defensive positions by the CAB601 helicopters, assisted by the Air Force Chinook and Bell 212.

On 12th April the ships of the South Georgia Task Group (TG317.9) left Ascension and sailed south to put into effect Operation 'Paraquat'. TG317.9 consisted of *Antrim* with a Wessex HAS3 (XP142), *Plymouth* with a Wasp HAS1 (XT429) and *Tidespring* with two Wessex HU5s of 'C' Flight 845 Squadron (XT464 and XT473 that had arrived from the UK on 6th April).

On the 12th *Endurance* rendezvoused with *Fort Austin* to be replenished with stores and ammunition. *Fort Austin*'s two embarked Wessex HU5s (XT468 and XT765 of 'B' Flight 845 Squadron) and *Endurance*'s two Wasp HAS1s moved troops and several tons of stores from the RFA to *Endurance* during the transfer process. Two days later, *Endurance* (which was overflown by two Soviet Tu-95 'Bear' maritime reconnaissance aircraft on the 12th) rendezvoused with the other ships of the Task Group before they all proceeded south for the week-long journey to South Georgia. The Task Group was later joined (on the 24th) by *Brilliant* with two Lynx HAS2s (XZ721, a Sea Skua-capable helicopter that had been collected at Ascension Island after being flown from the UK in a Hercules; and XZ729). Captain Brian Young of *Antrim* was appointed overall Task Group commander for the South Georgia operation.

Within the Carrier Battle Group the Sea Harriers and helicopters continued their busy training schedule. On the 12th 800 Squadron started five days of bombing and anti-shipping strike practise and also started to learn about ground attack and close air support – a new task for the Sea Harrier pilots and difficult to accomplish while flying over the sea! The helicopters practised ASW and other tasks and 820 Squadron's engineers designed and built a mounting for a GPMG to be fitted in the open doors of their Sea Kings. A similar mounting was also designed and fitted locally to the Lynx helicopters of the Task Force.

The Sea Harriers of 801 Squadron flew sorties to enable *Invincible*'s Sea Dart fire control radar to be fine-tuned; a useful exercise for all concerned as both of the Argentine Navy Type 42 destroyers were also fitted with Sea Darts and so it enabled the British fighter pilots to distinguish the Sea Dart radar's signature.

13th April (Tuesday)
The first of the more capable Nimrod MR2s (XV230) with its advanced Searchwater radar arrived at Wideawake airfield on the 13th to replace the 42 Squadron MR1s. The first 42 Squadron aircraft to return home (XV258) took off from Ascension Island on the same day and arrived at RAF St Mawgan on the 15th, routing via Dakar and Gibraltar. The same day saw the redeployment of Argentine maritime patrol aircraft as the two S-2E Trackers that had been based at Stanley airport since the 3rd departed for Espora, their survey work of the Falklands having been completed.

By the 13th Argentine ships, including the *Cabo San Antonio*, *Bahia Buen Suceso*, *Rio Iguazu*, *Islas Malvinas*, *Formosa*, and *Rio Carcarana* had delivered about 10,000 troops to the Falklands. However, after this date very few Argentine ships ran the blockade to the Falklands; some of those that did so did not return to the mainland.

14th April (Wednesday) –
1 (Fighter) Squadron Prepares for War
The 14th saw another operational deployment on the Argentine mainland when the first of 12 A-4B Skyhawks of Grupo 5 de Caza flew from their base at Villa Reynolds

to Rio Gallegos, on the southernmost tip of the Argentine mainland.

Meanwhile, on the Falklands the SAR helicopters of the Argentine Air Force, two Chinooks and two Bell 212s, moved from Stanley airport to the airstrip at Goose Green, recently renamed BAM Condor. Although belonging to the Escuadron de Helicopteros Malvinas and under the direction of SOBS, the helicopters spent much of their time on logistics and reconnaissance tasks, as there was little call for SAR at this stage of the conflict. The huge load-carrying capability of the Chinooks was particularly useful in deploying troops and equipment to remote parts of the islands.

Excitement was generated on board the ships of the British Task Force on the 14th when a Soviet Navy Tu-95 'Bear D' reconnaissance-bomber made two low passes over the ships. The aircraft was thought to have flown from Luanda in Angola or Conakry in Guinea on the West African coast and was one of several visits by the Russians. Whether information gained on these overflights was ever passed to Argentina is not known.

The Sea Harriers from each aircraft carrier took turns to mount strikes on the 'opposing' aircraft carrier during the day. On the 14th the five ships of the Advanced Group, less *Glamorgan*, which had been sent to meet the aircraft carriers, left Ascension Island for the last leg of their journey to the Falklands. Probably few on board these ships imagined that two of the Type 42

destroyers of this Group, *Coventry* and *Sheffield*, would not make the return journey to the UK.

By the 14th plans for the inclusion of RAF combat aircraft in the Task Force were progressing well. Wing Commander Peter Squire, the commanding officer of 1 (Fighter) Squadron, Royal Air Force, had received a warning order as early as 8th April that his unit would be deployed to the South Atlantic as part of Operation 'Corporate'. It was thought that the expected attrition of Sea Harriers could not be made good without the addition of Harrier GR3s from the RAF. As the RAF Harrier squadrons specialised in ground attack and battlefield air interdiction, 1 Squadron would also take over much of the air-to-ground tasking, leaving the Sea Harriers to the air defence role for which they and their pilots were optimised. The Harrier GR3s were to operate from *Hermes* and the deployment would mark the first occasion that RAF aircraft had flown operationally from a Royal Navy aircraft carrier since the Second World War.

Nimrod MR2 XV260 was one of several Nimrods deployed from Kinloss and St Mawgan to Ascension Island during the Falklands conflict. The aircraft is seen here at Wideawake airfield with a Sea King HC4 and a visiting VC10 and Hercules in the background. MoD

On the 14th plans for modification of the Harriers were finalised between British Aerospace and the Ministry of Defence. These modifications consisted of protecting the airframe against saltwater corrosion; fitting deck lashing points; fitting an I-band transponder to enable identification by ships' radar; finding a means of aligning the Harrier's inertial navigation system (INS) while on a moving deck; and improving self-protection and air defence capability. The problem of aligning the aircraft's INS was at least partially solved by the development of the Ferranti Inertial Rapid Alignment Equipment (FINRAE), which was a trolley-mounted system that could align the INS on a pitching, rolling deck in the middle of the ocean. Self-protection was afforded by modifications to enable the mounting and firing of a pair of AIM-9G Sidewinders, the first trial installation taking place on 21st April. The first modification was completed at Wittering on 28th April and live firing trials took place on the range in Cardigan Bay on 30th April.

Another modification was the replacement of the RAF's 68mm SNEB rockets with the Royal Navy's 2-inch rockets, which were more resistant to the high electromagnetic fields present on aircraft carriers. Some Harrier GR3s were also fitted with the Blue Eric ECM pod in one of the two Aden 30mm gun pod mountings and AN/ALE-40 chaff/flare dispensers in a modified ventral access panel. In the event neither the Blue Eric pod nor the Sidewinder AAMs were used in combat by the GR3s.

The initial plan was for the RAF Harriers to embark on the converted aircraft transport, SS Atlantic Conveyor at Plymouth on 22nd April. However, it was then decided that the aircraft would fly to Ascension Island to meet the ship, thereby allowing an extra ten days' work-up time. This extra training involved each pilot making at least two take-offs from the ski-jump at Yeovilton, commencing on the 14th. Air combat training was also very much on the agenda and five Harriers deployed to RAF Binbrook on 15th April to fly against the Lightning squadrons based there. More realistic training was provided by a French Air Force Mirage III two-seater, which spent two days based at RAF Coningsby, and by French Navy Super Etendards. Several Sea Harrier pilots from 809 Squadron flew in the back seat of the Mirage while the aircraft was at Coningsby.

Ground crews meanwhile prepared and modified the Harriers for the deployment but 1 Squadron was already well practised in 'bare base' deployments, having frequently deployed to Norway, Cyprus and other overseas locations. Eight of 1 Squadron's pilots ferried Harriers from RAF Germany to Goose Bay in Labrador for an

air combat exercise during the second week in April as the West Germany-based Harrier pilots were not current in air-to-air refuelling procedures. This long-range ferry mission would prove to be useful practise for what lay ahead.

15th April (Thursday)
On 15th April Task Force 79 of the Argentine Navy left port for a major exercise to prepare itself for the coming conflict with the Royal Navy. The aircraft carrier, 25 de Mayo, carried eight A-4Q Skyhawks of 3 Escuadrilla de Caza y Ataque, four S-2E Trackers of the Escuadrilla Antisubmarina, and three Sea Kings of 2 Escuadrilla de Helicopteros. Alouette III and Lynx HAS23 helicopters were embarked on some of the other vessels accompanying the aircraft carrier. Three of the A-4Qs were equipped with the VLF Omega navigation system for accurate navigation over the ocean. Task Force 79 would spend the next two weeks working-up its combat procedures in anticipation of combat with the Royal Navy.

Meanwhile the small British Task Group en route to South Georgia was overflown by a Nimrod MR2 (XV230), which dropped a package containing secret orders for the Task Group commander on board Antrim. The orders came from Admiral Sir John Fieldhouse and included the final instructions for putting Operation 'Paraquat' into action. On the 15th Admiral Woodward and his staff were flown by Sea King HC4 from Glamorgan to the flagship Hermes that was approaching Ascension Island.

16th April (Friday)
The two aircraft carriers and their four attendant destroyers and frigates (Glamorgan, Alacrity, Broadsword and Yarmouth), together with the tanker Olmeda, arrived at Ascension Island at midday on the 16th. The Sea King HC4s of 846 Squadron immediately set about assisting the two Wessex and another Sea King already temporarily based at Wideawake airfield in the huge logistic shuffle to distribute stores amongst the ships.

Meanwhile the Sea Harriers continued their training, 800 Squadron attacking splash targets offshore and one aircraft firing an AIM-9G Sidewinder, which scored a direct hit on a LEPUS flare. A plan to conduct a mock attack on Wideawake airfield, to provide a further training opportunity for the Sea Harrier pilots, had to be scrapped due to the large number of transport aircraft and helicopter movements that would have been disrupted by such an action. In fact it was claimed that on the 16th, Wideawake airfield was the busiest airfield in the world, primarily as a result of the helicopters shuttling to and fro between ships and the shore.

17th April (Saturday)
While the British Task Force was en route to the Falklands there were numerous exchanges of helicopters among the Lynx-equipped ships. This was necessary due to the fact that the new Sea Skua anti-ship missile was just being introduced into the Lynx fleet and had not even been released for operational service when the Argentine invasion took place. Some of the Lynx fleet had been modified to carry the Sea Skua but others had yet to be modified and could not use the missile. Fort Austin carried three Sea Skua-equipped Lynx HAS2s, which she distributed to ships of the Advanced Group on the 17th. Arrow, Coventry and Glasgow each received a single Lynx in exchange for their non-Sea Skua capable helicopter, which were flown across to Fort Austin. All three helicopters would later be issued to other ships of the Fleet.

Meanwhile at Ascension Island the arrival of HMS Fearless, the first amphibious ship to arrive, added another three Sea King HC4s to the 846 Squadron helicopters from Hermes that were already assisting in the massive HDS effort. Later in the day, RFA Stromness and five of the LSLs also arrived at Ascension. Along with other ships that would arrive at Ascension over the next week, these vessels formed the Amphibious Group that would eventually take troops into Falkland Sound and land them at San Carlos, the chosen landing site.

During the stay off Ascension Island the vessels, troops and helicopters undertook a wide range of amphibious training, usually employing the helicopters of 3 CBAS that were being carried on board some of the ships. Some of the Royal Marine Gazelle AH1s that were embarked on the LSLs were fitted with SNEB rocket pods while at Ascension Island. The first flight trials of a Gazelle fitted with a SNEB pod had taken place at Yeovilton on 11th April followed by successful test firings at Larkhill the next day. While the LSLs were at Ascension, aircrew of 3 CBAS took the opportunity to fire a number of SNEB rockets at sea targets.

One other arrival at Wideawake on the 17th was a Nimrod MR2 (XV255). This aircraft replaced the last 42 Squadron MR1 (XV244), which departed for St Mawgan the same day.

18th April (Sunday)
More Argentine helicopters reached the Falklands on the 18th as the first UH-1H to be airfreighted into Stanley arrived on board a C-130. Other CAB601 Hueys arrived on the 21st, 22nd, 23rd and 29th of April. Also by the 18th the fifth and final Puma and the first of two CAB601 Chinooks had been ferried to Stanley from the mainland. The second Chinook (AE-521) arrived on 30th

April, on the very eve of the air war; however, the other Chinook (AE-520) was promptly grounded on 2nd May with a serious engine problem and did not fly again until just a few days before the surrender. CAB601 had 11 helicopters in service at its base at Moody Brook by 18th April.

Having spent two days replenishing and training off Ascension Island the Carrier Battle Group prepared to sail for the Falklands on the 18th. At 1300Z *Hermes* left Ascension Island accompanied by the destroyer *Glamorgan*, the frigates *Alacrity*, *Broadsword* and *Yarmouth*, the tanker *Olmeda* and the replenishment ship RFA *Resource*, for the 3,900-mile journey south to their ultimate destination. The departure was hastened by a report from *Olmeda* of a periscope that could have been from an Argentine submarine. An RAF Nimrod later reported seeing a school of whales that was thought to have caused the 'periscope' sighting. This was just the first of several such scares caused by these huge marine mammals during the next few weeks.

Invincible spent much of the day replenishing at sea and taking on 80 helicopter-loads of supplies before setting sail at 1745Z to catch up with the rest of the Task Force. 846 Squadron left five Sea Kings behind at Wideawake to assist with HDS duties, leaving just five helicopters on board *Hermes*. The helicopters left at Ascension Island would travel south later on other ships to rejoin the rest of 846 Squadron prior to the amphibious assault.

As the Carrier Battle Group was leaving Ascension Island the first RAF Handley Page Victor K2 tankers began to arrive at Wideawake airfield. Requiring in-flight refuelling themselves for the nine-hour flight from Marham, the Victors (XL163, XL189, XL192, XL511 and XM715) were joined the next day by four more aircraft (XH671, XL164, XL188 and XL232). In addition to their primary task of air-to-air refuelling, several of the Victor crews had been training in photographic reconnaissance and maritime radar reconnaissance (MRR), roles that the Victor SR2-equipped 543 Squadron had specialised in until disbanded in May 1974. For these missions the Victor crews were supplemented by radar navigators who had served with the recently disbanded 27 Squadron, which had specialised in the MRR role with modified Vulcan SR2s.

A minor accident occurred at Wideawake airfield on the 18th when a 10 Squadron VC10 C1 (XV102) throttled-up prior to taxying out for take-off and blew a set of passenger steps into the wing of a chartered British Airways Boeing 707-336C. The damage was patched up and the airliner (G-ASZF) was later flown back to Heathrow for further repairs. Another VC10 C1 (XR807) flew from Ascension Island to Brize Norton on the 18th after collecting a group of 35 Falkland Islanders from Montevideo. Argentina had deported these islanders from the Falklands as 'undesirables'. Yet another VC10 C1 (XV106) was in the process of collecting from Montevideo a group of 22 Royal Marines who had been captured in South Georgia along with seven stragglers from the Falklands who had evaded capture for several days.

19th April (Monday) –
The Super Etendard and the Exocet:
A Deadly Combination
When the vigorous British response made armed conflict appear all the more likely, CANA's 2 Escuadrilla de Caza y Ataque began an intensive training programme. The squadron had received its first five Super Etendard strike aircraft at its base at Espora on 17 November 1981 and was still

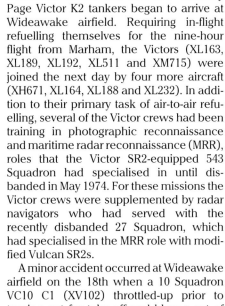

The Fleet replenishment ship Resource *is seen here on her way down south with one of her two 845 Squadron Wessex HU5s on the helicopter flight deck.* Cdr S Chelton

The importance of the Victor K2 tanker to the war effort is well illustrated by this photograph which shows a total of 12 Victors together with a solitary Phantom FGR2 on the pan of Wideawake airfield. All 12 Victors would be needed for a single 'Black Buck' mission. MoD

in the process of introducing the aircraft into operational service when the conflict broke out. By the end of March 1982 ten pilots had each achieved about 80 flying hours on the aircraft but still had a lot to learn about the Super Etendard and its AS39 Exocet anti-ship missile. Following the Argentine invasion, France immediately placed an embargo on the supply of arms to Argentina so the next five Super Etendards, although complete, were impounded and did not reach Argentina until six months after the end of the conflict. This also meant that 2 Escuadrilla de Caza y Ataque had just five AS39 Exocets for its Super Etendards. Despite strenuous efforts, Argentina was unable to obtain any more Exocets during the conflict.

From 1st April training was accelerated and focused on weapons delivery and using the Super Etendard's Agave radar. On the 19th two of the aircraft flew from Espora to Rio Grande, the squadron's temporary base for the duration of the conflict. Two more aircraft followed on the 20th while the fifth and final aircraft remained at Espora and was slowly cannibalised of parts to maintain the four aircraft at Rio Grande.

As soon as the unit was established at its new base it started to fly training missions which included a variety of mission profiles, most of them at very low level in radio and electronic emission silence. The missions were optimised to achieve maximum surprise by using the Super Etendard's performance and its advanced navigation system to approach the target and launch the Exocet before the aircraft could be detected. The Super Etendard, with its potent weapon, was the latest and most effective addition to Argentina's airborne armoury and would soon prove its value in combat. It says much for the skill, determination and training of the personnel of 2 Escuadrilla de Caza y Ataque that they were ready for action when required, despite receiving no help from the manufacturer in preparing the aircraft or its weapon after 1st April. Part of this training was a series of trials to see if the Super Etendard could be operated from runways as short as that of Stanley airport. The trials, undertaken on the mainland, proved that the aircraft could not land safely on a wet runway without the aid of runway arrester gear, which was not then available to the Argentines.

As the first two Super Etendards deployed to Rio Grande the two Grupo 1 KC-130H tankers deployed to nearby Rio Gallegos. The tankers had conducted a successful series of trials with the Super Etendards before the strike aircraft left Espora and it was anticipated that air-to-air refuelling would play a major role in the anti-ship missions. The two KC-130Hs were

the only tanker aircraft in service with the Argentine forces during the conflict and the limitations imposed by having just two such aircraft would become a major factor in the prosecution of Argentina's air campaign.

On the 19th the Argentine air bridge to the Falklands, the Punte Aereo, moved into high gear with military and civil transport aircraft bringing in troops, equipment and supplies that could not be brought by sea due to the threat of attack by Royal Navy submarines. Aircraft of the state airline, Aerolineas Argentinas, including Boeing 707s and 747s, transported troops to the mainland airheads at Comodoro Rivadavia and Rio Gallegos. From these bases Argentine Air Force, Navy and LADE transport aircraft ferried the men and equipment to Stanley airport. Between 19th and 25th April a total of 205 air transport flights arrived at Stanley from Comodoro Rivadavia (91 were flown by C-130s, 74 by F-28s, 36 by Aerolineas Argentinas Boeing 737s, and four by Austral BAC 1-11s). These flights brought in 1,544 tons of supplies and 2,844 troops. The air bridge operation ceased on 29th April when hostilities became imminent, but the C-130s carried on the vital resupply missions throughout the conflict.

One group of passengers flown into Stanley on the 19th consisted of 19 civilian members of the Cordoba Radio Club. These men had volunteered themselves and their equipment to help set up an air observers' network on the islands.

Meanwhile the nuclear-powered submarine *Conqueror* arrived off South Georgia on the 19th to reconnoitre the coastal waters prior to the arrival of the Task Group. The submarine sent a report back to Northwood for retransmission to the Task Group to report that no enemy shipping was visible around Leith or Cumberland East Bay.

20th April (Tuesday)
The Victor K2 detachment at Wideawake flew its first operational mission on 20th April, an MRR sortie to search for shipping and icebergs around South Georgia. Captained by Squadron Leader John G Elliott, XL192 took off at 0400Z, accompanied by three other Victor K2s to provide in-flight refuelling for the outbound leg of the flight. Elliott's aircraft was actually the reserve aircraft but he had to take over the mission when the lead aircraft developed equipment problems.

Elliott made his last tanker contact some 2,000 miles south of Ascension Island before climbing to 43,000ft to conserve fuel on the long journey south. On approaching South Georgia the Victor descended to 18,000ft as it commenced its radar sweeps of the ocean around the islands. Over 150,000 square miles was searched in 90 minutes before the aircraft climbed again

and headed north on its return journey to Ascension Island. Four more Victor tankers were launched to recover XL192, which flew over 7,000 miles in 14 hours and 45 minutes on this initial very long-range mission. At the time this was a record for RAF long-range air operations, but it was later beaten by several Vulcan, Hercules and Nimrod sorties. An important contribution to the long-range missions of all these aircraft was the fitting of Omega navigation equipment to enable accurate navigation over the sea. Elliot's mission confirmed that there were no Argentine ships or icebergs lying in wait for the South Georgia Task Group.

A VC10 C1 (XV106) of 10 Squadron visited Montevideo on the 20th to collect a party of 29 Royal Marines who had been captured on South Georgia and the Falklands together with 13 BAS scientists who had also been captured on South Georgia. The aircraft made a brief stop at Ascension Island before flying non-stop to Brize Norton on the 21st. Many of the Royal Marines captured early on in the conflict later returned to the South Atlantic to take part in the recapture of the islands.

Among the ships arriving at Ascension Island on the 20th were the P&O cruise liner RMS *Canberra*, the cargo ship MV *Elk*, and *Sir Tristram*, an LSL which had sailed direct from Belize.

Two days out from Ascension Island the Sea Harriers on board *Hermes* and *Invincible* were still flying training sorties but from the 20th two Sea Harriers, armed now with AIM-9L Sidewinders, were maintained on deck alert on each aircraft carrier, day and night. The AIM-9L all-aspect version of the Sidewinder had only just been introduced into the Royal Navy's inventory and stocks of the weapon were loaded onto the two aircraft carriers at Ascension Island to replace the rear-aspect only AIM-9Gs.

Since the 19th, throughout each day, fully armed Sea Kings flew ASW sorties ahead of the Task Force.

21st April (Wednesday) –
Operation 'Paraquat' Begins
The four ships that were tasked with the recovery of South Georgia (*Antrim*, *Plymouth*, *Endurance* and *Tidespring*) arrived off the islands in the midst of a storm force 10 on the morning of 21st April, after their seven-day transit from Ascension Island. The plan was for SBS troops to conduct a covert reconnaissance of the Grytviken/King Edward Cove/Cumberland East Bay area while troops of the SAS were to do the same around Leith, Husvik and Stromness. The main force of 'M' Company, Royal Marines would then be landed in response to the intelligence information gained by the Special Forces.

Antrim and *Tidespring* remained off-shore near Leith while *Endurance* and *Plymouth* sailed further south to conduct the SBS operations. Sixteen men of the SAS Mountain Troop were to be landed on top of the Fortuna Glacier from where they would trek about seven miles to observe Argentine troops at Leith and Stromness. This particular location was chosen as it was the least likely direction from which the Argentines would have expected an approach, but the site would pose tremendous difficulties for all the men involved.

At 0930 local Lieutenant Commander Ian Stanley took off from *Antrim* in a Wessex HAS3 (XP142, known affectionately as 'Humphrey') and flew a reconnaissance to ensure that conditions were suitable in the Fortuna Glacier area. The Wessex HAS3 was fitted with a computerised Flight Control System, which enabled it to be flown with greater precision and this, together with radar, Doppler and a better altimeter, enabled it to be used as a pathfinder for the more basic Wessex HU5 commando helicopters. Lieutenant Commander Stanley then returned to *Antrim* and at 1030 led the two 845 Squadron Wessex HU5s from *Tidespring* towards the selected landing point once they had picked up their load of troops from *Antrim*.

Wessex HU5 XT473 was flown by Lieutenant Mike Tidd, while XT464 was flown by an RAF pilot, Flight Lieutenant Andy Pulford. However, the first attempt to land the troops had to be abandoned as low cloud, driving rain and snowstorms made flying conditions impossible and the three helicopters had to return to their respective ships. At 1100 the weather improved sufficiently for a second reconnaissance flight to be made by XP142, this time carrying the two SAS commanders who had planned the reconnaissance mission and who now saw conditions on top of the glacier for themselves.

At 1145 the three helicopters started off on their second attempt to insert the 16 SAS soldiers of 'D' Squadron's Mountain Troop on the summit of the Fortuna Glacier. Despite appalling weather conditions the three helicopters threaded their way up the steep slope of the glacier, guided by the radar operator in XP142, and landed safely in the teeth of a gale with no discernible horizon and very little forward visibility. Once the soldiers had deplaned the three helicopters took off and made their way cautiously back down the glacier and out to sea to their ships. Unfortunately, weather conditions on the glacier deteriorated almost immediately, with storm force 10 winds gusting up to 70 knots which also caused minor damage to the ships at sea. By the morning of the 22nd it was obvious to the troops on the Fortuna Glacier that they could make little progress and could not remain there for much longer before they succumbed to exposure.

During the afternoon *Endurance*'s Wasp flew to a small hut at St Andrews Bay, a few miles south of Cumberland East Bay, to collect a BAS scientist who had valuable information about the area that the SBS were to reconnoitre. In the evening Lieutenant Commander Ellerbeck and Lieutenant Wells flew two sorties to Hound Bay to insert a section of SBS troops who were to make a reconnaissance of Cumberland East Bay and Grytviken. A further attempt to insert two more SBS soldiers in the early hours of the 22nd had to be aborted due to bad weather.

The decision to maintain Sea Harriers on deck alert from the 20th proved a wise one as the British Task Force received its first visit from an Argentine aircraft on the 21st. At 1130Z British radar picked up a contact at 160 miles range and Lieutenant Simon Hargreaves of 800 Squadron was scrambled in XZ460 to intercept the unidentified aircraft. The interception of an Argentine Air Force Boeing 707-389B (TC-91) took place at 35,000ft and a mutual photographic session then took place before the Boeing turned away to return to Argentina. The Boeing was flown by Vicecomodoro Jorge Ricardini, the most experienced pilot of Grupo 1 de Transporte Aereo's Escuadron II.

The Boeing's standard search pattern was a triangle starting from its temporary base at Ezeiza to Ascension Island in the north and South Georgia and the Falklands on the southern base of the triangle. Each flight would last up to 15 hours and was flown at 40,000ft for most of the way. The aircraft's standard weather radar was used to search for the British ships. On this first mission the Boeing found the Task Force about 1,400 miles east-northeast of Rio de Janeiro, just north of 20 degrees South, and radioed the information back to base before being intercepted by the Sea Harrier. The Boeing 707s turned up around dawn for the next few days until Argentina was told through diplomatic channels that the flights would no longer be tolerated.

Earlier in the day an RAF Hercules had flown from Ascension Island to make an airdrop to the Task Force. The load included a vital component for *Invincible's* Type 909 radar. This was the first of many long-range flights by RAF Hercules to airdrop equipment and personnel to the ships of the Task Force. Although still within range of Ascension Island, the Task Force would soon be out of range, leading to various modifications to extend the endurance of the Hercules. The loads dropped often included mail for the personnel on board the ships, an important factor in maintaining morale during the long weeks at sea.

Meanwhile at Ascension Island the five Sea Kings of 846 Squadron commenced amphibious operations training from *Canberra* and *Elk*, which had arrived off the island the previous day. The P&O cruise liner and the roll-on roll-off cargo ship had both been converted at Southampton and were now fitted with helicopter landing pads. *Canberra* carried over 2,000 troops of 3 Para, 40 Commando and 42 Commando while *Elk* transported Army vehicles and a few troops of HQ Company, 45 Commando.

22nd April (Thursday)

The Special Forces troops on the Fortuna Glacier radioed for evacuation on the morning of the 22nd as severe weather conditions made their position untenable. At 1050 local the weather conditions abated sufficiently for Lieutenant Commander Stanley in the Wessex HAS3 to lead off the two *Tidespring* Wessex HU5s to the glacier. Ian Stanley ordered the two helicopters to set down on flat ground at Cape Constance while he attempted to reach the troops on the glacier. However, he encountered thick cloud and very strong, constantly shifting winds and had to abandon the attempt. All three helicopters returned to their ships.

At 1330 the weather out at sea had improved enough for another attempt and Ian Stanley led Lieutenant Mike Tidd (in XT473) and Lieutenant Ian Georgeson (in XT464), each of whom flew with a crewman but no second pilot. In a brief spell of improved visibility the helicopters reached the glacier, picked up a SARBE signal and spotted smoke flares lit by the SAS troopers. The helicopters landed in high winds and quickly took on board the soldiers, six in each of the HU5s and four in the HAS3. However, the weather on the glacier was changing minute by minute and Tidd's Wessex took off just as a snow squall reached his position. Just moments after becoming airborne the helicopter was engulfed in a blizzard and Tidd was plunged into 'whiteout' conditions, unable to see anything outside, forwards or downwards. Seconds later the helicopter hit the ground, wiping off the port undercarriage leg and rolling onto its left side as it slid across the ice and snow. Miraculously the only injuries were a few cuts and bruises.

Seeing the crash, Ian Stanley and Ian Georgeson hover-taxied the half mile to the crash site as soon as the snow squall had passed and took on board the survivors. Ten minutes later the helicopters took off again, but just as they approached a ridge they encountered another snow squall. Ian Stanley cleared the ridge successfully and started to descend rapidly, relying on his radar altimeter and observer for ground clearance. Unfortunately, Ian Georgeson lost sight of the leading Wessex and was

Wessex HAS3 XP142 flown by Lieutenant Commander Ian Stanley made an immense contribution to the recapture of South Georgia. Having rescued the passengers and crew from two other Wessex, Ian Stanley then disabled the Santa Fe *and made several other rescues during the campaign. MoD*

engulfed in 'whiteout' conditions again. The Wessex HU5 hit a slight ridge and was twisted around before toppling over onto its starboard side. Once again, no one was seriously injured in the crash, but Ian Georgeson had to be cut free from his harness and extricated from the smashed cockpit.

This left only XP142 airborne so Ian Stanley took his load of troops to *Antrim* and took on blankets and medical supplies before lifting off again to fly back to the glacier. Carefully, he made his way up the side of the glacier in buffeting winds and poor visibility and although he contacted the survivors by radio he could not attempt a landing and so returned to *Antrim* after almost hitting a mountain and briefly losing tail rotor control. By 1630 the weather had improved a little and Stanley and his crew, together with the commanding officer of the SAS men who were trapped on the Fortuna Glacier, decided to attempt another rescue mission.

When they reached the glacier the weather was just as atrocious as it had been earlier. Nevertheless Stanley decided to climb up through the cloud, risking icing conditions, and eventually spotted the crashed XT464 lying on the ice. Realising that the survivors might not last a second night on the glacier and that a second mission that day was impossible because of the impending darkness, he decided to squeeze all 12 survivors into XP142. Overloaded by about 1,400lb, the helicopter took off and hugged the ground as it flew back down the glacier and out across the sea to *Antrim*. Despite a slightly heavy landing on *Antrim*'s heaving deck, the gamble paid off and very likely saved the lives of several men that day. Lieutenant Commander Stanley's outstanding flying skills won him a well-earned DSO while his crew of Sub Lieutenant S G Cooper (second pilot), Lieutenant C J Parry (observer), and Petty Officer Aircrewman D B Fitzgerald (crewman) all received a Mention in Dispatches.

Further south, the SBS patrol at Hound Bay had walked to the southeastern shore of Cumberland East Bay and one of *Endurance*'s Wasps airlifted two deflated Gemini boats and their engines to enable them to make a reconnaissance of the bay.

Reinforcements were on their way to South Georgia in the shape of *Brilliant* and her two Lynx helicopters. *Brilliant* had been

dispatched as soon as it was known that the two Wessex had been lost on the 22nd and headed for South Georgia at full speed. The ship had detached from the Advanced Group when 1,000 miles northeast of the Falklands on the 22nd after first swapping a Lynx HAS2 (XZ721) for a non-Sea Skua equipped example (XZ725) from *Sheffield*.

Another Victor K2 MRR sortie was flown to South Georgia from Ascension Island during the night of the 22nd/23rd by XL163, captained by Squadron Leader Martin D Todd. The aircraft was airborne for 14 hours and 5 minutes and plotted the position of British and Argentine ships in the area.

Meanwhile, the only excitement further north had occurred early in the morning at 0230Z, when the British Task Force detected an unidentified contact and Lieutenant Brian Haigh of 801 Squadron intercepted another Boeing 707 in the dark at 38,000ft some 60 miles from the aircraft carriers. Sixteen hours later, again in darkness, another Boeing 707 was intercepted, having been detected at a range of 120 miles. This time three Sea Harriers of 801 Squadron (flown by Lieutenant Commanders J Eyton-Jones and M Broadwater and Flight Lieutenant P Barton) were launched and they boxed-in the Boeing 707 in an attempt to emphasise the vulnerability of the Argentine aircraft should the British decide to take offensive action.

23rd April (Friday)

Following the aborted attempt to land SAS reconnaissance troops on the Fortuna Glacier, it was decided to use Gemini boats to take the troops to Grass Island in Leith harbour itself. Late on the 22nd *Antrim* edged her way into Stromness Bay and at 0330 local on the 23rd quietly launched five Gemini inflatable craft filled with men of the SAS's Boat Troop. *Antrim* then withdrew to the open sea but within minutes three of the Geminis suffered failures of their unreliable outboard motors and had to be towed by the remaining two in ever-worsening sea conditions

By morning, two of the Gemini boats had broken their tow and were missing, so Wessex XP142 was dispatched at 0810 local to search for them at first light on the 23rd. After about an hour and a half of anxious searching one of the boats was found drifting eight miles south along the coast. The occupants were quickly winched aboard the Wessex and returned to *Antrim*. The crew of the other boat was assumed to be missing believed drowned but miraculously turned up three days later!

Later during the morning of the 23rd an Argentine Air Force C-130 located three of the ships of the South Georgia Task Group. Another Hercules arrived over South Georgia about two hours later and started a low-level search of the northeast coast of the island. Later that afternoon electronic signals were picked up indicating that the *Santa Fe*, a patrol submarine, was in the vicinity of South Georgia. The *Santa Fe* had sailed from Mar del Plata on 16th April with 20 Argentine marines, reinforcements for the garrison on South Georgia. At this time *Tidespring* and *Plymouth* were well to the east and taking on fuel from RFA *Brambleleaf*, which had recently arrived direct from Mombasa, while *Antrim* was much closer to South Georgia.

Although a Second World War era diesel-powered boat and scheduled for retirement in July 1982, the *Santa Fe* represented a significant threat, so the tankers were ordered to stop fuelling and move further to the northeast. The two Wasps from *Endurance* flew a total of eight ASW sorties during the 23rd in an unsuccessful attempt to locate the enemy submarine.

With the discovery by Argentine C-130s and the submarine threat now apparent, it was decided to move forward plans to retake South Georgia. Operation 'Paraquat' had started off badly with the failure of the reconnaissance missions to both Leith and Stromness, and the loss of the only specialist assault helicopters available to the Task Group. It was decided that *Antrim* would move into Stromness Bay at first light on the 24th and put SAS troops ashore to capture Leith, while *Endurance* would return to

Hound Bay to support the SBS teams already ashore. However, the plan was scrapped when another Argentine C-130 was seen in the evening of the 23rd, thereby compromising *Antrim*'s position. Captain Young decided to take *Antrim* away from the coast to rejoin *Plymouth* and the RFAs and plan his next move.

Further north the British Task Force was once again visited by an Argentine Air Force Boeing 707 on a surveillance flight from Ezeiza. The aircraft was detected at 1100Z about 120 miles from the Task Force but the presence of Sea Harriers persuaded the Boeing to turn away before contact could be made. The same Boeing returned four hours later and approached to within five miles of *Invincible* despite being intercepted by a Sea Harrier.

On the same day, at around sunset, yet another unidentified contact was detected approaching the Task Group at high altitude from the southeast. Having by now had permission from Northwood to shoot down any Argentine surveillance aircraft that came too close, Admiral Woodward ordered *Invincible* to engage the target with her Sea Dart system. As the aircraft came closer to the Task Force, Admiral Woodward ordered that its route be checked and it was then realised that the aircraft was flying on a direct track between Rio de Janeiro and Durban and could be completely innocent. The launch of the Sea Dart was aborted just 20 seconds before the missile was due to be fired and a few minutes later a Sea Harrier intercepted the aircraft and confirmed that it was indeed a VARIG airliner on a regular commercial flight from Brazil. There was a good chance that if a Sea Dart had been fired it would have hit and destroyed the airliner, causing the sort of international furore that attended the Soviet shooting down of a Korean Air Lines Boeing 747-230B in September 1983 and the destruction of an Iran Air A300B2-203 by the USS *Vincennes* in July 1988. Luckily in this instance, sensible caution overcame the desire to rid the Task Group of an unwelcome shadower and reinforced the value of visual identification in such circumstances.

On the 23rd the British Task Force suffered its first aircraft loss and its first fatality. At 2113Z 846 Squadron Sea King HC4 ZA311 was returning to *Hermes* after a night VERTREP mission among other ships of the Carrier Battle Group when it crashed into the sea in bad weather and poor visibility. An 820 Squadron Sea King HAS5 (XZ574) located the Sea King's pilot, Flight Lieutenant R Grundy, in the water but, tragically, the aircrewman, Petty Officer Aircrewman K S Casey, was never found despite an extensive search by helicopters and three of the Task Force ships (*Yarmouth*,

Resource and *Olmeda*) that stayed in the area until well after daybreak. Sea King XZ574 was flown by Sub Lieutenant His Royal Highness The Prince Andrew, Sub Lieutenant C P Heweth, Lieutenant Commander I F McAllister and Leading Aircraftman T Arnull during the search for the crew of ZA311. *Yarmouth*'s Wasp HAS1 (XV624) was also involved in the search for the missing crewman.

24th April (Saturday)

Both of *Endurance*'s Wasps flew to Cumberland East Bay to recover the 12 men of the SBS observation teams, who had been unable to reconnoitre the bay as their inflatable boats were punctured by shards of flying ice blown from a nearby glacier by the fierce wind. Also on the morning of the 24th an Argentine Air Force Boeing 707 made a low-level reconnaissance of the South Georgia area and *Endurance*. As the ship was painted with a bright red hull (an aid to location in the Antarctic waters where the ship spent much of its time), it was not exactly difficult to see! Although it was not known at the time, *Endurance* was also seen by the *Santa Fe* on the morning of the 24th, but for some reason the submarine did not make an attack.

The Royal Navy Task Group that was assembled off South Georgia was about to be joined by the Type 22 frigate *Brilliant* during the night of the 24th, thereby completing all the elements required for the retaking of the island. However, the appearance of the Boeing 707 encouraged Captain Young to bring forward his new plan for the final assault on enemy forces on South Georgia, and *Antrim* and *Plymouth* headed back towards the coast at full speed.

Another Argentine Air Force Boeing 707 visited the Carrier Battle Group at 1550Z on the 24th and was once again intercepted by Sea Harriers from *Hermes* at a position about 80 miles to the east of the aircraft carrier. These surveillance flights were relaying valuable information about the composition and location of the British Task Force and after the interception on the 24th the Argentine Government was informed via Swiss diplomats than no further Boeing 707 overflights would be tolerated and that the aircraft would be shot down. The message was taken seriously and although the flights continued, they were flown much more cautiously in the future and usually kept a respectful distance from the British warships.

Soon after the Boeing 707 incident on the 24th the Carrier Battle Group joined up with the Advanced Group led by *Sheffield*. For much of the journey down south the Battle Group had fired chaff whenever an Argentine shadower approached them. This was done to delude the Argentines into thinking that the Battle Group was larger than it actually was and included the Amphibious Group, which was actually some weeks behind, and that an early landing could therefore take place. It is possible that the Argentines fell for this ploy as on 1st May they were initially convinced that an amphibious landing was taking place, even though there were no amphibious transports in the TEZ at the time.

Meanwhile on the Falklands the Argentine garrison continued to prepare its defences and receive reinforcements. On the 24th two Argentine Navy MB-339As and four T-34C-1 Turbo Mentors flew from Rio Grande to Stanley airport, with a Beech Queen Air 80 and a Beech Super King Air 200 respectively as navigational pathfinders. The first of ten MB-339As had been delivered to 1 Escuadrilla de Ataque at Punta Indio near Buenos Aires in 1980 and the type was still in the process of being bedded into service. Although classed as light attack and training aircraft, the MB-339As were at least able to operate from Stanley's short runway with safety – an advantage the type had over other jet combat aircraft in the Argentine inventory.

Neither the MB-339As nor the T-34C-1s were dispatched to Stanley with any clearly defined role and neither type possessed the firepower or performance to survive in a major conflict. There was almost certainly an element of Service rivalry involved in the decision to send these unsuitable aircraft to the Falklands as the Navy did not want the Air Force's Pucaras to be seen as the only aircraft involved in the occupation of the Malvinas. Under the command of Capitan de Corbeta Carlos Alberto Molteni, four MB-339As had deployed to Rio Grande as early as 2nd April to train closely with the 5th Marine Battalion in the close air support role and with Argentine Navy warships to practise anti-shipping operations. Other MB-339As were dispersed to the airfields at Comandante Espora, Trelew and Ushuaia to provide a surface attack capability if Royal Navy ships came close to Argentina's coast.

Earlier in the month Capitan Molteni had flown to Stanley several times in Navy transport aircraft to make preparations for the deployment of his aircraft. The MB-339As were to be dispersed near the eastern threshold of Stanley's runway and wooden planks were laid down so the aircraft could park away from the runway. Tents for air and ground crew were erected and ammunition and fuel were stored nearby so that the unit was almost completely self-contained. However, the tents were blown down in a gale on the first night and thereafter the crews moved to the more permanent accommodation of the FIGAS Beaver floatplane hangar on the far side of Stanley.

Fifteen T-34C-1s had been operated by the Escuela de Aviacion Naval at Punta Indio since 1978. The school was a component of 1 Escuadra Aeronaval and the T-34C-1s were operated by 4 Escuadrilla de Ataque, indicating that these aircraft also had a light attack role as well as their primary role of basic flying and weapons training. Four T-34C-1s had deployed from Punta Indio to Rio Grande on the 10th and they, like the 1 Escuadrilla detachment, spent the next two weeks training for the close air support role. The original intention was to deploy the four T-34C-1s to BAM Condor, the grass strip at Goose Green, but CANA objected to the state of the airstrip and instead decided to send the aircraft to the airstrip at Pebble Island. As it turned out, this airstrip was even more unsuitable and the decision to deploy there probably had as much to do with inter-service rivalry as it did with operational considerations.

The Argentine occupants renamed Pebble Island airstrip EAN Calderon as it was controlled by the Navy. The T-34C-1s did not deploy to Pebble Island until the 29th and were preceded there by a Prefectura Naval Short Skyvan 3M, which brought in CANA ground crews on the 24th to prepare the airstrip for the four aircraft. The Prefectura Naval, the military-run Argentine coastguard service, had deployed two Skyvan 3Ms and a Puma to the Falklands earlier in the month to fly coastal patrols and assist in the logistics tasks on the islands. It had been the intention to deploy the Pucara squadron at Stanley airport to Goose Green by 14th April to ease congestion at the airport. However, it was not until the 24th that the first Pucara visited BAM Condor; an event that merited giving the local residents a firepower demonstration against a small offshore island.

25th April (Sunday) –
The Recovery of South Georgia and the Capture of the *Santa Fe*

During the night of the 24/25th, another Victor MRR sortie was flown from Ascension Island to South Georgia to ascertain the precise location of Argentine ships prior to the action planned for later on this day. The Victor K2 involved (XL189), captained by Wing Commander Colin B Seymour, was airborne for 14 hours and 5 minutes on this mission. This, like the two previous MRR missions, was able to provide the South Georgia Task Group commander not just with the location of shipping but also the extent of the Antarctic pack ice and the positions of icebergs that could pose a danger to his vessels.

The intelligence section at Northwood estimated that the submarine *Santa Fe* would reach Grytviken during the night of the 24/25th and could therefore be

expected to sortie from there at first light, after having unloaded the troops and weapons she was carrying. Captain Young of *Antrim* planned his search for the *Sante Fe*, although his ship was still some 70 miles from the coast. His Wessex would search the Cumberland Bays while *Brilliant's* helicopters would search the coast to the north and the Wasps of *Endurance* and *Plymouth* would sit on deck alert armed with AS-12 missiles, ready to join the action as soon as the submarine was spotted.

At 0730 local a radio message from the *Santa Fe* was picked up and *Antrim's* Wessex and *Brilliant's* Lynx were prepared for take-off. At 0810 Lieutenant Commander Ian Stanley's Wessex HAS3 took off and flew towards Cumberland East Bay where it arrived at 0840 but found no sign of the submarine. The helicopter briefly turned on its radar and picked up a faint return outside Cumberland Bay and just north of Banff Point. The *Santa Fe* had just left Grytviken harbour and was heading out to the open sea on the surface when she was sighted by the crew of the Wessex. Ian Stanley raced towards the *Santa Fe* and dropped two Mk11 depth charges close to the submarine at 0900. The depth charges straddled the submarine and lifted its aft end out of the water. One of the depth charges exploded within 20ft of the port side, causing some damage to a ballast tank and rupturing a fuel tank. The *Santa Fe* reversed course and headed back towards Grytviken. The Wessex then flew round and round the submarine as Petty Officer Aircrewman Fitzgerald sprayed the boat with machine gun fire from the GPMG mounted in the helicopter's door.

Five minutes after the depth charge attack the first Lynx HAS2 from *Brilliant* (XZ725 flown by Lieutenant Commander B W Bryant and Lieutenant N A M Butler) arrived and launched a Mk46 homing torpedo set to shallow running which circled beneath the *Santa Fe*. The submarine's skipper, Capitan de Fregata H C Bicain, saw the torpedo drop and heard it circling underneath his boat so he knew he could not submerge, even if he was able to, as the torpedo would then intercept the submarine. The Lynx crewman also fired on the *Santa Fe* using the GPMG and, having exhausted his ammunition, then resorted to using small arms.

A few minutes later, at 0912, one of *Endurance's* Wasp HAS1s (XS527 flown by Lieutenant Commander Tony Ellerbeck and Lieutenant David Wells) joined in the fight and fired two AS-12 air-to-surface missiles. The first missile hit the conning tower but simply punched its way through the thin structure, wounding a sailor before exiting to explode harmlessly on the far side of the boat. The second missile fell about 30 yards

short. By now well into Cumberland East Bay, the *Santa Fe* was heading for the jetty at King Edward Point near Grytviken and was harried all the way by small arms fire from the Lynx.

About 0940, *Brilliant*'s other Lynx HAS2 (XZ729 flown by Lieutenant Commander J N Clark and Lieutenant P A McKay) arrived as XS527 returned to *Endurance* to re-arm. The Lynx was only armed with a GPMG, which it used to pepper the hull and conning tower, but few of the bullets penetrated. Tony Ellerbeck in XS527 then returned having re-armed with two more AS-12s. The first missile went rogue and veered way off course but the second punched another hole in the submarine's conning tower. *Plymouth*'s Wasp HAS1 (XT429 flown by Lieutenant Commander John Dransfield and Leading Aircraftman Joe Harper) then arrived on the scene carrying just a single AS-12 due to the distance the helicopter had to fly. The missile was launched successfully from 5,000 yards at 0953 and exploded close to the submarine's hull, causing a ballast tank to rupture and a serious leak inside the boat. By now the submarine was very close to shore and all the helicopters came under sustained small arms fire from the Argentine garrison at King Edward Point, but none were hit.

As *Plymouth*'s Wasp withdrew, its place was taken by *Endurance*'s second Wasp (XS539 flown by Lieutenant Tim Finding and Leading Aircraftman Bob Nadin), which was carrying two AS-12s. The crew fired their missiles just as the *Santa Fe* was rounding King Edward Point and although one missile missed by 50 yards, the other punched yet another hole in the conning tower, although once again the missile failed to explode. Ian Stanley then reappeared in the Wessex at about 1012, having been back to the *Antrim* to load two more depth charges, but in his assessment the submarine was no longer a threat and he called off the attack.

Just as the Wessex and the two Lynx turned back to their respective ships, Tony Ellerbeck in Wasp XS527 then returned with his third pair of AS-12s and attacked the submarine once more. *Endurance*'s Wasps had a different radio fit to the other

The Wasp/AS-12 combination proved itself to be a useful anti-surface weapon against the lightly defended Santa Fe *off Grytviken on 25th April when four of the nine missiles fired hit the target, causing severe damage.* MoD

A Wasp HAS1 from either Endurance *or* Plymouth *flies over the stricken* Santa Fe *in Grytviken harbour soon after the submarine was disabled as it tried to put to sea on 25th April.* MoD

helicopters in the Task Group so could not hear Ian Stanley's transmissions. One of the AS-12s failed to launch and had to be jettisoned but the other hit the conning tower and destroyed the periscope, a radio aerial and the snorkel. The submarine was actually tied up at the jetty when this final attack took place and Capitan Bicain was stood on the jetty as the missile smashed through his conning tower. By 1025 the battle was over and all the helicopters had returned to their ships. The fight had not been as one-sided as it may seem as the helicopters were under constant fire from Argentine troops based in and around Grytviken as well as receiving return fire by sailors on the submarine itself.

Of the nine AS-12s used, four had hit the target, four had missed and one had failed to launch. If either of *Brilliant*'s helicopters had been capable of carrying Sea Skuas the results of the attack on the *Santa Fe* might have been very different.

With the neutralisation of the main threat to the Task Group the landings at Grytviken

The 15,000-ton Atlantic Conveyor *is seen her prior to setting off for the Falklands. The Sea Harriers did not embark until the ship reached Ascension Island so this aircraft is probably involved in trials before the ship set sail.* MoD

commenced at 1415 following a bombardment by the guns of *Antrim* and *Plymouth* directed by naval gunfire observers airborne in *Endurance*'s Wasps. Prior to this, Tony Ellerbeck had flown an observer to Cumberland East Bay to spot for *Plymouth*. However, the visibility was poor so he landed the Wasp behind a hill at Dartmouth about four miles south of King Edward Cove and the observer targeted *Plymouth*'s gun from there.

The main group of Royal Marines of 42 Commando were on *Tidespring*, still some 200 miles away, so it was left to the 75 marines and Special Forces on board *Antrim* to make the assault. Once again Wessex HAS3 XP142 led the assault and landed troops on the shore opposite Grytviken, followed by the two Lynx from *Brilliant*. Each helicopter carried eight fully equipped troops and made several trips between the ships and the shore. The fight lasted just over two hours and the Argentine forces on South Georgia surrendered at 1715 as the naval gunfire barrage crept closer to Grytviken. Wasp XS527 landed to take Major Sheridan of the Royal Marines to King Edward Point to accept the surrender.

The formal surrender of all Argentine forces on South Georgia took place on board *Plymouth* on the 26th, by which time the news of the retaking of South Georgia

had provided much encouragement both in the UK and within the rest of the Task Force. South Georgia could now be used as a safe anchorage and staging point for RMS *Queen Elizabeth II*, which was too large and vulnerable to make the trip to the Falkland Islands.

As the drama at South Georgia was being played out the Argentine forces were preparing for the main event. On the 25th two squadrons of Dagger A fighter-bombers from Grupo 6 de Caza at Tandil in Buenos Aires province were deployed to their wartime bases. Escuadron II under Mayor Juan Sapolski flew its ten aircraft to the civil airport at San Julian to join the A-4C Skyhawks of Grupo 4 de Caza. Later the same day Escuadron III, commanded by Mayor Carlos Napoleon Martinez, deployed nine aircraft to Rio Grande on Tierra del Fuego. The Rio Grande detachment was designated Escuadron Aeromovil 1 and the San Julian detachment became Escuadron Aeromovil 2.

The Dagger was an Israeli-built version of the Mirage 5 and was the most recent addition to the combat inventory of the Argentine Air Force. The first aircraft had arrived from Israel in December 1978 but by April 1982 many Dagger pilots were still relatively inexperienced on the type; indeed some were converting to the Dagger as the con-

flict started. The 19 Dagger As that deployed on 25th April probably represented most of the serviceable aircraft available on that date, minus a few aircraft that were left at Tandil to continue pilot conversion.

Soon after arriving at Rio Grande, two Escuadron III Dagger As were supposed to fly a practise escort mission with the Super Etendards based there. However, the mission was a disaster, one of the aircraft aborting prior to take-off and the other returning early with a fuel leak. This early mission was a portent of the poor inter-service co-operation as far as the Super Etendard missions were concerned, although the Dagger As continued intensive training for anti-ship missions.

Meanwhile the air bridge continued to strengthen the Argentine position on the Falklands. On 25th April a total of 34 transport flights were planned to reach Stanley airport from the main airhead at Comodoro Rivadavia, although eight sorties could not be completed due to bad weather over West Falkland. These 34 sorties were to consist of 13 by C-130s, 13 by F-28s and eight by civil Boeing 737s.

Back in the UK, two more ships set sail for the South Atlantic. MV *Europic Ferry* was carrying stores and equipment for the Parachute Regiment along with three Scout AH1s of 656 Squadron, Army Air Corps. The 15,000-ton SS *Atlantic Conveyor* was one of two ro-ro container ships that had been requisitioned from Cunard/ACL. She and the SS *Atlantic Causeway* were converted to aircraft transports as their spacious flat decks were ideal for parking aircraft, with each ship destined to carry Harriers/Sea Harriers and helicopters to the South Atlantic. The ships were rapidly converted for their new role in Plymouth, the work taking just nine days in the case of the *Atlantic Conveyor*, and on the 24th the latter ship embarked six Wessex HU5s of 'D' Flight 848 Squadron (XS480, XS495, XS499, XS512, XT476 and XT483) and five Chinook HC1s of 18 Squadron (ZA706, ZA707, ZA716, ZA718 and ZA719). To provide some protection for the aircraft, which had to be stored on the main deck, a wall of containers was built up on either side and landing spots forward and aft were left free. 848 Squadron had been reformed at Yeovilton on 19th April by the simple expedient of upgrading the Wessex training unit, 707 Squadron, to operational status.

26th April (Monday)

Just before midnight on the 25th the Carrier Battle Group and the Advanced Group, having joined up earlier in the day, set course for the final leg of their voyage to enter the MEZ. The Task Force now consisted of the two carriers (*Hermes* and *Invincible*), four destroyers (*Coventry, Glamorgan, Glasgow*

and *Sheffield*), three frigates (*Alacrity, Arrow* and *Broadsword*) and the RFA *Appleleaf* with *Yarmouth* and *Olmeda* and *Resource* catching up from the north.

As part of the deployment of troops to strategic points within the Falklands, CAB601 Pumas and UH-1Hs started to move troops from Stanley airport to Port Howard on the Falkland Sound coast of West Falkland. This deployment took four days to complete and resulted in a sizeable garrison in the Port Howard area that included an air defence capability.

Since 1971 the long-range bomber force of the Argentine Air Force had consisted of a dozen ex-RAF Canberra B2s and T4s, redesignated as B62s and T64s. Grupo 2 de Bombardeo was based at Parana in Entre Rios but on 26th April seven aircraft (later augmented by two more) were deployed to EAN Trelew, a naval air base further south but still some 200 miles north of Comodoro Rivadavia. Trelew proved to be too distant for most combat missions to the Falklands (593 miles), so three of the Canberras were immediately redeployed to Rio Grande. The Canberras also operated from the airfield at Rio Gallegos during the conflict.

On the 26th the three Canberras of the Rio Grande detachment took off on Grupo 2's first combat mission of the conflict to search for and attack the British warships involved in Operation 'Paraquat' around South Georgia. For this long-range mission the Canberras were fitted with an auxiliary fuel tank in the bomb bay, thereby reducing the aircraft's bomb load to just two 1,000lb bombs each. The leading Canberra had to abort the mission and return to base when it was unable to release its wing-tip fuel tanks, so the remaining two aircraft continued on under the supervision of a Boeing 707, which provided navigation. In radio silence the Canberras simply followed the Boeing's vapour trails until it was time for it to turn back, at which point both bombers descended to low level. A KC-130H was on station near South Georgia and passed on the position of the British ships, but bad weather in the area and the proximity of the ships to the mountainous shoreline forced the Canberra crews to abandon the mission and return to base. The two aircraft had flown a round trip of 2,530 miles in a mission lasting 5 hours and 30 minutes.

The three SAS men who went missing on the 23rd when their Gemini boat's engine failed had very fortunately landed on a beach several miles down the coast. They had tried to get the boat's engine running during the following night but without much success. They then walked over Jason Peak and on the 26th they signalled to *Plymouth* in Stromness Bay and were rescued by Lieutenant Commander Tony Ellerbeck in Wasp HAS1 XS527. In the

evening one of *Brilliant*'s Lynx HAS2s (XZ729) made three trips to a small beach between Stromness and Leith in a blizzard and gale force wind to pick up an SAS patrol that had been ashore for five days and was running out of food and supplies.

At midday on the 26th the submarine *Conqueror* surfaced off the coast of South Georgia to offload some SBS troops that she had transported south. While the submarine was on the surface a large wave washed a sailor and an SBS man overboard into the freezing water. Fortunately, Lieutenant Commander Ian Stanley's Wessex was hovering close by as he was about to winch the SBS troops and their equipment off the submarine for transfer to *Plymouth*. Seeing what had happened, Petty Officer Aircrewman Fitzgerald directed Ian Stanley back to the two men in the water and lowered a lifting net. The SBS man grabbed the net and was towed towards the sailor who was in difficulty. Within minutes the men were on board *Antrim* and receiving medical attention to combat hypothermia.

27th April (Tuesday)

Grupo 2 attempted to fly its mission to South Georgia again on the 27th but as the Canberras were lined up on the runway, ready to go, the mission was suddenly cancelled. The Argentines had just received news of the surrender of their garrison on South Georgia, thereby making the highly risky mission unnecessary.

On the 27th *Brilliant*'s helicopters flew some of the 200 Argentine troops captured on South Georgia to *Tidespring* for the journey to Ascension Island and eventual repatriation. During the transfers one of the helicopters made the first landing of a Lynx on a Type 12 frigate when it landed on the confined helicopter deck of *Plymouth*. *Tidespring* left South Georgia for Ascension Island on 2 May with *Antrim* as escort.

28th April (Wednesday)

On the 28th it was announced that the British MEZ that extended from the Falkland Islands for 200 miles in all directions was to be renamed the Total Exclusion Zone (TEZ) to include air movements as well as ships at sea. The TEZ was to come into effect at 1100Z on the 30th but three days of stormy weather meant that the Task Force would not actually reach the TEZ until after the deadline. As part of the final preparations a Sea Harrier FRS1 from 800 Squadron dropped a BL755 cluster bomb unit (CBU) for practice, as this would be one of the main weapons used when attacking airfields.

An Argentine Air Force Boeing 707 was detected on radar and, despite poor weather, an 800 Squadron Sea Harrier CAP was put up which deterred the Boeing from approaching closer than 100 miles from the aircraft carriers.

Following mopping-up operations at South Georgia, *Brilliant* and *Plymouth* left the islands to join up with the Carrier Battle Group, which they met the next day, leaving *Endurance* behind to patrol the waters around South Georgia for the duration of the conflict.

29th April (Thursday) – Final Preparations for War

With the imminent arrival of the British Task Force and the likelihood of an all-out attack on Stanley airport, the Argentine air bridge operation was shut down at 2000Z on the 29th, although not before six C-130 and eight F-28 sorties had been flown to Stanley on that day. By this date a total of 452 sorties had reached Stanley airport from the Argentine mainland delivering 5,008 tons of cargo and 9,215 passengers, mostly troops. Many of the flights were made in atrocious weather and it is to the great credit of the Argentine military and civilian flight crews that such an effort was made without the loss or damage of a single aircraft. Although the air bridge ceased on this day, the C-130s resumed flying to Stanley on 6th May and continued to run huge risks to resupply the garrison for the rest of the conflict.

There was a general dispersal of aircraft from Stanley airport on the 29th to reduce their vulnerability to air attack. Under the command of Teniente de Navio Jose Maria Pereyra, the four T-34C-1s flew from Stanley to the airstrip at Pebble Island while the 12 Pucaras of the Escuadron Pucara Malvinas flew to Goose Green. Over the next couple of days the Pucaras made a few local flights to get used to their new and barely adequate airfield. The only aircraft left at Stanley by the 30th were the two MB-339As (which had nowhere to disperse to on the Falklands) and the resident civilian aircraft.

The Argentine aircraft and helicopters based in the Falklands were painted with a broad yellow band around the rear fuselage or tail boom to readily identify them to Argentine troops and hopefully avoid any 'friendly fire' incidents.

A significant arrival at Wideawake airfield on the 29th was two Vulcan B2 bombers (XM598 and XM607), which had flown for nine hours non-stop from RAF Waddington to Ascension Island with the aid of in-flight refuelling from Victor K2 tankers. The Vulcan would open the British air campaign to retake the Falkland Islands two days later.

The Falklands conflict occurred at a time when the RAF was undergoing a dramatic change as far as its offensive capability was concerned. The ageing Vulcan, long the RAF's primary strategic weapon that had helped to maintain the UK's nuclear deterrent, had served as a tactical nuclear and conventional bomber since the mid-1960s. In 1982 the aircraft was being replaced by the Tornado GR1, a state-of-the-art, multirole aircraft but without the range or load-carrying capability of the Vulcan. In March 1982 there were only three squadrons of Vulcans left serving with the RAF, all of them based at Waddington, and these squadrons were due to be disbanded and their aircraft scrapped by June. However, the rundown of 44, 50 and 101 Squadrons was interrupted on 9th April when Waddington was notified of the possibility of involvement in Operation 'Corporate'.

Six aircraft were selected from those still in service and these were quickly put through a modification programme to bring their in-flight refuelling system back up to operational capability. The Vulcan force had not used its in-flight refuelling capability for many years, and the system had to be reconnected and the crews trained in the technique. It was decided that each aircraft would carry an AAR instructor from the Victor squadrons who would direct the in-flight refuelling sessions from the co-pilot's seat on operational missions. Although the modification programme was a success, fuel leaks during in-flight refuelling remained a constant problem.

Another deciding factor on which airframes were selected was the need for an underwing stores-carrying capability. In the early 1960s it was planned that the Vulcan would carry the American Skybolt nuclear standoff weapon, one of which would have been carried under each wing. A number of Vulcans received special modifications to the wing to enable them to carry the missile. When the Skybolt programme was cancelled the wing hardpoints and associated ducting for the missiles were covered over and largely forgotten about. However, the need to carry an ECM pod and, as it later transpired, air-to-surface missiles meant that only the aircraft originally modified to carry Skybolt could be used. Two of the Vulcans selected, XL391 and XM654, were used only for training in the UK (XM654 did not even receive the modifications the other aircraft received), but the other four aircraft (XM597, XM598, XM607 and XM612) were deployed to Wideawake airfield at various times during the conflict, although normally only two aircraft were based there at any one time. Some of the five crews selected had gone through a Red Flag training exercise in the United States in February 1982 and this recent experience in a realistic air combat exercise proved invaluable.

The Vulcans were fitted with the Carousel inertial navigation system (removed from ex-British Airways VC10s that were stored ready for conversion to the tanker role) to obtain the improved navigational accuracy necessary for the long, overwater flights. Carousel was also fitted to the Victor tankers involved in Operation 'Corporate' and the Victor and Vulcan crews were trained on the use of the equipment by 51 Squadron personnel whose Nimrod R1s had been fitted with Carousel for some years. The Vulcans were also modified to carry the AN/ALQ-101 ECM pod (from the RAF's Buccaneer fleet), which was fitted on the wing pylon under the starboard wing, in order to combat the Argentine ground-based radar. Lastly, the Light Sea Grey undersides of each Vulcan were repainted in Dark Sea Grey to make the aircraft less visible from the ground at night.

Before the first two Vulcans were deployed to Ascension Island at the end of April, the crews spent much of their time practising in-flight refuelling in day and night conditions. They also flew low-level night navigation exercises, and dropped practise and live bombs on various ranges in the UK. The Vulcan force was trained primarily for the tactical nuclear strike role and the crews had to retrain for operations with a conventional bomb load. In fact no RAF crew had been trained to drop conventional bombs for the previous seven years. Additionally, when it was decided that the aircraft should be fitted with the Shrike anti-radar missile, the Vulcan crews received briefings and assistance from USAFE F-4G 'Wild Weasel' crews who visited Waddington from their base at Spangdahlem AB, West Germany.

Brilliant and *Plymouth* rejoined the Task Force on the 29th from their sortie to South Georgia, thereby increasing its strength to five frigates. The ships transferred the SAS and SBS troops who had been involved in the South Georgia operation to the two aircraft carriers. Some last-minute replenishments and transfer of stores took place within the Task Force on the 29th, but flying was greatly restricted due to fog.

During the night of the 29/30th the five LSLs (*Sir Galahad*, *Sir Geraint*, *Sir Lancelot*, *Sir Percivale* and *Sir Tristram*) left Ascension Island for the Falklands, escorted by HMS *Antelope* and RFA *Pearleaf*. *Sir Galahad*, *Sir Geraint* and *Sir Percivale* each carried three Gazelle AH1s of 3 CBAS while *Sir Lancelot* carried three of the squadron's Scout AH1s (another three Scouts were embarked on *Fearless*). *Sir Tristram* received one of the Scouts from *Fearless* before setting sail for the Falklands. One of the Gazelles almost did not sail with the rest as XZ326 had to be force-landed on the beach at Ascension Island by Sergeant S Congdon on the 29th due to fuel starvation. The helicopter was later airlifted on board its LSL by a Sea King.

A Sea Harrier FRS1 of 809 Squadron arrives at Ascension Island on 1st May having left Yeovilton the day before. 809 Squadron flew eight Sea Harriers from the UK to Ascension Island on 1st/2nd May for embarkation on the Atlantic Conveyor. MoD

Nimrod MR2 XV228 of the Kinloss Wing lands at Wideawake airfield on Ascension Island around 1st May. In the background can be seen three Nimrods, a USAF C-141B Starlifter and the two 'Black Buck 1' Vulcan B2s. MoD

30th April (Friday)

Poised to enter the TEZ on 1 May were 14 ships of Task Force 317 comprised of two aircraft carriers (*Hermes* and *Invincible*), four destroyers (*Coventry*, *Glamorgan*, *Glasgow* and *Sheffield*), six frigates (*Alacrity*, *Arrow*, *Brilliant*, *Broadsword*, *Plymouth* and *Yarmouth*) and two tankers (*Olmeda* and *Resource*). On board the 14 vessels that opened hostilities were 20 Sea Harrier FRS1s, 20 Sea King HAS5s and nine Sea King HC4s on *Hermes* and *Invincible*, and nine Lynx HAS2s, two Wessex, two Wasp HAS1s and two Sea Kings on board the other ships. There would be no reinforcements for these ships or aircraft until the arrival of the leading elements of the Amphibious Group, which were not expected until 16th May.

Reinforcements were, however, on their way to Ascension Island for eventual delivery to the Carrier Battle Group. When the two Sea Harrier squadrons deployed on board the carriers during the first week in April they left behind just a handful of aircraft in service with 899 Squadron, the Sea Harrier training unit. On 8th April a new Sea Harrier unit, 809 Squadron commanded by Lieutenant Commander Tim Gedge, was formed at Yeovilton to provide replacement

aircraft and pilots to balance the expected attrition rate of 800 and 801 Squadrons. Every available Sea Harrier pilot was immediately posted in from various non-flying or overseas exchange postings and were supplemented by two RAF ex-Lightning pilots, Flight Lieutenant S Brown and Flight Lieutenant J Leeming, from the Harrier squadrons in RAF Germany.

Sea Harriers themselves were also in short supply and a total of eight airframes were eventually made available for the new squadron. Five of these aircraft were taken out of storage at RAF St Athan, while another two were provided by 899 Squadron (leaving the squadron temporarily with no aircraft at all), and a brand-new Sea Harrier was received direct from BAe Dunsfold. The new squadron started working-up its aircraft, pilots and ground crew on 12th April although the aircraft had to undergo many modifications to bring them all up to operational service standard.

On 21st April 809 Squadron flew the first Sea Harrier air refuelling trials with Victors. The Sea Harriers were fitted with bolt-on in-flight refuelling probes and carried 100-gallon fuel tanks for the long ferry flight to Ascension Island where they would embark on the converted aircraft transport

Atlantic Conveyor. The ship had left Plymouth on schedule on the 25th and 809 Squadron received its eighth and final aircraft three days later.

On the 30th six Sea Harriers of 809 Squadron (XZ458, XZ491, ZA174, ZA176, ZA190 and ZA194) took off from Yeovilton on the ferry flight to Ascension Island via Banjul in The Gambia. Refuelled by Victor tankers along the way, all six aircraft arrived safely at Ascension Island on 1 May after a night-stop at Banjul. The last two 809 Squadron aircraft (XZ499 and ZA177) left Yeovilton on 1st May and arrived at Ascension Island on the 2nd. Each pilot flew a total of nine hours during the two-day ferry flight and refuelled a total of 14 times from the Victors.

The Argentine forces on the Falklands and on the mainland waited tensely for the expected British invasion, as they knew the Task Force was by now within Sea Harrier range of Stanley and they thought the amphibious ships were with the aircraft carriers. As if to illustrate the tension felt by all, on the evening of the 29th an unidentified radar target caused all the Skyhawks and Daggers at San Julian to be scrambled and evacuate to Comodoro Rivadavia. The radar contact turned out to be a false alarm, thought by at least one Argentine source to have been caused by British electronic countermeasures.

Chapter Four

The Shooting War from
1st May 1982 to the Surrender

1st May (Saturday) –
The Empire Strikes Back
British offensive air action to recover the
Falkland Islands commenced a few minutes before midnight on 30th April when
Operation 'Black Buck 1' swung into action.
The plan was for a single Vulcan to make a
pre-dawn strike on Stanley airport, hopefully rendering the airfield unusable, at least
for a short time. A Sea Harrier CAP would be
airborne at the time in the unlikely event of
the Vulcan being intercepted by Argentine
fighters. This was to be followed at dawn by
a strike by Sea Harriers on the airfields at
Stanley and Goose Green, while later in the
day the destroyer *Glamorgan* and the
frigates *Arrow* and *Alacrity* would open the
naval bombardment from just three miles
off Stanley. This dramatic opening day was
planned to convince the Argentines that the
British Task Force meant business and to
test the Argentine response.

Although no air opposition was
expected, the first air raids on Stanley
would test the Argentine ground-based air
defences on the Falklands. By 1st May the
air defences around Stanley and other
strategic points were quite formidable and
consisted of the following:

Argentine Army
The 601st Air Defence Artillery Group was
equipped with:
 1 Cardion TPS-44 long-range early
   warning radar
 6 Skyguard fire control radars
12 Oerlikon twin 35mm anti-aircraft guns
 1 Roland SAM fire unit
 3 Oerlikon twin 20mm anti-aircraft guns
 3 Tigercat SAM triple launchers

A single battery of the 101st Air Defence
Group was equipped with:
 8 Hispano HS-831 30mm anti-aircraft guns

Argentine Air Force
The Airfield Defence Group consisted of:
 1 Westinghouse TPS-43F long-range
   surveillance radar
 1 Superfledermaus fire control radar
 1 Elta short-range radar
 4 Oerlikon twin 35mm anti-aircraft guns
 9 Rheinmetall twin 20mm anti-aircraft guns
   Several SA-7 portable SAMs

Argentine Navy (CANA)
No.1 Marine Air Defence Battalion consisted of:
 3 Tigercat triple launchers
12 Hispano HS-831 30mm anti-aircraft guns

'Black Buck I' consisted of two waves of a
total of 11 Victor K2 tankers with two Vulcan B2s in the numbers 11 and 13 take-off
slots. Each Vulcan was loaded with 21
1,000lb HE bombs and the mission was
flown in complete radio silence and without navigation lights. With a full bomb and
fuel load each of the Vulcans was about
6,000lb over its normal maximum take-off
weight of 204,000lb, but its immense power
coupled with the very long runway at
Wideawake enabled a safe take-off. An
additional seven Victor sorties would be
required for the return phase of the mission
and the number of Victors involved underlines the critical importance of in-flight
refuelling to what were the most distant
bombing missions ever flown by the RAF.
With only 14 Victor tankers available at
Wideawake on the 1st, the 'Black Buck'
missions stretched the RAF's tanker force
to the limit.

The two-fold objective of this opening
raid was to cause damage to Stanley's runway, thereby denying it to Argentine Skyhawks, Mirages and Super Etendards and
also to demonstrate British resolve in no
uncertain way by commencing the air campaign of Operation 'Corporate' with an
impressive strategic air raid.

Squadron Leader R J Reeve and his crew
took off in Vulcan B2 XM598, the primary
aircraft, at one minute past midnight with
XM607 following two minutes later. The
second Vulcan was the airborne reserve
aircraft captained by Flight Lieutenant W F
M Withers and was due to return once
XM598 had made its first in-flight refuelling.
In the event the reserve aircraft had to take
over the mission almost immediately when
the direct-vision window of XM598 refused

*The capacious bomb bay of the Vulcan could
hold up to 21 1,000lb bombs and three times
during the conflict this load was hauled nearly
4,000 miles to Stanley from Ascension Island
during the 'Black Buck' missions. MoD*

to seal properly as the pilot tried to close it
after take-off, which meant that the aircraft
could not be pressurised and flown to high
altitude. As Squadron Leader Reeve reluctantly returned to Ascension Island, Martin
Withers took over the lead and climbed
XM607 to 27,000ft for the first of six in-flight
refuelling sessions en route to the Falklands. Soon afterwards one of the Victors
discovered that its hose would not deploy
and the spare Victor had to take its place,
thus demonstrating the wisdom of incorporating spare aircraft into the plan, especially
as the plan involved elderly airframes.

The Vulcan and the ten remaining Victors
proceeded south, the tankers progressively
breaking away from the formation and
heading back towards Ascension Island
after passing fuel to XM607 and to the last
two Victors that would accompany the Vulcan as far south as they could. Thunder-
storms and turbulence added to the
darkness to make the outbound journey
even more challenging for all the crews
involved. At the sixth and final refuelling
before the last two Victors had to turn back
the lead tanker (XH669 captained by Flight
Lieutenant Steve Bigland) ran into turbulence and had to break contact when its
probe was damaged while topping-up from
the second Victor. Flight Lieutenant
Bigland had to head back to Ascension

A Victor K2 streams its huge braking parachute as it lands at Ascension Island after another tanker sortie. Without the Victor tankers, none of the 'Black Buck' missions could have taken place. MoD

Island, leaving Squadron Leader Robert Tuxford (in XL189) to refuel the Vulcan. Although Bob Tuxford's aircraft took back some fuel from XH669 before it headed back north, XL189 was now dangerously short of fuel because of the switch around of the tankers. Bob Tuxford transferred as much fuel as he dared to XM607 before waving off the Vulcan prematurely and heading back to Ascension Island himself. Nevertheless the Vulcan was some 6,000lb of fuel short of what it should have had at this stage of the mission, which must have been a worrying predicament for the crew.

When some 300 miles out from the Falkland Islands the Vulcan commenced a descent to 250ft to avoid being picked up by the Argentine radar. With 40 miles to go Martin Withers put the Vulcan into a climb up to 10,000ft for the bombing run over Stanley airport. As the aircraft neared the target the radar navigator, Flight Lieutenant R D Wright, picked up the airport's position on the aircraft's H2S radar. In the final stages of the bomb run an Argentine Skyguard AAA fire control radar illuminated the Vulcan but was quickly jammed by the aircraft's AN/ALQ-101 ECM pod, although several of the 35mm guns did open fire after the Vulcan dropped its bombs.

At 0738Z Martin Withers dropped his 21 bombs diagonally across the runway to ensure that at least one bomb (as it happened it was the first) hit the runway's surface. The first thing that many of the Argentine troops stationed in and around Stanley (or Stanley's civilian residents for that matter) knew of the start of the air campaign was when the first bombs started exploding on the airport. Several of the bombs were fused with 30- or 60-second

delays to make it appear that more than one aircraft had been involved. The anti-aircraft guns did not open up until several minutes after the Vulcan had dropped its bombs by which time the aircraft was well out to sea and out of range. The Vulcan had flown 3,900 miles supported by 11 Victor tankers for those five brief seconds on the final bomb run over Stanley.

As soon as the bombs had been released the plan was for the Vulcan to drop to low level again to stay under enemy radar. However, because of the early break-off from the last refuelling, the Vulcan was now very short of fuel, so Martin Withers elected to climb to 41,000ft to conserve fuel until he could reach a tanker. Bob Tuxford in the Victor was in an even worse state. Heading back towards Ascension Island his navigator had worked out that they would run out of fuel some 400 miles from base unless they could be refuelled. Unwilling to compromise the mission by breaking radio silence early, Bob Tuxford waited until he heard the Vulcan transmit the code word 'Superfuse' for a successful bomb drop (at 0746Z) before he radioed Ascension Island and requested a tanker which reached the Victor just in time.

Meanwhile Martin Withers and his crew were sweating out the rendezvous with their own tanker, which had to be vectored much further south than planned to meet the Vulcan. The Victor was directed by a Nimrod that was flying as SAR and communication relay support for the 'Black Buck' mission. The refuelling was accomplished successfully despite a large amount of fuel spraying out over the Vulcan's windows, making visibility difficult. About 2,000lb of the 36,000lb of fuel pumped from the Victor

was lost during the transfer but this final refuelling enabled the Vulcan to touch down at Wideawake at 1452Z on 1st May after almost 16 hours in the air covering 7,860 miles.

The first Vulcan raid had been a great success, especially considering the immense difficulties it presented to those who had planned and executed it. One bomb had landed squarely midway down the runway thereby reducing its useable length by half. Other bombs had destroyed or damaged airfield facilities including the control tower and a small hangar that was used to store spares for some of the Argentine aircraft based at Stanley. The raid, the longest bombing mission ever flown up to that time (since eclipsed by the B-2A raids from the USA to Afghanistan during Operation 'Enduring Freedom' in 2001), involved two Vulcans and 16 Victor sorties (five Victors flew two sorties each) and a total of 18 refuellings, but the impact was wide-ranging. Not only did it open the air campaign in an impressive manner and create significant damage to Stanley airport, it also created an element of panic in Argentina as it demonstrated the British capability to strike from very long range. This meant that, theoretically at least, targets on the Argentine mainland were also vulnerable.

The immediate result in Argentina was the withdrawal of some of the Grupo 8 de Caza Mirage IIIEAs from southern bases to protect the mainland airfields and Buenos Aires itself. Eight Mirage IIIEA interceptors had been deployed to Comodoro Rivadavia soon after the invasion of the Falkland Islands, four of these aircraft later moving further south to Rio Gallegos, leaving just four operational aircraft to defend Buenos Aires. Although there was never any British plan to attack the capital, the Argentine junta could not leave the city unprotected and so recalled the Mirage IIIEAs, a move welcomed by the Grupo 8 pilots as they knew by the end of 1st May that they were outmatched by the Sea Harriers at low level.

An even more immediate effect of the first air raids on Stanley was the cancellation of sorties planned by the 1 Escuadrilla detachment for the next two days as the MB-339As could not take off until the hole in the runway was filled in and patched. Although the material damage was slight when compared to the immense effort of getting a single Vulcan overhead Stanley, the psychological impact of the raid should not be underestimated. Even though the Argentine defenders were expecting some sort of attack, the Vulcan raid was a major shock and a brilliant opening action by the British armed forces in the offensive to retake the Falklands.

For his part in the 'Black Buck 1' raid Flight Lieutenant Martin Withers was awarded the DFC while his crew, consisting of Flying Officer P L Taylor (co-pilot), Flight Lieutenant R D Wright (nav-radar), Flight Lieutenant C G Graham (nav-plotter), Flight Lieutenant H Prior (AEO) and Flight Lieutenant R J Russell (an AAR instructor from RAF Marham), each received a Mention in Despatches. Squadron Leader Bob Tuxford was awarded the AFC for his part in the mission and his crew were all awarded the Queen's Commendation for Valuable Service in the Air.

The Carrier Battle Group entered the TEZ at about 0530Z and took up position about 100 miles northeast of the Falklands. The Group was led by the three Type 42 destroyers *Coventry*, *Glasgow* and *Sheffield*, which formed an advanced air defence screen to protect the two aircraft carriers, which were now about to start their own air operations after the opening shot by the Vulcan.

At 0900Z four Sea Harriers of 801 Squadron took off from *Invincible* to take up CAP positions to the east and northeast of Stanley. *Invincible* served throughout the conflict as the Anti-Air Warfare Co-ordinator responsible for the overall air defence of the Fleet. After an uneventful hour the four aircraft were replaced by another four Sea Harriers from 801 Squadron so that the first flight could land, refuel and take off again in time to cover the first Sea Harrier strike of the conflict.

At 1048Z the first of all 12 800 Squadron Sea Harriers took off from *Hermes* (which was then positioned about 95 miles east-northeast of Stanley) to attack the airport at 1100Z. Nine aircraft, led by Lieutenant Commander Andy Auld, the commanding officer of 800 Squadron, headed for Stanley airport while the other three made for the airfield at Goose Green. The larger formation split up as it crossed the coast near MacBride Head, 20 miles north of Stanley, to enable four aircraft (each carrying three 1,000lb airburst bombs) to approach the target from the north and pull up to toss their bombs onto Argentine AAA positions that ringed the airport. Seconds after the first flight released its bombs and dived back to low level and sped away to the southeast, the other five aircraft made a low-level run over the airfield from the northwest, dropping cluster bombs on parked aircraft, airfield facilities and the runway. One aircraft, flown by Flight Lieutenant Bertie Penfold, carried three 1,000lb retard bombs, which were aimed at the

runway. Two of Penfold's bombs hit the runway, causing additional damage to that already caused by the earlier Vulcan attack.

Initially taken by surprise, the Argentine defences reacted vigorously as the second wave of Sea Harriers swept over the target area. The last aircraft to attack was that of Flight Lieutenant Dave Morgan (ZA192), which was the first Sea Harrier to receive battle damage in the conflict when it was hit by a 20mm shell that passed through the tailfin without exploding. Morgan also saw a Tigercat SAM streak past him and had to break the lock of an anti-aircraft gun radar by jinking and dropping chaff while escaping at low level. Another Tigercat missile was seen by Stanley residents to streak away at a low angle and hit the hallowed turf of the town's football pitch before ricocheting upwards and exploding. It seems that at least one Roland missile was also fired but the Argentine claim that two Sea Harriers were shot down, one by a Tigercat and one by a Roland, was patently fictitious.

The only Argentine aircraft on the airport at the time of the attack were the two MB-339As of 1 Escuadrilla de Ataque and these were fortunate to escape damage as they were parked well away from the airport buildings. Less fortunate were several of the civil aircraft based at Stanley. Three Cessna 172s (VP-FAR, VP-FAS and VP-FBA) received various degrees of damage but worst hit was the Britten-Norman Islander (VP-FAY) of the Falkland Islands Government Air Service, which had its tail severed by a direct hit from one of Dave Morgan's CBUs. The Islander has a good short take-off and landing capability and its destruction at least denied its further use by the Argentine forces who had already flown about 30 hours in the aircraft since the invasion. The three Cessnas were damaged in further air raids and naval bombardments and all three, including the Governor's aircraft (VP-FBA), had to be written off after the conflict.

A total of 15 1,000lb bombs and 12 CBUs were dropped on Stanley airport during this first attack. Following this first raid the Argentines sometimes piled earth on the runway during the day to give the impression that it had been damaged by bombs. When it became dark the earth was simply shovelled away, allowing Hercules from the mainland to land and take off.

The three 800 Squadron Sea Harriers that were targeted against Goose Green airfield met very little opposition as they swept over the airfield from the direction of Falkland Sound at extremely low level, dropping three 1,000lb bombs and six CBUs at 1125Z. Led by Lieutenant Commander Rod Fredericksen, the three aircraft escaped unharmed and returned to *Hermes* safely. There were nine Pucaras on the airfield at

Goose Green when the Sea Harriers arrived. Three Pucaras had taken off earlier in the morning to search for British troops but one of the aircraft (flown by Teniente Russo) rotated prematurely and hit a landing light and a fourth aircraft (A-506 flown by Teniente Calderon) had aborted its take-off from the muddy runway surface and ended up with its nosewheel collapsed, blocking the grass runway. The Pucaras had been dispatched on a fruitless three-hour search-and-destroy mission under the mistaken assumption that British forces had landed en masse on the islands and the aircraft were diverted to Pebble Island after Goose Green was bombed.

A second flight of Pucaras had been delayed by Calderon's accident and was just about to taxi out for take-off as the Sea Harriers attacked. Primer Teniente Antonio Jukic was taxiing A-527 along the grass when his aircraft was hit by a CBU and exploded, killing him instantly. Seven Air Force ground crew who were standing nearby were also killed and a further 14 were wounded in the raid. Another Pucara (A-517) was so badly damaged that it was not repaired and it, together with A-506, was propped up on empty oil drums as a decoy for future air raids. It is thought that a total of five Pucaras were damaged to some extent during the raid. According to an Argentine account, some of the cannon and machine guns and even a rocket pod from the damaged Pucaras were removed from the aircraft wrecked during the raids on Goose Green and mounted for airfield defence duties. A tractor was used to mount one of the guns to provide a measure of mobile airfield defence.

It was fortunate for the Argentine forces that the helicopters based at Goose Green (two Chinooks and two Bell 212s) had recently been flown from the airfield to be hidden among the settlement buildings of Goose Green itself, thereby escaping damage. Following the air raid, one of the Chinooks flew the wounded to Stanley and at dusk one of the Bells flew a SAR mission in the hope of finding Primer Teniente Ardiles, who had been shot down over Lively Island in his Dagger A (C-433) earlier in the day. During the afternoon the Argentine Army A-109A and UH-1H helicopters of CAB601 that were based at Moody Brook near Stanley were moved to a safer location near Mount Kent, about ten miles west of Stanley, to afford them better protection from air attack.

As the 800 Squadron raiders were hitting their targets the 801 Squadron CAP was also about to see some action. Two Grupo 6 Dagger As were being vectored by an Argentine radar operator at Stanley towards two Sea Harriers north of the islands. The Daggers of Toro flight, flown by Capitan

A Pucara is seen here lying in pieces on Goose Green airstrip. Judging by the degree of destruction, this is almost certainly A-527 in which Primer Teniente Antonio Jukic was killed on 1st May when the aircraft was hit by a cluster bomb dropped by a Sea Harrier of 800 Squadron. Wg Cdr P Lyall

Pucara A-517 was damaged during the first Sea Harrier raid on Goose Green on 1st May and was then used as a decoy on the airfield for the rest of the conflict. The aircraft was later sold to Grampian Helicopters International and is now thought to be in the Channel Islands. Sqn Ldr D Cyster

Moreno and Teniente H R Volponi, had taken off from their base at Rio Grande to provide an escort for a CANA Lockheed SP-2H Neptune of the Escuadrilla de Exploracion that was due to fly a radar search mission off Stanley in an attempt to locate the British fleet. In the event, the Neptune failed to take off but the Daggers took off anyway on a revised mission. The Royal Navy radar operators spotted the Daggers on their screens and passed vectors to the Sea Harrier pilots, Lieutenant Commander Robin Kent and Lieutenant Brian Haigh.

The four aircraft approached head-on with the Sea Harriers at 15,000ft and the Daggers at 20,000ft. The Sea Harrier pilots thought they saw the Daggers fire air-to-air missiles at them but what they actually saw was each Dagger jettisoning its drop tanks in readiness for combat. One of the Argentine pilots claimed that he saw an AIM-9

Sidewinder pass close to his aircraft but in fact neither side fired any missiles, as they were unable to achieve a radar lock. The Dagger pilots broke away as they became concerned about their fuel state, and so the first air combat of the conflict ended inconclusively. About an hour later two more Daggers (Foco flight flown by Capitan H M Gonzalez and Teniente J D Bernhardt as escorts to a flight of A-4 Skyhawks) had an inconclusive encounter with a Sea Harrier CAP before returning to Rio Grande.

Following this first contact, more Argentine aircraft were seen on radar later in the morning but most stayed over West Falkland at high altitude. One such late morning incidents involved four Grupo 5 A-4Bs which were vectored by Argentine radar by mistake towards a Sea Harrier CAP! Fortunately for the A-4 pilots, their Mirage IIIEA escorts, Capitan Gustavo Garcia Cuerva

and Primer Teniente Carlos Perona, realised the error and accelerated to get between the Skyhawks and the Sea Harriers. The Argentine aircraft were about 20,000ft above the Sea Harriers and were hidden by a layer of cloud, so Lieutenant Commander John Eyton-Jones and Flight Lieutenant Paul Barton of 801 Squadron wisely decided not to engage at high altitude where the Mirage had an advantage. Had they known that four of the 'Mirages' were actually Skyhawk bombers, they might have risked an engagement.

The behaviour of the Argentine pilots was perplexing to the British but was understandable as the Argentines thought they were experiencing a full-scale assault from the sea and were looking for the British ships to attack. This was the third pair of Mirage IIIEAs to reach the Falklands on the 1st. Two earlier sections had taken off from Rio Gallegos soon after the Vulcan and Sea Harrier raids on Stanley airport but had found nothing.

When Royal Navy destroyers and frigates started firing at shore targets in the afternoon the Argentine forces on the Falklands became convinced that this was the start of the invasion. Pucaras and Turbo Mentors were dispatched on armed reconnaissance missions to find the British fleet and search for signs of helicopter-borne landings on the islands. At 1545Z three 4 Escuadrilla Turbo Mentors, flown by Teniente de Navio Pereyra, Teniente de Fregata D Manzanella and Teniente M Uberti, took off from Pebble Island to search for signs of enemy activity on the north coast of East Falkland. About ten miles from Stanley the trio spotted a Royal Navy Sea King, which they manoeuvred to attack. However, just as they were about to open fire on the helicopter they were themselves attacked by two Sea Harriers flown by Lieutenant Commander

The Sea Harriers of 800 and 801 Squadrons were very active throughout 1st May flying bombing raids on Stanley and Goose Green and combat air patrols to defend against Argentine aircraft. MoD

Nigel Ward and Lieutenant Mike Watson. The Sea Harriers had been vectored towards the Turbo Mentors by the radar operator on board *Glamorgan* and the brief action ended when the Turbo Mentors escaped into low cloud, although not before one of the aircraft was hit in the cockpit and slightly damaged by cannon fire from 'Sharkey' Ward's Sea Harrier. At one stage in the incident, Ward's Sea Harrier came very near to colliding with one the Argentine aircraft as it tried to escape in cloud. Following their narrow escape all three Turbo Mentors flew back to Pebble Island at very low level and landed without incident, thus concluding 4 Escuadrilla's only experience of combat during the entire conflict.

A few minutes after losing the Turbo Mentors, Ward and Watson were vectored by *Glamorgan* towards two high-flying Mirage IIIEAs about 40 miles to the south of their position that were coming to assist the Turbo Mentors upon hearing of their predicament. One of the Grupo 8 Mirages was seen to fire a missile (said to be a Matra R530 fired by mistake without a radar lock-on) at the Sea Harriers before turning away and heading for home. Once more the engagement ended inconclusively and it

was not until about three hours later that the Sea Harriers achieved their first air-to-air kill of the conflict.

At 1910Z Flight Lieutenant Paul Barton (in XZ452) and Lieutenant Steve Thomas (in XZ453) of 801 Squadron were vectored by *Glamorgan* towards two enemy aircraft flying east at high altitude over West Falkland. The Argentine aircraft were the Grupo 8 Mirage IIIEAs of Dardo flight flown by Capitan Cuerva and Primer Teniente Perona, who were on their second mission of the day. The Mirages were also under radar control and the two pairs of fighters closed rapidly head-on. Paul Barton peeled off to the right before resuming his westerly course in an attempt to outflank the Mirages, which were concentrating on Steve Thomas's aircraft in their 12 o'clock position. As Thomas spotted the Mirages at five miles distance he thought he saw them fire their air-to-air missiles but more likely saw them jettison their drop tanks.

Thomas was unable to get a head-on lock on the Mirages as he passed dangerously close to them at a closing speed of well over 1,000 mph. Perona started to turn to try to get behind Thomas's Sea Harrier, but by this time Paul Barton had swept in unnoticed and fired a Sidewinder from

Grupo 8 de Caza had 16 Mirage IIIEAs and one Mirage IIIDA in service at the beginning of the Falklands conflict, but two were lost on their operational debut on 1st May. Thereafter the aircraft rarely engaged in air combat but flew a number of escort and decoy raids, luring Sea Harriers away from attack aircraft. Argentine Air Force

The Argentine forces in the Falklands were well equipped with anti-aircraft guns, including the Oerlikon 35mm cannon seen here with hundreds of spent rounds on the ground. Flt Sgt D W Knights

about one mile behind Perona's Mirage (I-015) as it tried to evade the Sea Harrier. At 1928Z the Sidewinder streaked away from the Sea Harrier with a good lock-on to its target and hit the Mirage, causing it to explode. Carlos Perona ejected from his disintegrating aircraft and parachuted on to the shore just north of Pebble Island. Perona was later evacuated back to the mainland in a C-130 and spent several weeks in hospital recovering from injuries received when he landed heavily on the rocky shore.

Having seen Barton shoot down Perona's Mirage, Steve Thomas then achieved a radar lock on Cuerva's aircraft (I-019) and launched a Sidewinder as the Mirage started a spiral descent. Cuerva spotted the missile coming and dived towards cloud followed by the Sidewinder. Steve Thomas could not see what happened and did not know until some time afterwards that he had achieved the second Sea Harrier kill of the conflict. The Sidewinder exploded close to the Mirage while it was still in cloud and severely damaged the aircraft's controls and caused a fuel leak. With no

chance of returning to the Argentine mainland, Cuerva headed toward Stanley to either eject over the airfield or attempt a highly risky emergency landing. However, he did not have the opportunity to do either as his aircraft was shot down by mistake by a jittery Argentine AAA site near Stanley. Although they had been warned of the approach of a friendly aircraft, the gunners thought the aircraft was dropping bombs as it cleared its pylons of stores before attempting an emergency landing. Sadly, Capitan Cuerva was unable to eject and was killed when his aircraft crashed into the water just south of Freycinet Peninsula in what was the first of several 'friendly fire' incidents of the conflict.

Grupo 8 had been tasked to provide 12 Mirage IIIEA escort sorties from their base at Rio Gallegos during the day, although only ten may have been flown, so the loss of two aircraft and one pilot for so few sorties was particularly devastating. The salutary experience of 1st May resulted in the Mirages playing only a minor role for the rest of the conflict. The aircraft had an even

shorter range than the Dagger A and could not afford to come down to low level to engage the Sea Harriers, which certainly had no intention of climbing to engage the Mirages at their optimum altitude. With no clear advantage it made little sense to risk the Mirages unnecessarily and so they were used mainly for base alert at Rio Gallegos, Comodoro Rivadavia and Mariano Moreno, and as escorts and decoys for certain missions. This was the only occasion when British and Argentine aircraft intentionally engaged in air combat as, after 1st May, Argentine aircraft never challenged the Sea Harriers but chose to evade or avoid contact whenever possible.

As the air battle north of the islands was ending another one was developing further to the east. Two 800 Squadron Sea Harriers flown by Flight Lieutenant Bertie Penfold and Lieutenant Martin Hale were scrambled from *Hermes* to intercept Argentine aircraft that were heading towards the carrier group at high altitude. Four flights of Dagger As had taken off from San Julian earlier in the afternoon, these consisting of three pairs of escorts and a flight of three (Torno flight) carrying bombs to attack any British shipping found. Another pair of aircraft (Rubio flight) was supposed to take off from Rio Grande but one aborted, leaving just Primer Teniente Jose Ardiles (a cousin of the famous Argentine footballer Osvaldo Ardiles) flying Dagger A C-433 to continue his escort mission alone.

As the Daggers started to arrive over East Falkland they and the Sea Harriers were vectored towards each other by their respective radar controllers until the two Sea Harriers engaged the single Dagger of Jose Ardiles at 1941Z. The Dagger was at 33,000ft with the Sea Harriers at 20,000ft and Ardiles fired first. A Shafrir missile sped towards Martin Hale's aircraft and he lost 15,000ft of altitude as he dived into cloud while dumping chaff to decoy the missile, which eventually fell harmlessly away as its motor ran out of fuel just short of its intended target. Meanwhile, as Ardiles made a climbing turn to maintain his altitude advantage, Bertie Penfold (in XZ455) had moved in behind the Dagger and from a range of three miles fired a Sidewinder. The missile homed onto the glowing tailpipe of the Dagger as the aircraft was still in full afterburner, providing a good infrared signature for the heat-seeking missile. At 1941Z the Dagger exploded in a huge ball of flame and the wreckage fell on Lively Island, killing Jose Ardiles. By now short of fuel, the remaining Daggers broke away and headed for home, as did the two Sea Harriers. Unfortunately, the dramatic sight of the Dagger exploding and killing its pilot so disturbed Bertie Penfold that he had to be withdrawn from flying soon afterwards and returned to the UK.

While this engagement was taking place the three Grupo 6 Dagger As of Torno flight from San Julian managed to evade the Sea Harrier CAPs and attack *Glamorgan*, *Alacrity* and *Arrow* at their position off Cape Pembroke, where they were firing at Stanley airfield. Capitan Dimeglio, Teniente Aguirre Faget and Primer Teniente Cesar Roman had expected to find ships near the mouth of Falkland Sound but seeing none there they continued towards Stanley at low level. The warships had not detected the enemy aircraft on radar and so were caught unawares and were lucky to escape serious damage as each aircraft aimed two 500lb parachute-retarded bombs at each vessel. *Glamorgan* and *Alacrity* were slightly damaged below the waterline by the explosion of nearby bombs while *Arrow* was hit by cannon fire (about eight rounds) from one of the Daggers. Taken by surprise, the only air defence put up by the ships was a single Seacat fired by *Glamorgan* and a few rounds of 20mm cannon fire from the frigates, but none of it managed to hit any of

the Daggers. A Sea Harrier gave chase as one of the Daggers climbed to altitude to conserve precious fuel but had to break off when within five miles of the enemy aircraft due to its own fuel state. Two of the Daggers dived down to low level to escape the Sea Harriers but Cesar Roman did not hear the warning from Argentine radar and continued on at high altitude, blissfully unaware of how close the Sea Harrier had come.

The British warships had just finished a brief bombardment of Stanley airfield and were about to withdraw when the air attack took place. *Alacrity*'s Lynx HAS2 (XZ736) piloted by Lieutenant Commander R G Burrows was in the air at the time of the attack, having been spotting for the warships' guns. The Lynx carried Captain C C Brown of 148 (Meiktila) Commando Forward Observation Battery, Royal Artillery to provide gunfire observation reports to the warships. The Lynx was escorted during the mission by a GPMG-equipped Wessex HU5 (XS483) from 'A' Flight 845 Squadron that had been detached from RFA *Resource* to *Glamorgan* for two days. As the Lynx approached Kidney Island, just four miles to the northeast of Stanley, it came under fire from two small Argentine vessels. The Prefectura Naval Z-28 patrol boat *Islas Malvinas* was slightly damaged when the Lynx fought back using its door-mounted GPMG but the other vessel, the commandeered Falkland Islands Government boat, *Forrest*, was undamaged.

The Argentine sailors on board the boats hit the Lynx, which received several bullet holes in the cockpit, rotor blades and fuel tank and Bob Burrows was forced to break off the attack and land the helicopter on the shore for a quick visual inspection of the damage. This was the first landing of a Task Force aircraft on the Falklands since the invasion, albeit unplanned. The damage turned out to be serious but the pilot decided to take off again and limp back to *Alacrity*. During the mission two Tigercat SAMs were fired at the Wessex from a position near Stanley airport but both helicopters returned to their ships safely. On the 3rd *Alacrity*'s Lynx made a short flight across to RFA *Fort Austin* for urgent repairs to its badly damaged tail rotor driveshaft. The Lynx remained under repair until the 8th, during which time its place was taken by XZ700 borrowed from the *Fort Austin*.

The final air-to-air engagement of the day took place as dusk approached at 2047Z during the last Argentine air attack of the day. *Invincible* was about 100 miles northeast of Stanley at the time when her Fighter Director started to track three enemy aircraft about 60 miles to the west of the aircraft carrier. He vectored Lieutenant Commander Mike Broadwater (in ZA175) and Lieutenant Alan Curtis (in XZ451)

towards the Argentine aircraft and just moments later the two Sea Harriers picked up the targets dead ahead on their Blue Fox radars at a range of 26 miles. The two Sea Harrier pilots spotted three Canberra B62 bombers flying at 100ft above the sea, heading east towards Stanley as they started to search for British shipping. The Sea Harriers quickly positioned themselves behind the formation and Al Curtis fired a Sidewinder at one of the aircraft, B-110 flown by Teniente Eduardo de Ibanez and Primer Teniente Mario Gonzalez. The missile detonated near the Canberra's wing root setting one wing on fire and damaging an engine, but the aircraft continued on its course for a few seconds and so Curtis fired his other missile. Before the second missile reached the Canberra its crew ejected a split second before the aircraft hit the sea.

Mike Broadwater fired both his missiles at another of the Canberras and although the first missile fell short, the second one exploded under the bomber, damaging its starboard wing and causing it to jettison its bombs before it returned to the mainland to make an emergency landing at San Julian. Unable to continue the fight due to a shortage of fuel, the two Sea Harriers then broke away to return to *Invincible*. As soon as he saw the Sea Harriers leave the area the leader of the Canberra formation, Capitan Alberto Baigorri, returned to search for his downed comrades but they were nowhere to be seen and their bodies were never found, despite an extensive search.

At 2054Z a Lynx from *Brilliant* spotted a Canberra some distance away, apparently with pieces falling off as it flew at low level. Although this gave rise to a British claim that a second Canberra had been shot down, what was seen was probably Baigorri's aircraft searching for the crew of B-110. This was the second Canberra bombing mission of the day. The first flight of three aircraft had failed to find any British warships and returned to their base at Trelew after a fruitless search. Canberra B62 B-110 had previously served with the RAF's 231 Operational Conversion Unit at RAF Bassingbourn before being sold to Argentina in 1970.

This concluded a very successful day for the British airmen and for the Sea Harrier pilots in particular. Despite several earlier inconclusive engagements, the Sea Harriers had succeeded in shooting down a Canberra bomber, a Dagger fighter-bomber and two Mirage III interceptors for no loss of their own. The success of the superior British tactics, training and weapons was immediately apparent and these initial results were demoralising to the Argentine aircrew. In addition the raid on Goose Green that disabled three Pucaras, together with the Vulcan and Sea Harrier raids that damaged Stanley airport, set the pattern for British airfield attacks throughout the conflict. The Argentine failure to engage the Sea Harrier in order to achieve air superiority had been a major mistake which was to have serious consequences for the duration of the conflict.

Not all the air operations around the Falklands involved air-to-air combat. On 1st May the Argentine Task Force with its aircraft carrier, *25 de Mayo*, was well to the northwest of the Falklands and 200 miles outside the British-imposed TEZ. In the early hours of the morning the carrier launched an S-2E Tracker flown by the unit commander, Capitan de Corbeta Hector Skare, in an attempt to locate the British fleet. The Royal Navy ships entered the TEZ at 0530Z but the Tracker failed to find them although it was made aware of their presence by picking up the British radar emissions on its recently installed radar homing and warning receiver equipment. It was not until 1500Z that another Tracker, flown by Capitan de Corbeta Alberto Dabini, located the British Carrier Battle Group at a distance of 55 miles. The Tracker was itself picked up by British radar as it climbed to make a radar sweep of the area, forcing the pilot to make a hasty exit as he was well within Sea Harrier range, although none were launched as they were being prepared for their pre-planned CAP missions. Another Tracker was launched from *25 de Mayo* at one minute past midnight to find the British fleet in preparation for a possible air strike at daybreak on the 2nd.

The A-4Cs of Grupo 4 at San Julian and the A-4Bs of Grupo 5 at Rio Gallegos had a busy if frustrating day on the 1st. Grupo 4 planned to put up four flights each of four aircraft during the day, the first of which took off at 1320Z but returned an hour and a half later having found nothing to attack. One of the Grupo 5 flights was vectored towards a Sea Harrier CAP by mistake (as has already been related) and all four aircraft were fortunate to return safely to Rio Gallegos. Another Grupo 5 flight did manage to find and attack a ship south of Stanley but the next morning the A-4Bs' pilots were reprimanded for attacking an Argentine vessel, the blockade-runner *Formosa*, which had left Stanley a few hours earlier to return to the mainland. The aircraft (flown by Capitan P Carballo, Primer Teniente Cachon and Teniente C Rinke) made numerous passes and hit the ship with at least two bombs, one of which lodged in the hold but failed to explode. Most Skyhawk flights on 1st May had top cover provided by either Mirage IIIEAs of Grupo 8 or Dagger As of Grupo 6. Several Skyhawks were turned back by the Argentine radar controllers at Stanley when Sea Harrier CAPs threatened.

While most of the ships of the Task Force stayed near the edge of the TEZ during the day, the frigates *Brilliant* and *Yarmouth* together with three 826 Squadron Sea King HAS5s were tasked with investigating the coastal waters north of East Falkland. It was suspected that an Argentine Salta class submarine might be lurking offshore. If the suspicion was correct, then this would be the *San Luis*, thought to be Argentina's only operational submarine at this time. The *Salta* herself set off for the Falklands in mid-April but was found to be too noisy underwater to be fit for combat duties as she could be easily detected by sonar; she also had problems with her torpedo fire control system. The problems were not solved before the end of hostilities and the *Salta* took no part in the conflict.

The *Santiago del Estero* had recently been decommissioned and was waiting to be broken up and cannibalised and her sister ship, *Santa Fe*, had been captured in South Georgia. However, even with only one operational submarine on the prowl, the British Task Force could take no chances and expended a tremendous effort on ASW in an attempt to safeguard the warships and the resupply vessels plying to and from Ascension Island. During the operation the helicopters used the HIFR refuelling system in action for the first time. This entailed the Sea King hovering over the stern of a frigate as the helicopter crew lowered a hook to hoist up a fuel line and take on fuel.

The unsuccessful search for the *San Luis* continued into the early hours of 2nd May and resulted in the Sea Kings involved dropping six Mk11 depth charges, launching two Mk46 torpedoes and refuelling ten times from the frigates. The crew of each Sea King was exchanged while the helicopter hovered over the ships and one of the helicopters (XZ577) flew for a total of 10 hours 20 minutes, a new world record for a continually airborne operational mission for helicopters up to that time. *Brilliant*'s Lynx and *Plymouth*'s Wasp were also involved in the search for the *San Luis*. However, despite intense activity throughout the day by the ships and the helicopters, no firm contact with the submarine was made, although it was almost certainly somewhere in the general area.

Although the Argentines eventually realised that there were no large-scale landings on the Falklands on 1st May, they were at least correct in assuming that British Special Forces were being inserted onto the islands covertly. In the evening of the 1st a Sea King HC4 of 846 Squadron flew from *Hermes* to land the first patrols of 'G' Squadron 22 SAS Regiment, who were tasked with gathering intelligence on Argentine positions. Some of these men

stayed close to Argentine positions, often in severe weather conditions, for up to 26 days. The first patrols were inserted near strategic points around the islands including Stanley, Bluff Cove, Darwin, Goose Green, Fox Bay and Port Howard. The helicopters usually routed inland well to the west of Stanley, often using Bombilla Hill as an initial point before using the valleys and hills to effectively mask their flight to the insertion points.

SBS patrols were inserted to overlook Berkeley Sound and other points along the north coast of East Falklands on 1st May. Two teams were flown to Ajax Bay and the Verde Mountains to keep an eye on San Carlos Water, the eventual landing place for the British forces. By the 3rd, eight four-man SAS patrols had been inserted into various locations in the Falklands and by the 18th a total of 25 night sorties had been flown by 846 Squadron to insert, recover and resupply Special Forces on the islands. Most of these missions involved the use of passive night-vision goggles (PNGs) by the Sea King crews which greatly aided their precise navigation and flying over the featureless, unlit terrain. However, there were only five sets of advanced PNGs available and this restricted the night effort that 846 Squadron could mount. The Special Forces flight of 846 Squadron had the most advanced version of night-vision goggles available, while other helicopter units used earlier versions. The extensive and vital night operations undertaken by the Sea Kings of 846 Squadron were greatly assisted by the use of this equipment and only three missions failed to reach their objectives.

The 1st of May had been a very busy day for both sides and the intense level of air activity would not be achieved again for another three weeks, during the first day of the amphibious landings at San Carlos.

2nd May (Sunday) –
The Sinking of the *General Belgrano*

Following the intense air activity of 1st May, the next day saw a marked reduction due to the onset of what turned out to be a prolonged spell of bad weather that blanketed most of the islands and the sea around the Falklands. However, following the opening of hostilities, tensions were running very high on both sides and the 2nd turned out to be even worse than the previous day for the Argentine forces, despite the marked lack of air action.

Virtually the entire Argentine fleet was preparing for action off the Falklands on the 2nd. The lone aircraft carrier, two Type 42 destroyers and two Exocet-armed frigates were approaching the islands from the northwest, while further north was a group of three additional Exocet-armed frigates. The third group, consisting of the cruiser

Argentine bombs are prepared for an attack on the British Task Force on 2nd May that never materialised. The Skyhawks were unable to take off from the 25 de Mayo *due to insufficient wind over the deck to launch the heavily-laden aircraft safely.* Argentine Navy

General Belgrano and two more destroyers were manoeuvring southeast of the Falkland Islands.

The day started with the *25 de Mayo* sending out another S-2E Tracker in an attempt to find the British Task Force. The aircraft took off at one minute past midnight for a night radar search of the area to the north and east of the Falklands. Flying eastwards at low level, Capitan de Corbeta Emilio Goitia eventually found four ships on his radar screen at some 60 miles distance. Having pinpointed their position he turned around to return to his aircraft carrier but was soon warned that an aircraft, presumed correctly to be a Sea Harrier, was on an intercept course towards the Tracker. Capitan Goitia descended as low as he dared in the darkness as he made for the safety of the Argentine Task Force.

Invincible had picked up radar emissions from the Tracker at 0312Z and assumed that it was an Argentine C-130 on a radar reconnaissance mission. Flight Lieutenant Ian Mortimer of 801 Squadron took off at 0331Z and headed west trying to locate the 'C-130' using only his own RWR. As he got closer to the Tracker, about 150 miles northwest of *Invincible*, Ian Mortimer began to receive warnings that he was being illuminated by a Sea Dart fire control radar (from the Argentine destroyer *Hercules*). He knew that the Argentine Type 42 destroyers carried Sea Darts and that the only British ships with Sea Dart missiles were some distance behind him, so he quite sensibly turned back before flying westwards again in an attempt to pick up the source of the emissions. At 0358Z he picked up five surface contacts on his Blue Fox radar at a distance of some 25 miles. Having found the Argentine Task Force he returned to *Invincible* at 0457Z to report.

By 0500Z Capitan Goitia had landed back on the *25 de Mayo* to deliver his information and a dawn raid by eight A-4Q Skyhawks of 3 Escuadrilla was quickly planned. By first light seven Skyhawks were each loaded with six Mk82 Snakeye bombs while the eighth aircraft was fitted with AIM-9B Sidewinders to provide a degree of air defence cover. However, the Argentine force commander needed more precise information on the location of the British carrier group, so another Tracker was dispatched at 0828Z to update Goitia's information. Unfortunately for the Argentine Navy, the Tracker's radar malfunctioned just minutes after take-off and the British position remained undetected, so the attack was cancelled.

The situation was complicated by the presence of a fleet of about 25 Soviet and Polish fishing trawlers situated almost midway between the two opposing fleets. It has also been suggested that the unusually calm wind conditions would have made launching the heavily laden A-4Qs dangerous. Whatever the reason, 3 Escuadrilla's mission was scrubbed at 0900Z and the Argentine Navy missed one of the few opportunities it would have to strike at the heart of the Task Force. Meanwhile the British Carrier Battle Group was preparing itself for such an attack, not knowing of the problems encountered by the opposing Task Force. Although CAPs were put up from both *Hermes* and *Invincible* and the aircraft carriers remained at action stations for most of the day, the flat calm and fog that developed later in the morning made any attack unlikely and what might have been a classic carrier battle was averted.

Following the failure of the Argentine Task Force to launch an early morning raid on the British aircraft carriers, any further attempts were abandoned at 1858Z in the afternoon when the cruiser *General Belgrano* was hit by two torpedoes from the submarine *Conqueror*. Launched in 1938 as the USS *Phoenix* and a survivor of the Japanese attack on Pearl Harbor, the cruiser later served as General MacArthur's flagship in the Pacific before being bought by Argentina in 1951. It was leading a detached element of the Argentine Task Force well to the south of the *25 de Mayo*'s group as part of a planned pincer movement when it was hit. The elderly ship sank within 15 minutes with the tragic loss of 321 crewmen, which caused a major furore in Argentina and a controversial legacy in the UK. Whatever the exact circumstances surrounding the sinking, the event effectively signalled the end of major Argentine naval operations around the Falklands. A number of aircraft including S-2E Trackers and SP-2H Neptunes took part in the search for survivors from the cruiser, some of whom were not rescued until 48 hours after the sinking. Task Force 79 sailed back into home waters and largely sat out the rest of the conflict. The CANA aircraft disembarked from the *25 de Mayo* and later flew missions from land bases.

When the *General Belgrano* went down 35 miles outside the TEZ and just over 200 miles south of the Falklands, it took with it the embarked Alouette III (0649/3-H-109) from 1 Escuadrilla. The Argentine Task Force suffered even more bad luck on the 2nd when a Lynx HAS23 (0735/3-H-142), based on board the Type 42 destroyer *Santisima Trinidad*, collided with the ship in bad weather, killing the helicopter's crew. The wreckage of the Lynx was salvaged and returned to port and was later displayed at the Museo Aeronaval de la Armada in Puerto Belgrano.

What might have been a much-needed success for the Argentine forces on the 2nd, an attempt by 2 Escuadrilla to mount its first Super Etendard mission against the British Task Force, also failed. Two aircraft took off from Rio Grande flown by the squadron commander, Capitan de Fragata Jorge Colombo and Teniente de Fragata Carlos Manchetanz, but a fuel transfer problem with one of the Super Etendards during inflight refuelling from the KC-130H tanker caused the mission to be abandoned. The Exocet's targeting information had to be reprogrammed if flown and not fired but the equipment to do this could not be moved from their main base, so this failed mission resulted in the two aircraft having to fly a 900-mile round trip from Rio Grande to Espora before they could be used in action again.

The sinking of the *General Belgrano* combined with the opening Vulcan raid on Stanley effectively imprisoned the Argentine garrison on the Falklands. With the Argentine Navy confined to mainland coastal waters and the Falklands garrison denied the use of Stanley as a main operating base for fighter aircraft, the Argentine forces' options began to narrow considerably. The Air Force and Navy were forced to fight the air war from their airfields on the mainland, none of which were closer than 380 nautical miles to the Falklands. In effect the Argentine Air Force was faced with a similar situation to that of the Luftwaffe during the Battle of Britain. Operating at extreme range, the fighters had insufficient endurance to stay in the combat zone for very long and their tactical use was therefore greatly restricted.

3rd May (Monday)

During the night of 2nd/3rd May the Argentine patrol vessel *Alferez Sobral* was still searching the sea north of East Falkland for the crew of the Canberra that had been shot down on the 1st. The *Alferez Sobral* was an 800-ton ex-US Navy auxiliary ocean-going tug that was being used by the Argentine Navy as a patrol vessel. At 0400Z Sea King HAS5 ZA129 from 826 Squadron, captained by Lieutenant Commander J S M Chandler, picked up a small contact on its radar and went to investigate. The helicopter was fired on by the *Alferez Sobral* as it approached the well-lit boat in the dark. Lieutenant Commander Chandler took the Sea King out of range and radioed for assistance that was soon forthcoming in the shape of two Lynx HAS2s sent by the Type 42 destroyers *Coventry* and *Glasgow*. However, *Glasgow*'s Lynx (XZ247) suffered a temporary radio failure so *Coventry*'s Lynx (XZ242) fired its two Sea Skuas first, marking the operational debut of the new anti-ship missile. Both Sea Skuas hit the *Alferez Sobral*, which was assumed to have sunk, the explosion being seen by British warships 30 miles away.

Glasgow's Lynx then regained the use of its radio but came under fire while searching for survivors or wreckage from the *Alfereze Sobral*. The Lynx fired its two Sea Skuas at what was thought to be a second patrol boat a short distance away. In fact it was the *Alferez Sobral* again, which was once more hit and badly damaged by the two missiles. Both Lynx had to return to their ships as their fuel reserves were running low and the crews were convinced that they had sunk two patrol boats. In fact no boat had been sunk as the *Alferez Sobral* struggled back to Puerto Deseado with her bridge totally destroyed and her captain and seven other crewmen dead. The devastated patrol vessel was later repaired but took no further part in the Falklands conflict. Many early post-war reports claimed that it was the *Comodoro Somellera* that was sunk but

Seen here wearing the markings of 706 Squadron, Sea King HAS5 ZA129 was transferred to 826 Squadron on board Hermes *on 2nd April 1982. It was ZA129 that located the* Alferez Sobral *on 3rd May. MoD*

On 5th May four Harrier GR3s left St Mawgan for the non-stop flight to Ascension Island. XZ132 developed a problem during the flight and had to divert to Banjul in The Gambia, where it is seen in this photograph with one of the Victor K2 tankers that had been refuelling the Harriers. Wg Cdr N Sharpe

in fact that vessel was nowhere near the scene of the action and it survived the conflict unscathed. Both tugs were still serving with the Argentine Navy in the late 1990s.

Thick fog curtailed most air operations by the British Task Force on the 3rd. A radar contact with what was thought to be a CANA SP-2H Neptune prompted *Invincible* to send an 801 Squadron Sea Harrier to investigate, but the aircraft found nothing and returned safely to the aircraft carrier.

Two Canberras from 2 Grupo took off from Trelew during the afternoon to attack shipping but upon reaching their target they discovered that the vessels were Argentine and so returned to base disappointed.

The weather on the Falkland Islands was not much better than it was out to sea. Three Pucaras were made serviceable at Goose Green and flown to Pebble Island, another aircraft arriving on the 4th. At 1806Z the two MB-339As, led by Capitan de Corbeta Molteni, took off from Stanley airport on a low-level armed reconnaissance flight after a ship had been reported 60 miles southeast of Stanley. The aircraft searched the designated area under low cloud but found no sign of any ships so returned to Stanley in radio silence. As the second aircraft (0764/4-A-113 flown by Teniente de Fregata Carlos Benitez) approached Stanley's runway from over the sea it drifted off the centreline and hit a rock, tearing off a wing. The aircraft cartwheeled onto the beach near the Cape Pembroke lighthouse, killing Carlos Benitez instantly. Later, during the afternoon, two more replacement

MB-339As were flown to Stanley from Rio Grande to bring the detachment strength up to three aircraft.

As night drew on, an Alouette III and a Puma from the *Bahia Paraiso*, now converted to the role of hospital ship since her participation in the South Georgia operation, searched for any more survivors from the *General Belgrano*. The *Bahia Paraiso* eventually picked up 74 survivors and 18 bodies from the sunken cruiser.

The ships of the South Georgia Task Group headed towards Ascension Island with their cargo of Argentine prisoners and were overflown by an Argentine Air Force Boeing 707 on the 3rd. *Antrim* later handed over her escort duties to *Antelope* with which she exchanged places to escort the LSLs to the TEZ.

On 1st May two RAF Hercules had left Wittering for Ascension Island with 40 members of 1 Squadron's ground crew. The next day five Harriers GR3s flew to St Mawgan, the most southerly RAF mainland airfield. On the 3rd three of the Harriers (XV789, XZ972 and XZ989 flown by the squadron commander Wing Commander Peter Squire, Flight Lieutenant Tony Harper and Flight Lieutenant Mark Hare respectively) set off on the 4,600-mile flight to Ascension Island. Two aircraft flew non-stop but the third (flown by Peter Squire) had to make a brief stop at Banjul in The Gambia as the tanker had used more fuel than planned. The Harrier and its tanker then flew on to Wideawake airfield later that night. The non-stop flight took nine hours and 15 minutes and was three hours longer than the previous record non-stop flight (transatlantic) for Harrier aircraft. During the deployment the Harriers were refuelled by Victor tankers operating from Marham and Ascension, and SAR coverage was provided by Nimrods operating from St Mawgan and Freetown. Each Harrier carried a pair of 330-gallon ferry tanks and

most of the ferry flights involved up to five in-flight refuellings to ensure that the Harriers had enough fuel to enable them to divert to an airfield if necessary.

Two more Harrier GR3s flew down to St Mawgan on the morning of the 4th as three more aircraft (XV787, XZ963 and XZ997) took off for the non-stop flight to Ascension Island. Unfortunately, XV787 flown by Flight Lieutenant John Rochfort developed a technical problem and had to divert to Madeira and was eventually flown back to Wittering, taking no further part in the deployment. The last four Harriers (XW919, XZ129, XZ132 and XZ988) left St Mawgan on the morning of the 5th on a non-stop flight to conclude 1 Squadron's initial deployment to Ascension Island. However, one of the aircraft (XZ132 flown by Flight Lieutenant Ross Boyens) had to divert to Banjul in The Gambia and did not complete the flight to Wideawake airfield on the 6th.

Although the 42 Squadron Nimrod detachment at Wideawake had returned to St Mawgan in mid-April, the unit was still heavily involved in Operation 'Corporate'. From 1st May, 42 Squadron deployed aircraft to Freetown, Sierra Leone to provide SAR coverage on the southern leg of the ferry route of the Harriers flying from the UK to Ascension. The first SAR sortie was flown by XV249 on the 3rd and further sorties were flown on the next three days.

4th May (Tuesday) – The Loss of HMS *Sheffield*

Three days after the initial Vulcan attack on Stanley airport the raid was repeated as 'Black Buck 2', but with less spectacular results. This time Squadron Leader Reeve's aircraft (XM607) did not let him down and he took off with the accompanying Victor tankers and Vulcan XM598 as reserve just before midnight on the 3rd. The raid involved a different sequence of in-flight refuellings from that used on 'Black Buck 1'

An aerial view of Stanley airport looking towards the southeast. The confined nature of the airport is plainly visible in this photograph. MoD

and the final bomb run was flown at 16,000ft as opposed to 10,000ft in order to give added protection from enemy ground-based air defences. The bombs were dropped successfully at 0830Z but, unfortunately, none of them hit the runway on this occasion although all fell on the airport and caused further damage as well as much consternation among Argentine troops based at Stanley. In contrast to the high drama of the first raid, 'Black Buck 2' was flown without incident and the Vulcan arrived back at Wideawake about 15 hours after take-off. Three days later XM598 and XM607 flew back to Waddington for minor modifications and to make space available at busy Wideawake. Both aircraft returned to Ascension Island a week later for the third 'Black Buck' mission.

During the night of 3rd/4th May, naval bombardment disabled the Prefectura Naval Skyvan 3M (PA-54) as it sat on Stanley racecourse, although its destruction was not completed until the night of 12/13th June when it was hit by 105mm artillery shells. The Prefectura Naval Puma (PA-12) was also damaged by naval gunfire during this night and its hulk was eventually canni-balised for spare parts for the Argentine Army Pumas based on the island.

The day dawned clear and bright, in con-trast to the low cloud and fog of the previ-ous day. The better weather meant that Argentine aircraft would be searching for the Task Force and at 1010Z an SP-2H Nep-tune (0708/2-P-112) reported the location of the British fleet while on a radar reconnais-sance mission. The last two operational Neptunes of the Escuadrilla de Exploracion had deployed to Rio Grande in April but the aircraft were nearing the end of their useful life and were due to be withdrawn from ser-vice in a matter of months. The Neptune was actually checking to see if it was safe for a flight of three C-130s to fly to Stanley airport and had taken-off from Rio Grande and flown to the south of the Falklands before turning north. The airlift mission was abandoned after the Vulcan raid on Stanley but the Neptune's pilot, Capitan de Corbeta Ernesto Proni Leston, was ordered to stay in the area to the southeast of Stanley and search for enemy shipping. The aircraft then picked up three ships on its radar and was itself detected by British radars, which illuminated the Neptune's RWR.

Although the Neptune approached to within 60 miles of the British ships it was not investigated and was therefore able to pass its vital information back to Rio Grande, where two Super Etendards were prepared for take-off. Retiring to the area where the *General Belgrano* had been sunk on the 2nd, in order to fool the British that the air-craft was part of the SAR operations, the Neptune climbed to 3,500ft at 1335Z for one last radar sweep to obtain precise locations of the British ships. This information was then passed to the Super Etendard pilots as they approached the Falklands. The Nep-tune then turned for home having played a vital and very dangerous part in the drama that was to follow. The Carrier Battle Group was indeed close to the islands, sailing west-southwest about 70 miles southeast of Stanley and was being led by the three Type 42 destroyers *Glasgow*, *Coventry* and *Sheffield*. The air defence picket line of Type 42s was followed 18 miles behind by *Glamorgan* and the ASW screen of the frigates *Alacrity*, *Arrow* and *Yarmouth*. Behind them were the fleet auxiliaries *Fort Austin*, *Olmeda* and *Resource* and then the two aircraft carriers and their attendant goalkeeper Type 22s (air defence close protection). The Battle Group had come in close to the Falklands in order to insert Special Forces by helicopter later that night and to probe the Argentine defences.

In response to the Neptune's discovery, two Super Etendards flown by Capitan de Corbeta Cesar Augusto Bedacarratz (in 0752/3-A-202) and Teniente de Fregata Armando Mayora (in 0753/3-A-203) took off from Rio Grande at 1245Z. The aircraft subsequently refuelled from a KC-130H and proceeded in radio silence. Two flights of Dagger As from Rio Grande provided an escort for the tanker. By 1330Z the Super Etendard pilots became aware of British radar transmissions and descended to less than 50ft to avoid being detected. The aircraft flew under a 500ft cloud base and passed through rain and snow showers. Five minutes later the Super Etendards received the last update from the Neptune before it left the area and the pilots decided to attack the largest of four ships that had been located, which was then about 115 miles away. At 1356Z the aircraft popped up to 150ft briefly to confirm the position of the target with their own Agave search radar; however, in doing so the Super Etendards briefly became visible on the radar screen of at least one British ship. To make matters worse there was no sign of the ships on the Super Etendard radars.

Glasgow spotted the two aircraft on her radar and immediately transmitted a warning to the rest of the Task Force. However, the Task Force had been overloaded with spurious reports of Super Etendard-type attacks in recent days and there was some confusion as to the veracity of *Glasgow*'s initial report, so the warning was downgraded by the Force Anti-Air Warfare Commander on board *Invincible*.

A short while later the Super Etendards popped up again and this time found the British ships on their radar and decided to attack the southernmost target. Again the Anti-Air Warfare Officer on *Glasgow* tried to convince *Invincible* that this was a real attack, but the Task Force remained at Air Raid Warning White, an alert state indicating that no enemy aircraft had been detected within 100 miles. At about 1402Z,

both pilots launched their Exocet missiles at less than 20 miles from their target. The two Super Etendards turned for home as soon as they had launched their missiles and quickly out-distanced two Sea Harrier CAPs that were airborne at the time. Meanwhile *Glasgow* started to fire chaff and later attempted, unsuccessfully, to engage the Exocets with her Sea Dart missile system. The missiles sped along a few feet above the waves and at 1404Z one missile slammed into the starboard side amidships of *Sheffield*. The Super Etendards then climbed to high altitude to conserve fuel once they were clear of the Sea Harriers and eventually landed at Rio Grande at 1510Z to a rousing welcome by fellow pilots and ground crew who were aware that the mission had been successful.

During the Super Etendards' approach, *Sheffield*'s electronic warning equipment was unusable as the ship's SCOT satellite uplink terminal was being used to contact London at the time, which largely prevented the interception of aircraft and missile transmissions. In a recent television documentary it was suggested that a breakdown in the command and control arrangements in *Sheffield*'s Operations Room was also a contributory factor. This was just one element in an unfortunate chain of events that led to *Sheffield* not detecting the Exocet missile, nor hearing *Glasgow*'s warnings and not reacting quickly enough when she did. However, the fundamental issue was that in 1982 the Royal Navy had very little defence against a sea-skimming missile such as Exocet. The missile punched through *Sheffield*'s skin just six feet above the waterline and although the missile warhead did not explode, there was enough kinetic energy and unspent rocket fuel to cause massive

damage and a major fire, which soon spread out of control. Unfortunately, the missile hit close to one of the ship's fuel tanks resulting in a fierce fire. The ship's water main and power supply had also been damaged by the Exocet so it was not possible to fight the fire effectively.

Confirmation that *Sheffield* had been hit by an Exocet and was in serious trouble was provided by an 826 Squadron Sea King HAS5 (XZ577 flown by Sub Lieutenant Phil Dibb). The helicopter was on an ASW patrol nearby and lowered a crewman to the ship's deck to find out what had happened. The Sea King then informed the flagship about ten minutes after the Exocet had struck. About an hour after the ship was hit, *Sheffield*'s Lynx HAS2 (XZ721) took off from the stricken vessel to take the AAWO to *Hermes* to report on the situation. After four hours of desperate fire-fighting on board *Sheffield* Captain Sam Salt reluctantly gave the order to abandon ship as the fire approached the Sea Dart magazine.

During the rescue *Yarmouth* reported that its sonar was picking up what it thought to be the noise of torpedoes running in the water. The ship was sufficiently concerned about the submarine threat that its helicopter dropped depth charges and the ship itself fired nine mortars. The reports of the presence of an Argentine submarine later proved to be false. The majority of the 266 survivors of *Sheffield*'s company were rescued by *Arrow*, which came alongside, although the last few were evacuated by a single Sea King of 826 Squadron, when *Arrow* mistakenly thought a torpedo had been fired at her and rapidly cleared the area to manoeuvre. The following day two Wessex from the *Resource* transferred the survivors from *Arrow* to the *Resource* and *Fort Austin*. Sadly, despite the rescue

The Prefectura Naval Puma PA-12 was found by British troops by the side of a road near the Governor's Residence in Stanley. The Puma did not appear to have been flown for some time and had probably been cannibalised for spares for the Argentine Army Pumas. PA-12 was brought to the UK and spent many years at RAF Odiham as a battle damage repair airframe until refurbished recently for use by 33 Squadron. Flt Sgt D W Knights

efforts, 20 men lost their lives on board *Sheffield*, the first casualties of the Royal Navy Task Force in action. The second Exocet is believed to have been deflected by chaff and was reportedly seen falling into the sea near *Alacrity*. Following the incident the Carrier Battle Group sailed east but later returned closer to the islands and the scheduled Special Forces insertion went ahead as planned.

Following evacuation, *Sheffield* continued to burn but did not sink and the ship was surrounded by a ring of passive sonars dropped by Sea Kings as it was thought that an Argentine submarine might try to finish off the destroyer with a torpedo. However, no submarine was detected and, after drifting for some time, *Sheffield* was eventually taken under tow by *Yarmouth* in the early hours of 9th May in the hope of taking the gutted vessel to South Georgia for salvage operations. However, this was not to be and on 10th May in a rough sea the towline had to be cut as *Sheffield* rolled over and sank well to the southeast of the Falklands. The loss of *Sheffield* marked the first time that a major warship had been sunk by an air-launched anti-ship missile since the Second World War, when a number of Allied vessels had been hit and sunk by German wire-guided glide bombs.

A few days after *Sheffield* was hit, *Exeter*, another Type 42 destroyer, was ordered to leave her guardship duties in the Caribbean and proceed to the South Atlantic via Ascension Island as a replacement. *Exeter* was the only Type 42 destroyer to be deployed to the Falklands that was fitted with the new Type 1022 radar that improved the Sea Dart's reaction time and enhanced its capability against aircraft flying near land. Another Type 42, *Cardiff*, was diverted to Gibraltar as she sailed through the Mediterranean while on her way home from patrol in the Persian Gulf. *Cardiff* was replenished at Gibraltar and prepared for action in the South Atlantic. Another action taken after the attack on *Sheffield* was to station two of the Royal Navy's nuclear-powered submarines off the major airfields (especially Rio Grande) to monitor Argentine aircraft as they took off for the Falklands. This was a dangerous venture for the submarines as they risked detection in the coastal waters and the information gained could only have been of general use as the flight paths could not be plotted.

About an hour after *Sheffield* was attacked a flight of three 800 Squadron Sea Harriers took off from *Hermes* for a raid on Goose Green airstrip. The raid had been postponed when *Sheffield* had been hit but the aircraft eventually took off at 1530Z.

Sea Harrier FRS1s XZ450 '50' (right) and XZ459 '25' (left) on board Hermes *with Broadsword in goalkeeper position close by. XZ450 was shot down at Goose Green on 4th May and its pilot, Lieutenant Nick Taylor killed.* MoD

Lieutenant Commander G W J Batt (in ZA192) led the raid and he and Lieutenant N Taylor (in XZ450) carried a load of CBUs to drop on parked aircraft while Flight Lieutenant E H Ball (in XZ460) was to drop three 1,000lb retard bombs on the grass strips. The two CBU-equipped aircraft made their run from the southeast along Choiseul Sound at low level and just as Gordy Batt dropped his bombs he saw Nick Taylor's Sea Harrier burst into flames, explode and hit the ground on the outskirts of the airfield. The aircraft had been hit by 35mm flak from a radar-controlled Oerlikon anti-aircraft gun and Lieutenant Taylor had no time to eject before his aircraft ploughed into the ground. Ted Ball also saw the explosion as he ran in from the southwest to drop his bombs on the airstrip. As well as the sad loss of a Sea Harrier pilot the raid achieved very little of effect as most of the serviceable Pucaras had already hastily departed the airstrip at Goose Green for the relative safety of Pebble Island.

The death of Nick Taylor led to a change of policy resulting in a move from low-level bombing of airfields (except when it was absolutely necessary) to medium/high-level bombing and toss-bombing, which exposed the aircraft to less risk although the accuracy of the bombing was more variable. Lieutenant Nick Taylor was buried with full military honours at the edge of Goose Green airstrip by troops of the Argentine garrison. His Sea Harrier (XZ450) had been used by British Aerospace in carriage trials of the Sea Eagle anti-ship missile and was still fitted with cockpit instruments for the Sea Eagle. At least one analyst suggests that the finding of this instrumentation in the Sea Harrier's cockpit might have been a contributory factor to the withdrawal to port of the Argentine fleet.

The 4th of May ended with the British Task Forces' first experience of battle casualties. Within a short space of time not only had the Royal Navy lost one of its most potent warships and 20 sailors on board, but 800 Squadron had lost the first Sea Harrier and its pilot in action. The result of the attack on *Sheffield* was that the Carrier Battle Group stayed well to the east of the Falklands from now on, except on special occasions. This meant that the Sea Harriers had a shorter time on their CAP stations than when the aircraft carriers operated closer to the islands. However, this was necessary, as the loss of a single aircraft carrier would almost certainly have meant the end of the conflict for the UK.

5th May (Wednesday)
Bad weather again curtailed much of the planned air activity on both sides. By the 5th most of the Argentine ships were within coastal waters when an S-2E Tracker that was still searching for survivors from the *General Belgrano* picked up an unidentified contact, thought to be a British submarine, about 45 miles from Bahia Camerone. Two Sea Kings and another Tracker were launched from the *25 de Mayo* to join in the hunt. Whatever was attacked by depth charges, no British vessel was damaged or sunk, although some Argentine accounts claim that the submarine was probably HMS *Onyx* engaged in clandestine operations. It was more likely that the South Atlantic whale population suffered another loss! Later in the day the *25 de Mayo* returned to port and her aircraft disembarked to shore bases from where they later took part in the conflict without the benefit of the aircraft carrier.

An Argentine submarine, the *San Luis*, was thought to have been detected and attacked near the British Carrier Battle Group during the 5th. An 820 Squadron Sea King HAS5 attacked the submerged contact but the submarine escaped undamaged.

Another 820 Squadron helicopter flew a team to the still smouldering *Sheffield* to ascertain the possibility of salvaging the vessel. The wreck was also visited by an 846 Squadron helicopter to retrieve fire-fighting equipment and helicopter stores from the hangar. The weather was very poor to the east of the Falklands on the 5th and the Sea Harriers flew few CAP sorties but maintained deck alert in case of an attack.

At Ascension Island the requirement for helicopter logistics support during the hectic period when ships were using the island as a staging post soon outstripped the available resources. Two Royal Navy Wessex had been based at Wideawake since 9th April to perform HDS and VERTREP tasks, and other helicopters from passing ships assisted in these duties as and when they could. However, more support was needed and as every available Royal Navy utility helicopter was already employed, the RAF was asked to provide assistance. The *Atlantic Conveyor* reached Ascension Island on the 5th with her load of Wessex HU5 and Chinook HC1 helicopters. One of the Chinooks (ZA707) was flown off to Wideawake airfield and commenced logistics duties straight away, its heavy-lift capability proving most useful. The Chinook stayed behind when the *Atlantic Conveyor* left on the 7th and remained at Ascension Island until it embarked on the *Contender Bezant* on 3rd June.

As well as the *Atlantic Conveyor*, HMS *Intrepid* also arrived at Ascension on the 5th. *Intrepid* had been taken out of service as a result of the 1981 defence review and it had taken several weeks to prepare her for service to join the Amphibious Group. Her two Wessex HU5s of 'E' Flight 845 Squadron flew ashore to assist in the logistics task and were then transferred to *Tidepool*, which sailed south the following day. The two 845 Squadron Wessex that had been based at Wideawake airfield since 9th April embarked on *Intrepid* as replacement aircraft and sailed with the ship for the Falkland Islands on the 7th. They would eventually be transferred to 847 Squadron.

6th May (Thursday)
The bad weather surrounding the Falklands continued into the 6th with fog, low cloud and very poor visibility. Nevertheless the Sea Harriers flew CAPs from dawn, especially over the wreck of *Sheffield*. Later in the morning a Sea King reported picking up a fleeting radar target to the south of the Carrier Battle Group, close to where *Sheffield* was drifting, and two 801 Squadron Sea Harriers that were already airborne but some 20 miles apart on separate CAPs were vectored to investigate. Lieutenant Al Curtis (in XZ453) and Lieutenant Commander John Eyton-Jones (in

XZ452) descended into the cloud tops at about 2,000ft from different directions. The two aircraft disappeared from radar as they descended to low level and no more radio transmissions were heard. Helicopters were sent to the area but there was no sign of the aircraft or their pilots and it was noted that the cloud base was very low in places. It was assumed that in a million-to-one chance the two Sea Harriers had probably collided in the cloud, although there also remained the possibility that the pilots (both highly experienced QFIs) had inadvertently flown their aircraft into the sea. Whatever the cause, neither wreckage nor the bodies of the pilots were ever found. The Sea Harrier force on board the aircraft carriers was now reduced to 17 from the original 20 and it would be 12 days before any reinforcements arrived. The loss was particularly hard felt as both pilots were highly experienced Air Warfare Instructors. In addition, Al Curtis had flown Mirage IIIs and A-4 Skyhawks while on an exchange posting in Australia and New Zealand and was therefore a useful source of intelligence on the opposition.

Soon after the two Sea Harriers disappeared the Lynx helicopters from *Arrow* and *Coventry* were loaded with Sea Skua anti-ship missiles and set off to investigate a surface contact in the same general area. In conditions of very poor visibility with patches of thick fog the unidentified contact was eventually located by using the helicopters' radar, but it turned out to be the drifting hulk of *Sheffield*. The ship was later taken under tow by *Yarmouth* to prevent any further confusion.

By 6th May nine of 1 Squadron's Harrier GR3s had reached Ascension Island and six of these (XV789, XZ963, XZ972, XZ988, XZ989 and XZ997) embarked on the *Atlantic Conveyor* later that day and were wrapped in specially designed rubberised canvas bags to protect them from saltwater corrosion. For most of the 1 Squadron pilots this was the first time they had landed on the deck of a ship in a Harrier. Also embarked on the *Atlantic Conveyor* were the eight Sea Harrier FRS1s (XZ458, XZ491, XZ499, ZA174, ZA176, ZA177, ZA190 and ZA194) of 809 Squadron that had arrived at Wideawake on the 1st and 2nd of May and flown out to the ship on the 5th. These, together with the Chinooks and Wessex already on board, made the *Atlantic Conveyor* a very crowded ship. Like the Harrier GR3s, all of the Sea Harrier FRS1s were wrapped in protective bags for the long journey south, except for one aircraft that was kept on armed deck alert in case the ship was intercepted by Argentine aircraft.

The remaining three Harrier GR3s (XW919, XZ129 and XZ132) were fitted with AIM-9 Sidewinders and remained behind at

Three of 1 Squadron's Harrier GR3s sit on the pan at Ascension Island surrounded by Victor K2 tankers. Six Harrier GR3s embarked on the Atlantic Conveyor on 6th May for the voyage south. MoD

The eight Sea Harrier FRS1s of 809 Squadron that flew to Ascension Island during the first week of May embarked on the Atlantic Conveyor for the Task Force on the 6th. MoD

Large rubberised bags provided excellent protection for the aircraft travelling south on the exposed deck of the Atlantic Conveyor, which left Ascension Island on 6th May. MoD

including two CAPs on the 8th that were vectored towards Argentine aircraft that were probing the British defences. An Argentine C-130 was thought to have attempted to land at Stanley on the 8th but flew off when Sea Harriers were launched.

The frigate *Brilliant* temporarily swapped one of her Lynx for *Glasgow*'s Sea Skua-equipped Lynx (XZ247), it being needed for a sea search for Argentine shipping during the night of 8/9th May. *Brilliant*'s helicopters then made an ESM sweep north of Falkland Sound but found no contacts as the ship entered the Sound to search for enemy supply ships. The helicopters then attacked Argentine troop positions at Port Howard on West Falkland with GPMG fire and also dropped flares to keep the enemy troops awake and unnerved. The two Lynx were swapped back again the next day.

An 801 Squadron Sea Harrier flown by Lieutenant Commander Nigel Ward also dropped flares over the Argentine garrisons at Goose Green and Fox Bay during the night as a harrying tactic. The mission was flown in very bad weather using the Sea Harrier's advanced radar and navigation computer to find the targets. Meanwhile

Sea Harriers and Sea Kings prepare for operations from HMS Hermes, *viewed from her goalkeeper, HMS* Broadsword. *The rust stains on the aircraft carrier's hull are noticeable in this photograph.* Cdr S Chelton

Alacrity fired some 90 shells at an Argentine encampment on Stanley Common. All this activity was designed, in part, to divert attention away from *Yarmouth* as she sailed to the southeast of the islands and took the stricken *Sheffield* under tow in the hope of salvaging the wrecked vessel.

9th May (Sunday) – Skirmishes

Although bad weather persisted around the Falklands there was a slight improvement on the 9th and a few sorties were flown by both sides, including several strike missions mounted from the Argentine mainland bases. However, the weather rapidly deteriorated and most flights were recalled before they reached the Falklands. For some reason one flight of A-4C Skyhawks from Grupo 4 de Caza continued towards the Falklands. The flight had taken off from San Julian to attack a group of British ships known to be to the east of Stanley. The Skyhawks were forced to fly very low under the cloud base and two of the aircraft disappeared en route to the target area. It was later discovered that Teniente Jorge Casco had flown his aircraft (C-313) into a northwest facing cliff on South Jason Island. This small island lies about ten miles off the extreme northwest tip of West Falkland. The wreckage was found by the Royal Navy some months after the end of the conflict. The bomb load was still intact, not having been dropped, and the remains of the pilot were found in the wreckage, indicating that

he had not had a chance to eject. The other Skyhawk (C-303), flown by Teniente Jorge Farias, simply vanished and neither the wreckage nor the pilot's body was ever found. It was presumed that the aircraft had flown into the sea in the poor visibility. Two flights of Dagger As, each of four aircraft, also took off on a strike mission, but they turned back upon encountering the bad weather near Jason Island.

The ships that the Grupo 4 flight was after were probably *Broadsword* and *Coventry*, which were about 12 miles to the east of Stanley at the time. *Broadsword* had been detached from her duties as goalkeeper for *Hermes* to accompany *Coventry* in the hope of shooting down any aircraft attempting to use Stanley airport. *Coventry* also bombarded shore positions with her 4.5-inch gun until it jammed. The ships did track an enemy formation on their radar and, at 1417Z, fired three Sea Dart missiles at what was presumed to be a C-130 with an escort of Mirage fighters. However, none of the missiles hit their target and the action took place on the opposite side of the Falkland Islands to that where the two Skyhawks were lost so it is unlikely that the Sea Darts were responsible for the demise of the two aircraft, especially as the Skyhawks were flying at very low level and would not have been seen on *Coventry*'s radar. However, it is possible that the launch of the Sea Darts caused the Skyhawk formation to abandon the mission and turn back. The

Several Argentine Army Bell UH-1Hs were found on Stanley racecourse on 14th June. This helicopter is AE-410 which, despite having suffered terminal damage on 9th May, was saved to eventually become a museum exhibit in the Falklands. Wg Cdr P Lyall

combination of a Type 42 (long-range Sea Dart) and a Type 22 (better radar and short-range Seawolf) to act as a radar picket was a bold experiment. The combination had some success when both ships' missile systems were working.

The improved weather allowed the two Sea Harrier squadrons to resume their regular CAPs and 800 Squadron attempted a medium-level raid on Stanley airport. However, the weather had not improved that much and when Lieutenant Commander Batt (in XZ460) and Flight Lieutenant Morgan (in ZA191) arrived over the airfield they found it obscured by cloud and could not drop their bombs as the risk to civilians in Stanley was too great. The change in policy to medium/high-level attacks since the loss of Lieutenant Taylor on the 4th required better weather to enable the pilots to see their target from altitude.

On the way back to *Hermes* Dave Morgan noticed a surface return on his Blue Fox radar about 60 miles to the southeast of Stanley. Gordy Batt and Morgan descended through the cloud to low level and spotted

a boat that they identified as the 1,400-ton Argentine stern trawler *Narwal*. This ship had been requisitioned by the Argentine Navy and had been warned to keep away from the British Task Force as early as 30th April when it was chased away by *Alacrity*, but it continued to shadow the Task Force to gather intelligence on its movements. At 1250Z *Coventry* gave Gordy Batt permission to attack the *Narwal* and both Sea Harriers made a strafing run across her bows in the hope that this would bring her to a halt while a boarding party was flown out to the vessel. However, the *Narwal* did not stop so the attack continued and both Sea Harriers dropped their single 1,000lb bombs on the vessel. Dave Morgan's bomb only narrowly missed the ship but Gordy Batt's bomb scored a direct hit and entered the engine room but failed to explode as the bombs had been fused with a seven-second arming delay for dropping from high altitude. Further strafing runs damaged the ship along the waterline and at 1330Z two more Sea Harriers, flown by Lieutenant M Hale and Sub Lieutenant A J George, turned up

and also made strafing runs with their 30mm cannon, causing more damage.

With the vessel now dead in the water, the 800 Squadron aircraft departed as Lieutenant Commander Ward arrived overhead to provide a CAP while a boarding party was flown to the *Narwal* in two Sea King HC4s of 846 Squadron accompanied by a Sea King HAS5 of 826 Squadron. An SBS team was lowered to the *Narwal's* deck and the Argentine crew, some of whom were wounded, were winched off and flown to *Hermes*. During the return journey Lieutenant Commander W A Pollock (flying ZA292 of 846 Squadron) had to refuel from *Glasgow* as the Carrier Battle Group had moved away from its planned position.

From the documents and equipment found on board it was obvious that the *Narwal*, under the command of an Argentine naval officer, was being used for gathering intelligence on the movement of British ships and aircraft. The *Narwal* was boarded by a prize crew from *Hermes* but the trawler sank in a storm on the 10th after the crew was removed by 820 Squadron Sea Kings.

Some hours after the *Narwal* was attacked a CAB601 Puma (AE-505) was tasked to search in the Choiseul Sound around Sea Lion Island, to look for survivors. The Prefectura Naval Puma (PA-12) had been damaged by naval bombardment by this time so an Army helicopter was tasked with the mission and was hastily equipped for rescue duties with inflatable dinghies and ropes. At the time, *Coventry* and *Broadsword* were over 30 miles away to the northeast bombarding Stanley when *Broadsword* picked up the helicopter on her radar. Firing instructions were passed to *Coventry* and at 1907Z she fired a Sea Dart which hit the Puma and destroyed it. The three crew members (Primer Teniente Roberto Fiorito, Primer Teniente Juan Buschiazzo, and Sargento Raul Dimotta) were all killed. The helicopter was thought to have come down in the sea near Sea Lion Island but CAB601 could not mount a search for four days due to extremely bad weather. No trace of the helicopter or its crew was ever found.

As night drew on the naval bombardment of targets in and around Stanley continued, during which the old Royal Marine barracks at Moody Brook was hit. The CAB601 helicopters had recently returned to Moody Brook from their temporary base near Mount Kent to where they had been evacuated after the initial air raids on 1st May. The unserviceable UH-1H (AE-410) was further damaged during this bombardment and was never repaired, and a Puma was slightly damaged but quickly made serviceable again. Soon afterwards the helicopters dispersed to the Mount Kent site again. The spotting for *Coventry*'s gun was performed by a naval gunfire observer of 148 (Meiktila) Commando Forward Observation Battery, Royal Artillery, flying in *Broadsword*'s Lynx. This unit deployed five small teams to the Falklands which provided all naval gunfire observation as well as forward air control in the latter stages of the conflict.

At sea the only other activity of note on the 9th was when *Alacrity*'s Lynx HAS2 (XZ736) flown by Lieutenant R E Sleeman launched a Mk46 torpedo at a sonar contact. Several Task Force ships detected a good sonar this day. However, the torpedo did not detonate and all that was found was a large mass of kelp. Huge, dense mats of this seaweed surrounded much of the Falklands and were often mistaken for a submarine on sonar, as were whales and unchartered rocks.

When the aircraft carrier *25 de Mayo* returned to port following the loss of the cruiser *General Belgrano*, the eight A-4Qs

The Type 21 frigates served well in the Falklands conflict despite being plagued by cracks in their superstructure caused by the severe weather they encountered. Two Type 21s were lost, both to bombing.
Flt Sgt D W Knights

of 3 Escuadrilla disembarked and flew to the unit's shore base at Comandante Espora, but the squadron deployed south to Rio Grande on the 9th. The squadron commander, Capitan de Corbeta Rodolfo Alberto Castro Fox, set his men to training in preparation for the expected British landings on the Falklands. The eight A-4Qs were later joined by two more aircraft that had been undergoing major servicing. No operational missions were flown until the 21st, the first day of the amphibious assault.

The RAF flew its first operational Nimrod MR2P sortie from Ascension Island on the 9th when XV227, captained by Flight Lieutenant D J Ford of 206 Squadron, flew 2,750 miles to the south to provide ASW cover for the Amphibious Group heading for the Falklands. The aircraft was refuelled in flight by three Victor K2s. On the same day another Nimrod MR2P (XV232) made the first AAR assisted deployment from Kinloss to Ascension Island. With a minimum of two MR2Ps, the Nimrod detachment was now capable of mounting long-range flights on a daily basis.

10th May (Monday)
With bad weather persisting around the Falklands the focus of activity on the 10th was in the UK. On that day the *Bristol* Group of ships set sail for the South Atlantic from Devonport and Portsmouth. This was the last major element of the Task Force to leave the UK during the conflict and it consisted of the destroyer HMS *Bristol*, the frigates HMS *Active*, HMS *Andromeda*, HMS *Avenger*, HMS *Minerva* and HMS *Penelope*, the helicopter support ship RFA *Engadine*, and the tanker RFA *Olna*. The *Engadine* had

embarked four Wessex HU5s of 'A' Flight 847 Squadron during the previous day. The squadron had been formed at Yeovilton on 7th May with the intention of becoming the garrison squadron on the Falklands after the conflict. A total of 27 Wessex HU5s were eventually transferred to the new squadron from various training squadrons and other second-line units. Under the command of Lieutenant Commander M D Booth the four 'A' Flight helicopters embarked on the *Engadine* while 20 Wessex of 'B' Flight awaited passage on the *Atlantic Causeway*.

On the 10th the frigate *Brilliant* and the destroyer *Glasgow* relieved *Broadsword* and *Coventry* on naval bombardment and radar picket duties off Stanley. As usual on this task a Lynx provided naval gunfire support (NGS) observation during the bombardment and occasionally came under fire from shore-based artillery. The two pairs of ships alternated this duty for several days. In the early hours of the 10th *Sheffield* finally sank 135 miles east of the Falklands while under tow by *Yarmouth* due to high seas flooding the ship's lower decks.

11th May (Tuesday)
Yet again bad weather curtailed air operations for much of the day but the weather did, however, prove to be of benefit in one respect. During the night of 10/11th May, *Alacrity* sailed close along the southern coast of both East and West Falkland and then up through Falkland Sound, which separates the two main islands. This was the first time in the conflict that a British ship had sailed the length of Falkland Sound and it represented a considerable risk, reduced somewhat by the poor

weather which kept Argentine aircraft grounded. The sortie was vital to see if the Sound had been mined, even if it meant the loss of a Type 21 frigate to find out. *Alacrity*'s Lynx took off during the passage through the Sound and probed the Argentine defences at Fox Bay and other harbours, thereby providing a diversion for the ship's transit through the Sound.

As the frigate was sailing north near Port King it came upon an Argentine Navy transport ship, the 2,684-ton *Isla de los Estados*. The ship had served with the Argentine Navy for just over a year and had taken part in the invasion during Operation 'Rosario'. She was engaged in carrying supplies to the islands from the mainland, one of the few ships to risk the passage through the TEZ. On the night of the 11th she appeared to be making for Port Howard on West Falkland (in fact she had left Port King bound for Port Darwin) when she was discovered near Swan Island by *Alacrity*. The frigate fired a starshell to illuminate the Argentine ship and then fired several rounds of 4.5-inch shells. The vessel was hit almost immediately and its cargo of 90,000 gallons of aviation fuel and ammunition exploded with great force. The ship sank very quickly and only two of the 22-man crew managed to survive. Argentine SAR operations continued in the Sound until the 16th in the hope of finding more survivors.

The crew of *Alacrity* was unaware that they themselves had actually come under attack as the ship sailed away from the Sound. As the frigate emerged from the northern mouth of Falkland Sound and headed back towards the Task Force in company with *Arrow*, they were seen by the Argentine submarine *San Luis* which fired a single torpedo from a range of 5,030 yards. Fortunately for *Alacrity* the *San Luis's* firing predictor had malfunctioned and the torpedo had to be fired manually. It failed to hit its target although it may have been responsible for damage to *Arrow's* towed torpedo decoy.

After *Arrow*'s narrow escape, the *San Luis*, which had been patrolling off the north coast of the Falklands for a month by this time, was ordered to return to port for repairs and did not put to sea again until after the end of the conflict. The *Salta* could not replace the *San Luis* due to noise problems that had proved fatal to the submarine in the ASW environment off the Falklands, so this was the last day that an Argentine submarine could have threatened British ships. But the Task Force was unaware of this at the time.

As the Amphibious Group continued on its journey south the main group caught up with the *Canberra*, *Elk* and *Tidepool* and their escorts *Ardent* and *Argonaut*, which had left Ascension Island five days earlier. The three Scout AH1s of '5' Flight (656) 3 CBAS from the *Europic Ferry* and XT629

from *Fearless* were flown to the *Elk* for storage below decks in an attempt to reduce the amount of saltwater corrosion the helicopters were suffering in their more exposed positions on the other ships. All the Scouts would be flown back to the *Europic Ferry* six days later.

The hospital ship SS *Uganda* arrived off the Falklands on the 11th and took up her position in an area about 30 miles north of the islands in what was termed the Red Cross Box, where both British and Argentine medical vessels could operate in safety. The *Uganda* was the main British hospital ship to where the wounded would first be taken. When the patients were ready and able to travel they would be flown across to one of the three ambulance ships, HMS *Herald*, HMS *Hecla* and HMS *Hydra*, which would take it in turns to sail to Montevideo in Uruguay. From here the British wounded would be flown on RAF VC10 C1s to Ascension Island and then on to the UK. When wounded Argentine troops were captured later in the conflict they were also repatriated to Montevideo by the ambulance ships. Although the

A Seawolf missile is launched from Broadsword. *Four Argentine aircraft are thought to have been brought down by Seawolf missiles, three of them launched by* Brilliant *on 12th May.* Cdr S Chelton

Uganda had a helicopter platform fitted on her stern, she had no embarked helicopter of her own but would receive casualties from shore-based and ship-based helicopters throughout the conflict.

12th May (Wednesday) –
Grupo 5's Day of Triumph and Tragedy
Although the weather was still poor the cloud lifted sufficiently for 800 Squadron to attempt a raid on Stanley airport during the morning of the 12th. At 1155Z the squadron flew the first of three raids on the airport during the day. All the raids were flown at medium level to avoid the Roland missiles that were known to be defending the target. Another raid was flown four hours later but none of the bombs, which were dropped from about 18,000ft, did any damage. The third raid was aborted when *Brilliant* (which was controlling the air strike) and *Glasgow* came under attack and had to defend themselves.

The Royal Navy Task Force lost a helicopter on the 12th when a Sea King HAS5

Both Sea King HAS2As of the 825 Squadron detachment on board the Queen Elizabeth II *are seen here on the liner's newly fitted helicopter deck. XV648 is in the foreground with XV677 behind. Both helicopters served with 706 Squadron at Culdrose before the conflict.* Wg Cdr P Lyall

(ZA132) of 826 Squadron was forced to ditch when it suffered an engine failure while in the hover. The helicopter landed in the water successfully but the sea was very rough and the Sea King was almost immediately rolled over onto its side by a large wave and sank. All four crew members (Lieutenant Commander J S M Chandler, Sub Lieutenant A J Moss, Sub Lieutenant K B Sutton, and Leading Aircraftman P W Coombes) escaped and were rescued from the sea about 20 minutes later. Another Sea King HAS5 (XZ578) was transferred from 820 Squadron on board *Invincible* to 826 Squadron on the 14th to replace ZA132, while a second replacement (XZ573) was transferred from *Invincible* to 826 Squadron on the 15th.

Despite the continuing poor weather the Argentine Air Force mounted a mission on the 12th to attack the two Royal Navy ships that were shelling Stanley on a daily basis. The ships had a secondary mission to entice Argentine aircraft into a missile trap as both *Brilliant* and *Glasgow* carried a formidable mix of Seawolf and Sea Dart missiles. Grupo 5 de Caza at Rio Gallegos was ordered to dispatch two flights, Cuna and Oro, each of four aircraft, and the first of these took off at 1600Z. Cuna flight was led by Primer Teniente Oscar Bustos with Tenientes Jorge Ibarlucea, Mario Nivoli and Alferez Jorge Vazquez. The A-4Bs were refuelled en route by a KC-130H flown by

Vicecomodoro A A Cano after which Cuna flight dropped to low level and headed straight for the warships, two of the aircraft attacking *Brilliant* and two *Glasgow*. At the time *Glasgow*'s gun had developed a fault and the two ships were withdrawing from their bombardment about 15 miles south of Stanley when the A-4Bs were detected 30 miles away. When the aircraft had closed to 17 miles it was discovered that *Glasgow*'s Sea Dart launcher also had suffered a malfunction, leaving air defence in the hands of *Brilliant*'s Seawolf operators who were about to make history by using the new missile for the first time in combat.

Cuna flight started its attack at 1644Z but even at very low level and high speed the A-4Bs were unable to avoid the deadly Seawolf. The aircraft of Bustos (C-246) and Ibarlucea (C-208) were both hit by missiles and both men were killed in the resulting explosions. Nivoli (in C-206) tried to evade the third Seawolf but inadvertently flew into the sea and was killed. Only Vazquez survived from Cuna flight and neither of his two 500lb bombs found their mark, although one bomb bounced off the sea and over *Glasgow*'s stern. Just as Vazquez was about to drop his bombs, *Glasgow*'s Oerlikon 20mm gun jammed, leaving the ship completely defenceless apart from several sailors firing small arms and machine guns. Vazquez's windscreen was so encrusted with salt after his low-level

flight over the sea that he was unable to see properly and consequently his aircraft ran off the side of the runway after it landed back at Rio Gallegos.

About 10 minutes later Oro flight arrived and began its attack on *Brilliant* and *Glasgow*. Oro flight was led by Capitan Zelaya with Primer Tenientes Fausto Gavazzi and Alferez Dellepiane and Teniente Juan Arraras as his wingmen. The attack commenced at 1715Z but due to a misunderstanding only one A-4B (flown by Arraras) attacked *Brilliant* while the other three made for *Glasgow*. Her Sea Dart system was still out of action but the 4.5-inch gun was now firing at the attackers. Unfortunately for the British ships, *Brilliant*'s Seawolf computer system became confused by the manoeuvring of the four aircraft and failed to fire any missiles at Oro flight.

Arraras dropped his two bombs and was dismayed to see them both hit the water, bounce over *Brilliant* and hit the sea on the far side of the ship without causing any damage. However, *Glasgow* did not get away so lightly. One of Gavazzi's bombs hit the ship just three feet above the waterline, passed through the auxiliary machinery room and hit a fuel tank before punching another hole in the hull as it exited and exploded harmlessly when it hit the sea. Bombs from Zelaya and Dellepiane came close to hitting *Glasgow* but did no further actual damage.

After surviving a hail of gunfire from the two ships and severely damaging one of the vessels, Oro flight then suffered a tragedy on its return journey when Gavazzi flew at low level over Goose Green airstrip and was shot down in error by one of the deadly Argentine radar-controlled Oerlikon 35mm anti-aircraft guns. Gavazzi's A-4B (C-248) hit

the ground and exploded moments after he ejected but he was at too low an altitude for a safe ejection and was killed, the second victim of Argentine 'friendly fire' during the conflict. *Glasgow*, with her Sea Dart system and main gun repaired but holed just above the waterline and taking in water, retired back to the Carrier Battle Group for further repairs. Daylight bombardments of Stanley's airfield and enemy positions around the town were suspended after this attack, although the nightly bombardments continued unabated.

Grupo 5 had tasted both success and defeat on the 12th. On the one hand it had so badly damaged a British destroyer that it soon had to be withdrawn for the rest of the conflict; but on the other hand it had lost four aircraft and four pilots, one of them to 'friendly fire' and one of them a highly experienced flight leader. The Argentine Air Force was confused as to which ship they had damaged on the 12th and claimed that *Brilliant* had been sunk during the engagement. *Glasgow* had been seriously damaged and was already suffering from engine problems. After spending two weeks trying to remain operational, it was withdrawn to the edge of the TEZ for repairs on the 25th. Effective repairs proved impossible with the resources available in the South Atlantic so the ship was dispatched back to the UK on the 27th with its engines and propellers under manual control for the entire voyage. The destroyer was later repaired but did not leave Portsmouth again until 6th September when it sailed for its second tour of duty in the South Atlantic.

The Skyhawk raids on the 12th should have been flown in conjunction with two flights of Dagger As but due to aircraft unserviceability and various communica-

tions problems, the Daggers never took off.

On the 12th RFA *Regent* became the first ship to enter the TEZ since the commencement of operations on 1st May. The ship started its replenishment duties throughout the Carrier Battle Group using its two Wessex HU5s (XS486 and XT756). These two helicopters had been fitted with GPMGs and 2-inch rocket pods during the *Regent*'s journey to the Falklands. The ship later sailed to meet the Amphibious Group to replenish those vessels before their arrival in the TEZ.

Meanwhile at Wideawake airfield, a Heavylift Belfast (G-BEPS) delivered two more Wessex HU5s on the 12th for the Base Flight. Allocated to 'D' Flight 845 Squadron, XS491 stayed until the 25th when it embarked on RFA *Engadine* to join 847 Squadron while XT761 remained at Ascension Island on HDS duties for the duration of the conflict and did not return to Yeovilton until December 1983.

Also on the 12th, Nimrod MR2P XV227 made a 14 hour 35 minute flight using in-flight refuelling and reached 45 degrees South. The aircraft was captained by Flight Lieutenant C Moncaster and his crew from 201 Squadron and searched the ocean around the *Fearless* and *Antrim* groups as the ships sailed south. During the night of

The VC10 C1s of 10 Squadron spent many flying hours shuttling troops and stores between the UK and Ascension Island but they also flew a number of missions to Montevideo to deliver Argentine prisoners and pick up captured and wounded British troops. Flights that were monitored by the International Committee of the Red Cross wore a large red cross on the forward fuselage. MoD

Hercules C1 XV291 was one of a small number of aircraft to be fitted with internal long-range fuel tanks in an effort to extend its range. The aircraft was later one of 16 to be fitted with an in-flight refuelling probe and redesignated Hercules C1P. MoD

For a Hercules to refuel from a Victor K2 required the formation to perform the procedure while in a gentle dive that resulted in the loss of several thousand feet of altitude. The view from the Hercules cockpit was actually much better than most aircraft involved in in-flight refuelling. MoD

12/13th May, a 202 Squadron Sea King HAR3 (XZ593) assisted other helicopters in transferring Argentine POWs captured on South Georgia from the *Tidespring* to Wideawake airfield prior to repatriation.

As San Carlos had by now been selected as the site for the amphibious landing, it was important to neutralise the airstrip at Pebble Island, just a few minutes' flying time away. If Pucaras were permitted to fly from Pebble Island during the landings they could wreak havoc among the troop transports and the troops ashore. The SAS under Lieutenant Colonel Michael Rose proposed a surprise attack on the airstrip but only had a few days in which to plan it and carry it out. Under cover of darkness and poor weather an 846 Squadron Sea King HC4 inserted an eight-man reconnaissance team from 'D' Squadron, 22 SAS Regiment near Port Purvis, east of Pebble Island on the night of the 12/13th. The SAS patrol crossed over to Pebble Island in canoes in the early hours of the 14th and observed Argentine activity on the island, particularly the airstrip, which by this date had 11 air-

craft based there. The SAS also located the airstrip's ammunition and fuel storage dump and planning was commenced for a commando raid on the airstrip, which took place on the 15th.

13th May (Thursday)

For the ninth consecutive day the weather surrounding the Falkland Islands limited air operations and very few sorties were flown by either side. The bad weather was also taking its toll on the ships at sea. On the 13th *Alacrity*'s Lynx slid into the side of its hangar when rough seas smashed against the side of the vessel. Two rotor blades and the radar scanner were badly damaged and a replacement radar had to be transferred from *Broadsword* to enable the Lynx's Sea Skua missile to be used if necessary. Another helicopter became unserviceable on the 13th when *Herald*'s Wasp was found to have a defective tail rotor drive shaft. The

problem was not rectified until the 29th and in the meantime *Herald* had to make use of the Wasps embarked on the other ambulance ships.

About 180 Argentine prisoners captured during the British reoccupation of South Georgia were flown to Montevideo from Ascension Island after arriving at the island on board the *Tidespring* the previous day. For this operation a 10 Squadron VC10 C1 was painted with a large red cross on a white square to indicate that the operation was being conducted under the supervision of the International Red Cross. The previous day, Argentine prisoners captured at South Georgia left Ascension Island aboard a chartered DC-10 bound for home.

14th May (Friday)

The 14th was the last day of a ten-day period of continuous poor weather around the Falkland Islands. The low cloud, storms and poor visibility had affected the air and sea operations of both sides, particularly the British air raids on Stanley airport and other Argentine targets on the Falklands. The bad weather had made operations more difficult and dangerous, but it had also assisted certain operations such as the covert insertion of Special Forces on the islands and the safe transit of *Alacrity* through Falkland Sound.

In an effort to further increase the range of the RAF's Hercules, a modification programme had been instigated to add an in-flight refuelling capability to some of the aircraft. Marshalls of Cambridge was responsible for major overhaul and modification of the RAF's Hercules fleet and they started work on the project on 15th April. Just two weeks later, on 28th April, XV200 made its first flight with the new probe. Eventually 16 Hercules were modified to C1P standard but only six aircraft (XV179, XV196, XV200, XV206, XV218 and XV291) had been modified before the end of the conflict. The first modified aircraft (XV200) arrived at Wideawake airfield on 14th May and flew its first sortie two days later. The speed differential of the Hercules C1P and the Victor K2 tanker made it necessary to conduct refuellings while the two aircraft were in a shallow dive so that the Hercules could maintain station with the Victor. The refuelling session had to start at about 23,000ft and it took about 20,000ft of altitude to transfer 25,000lb of fuel before the aircraft could separate, level off and climb back to cruising height.

Vulcan B2 XM612 was flown from Waddington to Ascension Island on the 14th in preparation for the next 'Black Buck' mission, planned for the 16th. The aircraft was one of the original six Vulcans modified but had not itself been deployed to Ascension Island before.

The destroyer *Exeter* arrived at Ascension Island from Antigua on the 14th. She had been on West Indies guardship duties

since March and was ordered to make her way to the Falklands via Ascension Island on the 7th following the loss of *Sheffield*. *Exeter*'s crew had been intrigued to read that the Argentines claimed that she had hit a mine on 29th April and sunk even before she had even set sail for the South Atlantic!

In the UK the second aircraft transport vessel, the *Atlantic Causeway*, left Plymouth bound for the Falklands. On board the 15,000-ton ship were 20 Wessex HU5s of 847 Squadron and eight Sea King HAS2As of 825 Squadron. The latter squadron had been formed at Culdrose on 7th May under Lieutenant Commander H S Clark, the then commanding officer of 706 Squadron. The new squadron's personnel were drawn mainly from the instructors and students of 706 Squadron despite the fact that some of the students were only part way through their course. Ten Sea Kings were transferred to 825 Squadron from 706, 819 and 824 Squadrons and were to operate as utility transports rather than in their normal ASW role. A strengthened freight floor was built into the Sea Kings and the sonar and other ASW equipment removed to make more room for troops and cargo. On the 12th two Sea Kings (XV648 and XV677) had embarked on the *Queen Elizabeth II* as she sailed down the Solent carrying troops of the 5th Infantry Brigade. The remaining eight Sea Kings embarked on the *Atlantic Causeway* on the 13th in preparation for the long journey south.

15th May (Saturday) – The Pebble Island Raid

Using the information acquired by the SAS reconnaissance patrol on Pebble Island, a Special Forces raid was put into action on the night of the 14/15th. On the 13th *Hermes*, *Broadsword* and *Glamorgan* had detached from the Carrier Battle Group and sailed around the north of the Falklands to position themselves for the raid. However, within a few hours the ships turned back as

nothing had been heard from the recce party already on Pebble Island, so the raid was delayed for 24 hours. The ships set off again at 2230Z on the 14th and this time the raid went ahead. With difficulty due to very stormy weather four Sea King HC4s of 846 Squadron took off from the carrier at 0225Z on the 15th with 45 men of 'D' Squadron, 22 SAS and their naval gunfire support team. The aircraft carrier had sailed to within 40 miles of the coast to reduce the helicopters' flight time and was unprotected for some of the time as *Broadsword* had been unable to keep up in the rough seas.

The SAS troops were landed on the southeast coast of Pebble Island about three miles from the airstrip. The helicopter crews used passive night-vision goggles and were assisted by the poor weather that kept most of the Argentine defenders under cover during the night. The main force met up with the reconnaissance patrol that had been inserted earlier and moved rapidly onto the airfield. Here they placed explosive charges among the aircraft and other equipment and stores which detonated at about 0740Z. The troops then withdrew under fire as *Glamorgan* provided covering gunfire. Four Sea Kings landed close to the airstrip to recover the SAS troops after the raid and the ships sailed northeast at high speed to be well away from the coast by daylight. In a single operation that had only been planned five days in advance, a substantial number of the Argentine aircraft based on the Falklands had been put out of action for the rest of the conflict for the cost of just two men wounded.

The raid resulted in the destruction or immobilisation of all 11 aircraft on the airstrip at the time. The aircraft involved were six Pucaras (A-502, A-520, A-523, A-529, A-552 and A-556), four T-34C-1 Turbo Mentors (0719, 0726, 0729 and 0730) and a Prefectura Naval Skyvan 3M (PA-50). The Skyvan and one of the Pucaras (A-502) were completely gutted by fire but the other aircraft were left more or less intact and had the Argentines had better facilities at Pebble Island, there is no doubt that at least some of the aircraft could have been repaired. Some of the pilots of the aircraft that were destroyed at Pebble Island in the early hours of the 15th were flown to Stanley later in the day by a Grupo 7 helicopter, probably a Chinook, to await a flight back to the mainland. According to the detachment

Four T-34C-1 Turbo Mentors were disabled at Pebble Island during the SAS raid on 15th May 1982. This aircraft, 0730 (412), was eventually moved to a weapons range near Rabbit Mount in East Falkland; another was brought to the UK for display at Yeovilton. MoD

While on board the Atlantic Conveyor *one of the 809 Squadron Sea Harrier FRS1s was kept armed and ready on the deck in case any Argentine aircraft or ship should come within range. On 15th May it was only bad weather that prevented the Sea Harrier from being launched to intercept an Argentine Boeing 707 on a surveillance flight.* MoD

leader, the T-34C-1 pilots of 4 Escuadrilla de Ataque were flown back from Stanley by a CANA Super King Air 200.

Another permanent grounding took place on the 15th when the last two CANA SP-2H Neptunes were finally withdrawn from service at Rio Grande and ferried back to their base at Espora to join two other Neptunes that were already being used for spares recovery. Although one of the aircraft had played a crucial role in the attack on *Sheffield*, all four were worn out and too vulnerable to risk the lives of the aircrews on further missions. Argentine Air Force C-130s took over some of the duties of the ageing Neptunes, one of which (0708) has been preserved at Museo Aeronaval de la Armada at Puerto Belgrano.

Following the devastating raid at Pebble Island the Grupo 3 Pucara detachment on the Falklands was reduced to just two serviceable aircraft from the original 12 and reinforcements were called for. On the afternoon of the 15th four Pucaras were flown from the mainland to Goose Green. Three more Pucaras arrived from the mainland a few days later but by then the Argentine Air Force considered that Goose Green was too vulnerable to a commando raid or air attack and so the aircraft were flown back to Stanley airport. On the afternoon of the 15th two MB-339As of 1 Escuadrilla de Ataque flew from Rio Grande to the Falklands, thereby increasing the number of MB-339As at Stanley to five.

By dawn on the 15th the weather had begun to improve and the Sea Harriers of 800 Squadron were able to fly the first of several raids on Stanley airport. The results of the first raids were disappointing so the squadron switched from high-level bombing to toss-bombing for the afternoon raid, resulting in a greater degree of accuracy. One of the bombs was seen to detonate at about 10,000ft and may have been hit by a Roland missile, as claimed by the Argentines after the conflict. From around this date, aircraft of both Sea Harrier squadrons took to carrying a single 1,000lb bomb as they set off on each CAP. The bombs were dropped on targets of opportunity, especially around Stanley, in the hope that continuous, apparently random, bombing would sap the morale of the Argentine troops and keep them at a constant state of alert, thereby inducing fatigue.

By early evening the carrier *Invincible* and her accompanying escorts had closed to within 80 miles of Stanley before moving further east again during the night. Also in the evening *Alacrity* set off to repeat her transit through Falkland Sound and *Brilliant* was sent to investigate a ship that had been seen at Fox Bay.

An Argentine Air Force Boeing 707 flew close to the Amphibious Group during the 15th and unknowingly had a lucky escape. One of the *Atlantic Conveyor*'s load of Sea Harriers was kept ready for action on the deck of the ship and it was only bad weather that kept the aircraft from getting airborne to intercept the Boeing.

In the early hours of the 15th a Nimrod MR2P (XV232) took off from Wideawake airfield for a long-range surveillance operation off the Argentine coast to make certain that the Argentine fleet was still within the 12-mile zone. Twelve Victor tanker sorties were needed to support the Nimrod, two of the Victors flying two sorties each, one on the outbound leg and one on the return leg. The Nimrod, captained by Flight Lieutenant J A Cowan of 201 Squadron, flew to a point about 150 miles north of Stanley before turning west and approaching to within 60 miles of the Argentine coast. The aircraft flew north and parallel with the coast at 7,000-12,000ft and used its Searchwater radar to plot the positions of Argentine Navy warships. The sortie, which lasted 19 hours and 5 minutes, confirmed that the Argentine Navy was still in port and the aircraft returned safely to Ascension Island after a flight of 8,300 miles.

For part of the mission the Nimrod was extremely vulnerable as it was within range of Argentine fighters and flying at medium altitude, where it could have been detected on Argentine radar. Miraculously however, the aircraft was not intercepted and returned to Ascension Island with much valuable information. This long-range sur-

veillance mission was followed by several more such missions at night to maintain a watch on the Argentine fleet to ensure that it did not put to sea to interfere with the the the Amphibious Group as it neared the Falkland Islands.

16th May (Sunday)
On 14th May another Vulcan B2 (XM612) had arrived at Wideawake airfield from Waddington in preparation for the third Vulcan raid, 'Black Buck 3'. On the 15th XM607 also returned from Waddington. These two aircraft were assigned to bomb Stanley airport and were due to take off just before midnight on the 15th when the mission was cancelled. The reasons for the cancellation were strong winds which would have reduced the fuel reserves to an unacceptable level and also the fact that the port underwing pylon had been removed from both Vulcans while they were at Waddington because the crews thought (incorrectly as it transpired) that the pylon was causing too much drag. Both aircraft returned to Waddington, XM607 on the 20th and XM612 on the 23rd, but Wideawake airfield had not seen or heard the last of XM607.

During the night of the 15/16th *Brilliant* sailed into Falkland Sound to investigate a large transport vessel that had been seen in Fox Bay East. This was the 5,000-ton *Bahia Buen Suceso* that had taken the Argentine 'scrap merchants' to South Georgia on 19th March. The two Lynx from *Brilliant* set off to identify and attack the ship. One of the helicopters carried two Sea Skua missiles while the other carried a home-made bomb with a short time fuse, the plan being to drop it directly onto the deck of the vessel. However, the harbour at Fox Bay East was well defended and neither helicopter was able to penetrate the defences to carry out the attack, so they returned to *Brilliant*, which then set off back to the Task Force.

At 1223Z two Sea Harrier FRS1s of 800 Squadron took off from *Hermes* on a photographic reconnaissance mission to Fox Bay and other harbours on either side of Falkland Sound. When the aircraft returned to *Hermes* it was discovered that not only was the *Bahia Buen Suceso* still berthed at Fox Bay East, but the *Rio Carcarana* was anchored in the Sound off Port King on Lafonia. The *Rio Carcarana* was a commercial cargo ship of some 8,482 tons and, like the *Bahia Buen Suceso*, was running the British naval blockade and resupplying the Argentine forces on the Falklands. At 1603Z Lieutenant Commander Gordy Batt (in XZ459) and Lieutenant Andy McHarg (in XZ494) took off and headed for Port King. The Sea Harriers arrived there about 20 minutes later and proceeded to bomb and strafe the *Rio Carcarana,* forcing the crew to abandon the ship when it caught fire. However, the stricken ship did not sink but remained abandoned until it was attacked again on the 21st (by Argentine aircraft), 22nd and the 23rd.

As Batt and McHarg were returning to *Hermes* Lieutenant Commander Andy Auld (in XZ500) and Lieutenant Simon Hargreaves (in ZA191) took off to attack the *Bahia Buen Suceso*. The vessel was berthed close to houses in Fox Bay and could not therefore be bombed. However, the Sea Harriers attacked with their 30mm cannon and during a single pass they damaged the ship's bridge and engine room and set fire to a diesel oil storage tank on the shore, very close to the ship. Simon Hargreaves's Sea Harrier was hit in the tail by Argentine AAA but both aircraft returned safely to Hermes. The *Bahia Buen Suceso* was not used again and remained tied up at Fox Bay East for the duration of the conflict. After the conflict it tore loose from its moorings during a storm and was beached further up the coast. It was later towed to San Carlos Water and then towed out to a deepwater area east of Stanley and on 21 October 1982, Trafalgar Day, was sunk by naval gunfire, cannon fire and rockets from Sea Harriers of 809 Squadron and a hit by a torpedo from the submarine *Onyx*.

Broadsword had been having trouble with water ingress into her forward Seawolf tracker so it was decided to test-fire the missiles against 4.5-inch shells on the 16th. *Yarmouth* provided the necessary gunfire and two shells were destroyed in flight by *Broadsword*'s Seawolfs, thereby proving the system.

On the 16th the CAB601 helicopters returned to Moody Brook Barracks but moved on a few days later to a dispersed site in the Two Sisters area, five miles west of Stanley, and then back to the Mount Kent site. On the north coast of East Falkland three Special Forces reconnaissance teams

were inserted by *Arrow*'s Lynx on the 16th in preparation for the forthcoming amphibious landings.

Sometime on the 16th an Argentine Air Force C-130 Hercules landed at Stanley airport carrying a 155mm gun, the first of several delivered to the islands. With this weapon the Argentine garrison at Stanley could fire back at the warships during their nightly bombardment of the airfield. These artillery weapons would also be well used during the final stages of the land battle for the Falklands in a few weeks' time.

The two elements of the Amphibious Group, led by *Fearless* and *Antrim*, joined up at sunset on the 16th resulting in a large group of 15 RFAs and merchant ships led and protected by *Fearless*, *Intrepid*, *Antrim*, *Ardent*, *Argonaut* and *Plymouth*.

Throughout the day an RAF Hercules C1P (XV200) had been slowly making its way south on the first air-refuelled mission from Ascension. Flight Lieutenant H C Burgoyne and his 47 Squadron crew took off at 0245Z on the 16th and refuelled from two Victors on the outbound leg. The aircraft then dropped 1,000lb of special stores and eight parachutists (Special Forces troops) to *Antelope* just within the TEZ. The Hercules was refuelled by three more Victors on the return leg of the 6,300-mile trip and landed back at Ascension Island at 0250Z on the 17th having been airborne for 24 hours and 5 minutes. This flight, for which Harry Burgoyne received the AFC and the rest of the crew were all decorated, was eclipsed by an even longer mission on the 18th.

17th May (Monday)

Both Sea Harrier squadrons were active on the 17th with 800 Squadron flying low-level photographic reconnaissance flights over selected areas of the Falklands in preparation for the amphibious landings, while a flight of aircraft from 801 Squadron was diverted from a CAP to meet an Argentine air attack, which never materialised. A potential replacement Sea Harrier was lost on this day back in the UK when XZ438, a trials and development aircraft, crashed as it attempted to take off from Yeovilton's ski-jump ramp. The aircraft was testing various combinations of underwing fuel tanks and was carrying two large 330-gallon tanks when it crashed. Luckily the pilot ejected and survived the accident.

As the Amphibious Group proceeded towards the TEZ, *Hermes*, accompanied by the RFAs *Fort Austin* and *Resource* sailed to meet it. With the arrival of the Amphibious Group the converted aircraft transport *Atlantic Conveyor* came within flying distance of the Carrier Battle Group. In preparation for the two aircraft carriers receiving additional Harriers and Sea Harriers, there was some shuffling of helicopters between

ships. Four Sea King HAS5s (XZ577, ZA130, ZA133 and ZA137) of 826 Squadron were flown from *Hermes* to *Fort Austin* on the 17th. This detachment was to provide ASW coverage of Falkland Sound during the amphibious landings. *Fort Austin*'s four Lynx HAS2s were dispersed, three of them (XZ240, XZ700 and XZ720) to *Hermes* and one (XZ725) to *Invincible* to provide the aircraft carriers with an anti-Exocet ESM capability. As soon as XZ725 arrived on board *Invincible* however, both of its engines had to be changed. *Fort Austin* also transferred a Wessex HU5 (XT468 of 'B' Flight 845 Squadron) to *Hermes*. During the evening of the 17th two Sea King HC4s (ZA290 and ZA292) of 846 Squadron were flown over to *Invincible* for a special long-range covert operation which ultimately gathered more publicity than was intended.

Another helicopter transfer on the 17th saw the return of the four 3 CBAS Scout AH1s from the *Elk*, where they had been sheltering below decks since the 11th. All four helicopters flew to the *Europic Ferry* in readiness for their part in the amphibious landings. One of the few British helicopters to see any action on the 17th was Lynx HAS2 XZ736 from *Alacrity* which dropped flares over Port Howard as a diversion to the landing of NGS spotting teams who dug themselves in to wait for the landings.

2 Grupo flew its first operational mission since 3rd May when one of it's Canberras flew a reconnaissance mission searching for British ships. Additional single-aircraft reconnaissance missions were flown by the Grupo on the 20th, 21st, and 25th May and on 11th June, all without success.

18th May (Tuesday) – Clandestine Missions

The British Task Force lost two Sea Kings on the 18th, one of them in unusual circumstances. In the early hours of the morning an 826 Squadron Sea King HAS5 (XZ573) suffered a radio altimeter failure while in the hover and ditched in the sea about two miles from *Hermes*. The crew of four were rescued safely by another of the squadron's Sea Kings and the stricken helicopter remained afloat. *Hermes* was about to haul the Sea King onto its deck using one of the ship's cranes when it was realised that if the helicopter should suddenly sink, the Mk11 depth charges it was carrying would detonate and damage the aircraft carrier. The result was that *Hermes* moved away and the Sea King was sunk by small arms fire as it represented a hazard to shipping. As the helicopter sank beneath the waves the depth charges did indeed detonate at the appropriate depth!

Soon after the two Sea King HC4s of 846 Squadron had been flown to *Invincible* from *Hermes* late on the 17th, the carrier and its escort, *Broadsword,* detached from the Carrier Battle Group and headed west at high speed in radio and radar silence and with all lights extinguished. At 0315Z on the 18th Lieutenant Richard Hutchings lifted off ZA290 from the deck of *Invincible* carrying an SAS team. As the helicopter headed west towards the Argentine mainland the two ships turned about and headed back east towards the Task Force. However, the Sea King was detected on radar as it flew towards Rio Grande and the airfield was lit up by flares in an attempt to spot the helicopter. With the element of surprise lost, the Sea King deposited its load of soldiers and sometime during the evening of the 18th landed on a beach at Agua Fresca, 11 miles east of Punta Arenas on the very southern tip of mainland Chile and just 110 miles west of the Argentine Navy base at Rio Grande. The Sea King crew then set fire to the helicopter and disappeared into the hills before giving themselves up to the Chilean authorities a few days later.

The discovery of the wreckage of ZA290 caused a media sensation and inevitably led to speculation that the helicopter had delivered a Special Forces team near to Rio Grande to monitor or perhaps sabotage the Super Etendards based there. Certainly the Argentines were extremely worried about an attack on Rio Grande and the base was very tightly guarded but, as far as is known, no attack ever took place on the airfield. Whatever the precise details of the Sea King's mission the crew were repatriated and later decorated, with Lieutenant Hutchings and Lieutenant Alan Bennet receiving DSCs and Leading Aircraftman P B Imrie receiving a DSM.

A television documentary has since claimed that this was not the only attempt to destroy the Super Etendards. A highly risky plan to airland 60 men of 'B' Squadron, SAS on Rio Grande airfield (some sources say Stanley airfield) in a one-way mission by two RAF Hercules flying from Ascension Island was stopped shortly before the aircraft were due to take off. The raid would almost certainly have been suicidal and it was to the great relief of all involved that the mission was aborted. It is possible that the Sea King was to land a reconnaissance party near Rio Grande prior to the main force arriving, but the mission was compromised when the Sea King was spotted and forced to escape to Chile and the Hercules never took off.

Other stories have surfaced in recent years claiming that the Chileans had a much greater involvement in the conflict than was publicly acknowledged. Reports have claimed that several RAF Canberra PR9s from 39 Squadron were flown from Wyton to Belize in mid-April and then, having been repainted in Chilean Air Force

On 18th May 826 Squadron Sea King HAS5 XZ573 suffered a radio altimeter failure and ditched in the sea about two miles from HMS Hermes. The crew of four were quickly rescued by another Sea King but XZ573 had to be sunk by gunfire as it refused to sink of its own accord and was a considered to be a hazard to shipping. MoD

markings, were flown on to Punta Arenas air base. Here the aircraft were said to have been flown by RAF crews over mainland Argentina and the South Atlantic, gaining valuable intelligence about the Argentine forces and their dispositions. Four of the older Canberra PR7s from 100 Squadron were also said to have operated from Chile during the conflict.

It is true that Chile received three Canberra PR9s from the RAF in October 1982 but whether any Canberras were actually used during the conflict has not been confirmed by British official sources. Other aircraft sold to Chile included 12 ex-RAF Hunters that were flown to Chile as airfreight in April, May and November 1982. Also unconfirmed is a claim that two RAF Hercules C1s (XV192 and XV292) were repainted in Chilean Air Force markings and operated clandestinely from Punta Arenas. Apparently the aircraft were seen at Lyneham after the conflict still bearing faint traces of Chilean Air Force markings.

As *Invincible* was returning to the Task Force in the early hours of the 18th two 801 Squadron Sea Harriers flown by Lieutenant Commander 'Sharkey' Ward (in XZ498) and Flight Lieutenant Ian Mortimer (in XZ495) dropped flares over selected locations in the Falklands as a diversionary tactic. Sea Harriers of 801 Squadron also flew

a number of CAPs during the morning of the 18th, dropping bombs on Stanley airfield from high altitude in the process.

When the *Atlantic Conveyor* and *Hermes* rendezvoused just outside the TEZ, the Sea Harriers and Harriers started to leave for their assigned aircraft carriers. First to leave were four Sea Harriers (XZ499, ZA176, ZA177 and ZA194) which took off vertically from the deck of the *Atlantic Conveyor* and flew to join 800 Squadron on board *Hermes.* Later in the day the fifth Sea Harrier (ZA190 flown by Lieutenant Commander Tim Gedge) flew to join 801 Squadron on board *Invincible.* All the pilots who flew these much-needed reinforcements to the two aircraft carriers were from 809 Squadron and although the squadron did not fight as a unit, its contribution in terms of men and aircraft was considerable.

Also departing the *Atlantic Conveyor* on the 18th were four RAF Harrier GR3s of 1 Squadron. Wing Commander Peter Squire (in XZ972) led Squadron Leader Peter Harris (XZ988), Squadron Leader Jerry Pook (XZ997), and Flight Lieutenant John Rochfort (XV789) off the ship on the ferry flight to *Hermes.* Two Harriers had minor unserviceabilities and did not leave the *Atlantic Conveyor* until the following two days. The newly arrived pilots, who had been inactive for two weeks while on board the *Atlantic Conveyor,* were flying familiarisation sorties within three hours of arriving on *Hermes* and *Invincible.*

During the night of the 18/19th the Sea King HC4s of 846 Squadron flew the last of the squadron's Special Forces insertion flights prior to the amphibious assault. The squadron had flown a total of 26 sorties in support of the SAS and SBS in 12 nights since 1st May.

A Sea King hovers above the Atlantic Conveyor *as a Sea Harrier is unbagged and prepared for flight.* MoD

Wing Commander Peter Squire lifts off in Harrier GR3 XZ972 from the Atlantic Conveyor *on 18th May 1982 en route to* Hermes. *This was the aircraft in which Flight Lieutenant Jeff Glover was shot down near Port Howard on 21st May.* MoD

The *Bristol* Group of eight ships arrived at Ascension Island on the 18th and left on the following day, while *Ardent* joined up with the Carrier Battle Group at night after having escorted the ships of the Amphibious Group for several days.

HMS *Leeds Castle*, a North Sea fishery protection vessel armed with a 40mm gun, was en route to the TEZ as a dispatch vessel on the 18th when she experienced engine problems. At 0735Z Hercules C1 XV291, one of the aircraft fitted with auxiliary fuel tanks in the fuselage, took off from Ascension Island to airdrop a new camshaft to the vessel. The repair work was completed 32 hours later and the *Leeds Castle* continued her journey thanks to the 47 Squadron crew who had made the 16 hour 40 minute trip from Ascension Island.

19th May (Wednesday)
At 1215Z four 801 Squadron Sea Harriers took off from *Invincible* for a raid on the Argentine Army forward helicopter base near Mount Kent. The raid was originally scheduled for just before dawn but was postponed, primarily because of low cloud. The four aircraft, flown by Lieutenant Commander Ward (ZA175), Flight Lieutenant Mortimer (XZ498), Lieutenant Commander Kent (XZ495) and Flight Lieutenant Barton (XZ451), dropped VT-fused bombs from high level above a cloud base. However, the combination of high altitude and cloud cover resulted in the bombs missing their target with the result that none of the helicopters on the ground were damaged.

Shortly before the Sea Harriers took off from *Invincible*, the next batch of aircraft

started their ferry flight from the *Atlantic Conveyor* when the final three Sea Harrier FRS1s (XZ458, XZ491 and ZA174 flown by 809 Squadron pilots Lieutenant Commander D D Braithwaite, Lieutenant D Austin and Lieutenant A Craig respectively) were flown to *Invincible* as replacements and reinforcements for 801 Squadron. Also departing from the *Atlantic Conveyor* on the 18th was a Harrier GR3 (XZ963), flown to *Hermes* by Flight Lieutenant Tony Harper, which had been delayed due to a minor technical problem.

The Harrier GR3s of 1 Squadron commenced their first operational missions from *Hermes* on the 19th, each pilot flying at least two air combat training and familiarisation sorties during the day carrying AIM-9Gs as part of the theatre indoctrination and final work-up. On the first mission Wing Commander Squire and Flight Lieutenant Jeff Glover were airborne when an Argentine Air Force Boeing 707 was picked up on radar, some 180 miles northeast of the Task Force. Fortunately for the Boeing it turned back before the Harriers were able to make positive contact. After the 19th the AIM-9Gs were removed from the Harrier GR3s which then reverted to their primary roles of ground attack, battlefield air interdiction and armed reconnaissance, leaving air defence duties to the more suitable Sea Harriers. By the end of the day the Harriers had flown a total of 16 sorties, while 800 Squadron's Sea Harriers flew a further 25 as the new pilots quickly familiarised themselves with shipboard operations.

The only other Argentine air movement recorded on the 19th was a resupply flight by a Grupo 1 Hercules. The resupply of the more remote garrisons on the Falklands was always a problem for the Argentines. In an effort to reduce the need for helicopters or small boats to redistribute the supplies from Stanley, it was decided that C-130s would fly direct to the remote garrisons and airdrop the supplies. At 1621Z the C-130H (TC-68), captained by Mayor Ruben Palazzi, took off from Comodoro Rivadavia and flew at low level (rarely higher than 100ft despite poor visibility and light rain) to the Falklands. As the aircraft approached Darwin it climbed to 600ft and dropped eight tons of supplies in containers to the troops waiting below. The mission once again illustrated the proficiency and courage of the Argentine Air Force C-130 crews who daily risked their lives to keep their comrades in the Falklands resupplied.

The large Amphibious Group had finally rendezvoused with the Carrier Battle Group late on the 18th and spent much of the next day outside the TEZ repositioning helicopters, troops and stores in preparation for the assault on the Falklands. The Amphibious Group had all the appearance of a Second World War convoy and consisted of the following vessels: *Fearless, Intrepid, Antrim, Antelope, Sir Galahad, Sir Geraint, Sir Lancelot, Sir Percivale, Sir Tristram, Norland, Elk, Europic Ferry* and *Atlantic Conveyor*. The commanders at Northwood had decided that it was too risky to have most of the troops who would be involved in the initial landings all together in one ship so it was decided, almost at the last moment, to disperse some of those aboard the heavily laden *Canberra* to other ships. Throughout the 19th troops from the *Canberra* were airlifted to other ships to spread the load more evenly, especially as the threat of Argentine submarine and air attack was increasing.

Men of 40 Commando were redeployed to *Fearless* while 965 paratroopers of 3 PARA were taken across to *Intrepid*. A large amount of stores also had to be redistributed and the assault ships' landing craft and helicopters were busy shuttling men and stores throughout the day.

As space was at a premium on board *Hermes*, thanks to the arrival of Harriers and Sea Harriers and because the SAS troops were needed on board *Intrepid*, it was decided to send the last three 846 Squadron Sea King HC4s to *Intrepid*. In short flights, the helicopters moved troops and equipment across to *Intrepid* but at 2215Z disaster struck. Sea King ZA294 was transporting a group of SAS soldiers to *Intrepid* and was circling the ship waiting its turn to land when the crew heard a loud thump and the engine failed. The helicopter hit the sea hard, rolled inverted and sank within minutes. The two pilots, Lieutenant R Horton and Sub Lieutenant P Humphreys, managed to scramble through the cockpit windows with difficulty but 21 men drowned as the helicopter sank beneath the waves.

For 30 minutes the nine survivors clung onto a dinghy in the freezing water until they were rescued by one of *Brilliant's* sea boats and a Sea King of 826 Squadron from *Hermes*. Among the dead were the Squadron Sergeant Majors from both 'D' and 'G' Squadrons of the SAS, the Sea King's crewman, Corporal Aircraftman Michael D Love, RM, and Flight Lieutenant G W Hawkins and his signaller, Corporal D F McCormack, Royal Signals. The latter two men were attached to the SAS as a for-

ward air control team and Garth Hawkins was the only member of the RAF to lose his life during the conflict.

The cause of the accident was never ascertained but it was thought possible that the helicopter might have collided with an albatross or another large sea bird as bird remains were later found in the area. Whatever the cause, the accident was a tragedy that was sorely felt by the small, close-knit SAS fraternity in the South Atlantic. The loss of 20 soldiers represented the greatest loss of life in a single incident to affect the SAS since the Second World War.

The shuffle of helicopters among the Amphibious Group continued despite the tragic accident. The two remaining 846 Squadron Sea Kings from *Hermes* transferred to *Intrepid* as planned, while ZA291 was flown from *Intrepid* to the *Canberra*. The two Sea Kings on board the *Elk* were also transferred, ZA295 to the *Norland* and ZA312 to *Fearless*. Another movement was that of 'B' Flight 845 Squadron Wessex HU5 XT765, which had been on *Invincible* since the 9th. It flew across to the *Atlantic Conveyor* on the 19th to make more room for the additional Sea Harriers on *Invincible*. Lastly, 'E' Flight 845 Squadron Wessex HU5 XT449 flew from *Tidepool* to *Antrim* to assist the ship's own Wessex in a Special Forces insertion the following day.

Apart from the *Bristol* Group of ships leaving Ascension Island the only movement of note on the 19th was the arrival from Lyneham of a Hercules C1P (XV179), the second C1P to deploy to Wideawake. The aircraft flew its first long-range mission two days later.

A solitary Harrier GR3 of 1 Squadron, RAF sits among five Sea Harrier FRS1s on the deck of Hermes. This photograph must have been taken after 18th May when ZA176, the third aircraft from the camera, was flown to Hermes from the Atlantic Conveyor. MoD

20th May (Thursday)

Even after the initial clashes on 1st May, diplomatic efforts had been continuing in Washington, London, Buenos Aires and at the UN at New York. However, with all hope of a last-minute diplomatic solution by now lost, the 20th was spent in final preparation for the amphibious landings that were to take place the following day. Neither of the

Sea Harrier squadrons did much flying so as to conserve themselves for a very busy day on the 21st. However, the Harriers of 1 Squadron flew their first offensive mission of the conflict on the 20th despite the fact that the FINRAE alignment equipment had not yet arrived on board *Hermes*, which meant that the Harriers' inertial navigation system could not be used.

At 1430Z Wing Commander Squire, Squadron Leader Bob Iveson and Flight Lieutenant Jerry Pook took off from *Hermes* for a cluster bomb attack on a fuel dump at Fox Bay East on West Falkland, at the southern end of Falkland Sound. A large number of petrol and oil drums exploded spectacularly as the Harriers swept in and dropped their BL755 CBUs on target and

A Sea Harrier FRS1 is about to touch down on the deck of HMS Hermes *as an RAF Harrier GR3 awaits its turn to come aboard. The Falklands conflict marked the first occasion that RAF aircraft had flown from the deck of an aircraft carrier operationally since the Second World War. MoD*

A Gazelle AH1 of 3 CBAS flies over the barren terrain that is typical of much of the Falklands. Two of these helicopters were shot down by small arms fire on 21st May during the opening phase of the landings. MoD

escaped without encountering any opposition fire. The only Sea Harrier mission flown over the Falklands on the 20th involved a single aircraft that provided navigational assistance to the 1 Squadron Harriers and then flew a photographic reconnaissance sortie over selected positions in the islands.

At 1400Z 1 Squadron had received its final Harrier when Flight Lieutenant John Rochfort took off from the *Atlantic Conveyor* in XZ989 having being delayed by an unserviceable radio. By this date *Hermes* was out of flying range of the *Atlantic Conveyor* so Rochfort had to land on *Invincible* for a short stop to refuel before continuing on to *Hermes*. The Task Force now had a total of 25 Sea Harrier FRS1s and six Harrier GR3s on hand, with 21 of the jets being based on board *Hermes*.

The only Argentine air activity of note on the 20th was the second, and final, Hercules resupply flight from the mainland direct to an outpost on the Falklands. The destination this time was Fox Bay East and the mission was flown by a C-130H (TC-64). The aircraft was guided in by an Air Force controller who had been flown into Fox Bay by a Grupo 7 Bell 212. The Hercules arrived over the settlement and dropped ten containers consisting of 9.5 tons of supplies for the Army garrison. Unfortunately, the local garrison showed its gratitude by then trying to shoot down the Hercules! Several anti-aircraft guns opened fire on the aircraft but the pilot made a steeply banked turn and dived back down to low level to make his escape back to the mainland. This eventful sortie marked the last time that the direct resupply of an Argentine garrison outside of Stanley was attempted.

On the 20th two Embraer EMB-111 Bandeirante maritime patrol aircraft arrived at Rio Gallegos on loan from Brazil. These two aircraft supplemented the small number of S-2E Trackers operated by the Escuadrilla Antisubmarina and the withdrawn SP-2H Neptunes of the Escuadrilla de Exploracion in conducting a series of maritime surface surveillance missions off the coast of Argentina for the rest of the conflict, but their short range was a limiting factor. The two Bandeirantes flew a total of 39 sorties and accumulated approximately 200 flying hours during the conflict.

Meanwhile some of the Task Force helicopters shuttled back and forth between the ships, ensuring that the correct stores were on the right ships for the big day. There were also more helicopter transfers between ships on the 20th. Having lost a PNG-equipped Sea King HC4 when ZA294 crashed the previous day, one of *Intrepid*'s two remaining Sea King HC4s (ZA313) was exchanged for ZA295 which was PNG-equipped and which had been transferred from the *Elk* to the *Norland* on the 19th.

Because *Hermes* was becoming overcrowded due the arrival of fresh Harriers and Sea Harriers, one of RFA *Fort Austin*'s Wessex HU5s (XT468) that had been transferred to *Hermes* on the 17th was flown across to the *Atlantic Conveyor* on the 20th. Some of the 3 CBAS helicopters were also moved around to ensure that helicopter support was available to each element of the brigade. Scout AH1 XP902 from the *Sir Tristram* and XT629 from the *Europic Ferry* both flew across to the *Stromness* where they joined 45 Commando, while the squadron's 'A' Flight Gazelles AH1s (XZ326, ZA730 and ZA776) moved from the *Sir Geraint* to the *Sir Tristram*.

The only movements of interest at Ascension Island during the day were the departure of Vulcan B2 XM607 to Waddington and the arrival of the *Baltic Ferry* and the *Nordic Ferry*, both of which left later the same day. However, on the night of the 20th Nimrod MR2P XV232 took off on a long-range sortie to monitor enemy activity around the Falklands as the Amphibious Group made its way towards the islands. Captained by Flight Lieutenant D J Ford of 206 Squadron, the aircraft returned to Wideawake airfield 18 hours and 50 minutes later having flown a record 8,453 miles. A total of 14 Victor K2 tanker sorties were required to support the Nimrod on its flight. Although by no means the longest-duration flight to the Falklands (that honour belongs to the Hercules fleet), this was the longest-distance flight to take place during the conflict and is still to this day the longest-range operational flight ever undertaken by an RAF aircraft.

By mid-May there were so many of the RAF's Victor K2s based at Wideawake airfield (15 rising to a peak of 17) that, from the 18th, USAF Boeing KC-135 Stratotankers took over much of the UK's in-flight refuelling support that was required during air defence operations over the North Sea.

The Task Force re-entered the TEZ shortly after dawn on the 20th and at 1415Z the two main groups split up. The two aircraft carriers, escorted by *Coventry*, *Glamorgan*, *Glasgow*, *Alacrity* and *Arrow*, along with eight RFAs and STUFT vessels, headed southwest while the Amphibious Group and its escorts (including the two Type 22 frigates) split away to head due west in readiness for its final approach to Falkland Sound and San Carlos Water. From now on Commodore Clapp in his capacity as Commodore Amphibious Warfare was in charge of the landings in what was referred to as the Amphibious Operating Area (AOA) and the focus of attention shifted from the open sea to San Carlos Water. On the eve of the landings the disposition of aircraft on board Task Force ships was finalised and is presented in the accompanying table.

Ships assigned to Operation 'Sutton', the Landings on the Falklands
(including those in supporting roles):

HMS *Antrim*
Wessex HAS3 of 737 Squadron (XP142)

HMS *Ardent*
Lynx HAS2 of 815 Squadron (XZ251)

HMS *Argonaut*
Lynx HAS2 of 815 Squadron (XZ233)

HMS *Brilliant*
Lynx HAS2 of 815 Squadron
(XZ721 and XZ729)

HMS *Broadsword*
Lynx HAS2 of 815 Squadron
(XZ728 and XZ732)

HMS *Plymouth*
Wasp HAS1 of 829 Squadron (XT429)

HMS *Yarmouth*
Wasp HAS1 of 829 Squadron (XV624)

HMS *Fearless*
Sea King HC4 of 846 Squadron
(ZA296, ZA298, ZA310, ZA312)

HMS *Intrepid*
Sea King HC4 of 846 Squadron
(ZA292, ZA293, ZA295, ZA297)

RFA *Sir Galahad*
Gazelle AH1 of 'C' Flight 3 CBAS
(XX402, XX411, XX412)

RFA *Sir Geraint*
No helicopters embarked

RFA *Sir Lancelot*
Scout AH1 of 'B' Flight 3 CBAS
(XV140, XW615, XW616)

RFA *Sir Percivale*
Gazelle AH1 of 'M' Flight 3 CBAS
(XX376, XX380, XX413)

RFA *Sir Tristram*
Gazelle AH1 of 'A' Flight 3 CBAS
(XZ326, ZA730, ZA776)

RFA *Fort Austin*
Sea King HAS5 of 826 Squadron
(XZ577, ZA130, ZA133, ZA137)

RFA *Stromness*
Scout AH1 of 'B' Flight 3 CBAS
(XP902, XT629)

SS *Canberra*
Sea King HC4 of 846 Squadron
(ZA291, ZA299)

MV *Europic Ferry*
Scout AH1 of '5' Flight (656) 3 CBAS
(XR627, XR628, XT637, XT649)

MV *Norland*
Sea King HC4 of 846 Squadron (ZA313)

Ships not directly involved in the landings

Carrier Battle Group

HMS *Hermes*
Sea Harrier FRS1 of 800 Squadron
(XZ455, XZ457, XZ459, XZ460, XZ492,
XZ494, XZ496, XZ499, XZ500, ZA176,
ZA177, ZA191, ZA192, ZA193, ZA194)
Harrier GR3 of 1 Squadron
(XV789, XZ963, XZ972, XZ988, XZ989,
XZ997)
Sea King HAS5 of 826 Squadron
(XZ571, XZ577, XZ578, ZA129, ZA130,
ZA131, ZA133, ZA136, ZA137)
Lynx HAS2 of 815 Sqn (XZ240, XZ720)

HMS *Invincible*
Sea Harrier FRS1 of 801 Squadron
(XZ451, XZ456, XZ458, XZ491, XZ493,
XZ495, XZ498, ZA174, ZA175, ZA190)
Sea King HAS5 of 820 Squadron
(XZ574, XZ918, XZ920, XZ921, ZA126,
ZA127, ZA128, ZA134, ZA135)
Lynx HAS2 of 815 Squadron (XZ725)

HMS *Coventry*
Lynx HAS2 of 815 Squadron (XZ242)

HMS *Glamorgan*
Wessex HAS3 of 737 Squadron (XM837)

HMS *Glasgow*
Lynx HAS2 of 815 Squadron (XZ247)

HMS *Alacrity*
Lynx HAS2 of 815 Squadron (XZ736)

HMS *Arrow*
Lynx HAS2 of 815 Squadron (XZ730)

Other ships in or close to the TEZ

HMS *Exeter* (arrived on the 21st)
Lynx HAS2 of 815 Squadron (XZ733)

HMS *Hecla*
Wasp HAS1 of 829 Squadron (XT420)

HMS *Hydra*
Wasp HAS1 of 829 Squadron (XT432)

HMS *Leeds Castle* (arrived on the 21st)
No helicopters embarked

RFA *Appleleaf*
No helicopters embarked

RFA *Olmeda*
Sea King HAS2A of 824 Squadron
(XV649, XV660)

RFA *Pearleaf*
No helicopters embarked

RFA *Regent*
Wessex HU5 of 848 Sqn (XS486, XT756)

RFA *Sir Bedivere*
No helicopters embarked

RFA *Tidepool*
Wessex HU5 of 845 Sqn (XT449, XT461)

SS *Atlantic Conveyor*
Chinook HC1 of 18 Squadron
(ZA706, ZA716, ZA718, ZA719)
Lynx HAS2 of 815 Squadron (XZ700),
Wessex HU5 of 845 Squadron
(XT468, XT765)
Wessex HU5 of 848 Squadron
(XS480, XS495, XS499, XS512, XT476,
XT483)

MV *Elk*
No helicopters embarked

SS *Uganda*
No helicopters embarked

21st May (Friday) –
The Initial Landings at San Carlos

As the Amphibious Group started its run-in towards the Falkland Islands and its final destination of San Carlos Water, *Antrim* and *Ardent* were detached and sent ahead to pave the way for the main force. At midnight on the 20th *Ardent* entered Falkland Sound through a narrow passage opposite Fanning Head and proceeded to Grantham Sound to take up a position from where she could assist an SAS diversionary attack on Goose Green and Darwin during the landings. Two hours later, *Antrim* entered Falkland Sound to insert an SBS patrol equipped with night-vision equipment to report on enemy positions on Fanning Head. The weather was ideal for the operation with fog, low cloud and strong winds that prevented Argentine air operations and helped the Amphibious Group to avoid detection. As the ships approached Falkland Sound two Sea King HAS5s of 826 Squadron began sonar sweeps of the northern approaches of the Sound on the lookout for the submarine *San Luis*.

At dusk on the 20th Special Forces teams had been landed on the Falkland Islands. *Intrepid*'s four PNG-equipped Sea King HC4s airlifted 40 men of 'D' Troop, SAS to the north of Darwin and Goose Green and to the south of the Sussex Mountains. Under the code name Operation 'Tornado', the troops were to carry out diversionary operations as the main force landed. As part of this plan, *Glamorgan* took up position off the east coast of East Falkland and fired 100 rounds of 4.5-inch shells towards Berkeley Sound. The ship's Wessex HAS3 flew spoof missions towards the coast to reinforce the Argentine high command's suspicion that the amphibious assault was taking place near Stanley. Similarly, *Antrim*'s Wessex HAS3 (XP142, 'Humphrey' of South Georgia fame) and an 845 Squadron machine (XT449) on detachment to the ship, landed 32 men from 3 SBS at Fanning Head at the mouth of Falkland Sound. This party, with supporting gunfire from *Antrim*, later captured or killed many of the occupants of the

Argentine observation post. The rest of the Carrier Battle Group sailed to the south of the Falklands in an attempt to divert attention away from the Amphibious Group's approach.

In the early hours of the 21st the other ships of the Amphibious Group and their close escorts entered Falkland Sound, which was designated as the AOA. The troop transports then arrived, the *Canberra* being the first to enter San Carlos Water while the escorting frigates and destroyers remained close by in the Sound to defend the amphibious ships from air attack. The assault ships *Fearless* and *Intrepid* both launched their 16 landing craft to collect troops from the transports and deliver 40 Commando to San Carlos, 2 PARA and 45 Commando to Ajax Bay and 3 PARA to Port San Carlos. *Antrim* was placed in charge of air operations over the AOA. While the amphibious ships unloaded their precious cargoes of men and equipment, the warships *Antrim*, *Ardent*, *Argonaut*, *Brilliant*, *Broadsword* and *Yarmouth* stood guard in Falkland Sound, with *Plymouth* in San Carlos Water itself, ready for the expected enemy counterattack.

It was estimated that the landings would continue for about five days before any breakout from the San Carlos area could be attempted. During these five days supplies would be built up at the beachhead and troops would dig themselves in, ready to defend themselves against the expected Argentine air raids. The breakout was originally intended to be in only one direction, towards Douglas and Teal Inlet on the north coast before making for the hills to the west of Stanley. However, following pressure from London it was decided to conduct a raid on Goose Green that developed into a major battle, after which a southern arm of a pincer movement could take place before the final assault on Stanley itself. However, for the plan to work the initial landing in San Carlos Water had to succeed and the 21st was probably the most critical day of the entire conflict in this respect. For over six hours the Task Force ships would have to withstand Argentine air raids flown in perfect flying weather with the protection of only a handful of Sea Harriers and the ships' own air defence weapons.

Antrim opened hostilities in Falkland Sound at 0452Z by firing 4.5-inch shells at Argentine positions located on Fanning Head, following which the SBS troops captured the positions, although a few enemy troops escaped. With Fanning Head secured, the landing craft started bringing the main force ashore at 0530Z. British aerial activity early in the day included armed reconnaissance flights by Gazelle AH1s of 3 CBAS fitted as gunships with a GPMG and SNEB rockets. Two 'A' Flight Gazelles took

The Nimrod detachment based on Ascension Island flew many long-range maritime patrol flights over the South Atlantic, including a record-breaking flight of 8,453 miles by XV232 on 20/21st May. XV260 was one of 16 aircraft fitted with an in-flight refuelling probe to extend its range. MoD

Gazelle AH1 XX412 of 'C' Flight 3 CBAS was hit by small arms fire early in the morning of 21st May during the initial landings at San Carlos. When XX412 was put on display at the Army Air Day at Middle Wallop on 24th July 1982, it was still fitted with SNEB rocket pods and a GPMG and had bullet holes in the canopy and tail boom. This Gazelle was the first British aircraft to land at Stanley following the Argentine surrender on 14th June. C M Hobson

off from the *Sir Tristram* before dawn to support the attack on Fanning Head by the SBS teams that had been inserted during the night.

It was imperative that the Rapier fire units be set up on high-ground positions around San Carlos as soon as possible to help the warships to provide air defence against the expected Argentine air raids. Although 846 Squadron Sea King HC4s would transport the Rapier units, it fell to the Gazelle AH1s of 'C' Flight 3 CBAS to recce the proposed sites and escort the Sea Kings with their underslung loads. Just as dawn was breaking at 1100Z (0800 local), two Gazelles took off from the *Sir Galahad* to ensure that the selected positions were clear of Argentine troops so that Rapier sites and artillery positions could be set up. When this task was

completed the Gazelles then flew back to the amphibious ships to escort Sea Kings to the landing sites. Sergeant A Evans and Sergeant E R Candlish in Gazelle AH1 XX411 left first with Sea King HC4 ZA296 of 846 Squadron carrying an underslung load of mortar ammunition. The two helicopters crossed the coast and flew past Hospital Point towards Port San Carlos. They then inadvertently overtook the forward troops of 3 PARA, who had landed earlier and were moving inland, and flew on towards Cameron's Point. The helicopter crews then realised that they had overshot their

destination and started to turn around to head back towards friendly troops.

As the Gazelle was making its turn at 1141Z it was hit by small arms fire from troops of Equipo Combat 'Guemes', the platoon garrisoned in the Port San Carlos area under the command of Primer Teniente Carlos Estaban of the Regimiento de Infanteria 25. The Argentine troops from Port San Carlos and Fanning Head were retiring inland when the helicopters appeared, flying at low level towards their positions. The bullets hit the Gazelle's tail rotor and engine gearbox causing the helicopter to pitch and yaw violently. As it was only flying at about 40ft above the ground at the time, the pilot, who was wounded, barely had time to ditch the aircraft just offshore. Both the crew exited the helicopter before it sank and Edward Candlish helped his pilot to reach the shore where Andrew Evans died of gunshot wounds a few minutes later. Sergeant Candlish later reported that they had been fired at by Argentine troops when he was struggling to reach the shore while trying to save his pilot.

Five minutes after XX411 was shot down a second 'C' Flight Gazelle AH1 (XX402 flown by Lieutenant Kenneth Francis and Lance Corporal Pat Giffin) crossed the coast while leading another Sea King and flew over Cameron's Point, close to where XX411 had been hit. As the helicopter was turning over Clam Creek at about 70ft above ground level it too was hit by small arms fire. The pilot was hit in the head and the chest and probably died instantly; the helicopter crashed into a hillside, killing the aircrewman. The bodies of the crew were later recovered by a Wessex HU5 (XT449) of 'E' Flight 845 Squadron and flown to San Carlos for burial. 'C' Flight's third Gazelle (XX412) was also hit by small arms fire near Port San Carlos during the morning. However, it managed to return safely to the Sir Galahad for repairs to its tail rotor and boom and was airborne again two hours later, despite having sustained 12 hits, including several that passed through the cockpit bubble glazing.

The loss of two helicopters and three aircrew so early on during the landings was a blow but by and large the landings went smoothly, thanks in part to the intense activity of the reconnaissance and transport helicopters that flew throughout the day. Although the Gazelles of 3 CBAS returned to their respective ships at the end of the day, six of the squadron's Scouts remained overnight at a landing site near the Ajax Bay refrigeration plant and 3 CBAS thereby became the first British aviation unit to deploy ashore in the Falkland Islands during the conflict. The three Scout AH1s of '5' Flight 3 CBAS were also busy, flying support missions from the Europic Ferry during the 21st (the fourth helicopter was transferred to 'B' Flight 3 CBAS on the 21st). Two of the helicopters worked with 2 PARA as it came ashore at first light while the third helicopter was allocated to 3 PARA but was not needed and so flew on other tasks. All three Scouts helped to recover the 40 SAS soldiers who had been conducting diversionary attacks near Goose Green.

The Sea Kings of 846 Squadron operated from dawn throughout the day from the Norland, Canberra and Fearless, bringing ashore troops and equipment including several 105mm guns and Rapier fire units.

However, because the Rapier equipment had been loaded on the Sir Geraint early during the loading process and was fairly inaccessible, it was noon before the first fire unit could be unloaded. By then Argentine air attacks on the ships in San Carlos Water and Falkland Sound had already commenced. Most of the 30 105mm guns and 10 out of 12 Rapier fire units of 'T' Battery of 12 Air Defence Regiment, Royal Artillery were in position by the end of the day. The Rapiers alone required 63 helicopter sorties to offload and position the equipment. The fire units and their sensitive equipment had suffered during the long journey by ship and the subsequent unloading and it took several days before all 12 units were operational; and even then problems with generators took a toll on serviceability.

The 846 Squadron helicopters ended the day by flying casualties out to the Canberra for medical treatment. Each of the 11 Sea Kings flew an average of nine and a half hours during the 21st and the seven non-PNG equipped helicopters moved a grand total of 912,000lb of stores and 520 troops in 288 loads. The four PNG-equipped helicopters were reserved mainly for nocturnal work that involved moving Special Forces and performing other tasks.

Since the early hours of the 21st two Sea Kings from the 826 Squadron detachment on board the Fort Austin had provided sonar cover to the north of Falkland Sound, on the lookout for Argentine submarines. During the day two Sea Kings were unsuccessfully attacked by Dagger As and one helicopter was reportedly fired at by an Argentine Blowpipe man-portable SAM near Port Howard as the Sea King searched for the location of an emergency SARBE beacon.

The Harriers of 1 Squadron had a day of mixed fortunes on the 21st. The FINRAE equipment had now arrived enabling the pilots to use their head-up displays and improve navigation and weapons aiming accuracy. The first mission took off at 20 minutes before sunrise and was very successful, involving an attack on Argentine Army helicopters encamped at a FOB just to the north of Mount Kent. Acting on intelligence information received from an SAS forward patrol, Squadron Leader Jerry Pook (XZ988) and Flight Lieutenant Mark Hare (XZ963) approached the target area soon after dawn and spotted several helicopters on the ground. The helicopters had been dispersed to this position due to the danger of bombardment from sea or air at Stanley and were waiting to take reinforcements to wherever the British landed.

The Harrier pilots did not see the helicopters until they were almost over the top of them, so they swept around Mount Kent

to make another run from a different direction, thinking the area was undefended. Their first pass using CBUs was unsuccessful (Pook's bombs were dropped too early and Hare's bombs hung up) so they made a second attack using their Aden 30mm cannon. The shooting was more accurate and Mark Hare hit a Chinook (AE-521) while Jerry Pook hit a Puma (AE-501). On the third pass both the Harriers hit the Puma and also inflicted some slight damage on a UH-1H (AE-417) as it was about to lift off. Another Puma was also damaged during the attack. The Chinook caught fire and was completely destroyed but Puma AE-501, although badly damaged, was probably repairable. After the third pass Mark Hare felt a hit and the two aircraft set off back to Hermes, Hare jettisoning his CBUs en route. Both the Harriers returned safely to the aircraft carrier, although Hare's wing tank had indeed been holed by small arms fire during the attack. However, Puma AE-501 did not survive to fly again, as it was later destroyed where it sat during another Harrier attack on the 26th.

Following the Harrier raid on the 21st, which significantly reduced the Argentine capability to fly reinforcements to San Carlos, the CAB601 helicopters evacuated their encampment near Mount Kent yet again and moved back to the relative safety of Stanley. Here they could at least come under the air defence umbrella of the many AAA sites positioned around the town and the airport.

During the night one of the Operation 'Tornado' diversionary attacks by Special Forces troops had resulted in damage to a Pucara at Goose Green. However, it is thought that the aircraft in question was A-517, one of the Pucaras that had been grounded and used as a decoy at Goose Green since the first Sea Harrier attack on 1st May. By 1130Z six Pucaras had been readied for flight at Goose Green and four of the aircraft started to take off just as the first shells from Ardent started to fall on the airfield, fired from a full 12.5 miles away in Grantham Sound. The first aircraft (A-531), flown by Capitan Jorge Benitez, took off safely but the next one was unable to do so, although the second pair did eventually get away some minutes later. Benitez flew to the vicinity of Bombilla Hill and from there saw the British warships in San Carlos Water and spotted troops on the beach. As he circled to choose a suitable target his aircraft was hit in the starboard engine by a missile.

The Pucara had been seen by a forward patrol and a soldier of 'D' Squadron, 22 SAS fired a Stinger man-portable shoulder-mounted SAM. The Pucara pitched up and then began to spin violently as Benitez ejected safely. The aircraft crashed near to the Flats Shanty settlement and Jorge Benitez evaded capture successfully and eventually made contact with Argentine troops some ten hours later. Apparently, a small number of Stingers had been brought back from the United States by an SAS contingent which had just returned from a training course there. The only trained Stinger operator, Staff Sergeant P O'Connor, had been killed in the Sea King crash on the 19th, so another soldier took his place; but due to his lack of training on the system, Benitez's aircraft was the only one that he hit, despite firing five more Stinger SAMs later during the day.

The second mission of the day for the Harrier GR3s of 1 Squadron almost ended in tragedy. Wing Commander Peter Squire (in XZ997) and Flight Lieutenant Jeff Glover (XZ972) took off from *Hermes* at 1156Z and set off on a close air support mission to the San Carlos area. However, XZ997's undercarriage would not retract so Peter Squire had to return to the aircraft carrier. Jeff Glover continued with the mission but en route to San Carlos he was informed that there was no worthwhile target for his load of CBUs and was instead asked to make a reconnaissance run over enemy positions at Port Howard on the east coast of West Falkland. His first run was uneventful but when he was asked to return for a second run over the target area to take photographs 15 minutes later, the Argentine defenders were waiting for him. As the Harrier swept low over Port Howard it was hit and started to roll out of control. Jeff Glover thought that the aircraft had been hit by at least two anti-aircraft shells but the Argentines claimed that the aircraft was shot down by a Blowpipe SAM, fired by Primer Teniente S Fernandez of Compania de Comandos 601, an Argentine Special Forces unit based at Port Howard. Whatever hit it, the Harrier immediately began a rapid roll and a wing folded as Jeff Glover ejected at 600mph at very low level. He passed out due to the violence of the high-speed ejection and hit the water before his parachute had time to deploy fully, but the deceleration provided by the parachute was enough to save his life. His injuries included a broken left arm, shoulder and collar bone, severe shock and facial bruising. He was rescued from the water by Argentine soldiers, treated for his wounds at Port Howard and flown in a UH-1H the next day to Goose Green and then to Stanley on the 23rd. He was evacuated to Comodoro Rivadavia by a C-130 on the evening of 24th May but was not released from Argentina until 8th July as Argentina's only British POW since the initial occupation.

The two Sea Harrier squadrons were in action throughout the day, maintaining almost continuous CAPs at the northern and southern ends of Falkland Sound as well as over West Falkland in an attempt to stop any Argentine strike aircraft from reaching the ships in the Sound. The three CAPs had a combined total of six aircraft on station at any one time; precious few to cope with the expected waves of enemy aircraft. 801 Squadron flew the first of its 28 sorties during the day when two of its Sea Harriers were launched half an hour after dawn, but it was too early at that stage for any Argentine air opposition. In fact the first enemy air activity to threaten the ships in Falkland Sound came from an unexpected direction.

A two-aircraft mission over Falkland Sound had been planned by the 1 Escuadrilla de Ataque detachment at Stanley airport the previous day but at about 1300Z only one MB-339A took off as the other aircraft (to be flown by Teniente Horacio Talarico) was found to have a flat tyre. Teniente de Navio Guillermo Crippa (in 0766/4-A-115) was aware that British ships were in the Sound and that landings were being made in San Carlos Water so it was vital that he obtain up-to-date information on the disposition of the British forces. At about 1315Z Crippa approached from the north and saw several warships in the Sound but continued at 500ft towards San Carlos Water. He spotted a Lynx and was just about to make an attack on it when he saw the distinctive shape of a Leander class frigate ahead. He made a hasty attack on *Argonaut*, firing his eight Zuni rockets and his 30mm cannon and caused minor damage to the ship's Seacat deck.

Three men were wounded in the attack and later evacuated to the *Canberra*. The attack also left a hole in the ship's Type 965 radar antenna, after which the radar actually seemed to work better! This was just as well as *Argonaut*'s Type 965 was one of the few long-range radars available close in to the Falklands. Amazingly, Crippa's aircraft escaped the return fire from several ships, including a Seacat fired from *Intrepid* and a Blowpipe SAM fired by a soldier on board the *Canberra*. Crippa stayed at low level and jinked his aircraft all the way up Port San Carlos valley to escape unharmed. He returned briefly but remained some distance away as he counted the British ships before heading back to Stanley. His information was immensely useful to the Argentine commanders at Stanley and Teniente Crippa was subsequently decorated for his bravery in persisting with his one-man mission. By coincidence, three more MB-339As were being prepared for the ferry flight from Rio Grande to Stanley at the time of Crippa's sortie, but the reinforcement was cancelled until information about the British amphibious landings could be analysed.

Even before Teniente Crippa's sortie in his MB-339A, Grupo 6 started sending off flights of Dagger As (with Learjets as pathfinders) from Rio Grande and San Julian from about 1245Z, the intention being that the flights would arrive over San Carlos Water close together and thereby swamp the British air defences. Cuna flight, consisting of Capitan Dimeglio and Teniente Carlos Castillo from San Julian, approached Falkland Sound from the northwest at low level and surprised *Antrim* off Fanning Head at 1325Z. Although the ship was hit by several rounds of cannon fire the bombs missed their mark and the Daggers escaped without damage. *Antrim*, *Argonaut* and *Broadsword* were stationed off the mouth of San Carlos Water throughout the 21st to form an air defence barrier against air attacks on the amphibious ships that were unloading troops and equipment behind them.

Just minutes after *Antrim* was attacked, two flights consisting of six Dagger As from Rio Grande arrived over Falkland Sound. Seeing ships in the Sound and in San Carlos Water in the distance, the first flight leader, Capitan Rohde, decided to go for a group of three ships in the Sound. *Broadsword* and *Argonaut* were both hit by cannon fire during the attack but no serious damage was done. One one of *Broadsword*'s Lynx (XZ732) suffered shrapnel damage and the ship had to be loaned a replacement (XZ729) from *Brilliant*. However, this time the Daggers did not get away so lightly. Teniente Pedro Bean was killed when his aircraft (C-428) was hit by a SAM and destroyed as it made its bombing run at low level. Although the Argentine Air Force and the Royal Navy initially claimed that the aircraft had been shot down by a Seacat from either *Argonaut* or *Plymouth*, it is probable that it was destroyed by a Seawolf fired by *Broadsword*, which was slightly damaged by cannon fire in the attack.

The second flight of three Daggers, led by Capitan Moreno, concentrated on *Antrim* and one of the aircraft hit the ship with a 1,000lb bomb and about 40 rounds of cannon fire. Luckily for *Antrim*, the bomb bounced off the flight deck and passed through several compartments (including the Seaslug magazine, missing an armed missile by just three feet) before coming to rest in one of the ship's heads and failing to explode. The ship's Wessex HAS3 (XP142) was slightly damaged by bomb splinters during the raid and several fires broke out on board the ship. During the attack the ship fired a Seaslug missile at the Daggers but they were too low and managed to avoid being damaged.

A bomb disposal team was flown to *Antrim* by *Yarmouth*'s Wasp later in the day and the bomb was defused and lowered into the sea before *Antrim* left Falkland

Sound for the Carrier Battle Group later that night. Because her Seaslug system was out of action, *Antrim* was assigned to escort duties in the replenishment area following essential repairs. The bomb disposal team was led by Fleet Chief Petty Officer M G Fellows, who was awarded the DSC for his efforts.

Capitan Moreno's flight escaped south down Falkland Sound before turning west for home but at that point (at 1340Z) they were intercepted by two 800 Squadron Sea Harriers flown by Lieutenant Commander R Fredericksen and Lieutenant M Hale, who had been vectored towards the enemy aircraft by *Brilliant*. When *Antrim* was damaged early on in the raid, *Brilliant* had immediately taken over the role of air defence control ship and her more modern radar proved very useful in the next few hours. As the Daggers accelerated away at very low level, Martin Hale launched a Sidewinder at extreme range but it failed to reach the enemy aircraft, which returned safely to base minus Teniente Bean's aircraft. Later, two more flights of Daggers arrived and attacked *Brilliant* and two other vessels without causing much damage.

Five minutes after the last of the Daggers had attacked the warships in Falkland Sound, two flights of Grupo 5 A-4B Skyhawks swept down the Sound undetected. The six aircraft had taken off from Rio Gallegos at 1200Z and each carried a single 1,000lb bomb. At 1330Z the six A-4Bs of Leo and Orion flights bore down on *Argonaut*, which had been attacked by Teniente Crippa's MB-339A just a short while earlier and was hugging the rocky shoreline to make herself as difficult a target as possible for the Skyhawks. Using the hills close to

the shore for terrain masking, the Skyhawks made a successful attack on the frigate, which was hit by two bombs. One bomb penetrated the boiler room, causing a boiler to explode, while the other entered the forward magazine below the waterline where Seacat missiles were stored. Two of the missiles partially exploded with the force of the impact, causing a major fire and heavy flooding. Fortunately neither of the bombs detonated, but the damage of the impact was severe enough to effectively cripple the ship. *Argonaut*'s engines failed to respond, her steering was lost and several fires broke out and caused considerable damage before being brought under control.

The ship headed towards Fanning Head out of control but stopped with only yards to spare when the anchor was dropped. Unfortunately, two seamen who had been loading Seacats in the magazine were killed during the attack. In the evening the vessel was towed by *Plymouth* from its position off Fanning Head to a safe anchorage in San Carlos Water and remained in this position for eight days as repairs were carried out and the two bombs removed. Lieutenant Commander B F Dutton was awarded the DSO for leading the team that defused and removed *Argonaut*'s bombs. During this time *Argonaut* was capable only of static air defence and although she returned to action on the 26th, she was relieved three days later having been all but put out of action by the Grupo 5 attack on the 21st. All six Skyhawks from Leo and Orion flights returned safely to base despite running the gauntlet of anti-aircraft fire and at least one Seacat missile launch during the attack.

The next raid on the ships in San Carlos Water should have been by two flights each of three A-4Q Skyhawks from CANA's 3 Escuadrilla, which took off from Rio Grande at 1315Z. However, the raid seems to have been launched prematurely with little in the way of hard information on the location of targets. As a consequence, the flights were recalled before they reached the Falklands and returned to base.

At 1345Z, about 45 minutes after Jeff Glover was shot down, Squadron Leader Peter Harris (in XZ988) and Flight Lieutenant John Rochfort (XZ997) set off on an armed reconnaissance of the beachhead around San Carlos and an airstrip at Dunnose Head on West Falkland. They found no targets and so they returned to *Hermes* still carrying their CBUs. As John Rochfort landed close to the edge of the deck, his Harrier's port outrigger wheel left the deck and fell into the catwalk, leaving the aircraft at a precarious angle overlooking the sea below. Fortunately the aircraft was quickly hauled back onto the deck with no real damage done. In fact XZ997 was back in the air just a few hours later when Flight Lieutenant Mark Hare and Flight Lieutenant Jerry Pook (in XZ989) flew another armed reconnaissance mission.

Meanwhile the second pair of Pucaras that took off from Goose Green at about 1145Z were, like Capitan Benitez, also sent to look for signs of British activity around the Bombilla Hill area. Mayor Carlos Tomba and Primer Teniente Juan Micheloud then proceeded west and were targeted by machine-gun fire and at least two SAMs. The two aircraft were recalled to Goose Green to attack a British observation post manned by 'D' Squadron, SAS near the airfield that was directing *Ardent*'s gunfire onto the airfield. When the Pucaras arrived back over Goose Green they started to approach *Ardent* so she fired a Seacat SAM and several 4.5-inch shells at the two aircraft, so deterring any further interest. The Pucaras then made a rocket attack on an empty house which the Argentines suspected housed an SAS observation post and were then directed to another observation post near the airfield. At this point three 801 Squadron Sea Harriers, flown by Lieutenant Commanders 'Sharkey' Ward (in XZ451) and Alisdair Craig (XZ495) and Lieutenant Steve Thomas (XZ456) were vectored towards the Pucaras by *Brilliant*.

The two Pucaras were intercepted about

seven miles to the southwest of Goose Green, but the Sea Harriers overshot at first as the speed differential was too great. Juan Micheloud flew his manoeuvrable little aircraft down a narrow valley to escape from the Sea Harriers and later landed safely at Goose Green. However, Carlos Tomba (in A-511) was unable to shake off his pursuers despite flying within 40ft of the ground. 'Sharkey' Ward slowed his aircraft right down and made three firing passes at Tomba's Pucara, damaging the fuselage, canopy, port engine and port aileron. After the third pass (at about 1510Z), Carlos Tomba was forced to eject from his crippled aircraft and parachuted to safety near Drone Hill, about ten miles southwest of Goose Green. He was rescued about five hours later by an Argentine helicopter. At dusk on the 21st the remaining flyable Pucaras at Goose Green were evacuated to the relative safety of Stanley airport.

Tomba and some of his fellow pilots later became prisoners when Goose Green and Darwin were captured. Tomba's flying helmet eventually found its way to the Fleet Air Arm Museum at Yeovilton. Mayor Tomba later acted as an interpreter at the Ajax Bay field hospital and thereby helped the medical surgeons to treat many of his wounded countrymen.

In the afternoon the Argentine Air Force Skyhawks returned to attack ships in Falkland Sound and San Carlos Water again. Two flights, one of four A-4Bs from Grupo 5 followed closely by a flight of four A-4Cs from Grupo 4, took off from their bases to arrive over Falkland Sound about 1600Z. One of the Grupo 5 aircraft dropped out when it was unable to take on fuel from a KC-130H tanker due to an iced-up refuelling probe, but the remaining three continued towards the Falklands. Grupo 5's Mula flight flew across West Falkland to attack down the Sound from the north. At this point another Skyhawk of the flight suffered a fuel transfer problem from its drop tanks and was ordered to return to base, despite being so close to the target.

The two remaining Skyhawks, flown by Capitan Pablo Marcos Carballo and Primer Teniente Alferez Carmona, were unable to find a way through low cloud and had to turn south before breaking cloud and crossing over Falkland Sound near Swan Island. Ahead of them they saw a cargo ship close to the shore of West Falkland and commenced an attack. At the last moment Capitan Carballo realised that something was wrong as there was no sign of anti-aircraft fire, but by that time it was too late as Carmona had dropped his bomb. The ship was the *Rio Carcarana*, which had already been attacked and damaged by Sea Harriers five days earlier. This left just Capitan Carballo with his one 1,000lb bomb and so he turned

northeast up Falkland Sound until he came across a frigate in Grantham Sound, south of San Carlos Water.

At 1555Z *Ardent* was having a break from her lengthy bombardment of the airfield at Goose Green when Carballo attacked, his bomb narrowly missing the ship and causing no damage other than knocking the ship's Type 992 radar antenna 30 degrees out of alignment. The attack was very sudden, there being no radar warning due to Carballo's low-level approach, and *Ardent* only had time to return fire with her Oerlikon 20mm guns. Carballo turned for home just in time to avoid a pair of 800 Squadron Sea Harriers that were being vectored towards him and he returned safely to Rio Gallegos. During the action Carballo twice inadvertently lowered his undercarriage when he nudged the undercarriage lever as he pushed his throttle forward as far as it would go to get every ounce of speed out of the Skyhawk.

Soon after Capitan Carballo's attack on *Ardent* a flight of four Grupo 4 A-4Cs approached the coast of West Falkland en route to Falkland Sound. However, the two Sea Harriers directed by *Brilliant* to intercept Carballo spotted the new flight as it approached Chartres Settlement. The Skyhawks' pilots saw the Sea Harriers, immediately jettisoned their wing tanks and bombs and turned south as fast as they could go. The two Sea Harriers, flown by Lieutenant Commander Mike Blissett (XZ496) and Lieutenant Commander Neill Thomas (XZ492), closed on the Skyhawks and each fired a Sidewinder at 1605Z. Mike Blissett's missile hit one of the Skyhawks, the tail of which broke off before it crashed into the ground south of Christmas harbour. Neill Thomas's missile followed a Skyhawk as it flew into cloud and must have hit its target as the aircraft was then seen tumbling in flames as it crashed close to the first Skyhawk. Both pilots were killed and it is thought most likely that Blissett had shot down Primer Teniente Daniel Manzotti (in C-325) while Thomas had accounted for Teniente Nestor Lopez (in C-309). Lopez ejected shortly before his aircraft crashed but he was too low for his ejection to be survivable. Mike Blissett also attacked another Skyhawk in the formation using only his cannon but the aircraft escaped trailing smoke, having sustained minor damage.

In the afternoon Grupo 6 attempted to repeat the morning's raid on the British ships and planned to launch six Dagger As (Laucha and Raton flights) from San Julian at 1645Z and six more (Cueca and Libra flights) from Rio Grande at 1655Z, the intention again being to attack almost simultaneously in an attempt to swamp the British defences. In the event it was the two Rio Grande flights that left first but only five aircraft took off as one aborted with a technical problem. The target was a ship that was reported to be in Falkland Sound to the south of San Carlos Water and was, in fact, *Ardent*, which had been operating alone in Grantham Sound all day, firing at Goose Green airfield and enemy positions located at Darwin.

A second Rio Grande Dagger A dropped out with an oil problem and returned safely to base trailing black smoke. The third and final aircraft of Libra flight (flown by Capitan Robles) then joined the three aircraft of Cueca flight to continue the mission. The two flights of Daggers from San Julian were about 15 minutes behind the first flight and their target appears to have been ships in San Carlos Water itself.

As the Cueca flight aircraft approached the Falklands and started their final descent to low level for the approach to the Sound, they were picked up on *Brilliant*'s radar and a pair of 800 Squadron Sea Harriers was vectored towards them. The Daggers flew over Jason Island and crossed the coast of West Falkland at King George Bay before heading east towards Falkland Sound at very low level, beneath cloud and through valleys in what resembled a high-speed tailchase. As the four aircraft approached Chartres Settlement they were spotted by the Sea Harriers of Lieutenant Commander Rod Fredericksen (XZ455) and Sub Lieutenant Andy George (ZA176). With Andy George covering his tail, Rod Fredericksen swept in behind the last Dagger and launched a Sidewinder, which hit the aircraft of Primer Teniente Hector Luna (C-409) at 1735Z. The Dagger began to roll violently and Hector Luna ejected at low level moments before his aircraft crashed near Teal River Inlet close to Mount Maria on West Falkland. Luna broke his shoulder and dislocated his knee during the ejection and subsequent landing and was found the next day by some of the local islanders who radioed Stanley to report that he was safe. Luna was picked up by a Bell 212 and flown to Goose Green before being flown back to Argentina in a C-130 on the 25th.

The remaining Dagger As flew on, the pilots concentrating on their low-level flight across West Falkland and oblivious to the fact that one of their number had just been shot down and that they themselves had been under attack by cannon fire from the two Sea Harriers. As the three remaining Daggers threaded their way through the hills of West Falkland they crossed the coast out into Falkland Sound and saw a British warship in Grantham Sound. *Ardent* had completed her bombardment of shore positions and was on her way to join the other warships in Falkland Sound when she was attacked. The Daggers manoeuvred over Falkland Sound to identify the best approach position; then, at 1744Z, Capitan Horacio Mir Gonzalez led the flight into the attack. Unable to make use of her 4.5-inch gun because the aircraft approached from behind and unable to fire a Seacat due to a problem with the missile control, *Ardent*'s defence comprised two Oerlikon 20mm guns and some light machine guns.

Gonzalez's 1,000lb bomb hit the water and bounced up into *Ardent*'s hull but did not explode. Teniente J D Bernhardt was more successful as his bomb hit the frigate squarely near to the hangar deck and exploded on impact. Several of the ship's crew were killed or injured by the bomb explosion and the ship's hangar and its Lynx HAS2 (XZ251) as well as the Seacat launcher were completely destroyed in the blast. Fires broke out and the ship's gun was rendered useless when power cables were severed. The last Dagger, flown by Capitan Robles, missed its mark but *Ardent* had been badly damaged and made her way slowly towards the ships at the mouth of San Carlos Water for protection.

The two San Julian flights of Dagger As reached the Falklands intact and carried out an attack on a group of ships at the mouth of San Carlos Water at about 1750Z. This was the first time during the day that Argentine aircraft were able to penetrate San Carlos Water. Two aircraft of the first flight (flown by Primer Teniente Cesar Roman and Mayor Luis Puga) bypassed the *Canberra* and attacked *Brilliant*, causing minor shrapnel and cannon shell damage to the ship's Seawolf and Exocet launchers and sonar equipment. *Brilliant*'s Seawolf was unable to obtain a lock-on as the Daggers swept through the entrance into San Carlos Water, but *Broadsword* fired a missile at a Dagger although it missed its target. Several of *Brilliant*'s crew were wounded during the attack including the First Lieutenant, Lieutenant Commander Lee Hulme, who was in the midst of directing a Sea Harrier CAP at the time and who carried on regardless of his wound.

During the run-in on the target one of the Daggers was enveloped in a wall of spray thrown up by *Brilliant*'s return fire. The pilot of the third Dagger, Primer Teniente M Callejo, was lucky to escape when his windscreen was crazed by shrapnel during his bombing run. Despite a hail of gunfire and SAMs, all three Daggers of Laucha flight escaped at low level before climbing to 35,000ft to return to San Julian.

The second group of San Julian Daggers, Raton flight, was picked up by *Brilliant*'s radar operator and an 801 Squadron Sea Harrier CAP was vectored from overhead Port Howard towards them. As Raton flight passed through the valleys north of Mount Maria the Sea Harriers, flown by Lieutenant Commander 'Sharkey' Ward (ZA175) and

Lieutenant Steve Thomas (ZA190), spotted two of the Daggers. At about 1750Z Primer Teniente Jorge Senn saw the Sea Harriers and called a warning to his leader. Capitan Guillermo Donadille and Mayor Gustavo Piuma dropped their wing fuel tanks, jettisoned their bombs and turned to meet 'Sharkey' Ward's Sea Harrier head-on. However, as they fired their cannon at Ward's aircraft, they failed to see Steve Thomas's Sea Harrier as he manoeuvred behind the Daggers. In quick succession Steve Thomas fired two Sidewinder missiles at the two Daggers that were flying close together. The first missile hit Mayor Piuma's aircraft (C-404), which started to disintegrate a few moments after the pilot ejected. The second missile then exploded close to the wing of Capitan Donadille's aircraft (C-403), causing it to roll and then spin. Again the pilot was fortunate enough to be able to eject before the aircraft hit the ground and was destroyed.

The remaining Dagger (C-407), that of Primer Teniente Senn, which had become separated from the other two aircraft at an early stage in the fight, then attacked but overshot the Sea Harrier of 'Sharkey' Ward who fired a Sidewinder at it. The missile hit the Dagger, which promptly exploded and cartwheeled into the ground. Miraculously, Senn was able to eject from his disintegrating aircraft. The fact that all three pilots survived being shot down at low level and high speed is testimony to the efficacy of the Martin-Baker ejection seats that were fitted to the Daggers.

Donadille and Piuma were shot down near Green Hill Bridge while Senn was shot down about four miles to the west and just two miles south of Mount Caroline. All three pilots were taken to Port Howard before eventually being flown back to the Argentine mainland in a C-130. Pieces of Piuma's aircraft were recovered after the conflict and put on display in a war museum at Port Howard run by the settlement manager, Robin Lee. Steve Thomas, one of the least experienced Sea Harrier pilots with less than 200 hours on the aircraft, had now shot down three Argentine fast-jet aircraft, the only British pilot to do so during the conflict.

Following the first abortive mission in the morning, CANA's 3 Escuadrilla mounted another mission in the afternoon, again with two flights each of three A-4Q Skyhawks. The aircraft took off between 1730Z and 1745Z and were targeted at the frigate that was operating alone in the Grantham Sound area – *Ardent*. The first flight, call sign Tabano, was led by Capitan de Corbeta Alberto Jorge Philippi. As Tabano flight approached the Falklands it descended to low level from its cruise altitude of 27,000ft and flew up Falkand Sound from the south. The badly damaged, burning and almost

defenceless *Ardent* was making her way slowly towards the other ships and was off North West Island when the Skyhawks found her at 1806Z. Philippi and Teniente de Navio Jose Cesar Arca attacked *Ardent* from the rear quarter and each aircraft dropped four 500lb Snakeye bombs, several of which hit the stern of the ship, causing further devastation and more serious fires. The third Skyhawk, flown by Teniente de Fregata Gustavo Marcelo Marquez, also attacked *Ardent* but appears to have missed the vessel; the aircraft may have been damaged by 20mm cannon fire from one of the ship's Oerlikons.

The second flight of A-4Q Skyhawks from 3 Escuadrilla (flown by Tenientes Benito Rotolo, Roberto Sylvester and Carlos Lecour) followed up Tabano flight's attack and may have caused further damage to *Ardent*. Two of the Skyhawks received slight shrapnel damage, possibly from their own bombs, but all three aircraft returned home safely.

Tabano flight had been spotted by 'Sharkey' Ward and Steve Thomas as were returning to *Invincible* following their fight with the Grupo 6 Daggers. The two 801 Squadron Sea Harriers were too far away to engage and could not give chase due to their fuel state. However, shortly after the attack the Skyhawks were seen by a pair of 800 Squadron Sea Harriers flown by Lieutenant Clive Morrell (XZ457) and Flight Lieutenant John Leeming (XZ500), who were en route to the southern end of Falkland Sound to take up their CAP positions. The Sea Harriers immediately dived through a scattered cloud layer and caught up with the slower Skyhawks, which were flying at very low level about ten miles south of *Ardent*'s position, off the east coast of Swan Island. Marquez spotted the two Sea Harriers and warned the other members of the flight. They immediately dropped their wing tanks in the vain hope of outrunning the British aircraft. Clive Morrell's first Sidewinder homed onto the tailpipe of Capitan Philippi's aircraft (0660/3-A-307), which disintegrated as he ejected to safety. Morrell's other Sidewinder failed to launch at first so he used his 30mm cannon on the next Skyhawk, that of Jose Arca (0665/3-A-112). The Skyhawk was hit several times in the wings and was almost hit by Morrell's second Sidewinder when it suddenly launched of its own accord. However, the missile appeared to malfunction as it fell short of its target.

Marquez's aircraft (0667/3-A-314) was also hit by cannon fire as John Leeming had problems launching his Sidewinders and had to rely on his two cannon to attack the remaining Skyhawk of the flight. Marcelo Marquez was less fortunate than his compatriots and was killed when his aircraft exploded at low level over Falkland Sound. This was one of the few occasions when the Sidewinder malfunctioned during the conflict, spoiling an otherwise impressive operational record.

Jose Arca ejected from his badly damaged A-4Q almost immediately after Clive Morrell's attack, but although he regained control he realised that he would never reach Rio Grande as his aircraft was losing fuel rapidly. He therefore headed for Stanley with the intention of making an emergency landing there. Upon arriving over Stanley, Arca was told that his port main undercarriage leg was missing and that he had to eject as it was too dangerous for him to land on the short runway. He ejected over the coast and was rescued from the sea by a CAB601 UH-1H flown by Capitan Jorge Svensen, the commander of the UH-1H detachment. The rescue was not without difficulty as the helicopter was not

Ardent burns in Falkland Sound as Yarmouth *stands by to evacuate her crew following a series of air attacks throughout 21st May. The scene is viewed from* Broadsword, *whose forward Seawolf and Exocet launchers are plainly visible.* Cdr S Chelton

equipped with a rescue hoist. Arca's aircraft refused to fly out to sea and crash as intended but instead flew round in circles until it was brought down just south of the airfield by Argentine anti-aircraft fire.

Capitan Philippi had parachuted into the sea in King Bay not far from the wrecked *Rio Carcarana*. He then swam ashore and walked inland for two days until he was discovered by a Falklands farm manager who took Philippi to his farm and looked after him until he was collected by Argentine forces. Philippi was taken by helicopter to Stanley via Darwin and was flown back to the mainland by a C-130 on the 30th. He later took command of 3 Escuadrilla.

There is a postscript to this complex and intense engagement. As 'Sharkey' Ward was busy talking to the Fighter Direction Officer of *Brilliant* on his way back across West Falkland en route to *Invincible*, he realised that he had lost visual and radio contact with Steve Thomas. After a brief search, Lieutenant Commander Ward reported that he thought Thomas's aircraft had been shot down by AAA. He then flew back to the aircraft carrier only to find Steve Thomas already on board and waiting for him. Thomas's aircraft had indeed been hit by anti-aircraft fire as they passed over Port

Howard and his TACAN and radio had been put out of action, so he was unable to report to his leader or to *Invincible*. This was the first battle damage to an 801 Squadron Sea Harrier since the conflict began.

Ardent had been dealt several mortal blows during the air raids on the 21st and, in retrospect, it was probably a mistake to send a lone ship so far south from the protection of the others for so long to shell a small airfield that had already been bombed several times and only held a handful of Pucaras. After the final attack by the Skyhawks the ship was ablaze aft of the funnel and had lost its steering. Captain Alan West dropped anchor and the ship started to list as the lower decks became flooded. The decision was made just before dusk to abandon ship and it finally exploded and sank on the evening of the 22nd. It was assessed that nine bombs had hit *Ardent* during the day, two of which failed to explode.

HMS *Yarmouth* took off the survivors and transferred them to the *Canberra*, but 22 men had died and over 30 were injured. Two men were rescued from the sea by Surgeon Commander Rick Jolly, a Royal Marine doctor who was tasked to set up a field hospital at the Ajax Bay refrigeration

plant. He was on board a Wessex flown by Lieutenant Mike Crabtree of 'E' Flight 845 Squadron at the time of the air raid and they flew across to *Ardent*, after quickly refuelling from *Fearless*. Rick Jolly was twice lowered on the helicopter's winch into the freezing sea to recover two men who had been forced to jump overboard from the ship. Among the dead on board *Ardent* were the pilot and observer of the ship's Lynx, Lieutenant Commander John M Sephton and Lieutenant Brian Murphy, who were last seen firing small arms from the stern railings as the ship was bombed by the Grupo 6 Dagger As in the 1744Z attack.

Yarmouth's Wasp airlifted EOD equipment over to *Ardent* but the stricken vessel was beyond saving. Sea Kings from 846 Squadron and an 'E' Flight 845 Squadron Wessex from the *Canberra* flew numerous casevac missions for the wounded from *Ardent*. Later, *Yarmouth* took *Ardent* in tow but the frigate sank off North West Island on the evening of the 22nd, the second of the Task Force's ships to be lost. The arrival in the TEZ of HMS *Exeter* on the 21st helped to balance the loss of *Ardent*, but *Exeter* remained with the Carrier Battle Group for much of the conflict.

Some time during the day, no less than eight Canberra B62s of 2 Grupo escorted by Mirage IIIEAs took off from Trelew, but the

force was recalled before it reached the Falklands due to intense Sea Harrier activity, which would have posed an unacceptably high risk to the elderly bombers.

At the end of the day some of the transport vessels were sent out to the relative safety of the open sea, even though they had not finished unloading. The *Norland* left San Carlos Water late in the evening and sailed to a holding area about 170 miles northeast of Stanley. The *Canberra* and the *Europic Ferry*, escorted by the damaged *Antrim*, also left Falkland Sound in the early hours of the 22nd and joined the *Norland* in the morning. It was originally intended that the *Canberra* should remain in San Carlos Water for several days as a floating rest ship and hospital but after the air raids on the 21st it was felt prudent to remove this large vessel from the line of fire.

In the evening a Lynx from *Brilliant* attempted to insert an SBS patrol at Chartres Settlement and Dunnose Head on the west coast of West Falkland. However, lights were seen at the landing site and the attempt was abandoned.

Despite the loss of *Ardent* and the serious damage sustained by *Antrim* and *Argonaut*, the landings had been a great success, with not one member of the forces put ashore killed or injured. The 21st had been a day of intense and often very confused combat.

Although the ships had endured about six hours of air raids, the air defence screen of ships in Falkland Sound had done its job admirably; none of the amphibious ships had been harmed. The Argentine pilots, limited by the endurance of their aircraft and a serious lack of tankers, nevertheless proved to be determined and resourceful and were as successful as could be expected under the circumstances. However, in concentrating on the warships rather than going for the more vulnerable and more critical troop transports, they had missed a major opportunity.

Of the 63 Argentine Air Force sorties planned from mainland bases on the 21st, 54 had taken place but only 44 (17 Dagger and 27 Skyhawk) had reached the target area. Ten Argentine Air Force aircraft were shot down during these raids, representing a prohibitive loss rate of 23 per cent of the aircraft reaching the target. The Daggers of Grupo 6 had suffered worst with five aircraft

As the Queen Elizabeth II *approached Ascension Island on 21st May the transfer of stores commenced to and from the ship. Chinook HC1 ZA707 'BP' of 18 Squadron was flown off the* Atlantic Conveyor *on 5th May and spent a month at Ascension Island assisting with the massive logistics task.* Wg Cdr P Lyall

lost from 23 sorties, a loss rate of 23.5 per cent. The Argentine Navy had suffered an even worse loss ratio: three Skyhawks lost in the six sorties that reached the Falklands. Ten of the total of 13 Argentine aircraft destroyed on the 21st fell to Sea Harriers. Disappointingly, only one aircraft had been shot down in San Carlos by a SAM as even the Seawolf radar was having difficulty picking up targets against the backdrop of surrounding high ground.

The Argentine air attacks had been largely blunted by the Sea Harrier CAPs and those that did get through had not penetrated the outer layer of warships, which protected the vulnerable transports and amphibious ships within San Carlos Water itself. The fact that such a huge, lucrative and visible target as the gleaming white *Canberra* spent the whole day in San Carlos Water without a scratch is testimony to the effectiveness of the British air and surface defences against enemy air attack. By the end of the 21st nearly 1,000 tons of supplies and more than 3,000 British troops were safely ashore, largely unopposed. They established a beachhead four miles wide that was quickly extended and by the 27th the number of British troops ashore had almost doubled to 5,600.

Back in the UK another batch of aircraft reinforcements set sail on board the container ship *Contender Bezant*, which left Start Point carrying three Chinook HC1s (ZA705, ZA713 and ZA715), two Wasp HAS1s (XS562 and XT427) and a Sea King HAS2A (XZ579).

22nd May (Saturday)
If the Argentines ever had any real chance of halting Operation 'Sutton', then these plans must have been scuppered on the 22nd when bad weather on the mainland grounded most aircraft and resulted in just a single ineffectual bombing raid at last light by two unidentified Skyhawks. Nevertheless, as the weather over the Falkland Islands was considerably better than that over Argentina, the Sea Harriers maintained their CAPs throughout the day, flying a total of 60 sorties, ten more than on the previous day. As a precaution, most of the warships in Falkland Sound were brought into San Carlos Water during the day to enhance their mutual protection and to take advantage of the 12 Rapier fire units that now ringed the San Carlos area and which were becoming operational.

With the sudden departure of several of the transport vessels during the night before a good deal of their cargo had been unloaded, the meticulously worked-out unloading plan had to be scrapped and the transports brought back and unloaded as and when conditions permitted. Those vessels remaining were the two assault ships

(*Fearless* and *Intrepid*), *Brilliant* (with an unserviceable Seawolf launcher that was being fixed by a civilian computer expert from Marconi who had been 'smuggled' on board at Ascension Island!), *Broadsword*, *Argonaut*, *Plymouth*, *Yarmouth*, the five LSLs and the replenishment ship *Fort Austin*. However, although there was no air combat during the 22nd, there was plenty of air activity over the Falkland Islands and within the TEZ.

RAF Hercules from Ascension Island continued their long-distance flights to enable them to make airdrops to the ships of the Task Force. On the night of the 21st/22nd a Hercules C1P (XV179), refuelled by Victor K2 tankers, flew over the Carrier Battle Group and dropped supplies for *Alacrity*, and several soldiers from 'B' Squadron, SAS to *Andromeda*. Meanwhile a non-AAR capable Hercules C1 (XV297) made an airdrop to *Avenger*, part of the *Bristol* Group of ships, which was still four days away from reaching the TEZ. During the 22nd the *Bristol* Group was found by an Argentine Air Force Boeing 707 on a surveillance flight. The rules of engagement had changed drastically since the 707s had first visited the British fleet as it sailed south from Ascension Island in April. The aircraft was captained by Vicecomodoro O Ritondale and was flying at 30,000ft as it approached the warships. At about 1510Z, having verified that the target was not on a commercial airway, *Bristol* and *Cardiff* both fired two Sea Darts at the Boeing 707. Vicecomodoro Ritondale saw the missiles being launched and closed the throttles, deployed the spoilers and pushed the nose hard down and into a steep spiral dive. The crew clearly saw the Sea Darts explode very close to their aircraft as the Boeing dived towards the sea before levelling out and leaving the area at high speed and low level. Once out of Sea Dart range the pilot and his severely shaken crew climbed back to high altitude and headed back home to Buenos Aires.

The Argentine Air Force also came very close to losing a C-130 Hercules while on a resupply flight to Stanley on the 22nd. The aircraft was seen on British radar at 0645Z and it was estimated that its track would bring it close to *Coventry* and *Broadsword*, both of which were on picket duty to the north of Pebble Island, preparing a missile trap for any Argentine air raid approaching from the north. At the worst possible moment *Coventry*'s Sea Dart system malfunctioned and the Hercules passed within eight miles of the ship, the aircrew presumably being oblivious to their lucky escape. The problem was that after being constantly swamped with sea water, the flash doors of *Coventry*'s Sea Dart magazine had become encrusted with salt and were

jammed shut, so the missile could not reach the launcher. However, the Hercules did not reach Stanley as an 801 Squadron Sea Harrier CAP was scrambled, which prompted the Argentine radar controllers at Stanley to order the Hercules to turn back. For the second time that morning the C-130 crew cheated death and returned safely to the mainland.

800 Squadron's first CAP of the day took off from *Hermes* in the dark at 1053Z to take up station at the southern end of Falkland Sound. As the two Sea Harriers of Lieutenant Commander Rod Fredericksen (XZ460) and Lieutenant Martin Hale (XZ499) passed over Choiseul Sound, they came upon a small ship. The vessel, identified as the Z-28 Type patrol boat *Rio Iguazu* of the Prefectura Naval, was making its way towards Goose Green from Stanley with a cargo of ammunition and other supplies for the garrison. Martin Hale attacked the boat with his 30mm cannon as Rod Fredericksen provided top cover for him. The *Rio Iguazu* was badly damaged in the attack and was beached and then abandoned at Button Bay near Bluff Creek House. The boat's crew (one of whom later died) were rescued by CAB601 UH-1Hs and some of its cargo, which included two 105mm guns and spare parts for the Pucara still left at Goose Green, was recovered by Argentine divers. The guns were later airlifted to Goose Green and were used in the defence of the settlement against 2 PARA's assault.

Other helicopters of CAB601 were also busy on the 22nd flying logistics missions throughout the islands. During the day a flight of three Pumas and one A-109A (the latter flying as an armed escort) attempted an ill-fated mission to take some much-needed ammunition from Stanley to Port Howard. The ammunition included mortar shells and Blowpipe SAMs for the Port Howard garrison. The Puma detachment commander flew in AE-508, leading AE-500 and AE-503; CAB601's deputy commander flew in the A-109A (AE-337). The flight left Stanley in mid-afternoon but was delayed for a short while when it reached Darwin as Sea Harriers had been reported in the area. The flight commander decided to press on and the formation flew down the coast of Lafonia until all four helicopters reached Port King where they saw a large ship anchored just offshore. Unable to identify the vessel in the poor light conditions the flight commander decided not to risk an engagement and turned back to remain at Darwin overnight. Upon reaching Darwin the aircrew were understandably upset when they were told that the ship they had seen was in fact the Argentine cargo ship *Rio Carcarana*, which had lain abandoned at Port King since the 16th!

The Sea Kings of 846 Squadron were again very busy on the 22nd, with all four of the PNG-equipped helicopters deployed ashore from *Intrepid* during the day to reduce the risk from Argentine air attack. Each helicopter was hidden at what was called an Eagle Base; a temporary site for one helicopter, its aircrew and ground-crew. The Sea Kings were hidden beneath camouflage netting and remained unde-tected throughout the campaign. The four Sea Kings from *Fearless* moved stores to the men of 2 PARA in their positions in the Sussex Mountains and assisted in building up the encampment at San Carlos.

The process of moving stores and equip-ment ashore was occasionally interrupted by air raid warnings, almost all of which proved to be false. The very real problem of identification was ever-present, even in the electronic environment of the Falklands conflict and one of *Fearless*'s Sea Kings (ZA296) was almost fired at on the 22nd when *Intrepid* reported it as an enemy air-craft. The three 846 Squadron helicopters on board the *Canberra* and the *Norland* transferred stores across to the *Stromness*, which was to remain in San Carlos Water, as the two civilian vessels left San Carlos and set sail for South Georgia in the very early hours of the 22nd to collect troops from the *Queen Elizabeth II* when the troopship arrived.

Other British helicopters were also busy on the 22nd and several joined those already ashore. A Wessex HU5 (XT765) of 'B' Flight 845 Squadron deployed from the *Stromness* to 'Red Beach' near the Ajax Bay refrigeration plant in support of 45 Com-mando. The headquarters of 3 Commando Brigade came ashore by landing craft at first light; its three Gazelle flights onboard the *Sir Galahad*, *Sir Percivale* and *Sir Tristram* flew ashore later in the day. The Gazelles of 'A' Flight flew to the foothills of the Verde Mountains to support 40 Commando, while 'M' Flight deployed to Ajax Bay, which was rapidly becoming a centre of intense heli-copter activity. The last remaining Gazelle of 'C' Flight deployed to a site near Bonners Bay and was joined by XX376, which was transferred from 'M' Flight. Also during the 22nd, *Plymouth*'s Wasp inserted SBS teams at locations in West Falkland.

The Harrier GR3s of 1 Squadron flew two missions on the 22nd. At 1701Z Squadron Leaders Iveson (XZ963), Harris (XZ989) and Pook (XZ997) and Flight Lieutenant Rochefort (XV789) took off on a four-ship armed reconnaissance mission to search for Pucaras thought to be present at the airstrip at Goose Green. The Harriers ran into heavy AAA as they bombed Goose Green with CBUs and caused additional damage to the fuel dump and to several Pucaras that had already been hit during

Sea Harrier FRS1 XZ499 was one of the replacement aircraft that travelled south on the Atlantic Conveyor *in May 1982 and flew to* Hermes *for transfer to 800 Squadron on the 18th. Lieutenant Martin Hale was flying this aircraft on 22nd May when he damaged the* Rio Iguazu *in Choiseul Sound. XZ499 is seen here at the Abingdon Battle of Britain display on 15th September 1984 while serving with 801 Squadron and is one of only five Sea Harriers that took part in the conflict still in service today.* C M Hobson

previous raids. Pete Harris's CBUs failed to drop as he attempted to bomb a stores dump on the airfield and he dropped chaff to break the lock of a fire control radar sited nearby. At 1924Z Wing Commander Squire and Flight Lieutenant Harper took off on an armed reconnaissance of the airstrips on Weddell Island and Dunnose Head on the west coast of West Falkland in preparation for a strike that was being planned for the next morning.

The Task Force received fresh reinforce-ments on the 22nd when the frigates HMS *Ambuscade* and *Antelope* entered the TEZ after their ten-day journey from Ascension Island. The two Type 21s joined two more of their class, *Alacrity* and *Arrow* as escorts to the aircraft carriers. On the same day the troopship *Queen Elizabeth II* passed close to Ascension Island and rendezvoused with the aircraft transport *Atlantic Causeway* while they were both on their way to the South Atlantic. Throughout the 21st and 22nd one of the embarked 825 Squadron Sea King HAS2As and an Ascension-based Chinook HC1 and Wessex HU5 airlifted stores to the liner.

23rd May (Sunday) – More Losses on Both Sides

On Argentine Air Force Day and with a general improvement in the weather the air attacks on the ships in San Carlos Water and Falkland Sound resumed, with mixed results for the Argentine pilots.

The reconnaissance mission to Dunnose Head by two Harrier GR3s of 1 Squadron on the 22nd had located and photographed an airstrip that was to be attacked at first light on the 23rd. It had been noted that Argentine C-130s disappeared from British radar screens in the vicinity of Dunnose Head and it was thought that transport aircraft might be using the airstrip on their resupply flights from the mainland. At 1216Z four Harriers flown by Wing Commander Squire, Squadron Leader Harris, and Flight Lieutenants Hare and Harper, took off from *Hermes* and dropped four CBUs and six 1,000lb retard bombs on the airstrip. Unfortunately, during the attack one of Mark Hare's bombs fell near the settlement, damaging several buildings, including the settlement stores and school and injuring two local residents. To make matters worse, it was later discovered that the C-130s were not landing at Dunnose Head at all; they disappeared from radar screens simply because they dropped to low level as they crossed the coast in this area and used low-level terrain masking all the way to Stanley airport.

Three hours after the Dunnose Head raid, Flight Lieutenants Pook and Rochfort flew an uneventful armed reconnaissance in the region around Chartres and Port Howard, on opposite coasts of West Falkland. At 1854Z three Harriers took off on a raid on the airstrip at Pebble Island, dropping CBUs and parachute-retarded 1,000lb bombs on the airstrip to prevent its use by resupply aircraft and Pucaras.

The flight of three CAB601 Pumas and an A-109A that had set off from Stanley on a resupply flight to Port Howard on the 22nd only to return to Darwin, attempted to complete the mission on the 23rd. The helicopters left Darwin early in the morning and retraced their route to Port King, this time passing the abandoned *Rio Carcarana* before crossing Falkland Sound at low level and making landfall near Shag House Cove on West Falkland at about 1330Z. The helicopters then turned northeast for the ten-mile run to Port Howard. However, the flight's luck then changed dramatically as the lead Puma (AE-503) was spotted by a pair of patrolling Sea Harriers. Flight Lieutenant Dave Morgan of 800 Squadron was lucky to see the camouflaged helicopter as it crossed a short stretch of water, thereby providing some visual contrast. He dived his Sea Harrier (ZA192) at high speed to make a head-on pass in order to visually identify the helicopter as Argentine before making his attack. As he did so the crew of another of the Pumas (AE-500) saw the Sea Harrier and radioed a warning to the rest of the formation.

As Dave Morgan and Flight Lieutenant John Leeming (in ZA191) flew through the formation the helicopters scattered in all directions. The pilot of AE-503 was so unnerved by the warning and the sudden appearance of the Sea Harriers that he lost control while trying to take evasive action (possibly exacerbated by wake turbulence from the Sea Harrier) and flew the helicopter into the ground. Luckily all the crew survived the crash and managed to extricate themselves from the wreck before it burst into flames and its cargo of mortar bombs exploded.

The other two Pumas managed to find some hidden ground a few hundred yards away and set down to unload their precious cargo. The A-109A (AE-337) was less fortunate as it landed in a small ravine just over a mile away from the burning wreck of the lead Puma and tried to hide. John Leeming saw it as Dave Morgan overflew the burning Puma and both Sea Harriers then attacked the luckless helicopter with cannon fire. After a couple of passes Dave Morgan's 30mm cannon shells hit the mark and the A-109A exploded in a ball of flames. The crew had already exited the helicopter and were watching the attack from a few hundred yards away.

Having unloaded its cargo the pilot of Puma AE-500 then made the mistake of flying over to the wreck of AE-503 to look for survivors. However, the two Sea Harriers were still in the area, waiting for the Pumas to reappear and Dave Morgan used up the last of his ammunition to disable AE-500 which force-landed just 200 yards away from the wreck of AE-503. The remaining Puma (AE-508) almost met the same fate as it also took off from its hiding place to search for survivors. Although it was seen by Morgan and Leeming they were by now short of fuel and had used up all their ammunition, so all they could do was to call for another CAP to finish the job.

Within 20 minutes an 801 Squadron CAP arrived overhead Shag House Cove in response to Dave Morgan's report of his attack on the Argentine Army helicopters. Lieutenant Commanders Dave Braithwaite (ZA190) and Tim Gedge (XZ494) had taken off from *Invincible* at 1328Z on a routine CAP when they were diverted to Shag House Cove to complete the destruction of the CAB601 helicopters. On arriving they spotted the disabled AE-500 and attacked it

On 23rd May four Harrier GR3s of 1 Squadron dropped bombs on the airstrip at Dunnose Head under the mistaken assumption that the strip was being used by Argentine C-130s on their resupply flights from the mainland. One of the settlement's buildings was totally destroyed, as illustrated by this photograph taken on 30th June. Fortunately, the house was unoccupied at the time. Wg Cdr P Lyall

with cannon fire, resulting in its complete destruction. An Argentine claim that the Puma was destroyed by its own crew after all the cargo had been removed seems unlikely as the Sea Harrier pilots were able to make an unhurried attack with their devastating Aden 30mm cannon. The last remaining Puma of the unfortunate flight picked up all 12 aircrew from the three destroyed helicopters and finally left for Port Howard at 2030Z. Despite the loss of three helicopters the mission demonstrated the courage and resourcefulness of the Argentine helicopter crews; they even managed to salvage some of the ammunition, including several Blowpipe SAMs.

The Lynx from the crippled *Argonaut* was dispatched to attack the cargo ship *Rio Carcarana*, which had been damaged during a Sea Harrier attack but had been reported, probably erroneously, to be leaving Port King. The vessel had been shelled by a British ship the previous night and was almost certainly still abandoned. As *Argonaut*'s Lynx approached the ship the crew were unable to obtain a lock-on from either of the helicopter's two Sea Skuas so *Antelope*'s Lynx (XZ723) was called in. *Antelope* had entered Falkland Sound early on the 23rd as escort to the transport ships that were returning to San Carlos Water. The Lynx took off from *Antelope* at 1600Z and Lieutenants T J McMahon and D H Hunt made their way to Port King. The helicopter fired both of its Sea Skuas, which hit the *Rio Carcarana* and exploded, setting the ship on fire. The 8,482-ton cargo vessel was then seen to settle in the water and later sank.

Another Argentine ship (in this case a captured Falkland Islands vessel) was also accounted for on the 23rd. *Brilliant* and *Yarmouth* sailed south out of Falkland Sound to follow the coast of East Falkland in an attempt to catch any more attempts at resupplying Goose Green. The tiny 230-ton coastal freighter *Monsunen* had been seen making her way south from Falkland Sound to Stanley on the 22nd. In the early hours of the 23rd *Brilliant*'s Lynx (XZ721) took off with an SBS team on board to search for the vessel. As the helicopter approached a surface contact in Choiseul Sound it came under heavy machine gun fire from the *Monsunen*. The Lynx crew did not launch their Sea Skua missile in case there were civilians on board the boat so they alerted their parent ship. *Brilliant* and *Yarmouth* then set off in pursuit and the *Monsunen* was run aground in Lively Sound as the frigates started firing starshells over the vessel. The next day the boat was towed into Darwin by the *Forrest*, another captured Falkland Islands vessel. Later on the 23rd, *Yarmouth* returned to Falkland Sound while *Brilliant* sailed to join the Carrier Battle Group to have her Seawolf launcher

repaired of the damage it had sustained as a result of the attack on the 21st.

The weather on the Argentine mainland cleared sufficiently by midday for several raids to be launched on the ships in San Carlos Water. Although 46 sorties were planned during the 23rd, only about 20 aircraft actually reached their targets as the combination of Sea Harrier CAPs and bad weather forced many aircraft from Grupos 4, 5 and 6 to turn back. Two flights of Daggers from Rio Grande had attempted to reach the islands in the morning but had to turn back due to low cloud and poor visibility. Some Argentine aircraft even failed to find the KC-130H tankers and thus were forced to return to base.

The first group of Argentine aircraft to reach the British warships was also the most successful of the day. Two flights each of three A-4B Skyhawks of Grupo 5 were planned to take off but in the event only four aircraft departed from Rio Gallegos. One pilot slipped off the wing of his aircraft and injured his arm during his pre-flight check, while another had a technical problem and was unable to take off. The four aircraft flew as a single group and refuelled in cloud close to the coast of West Falkland due to an oversight during flight planning. The Skyhawks flew into Falkland Sound and headed towards San Carlos Water from the southwest. As they crossed Grantham Sound they actually flew over *Antelope*'s Lynx as it was flying back to the ship following its attack on the *Rio Carcarana*. Capitan P M Carballo tried to shoot down the helicopter but his cannon jammed. The formation passed the Lynx and then flew to the northern end of the anchorage before turning south to approach San Carlos Water from behind the Verde Mountains at 1650Z.

The first ship they encountered was the frigate *Antelope*, close to Fanning Island in San Carlos Water and the flight leader Capitan Carballo and his wingman, Primer Teniente Alferez Gomez, made a fast low run on the ship. A 1,000lb bomb from one of the Skyhawks hit the aft end of *Antelope* on the starboard side but failed to explode. Carballo's aircraft was badly damaged by anti-aircraft fire and the blast from a SAM fired from a nearby vessel turned the aircraft on its back and damaged the drop tank on the starboard wing. Carballo almost ejected but regained control as he was missed by a second SAM, probably a Seacat fired by *Antelope*.

The other two aircraft, flown by Primer Tenientes Guadagnini and Cachon, attacked next as Carballo and Gomez escaped. The attack resulted in *Antelope* being hit again by another 1,000lb bomb, which struck below the bridge on the port side and, once more, failed to explode. One sailor was killed in the bomb attack. During the attack,

Guadagnini's Skyhawk (C-242) was hit by a SAM and crashed into the sea. An Argentine Air Force report on the mission claims that Guadagnini dropped the bomb that hit the ship and that his aircraft was also hit by 20mm gunfire before clipping the mast of *Antelope* and crashing. The precise circumstances of Guadagnini's demise are confused and his aircraft has been claimed by *Broadsword* with a Seawolf, *Antelope* with 20mm cannon fire and by a Rapier fire unit on a hillside overlooking the bay. Two bombs straddled *Broadsword*, exploding very close to the ship. *Antelope*'s mainmast had been struck a glancing blow by a low-flying Skyhawk during the raid, but it may not have been Guadagnini's.

A witness to the attack on *Antelope* was Commander Simon Chelton (at the time, Lieutenant Chelton, Captain's Secretary and Flight Deck Officer of *Broadsword*):

'*Sunday morning in San Carlos Water was still, cool and with high and nearly complete cloud cover. Broadsword was stationed towards Falkland Sound, not too far from Hospital Point. Antelope was nearby, about half a mile or so further into San Carlos and nearer the landing area. Some but not all of the landing ships were visible to us. The ships were working in "Zulu" time and sunrise did not occur, therefore, until mid-forenoon. We had been at Air Raid Warning Red for some time, but there had been little action in our vicinity and it was noticeably quiet.*

'*I was on the Flight Deck, as Flight Deck Officer with some of the flight maintenance crew. (If I remember correctly, one of our two Lynx was airborne at this stage.) The first indication we had of an attack was the sound of the Bofors anti-aircraft gun, firing single shots, then of a Seawolf missile or two being launched. At this stage, this was not unprecedented and we knew it would be supplemented by small arms fire if an attacking aircraft came sufficiently close. Not surprisingly, we ran extremely quickly off the Flight Deck at the sound of the first guns and took shelter in the hangar. I think there were two attacks and I do remember at least one, if not two bombs narrowly missed us and exploded in the water just beyond the ship, causing no damage. From our position, we were not aware of the damage that had occurred to Antelope but I remember clearly noticing that, after one attack, the top of her mainmast had been broken off. I had taken a photograph of her before the attack, and took one afterwards which clearly showed the damage.*'

Grupo 5 had to wait until the following day to hear that, despite the loss of one of their number, their attack had indeed been successful and *Antelope* had later sunk after one of the bombs exploded during an attempt to defuse it. The ship was sailed into Ajax Bay so that an EOD team could attempt to defuse the bombs. Staff Sergeant James Prescott of the Royal Engineers was killed and Warrant Officer John Phillips badly injured in the explosion. All the frigate's crew of 175 men abandoned the ship safely and were picked up by other vessels after the bomb exploded and fires spread rapidly through the ship. Fires raged on board the ship throughout the night until another large explosion, probably from the second bomb, broke the ship's back and it settled slowly into San Carlos Water in two sections at 1100Z on the 24th, providing yet another hauntingly memorable image of the Falklands conflict. *Antelope* had been in the war zone for less than 48 hours. The ship's Lynx, which had landed back on board following the attack by the Grupo 5 Skyhawks, later deployed ashore to Ajax Bay and then flew on to the assault ship *Fearless* later that night.

The next raid on San Carlos Water, or 'Bomb Alley' as it was now being dubbed, occurred around 1705Z, just 15 minutes after the Grupo 5 attack. The CANA's 3 Escuadrilla had just four serviceable A-4Q Skyhawks available on the 23rd so all four aircraft took off from Rio Grande at 1535Z led by the squadron commander, Capitan

This is the sort of view that an Argentine pilot would have had of British ships in San Carlos Water soon after the landings. One of the assault ships, Fearless, *is seen here with an LSL and the ferry* Norland. *Cdr S Chelton*

de Corbeta Castro Fox. Three of the four aircraft successfully refuelled from a KC-130H some 200 miles to the east of Rio Grande but one aircraft, flown by Teniente de Navio Oliveira, had to return to Rio Grande when it encountered problems in taking on fuel. The remaining three aircraft flew over West Falkland at low level and entered the northern end of the Sound from the direction of Mount Rosalie, almost directly opposite the mouth of San Carlos Water. Each pilot selected a ship (*Broadsword, Antelope* and *Yarmouth*) as a target but Capitan Fox and Teniente de Navio Marcos A Benitez both missed and Capitan de Corbeta Carlos M Zubizarreta (the squadron executive officer) was unable to drop any of his four 500lb Snakeye bombs due to an electrical malfunction. All three of the aircraft escaped serious damage despite a large amount of anti-aircraft fire directed at them from the ships in San Carlos Water.

Soon after the attack, Castro Fox realised he had a problem when the fuel flow stopped from one of his drop tanks. He had to jettison his remaining stores, climb to altitude to conserve fuel and return to base independently. When the other two aircraft returned to Rio Grande Zubizarreta landed heavily on the wet runway, missed the arrester wire and lost control of his aircraft, which slewed to one side of the runway. Realising that the aircraft was about to leave the runway and that he still had a full load of bombs on board, Zubizarreta ejected but was killed when he hit the runway hard before his parachute had time to deploy. It was claimed that the rocket

boosters fitted to the ejection seats of CANA Skyhawks were mostly time-expired and that Zubizarreta was killed because his seat was not lifted high enough to allow time for his parachute to open. In the event the ejection was unnecessary as the bombs did not explode and the aircraft (0662/3-A-309), one of the squadron's VLF Omega-equipped A-4Qs) only received minor damage, which was quickly repaired. However, the aircraft subsequently crashed on 11th November 1982, six months after the conflict, killing another pilot.

Three flights of Dagger As from San Julian and Rio Grande were dispatched on the 23rd but with little success. Two Daggers attacked *Broadsword* and missed as did *Broadsword*'s Seawolf fired in response. Two aircraft from Rio Grande's Punal flight arrived over the northern end of Falkland Sound just before 1900Z but received a warning of the proximity of a Sea Harrier CAP, so they jettisoned their bombs and turned about to head for home. As they flew over Pebble Island they were spotted by a pair of Sea Harriers flown by Lieutenant Commander Andy Auld (ZA177) and Lieutenant Martin Hale (ZA194). The leading Dagger, flown by Mayor Martinez, was out of range but the other aircraft (C-437), flown by Teniente Hector Ricardo Volponi, was over a mile behind. Martin Hale got behind the Dagger as it started to accelerate away and from 1,000 yards distance fired a Sidewinder, which guided into the engine exhaust. The Argentine aircraft exploded at low level and the pilot was killed instantly as the wreckage fell on the western side of

Elephant Bay in the middle of Pebble Island. The other two flights, both from San Julian, returned to base without engaging in combat.

On the 23rd the Super Etendards of 2 Escuadrilla launched on their third mission of the conflict in the hope of achieving another success in the wake of their earlier attack on *Sheffield*. Two Super Etendards, flown by Capitan de Corbeta Roberto Agotegaray and Teniente de Navio Juan Rodriguez Mariani, took off in the early afternoon and headed for the Task Force aircraft carriers that were thought to be to the northeast of the Falklands. Nothing was found and at 2030Z the mission was abandoned and the two aircraft flew back to base to start the laborious procedure of downloading their Exocets. On their way around the south coast of East Falkland they were illuminated by British fire control radars and both aircraft dropped to low level in the dark as they made their escape. Other aircraft, including a flight of A-4Cs from Grupo 4, also failed to find their targets during the 23rd.

As night fell 800 Squadron prepared to carry out a Sea Harrier raid on Stanley airport. Reconnaissance reports suggested that runway arrester gear was being fitted at the airport, indicating that the Argentines might be planning to base jets there, in addition to the five MB-339As already on the

airfield. Each Sea Harrier carried three VT-fused 1,000lb bombs all of which would be tossed onto the runway from some distance away, thereby reducing each aircraft's vulnerability during the attack. The launch of the four aircraft was delayed for almost three hours until they finally took off in the dark at 2250Z as *Hermes* was about 90 miles northeast of Stanley.

Three aircraft flown by Lieutenant Commanders Neill Thomas, Mike Blissett and Andy Auld took off successfully, followed by Lieutenant Commander Gordy Batt (in ZA192). However, Gordy Batt's aircraft then flew into the sea about a mile ahead of the carrier and exploded in a huge fireball as he was trying to join up in the dark after take-off. *Brilliant* searched the area but found no trace of the aircraft or its unfortunate pilot. The cause of the accident could not be established with certainty (engine failure and pilot fatigue or disorientation have been suggested) but the loss of an experienced pilot who was on his 30th mission at the time was keenly felt. The other three Sea Harriers delivered their bombs on Stanley airport despite heavy anti-aircraft fire.

As usual, 846 Squadron had a busy day on the 23rd. The *Stromness*, *Europic Ferry* and *Norland* returned to San Carlos Water to unload more troops and stores. The *Norland*'s two Sea King HC4s (ZA291 and ZA313) flew ashore to set up Eagle bases

The Argentine Navy's 3 Escuadrilla de Caza y Ataque had little opportunity to mount missions from the 25 de Mayo and deployed its A-4Q Skyhawks to Rio Grande on 9th May. Skyhawk 0659/3-A-306 survived the conflict but crashed at Espora on 11th November 1982. Argentine Navy

like those of the four PNG-equipped helicopters that had already done so. The Eagle bases were clustered around a FOB that was being established at Old House Creek located just over two miles north of San Carlos Settlement.

One of the PNG Sea Kings from *Fearless*, ZA310 flown by Lieutenant D A Lord, was put out of action on the 23rd. The helicopter had flown to a position north of Fanning Head to pick up some casualties from a patrol that had been the victim of 'friendly fire' but as it landed its tail rotor hit the ground and the helicopter could not take off again. It took no further part in the conflict as it had to be left where it sat until it was airlifted out by a Chinook on 7th June.

Another Sea King HC4 (ZA312) from *Fearless* came ashore on the 23rd for repairs to its hydraulics, while others flew casevac sorties to and from the Ajax Bay field hospital. Two of the PNG-equipped helicopters took a company of troops of 2 PARA to Camilla Creek House as part of the preparation for a night assault. Some of 846 Squadron's helicopters also took part in the SAR and evacuation operation after *Antelope* was bombed.

Out towards the edge of the TEZ the troopship *Canberra* had rendezvoused with the *Resource* during the 23rd, after which the two Wessex HU5s of 'A' Flight 845 Squadron moved tons of stores and ammunition from the troopship to the RFA, as the latter was to sail back into San Carlos Water the next day. Two days later the *Canberra* set sail for South Georgia and her rendezvous with the *Queen Elizabeth II*.

A Hercules C1P (XV200) made an AAR-assisted, long-range airdrop on the 23rd to RFA *Olna* in the *Bristol* Group of ships and to the MV *Anco Charger*. The four loads dropped by the Hercules for the *Olna* were recovered by the ship's Wessex HU5s of 'B' Flight 848 Squadron.

24th May (Monday)

Harrier GR3s of 1 Squadron made their first attack on Stanley airport on the 24th, taking off at 1203Z. Four aircraft took part and were supported by two Sea Harriers from 800 Squadron, which provided a degree of defence suppression. The two Sea Harriers, flown by Lieutenant Commanders Neill Thomas (XZ496) and Mike Blissett (ZA191), approached the airfield from the northeast and pulled up to toss 1,000lb air-burst VT-fused bombs at the defenders. This kept the AAA and SAM sites occupied long enough to distract them from seeing the first pair of Harriers, flown by Squadron Leader Bob Iveson (XZ997) and Flight Lieutenant Tony Harper (XZ989), as they came in low from the northwest to drop their parachute-retarded bombs on the runway. The first pair was followed about 20 seconds later by Wing Commander Peter Squire (XZ988) and Flight Lieutenant Mark Hare (XV789) who came in from the west to drop more 1,000lb retard bombs in the face of intense flak. The approach of each element from a different direction initially took the defenders by surprise.

Although the runway was hit by three of the 12 bombs dropped, it remained operational as all of the bombs bounced before exploding and failed to penetrate deep enough to cause much damage. All four Harrier GR3s returned safely to *Hermes* although the second pair incurred some light damage from small arms fire and possibly from debris from the first pair's

bombs. The squadron knew that low-level retard bombs could not hope to penetrate Stanley airport's runway and was looking forward to using the new laser-guided bombs (LGBs), but these could not be used until trained forward air controllers and laser marking equipment became available. The first Paveway II adapter kits to convert 'dumb' 1,000lb bombs into 'smart' weapons were airdropped to *Hermes* on this day by a Hercules from Ascension Island. However, for a variety of reasons 1 Squadron was not to achieve success with the LGB until the penultimate day of the conflict.

The Argentine Air Force changed its tactics on the 24th by sending most of its raids south of West Falkland to approach San Carlos Water from the southern end of Falkland Sound, and by making better use of the terrain to limit the ships' ability to detect the raids on radar early enough to be prepared. The stationing of a radar picket or 'missile trap' (a Type 22 and a Type 42 combination) to the north of Falkland Sound may also have influenced this decision.

Grupo 6 flew several raids on the transport ships in San Carlos Water on the 24th, the first wave of Daggers arriving at about 1400Z. A flight of four aircraft led by Capitan Mir Gonzalez from Rio Grande approached San Carlos Water from the southern end of Falkland Sound. The Daggers of Azul flight flew fast (550 knots) and low up the Sound, hopped over the Sussex Mountains and dived down towards San Carlos Water. Although they were the subject of many well publicised photographs as they passed low over and between the ships, they did no serious damage to any vessel. There was not enough time for the pilots to line up on a target and drop their bombs accurately in the confined space of San Carlos Water. On the other hand the British defences were also restricted by the terrain and the fact

that there were so many ships at anchor that missiles and guns had to be fired with caution.

Capitan Carlos A Maffeis (C-431) was unable to drop his bombs due to an electrical generator failure, so he simply fired at the ships with his two 30mm cannon. Gonzalez, Capitan Robles and Teniente Bernhardt all managed to drop their bombs. Three of the Daggers were damaged by anti-aircraft fire but all four aircraft subsequently returned safely to Rio Grande.

A short while later Plata flight, also from Rio Grande, attacked the warships in San Carlos Water using parachute-retarded bombs. The Dagger As of Capitan Dellepiane, Primer Teniente Musso and Teniente Callejo all escaped safely although they reported that two SAMs, thought to be Sea Darts, were fired at them by warships north of Pebble Island (most probably *Coventry* on radar picket duty with *Broadsword*). *Coventry* was co-ordinating the overall air defence for the AOA and *Broadsword* was providing close air defence for *Coventry*.

Unlike their compatriots, three Daggers from Oro flight from San Julian then approached Falkland Sound from the north, but this flight ran into a Sea Harrier CAP that was orbiting north of Pebble Island at 10,000ft under the control of the radar picket. The Sea Harriers of Lieutenant Commander Andy Auld (XZ457) and Lieutenant Dave Smith (ZA193) were vectored towards the Daggers by the radar operator on board *Broadsword*. On this occasion it appears that the Dagger pilots were not warned by their own radar operator at Stanley and did not see the Sea Harriers until the last moment as they dived in behind them. As the Daggers approached Pebble Island low and fast, Andy Auld fired his two Sidewinders in quick succession. Each missile hit a Dagger, both of which exploded and crashed into the sea. Both Argentine

Fearless, the headquarters ship of the Amphibious Group, comes under attack in 'Bomb Alley', as San Carlos Water came to be known. Fearless *lived up to her name and escaped being damaged in any of the air raids she experienced.* MoD

An Argentine Air Force Dagger A flies low over the LSL Sir Bedivere *in San Carlos Water. The Daggers of Grupo 6 de Caza had the highest attrition rate of any type in the Argentine Air Force during the conflict.* MoD

pilots, Mayor Luis Puga (C-419) and Capitan Raul Diaz (C-430), ejected safely and came down in the sea just off the north coast of Pebble Island and both were later rescued by an Argentine patrol.

Meanwhile Dave Smith chased the other Dagger (C-410), the pilot of which, having seen his two comrades' aircraft explode, knew he was in mortal danger. The Dagger turned hard to the west and jettisoned its bombs and fuel tanks. However, Dave Smith closed on the aircraft and at a very high angle off fired a Sidewinder that hit the aircraft as it turned, blowing it apart. The remains of the Dagger fell on the slopes of First Mount, on the western edge of Elephant Bay and the pilot, Teniente Carlos J Castillo, was killed. Although both of the Sea Harriers briefly chased another Dagger (from Plata flight), it was too far away and it escaped the fate of Oro flight. It was not until 1998 that the wreckage of C-410 and the remains of its unfortunate pilot were found by an islander.

About 45 minutes after the Daggers reached the Falklands a formation of five A-4B Skyhawks of Grupo 5 arrived from Rio Gallegos. Two flights each of three aircraft had taken off at 1400Z but one of the flight leaders inadvertently armed and jettisoned his bombs soon after refuelling. The formation leader, the commander of Grupo 5, Vicecomodoro Mariel, led the aircraft to the south of West Falkland and flew up the eastern coast of East Falkland before turning west to attack San Carlos from an unexpected direction. The flight descended to low level for the final run-in to San Carlos, using terrain masking to shield them from radar and achieve an element of surprise.

At 1500Z the five Skyhawks swept into San Carlos Water over the Sussex Mountains from the southeast and attacked the ships anchored there. All of the ships were caught unawares and were extremely lucky to suffer no real damage during the attack. Bombs were dropped close to several ships, including the *Fort Austin*, but no hits were sustained. A large amount of gunfire and several missiles were fired at the attackers and some minor damage was done to at least one aircraft, but all five Skyhawks escaped the inferno and climbed away for the flight back to Rio Gallegos. Minimal damage had been done to either side but the raid was a nasty shock to the ships in San Carlos Water as it came without any warning. The results could have been much worse.

Hot on the heels of the Grupo 5 attack was a raid by six A-4C Skyhawks of Grupo 4 from San Julian following the same route as the Grupo 4 aircraft. The first flight of three aircraft, led by Teniente Ricardo Lucero, managed to avoid a Sea Harrier CAP and arrived over San Carlos Water at 1615Z. Having been raided by the Grupo 5 aircraft earlier, the British air defences on board the ships and on land were now alerted and the first flight of A-4Cs was fortunate to survive the attack. The second flight, led by Primer Teniente Jose Vazquez, was not so lucky. Although the *Sir Lancelot* and *Sir Galahad* were hit by bombs (which failed to explode and took several days to remove), all three A-4Cs in the second flight were hit by gunfire and shrapnel as they made their attack and were fortunate to escape from the San Carlos area. The aircraft climbed to 21,000ft while over West Falkland but those flown

by Vazquez and his number two, Teniente Alferez Martinez, were losing fuel.

Teniente Jorge Bono's A-4C (C-305) was more badly damaged, could not maintain altitude and was also losing fuel. Bono's radio was probably damaged as Vazquez and Martinez received no response to their calls telling him to eject while still over land. The pair watched in horror and frustration as Bono's aircraft descended in a smooth left-handed turn until it hit the sea in King George Bay on the west coast of West Falkland. It is not known for certain what caused the damage to Jorge Bono's aircraft although the *Sir Bedivere* claimed to have hit a Skyhawk with a Blowpipe missile during the raid. Bono was not seen to eject and Vazquez and Martinez could not spend time searching as they were losing fuel and had to rendezvous with the tanker. Even after refuelling safely their aircraft were in such a state that they had to be escorted all the way back to San Julian by the KC-130H. During the flight back Vazquez's aircraft received 5,000 gallons of fuel, most of which must have vented straight out of the fuel tanks as the Skyhawk has a fuel capacity of just 666 gallons.

A search was mounted for Jorge Bono but his body was never found. An Argentine source claimed that Bono's aircraft had been hit by a Sea Dart fired by *Coventry* but there is no corroborating evidence to confirm this.

Of the 20 Argentine aircraft dispatched on the 24th only 15 had actually reached the anchorage at San Carlos Water and no terminal damage was done to any of the British vessels for the loss of four of the Argentine attackers. The *Sir Galahad* had been hit by a bomb, which had first bounced off the *Sir Bedivere* and failed to explode and the *Sir Lancelot* had been struck by two bombs, neither of which exploded. The *Sir Galahad* was abandoned overnight while the bomb was removed and defused. Luckily, the RFA *Fort Austin*, *Stromness* and *Norland* had all been missed by bombs (albeit narrowly) during the attacks and *Fearless* had been strafed but with no real damage done. The Argentine aircraft were attacking from such a low altitude in an attempt to avoid the SAMs and AAA that many of the bombs they dropped simply did not have time to arm before they hit the ships or the water.

The volume of anti-aircraft fire from guns and missiles on the ships and on the shore together with the Sea Harrier CAPs effectively defeated the Argentine air offensive against the amphibious operation. The loss of three more Dagger As on the 24th prompted Peru to offer 10 of its own Mirage 5Ps as replacements, but although the aircraft were quickly delivered to Argentina they were not used during the conflict and were not brought into Argentine Air Force service until several months after the end of hostilities, when they were allocated serial numbers of Daggers lost in the conflict.

The attacks on the 24th did not stop the continued build-up in the San Carlos area and by the end of the day a total of 5,500 British troops were ashore along with over 5,000 tons of equipment and stores.

As well as the Pucaras of Grupo 3 based at Stanley during the conflict, the aircraft of Grupo 4 de Ataque based at Comodoro Rivadavia also played a part in the conflict. The Grupo 4 Pucara squadron was tasked with coastal surveillance should any Task Force ship(s) attempt operations close to Argentina's shoreline. On the 24th a Grupo 4 Pucara (A-540) crashed into the sea killing the pilot, Teniente Alferez Mario Valko.

The remains of Antelope *sink slowly in San Carlos Water on 24th May as the* Resource *and the ferry* Norland *look on. The ship had been attacked by Skyhawks from Grupo 5 the previous day and had been hit by two bombs, one of which exploded as a bomb disposal team was trying to defuse it.* MoD

The situation at Darwin and Goose Green was growing more dangerous every day for the Argentine forces. On the 24th the two Grupo 7 Chinooks moved to the relative safety of Stanley airport. The only remaining operational aircraft left at Goose Green were now the two Bell 212s and they too would depart for Stanley a few days later.

The British transport helicopters continued their daily movement of troops and stores and the resupply of forward positions. 846 Squadron had to cancel a night PNG mission to Camilla Creek to reinforce 2 PARA when low cloud covered much of the Sussex Mountains. The Sea Kings were reinforced on the 24th by two more Wessex HU5s (XS483 and XT484) of 'A' Flight 845 Squadron, both of which deployed to Old House Creek after unloading stores from the *Resource* following its re-entry into San Carlos Water. 845 Squadron set up a FOB at Old House Creek in preparation for the arrival of more of its helicopters.

Antelope's Lynx had remained on board *Fearless* overnight but flew to the San Carlos FOB in the morning and spent the day flying in support of 3 Commando Brigade, before returning to *Fearless* again in the evening. After *Antelope* blew up and sank on the evening of the 24th the Lynx's flight crew were flown over to the *Norland* to return to the UK. The Lynx remained on *Fearless* until it was transferred to *Brilliant* on 30th May. The *Norland*, *Sir Bedivere* and *Sir Tristram* left San Carlos Water in the evening to return to the edge of the TEZ.

Since the first week of May a detachment of three Harrier GR3s of 1 Squadron had been stationed at Wideawake airfield to provide local air defence. An Argentine air attack or commando assault on this vital base could not be completely ruled out, so some form of protection was needed. However, the basing of Harriers on Ascension Island was only a stop-gap measure and on 24th May two Phantom FGR2s (XV468 and XV484) of 29 Squadron arrived from RAF Coningsby to take over the air defence commitment. The aircraft were refuelled on the nine-and-a-half-hour non-stop flight by Victors operating from Marham and Dakar. A third Phantom (XV466) arrived on the 26th to complete the detachment.

The Phantoms sat on QRA day and night, ready to investigate unidentified aircraft and ships and were scrambled on several occasions. The most interesting visitors were two Soviet Navy Tu-95 'Bears', which were intercepted by the detachment commander, Squadron Leader P R Morley, on 11th July when the Soviet aircraft were monitoring the aircraft carrier *Hermes* while it was on its way home to the UK. The QRA was stood down three days later and the three aircraft returned to Coningsby on the 18th, 19th and 20th of July. When 29 Squadron took over the air defence of the Falkland Islands in October 1982, XV484 was one of the first aircraft to be deployed, but it crashed into Mount Usborne during an air combat training mission on 17th October 1983, killing both crew.

25th May (Tuesday) –
The Loss of HMS *Coventry* and
the *Atlantic Conveyor*

The British Task Force expected an all-out effort from the Argentine armed forces on the 25th as it was Argentina's national day, a day when patriotic pride and fervour could be expected to be at fever pitch. The day did indeed turn out to be traumatic for the Task Force, with the loss of two important ships; however, the 25th also marked the last real attempts by Argentine forces to interfere with the landings at San Carlos and with it, Argentina lost any real hope of stopping an almost inevitable defeat on the Falkland Islands.

In anticipation of increased attacks on the beachhead, Rear Admiral Woodward moved the Task Force to within 80 miles east of Stanley and just 130 miles from Falkland Sound to permit the Sea Harriers a longer time on their CAPs. This was the closest the Carrier Battle Group had come to the Falklands since the sortie on 4th May when *Sheffield* was lost.

The day started with a rare pre-dawn take-off from Rio Gallegos of a flight of A-4B Skyhawks from Grupo 5, led by Capitan H Palaver. Their mission was to attack two ships, *Coventry* and *Broadsword*, which were stationed a few miles north of Pebble Island as radar pickets to track and, if in range, engage any raids approaching from the north and west. The Skyhawks were probably guided by a C-130 that passed the precise location of the two ships as Capitan Palaver's flight approached the Falklands.

The Skyhawks had refuelled from a KC-130H en route just as it was getting light and were approaching over West Falkland

at high level at 1130Z when, without warning, the leading aircraft (C-244) exploded as it was hit by a Sea Dart missile. *Broadsword* and *Coventry* had tracked the flight on their radar and *Coventry* had launched a Sea Dart at long range, achieving a hit. Capitan Palaver was killed in the incident and the remaining pilots abandoned the mission and returned to Rio Gallegos without their leader. Back at Rio Gallegos the incident spurred both the aircrew and the ground-crew to renew their efforts and another mission was planned for the afternoon.

Grupo 6, still smarting from the mauling it received on the 24th, dispatched two flights of Dagger As on armed reconnaissance missions to the southern part of the Falkland Islands. All the aircraft returned home safely having found nothing to attack. During the morning a Learjet 35A of Grupo 1 de Aerofotografico conducted a high-altitude reconnaissance over Falkland Sound and obtained photographs of the shipping in the Sound and in San Carlos Water and the troop positions ashore. The aircraft completed its task and turned for home before *Coventry* was able to launch a Sea Dart.

The first action for the British attack aircraft on the 25th was another combined Royal Navy/Royal Air Force raid on Stanley airport. At 1415Z, two Sea Harriers flown by Lieutenant Commander Neill Thomas (XZ455) and Lieutenant Clive Morrell (ZA191) took off from *Hermes*, followed soon after by four Harrier GR3s flown by Wing Commander Peter Squire (XV789), Squadron Leader Peter Harris (XZ989), Squadron Leader Jerry Pook (XZ988) and Flight Lieutenant John Rochfort (XZ997). In a change of tactics from the previous day

the Harriers toss-bombed the airfield, one Sea Harrier each leading a pair of Harriers. Each Sea Harrier used its Blue Fox radar to measure distance to the airfield and the formation pulled up and released its bombs simultaneously. Jerry Pook continued his climb to see where the bombs had fallen and as he came close to the airfield a Roland and a Tigercat missile were launched, but both SAMs fell away before they could reach his aircraft.

The raid had caused some damage but the runway once more survived and all the aircraft returned to *Hermes* by 1456Z. After a quick briefing and the re-arming of the aircraft, Peter Squire (now in XZ989) and John Rochfort (still in XZ997) took off from the aircraft carrier at 1631Z for an uneventful armed reconnaissance.

Meanwhile a flight of five Grupo 4 A-4Cs had taken off from San Julian and were heading for the Falklands. Led by Capitan Garcia, the flight was soon reduced to four aircraft when one of them had to abort due to smoke in the cockpit. Toro flight now consisted of Garcia leading Tenientes Lucero, Paredi and Alferez Gerardo Isaac. The flight reached the San Carlos area at about 1530Z and ran into a wall of gunfire and SAMs as they attacked the ships. Teniente Lucero's aircraft (C-319) was seen to disintegrate at low level and he was very lucky to eject successfully from the wreckage. He injured his knee on ejection but

Coventry burns fiercely just moments after being hit by three 1,000lb bombs dropped by the Skyhawk of Primer Teniente Mariano Velasco of Grupo 5 de Caza. Cdr S Chelton

As well as leaving a large hole in the flight deck the 1,000lb bomb that hit Broadsword *on the 25th also destroyed the nose of Lynx HAS2 XZ729, which was on loan from* Brilliant *at the time. After the conflict the Lynx was repaired and returned to service.* Cdr S Chelton

was soon plucked out of the water and brought on board *Fearless* in full view of British television cameras. His aircraft had probably been hit by numerous machine gun and cannon rounds and may also have been damaged by the nearby explosion of a Rapier SAM; but it was also claimed by *Yarmouth*, which fired a Seacat. Lucero was then flown to the British field hospital at Ajax Bay and endured several days of bombing alongside British patients.

Garcia was also in trouble as he had at least one hung bomb after completing his run over the ships. He joined up with Paredi and Isaac and they headed northwest, away from the Task Force. However, like Palaver before him, Garcia's A-4C (C-304) was suddenly hit by a Sea Dart missile fired by *Coventry* from her position north of Pebble Island. Once again *Broadsword*'s radar had detected the Skyhawk formation at long range and had passed the radar picture to *Coventry* via a data link so that the destroyer could target its Sea Dart system at the Argentine aircraft.

Garcia's Skyhawk crashed in the sea and as no one saw him eject, no rescue mission was mounted by either side. However, Garcia did eject from his aircraft and managed to get into his dinghy but tragically he died of exposure as his dinghy was found, with his body still in it, washed ashore on Golding Island, to the south of Pebble Island, over a year later. Meanwhile Alferez Isaac also had a major problem. His Skyhawk had been hit by 20mm cannon fire during the attack and was leaking like a sieve. With Paredi in attendance he flew west and just reached the KC-130H tanker before his tanks ran dry. Even so, he had to remain plugged into the tanker almost all the way to San Julian as the Skyhawk was losing fuel almost as fast as it could be received. Although Isaac's aircraft was later painted with the silhouette of a Type 22 frigate, none of the Grupo 4 flight had done any damage to any ship during the raid.

At 1728Z two Harriers of 1 Squadron flown by Squadron Leader Peter Harris (XZ988) and Flight Lieutenant Mark Hare (XV789) took off from *Hermes* for another raid on Stanley airport, this time dropping their bombs onto the airfield from 20,000ft. Again a Roland missile was fired at the Harriers but missed. However, only three of the six bombs hit the target and another mission was quickly planned. Three aircraft took off on the next mission at 1927Z, Peter

Harris (again in XZ988) being accompanied by two 800 Squadron Sea Harriers flown by Lieutenants Clive Morrell (ZA194) and Andy McHarg (XZ460), who tossed their 1,000lb bombs onto Stanley airport. When the pilots returned to *Hermes* at 2041Z they reported that swept-wing aircraft were visible on the airfield, but the report was in error and what they had presumably seen was the MB-339As of 1 Escuadrilla.

The afternoon raid by Grupo 5 was, like the aborted morning mission, targeted at the two radar pickets, *Coventry* and *Broadsword*, which were now only about 15 miles north of Pebble Island and in full view of the Argentine observation posts onshore. The tactics would be different and each aircraft would carry a maximum warload of three 1,000lb bombs. Two flights, each of three aircraft, were planned but one aircraft from each flight dropped out, leaving four Skyhawks to fly the mission, still as separate flights. The mission was aided by a C-130, which passed precise information on the location of the two ships to the Skyhawks en route. The first flight, consisting of Capitan P M Carballo and Teniente Carlos Rinke, followed a southerly route up Falkland Sound to Pebble Island while the second flight, of Primer Tenientes Mariano Velasco and Alferez Jorge Barrionuevo, flew a more northerly route.

While still some distance from the Falklands the Skyhawks were warned of a Sea Harrier CAP heading their way and immediately dived to low level to approach the ships. The Skyhawks were lost on radar when they descended to low level over the islands, but at about 1800Z Carballo and Rinke were spotted flying up Falkland Sound only to turn inland over West Falkland rather than attack the ships in San Carlos Water. Lieutenant Commander Neill Thomas (XZ496) and Lieutenant Dave

Smith (XZ459) spotted the leading flight of Skyhawks, got to within three miles of them and were just about to launch their Sidewinders when they were ordered to break off at 1820Z. *Coventry* was tracking the Skyhawks with its Sea Dart system and pulled the Sea Harriers off to give the Sea Darts a clear target. If the Sea Harriers were too close behind the Skyhawks there was a distinct possibility that a Sea Dart might lock onto it rather than its intended Skyhawk target. Unfortunately, the Sea Dart failed to acquire the Skyhawks as they came in fast and low from behind Pebble Island and the Sea Dart radar could not distinguish the aircraft from the coastline and hills in the background. *Broadsword*'s Seawolf system also became confused when one radar target split into two as the two aircraft flying in close formation came nearer to the ship. Unable to resolve the problem the Seawolf's computer crashed and had to be reset, a process that took valuable seconds.

The two Skyhawks made their attack on *Broadsword* opposed only by *Coventry*'s 4.5-inch gun and light anti-aircraft fire, and the frigate was lucky that only one of the bombs dropped actually hit the target. The bomb struck the surface of the sea and bounced up into the aft hull on the starboard side and out through the flight deck, smashing the nose of Lynx HAS2 XZ729 (on loan from *Brilliant*), before exiting the ship on the far side and splashing into the water some distance away, still without exploding! The bomb left a huge hole measuring 8ft x 14ft in the hangar deck but the ship's other Lynx in the hangar was untouched.

As Carballo and Rinke were making their run on *Broadsword* the second flight of Skyhawks was manoeuvring to start its attack on the ships just over a minute later. Once again the Sea Harrier CAP was well placed to engage but was ordered to stay away so

that the ships could launch their missiles at the attacking aircraft. However, once again *Coventry*'s Sea Dart system was unable to acquire the targets and a missile was fired blind (without radar guidance) as a deterrence but was easily evaded by the Skyhawk pilots, so *Broadsword*, her Seawolf system having been reset, prepared to launch her missiles at the Skyhawks. Not wishing to take any chances this time, *Broadsword*'s missile operator switched to TV mode so that he could control the launch himself and not rely solely on the radar for target acquisition. However, unsure of Seawolf's protection, *Coventry* then turned to port to present as small a cross-section as possible to the Skyhawks. Unfortunately, by doing so she placed herself directly between *Broadsword* and the Skyhawks and thereby broke the radar lock that the Seawolf missile system had on the enemy aircraft.

With no missiles to bother them, Velasco and Barrionuevo were able to complete their bomb run. Barrionuevo's bombs hung up, but Velasco (in C-207) put all three of his 1,000lb bombs deep into *Coventry*'s flank. The bombs exploded in the bowels of the ship and caused massive damage, killing all the occupants of the computer room instantly. Rapidly flooding and on fire, the

The attack on Broadsword *north of Pebble Island on 25th May by a flight of Skyhawks from Grupo 5 de Caza left a gaping hole in the ship's flight deck. The hole was later repaired by the* Stena Seaspread. *Cdr S Chelton*

Coventry's *Lynx HAS2 XZ242 can be seen on the flight deck and was lost when the ship capsized a few minutes after this photograph was taken from* Broadsword. *Cdr S Chelton*

During the attack on the Atlantic Conveyor, Invincible *fired a salvo of six Sea Dart missiles, but it was thought unlikely that any of them hit an incoming Exoce missile.* MoD

ship keeled over onto its side within 15 minutes of being hit and turned completely upside down another 15 minutes later. The four Skyhawks escaped and headed back to Rio Gallegos while the Sea Harriers, by now short of fuel, left for their carrier. Another pair of Sea Harriers from 800 Squadron, flown by Lieutenant Commander Andy Auld (ZA177) and Flight Lieutenant Ted Ball (ZA176), arrived over *Coventry* to mount a protective CAP as the ship was abandoned at 1848Z and the rescue operation got under way. The ship sank at 1922Z, taking with it Lynx HAS2 XZ242. Primer Teniente Velasco's aircraft is now preserved in the Museo Nacional de Aeronautica Aeroparque in Buenos Aires.

When *Coventry* was hit a call went out for every available helicopter to assist in the rescue operation, many of them arriving before the destroyer had fully capsized. All 10 operational 846 Squadron Sea King HC4s responded and were soon winching up survivors to take them to *Broadsword* or the *Fort Austin* or, if needing medical attention, straight to the hospital ship *Uganda* or the field hospital at Ajax Bay. The commando Sea Kings were joined in the rescue by the four Sea King HAS5s of the 826 Squadron detachment on board the *Fort Austin*. In all, 234 men were safely recovered from *Coventry*, 170 of them by *Broadsword*, but 19 men died in the attack and many more, including Captain D Hart-Dyke, were badly injured, mostly during the initial explosions.

The tragic sinking of *Coventry* effectively marked the end of the battle for San Carlos. It also marked the end of the Type 22/Type 42 combination as radar picket and missile trap. Although the system did have some success, it had proved too vulnerable. Yet despite the loss of *Coventry*, *Ardent* and *Antelope*, the landings had been successful and had placed the ground forces where they needed to be in strength. The combined efforts of the Argentine Air Force and Navy had failed to halt the operation although they had made it more costly for the Royal Navy than had been anticipated. The 24 Sea Harriers from the two aircraft carriers had flown a total of 63 sorties during the 25th, the highest number for a single day during the conflict.

Between the 21st and the 25th the Argentine Air Force and Navy mounted approximately 180 sorties to oppose the landings, of which 117 are claimed to have reached the target area. However, according to British sources only about 80 aircraft were encountered during these five days, so

there is a discrepancy of about 37 sorties that did not reach the AOA. During the Battle of San Carlos nine Daggers, seven Air Force Skyhawks and three Navy Skyhawks were lost, giving a combined loss rate of 10.5 per cent of sorties dispatched and 23.75 per cent of the aircraft that actually reached their targets, assuming that only 80 aircraft did so. This rate of attrition could not be sustained for long. However, while the landings may have been drawing to a successful conclusion on the 25th, the day was not yet over.

Nine minutes after *Coventry* slipped beneath the waves, two Super Etendards were detected by *Exeter* and *Ambuscade* from the Carrier Battle Group's position, now just some 60 miles northeast of Stanley. The Carrier Battle Group had come much closer to the Falkland Islands than normal to reduce the transit time to and from CAP positions for the Sea Harriers and to ensure that more fighters would be available throughout the day. The Group was also covering the *Atlantic Conveyor*, which was due to enter San Carlos Water later that evening and unload its Chinook HC1 and Wessex HU5 helicopters that were needed for the first stage of the ground war. The *Atlantic Conveyor* was placed on the northern edge of the Carrier Battle Group, away from what was thought to be the most likely direction of threat from air attack.

The Super Etendards were detected at about 25 miles range and anti-Exocet measures were immediately instigated. Within another four minutes all the available Sea Harriers had scrambled from the decks of both aircraft carriers and set off to search for the Argentine aircraft. The Lynx helicopters from both *Hermes* and *Invincible* also took off to try to jam the Exocets; chaff rockets were fired continuously. However,

by this time the Super Etendards had already launched their Exocets and turned away from the Task Force. At 1841Z the *Atlantic Conveyor* was hit by an Exocet that had been launched from a position about 30 miles to the north of the ship. The ship had started to turn to present its stern to the missile but the Exocet punched through the hull about 10ft above the water line. At the time it was hit the *Atlantic Conveyor* was less than two miles from *Hermes* with *Invincible* another eight miles further south and it was thought that the Exocet had been successfully decoyed by chaff fired by *Ambuscade* – only for it to hit the *Atlantic Conveyor*. For the chaff to have worked it would have had to float down close to the surface of the sea, so the Exocet probably aimed for a cloud of chaff but, having passed through it, then located a fresh target dead ahead, which happened to be the *Atlantic Conveyor*.

Moments after the *Atlantic Conveyor* was hit, a fast and low radar target was observed possibly approaching the aircraft carriers. *Invincible* fired a salvo of six Sea Darts at the target. The radar blip then disappeared but if it was the other Exocet, which is unlikely, it remains unconfirmed whether or not it had been hit by one of *Invincible*'s Sea Darts or had been decoyed and deflected by a combination of chaff and jamming. Some observers think that the *Atlantic Conveyor* was hit by both Exocets but most references confirm only one hit. Some of the Sea Darts that *Invincible* fired were thought to have homed onto the numerous chaff clouds developing above the Task Force.

The original plan called for 2 Escuadrilla to launch both of the Super Etendards at 1200Z, but the mission was delayed due to the non-availability of the KC-130H tanker. The position of the Carrier Battle Group had

ZA718 'BN' of 18 Squadron was the only Chinook HC1 to survive the sinking of the Atlantic Conveyor *on 25th May and performed sterling work for the rest of the war despite major problems caused by the loss of specialist tools and stores when the ship was sunk.* MoD

been accurately plotted by the radar operators at Stanley who monitored the launch and return of Sea Harriers and helicopters, even though the aircraft flew at low level when within a certain distance of the aircraft carriers. The two Super Etendards eventually took off from Rio Grande at 1730Z and were flown by Capitan de Corbeta Roberto Curilovic (0753/3-A-203) and Teniente de Navio Julio Hector Barraza (0754/3-A-204). The aircraft flew northeast from their base to a position 160 miles east of Puerto Deseado and well to the north of the Falklands, where they refuelled before heading southeast. They descended to less than 100ft above the sea for the last 150 miles of the run-in to the target and with the first sweep of their radar found the Task Force ships, which they approached from the northwest.

When the aircraft popped up for their brief radar sweep they were immediately detected by *Exeter* and *Ambuscade*. The aircraft were flying just 200 yards apart when they both launched their Exocets simultaneously at the largest of the three radar targets they could see. This was probably *Ambuscade*, which was the nearest ship to the Super Etendards at the point of launch. The two aircraft turned back and refuelled from the KC-130H again before heading back to Rio Grande, where they landed at 2137Z having been airborne for four hours and seven minutes. The Super Etendard attack came as a surprise to the British fleet, especially as it came from an unexpected direction. Sea Harrier CAPs were occupied with *Coventry* and the two Argentine aircraft escaped at high speed without being intercepted.

As soon as the *Atlantic Conveyor* was hit a massive rescue operation swung into action. The ship immediately caught fire as the Exocet punched a huge hole in her starboard hull and exploded in a large open deck crammed with 4-ton trucks with full

fuel tanks and other flammable material. A Wessex HU5 (XT468) and several Sea Kings from both *Invincible* and *Hermes* rushed to the burning ship and picked up 13 men who had been cut off on the forward deck of the vessel as the fire spread rapidly through the ship. *Alacrity* and *Brilliant* picked up many survivors from life rafts and 133 men were rescued in total but 12 men died, including the Ship's Master, Captain Ian North, who drowned before he could reach a lifeboat despite an heroic effort by Captain Mike Layard (Senior Naval Officer on board the *Atlantic Conveyor*) to save him.

As well as the loss of lives, the loss of much valuable equipment, including helicopters, spare parts and bombs, was also a major blow. The destruction of the helicopters would delay the advance to Stanley as many troops would now have to travel on foot rather by air. A huge amount of tents and kitchen, sanitary and laundry equipment was also lost, causing great hardship in the weeks to come. Also serious was the loss of a large number of CBUs and 1,000lb bombs destined for 1 Squadron as well as metal sections for a temporary Harrier airstrip. Three of the five Chinook HC1s (ZA706, ZA716 and ZA719) that embarked were still on board as were six Wessex HU5s (XS480, XS495, XS499, XS512, XT476 and XT483) of 'D' Flight 848 Squadron and a Lynx HAS2 (XZ700). *Fort Austin*'s peripatetic 'B' Flight 845 Squadron Wessex HU5 (XT468), which was temporarily residing on the *Atlantic Conveyor*, was airborne on a test flight when the container ship was hit and, after taking part in the rescue operation, flew to *Hermes* where it stayed for 10 days before moving yet again.

However, the luckiest escape was that of Chinook HC1 ZA718 of 18 Squadron. Work had started early on the 25th to fit the rotor blades to two of the four Chinooks (ZA706 and ZA718) that were stored on the deck of the *Atlantic Conveyor*. The fitting of the

blades was a difficult and dangerous task on the heaving deck without specialist lifting equipment and work on ZA718 was not finished until late afternoon. The helicopter was flown off the ship by Flight Lieutenant John Kennedy and had commenced resupply flights to other ships of the Task Force shortly before the attack took place. The Chinook flew to *Hermes* and stayed on the aircraft carrier overnight before flying ashore to the 845/846 Squadron FOB at Old House Creek near San Carlos on the 26th. The 18 Squadron main party had travelled to the Falklands on the *Norland* but had been transferred to *Fearless* for the landings at San Carlos. Without their helicopters most of the squadron personnel were taken back to Ascension Island, leaving a small detachment on the Falklands commanded by Squadron Leader R U Langworthy and consisting of two night-qualified crews, 13 ground crew and four Joint Helicopter Support Unit loading/rigging specialists.

The stricken *Atlantic Conveyor* was later reboarded and then taken under tow by the tug *Irishman* on the 28th, the intention being to salvage what had not been destroyed by the fire. However, seriously weakened by the fire, the ship broke its back during a storm on the 30th. The forward section of the vessel sank almost immediately but the aft section remained afloat and had to be sunk by naval gunfire to prevent it from becoming a hazard to the rest of the Task Force.

A planned night insertion of Special Forces troops onto Mount Kent and Mount Challenger by the four PNG-equipped Sea King HC4s of 846 Squadron had to be cancelled on the 25th due to the extra tasking required following the loss of *Coventry*. These two mountains, less than 10 miles west of Stanley, were only lightly defended and provided excellent observation points from which to view the Argentine positions in the hills near the town. A British presence on Mount Kent would also plug the huge gap between the northern and southern advances that would develop over the next few days and weeks. Welcome reinforcements in the shape of two Wessex HU5s (XT449 and XT461) from 'E' Flight 845 Squadron deployed ashore from the *Tidepool* to Ajax Bay on the 25th. Both helicopters moved on to the FOB at Old House Creek the following day.

The report following 1 Squadron's raid on Stanley airport suggesting that swept-wing jets had been seen there, coupled with a 23rd May report of arrester gear having been seen on the runway, lent itself to the possible conclusion, albeit unlikely, that the Super Etendards that had hit the *Atlantic Conveyor* might make for Stanley instead of their mainland base. Consequently three Sea Harriers flown by Lieutenant Commander Mike Blissett, Lieutenant Clive Morrell and Lieutenant Andy McHarg took off from *Hermes* at 2155Z for another toss-bombing raid on the airfield at Stanley. They returned safely to the aircraft carrier an hour later, unaware of the results of their raid.

Late on the 25th the *Bristol* Group of ships (*Bristol*, *Cardiff*, *Active*, *Andromeda*, *Avenger*, *Penelope*, and the RFAs *Bayleaf* and *Olna*) arrived in the TEZ. The timely arrival of these eight ships, which joined the Carrier Battle Group on the 26th, helped to make up for the loss of *Coventry*, *Sheffield*, *Antelope* and *Ardent*. *Andromeda* was particularly useful because although she was an elderly Batch 3 Leander class frigate, she was equipped with just a single Seawolf launcher (as opposed to the two launchers fitted to the Type 22s) and spent most of the conflict supplementing both *Brilliant* and *Broadsword* as goalkeeper for the aircraft carriers. However the *Atlantic Causeway*, which carried replacement helicopters, was still some four days away from the Falklands.

Meanwhile, the last major warship in transit via Ascension Island arrived there on the 25th. RFA *Engadine* was the Royal

Navy's helicopter support ship and carried the headquarters and 'A' Flight of 847 Squadron with four Wessex HU5s, the rest of the squadron being embarked on the *Atlantic Causeway*. At Ascension 'A' Flight exchanged one of its helicopters (XT764) that had been experiencing technical problems for a Wideawake-based Wessex HU5 (XS491) of 'D' Flight 845 Squadron that had been on the island since the 12th.

26th May (Wednesday) –
The Breakout from San Carlos Begins
After the momentous events of the day before, the 26th proved to be something of an anti-climax. The Carrier Battle Group, shaken by the Super Etendard attack that had caused the loss of the *Atlantic Conveyor*, moved towards the edge of the TEZ to a position about 200 miles east of the Falklands. *Broadsword* returned to the Carrier Battle Group and then set off for repairs by the converted offshore support vessel MV *Stena Seaspread*, after which she spent the rest of the conflict protecting *Hermes*. There were no Argentine raids on the 26th but the Sea Harrier squadrons maintained CAPs throughout the day.

The only Argentine action on the 26th took place on the Falkland Islands themselves and involved helicopters of CAB601. Puma AE-508, the last surviving helicopter of the resupply mission to Port Howard, set off back to Stanley two hours before dawn. The Puma carried all the crews from the three CAB601 helicopters that had been lost on the ill-fated mission, as well as Capitan Donadille who had been shot down in his Dagger on the 23rd and a number of Argentine Army commandos. The helicopter flew back to Stanley via Darwin and at one stage became lost during the 45-minute flight.

The CAB601 helicopters were very busy in the days following the British landings, airlifting troops to forward positions.

Although the Sea Harriers saw no action on the 26th, the 1 Squadron Harriers were very active. The squadron's first mission involved two aircraft flown by Squadron Leader Jerry Pook (XZ988) and Flight Lieutenant John Rochfort (XZ963), which took off from *Hermes* at 1233Z for an armed reconnaissance around Stanley. Unfortunately, Jerry Pook's IFF transmitter failed, leaving him vulnerable to attack by the British air defences as well as Argentine missiles and radar-controlled guns, so he had to abort the mission and return to *Hermes*. Squadron Leader Bob Iveson and Flight Lieutenant Tony Harper took off at 1240Z for an uneventful CBU attack on enemy troop positions at Port Howard. The squadron commander, Wing Commander Peter Squire, took off at 1659Z for a solo toss-bombing raid on Stanley airport but he too suffered a technical problem when one of his bombs hung up and had to be jettisoned before he returned to *Hermes*. As with so many raids during the conflict, low cloud prevented the results of the bombing being reported.

At 1756Z Jerry Pook (this time flying XZ989) took off again for another mission, along with Flight Lieutenant Mark Hare (XZ988) on an armed reconnaissance from Teal Inlet to the Stanley area. The pair came upon a Puma sitting on the ground near Mount Kent and after coming under ground fire Jerry Pook flew off and returned from a different direction to score a direct hit on the helicopter with his CBUs. However, these two pilots were simply completing a task they had started earlier as the Puma was AE-501 – the same helicopter that Mark

After the air attacks on Broadsword *on 25th May the ship sailed to the TRALA for repairs by the* Stena Seaspread. Broadsword *was operational again by 1st June. Cdr S Chelton*

Hare had disabled during a mission with Jerry Pook on the 21st. Although the Puma had been badly damaged in the previous attack, it was repairable and was presumably waiting to be recovered or repaired in the field when it was finally destroyed on the 26th. During the mission the Harriers were locked up by a Superfledermaus fire control radar and a Blowpipe missile was fired at them but missed.

The orders for the breakout from San Carlos were issued on the 26th. Although the original plan was for the Commando Brigade to await the arrival of the 5th Infantry Brigade, the loss of ships and increasing impatience in the UK forced a move earlier than was strictly desirable. A northern thrust would see 45 Commando advance to Douglas and 3 PARA to Teal Inlet on the north coast while 2 PARA would head south and neutralise the strong Argentine garrison at Darwin and Goose Green. The San Carlos base area was left to the defence of 40 Commando; 42 Commando was held at San Carlos in reserve. The British helicopters ashore continued to support the troops in any way they could but the loss of the Chinooks and Wessex on the *Atlantic Conveyor* meant that there were not enough helicopters to complete all the planned tasks at this stage of the conflict. The reduced helicopter availability certainly slowed down the British advance as most of the troops had to walk instead of being flown to new positions by helicopter. 'Yomping' became a new word in the vocabulary of the British press to describe the hard slog of walking over rough or boggy terrain while carrying heavy packs. The total number of British helicopters available to the ground forces on the 26th was just 32, of which only 16 were the vitally needed transport helicopters.

British Helicopters Available for Operations Ashore on 26th May

Ajax Bay
'B' Flight 3 CBAS:
Scout AH1(XP902, XR627, XT629, XV140, XW615, XW616)
'M' Flight 3 CBAS:
Gazelle AH1 (XX380, XX413)

Clam Valley
'A' Flight 3 CBAS:
Gazelle AH1 (XZ326, ZA730, ZA776)

Head of the Bay
'5' Flight (656) 3 CBAS:
Scout AH1 (XR628, XT637, XT649)

Old House Creek
845 Squadron 'A' Flight:
Wessex HU5 (XS483, XT484)
845 Squadron 'B' Flight:
Wessex HU5 (XT765)

845 Squadron 'E' Flight:
Wessex HU5 (XT449, XT461)
846 Squadron:
Sea King HC4
(ZA291, ZA299, ZA312, ZA313)

18 Squadron:
Chinook HC1 (ZA718)

Unnamed FOB near Ajax Bay
'C' Flight 3 CBAS:
Gazelle AH1 (XX376, XX412)

Eagle Bases/HMS *Intrepid*
846 Squadron:
Sea King HC4
(ZA292, ZA293, ZA295, ZA297)

HMS *Fearless*
846 Squadron:
Sea King HC4 (ZA296, ZA298)

The PNG-equipped Sea King HC4s of 846 Squadron remained busy during the 26th but the second attempt to insert Special Forces near Mount Kent and Mount Challenger failed due to a combination of bad weather, difficult terrain and navigational problems. The mission was postponed, once more, to the 27th. The single Wessex HU5 of 'B' Flight 845 Squadron that had been working with 45 Commando from Ajax Bay since the 22nd moved to 845 Squadron's FOB at Old House Creek. The advanced detachment of 656 Squadron (operating as '5' Flight 3 CBAS) flew ashore on the 26th and set up a temporary FOB at the base of the Sussex Mountains near Head of the Bay House, at the furthest point inland reached by San Carlos Water.

Late on the 26th the breakout from the San Carlos area commenced. During the night the men of 2 PARA walked the nine miles from the Sussex Mountains to Camilla Creek House where they prepared for the assault on the Argentine garrison at Darwin and Goose Green. No opposition was encountered during this advance. Although not originally part of the plan for the ground offensive, the neutralisation of the strongpoint at Darwin/Goose Green before the main advance to Stanley would certainly be an advantage as it would remove a potential flanking threat, even though it tied up precious helicopter resources.

Meanwhile the ships of the *Bristol* Group were integrating themselves with the rest of the Task Force, providing much-needed replacements for lost or damaged vessels. On the 26th *Glasgow*, which had been holed by a 500lb bomb on the 12th but had been forced to remain operational until the arrival of the *Bristol* Group of ships, sailed to the Tug, Repair and Logistic Area (TRALA) for temporary repairs alongside the *Stena Seaspread*. However, it was soon decided that *Glasgow* was too badly damaged even

for the resources of the *Stena Seaspread* and so the destroyer left for the UK on the 27th, arriving at Portsmouth on 20th June having sailed most of the way using only her secondary engines.

Argonaut, which had suffered major damage and was rendered immobile during an air raid on the 21st, was declared operational on the 26th following repairs by the ship's company. The main problem had been disposing of one of the two unexploded bombs, which had to be carefully lifted from the shambles of the Seacat magazine and passed through holes cut into two decks before being lowered into the sea. *Argonaut* subsequently resumed air defence duties in San Carlos Water but was replaced a few days later by the newly arrived *Minerva*, freeing *Argonaut* to depart and rendezvous with the *Stena Seaspread*.

The hulk of the *Atlantic Conveyor* was visited on the 26th and 27th by a Sea King HAS5 from 820 Squadron that carried teams which assessed the possibility of salvaging the ship or some of its contents.

Meanwhile, in preparation for further 'Black Buck' missions, Vulcan B2 XM598 flew from Waddington to Ascension Island on the 26th. The two main Argentine radar units on the Falklands, the Air Force's Westinghouse AN/TPS-43F and the Army's Cardion TPS-44, were providing the Argentine aircraft with early warning of Sea Harrier CAPs, enabling them to be avoided. The destruction of these radars by conventional bombs would be difficult and dangerous as they were sited close to civilian houses in Stanley itself. What was required was a specialised and precision-guided weapon, together with a means of delivering it. All the available anti-radar missiles were considered to be too large to be carried by the Sea Harriers/Harriers, which in any case would have had to be diverted from their primary tasks to deliver them. However the Vulcan, which had already proved the feasibility of long-range attack during the earlier 'Black Buck' bombing raids, could be adapted to carry the missiles. Accordingly, Vulcan B2 XM597 was fitted with Martel anti-radar missiles (already in use with RAF Buccaneer squadrons), these being carried on underwing pylons that were engineered specifically for the task.

The aircraft made its first flight with a Martel attached on 4th May and conducted the first test-firing over the Cardigan Bay weapons range on the 6th. However, there were concerns over the Martel's ability to withstand a long flight in the freezing cold of high altitude. The RAF was also worried that the large size of the missile's warhead might cause collateral damage to nearby civilians and buildings in Stanley. It was subsequently decided that the Vulcan would carry the US-built AGM-45A Shrike

The Martel anti-radar missile was not used operationally, although it was flight-tested by Vulcan B2 XM597. The Martel was replaced by the Shrike due to concerns over the Martel's ability to withstand cold temperatures for extended periods and the risk to civilians from the missile's large warhead. MoD

anti-radar missile instead and a number of these missiles were duly supplied by the USAF. Several Shrike-equipped F-4G 'Wild Weasel' Phantoms from the 52nd Tactical Fighter Wing at Spangdahlem AB visited Waddington from 19th to 23rd May so that the Vulcan crews and engineers could be briefed on the missile and its operation. Two Vulcans (XM597 and XM598) were selected for conversion and deployment; each was fitted with pylons to carry up to four Shrikes. XM598 flew from Waddington to Wideawake on 26th May, followed by XM597 the next day.

27th May (Thursday)
Fine weather on the morning of the 27th enabled a Learjet 35A of Grupo 1 de Aero-fotografico to make another high-altitude photographic run over Falkland Sound to take pictures of the beachhead positions and ships in the area.

The Harriers of 1 Squadron were busy again on the 27th and during the course of the day the squadron suffered its second loss of the campaign during the preparation for the battle of Goose Green. The small air-field at Goose Green was well protected by six Rheinmetall 20mm anti-aircraft guns with Elta fire control radar and two Oerlikon 35mm guns with their Skyguard radar. Blowpipe and SA-7 hand-held SAMs were also available to the Argentine defenders at Goose Green making air attack on the air-field a very dangerous proposition. SA-7 Strela missiles, the Russian equivalent to the Blowpipe or Stinger, were thought to have been delivered to Argentina during the conflict from Peru and Libya. However, the first mission of the day for 1 Squadron was another toss-bomb attack on Stanley airport by Squadron Leader Peter Harris and Flight Lieutenant Tony Harper.

After the Stanley raid the squadron switched its attention to Goose Green. Squadron Leader Bob Iveson (XZ988) and Flight Lieutenant Mark Hare (XV789) took off from *Hermes* at 1400Z. Two Argentine 155mm guns were threatening the British advance and were the primary target for the Harriers but detailed information as to their location was lacking. Visibility was poor and the Harriers were unable to follow the FAC's instructions as cloud covered their Initial Point, so on the first pass over the area Bob Iveson did not see the guns until it was too late. However, Mark Hare was able

to drop his CBUs on one of the guns as Bob Iveson came around for another pass only to see the target too late again for an accurate drop. Bob Iveson then made a third pass and dropped his BL755 cluster bombs on what looked like a company-size troop emplacement.

The two Harriers then returned to *Hermes* and were quickly re-armed for another attack on the Argentine defences at Goose Green. The aircraft took off again at 1612Z and once more the target was an artillery emplacement. Again the pair could not see the well-camouflaged gun on their first pass. They decided to attack a troop position instead and dropped CBUs on the target. In the mistaken belief that the Paras were in dire straits at this time (the main attack had not commenced but forward patrols had come under fire), Bob Iveson then decided to return to strafe the target area. During his third pass over the target he used up all his 30mm ammunition and was exiting over Goose Green airfield at about 100ft when his aircraft was hit twice by anti-aircraft fire, probably from one of the 35mm Oerlikon guns. The Harrier caught fire and the controls froze as the hydraulic pressure fell rapidly. Although the engine continued to run normally, Iveson knew he was losing control as the fire burnt its way through control cables and so, less than a minute after being hit and with flames now enter-ing the cockpit, he ejected near Paragon House, about seven miles west of Goose Green. The Harrier exploded as it hit the ground and although Iveson landed safely, the violence of his high-speed ejection resulted in cuts and lacerations to his face and temporarily blurred vision.

Unable to see properly, Iveson thought that Argentine troops were approaching his position so he abandoned his survival pack and evaded as fast as he could, only later

realising that the 'troops' had probably been sheep! Just before dark he came across an apparently deserted farmhouse; to make sure, he remained in hiding until dusk and collected blankets and food before leaving the house again in case enemy troops decided to search it during the night. He saw a UH-1H in the distance using a searchlight to look for him but the commencement of the British night attack on Goose Green curtailed the Argentine search effort. He returned to the farmhouse the next day to shelter from the cold and wind but decided not to stay for long as it was an obvious place for him to hide and he assumed that Argentine troops would be out looking for him. Bob Iveson spent the day hiding from enemy troops and shelter-ing from the wintry weather in whatever cover he could find.

At 1920Z Squadron Leader Jerry Pook took off in XV789 on a solo reconnaissance mission to try to find Bob Iveson or at least contact him by radio. However, Pook could not locate him and was fired on by AAA while flying at 15,000ft near Goose Green, so he returned to the aircraft carrier about an hour later.

Twenty minutes before Jerry Pook left *Hermes*, two flights of Grupo 5 A-4B Sky-hawks had taken off from Rio Gallegos on what is thought to have been the first Argen-tine air attack on a land target from the mainland during the conflict. Photographic reconnaissance by high-flying Learjets of Grupo 1 Aerofotografico had located the troop concentrations and headquarters at Ajax Bay. One Skyhawk dropped out of each flight so that only four aircraft took off from Rio Gallegos at 1900Z, each aircraft carrying several 400kg parachute-retarded anti-personnel bombs. Veterans Capitan Carballo and Teniente Rinke comprised the first flight, call sign Truco, while Primer

Teniente Velasco and Teniente Osses comprised Poker flight. After refuelling from a KC-130H the two flights made their way up Falkland Sound at low level, passed over Grantham Sound from the southwest and climbed to clear the Sussex Mountains before diving down towards San Carlos Water and heading for Ajax Bay on the western shore, arriving at 1950Z. Truco flight fired their cannon and dropped their bombs on 40 Commando's encampment, then escaped to the north through a hail of gunfire from troops on the ground and from the ships in San Carlos Water.

Poker flight attacked the Ajax Bay refrigeration plant, which, unbeknown to the Argentine pilots, housed a British field hospital as well as a stores dump. However, by then practically every gun in the San Carlos area was firing at the two Skyhawks (at least two SAMs were also fired, which narrowly missed the Skyhawks) and Velasco's aircraft was hit moments after all its anti-personnel ordnance had been released. Velasco's Skyhawk (C-215) had been hit in the wing by 40mm shells fired by *Fearless* and *Intrepid* and the aircraft soon began to lose hydraulic pressure as it turned west over Falkland Sound. Teniente Osses warned Velasco that his aircraft was on fire near the port wing root and Carballo advised him to eject immediately. Mariano Velasco waited until he reached the coast of West Falkland and ejected close to Port Howard, landing close to the wreckage of his aircraft. He injured his ankle and was eventually found by some local civilians but it took until 1st June for him to reach Argentine forces in Port Howard, by which time he had been given up for lost by his comrades in Grupo 5.

After the conflict, pieces of the wreckage of C-215 were salvaged from the crash site

and returned to the UK for display in the Fleet Air Arm Museum at Yeovilton. One piece of metal from the fuselage showed a silhouette of a British ship, presumably representing *Coventry*, which Velasco had sunk on the 25th. During the attack on the Ajax Bay refrigeration plant two bombs pierced the roof but failed to explode. Because the bombs were in a difficult position to defuse and were not thought to have armed, vital surgical operations continued throughout the conflict with the bombs in situ! To reassure medical staff and patients alike, Flight Lieutenant A Swan, an RAF bomb disposal expert, examined the bombs, declared them to be dud and slept beside them each night until they were eventually removed.

The raid on Ajax Bay resulted in eight soldiers being killed and 26 wounded. It also caused damage to the stores dump at the plant and some ammunition was lost in the subsequent fire. The raid had narrowly missed the Commando Brigade headquarters and the dispersed helicopters of 'A' and 'B' Flights 3 CBAS. A Scout AH1 (XR627) was damaged by shrapnel from the ammunition dump fire while it was undergoing maintenance at Ajax Bay but it was repaired within a few days.

The Skyhawks of Carballo and Osses had also been damaged during the attack on Ajax Bay. Carballo's aircraft was in a very bad way and only just made it back to Rio Gallegos. Carballo had to rely on Rinke as his radio and VLF Omega were unserviceable. His aircraft had been hit six times and was later found to have a cannon shell lodged in the port mainwheel and a gaping hole in the nose. Osses' aircraft suffered less damage but both drop tanks had been punctured by bullets or shrapnel. Once again it appears that the loss of an aircraft

and the damage to two more dissuaded the Argentines from pursuing this form of attack. In fact, this was the last low-level attack on British forces in the San Carlos area and the only low-level attack on the forces ashore at the beachhead.

Future raids on well-defended British positions on land were mostly confined to medium-level attacks by Canberras at night. The first (night) raid by Canberras was planned for the 26/27th but the three aircraft turned back before reaching the Falklands due to bad weather over the target area. Although Sea Harrier CAPs were flown throughout the day (801 Squadron flew 16 sorties on the 27th), no contact was made with any of the Argentine attackers.

At dusk on the 27th two replacement Pucaras were flown from Santa Cruz to Stanley airport to reinforce the dwindling number of Pucaras available on the islands. The two aircraft were guided to within visual distance of West Falkland by a civilian Mitsubishi Mu-2B, which had been impressed into military service as part of Escuadron Fenix. The Mu-2B possessed better navigational equipment than the Pucara and flew at 10,000ft while the Pucaras remained at low level throughout the ferry flight. The Pucara flight, led by Teniente Arganaraz, became lost soon after crossing the coast and had to be guided to Stanley by radar, landing at about 1945Z.

Escuadron Fenix was a temporary unit formed from impressed civilian aircraft and their crews, who were given military ranks for the duration of the conflict. The aircraft included business jets such as Learjets, British Aerospace 125s and a Cessna Citation as well as Rockwell Aero Commanders, Aerostar 601s, Mu-2Bs, a Swearingen Merlin IIIA, and several light helicopters. These aircraft flew mostly on communications and courier duties within Argentina but some also flew search and rescue, navigational pathfinder (especially for the poorly equipped Dagger As) and radio relay missions for the combat forces.

One of the two Argentine Air Force Chinooks took 67 troops to Darwin to reinforce the garrison there as the British assault on the Argentine stronghold commenced. The helicopter returned safely to Stanley carrying Argentine Air Force personnel, including a few pilots who had been shot down in the preceding days and others who had been evacuated to Darwin from Pebble Island following the Special Forces attack on the 15th.

As 2 PARA's advance on Darwin and Goose Green continued during the day and culminated in a night attack on Argentine positions, 45 Commando and 3 PARA set off at dawn on foot for Douglas Settlement and Teal Inlet in the north of East Island. This was the start of the intended advance through Douglas and Teal towards the Mount Kent area to link up with the advance from the south for the final assault on Stanley itself. The 2 PARA advance on Goose Green was supported by two Gazelle AH1s (XX380 and XX413) of 'M' Flight 3 CBAS and two Scout AH1s (XP902 and XT629) of the squadron's 'B' Flight. These helicopters moved ammunition, food and other supplies up to the 2 PARA positions from San Carlos throughout the day in readiness for the night assault. After dark, Sea King HC4 ZA292 flown by Lieutenant N J North of 846 Squadron moved three 105mm guns of 8 (Alma) Commando Battery, Royal Artillery up to Camilla Creek House to support the attack, complementing the 4.5-inch gun of the frigate *Arrow*, which would provide naval gunfire support.

All the British helicopters ashore on the islands were particularly active on the 27th. The delayed insertion of Special Forces

On 27th May the two Sea King HAS2As of 825 Squadron's detachment on board the Queen Elizabeth II *transferred Major General Jeremy Moore and his staff from the liner to* Antrim *near South Georgia. XV677 is seen here in the foreground with a cargo strop hanging under its fuselage ready for the next lift while XV648 waits its turn.* Wg Cdr P Lyall

onto Mount Kent by 846 Squadron was attempted yet again in the early morning but, although successful, the troops soon had to be taken off due to severe weather. The two remaining Sea King HC4s on board *Fearless* (ZA296 and ZA298) deployed ashore to a new FOB that had been set up at Fern Valley Creek, just one and a half miles south of the Old House Creek FOB. *Fearless* (with the 'B' Flight 845 Squadron Wessex HU5 XT765 on board from the Old House Creek FOB) then sailed from San Carlos Water to rendezvous with *Antrim* to collect Major General Jeremy Moore, the Commander Land Forces Falkland Islands, Brigadier M J A Wilson, commander of the 5th Infantry Brigade, and their staffs.

The Sea King HC4s of 846 Squadron also flew casualties from the Grupo 5 raid and other actions from Ajax Bay to the hospital ship *Uganda* in the designated Red Cross Box to the north of the Falklands. On the night of the 27th the long-delayed deployment of virtually the whole of 'D' Squadron, SAS to Mount Kent and Mount Challenger was finally completed by 846 Squadron, thereby making British occupation of this strategic position more secure.

As a diversion from the attack on Goose Green the Royal Navy carried out the largest shore bombardment of the conflict so far. Three ships (*Glamorgan*, *Alacrity* and *Avenger*) fired over 250 rounds at enemy positions around Stanley on the night of the 27/28th. The ships' helicopters provided much valuable targeting information for the gunners as they carried the naval gunfire observers. *Glamorgan* even fired a Seaslug missile at Stanley airfield in its ship-to-shore mode. The huge missile was unguided in this mode but it was hoped that the sight of it would affect Argentine morale that must

already have been in decline. Meanwhile, *Yarmouth* fired 300 rounds at positions in the Port Howard area. The Harriers of 1 Squadron had opened the bombardment on Stanley airfield earlier in the day when two aircraft tossed six delayed-action 1,000lb bombs at the runway at noon.

During the 27th *Cardiff* relieved *Brilliant*, which sailed to the TRALA to come alongside the *Stena Seaspread* so that damage to her weapon system incurred during the 21st could be repaired. The two ships swapped Lynx helicopters and their crews as *Cardiff*'s Lynx was not one of the Sea Skua-equipped helicopters. Before the two ships exchanged the helicopters back again on the 30th *Cardiff*'s flight crew were briefed on Sea Skua operations, although *Cardiff*'s Lynx never had an opportunity to use the missile during the conflict.

Further away from the Falklands the *Queen Elizabeth II* arrived off Grytviken on South Georgia on the 27th. Over the next two days the ship disembarked about 3,000 troops of the 5th Infantry Brigade (including men from 1st Battalion Welsh Guards, 2nd Battalion Scots Guards and 1st/7th Gurkha Rifles) to the *Canberra* and the *Norland* as it was considered far too risky to send Cunard's flagship into San Carlos Water. Also transferred to the *Canberra* was the main party of 656 Squadron. The cross-decking was performed by five STUFT trawlers, a tug and the two 825 Squadron Sea King HAS2As (XV648 and XV677) that had sailed on board the giant liner. The helicopters then embarked on the *Canberra* on the 28th for the journey to San Carlos Water. The two helicopters also transferred Major General Moore and his staff from the *Queen Elizabeth II* to *Antrim* for the next leg of his journey to the Falklands.

With the arrival of the second Vulcan B2 (XM597) at Ascension Island, Wideawake airfield was near to its capacity. On the 27th, as well as the two Vulcans, the airfield was host to 17 Victors, two Harriers, three Nimrods, three Hercules, three Phantoms, one Chinook, one Sea King, and two Wessex.

On the 27th two VC10 C1s (XR807 and XV103) of 10 Squadron flew from Ascension Island to Brize Norton with survivors from *Sheffield*. The survivors had been brought to Ascension Island on board the tanker *British Esk* after *Sheffield* had been sunk on 4th May.

28th May (Friday) –
The Battle for Goose Green

The battle for Darwin and Goose Green started in earnest at 0700Z on the 28th with *Arrow* firing the first of 22 rounds of starshell and 135 rounds of high explosives in support, resulting in the withdrawal of Argentine troops towards the airstrip. Soon after first light the Scout AH1s of 'B' Flight 3 CBAS evacuated the wounded from the night's action from the Regimental Aid Post after first delivering mortar ammunition. The position was subjected to intense Argentine artillery and mortar fire but helicopter evacuation was simply the only option for badly wounded troops. Air power might have played a more important role in the battle had it not been for atrocious weather that limited air operations in support of either side. Operations from the mainland were particularly disrupted as for example when four Grupo 6 Dagger As set off on a raid but had to return when they encountered bad weather before reaching the islands.

The last remaining operational Argentine aircraft to be based at Goose Green, the two Air Force Bell 212s, left for Stanley at dawn, bringing information on the plight of the defenders to the commanders at Stanley. The first air action of the day appears to have been a mission flown by three Pucaras from Stanley airport to Darwin and Camilla Creek. Led by Capitan Roberto Villa with Tenientes Cimbaro and Arganaraz, the flight arrived over Darwin under a low cloud base at about 1200Z, about one hour after dawn. Villa and Arganaraz attacked British troop positions near Camilla Creek House with 2.75-inch rockets, but to little effect. Cimbaro and Arganaraz then flew towards the three British 105mm guns that were supporting the attack but Cimbaro reported that a SAM (a Blowpipe fired by a soldier from 43 Air Defence Battery, Royal Artillery) had been fired at his aircraft and had only just missed. Another missile then misfired and exploded on the ground just in front of Arganaraz's low-flying aircraft, which was flipped inverted and out of control. The Pucara righted itself but it was obviously damaged, and Arganaraz flew very steadily

back to Stanley, closely escorted by his two companions. At this stage of the conflict it appears that there was a maximum of seven Pucaras still operational at Stanley, although never all at the same time.

As the position of the Argentine ground forces at Darwin and Goose Green became critical, a maximum effort mission was planned by CAB601 to fly in reinforcements from the Regimento de Infanteria 25. Six UH-1Hs, two A-109As and the last surviving Puma started to airlift troops to Goose Green during the morning. During the afternoon another mission was flown, taking more troops from the same regiment from Mount Kent to Goose Green. On this occasion the helicopters were assisted by one of the Grupo 7 Chinooks. The Puma and the Chinook, escorted by an A-109A gunship, flew ahead of the slower UH-1Hs. The Huey flight left Stanley at 1945Z and reached the Darwin area at 2030Z after almost colliding with a solitary Pucara that flew through the formation of six helicopters, apparently in difficulty. However, it had taken too long to collect the troops from Mount Kent and fly them to Goose Green, with the result that they played little part in the action before the surrender. Several of the helicopters then flew across to Darwin to evacuate wounded troops back to Stanley.

The only air raid from the mainland known to have reached the Falklands on the 28th was made by a flight of Grupo 5 A-4B Skyhawks and almost resulted in tragedy. The flight was tasked with finding and attacking an unidentified ship that had been spotted in Grantham Sound to the south of San Carlos Water. One of the six Skyhawks was flown by Vicecomodoro Dubourg, commanding officer of V Brigada. However, when the Skyhawks arrived over Falkland Sound at about 1420Z very low cloud covered the area and no ships were seen. Three of the aircraft turned back to the south while the other three exited Falkland Sound to the north and came across a vessel which, fortunately, they correctly identified as the hospital ship *Uganda*. Both sides recognised the designated hospital ships, which were painted with large red crosses, and they were left alone. On this occasion it is thought that the Skyhawk flight was guided to the target by an airborne controller, probably Mayor Medina of Grupo 5, who was airborne in the vicinity in either a C-130 or a Learjet.

The next attempt by the Argentine Air Force to assist the defenders of Darwin and Goose Green involved a pair of Pucaras flown by Tenientes Miguel Gimenez and Cimbaro. The aircraft arrived in the vicinity of Camilla Creek House at 1455Z and saw two Scouts of 3 CBAS, which were engaged in casevac duties to and from the battlefield. Four 3 CBAS helicopters of 'B' and 'M'

Flights had started their support work with 2 PARA the previous day. The Scouts were moving up stores and ammunition when, at 1445Z, a call was put out that Colonel H Jones, the commanding officer of 2 PARA, and others had been severely wounded during an assault. The two Scouts quickly had their small arms ammunition boxes unloaded and replaced by stretchers. The helicopters then took off to reach the forward position where 2 PARA's Tactical Headquarters was known to be. The two Scouts were flown by Captain J P Niblett with Sergeant J W Glaze as his air gunner/observer (in XP902) and Lieutenant R J Nunn with Sergeant A R Belcher (in XT629).

As the Scouts were flying at very low level towards the British lines they were spotted by Gimenez and Cimbaro. The Pucaras split up to each take on a Scout but the helicopters successfully evaded the Pucaras' first pass and hurriedly tried to find somewhere to set down. Teniente Gimenez (A-537) then made another head-on pass at XT629 and hit the cabin with 20mm cannon and 7.62mm machine gun fire, killing Richard Nunn instantly. The Scout crashed about a mile southeast of Camilla Creek House, further injuring Sergeant Belcher who had been wounded in the legs by a 20mm cannon shell and 7.62mm bullets. Despite terrible injuries Sergeant Belcher managed to crawl clear of the burning wreckage and inject himself with morphine to await rescue. Meanwhile Teniente Cimbaro had been unable to shoot down the other Scout before being driven off by small arms fire from troops on the ground as he followed the helicopter towards Camilla Creek House.

Captain Nick Pounds with Corporal J C Wood immediately took off in Gazelle AH1 XX413 to search for the wreck site of XT629. When it was found Jeff Niblett flew XP902 to the site and evacuated the badly injured Sergeant Belcher to the Ajax Bay field hospital where his right leg had to be amputated. Both Scout pilots were later award the DFC, posthumously in the case of Richard Nunn, for flying forward during the height of the battle for Goose Green. Jeff Niblett later reported that the Pucaras were very skilfully handled and used their great speed range and manoeuvrability to attack the Scouts from all angles, altitudes and speeds and were much more difficult to evade than a fast jet aircraft.

En route to Ajax Bay Captain Niblett radioed ahead to 2 PARA to report on the progress of the battle at Goose Green/Darwin. As a result of this report, two 656 Squadron Scout AH1s (XT637 and XT649) were dispatched to fly casevac missions. After delivering Sergeant Belcher, Jeff Niblett led the two casevac Scouts and two SS-11-armed Scouts (XW615 and XW616) of 3 CBAS back to Camilla Creek. In the event the British assault on Goose Green had regained momentum and the two SS-11-equipped Scouts were not required, so they returned to Ajax Bay.

Following the successful attack on Scout XT629, the two Pucaras rejoined and left Goose Green for the return flight to Stanley at low level. Soon afterwards the aircraft entered low cloud and Gimenez and Cimbaro became separated. Despite repeated radio calls, neither Cimbaro nor the Stanley radar controller could reach Gimenez and his aircraft simply vanished. At the time it was not known whether he had been shot down, crashed into high ground or become lost in cloud and flown out to sea and crashed. In fact the mystery was not solved until September 1986 when the wreckage of the Pucara and the body of Teniente Gimenez were found in the Blue Mountains, near Flats Shanty. The aircraft had crashed into the mountainside, probably while flying in very poor visibility, some 12 miles north-northeast of Goose Green while trying to return to base. Gimenez's relatives became the first Argentines to visit the Falklands after the end of the conflict when they attended his burial in the Argentine war cemetery near Goose Green.

The Harriers of 1 Squadron had started the day with an armed reconnaissance over Douglas settlement in the north of East Falkland. This was followed by a raid flown by Wing Commander Squire, Squadron Leader Harris and Flight Lieutenant Harper using 2-inch rockets on an Argentine storage dump on Mount Kent. On returning from the raid on Mount Kent, Peter Squire

A Victor K2 arrives back at Ascension Island after yet another tanker sortie. Between 26-28th May there was a total of 17 Victors based at Ascension Island, leaving just six available back in the UK. MoD

heard Bob Iveson's voice as he tried to contact them on his emergency radio. A helicopter rescue was suggested but there were concerns that it might be an Argentine trap and so the rescue did not go ahead. The bad weather that restricted Argentine air operations in the battle for Goose Green and Darwin also limited British air support and it was not until dusk that 1 Squadron was able to fly a mission to Goose Green. British troops at Goose Green were under fire from two Argentine 35mm anti-aircraft guns that were being used as conventional artillery and were holding up the advance. The guns were situated on a promontory on the far side of the settlement and the only way to knock them out was by an air strike as the Paras did not want to fight their way through the settlement, which was still occupied by many civilians.

As the weather at Goose Green cleared slightly, so Squadron Leader Peter Harris (XZ989), Squadron Leader Jerry Pook (XV789) and Flight Lieutenant Tony Harper (XZ997) took off from *Hermes* at 1905Z and were briefed on their targets en route by Captain Kevin Arnold, the naval gunfire officer of 148 (Meiktila) Commando Forward Observation Battery, Royal Artillery. Kevin Arnold's team was attached to 2 PARA but from first light he acted as a forward air controller as the RAF's controller, Squadron Leader Penman had been injured and had to be evacuated. Making their way down Falkland Sound under a low cloud base, the Harriers accelerated to maximum speed for the low-level attack from the north. Peter Harris and Tony Harper dropped CBUs while Jerry Pook fired 72 2-inch rockets at the Argentine positions. This devastating mission, in full view and very close to the troops of 2 PARA, greatly encouraged the British troops nearby and hastened the surrender of the Argentine defenders early the next morning.

In addition to the Pucaras based at Stan-

ley airport, the only other attack aircraft available on the Falklands to support the Argentine ground forces at Darwin and Goose Green were the five MB-339As of the CANA's 1 Escuadrilla de Ataque. So far the MB-339As had seen little action, apart from Teniente Crippa's successful attack on the frigate *Argonaut* on 21st May, and they were lucky to have survived the numerous bombing raids on Stanley airport. However, during the 28th the situation on the ground at Goose Green was so desperate that it was decided to use the MB-339As, despite very poor flying weather of low cloud and rain. Capitan de Corbeta Molteni and Teniente de Fregata Daniel Miguel took off for Darwin soon after noon (another aircraft failed to start due to a cold battery) but were told to abandon the mission shortly before they arrived overhead as the cloud was too low and the visibility too poor to make an attack. Both returned to Stanley to await an improvement in the weather.

The weather in the Goose Green/Darwin area improved slightly and the aircraft were refuelled and ready to take off by 1830Z, but strong crosswinds prevented the MB-339As and a pair of Pucaras from leaving Stanley for another hour. The MB-339As eventually took off, flown by the same pilots who had flown the first mission, and flew at low level to Darwin and there made fast passes on British positions near Darwin School, using both cannon fire and Zuni rockets. Ground fire was heavy and Teniente Miguel's aircraft (0765/4-A-114) was hit by a Blowpipe SAM as he made a rocket attack. The aircraft dived into the ground near Goose Green airstrip and Miguel was killed in the crash. The aircraft exploded close to British troops, several of whom were actually hit by debris. Capitan Molteni was told by the ground controller that his wingman had been shot down so he flew back to Stanley at low level and high speed as a precaution against Sea Harrier attack.

The Blowpipe missile that brought down Miguel's MB-339A was fired by Marine Strange of 3 Commando Brigade Air Defence Troop. A recent article by Capitan Molteni, commander of the MB-339A detachment at Stanley, indicates that when operating in support of the Army, the unit had to use the unfamiliar Air Force close air support procedures rather than the proven system that the unit had established with the Argentine marines. The loss of the MB-339A, just half an hour after the devastating Harrier raid, lowered the morale of the Argentine troops in Goose Green and Darwin still further.

The loss of Gimenez's Pucara earlier in the day was more than made up for by the welcome arrival of three more aircraft from the mainland during the afternoon, which enabled another Pucara mission to be flown in support of the Argentine troops at Goose Green and Darwin. When the cross-wind at Stanley abated enough to permit flying, two more Pucaras took off to conduct another mission against British forces at Darwin/Goose Green. Primer Teniente Micheloud and Teniente Cruzado were ordered to attack British mortar positions, for which Micheloud would carry napalm and Cruzado rockets and incendiary bombs. Although they took off at 1930Z, before either of the MB-339As, the faster jets reached the battlefield before the Pucaras, which arrived in the Darwin area about 2009Z, soon after Teniente Miguel's MB-339A had been shot down.

The Pucaras dropped and fired their ordnance but did not cause any British casualties, even though Micheloud's napalm canisters fell within 160ft of a platoon of troops. The aircraft flew through a hail of ground fire and Cruzado's Pucara (A-555) was hit many times by small arms fire resulting in loss of control. Cruzado ejected at very low altitude just moments before his aircraft crashed into a paddock known as 'Peter's Park' near to Darwin settlement, showering some men of 'B' Company with aviation fuel. Cruzado was taken prisoner and later returned to Argentina at the conclusion of hostilities. Micheloud's Pucara had also been hit by ground fire during the attack and he only just managed to fly his battered aircraft back to Stanley and land safely. Several napalm canisters, some of them apparently home-made, were found at Goose Green airstrip after its capture, which caused consternation among British troops, but its use during the conflict was rare and largely ineffectual. As night fell the fighting at Goose Green died down and later, during the night, surrender negotiations commenced.

Despite poor visibility, high winds and a rising sea state, 18 Sea Harrier CAP sorties were flown throughout the day but with no success. Four of the Sea Harriers dropped 1,000lb bombs on Stanley airfield at the start of their CAPs. The Sea King HC4s of 846 Squadron flew many sorties throughout the day bringing up ammunition in support of 2 PARA's attack on Goose Green, although resupply flights had to be curtailed due to a shortage of aviation fuel after Fearless left San Carlos Water for the open sea. The ship was to rendezvous with Antrim to collect Major General Moore and his staff.

Lieutenant Nigel North flew ZA292 into Darwin during the night of the 28th to pick up casualties while under the mistaken impression that a local cease-fire had been agreed. The helicopter was hit by a round of 7.62mm ammunition, which only just missed a vital hydraulic line. The other three PNG-equipped Sea King HC4s moved over 800 Bergen back-packs to Douglas for 45 Commando. The support helicopters also moved elements of 3 Commando Brigade forward to Teal Inlet as part of the northern advance towards Stanley. Among the forces moved forward were four Rapier fire units of 'T' Battery of 12 Air Defence Regiment to provide local air defence for the troops congregating at Teal Inlet before the next push forward. Chinook HC1 ZA718 (by now becoming well known as 'Bravo November' after its code letters 'BN') flew a load of patients who had been wounded during the attack on Ajax Bay on the 27th out to the Uganda in the Red Cross Box.

The only ship movement of note on the 28th was the departure of Active to the TRALA for a brief spell of repairs after escorting the Sir Geraint and the Europic Ferry out of San Carlos Water to the Task Force. The frigate had only joined the Task Force a few days earlier and while being repaired her Wasp HAS1 flew HDS sorties between the ships stationed in the TRALA before Active sailed for San Carlos Water on the 30th.

During the night of the 28/29th a de Havilland Canada DHC-6 Twin Otter 200 (T-82) flown by Capitan M N Uriona and Teniente J Poza of Grupo 9 de Transporte Aereo made a daring flight from Rio Gallegos to Pebble Island to evacuate a small number of wounded Air Force personnel and a couple of pilots (Mayor Puga and Capitan Diaz) who had ejected near Pebble Island in recent days. The body of Teniente Volponi was also loaded into the Twin Otter for return to the mainland. The flight was made entirely in darkness and mostly at low level to avoid detection by British radar.

The Twin Otter was accompanied by an F-27, flown by Capitan H D Mino, which provided navigational and radio communication assistance. The F-27 did not land at Pebble Island but remained out over the sea at low level as the Twin Otter loaded up. However, as it was carrying more passengers than originally planned, the Twin Otter had to be defuelled in order to take off from the boggy grass runway, with the result that the aircraft was on the ground for nearly two hours. The aircraft landed at Puerto Deseado before refuelling and flying on to Comodoro Rivadavia. After the conflict this Twin Otter was seen wearing a Malvinas silhouette on the port side of its nose with the inscription '28-29 De Mayo De 1982 – Isla Bourbon – Recuperacion Al Continente De Tripulantes Eyectados y Meridos En Combate'. Isla Bourbon is the Argentine name for Pebble Island.

29th May (Saturday)

At 1450Z on the 29th the Argentine garrison commander at Goose Green surrendered to 2 PARA. About 1,100 Argentine troops, many of whom were young conscripts and some who had been flown in less than 24 hours previously as reinforcements, were taken prisoner. Men of 2 PARA also captured the Argentine positions at Port Darwin during the day. Tons of ammunition was found at Goose Green including napalm canisters, bombs and Blowpipe and SA-7 SAMs. Several of the Argentine artillery and anti-aircraft guns that still worked were taken over and used by the Paras.

'Black Buck 4', the first anti-radar mission, was scheduled to commence just before midnight on the 28th and Vulcan B2 XM597, captained by Squadron Leader C N McDougall, took off and set course for the Falkland Islands. Unfortunately, some five hours into the mission the lead Victor's HDU failed and Neil McDougall had no option but to return to Ascension Island. The mission was flown successfully two days later.

Having been largely absent from the war zone since their initial missions on 1st May, the Canberras of Grupo 2 de Bombardeo returned to the Falklands in the early hours of the 29th. Realising that it was suicide to send the vulnerable bombers on daylight missions, especially against missile-armed warships protected by Sea Harrier CAPs, the aircraft had played no part in the anti-shipping campaign. Instead the Canberra crews were now targeted against British troop positions, especially known encampments, and would bomb from high or low altitude during the hours of darkness. With only rudimentary navigation and bomb-aiming equipment, the chances of hitting these small targets at night, and often in poor weather, was slim. However, the raids certainly had some nuisance value and must have reduced the overall efficiency of the ground forces by keeping troops awake and alert during the cold nights. The first Canberra raid dropped bombs east of the Port San Carlos area at 0500Z on the 29th but did no damage. Two Canberras were involved, each dropping four Mk17 1,000lb bombs from medium altitude above cloud.

From the 29th onwards, both Sea Harrier squadrons started bombing Stanley airport at irregular intervals during the hours of daylight. It was hoped that, apart from actually inflicting material damage on the aircraft, runway or installations on the airfield, the irregular raids during daylight hours would discourage the use of Stanley airport by jet aircraft and disrupt the C-130 resupply flights.

Although bad weather covered the Falklands on the 29th, the first 800 Squadron raid on Stanley commenced at 1208Z when Lieutenant Commander Mike Blissett (in XZ455) and Lieutenant Bill Covington (in XZ496) took off from *Hermes*. After making their toss-bomb attack they returned to the aircraft carrier at 1305Z. Just 30 minutes later, two more aircraft flown by Lieutenant Commander Andy Auld (XZ500) and Lieutenant Andy McHarg (XZ460) took off to drop bombs on the airstrip at Pebble Island to discourage its use.

At 1430Z Lieutenant Commander Neill Thomas (XZ496) and Lieutenant Clive Morrell (XZ455) took off for another raid on Stanley airport and were followed at 1555Z by Mike Blissett (XZ500) and Bill Covington (XZ460) on another toss-bomb attack on the airport. At 1735Z Andy Auld (XZ496) and Andy McHarg (XZ455) left *Hermes* to bomb Pebble Island once again. In addition 801 Squadron sent two aircraft, each carrying three 1,000lb VT-fused bombs, to attack Stanley airport.

The mounting pressure, not just from Harrier and Sea Harrier raids but also from the bombardment at night by warships, gradually ground down the resolve of the Argentine defenders and, while never actually closing the airfield for any length of time, it made effective operations from there almost impossible.

801 Squadron lost an aircraft in unusual circumstances during the evening of the 29th. At 1847Z *Invincible* was about 160 miles northeast of Stanley in heavy seas and was making a turn to starboard to head into wind. Lieutenant Commander Broadwater was taxying Sea Harrier FRS1 ZA174 across the deck, preparing to take off from the ski-jump when the aircraft carrier listed heavily during the turn due to a strong side wind and huge waves. The angle of list, combined with a wet deck and a heavily laden aircraft, caused the Sea Harrier to skid sideways off the edge of the deck. Mike Broadwater ejected just before the aircraft fell into the sea and was lucky to survive such a low-level ejection and be rescued from the stormy sea by one of the aircraft carrier's helicopters. Also on the 29th, Lieutenant Commander Ward fired a Sidewinder by mistake as he was bombing Stanley airport.

Due to the accumulated fatigue of continuous operations, he had forgotten to change his armament switch from missiles to bombs and when he pressed the button to drop his bombs he was surprised to see an unguided AIM-9L streak away from his aircraft instead!

Following the mission that resulted in the loss of the *Atlantic Conveyor* on the 25th, 2 Escuadrilla was left with only one Exocet, with little hope of obtaining more. With the French embargo in place the Argentines made every effort to purchase further missiles from whatever source available, including the black market. However, an MI6 deception operation is claimed to have thwarted the procurement of more missiles until after the cessation of hostilities. Although the Argentine Navy possessed Exocets on board several of its destroyers, these missiles could not be adapted for launching from aircraft.

To make the best use of the last airborne Exocet a new mission profile was worked out. The target was still the British aircraft carriers, although 2 Escuadrilla believed that they had damaged or possibly even sunk *Hermes* during the 25th May attack. Two Super Etendards would take off from Rio Grande and first fly southeast before turning east to rendezvous with a KC-130H tanker and then, along with the tanker, skirt around the southern coast of the Falklands and approach the Carrier Battle Group from the southeast. It was thought that the British would expect any attack to come from the north or the west and might therefore be vulnerable to attack from the southeast.

The 2 Escuadrilla mission was planned for the 29th. Capitan de Corbeta Alejandro Francisco would fly the missile-armed Super Etendard while Teniente de Navio Luis Collavino would fly the accompanying unarmed aircraft. At 1500Z on the 29th the two aircraft were waiting at Rio Grande for the tanker to report that it was approaching its station when suddenly the 2 Escuadrilla commander, Capitan de Fregata Columbo, announced a notable change of plan. He had just been informed that four Grupo 4 A-4C Skyhawks would accompany the Super Etendards and that they would arrive at Rio Grande in 15 minutes' time. The Skyhawks would follow the Super Etendards and attack the aircraft carrier with 500lb bombs soon after the Exocet had hit its target. The change of plan caused an uproar among the naval personnel at Rio Grande as the Skyhawks would slow down the Super Etendards and there was insufficient tanker support for them as well as the two naval aircraft.

The outcome of this farcical situation was that by the time it had been agreed between Air Force and Navy commanders that the mission would go ahead without

the Skyhawks, the tanker could no longer stay on station and the mission had to be abandoned for the day. It was rescheduled for the following day and 2 Escuadrilla were told that this time the Grupo 4 Skyhawks would definitely accompany them.

A mission that did go ahead on the 29th was a Grupo 6 raid on the ships in San Carlos Water. The first aircraft to arrive were two Dagger As of Limon flight flown by Capitan Mir Gonzalez and Teniente Juan Doming Bernhardt from Rio Grande. Each aircraft was carrying three 500lb parachute-retarded bombs. The Daggers evaded a Sea Harrier CAP and reached the target area but ran into a wall of anti-aircraft fire from guns and missiles. Teniente Bernhardt's aircraft (C-436) was shot down by a Rapier SAM – the first and only confirmed Rapier kill of the conflict – and the aircraft crashed into the sea. Bernhardt is thought to have ejected but his body was never recovered and he became the fifth Grupo 6 pilot to die in the conflict in what was the eleventh and last Dagger to be shot down. A second flight of Dagger As jettisoned its bombs near to Pebble Island and turned back when they thought they were about to be intercepted by Sea Harriers, while a third flight aborted its mission altogether before even reaching the islands.

Another unusual Argentine air mission took place on the 29th. A C-130H (TC-68) from Grupo 1 found the MV *British Wye*, one of the STUFT tankers, stopped in an isolated position 400 miles north of South Georgia and about 700 miles east of the Falklands. This ship was one of eight 15,000-ton tankers that were chartered by the Ministry of Defence from BP to supplement the RFA fleet tankers. The Hercules made a low pass over the ship for identification purposes. The aircraft then returned about 15 minutes later at about 150ft above the sea and dropped eight 500lb bombs from the open ramp at the rear of the aircraft. Fortunately, only minor damage was done to the vessel as four of the bombs fell into the sea without exploding, three exploded off the port side of the ship and one actually hit the ship's foredeck but bounced off into the sea without exploding. While an enterprising, albeit unsuccessful, attempt to give teeth to a transport aircraft engaged in long-range reconnaissance, the attack was not without precedence and it did have the effect of ensuring that other British supply ships sailed further to the east in future.

Another attempt to bomb a British ship may have been made on 31st May when the *Fort Grange*, then some 1,000 miles north of the Falklands, was approached by a C-130, which broke away when about a mile from the ship. It was conjectured that the Argentine pilot (assuming it was actually an

Argentine Air Force Hercules) may have been deterred by the more warlike appearance of the undefended *Fort Grange*.

Despite poor weather, 1 Squadron flew several sorties on the 29th. Wing Commander Peter Squire (XZ989) and Flight Lieutenant Mark Hare (XZ997) took off at 1545Z to make a rocket attack on Argentine troops near Mount Kent, while Squadron Leader Peter Harris made an unsuccessful search for radar sites that had been reported to the north of Stanley. Replacement Harrier GR3s left the UK on the 29th on the long delivery flight to Ascension Island. Five aircraft flew from Wittering to St Mawgan on the 28th and four of them (XV778, XW767, XZ133 and XZ992) left for Ascension Island the next day. Two more aircraft (XV762 and XW924) left St Mawgan on the 30th so by the end of that day there were nine Harriers at Wideawake airfield (three were already there on air defence duties) ready for the next stage of the journey to the Task Force. Needless to say the Harriers had to make extensive use of the Victor tankers during their long overwater flights. A Nimrod MR2 (XV249) flew from Dakar to provide SAR support if needed by the Harriers.

More helicopters deployed ashore to the Falklands during the 29th when the *Atlantic Causeway* arrived in the TEZ with her load of 28 helicopters. While still some distance away from the Falklands, four of the eight Sea King HAS2As from 825 Squadron flew ashore from the container ship on the 29th to set up the squadron's FOB at San Carlos. The flight took four hours to complete and

the helicopters had to land on the aircraft carriers to refuel, arriving ashore at dusk. The helicopters would be a most welcome addition to the overworked Sea King HC4s of 846 Squadron and the handful of Wessex HU5s belonging to 845 Squadron. 846 Squadron was very busy during the 29th moving up troops, stores and ammunition for 3 PARA and 45 Commando as they advanced and secured their positions at Douglas and Teal Inlet. The four PNG-equipped Sea King HC4s that had been operating from *Intrepid* with the Special Forces, finally moved ashore on the 29th. Their FOB was a small river gully about one and a half miles north of the Ajax Bay refrigeration plant and it was soon named 'Pollock's Passage' after Lieutenant Commander W A Pollock, 846 Squadron's Senior Pilot. The PNG Sea Kings were tasked with moving men of 42 Commando from Port San Carlos to Mount Kent as the SAS found the Argentine positions there largely empty, but heavy snow showers made the operation impossible.

One of the Scouts of '5' Flight (656) 3 CBAS was involved in a dramatic rescue in the early morning of the 29th. At 0200Z Lieutenant J Young of 'B' Company, 2 PARA was badly wounded close to the Argentine lines. Captain J G Greenhalgh and his crew of Sergeant R J Walker and Lance Corporal J Gammon flew Scout AH1 XT649 up to the front line in total darkness and extremely cold temperatures. There they located Captain Young, strapped him to a stretcher and flew him back to the surgical team at the

Three 825 Squadron Sea King HAS2As sit at their Eagle Base at San Carlos, waiting for their next tasking. The helicopter aircrew and ground crew must have felt very exposed to air attack in such open positions. Wg Cdr P Lyall

Ajax Bay field hospital to make a tricky night landing, thereby saving his life, for which Captain Greenhalgh was awarded the DFC.

The frigate *Minerva* entered San Carlos Water on the 29th to replace the damaged *Argonaut* on air defence duties. *Argonaut* was inspected when she rendezvoused with the *Stena Seaspread* in the TRALA, but she was found to be too badly damaged to be repaired at sea and so was dispatched back to the UK on 5th June, exchanging her Sea Skua-equipped Lynx HAS2 (XZ233) for *Cardiff*'s non-Sea Skua helicopter (XZ254) before departing. *Avenger* borrowed Lynx HAS2 XZ247 from *Ambuscade* during the day to insert SBS teams at Volunteer Bay just north of Berkeley Sound. RFA *Tidepool* left the Carrier Battle Group on the 29th and set sail for San Carlos Water carrying two Sea King HAS5s (XZ920 and XZ921) of 820 Squadron from *Invincible* to conduct ASW sweeps for the ship while on its way to the Falklands.

The three naval hospital ships that operated in the Red Cross Box each had a Wasp embarked. However, *Herald*'s Wasp HAS1 (XT794) had been unserviceable since 13th May and it had to borrow parts from *Hecla*'s helicopter (XT420) to enable it to become operational again. *Hecla* was sailing to

Montevideo in Uruguay with casualties for repatriation and so did not require its Wasp for the journey. The Wasps were used to transfer medical stores, supplies and casualties between ships and from the shore. The *Uganda*, although the largest vessel used as hospital ship, did not have a helicopter embarked, but it did have a helicopter landing pad fitted before the ship departed the UK.

30th May (Sunday) –
2 Escuadrilla's Last Mission
The day started off badly for the Argentine forces on the Falklands with the loss of the last surviving Puma (AE-508) of CAB601. Several helicopters, presumably UH-1Hs as well as the Puma, were evacuating troops from the Mount Kent area soon after dawn when the Puma was shot down by a SAM. The helicopter was carrying several men of a Gendarmeria Nacional unit that had been deployed to the islands and came down near Murrell Bridge sometime between 1200Z and 1300Z. Six of the passengers were killed, although the crew survived. Argentine reports are vague about the incident and simply refer to the helicopter being brought down by a 'British missile'. Curiously, although there were certainly British troops in the area at the time, no British unit has claimed the destruction of the Puma and it is possible that it was another victim of Argentine 'friendly fire'.

The four remaining Harrier GR3s of 1 Squadron were very busy on the 30th, which turned out to be a day of mixed fortunes for the squadron. Early in the morning (1150Z), two pairs of aircraft were dispatched to the Stanley area to attack Argentine positions on Mount Kent, Mount Round and Mount Low. The next raid, which began at 1435Z, was momentous as it was the first time that the Harriers carried the Paveway LGB during the conflict. All four aircraft took part in the mission to the Stanley area and the raid was flown by two pairs consisting of Squadron Leader Peter Harris (XZ989) and Flight Lieutenant Tony Harper (XZ997), with Squadron Leader Jerry Pook (XZ963) and Flight Lieutenant John Rochfort (XV789). Only XZ989 and XZ997 carried the LGBs, while the other two aircraft carried 2-inch rocket pods and were tasked with searching for Argentine artillery that had been spotted near Mount Wall to the west of Stanley.

In the event the inauguration of the LGBs in combat was something of an anti-climax as there was no ground-based FAC yet available to mark the target, so the Harriers' laser rangefinder was used but without any real success. The target was Stanley's runway and the aircraft made a 60-degree dive from 35,000ft but the results could not be seen. Even worse was to follow.

Jerry Pook and John Rochfort's mission was changed en route to look for helicopters on the ground closer to Stanley, instead of artillery on Mount Wall. As they flew over a road they came under small arms fire from Argentine troops. Jerry Pook felt a hit but everything appeared normal so he continued. Pook and Rochfort did not find any helicopters but they did spot an artillery battery which they attacked with rockets. As they left the target area Pook's aircraft was seen to be streaming fuel. Once clear of land the pair climbed to 25,000ft. Pook's aircraft still had 4,000lb of fuel left, which was enough to reach the aircraft carrier. However, the fuel leak became much worse so Pook jettisoned his rocket pods and empty wing tanks in an attempt to lighten the aircraft. Unfortunately, it soon became all too obvious that the Harrier would not be able to reach the aircraft carrier.

As the last of the fuel was used up and the engine began to wind down, Jerry Pook ejected at 10,000ft, still about 30 miles away from *Hermes* and about 15 minutes after his aircraft was hit. Pook had been unable to report his problem as his radio had partially failed soon after take-off but John Rochfort had seen Pook's Harrier streaming fuel, flew alongside him and alerted *Hermes*. Immediately upon hearing of the likelihood of an ejection *Hermes* had dispatched a Sea King HAS5 (XZ571) of 826 Squadron to rescue the downed pilot.

Jerry Pook landed in the cold sea in a force 5 wind which had whipped up waves to 15ft in height. He got into his life raft with some difficulty and was picked up within 10 minutes of ejecting. The Sea King was piloted by Sub Lieutenant K B Sutton who had been guided towards the downed pilot by *Exeter*'s Lynx which was returning from an ESM mission at the time and actually saw Jerry Pook parachute into the sea.

The last 1 Squadron mission of the 30th was flown by Wing Commander Squire and Flight Lieutenant Hare who took off at 1750Z to attack the troops who had shot at Jerry Pook and John Rochfort. However, the troops had moved on by the time the Harriers arrived so the pair attacked dug-in positions on the northern slopes of Mount Kent instead.

Jerry Pook was not the only 1 Squadron pilot to be rescued on the 30th following an ejection. Squadron Leader Bob Iveson had successfully evaded capture since being shot down near Paragon House on the 27th. Although he had found a deserted farmhouse, he spent about 60 hours living rough as he thought that Argentine troops might search the house if they were looking for him. He was cut about the face and his vision was temporarily impaired, and he was also suffering from back pain as a

result of an injury sustained when he ejected. During his three days in the wilderness, he had been seen by some of the islanders who were later liberated when 2 PARA recovered the settlement of Goose Green. With the information that Iveson was somewhere in the vicinity but probably unaware that the area was now in British hands, 3 CBAS sent Gazelle AH1 XX380 flown by Lieutenant W L Scott and Sergeant K Priest, to search isolated farmhouses and other buildings for the pilot. Bob Iveson was eventually found hiding in Paragon House, about seven miles northwest of Goose Green, and was soon flown back to San Carlos and arrived on board *Hermes* just a few minutes before Jerry Pook was brought back. For his successful evasion under most difficult conditions, Squadron Leader Bob Iveson was awarded the RAF Escaping Society Trophy for 1982.

800 Squadron mounted another toss-bombing raid on Stanley airport when Lieutenant Commander Neill Thomas (XZ500) and Flight Lieutenant Ted Ball (XZ496) took off from *Hermes* at 1717Z, just a few minutes before the Carrier Battle Group went to Air Raid Warning Red when two Super Etendards were detected.

Following the debacle of the failed joint raid that had been hastily arranged for the 29th, Argentine Air Force and Navy planners got together to work out a more feasible mission for the 30th. The Carrier Battle Group had approached closer to the Falklands than normal to cover the approach of the transports that were bringing in the 5th Infantry Brigade. The two Super Etendards, to be flown by Capitan de Corbeta Alejandro Francisco (0752/3-A-202) and Teniente de Navio Luis Antonio Collavino (0755/3-A-205), would lead four A-4Cs from Grupo 4 to the target. As soon as Francisco launched the final Exocet, the Super Etendards would turn away, leaving the Skyhawks to follow the sea-skimming missile and attack the ships themselves.

At about 1530Z the Super Etendards took off from Rio Grande, followed five minutes later by the four Skyhawks. Climbing to 12,000ft initially the aircraft rendezvoused with two KC-130H tankers captained by Vicecomodoros J L Litrenta and R Noe some 50 minutes after take-off and made the first refuelling. The tankers flew with the formation for 190 miles, giving each aircraft a final top-up before turning back. During the long outbound leg the KC-130Hs and the accompanying fighter-bombers stayed well south of the Falklands but could have been visible to British radars, so the Argentine aircrew kept a constant lookout for Sea Harriers. At one point, before the actual rendezvous with the jets, the Hercules started to make vapour trails and had to descend to become less visible.

After refuelling, the six attack aircraft descended to low level under a low cloud ceiling with rain showers. However, the Super Etendards were detected on British radars at 1645Z when they made their first pop-up and radar sweep, although at first the British radar operators thought that they might be looking at a false radar return. After the Super Etendards popped up for the second time to confirm the position of the Task Force, the radar operator on board *Exeter* realised that an attack was indeed under way and chaff and decoys were launched and helicopters scrambled to try to jam the Exocet's homing head. Capitan Francisco launched the Exocet at about 1732Z, some 24 miles away from the target. The missile soon outdistanced the following Skyhawks as the two Super Etendards turned back to return to Rio Grande.

There is some confusion as to the exact target of the final air-launched Exocet. From available evidence it would appear that *Exeter* was the most likely target, despite persistent Argentine claims that not only was *Invincible* the target, but that the missile actually hit the carrier! *Cardiff* and *Exeter* were situated about 20 miles west of the Carrier Battle Group as radar pickets and *Avenger* was about 10 miles south of *Exeter*, heading towards East Falklands for a shore bombardment session. *Invincible* was at least 40 miles away from the Super Etendard when it launched the Exocet and was therefore out of range.

Whatever the identity of the Exocet's intended victim, the missile failed to hit anything and fell harmlessly into the sea between *Exeter* and *Avenger*, probably as a result of being deflected off course by chaff and then running out of fuel, although *Exeter* fired Sea Darts and *Avenger* fired her 4.5-inch gun at the missile as well. A pair of 801 Squadron Sea Harriers was sent to intercept the Super Etendards but the Argentine aircraft accelerated away and soon outdistanced the British aircraft. To add to the confusion, two 820 Squadron Sea Kings detached to provide ASW protection to the *Tidepool* as she arrived in the AOA landed back on *Invincible* just as the Exocet attack was taking place.

The Argentine claim to have hit *Invincible* appears to stem from the evidence provided by the surviving Skyhawk pilots who attacked a 'burning warship'. The Skyhawk flight was led by Primer Teniente Jose Vazquez (C-301) and consisted of Primer Tenientes Ernesto Ureta, Omar Castillo and Alferez Isaac, each of whose aircraft carried two 500lb bombs. Vazquez soon spotted a warship on the horizon, apparently with smoke coming from her hull (the ship was actually making smoke as it was travelling at speed). The 'burning' ship was not the aircraft carrier *Invincible*, but the much

smaller frigate *Avenger*. What the Skyhawk pilots could not see at that moment was *Exeter*, some 10 miles to the northwest of *Avenger*. Using her new Type 22 radar, *Exeter* fired a Sea Dart at the Exocet but believed it to have missed. *Avenger* then started firing her 4.5-inch gun at the flight of Skyhawks, which were misidentified as Super Etendards. When the Skyhawks were within nine miles of *Avenger*, *Exeter*'s second Sea Dart missile suddenly hit the leading aircraft of Jose Vazquez. The Skyhawk's port wing was blown off and the aircraft exploded, killing the flight leader instantly.

Although shocked by the explosion of their leader's aircraft the remaining three pilots continued towards *Avenger*. However, the horrifying spectacle of a disintegrating Skyhawk was repeated when the formation was just two miles from *Avenger*, as *Exeter*'s third Sea Dart slammed into Castillo's aircraft (C-310). Ureta and Isaac bravely continued with their bomb run but despite overflying the frigate, their bombs missed, causing no damage to *Avenger*. The two Skyhawks departed the area as fast as they could go and headed southwest. Understandably, both pilots were badly shaken by their experience and had difficulty refuelling from the tankers until they calmed down enough to get their probes into the tankers' drogue baskets. The two KC-130Hs landed back at base in very poor visibility after an eight-hour flight in support of the mission.

Ureta and Isaac were convinced that they had hit and damaged *Invincible* and were treated to a hero's welcome when they returned to Rio Grande and later to their own base at San Julian. One Skyhawk (C-321) was even painted with the silhouette of the aircraft carrier and the date 30.5.82, despite the fact that *Invincible* was still afloat and undamaged! In reality, the Skyhawks never came within visual distance of the main force of the Carrier Battle Group, including *Hermes* and *Invincible*, which was 20 miles further north of *Exeter*.

Following the Super Etendard/Skyhawk attack on the Task Force, normal operations quickly resumed on board the aircraft carriers and two Sea Harriers were dispatched from *Hermes* at 1915Z on a photographic reconnaissance mission to East Falkland. Lieutenant Commander Rod Fredericksen (XZ499) and Lieutenant Clive Morrell (ZA176) returned to *Hermes* at 2005Z after an uneventful mission.

While the drama of the attack on the Task Force was unfolding at sea, the momentum of the ground war continued to be supported by British helicopters ashore. Although the weather at sea was poor for much of the 30th, the weather on the Falklands was reasonable and permitted 846

Squadron to move troops and equipment to forward positions throughout the day. Sea Kings moved forward staff of 3 Commando Brigade from San Carlos to Teal Inlet. Three PNG-equipped Sea King HC4s completed the move of 'K' Company, 42 Commando to Mount Kent during the late evening to take over the positions occupied by the SAS. The Sea Kings were assisted by the 18 Squadron Chinook HC1 which flew in 22 troops and three 105mm field guns – two of the guns being carried internally and one underslung – in a single flight. The heavily laden helicopter sank in the peaty ground as it touched down and the pilot had to lift off and keep power applied to keep it from sinking too deeply as the rear ramp was lowered. The unloading proceeded in the midst of a fire-fight between the SAS troops and an Argentine patrol.

On the return flight to the FOB at Port San Carlos the Chinook, flown by Squadron Leader Dick Langworthy and Flight Lieutenant Andy Lawless, both using night-vision goggles, encountered a snow storm that temporarily made the goggles useless. In the few seconds that their vision was impaired the Chinook hit the surface of a creek near Estancia House. The helicopter skimmed the water for about ten seconds before the pilots could raise the nose and climb away having caused a huge amount of spray, some of which was sucked into the engine intakes causing a temporary loss of power. Despite this very narrow escape the Chinook was little damaged and was flown back to the FOB at a higher altitude. Unable to contact anyone by radio, Dick Langworthy put out an emergency call and switched on the helicopter's navigation lights as it entered the missile engagement zone around San Carlos. Fortunately, the radio messages had been picked up and the Rapier batteries and Blowpipe operators held their fire as the helicopter landed at Port San Carlos with a much-relieved crew!

Fearless re-entered San Carlos Water with Major General Moore and an advance party of the 5th Infantry Brigade on board. Major General Moore and his headquarters staff remained on board *Fearless* until a Tactical Headquarters came ashore on 10th June. The ship also carried Wessex HU5 XT765, which disembarked to 845 Squadron's FOB at Port San Carlos. Two more 845 Squadron helicopters arrived at the FOB on or around this date when 'D' Flight's XT451 and XT460 disembarked from *Intrepid*. Originally intended as replacements, both Wessex were useful additions following the loss of the helicopters on board the *Atlantic Conveyor*.

Another move of helicopters involved the Gazelle AH1s of 'M' Flight 3 CBAS, which moved to Teal Inlet on the 30th in support of 3 PARA and 45 Commando, which had yomped the 50 miles from San Carlos. Helicopters from all of 3 CBAS's flights had assisted in moving the troops and their equipment forward to Teal during the day. On the same day troops of 42 Commando and 105mm ammunition were flown forward to secure positions on Mount Kent and Mount Challenger that had been taken by SAS patrols inserted a few days earlier.

31st May (Monday)
The last day of May started with two early morning bombing raids on the Falklands, one British and one Argentine. The first raid took place at 0530Z when a Grupo 2 Canberra B62 dropped four 1,000lb bombs from 600ft on 846 Squadron's FOB at Fern Valley Creek. The damage was light with just a tent and the telephone exchange destroyed but Lieutenant Commander R C Harden, the Air Engineering Officer, was wounded and was flown to Ajax Bay and then to the SS *Uganda* for medical treatment. Fortunately four Sea Kings had embarked on board *Fearless* for the night when had she re-entered San Carlos Water on the 30th. However, as a result of the raid, some of the helicopters based in the San Carlos and Port San Carlos area were subsequently dispersed to other sites. Two Canberra B62s had set out on the raid but the pilot of B-101 lost the other aircraft (B-108) and returned to base without attacking.

Following the cancellation of the RAF's first Vulcan anti-radar mission on the night of the 28th, 'Black Buck 5' was mounted just before midnight on the 30th. Like the earlier mission, the primary objective was the Westinghouse AN/TPS-43F radar at Stanley, which was thought to be responsible for giving Argentine aircraft early warning of the approach of Sea Harriers. Once again Squadron Leader Neil McDougall captained his crew in XM597 and flew at high level until some 200 miles distant from the Falklands. He then let down to 300ft to avoid being picked up on radar before climbing again to 16,000ft 20 miles from the islands. As the Vulcan approached the Falklands a Sea Harrier strike on Stanley airport was arranged to take place in an attempt to keep the Argentine radars on the air and occupied. Two aircraft from 801 Squadron toss-bombed the airfield, followed by another pair of Sea Harriers which repeated the raid about an hour later.

As the Vulcan climbed its RWR picked up transmissions from the TPS-43F radar, but the signal was soon lost as the radar signal strength was reduced in an attempt to trick the Vulcan crew into thinking the radar was further away than it was, thereby luring them towards the AAA defences around Stanley. Neil McDougall spent the next 40 minutes circling off the coast as his crew tried to pick up the enemy radar signal again. Eventually a signal was detected and the target was pinpointed as the aircraft launched its two Shrikes at 0845Z. The radar went off the air abruptly as the missiles impacted, one of them hitting the ground just 30-45ft away from the radar aerial and causing minor damage.

Although it seemed to be a successful mission at the time to the Vulcan crew, in fact the TPS-43F was operational again 24 hours later after repairs to the aerial. A solid earth revetment was built around the radar to protect the operators from further attack. However, the mission had the effect of reducing the amount of time the Argentines left the radar switched on, thereby reducing its effectiveness. For the anti-radar attacks the Vulcans carried an extra 16,000lb of fuel in auxiliary tanks fitted in the bomb bay, and so they required only four en route in-flight refuellings from the Victor K2 tankers rather than the six needed on the earlier bombing missions.

At 1130Z, just after dawn, 1 Squadron attacked Stanley airport with its three remaining Harriers, each of which carried different ordnance; Squadron Leader Peter Harris (XZ989) carried 1,000lb bombs, Flight Lieutenant Tony Harper (XV789) carried LGBs, and Flight Lieutenant John Rochfort (XZ997) carried 2-inch rocket pods. Once again, an attempt to steer the LGBs using the laser rangefinder failed and the results were disappointing. The trio made a low-level reconnaissance to the east of Stanley on their way back to the aircraft carrier.

At 1430Z an 801 Squadron CAP returned to *Invincible* with yet another report of

swept-wing aircraft being seen at Stanley airport. Such reports were not uncommon but there is no evidence that Super Etendards or any other Argentine jet aircraft other than the MB-339As were ever present at Stanley. However, such was the threat that the Super Etendards might have deployed to Stanley (the Task Force commander thought that 2 Escuadrilla had fired its last Exocet on the 30th but Argentina was still attempting to acquire more missiles on the black market) that each report had to be taken seriously.

A raid was hurriedly put together consisting of two 1 Squadron Harriers with 800 Squadron Sea Harriers providing defence suppression. A pair of 801 Squadron Sea Harriers returning from a CAP were directed to fly over Stanley to see if there were any jets on the airfield and when this was confirmed a raid was quickly mounted. Two Harrier GR3s (Wing Commander Peter Squire in XV789 and Flight Lieutenant Mark Hare in XZ997) and two Sea Harriers (Lieutenant Bill Covington in XZ496 and Lieutenant Commander Mike Blissett in XZ500) took off from *Hermes* at 1452Z. The aircraft attacked the airfield with rockets and bombs but a subsequent photographic reconnaissance sortie confirmed that the aircraft at Stanley were indeed MB-339As and that none had been significantly damaged during the attack. Both Harriers returned from the raid on Stanley having received considerable battle damage, with the result that 1 Squadron had just one airworthy aircraft (XZ989) in service for a day or two. One of the Harriers (XV789) needed an engine change and the only available Pegasus 103 had to be airlifted by helicopter from *Intrepid*, where it had been stored, to *Hermes*. The only other Pegasus 103 had been lost on the *Atlantic Conveyor*. Due to the immense difficulties of such a complicated maintenance procedure for an RAF aircraft on board a Royal Navy aircraft carrier, the engine change took 60 hours to complete.

The empty pylons for the Shrike anti-radar missiles can just be seen under the starboard wing of Vulcan B2 XM597. The ducting and cabling for the pylons was originally intended for the Skybolt nuclear missile that was cancelled before it entered service. MoD

The four Super Etendards of 2 Escuadrilla returned to Comandante Espora a few days after launching their last Exocet and took no further active part in the conflict, although they started training for conventional attack operations. Argentina was still hopeful of obtaining a further batch of Exocets and 2 Escuadrilla practised night low-level strikes from 2nd June until the end of the conflict in the hope of making more devastating raids on the Task Force.

At 1647Z Squadron Leader Peter Harris took off in the only available Harrier GR3 accompanied by three 800 Squadron Sea Harriers flown by Lieutenant Commander Rod Fredericksen (XZ460), Lieutenant Andy McHarg (XZ455), and Lieutenant Clive Morrell (ZA191). This raid was something of an experiment as Clive Morrell's Sea Harrier carried LGBs for which Peter Harris tried to illuminate a target with the Harrier GR3's laser rangefinder. Unfortunately, the original target, near Mount Usborne, was found to be too close to British troop positions to attempt the experiment so another target was selected near Stanley. However, the laser rangefinder was found to be incompatible with the Paveway bomb and so could not achieve a lock. The experiment was not repeated.

Apart from the early morning Canberra raid, the only Argentine air operation of note was a daring rescue mission flown by two CANA Sea Kings from the mainland to Pebble Island. Following the successful rescue of several men from Pebble Island by an Argentine Air Force Twin Otter on 28/29th May, the CANA decided to do the same. Two Sea Kings were stripped of unnecessary equipment and fitted with long-range fuel tanks in the fuselage and one was fitted with VLF Omega navigation equipment. The Sea Kings (0677 and 0678 of 2 Escuadrilla de Helicopteros) took off from Rio Grande at 1730Z on the 31st on the 350-mile overwater flight. For the first 120 miles the helicopters were accompanied by a Prefectura Naval Puma that helped to calibrate their VLF Omega equipment.

After a three-hour flight at low level in extreme cold and darkness, the two helicopters landed at Pebble Island at 2036Z to pick up 10 CANA personnel. As the Sea Kings departed Pebble Island at 2115Z, the Omega failed, leaving the crew to navigate by dead reckoning and map reading. As the night was dark and fog covered much of the ground and the NVGs which the pilots used were of limited use, the flight was extremely difficult and dangerous. The two helicopters, flown by Capitan de Corbeta Norberto Barro and Teniente de Navio Guillermo Iglesias, arrived safely back at Rio Grande at 0055Z on 1st June. This mission was to have an unexpected result the following day when Pebble Island was attacked because the British thought that the Sea Kings might be equipped with Exocet missiles.

The movement of British troops, artillery and supplies to Teal Inlet continued throughout the 31st with 846 Squadron's Sea King HC4s being heavily involved. The 3 Commando Brigade headquarters moved to Teal Inlet on the 31st and 'B' Flight 3 CBAS joined 'M' Flight there the same day. As night wore on, 846 Squadron's PNG-equipped helicopters moved men of 42 Commando and half a battery of artillery to Mount Kent as the British assault on the Argentine positions continued. A group of Argentine Special Forces from Compania de Comandos 602 had been spotted at Top Malo House near Mount Simon, about five miles south of Teal Inlet. Sea King HC4 ZA291 flew 19 men of the Royal Marine Mountain and Arctic Warfare Cadre to the vicinity. In the ensuing fighting on 1st June all the Argentine troops were killed or captured. The first battalions of the 5th Infantry Brigade started coming ashore at San Carlos on the night of the 31st as 45 Commando moved up from Douglas to Teal Inlet and 3 PARA moved to Malo Bridge.

There was little change among the ships of the Task Force on the 31st. *Active* and *Avenger* (the latter ship fresh from her encounter with the Super Etendard/Skyhawk raid the previous day) entered San Carlos Water. The Lynx from both *Arrow* and *Minerva* were sent off to locate the Argentine ship, the *Bahia Paraiso*, which had played a prominent part in the invasion of South Georgia but which had since been converted to a hospital ship. There was some suspicion that the *Bahia Paraiso* was not just engaged in medical duties and, as was permissible under international law, the Royal Navy wanted to board and inspect the vessel. When the ship was found *Arrow*'s Lynx remained airborne to provide a radio link with the Carrier Battle Group while *Minerva*'s Lynx landed on to inspect her. However, nothing suspicious was found and so both of the helicopters returned to their respective ships. The *Bahia Paraiso* carried an Argentine Army Puma painted overall white with a large Red Cross on each side of the fuselage.

The container ship *Contender Bezant* arrived at Ascension Island on the 31st from the UK. On board were three Chinook HC1s (ZA705, ZA713 and ZA715), two Wasp HAS1s (XS562 and XT427), and a single Sea King HAS2A (XZ579). While at Ascension the ship loaded four Harrier GR3s (XV762, XW767, XW924 and XZ129) that had flown in from the UK, two Gazelle AH1s (XW893 and XX444) and a Chinook HC1 (ZA707), the latter having been employed on HDS tasks there since 5th May.

1st June (Tuesday) –
The Death of a Hercules
In the early hours of 1st June, Grupo 2 made its first bombing raid on the British forces that were now fully in occupation of the Mount Kent area. Three Canberras, led by Capitan Garcia Puebla in B-109, took off from Rio Gallegos at 0700Z and climbed to 25,000ft for the flight to the Falklands. However, one of the aircraft had to return to base with a mechanical problem and before the remaining two aircraft started their descent to low level, they were detected by the frigate *Minerva*. At 0739Z, Lieutenant Andy McHarg (in ZA177) was scrambled from *Hermes* and vectored towards what was thought to be a flight of four aircraft heading towards East Falkland

At least one Argentine Army Puma was painted white overall and used as an ambulance helicopter on board the Bahia Paraiso. *It was the only Argentine Army Puma to visit the Falklands and survive the conflict.*
MoD

from the southwest. However, the two Canberras descended to 160ft and made their bombing attack on the British positions, narrowly missing the summit of Mount Kent in the process. The Argentine radar then warned the Canberra crews of the approaching Sea Harrier so Puebla and his wingman dropped their empty wing-tip fuel tanks and fired off chaff as they made their getaway.

By the time McHarg was getting close to the Canberras he was reaching the limit of his fuel (*Hermes* was on the extreme edge of the TEZ at the time) and he had to break away and head back to the aircraft carrier without engaging, although he did get close enough to see them drop their tanks and fire chaff. Unaware that the Sea Harrier had given up the chase the Canberras continued at maximum speed for some time and exceeded the airframe limits during their escape.

Since late May Argentine Air Force C-130 Hercules had been flying maritime reconnaissance flights to locate targets for strike aircraft. The CANA's SP-2H Neptunes had been retired on 21st May as they were in too poor a shape to continue so the Hercules was the only viable alternative at the time. There were several instances when C-130s were thought to have provided targeting information to strike aircraft as they were en route to the Falklands. The procedure for the C-130 reconnaissance flights was highly risky, considering the air defence environment in which they were forced to operate. The C-130 would fly at low level until it reached a point just 16 miles north of San Carlos Water, usually at dawn. At this point the aircraft would climb rapidly to 10,000ft and conduct a quick radar sweep of the area to plot British ships in the vicinity. After a maximum of 90 seconds, the aircraft would descend rapidly back to low level and then, if nothing had been found at this stage, fly a zigzag course to the north, climbing every 34 miles to repeat the radar search. The radar search would be made five times during each sortie before departing for home.

On the 1st a C-130E (TC-63) took off from Comodoro Rivadavia on a reconnaissance flight with the flight crew of Capitan Ruben Mertel, Capitan Carlos Krause and Vicecomodoro Hugo Meisner and four other crewmembers. The Hercules climbed to start its first radar sweep north of Pebble Island almost immediately it was detected by *Minerva* in San Carlos Water. At that point two Sea Harriers of 801 Squadron flown by Lieutenant Commander 'Sharkey' Ward (in XZ451) and Lieutenant Steve Thomas, had just finished a CAP near Port Howard and were climbing to high altitude to return to the ship. They were quickly diverted towards the enemy aircraft, 40 miles to the northwest of them, although they had little fuel to spare. The Sea Harriers quickly detected the target on their Blue Fox radars and intercepted the Hercules as it sped along at low level under a cloud base, heading towards the mainland, possibly after being warned of the Sea Harriers' approach by Stanley radar.

Steve Thomas remained above the cloud layer at 3,000ft in case the enemy aircraft climbed through the cloud while 'Sharkey' Ward descended through the cloud to find that the enemy aircraft was a Hercules and was less than six miles ahead, flying flat out at 200ft. Calling for Steve Thomas to join him, 'Sharkey' Ward then fired his first Sidewinder at the Hercules at extreme range at 1346Z. The first missile fell just short but the second one hit the starboard wing between the engines, causing a fire. The Hercules continued to fly until Ward made a cannon attack on the aircraft, putting all 240 rounds of his 30mm ammunition into the aircraft's tail and rear fuselage. The Hercules suddenly banked to the right and dived into the sea, about 50 miles north of Pebble Island.

Ward and Thomas could not linger to see if anyone had survived as they were getting short of fuel so they returned to *Invincible*. *Fearless* and *Intrepid* had cleared their decks of helicopters in case the Sea Harriers had to divert to them but a tailwind enabled both aircraft to reach *Invincible* comfortably. All seven men on the Hercules were killed in the crash and no more C-130 reconnaissance sorties were attempted by Grupo 1 after this tragedy.

At 1700Z Wing Commander Peter Squire took off from *Hermes* in XZ989, 1 Squadron's sole remaining serviceable Harrier GR3, on a reconnaissance flight between Bluff Cove and Goose Green escorted by Flight Lieutenant Ted Ball of 800 Squadron in Sea Harrier XZ457. The pair arrived back on *Hermes* at 1810Z after attacking a suspected radar position on Mount Usborne.

While the aircraft were away 1 Squadron was reinforced by the arrival of two new aircraft. Flight Lieutenant Mike Beech (XV778) and Flight Lieutenant Murdo MacLeod (XZ133) had taken off from Ascension Island 8 hours and 20 minutes earlier and refuelled numerous times from four Victors on the 3,900-mile flight to the aircraft carrier. If either of the aircraft had a problem their only hope of a landing was the deck of the helicopter ship *Engadine*, which was en route from Ascension Island to the Falklands. However, the only minor problem encountered was that one of the Victors had to complete its sortie on three engines after one of its Conways had to be shut down. The Harrier pilots suffered from heat stress as they were wearing full cold-weather immersion suits inside their warm cockpits in case of a ditching, but the main problem was boredom and muscle cramp on the long flight.

The two Harriers were escorted the last 200 miles by Flight Lieutenant John Leeming of 800 Squadron who guided them to the *Hermes*. The Harriers touched down on the carrier at 1732Z and increased the number of available Harriers by 300 per cent. Neither Mike Beech nor Murdo MacLeod had ever landed a Harrier on a ship's deck before this mission, although Murdo MacLeod did have carrier experience as he had flown Phantoms on an exchange posting with 892 Squadron and flew the last Phantom FG1 ever to be launched from HMS *Ark Royal* in 1978. This impressive demonstration of 1 Squadron's long-range deployment capability was to be repeated a week later by two more aircraft.

A few minutes after the RAF Harriers landed on board *Hermes*, the Royal Navy lost one of its Sea Harriers. Flight Lieutenant Ian Mortimer was flying XZ456 on an armed reconnaissance to the south of Stanley when his aircraft was hit by a Roland SAM. Mortimer's wingman had returned to the aircraft carrier with a defective AIM-9 system so Mortimer was alone at 10,000ft looking for any signs of aircraft movement on Stanley airport, four miles in the distance, when he noticed a flash as the Roland was launched. Although he estimated that the missile could not reach his altitude, he put the Sea Harrier into a steep climb and thought that he had safely outdistanced the Roland until an explosion in the aircraft's rear fuselage indicated otherwise. Ian Mortimer ejected before the aircraft broke up and he landed in the sea at 1750Z about five miles east of Stanley airport. He quickly climbed into his dinghy and made two brief voice transmissions on his survival radio in the hope that British aircraft might hear him. In fact he had been heard by other Sea Harriers on CAP and they alerted *Invincible*, which dispatched several Sea King HAS5s of 820 Squadron to Mortimer's location.

Mortimer then spotted a Pucara and a Grupo 7 Chinook searching for him about five miles to the west, in the position that his aircraft had hit the sea. He reported the position of the enemy aircraft as they flew over him, but either the aircraft failed to spot him or they had been warned of other Sea Harriers in the area as they quickly returned to Stanley. Mortimer settled down to wait for the Royal Navy helicopters, but his wait turned out to be longer than he had expected because the Sea Kings could not locate him as he had turned off his radio and SARBE emergency location beacon in case the Argentines should locate him by his transmissions. After dark, *Exeter*'s Lynx joined in the search, but as it had been unable to pinpoint Mortimer's location before he went off the air, the Lynx was also looking in the wrong area and found nothing. However, an Argentine radio report was picked up saying that a parachute had been seen after the Sea Harrier was shot down so the search continued apace with fresh hope.

The presence of the two CANA Sea Kings on Pebble Island had been noticed and reported to the Task Force. There was an immediate concern that the helicopters might have been carrying Exocet missiles. The Task Force commander could take no chances and therefore ordered a reconnaissance of Pebble Island airstrip on the 1st. Lieutenant Commander Rod Fredericksen (XZ500) and Flight Lieutenant Dave Morgan (ZA193) of 800 Squadron took off from *Hermes* at 1816Z to take a look at Pebble Island. The pair was followed 30 minutes later by Lieutenant Commanders Dave Braithwaite (in XZ491) and Alisdair Craig (XZ495) of 801 Squadron with orders to strafe the helicopters if present.

Although the 800 Squadron pair reported no sign of the helicopters at Pebble Island, the 801 Squadron aircraft strafed the airstrip anyway. *Avenger* fired 273 rounds of high explosives and 20 starshells at Pebble Island during the night and her Lynx, which was airborne spotting for the ship's gun, came under fire from the shore. Another pair of 800 Squadron Sea Harriers flown by Lieutenant Commander Neill Thomas (XZ492) and Lieutenant Andy McHarg (ZA177) took off from *Hermes* at 1936Z but again found nothing of interest at Pebble Island. This was hardly surprising as the Sea Kings, which were merely evacuating stranded personnel, had spent less than an hour on the ground at Pebble Island the

previous evening. Even so, the ships entering or leaving Falkland Sound proceeded more cautiously as the threat from Exocet missiles was always taken very seriously.

The main task for the Sea King HC4s of 846 Squadron on the 1st was to move gun batteries together with ammunition and other supplies up to Teal Inlet and Mount Kent. As 846 Squadron was fully occupied with these tasks they were unable to assist the unloading of the transport vessels that arrived in San Carlos that day, so the ships had to be laboriously unloaded by small craft. However, at this stage of the conflict, there was thought to be little threat from Argentine air raids on the shipping in San Carlos Water so the extra time required for unloading was not critical. After dark, three of the PNG-equipped Sea Kings flew Special Forces troops onto Mount Vernet near Estancia House, just 14 miles west of Stanley. Following this task, all four PNG helicopters resupplied the troops of 41 Commando in position on Mount Kent and Mount Challenger.

A welcome arrival in San Carlos Water during the early hours of the 1st was the *Atlantic Causeway* with her cargo of helicopters and Rapier missiles. The loss of her sister ship, the *Atlantic Conveyor*, with her precious cargo of Chinook and Wessex helicopters had been keenly felt by the ground troops who had to foot march, or 'yomp', across much of East Falkland, rather than take a short helicopter flight. The *Atlantic Causeway* carried the bulk of 847 Squadron, comprised of 20 Wessex HU5s (the squadron's other four Wessex were on board the *Engadine*, still en route to the Falklands) and four Sea King HAS2As of 825 Squadron.

Although the *Engadine* had left the UK four days ahead of the *Atlantic Causeway*, the RFA stopped off at Gibraltar and arrived at Ascension Island three days behind the larger vessel. 847 Squadron had been able to fly training sorties from the *Atlantic Causeway* using two of its Wessex during the early stages of the long voyage south via Freetown and Ascension Island. Upon arrival in San Carlos Water 12 of the Wessex disembarked and set up base at the Port San Carlos FOB, alongside the Wessex of 845 Squadron. Two of 'D' Flight 845 Squadron's Wessex HU5s (XT451 and XT460) were transferred to 847 Squadron control when 847 Squadron arrived at the FOB. The 847 Squadron Wessex immediately set to work supporting the ground troops in their advance towards Stanley.

Also disembarked from the *Atlantic Causeway* on the 1st were the remaining four Sea King HAS2As of 825 Squadron, another four having been flown to San Carlos on the 29th while the ship was still some distance offshore. Another two 825 Squadron Sea Kings had temporarily transferred from the *Canberra* to the *Atlantic Causeway* on the 31st to assist in taking ashore the 1st/7th Gurkha Rifles. The newly arrived helicopters took over much of the logistical effort in the San Carlos area and moved about 800 Argentine prisoners from

The Cunard/ACL container ship Atlantic Causeway *was a sister ship of the ill-fated* Atlantic Conveyor *and is seen here unloading in San Carlos Water, probably on 1st June. A Sea King can just be seen on her forward spot and her rear ramp is lowered for unloading.* Wg Cdr P Lyall

Darwin and Goose Green to RFA *Sir Percivale*, as well as moving up artillery pieces and ammunition from San Carlos to the Mount Kent area. The latter task occupied six of 825's helicopters for three hours during the morning of the 1st. During the resupply operation three Sea Kings crossed a ridge between Mount Kent and Mount Challenger, flew too far to the east and came within about six miles of Stanley before the lead pilot realised the mistake and turned the formation around. Miraculously, although the helicopters flew near several Argentine positions, none were hit by ground fire.

Also unloaded from the *Atlantic Causeway* on the 1st were eight Rapier fire units of 63 Squadron, RAF Regiment. The Rapiers would replace the 12 fire units of 'T' Battery of 12 Air Defence Regiment in the San Carlos beachhead thereby allowing the Army Rapiers to move forward. Although the RAF Regiment's missile fire units had been loaded onto the *Atlantic Causeway* the squadron personnel had sailed on the *Queen Elizabeth II* but had then been split up at South Georgia so that some travelled on the *Norland* and some on the *Canberra*. The result was a slow start to their deployment at San Carlos.

Another arrival in San Carlos Water on the 1st was the *Baltic Ferry*. The three 656 Squadron Scout AH1s (XV130, XV139 and XW282) flew off to join the 656 Squadron Advanced Section near Head of the Bay House. The Advanced Section had been assigned to 3 CBAS control as '5' Flight (656) since 7th May but on the 1st the Flight reverted to 656 Squadron control once more, as 2 PARA, which '5' Flight had been supporting, reverted back to the control of the 5th Infantry Brigade.

During the day an RAF Hercules C1P (XV179) flew another long-range mission (these were code named 'Cadbury') from Ascension Island to make an airdrop to the frigate *Penelope* on the edge of the TEZ. As well as high-priority freight, a number of personnel also parachuted into the cold waters of the South Atlantic including Lieutenant Colonel D R Chaundler, the new commanding officer of 2 PARA, who replaced Lieutenant Colonel H Jones who had been killed at Goose Green.

2nd June (Wednesday)
The search for Sea Harrier pilot Flight Lieutenant Ian Mortimer continued through the night but it was not until 0230Z that he was spotted by a Sea King HAS5 (XZ574) of 820 Squadron flown by Lieutenant Commander K Dudley. Mortimer had switched off his SARBE transmitter and was only located by the helicopter crew spotting a small light fixed to the pilot's helmet. The rescue was a major triumph in that it was carried out under very difficult conditions 120 miles

from *Invincible* and right under the noses of the Argentine forces on the coast. After more than eight hours in a life raft Ian Mortimer was very glad to be on his way back to his carrier!

Bad weather restricted flying for much of the 2nd and there were no Argentine air attacks either on the Task Force or the troops on the Falklands. Sea Harrier CAPs were maintained over the islands to protect both the *Canberra* and *Norland* as they unloaded troops of the 5th Infantry Brigade in San Carlos Water. The Harrier GR3s of 1 Squadron managed to fly a mission during the morning when Squadron Leader Jerry Pook (XZ989) and Flight Lieutenant Murdo MacLeod (XZ133) used rockets to support troops on the ground. This was Jerry Pook's first mission since his successful ejection on the 30th and Murdo MacLeod's first mission since arriving from Ascension Island the previous day.

A more momentous event on the 2nd was the completion of a temporary airstrip for use by Harriers and Sea Harriers on a hill just to the west of Port San Carlos. For several days men of 11 and 59 Squadrons, Royal Engineers had been preparing a patch of ground near the settlement and laying by hand hundreds of sections of 10ft by 2ft aluminium planks to make a runway some 850ft in length. The *Stromness* had begun unloading 11,000 aluminium planks on the 22nd together with rubber fuel bladders and associated equipment, and on 1st June the *Atlantic Causeway* unloaded special VTOL pads to be used as hardstandings for the strip. The runway was built on a slight slope that was noticeable but didn't quite reach ski-jump proportions! A small metal pad was also constructed to allow vertical take-offs and landings and a parking area for up to four Harriers. There was a taxying loop at either end of the strip, although one of these loops was soon removed. The strip was originally intended to be longer but a large quantity of aluminium planks was lost when the *Atlantic Conveyor* was sunk. Aviation fuel was stored in floating rubberised bags that were moored offshore and the fuel pumped through a small pipeline that stretched to the airstrip. The commanding officer of the airstrip was Squadron Leader Sid Morris and the airstrip became known to 1 Squadron as 'Sid's Strip', but the Sea Harrier pilots who would come to use it christened it HMS '*Sheathbill*'.

The *Canberra* arrived in San Carlos Water on the 2nd to disembark the men of the two Guards battalions of the 5th Infantry Brigade, as well as the main party of 656 Squadron's personnel that the *Canberra* had received from the *Queen Elizabeth II* off South Georgia. As the *Canberra* arrived, so the *Atlantic Causeway* left for the TRALA,

taking with her the eight remaining Wessex HU5s of 847 Squadron to hold as a floating reserve. The two Sea Kings that transferred from *Canberra* to the *Atlantic Causeway* on 31st May, moved back again to *Canberra* as she entered San Carlos Water and assisted the unloading.

On the 2nd five of 656 Squadron's Scout AH1s assisted troops of 2 PARA to occupy Swan Inlet House midway between Goose Green and Fitzroy, on the coast. Two Scouts (XR628 and XT649) were fitted with SS-11 missiles while the other three (XV130, XV139 and XW282) provided support, each carrying four paratroopers. Each of the missile-equipped helicopters fired two SS-11s during the early stage of the assault but only one missile functioned correctly and scored a hit. In the event Swan Inlet House was found to be unoccupied, the Argentine troops having withdrawn from there some time earlier.

Under a low cloud ceiling during the afternoon of the 2nd, Chinook HC1 ZA718 was diverted from its resupply tasks and flew troops of 2 PARA from Goose Green to Fitzroy in a highly opportunistic move. The knowledge that Fitzroy was unoccupied and safe for helicopters to enter was obtained by the simple expedient of telephoning one of the residents there. When he had entered Swan Inlet House, Major John Crossland discovered that the civilian telephone line was still working and so he simply rang up a resident of Fitzroy to enquire about the disposition of Argentine troops!

Flown by Flight Lieutenant N J Grose and Flying Officer C Miller, the Chinook was packed with 81 fully armed troops on the first flight to Fitzroy Ridge and 75 on the second mission, both considerably more than was recommended. The Chinook was escorted by two Scouts of 656 Squadron, flown by Captain John Greenhalgh and Sergeant Dick Kalinski, who searched the area for enemy troops to confirm that it was safe for the Chinook to proceed. This bold move placed an advanced party of British troops within about ten miles of Stanley. From Fitzroy Ridge a Scout then flew a reconnaissance platoon to Bluff Cove, while other Scouts moved more troops of 2 PARA forward from Goose Green.

Herald's Wasp (XT794) and *Hydra*'s Wasp (XT432) were also busy on the 2nd but in a more peaceful role, both helicopters flying casevac missions to and from the Red Cross Box before *Hydra* set off on the four-day journey to Montevideo to offload a number of casualties. *Herald*'s Wasp also helped to search for possible survivors from the Argentine Air Force Hercules that had been shot down the previous day, but no survivors or bodies were ever found despite the search continuing into the following day.

The only ship movement of any consequence on the 2nd was *Alacrity*, which left the TEZ en route to Ascension Island for much-needed repairs to her main engine. As soon as *Hecla* arrived at Montevideo on the 2nd with a load of British and Argentine wounded a 10 Squadron VC10 C1 (XV108) collected the British and flew them home, arriving at Brize Norton on the 3rd. This was one of several such repatriation flights that were monitored by the International Red Cross, the aircraft on which carried the red cross markings that had first been used when flying Argentine POWs to Montevideo on 13th May.

3rd June (Thursday) – Flying Down to Rio

'Black Buck 6', a repeat of the previous Vulcan anti-radar mission, commenced on the night of the 2nd. Squadron Leader Neil McDougall and his crew again flew XM597 in search of the TPS-43F surveillance radar that was sited in Stanley town. Following the same mission profile as the earlier raid the Argentine radar operators again reduced their signal strength and, once more, Neil McDougall had to spend 40 minutes trying to find a radar signal and even overflew several of the known radar positions in an attempt to make them illuminate the aircraft. Poor visibility grounded a Sea Harrier strike designed to maintain the interest of the radar operators, so the Vulcan was on its own. Only after the Vulcan started a feint towards Stanley airport did a radar finally illuminate the aircraft as it started to descend, but it was an Argentine Army Skyguard anti-aircraft gun-control radar rather than the TPS-43F surveillance radar that the crew was after. Unable to waste more fuel on what could have been a fruitless search for the TPS-43F and now under fire from 35mm AAA, Flight Lieutenant Rod Trevaskus, the air electronic officer, fired two of his four Shrikes at the Skyguard radar, destroying the radar and killing four Argentine soldiers. Waiting for a few minutes to see if the TPS-43F came up, Neil McDougall was then forced to head north to rendezvous with a Victor tanker.

Vectored to the tanker by a Nimrod, XM597 started to take on fuel while still some 2,000 miles south of Ascension Island. Unfortunately, just as the refuelling started the Vulcan's probe broke off leaving it unable to take on any more fuel and without enough to reach Wideawake airfield. The Vulcan's navigators worked out that the nearest airfield they might stand a chance of reaching from their position was at Rio de Janeiro in Brazil. Neil McDougall had to climb the aircraft from 20,000ft to 40,000ft to burn fuel more economically and reach Rio. Not wanting to land in a neutral country carrying two American-supplied missiles, he attempted to fire them both off, but only one of them launched successfully. The crew meanwhile crammed all their classified documents and maps into a weighted bag and, once the aircraft was depressurised and the crew had donned oxygen masks, they opened the crew door and threw the bag out over the sea. A few more anxious moments were caused when the door refused to close properly during the first attempt.

Meanwhile Neil McDougall had told Wideawake of their predicament and hasty telephone calls were made by diplomats in the FCO to their counterparts in Brazil to smooth the arrival of an armed British military aircraft. Following an 'interesting' radio conversation with Brazilian air traffic control the Vulcan was cleared for a straight-in approach to Rio Galeao airport. To conserve fuel Neil McDougall remained at 20,000ft until just six miles from the airport and then made a spectacular steeply banked, spiral approach to touch down perfectly with just 2,000lb of fuel on board; not even enough for an overshoot and go-around!

The last remaining Shrike was made safe by the crew but the aircraft was impounded by the Brazilian authorities. The crew remained with their aircraft in Rio until 10th June when the Brazilians allowed the Vulcan to leave for Ascension Island, having first removed the Shrike. XM597 was fitted

with a new refuelling probe at Wideawake and flew back to Waddington on 13th June. Squadron Leader Neil McDougall was later awarded a well-earned DFC for his superb flying skills and his leadership in a very difficult situation.

The problem of recovering the Vulcan from Rio once diplomatic clearance for its departure had been granted caused problems for the RAF's logisticians. Wing Commander Nigel Arnold, then commanding the Technical Supply Flight at Waddington recalls:

'As a Pilot Officer serving a first tour at Waddington in 1982 life seemed very exciting, and never more so when, as the duty supply officer in the Ops Wg HQ on an otherwise quiet Saturday afternoon, a phone call from Strike Command duty supply officer (a squadron leader no less) directed that there was a need to ship a number of spares and other items to Rio in order to ensure the aircraft would be in a serviceable state and ready to depart at the first opportunity once given diplomatic clearance. Exactly what was required was not specified, but a phone call to the duty engineering officer (fortunately, a hugely experienced warrant officer) established the most likely requirement was the means to replenish engine oil and some associated seals. A quick expedition to the 101 Squadron stores rapidly demonstrated a flexible approach to equipment accounting that had not been taught on any supply course and resolved the question of what to send to Brazil; more problematic was how to send it there.

The all-knowing Strike Command duty supply officer had offered two solutions: a British Airways flight departing Heathrow for Rio that evening or a VARIG (Brazilian Airlines) flight the following morning. It was however made quite clear that the preferred solution was the British Airways flight, as it was believed that potential problems with customs were less likely, the only snag being that the items were required at Heathrow by 1830 and it was now 1530 and the items were at Waddington. Getting the items packed and prepared for air carriage was relatively straightforward as the people to do this were already working on the airfield, dismantling and preparing the station's stock of runway repair mats for shipping to the South Atlantic to replace similar items lost when the Atlantic Conveyor *was sunk. Road and rail transport were rapidly*

Vulcan B2 XM597 is today preserved at the Royal Scottish Museum of Flight at East Fortune and is the aircraft that had to divert to Rio de Janeiro during the 'Black Buck 6' raid on 3rd June. C M Hobson

ruled out as they could not meet the required timescale, so air transport from Waddington to Heathrow offered the only realistic solution.

A request made through the duty ops officer to the duty commander at Waddington produced the wholly pragmatic answer of 'Fine, how big an aeroplane do you need?'. A Hercules was unnecessarily large so access to the high-priority item shuttle service being operated using Jetstream aircraft (from 6 FTS Finningley) was arranged. By 1700 on Saturday evening a Jetstream was standing, engines running, outside Ops Wg HQ at Waddington and the spares required for the aircraft in Rio, suitably packaged and with the paperwork essential for a smooth transit through customs were delivered into the hands of the crew for onward transit to Heathrow. The loop was then closed with the duty officer at HQSTC who was informed that the items were in transit and would be at Heathrow in time for the British Airways flight that evening.'

The Jetstreams of the Multi-Engine Training Squadron of 6 FTS had been flying regular communications and light transport missions in the UK and on the Continent in connection with Operation 'Corporate' since 1st May. Three of the squadron's 11 aircraft were available for shuttle service tasking each day and much of the work involved flying high-priority passengers and cargo to Brize Norton and Lyneham for onward transit to the South Atlantic. By the time the commitment finished on 26th July 1982, the Jetstreams had flown a total of 492 hours on Operation 'Corporate' support.

Apart from the 'Black Buck' raid, offensive air operations over the Falklands on the 3rd were greatly restricted by poor visibility with low cloud and patches of fog. Due to the bad weather Argentine aircraft were unable to mount any raids against the ships that were unloading the 5th Infantry Brigade at San Carlos. Neither the Harriers nor the Sea Harriers flew any sorties during the day but the helicopters were less affected. Argentine positions did however come under attack from naval gunfire as *Avenger* fired at Pebble Island, *Active* at Fitzroy Settlement and *Ambuscade* at Diamond Mountain.

During one of the frequent replenishments between an RFA and *Invincible*, a Gnome engine that was required for a sick Sea King fell from the sling on the cable between the two ships and was lost in the South Atlantic.

At 1030Z on the 3rd the *Nordic Ferry* arrived in San Carlos Water with the six Gazelle AH1s of 656 Squadron. A few hours later, in appalling weather, the helicopters flew off on the short flight to a new FOB at Clam Valley, southeast of San Carlos Settlement. New arrivals at the San Carlos FOB

were two Sea King HAS2As (XV649 and XV660) of 'A' Flight 824 Squadron. These helicopters were deployed ashore at short notice from the Fleet tanker *Olmeda*, which remained with the Carrier Battle Group. It was originally intended that the helicopters should assist with the unloading of ships in San Carlos Water during the day and then return to *Olmeda* in the evening. However, in the event the two Sea Kings stayed at the FOB for three days, assisting at San Carlos and Teal Inlet before returning to their ship.

Four more Sea King HAS2As arrived on the 3rd as the detachment of four 826 Squadron helicopters that had been on board the *Fort Austin* since 17th May, flew to the San Carlos FOB. These helicopters also stayed for three days until the bulk of unloading and moving forward of troops and supplies had been done. These shore deployments were necessary due to the loss of the Chinook and Wessex helicopters on board the *Atlantic Conveyor* and the need now to support two brigades onshore. Two more 826 Squadron helicopters transferred temporarily from *Hermes* to the *Atlantic Causeway* on the 3rd to make more room for the Harriers arriving from Ascension Island.

One of the eight 847 Squadron Wessex HU5s (XT471) on the *Atlantic Causeway* was swapped for a machine of 'B' Flight 845 Squadron (XT468), which was fitted out as a gunship and therefore had a reduced load-carrying capacity. This was the helicopter that had escaped destruction when the *Atlantic Conveyor* was hit and had been assisting in HDS duties on board *Hermes* since then. Meanwhile the Sea Kings of 846 Squadron moved artillery from Teal Inlet to Mount Estancia in poor visibility.

As dusk was approaching, Lieutenant P J Sheldon and Sub Lieutenant P Lyall of 825 Squadron were moving Rapier fire units among the hills in the San Carlos area in XV696 when they landed on the summit of Lookout Hill, just north of San Carlos settlement. Unfortunately, the ground was very boggy and as the helicopter sank into the soft ground all the main rotor blades hit the ground causing minor damage. The aircrewman, Chief Petty Officer P Withell, was almost catapulted out of the open cabin door as the helicopter came to a rest abruptly. Although the damage would have been easily repairable under normal circumstances, the lack of spares made this impossible at that time. The crew was picked up by an 846 Squadron Sea King but XV696 had to be left where it was and was subsequently cannibalised for spares for other Sea Kings with the intention of recovering it when possible. In fact the Sea King was airlifted out by Chinook three days later and flown to the San Carlos FOB where it

stayed until being loaded onto the *Engadine* on 7th July for the journey home.

The recent arrivals in the San Carlos area brought to 68 the number of British helicopters based ashore on the Falklands by 3rd June. This total consisted of 26 Sea Kings, 17 Wessex, a single Chinook, 11 Scouts and 13 Gazelles.

British Helicopters Available for Operations Ashore on 3rd June

Ajax Bay
'B' Flight 3 CBAS
Scout AH1 (XR627, XV140, XW615)

Clam Valley
656 Squadron
Gazelle AH1 (XX377, XX409, XZ290, XZ314, XZ321, ZA728)

Fern Valley Creek
846 Squadron
Sea King HC4 (ZA291, ZA296, ZA298, ZA299, ZA312, ZA313)

Head of the Bay
656 Squadron
Scout AH1 (XR628, XT637, XT649, XV130, XV139, XW282)

'Pollock's Passage'
846 Squadron PNG detachment
Sea King HC4
(ZA292, ZA293, ZA295, ZA297)

Port San Carlos
'A' Flight 824 Squadron
Sea King HAS2A (XV649, XV660)
826 Squadron detachment
Sea King HAS5
(XZ577, ZA130, ZA133, ZA137)
'A' Flight 845 Squadron
Wessex HU5 (XS483, XT484)
'B' Flight 845 Squadron
Wessex HU5 (XT765)
'C' Flight 845 Squadron
Wessex HU5 (XT449, XT461)
'B' Flight 847 Squadron
Wessex HU5 (12 serials unknown)
18 Squadron
Chinook HC1 (ZA718)

San Carlos Settlement
825 Squadron
Sea King HAS2A
(XV648, XV654, XV656, XV659, XV663, XV677, XV696, XV700, XV714, XZ580)
'A' Flight 3 CBAS
Gazelle AH1 (XZ326, ZA730, ZA776)

Unnamed FOB near Ajax Bay
'C' Flight 3 CBAS
Gazelle AH1 (XX376, XX412)

Teal
'B' Flight 3 CBAS
Scout AH1 (XP902, XW616)
'M' Flight 3 CBAS
Gazelle AH1 (XX380, XX413)

More reinforcements were on their way as the *Contender Bezant* headed for the South Atlantic from Ascension on 3rd June with her cargo of Harriers and helicopters.

Minerva's Lynx HAS2 (XZ698) had a close shave on the 3rd when an Argentine SAM was fired at it as the helicopter was flying about two miles southeast of Cape Pembroke. The missile, claimed to have been a Roland, but more likely a Tigercat or a Blowpipe, missed and the helicopter landed safely back on the ship before *Minerva* sailed out of Falkland Sound to rejoin the Carrier Battle Group that night. Another arrival with the aircraft carriers on the 3rd was the *Fort Grange* with three 'C' Flight 824 Squadron Sea King HAS2As on board.

4th June (Friday)
For the second day running, air operations were restricted by bad weather, with no Harrier or Sea Harrier sorties. However, the weather to the west of the Falklands was a little better and a flight of four Daggers from Rio Grande is reported to have dropped parachute-retarded bombs on British positions around Mount Kent by dive-bombing through cloud cover. One of the aircraft was flown by Comodoro Villar, the other pilots being Capitan Demierre, and Primer Tenientes Musso and Roman.

A worrying intelligence report had recently been received suggesting that the Argentines had removed at least one of the Exocet launchers from one of their Type 42 or A69 destroyers and flown it to Stanley for use against the ships that were regularly bombarding the airfield and other positions. In fact the Exocets may not actually have reached Stanley until the 5th and it then took several days for the missiles to be readied for use. In an attempt to lure a shore-based Exocet to reveal itself, *Exeter*'s Lynx HAS2 (XZ733) was fitted with radar reflectors to give it a signal that might be taken for a ship and was then flown slowly along the coast but out of sight of land. The helicopter was tracked by various fire control radars but no missile was fired and the results of the sortie were disappointing.

Another ship's Lynx HAS2, XZ730 from *Arrow*, flew to the Port San Carlos FOB on the 4th so that its tail rotor hub could be changed. The ship had been in Fox Bay since the 2nd and the Lynx had been carrying out observation for naval gunfire support. The support helicopters were also affected by the fog but still 845 and 847 Squadrons managed to establish a joint FOB at Teal Inlet during the day in support of the advance along the northern route towards Stanley. 825 Squadron's Sea Kings assisted the Wessex in moving guns and ammunition to Teal Inlet during the day.

Meanwhile, on the southern advance to Stanley the three Scouts of 'B' Flight 3 CBAS that had remained at Ajax Bay flew to Estancia House and were joined by two more Scouts from Teal Inlet, thereby making 'B' Flight complete once again. Estancia House was to be 'B' Flight's base until the end of the conflict and they were joined there by 'A' Flight on 7th June.

The weather was so bad on the 4th that 846 Squadron had to abandon the move of an artillery battery from Port San Carlos to Estancia House when heavy rain started to damage the helicopter's rotor blades. Night missions for the Special Forces were also cancelled due to bad weather.

Another Argentine daylight air raid was reported during the afternoon of the 4th. Three aircraft, possibly Daggers of Grupo 6, appeared over the islands at high level, bypassed San Carlos and dropped three bombs near Green Patch in Berkeley Sound. No damage was caused and the object of the raid was a mystery. Another raid, of four aircraft (probably Skyhawks), was later reported in the Mount Kent area, where ten bombs fell near the British positions but caused no casualties.

The Red Cross Box was shared by hospital and ambulance ships of the Royal Navy and the Argentine Navy. On the 4th *Herald*'s Wasp flew a party of observers from the International Committee of the Red Cross from the *Uganda* to the *Bahia Paraiso*, her Argentine counterpart. The ICRC was entitled to inspect the hospital ships to ensure that they conformed to their non-combatant role.

The men of 3 PARA moved into positions to the northwest of Mount Longdon during the day as 42 Commando was engaged in fierce fighting in the Mount Kent area. 45 Commando was moving up to reinforce 42 Commando in preparation for an assault on the Two Sisters mountains in the next few days. Elements of 2 PARA were moved up to Bluff Cove by helicopter and the Guards battalion was expected to join them soon. By the 4th the eight Rapier fire units of 63 Squadron, RAF Regiment had been set up in the San Carlos area to protect the base area and shipping.

At 2030Z, just as day was turning into night, *Invincible* sailed southwest to a position just south of Falkland Sound. The reason for this bold move was an attempt to catch one of the early morning Argentine Canberra bombing raids or one of the elusive C-130 resupply flights. From this position 801 Squadron could launch a Sea Harrier CAP that would be well placed to catch any intruders and not have to worry so much about fuel problems as *Invincible* would be much closer to the CAP.

Soon after *Invincible* set off on her mission, two Canberras were picked up on *Bristol*'s radar. Unfortunately, the fog was too thick for the Sea Harriers to launch at that time and the Canberras dropped their bombs on Mount Kent without causing any casualties. Later during the night, at 0300Z on 5th June, the first of two pairs of Sea Harriers was able to get airborne, but there was no sign of any enemy aircraft by then. *Exeter* had been dispatched to a corresponding position north of Falkland Sound in the hope of trapping any Canberras or Hercules that attempted to approach the San Carlos area from the northern route. As soon as the Sea Harriers landed on *Invincible* she sailed back to the eastern edge of the TEZ to await another opportunity.

Having transferred the troops of the 5th Infantry Brigade to other ships at South Georgia, the *Queen Elizabeth II* arrived off Ascension Island on the 4th. The ship still had some stores on board that could be useful to the Task Force and several personnel had to be taken off to fly back to the UK by RAF VC10. The Sea King HAR3 of the 202 Squadron detachment was used to unload the stores as it had a greater load-lifting capability than the Wessex of Base Flight Ascension. During the unloading, the Sea King was refuelled at sea using a hose (similar to the Navy's HIFR system) from the deck of the small HMS *Dumbarton Castle*, the first time an RAF helicopter had used this system.

5th June (Saturday) –
Another Tragic 'Friendly Fire' Incident
With *Invincible* sailing back to her daytime position towards the eastern edge of the TEZ, an 801 Sqn Sea Harrier was dispatched at 0840Z, despite poor visibility in fog and low cloud, to investigate a possible target near Stanley. *Exeter* had reported a possible enemy aircraft but Lieutenant Charlie Cantan found nothing and so returned to the carrier. By this time *Invincible* was shrouded in a thick bank of fog and Lieutenant Cantan had to be guided in by the radar operators on board the carrier. Flares were fired off the stern on his first attempt to land but the pilot could not see them even though he was only yards away from the ship, so he went around for what would have to be his last approach as, by now, he was extremely short of fuel. Guided by a vertical searchlight beam from the carrier, Charlie Cantan inched his way forward in the hover at 200 feet through the dense fog until he landed safely on the deck, more through instinct than by sight. Certainly no one on the deck saw the Sea Harrier until it was almost over the landing spot. The aircraft was found to have a mere 150lb of fuel left, enough for just two more minutes of flying time.

The fog and low cloud persisted into daylight and disrupted offensive air operations once more throughout much of the 5th. No Argentine air raids took place and the Sea

Harriers and Harriers only flew a few sorties during brief spells of improved visibility. Two flights, each consisting of a pair of Canberras, took off from Rio Gallegos at about 0800Z to attack British troop positions but reports of British SAM's being fired forced the Canberra crews to turn back before reaching the Falklands. One of the Canberras (B-101) returned to Rio Gallegos on one engine and its starboard undercarriage collapsed on touchdown, causing it to veer off the runway and sustain further damage.

Two flights of Daggers flew armed reconnaissance missions over West Falkland armed only with their internal 30mm cannon, but none of the aircraft engaged in combat or reported seeing any British warships.

The first Sea Harrier CAP took place soon after 1100Z when Lieutenant Commander Andy Auld and Lieutenant Simon Hargreaves took off from *Hermes*. However, by the time they were due to return to the carrier the fog had closed in once again and the pair were forced to divert to Port San Carlos and so became the first fixed-wing pilots to use the newly constructed FOB there. The two Sea Harriers flew four sorties from the FOB during the day before returning to *Hermes* at 1730Z when the fog had lifted enough to permit a safe landing. Use of the forward strip enabled Sea Harriers to remain at their CAP stations for at least 35 minutes rather than just ten minutes when operating from the carriers.

Auld and Hargreaves were soon joined at the Port San Carlos FOB by a pair of 1 Squadron Harriers, led by Squadron Leader Bob Iveson, who had taken off from the carrier at 1200Z and was also caught out by the foggy conditions. Iveson, who had just returned to flying following his ejection and subsequent evasion and rescue, lost his IFF during the sortie and was illuminated by several British radars as he approached San Carlos. He and Flight Lieutenant Tony Harper stayed at the FOB for two days before returning to *Hermes*. During the afternoon of the 5th Squadron Leader Peter Harris and Flight Lieutenant John Rochfort also visited the FOB and then attacked Argentine positions on the Two Sisters on their way back to the carrier.

Like all Grupo 2 de Bombardeo Canberras, B-101 originally served with the RAF. The aircraft was damaged when returning to Rio Gallegos from a raid on 5th June. The aircraft survived the conflict and was retired from Argentine Air Force service as recently as 2000.
Argentine Air Force

The Port San Carlos Harrier FOB came into operation on 5th June, resulting in longer CAP times and shorter transit times for the Harriers.
MoD

The intelligence information regarding the possibility of land-launched Exocet missiles being used from Stanley obviously generated a great deal of interest. Squadron Leader Jerry Pook and Flight Lieutenant Mark Hare took off at 1650Z for a low-level reconnaissance of the coast to the south of Stanley in search of the Exocet launcher but nothing was found. In fact the launcher was there by this date, probably parked somewhere within Stanley itself when this mission was flown. The launcher was mounted on a trailer but it took several days for the missile to be set up and for a suitable target to come within range, so the Exocet would not be used for some time yet.

At about 1850Z two Harrier GR3s flown by Wing Commander Peter Squire (XZ997) and Flight Lieutenant Mike Beech (XZ989) took off on an armed reconnaissance over the islands. The aircraft flew over Keppel Island, Rat Castle Shanty, Dunnose Head, Spring Point and, lastly, Pebble Island, where they again attacked the Pucaras that

had been disabled during the SAS nocturnal raid on 15th May.

The poor weather affected the helicopters flying in support of the ground forces to a lesser extent than it did the fixed-wing aircraft and so the Wessex, Sea Kings and Chinook continued with their ceaseless work of resupply and relocation of troops, stores and ammunition. Chinook HC1 ZA718 made up to 15 round trips each day carrying artillery ammunition from Teal Inlet to the batteries on Mount Kent. The Sea Kings of 846 Squadron moved two artillery batteries and a Rapier battery to Teal Inlet on the 5th and flew several night sorties in support of Special Forces despite fog and low cloud, which made the flying dangerous. The two Gazelles (XX376 and XX412) of 'C' Flight 3 CBAS moved up from San Carlos to Teal Inlet to join the two Gazelles of 'M' Flight in support of 3 PARA.

656 Squadron also became involved in the hunt for the suspected land-based Exocet launcher, Captain J G Greenhalgh in

Scout XT649 being tasked to search the many small islands to the east of Bluff Cove. The fear was that the missile might be used against the LSLs that were going to deliver the Guards from San Carlos to this area in the next few days. Once again, nothing was found during the search. During the day the Gazelle and Scout flights of 656 Squadron moved to Goose Green from the San Carlos FOBs, although the squadron headquarters remained at Clam Valley Creek FOB for the time being and the helicopters were flown back there for maintenance by 70 Aircraft Workshop's detachment as required.

Communications in the forward area of the southern advance was becoming a problem so a number of Relay-Broadcasting (REBRO) Stations were set up, often on summits, to improve the situation. It was while flying a sortie to set up a REBRO Station on Mount Pleasant Peak that 656 Squadron suffered the tragic loss of a helicopter and its occupants. Gazelle AH1 XX377 was flown by Staff Sergeant C A Griffin and Lance Corporal S J Cockton and it took off at 2030Z to carry some Signals Squadron personnel to Mount Pleasant to set up the equipment. The sortie was completed and the helicopter then returned to Goose Green for further tasks. However, about six hours later, at about 0200Z on the 6th, the station stopped working so another sortie to Mount Pleasant Peak was planned. The Signals Squadron commanding officer, Major M Forge and Staff Sergeant J I Baker boarded the Gazelle at Goose Green and the helicopter took off at 0350Z. Eighteen minutes later a missile hit the helicopter, blowing its tail boom off two miles south of Mount Pleasant Peak and killing all on board.

The wreckage of the Gazelle was found on the morning of the 6th by an 846 Squadron Sea King, despite poor visibility and heavy rain. There was speculation at the time that the Gazelle had been shot down by a Sea Dart fired by a British warship but it was not until June 1986 that it was officially admitted in the House of Commons that *Cardiff* had indeed fired the missile. *Cardiff* and *Yarmouth* had come close inshore off the Port Fitzroy area that night so as to provide naval gunfire support to the advance near Mount William, Tumbledown and Moody Brook. The helicopter was flying over ground that had not yet been declared fully clear of enemy troops and *Cardiff* saw an unidentified target on its radar screen heading east towards Stanley and fired three Sea Darts within the existing rules of engagement. The helicopter was flying higher and faster than the locally imposed limits of 100ft and 100 knots for British helicopters. Any helicopter flying higher or faster than this was assumed to be Argentine and was automatically engaged.

As far as *Cardiff* was concerned, the helicopter was not flying in the previously agreed 'safe' airspace for British aircraft and was therefore considered to be a perfectly legitimate target.

This was the most serious case of several 'friendly fire' incidents on the British side during the conflict and the root cause was a rare breakdown in communications between the British forces on the Falklands and the Task Force at sea. This tragedy was almost compounded later that night when *Cardiff* was about to open fire on unidentified vessels that later turned out to be *Intrepid's* landing craft, which she had not been notified were in the area.

Cardiff's Lynx HAS2 itself almost become a victim of 'friendly fire' during the night of the 5th. The helicopter (XZ233) was flying in support of naval bombardment of shore positions when it suffered an oil leak from the main rotor gearbox. The Lynx had to land quickly and so diverted to the nearest ship, which happened to be *Arrow*. During the emergency diversion the Lynx was tracked and locked onto by the fire control radars of several Royal Navy vessels, but fortunately the helicopter was then correctly identified and so no missiles were launched.

Meanwhile, at Wideawake airfield on Ascension Island, Nimrod MR2P XV232 arrived on the 5th, introducing a new modification for the type. The threat of interception by Argentine fighters, although remote on most sorties, was a distinct possibility when the Nimrods were flown close to the Argentine coast to monitor the ships of the Argentine Navy. As a fighter escort was out of the question, an attempt was made to give the Nimrods a degree of self-protection by fitting them with AIM-9 Sidewinders. As Nimrod crews practised air combat defensive tactics against RAF fighters from early May, a quick modification programme was worked out to fit pylons to the underwing hardpoints that all Nimrods were fitted with, but had never used operationally before. The first modified aircraft (XV229) made its first flight with the new pylons on 26th May and XV232 became the first modified aircraft to enter operational service before deploying south to Ascension Island on 5th June.

Although the Sidewinder was never used operationally by the Nimrods during the conflict and the chance of them being used effectively must remain doubtful, the addition of the missiles must have given the crews an added degree of confidence on their long, unprotected missions.

Another arrival at Wideawake airfield on the 5th was Hercules C1P XV196, the third of the probe-equipped long-range Hercules to be based at Ascension Island. Its first operational flight, an airdrop to the frigate

Minerva, commenced at 0405Z on the 6th and lasted for 24 hours and five minutes.

6th June (Sunday)

The bad weather over and around the Falklands continued for yet another day. Despite the poor weather, two Harrier GR3s of 1 Squadron were dispatched from *Hermes* to the Port San Carlos FOB at 1200Z on the 6th, but strong winds halted flying later in the day. The carrier was actually outside the TEZ, some 240 miles east of Stanley, when the aircraft were launched. The squadron flew several sorties during the day including ground attacks in support of British troops and an armed reconnaissance looking for the ground-based Exocet in the Stanley area. Such was the state of the weather that 800 Squadron only managed to launch a single Sea Harrier CAP, at 1415Z, during the entire day.

The failure of the Sea Harriers to engage the night-time Canberra raids led to a plan known locally as 'Operation Canbelow'. At dusk each evening *Invincible* and its attendant frigate, *Brilliant*, would detach themselves from the Carrier Battle Group and sail to within 100 miles of the coast of East Falkland. Here they would be able to launch CAPs and have alert aircraft sitting on the deck in readiness for the Canberras or the C-130 resupply flights, which were still eluding every effort to stop them. *Brilliant's* Lynx would fly ESM barrier patrols during the deployment as part of the frigate's role as goalkeeper for the carrier. 'Operation Canbelow' was put into action at dusk on the 6th but no enemy aircraft were detected on the first night. Meanwhile *Exeter* was again detached to the north of the islands in an attempt to intercept any Canberras attempting to approach from that direction.

Two of 846 Squadron's PNG-equipped Sea Kings flew a naval gunfire support team to Beagle Ridge to the north of Stanley during the night, where a patrol from 'D' Squadron, SAS had been located for almost three weeks. The observers targeted the Royal Navy's guns onto Argentine positions around Stanley. *Avenger's* Lynx HAS2 (XZ249) inserted an SBS team on Sea Lion Island in Choiseul Sound on the 6th. As *Active* started a spell of night naval gunfire bombardment in the Stanley area, her Wasp HAS1 (XT779) flew spotting missions in support of its parent ship.

Still numbed by the loss of two of its aircrew, 656 Squadron headquarters moved from the Clam Valley FOB to Goose Green on the 6th, to be closer to its deployed Gazelle and Scout flights. On the same day a Gazelle flew a reconnaissance to Button Bay on the north coast of Choiseul Sound to take a look at the beached Argentine patrol boat, the *Rio Iguazu*, which had been damaged in a Sea Harrier attack on 22nd May. On the 6th a 3 CBAS helicopter flew a casevac mission to recover a 42 Commando marine from Mount Kent after he had been injured by an Argentine land mine.

More troops arrived in the southern line of advance on the 6th when the 2nd Battalion Scots Guards were landed by *Intrepid*'s landing craft in rough weather at Bluff Cove during the early hours of the morning. The Guards relieved men of 2 PARA who were moved back to Fitzroy.

Meanwhile at Stanley airport, the last remaining operational MB-339A of 1 Escuadrilla (0766/4-A-115) took off and was flown back to Rio Grande on the mainland by Capitan de Corbeta C A Molteni. This left three unserviceable MB-339As on the airfield and these aircraft were not used again during the conflict, probably due to a shortage of spares as well as battle damage from the numerous air raids and bombardments on the airfield. These three aircraft were captured more or less intact when British forces entered Stanley on 14th June. A 1998 article in *Air Enthusiast* quotes Capitan Molteni's claim that another MB-339A (0769/4-A-119) had been delivered to Stanley and was also flown back to Rio Grande on this date by Teniente de Fregata G

HMS Exeter fires a Sea Dart from her patrol line in Falkland Sound. It is thought that this photograph shows the firing of the missile that destroyed Learjet 35A T-24 of Grupo 1 de Aerofotografico on 7th June. MoD

Henry, but this has not been corroborated by any other source.

There is considerable confusion here as Molteni states that three aircraft (misidentified as 'MB-326As' in the article) had deployed from Rio Grande to Stanley on 26th May together with an F-28 in support, but again this has not been corroborated and the number of MB-339As does not add up to those known to have been at Stanley and accounted for. However, the detachment commander was in the best position to know the situation so it should be accepted that two MB-339As escaped back to Argentina rather than just one aircraft.

7th June (Monday)
After five days of very bad weather, the 7th dawned a fine, clear day allowing unrestricted air operations to resume. Despite the fact that *Hermes* had sailed east out of the TEZ for some much-needed engine maintenance, 800 Squadron flew an early morning CAP in the hope of catching an Argentine C-130 on its way to or from Stanley. The Sea Harriers made use of the Port San Carlos strip to fly a CAP en route from and to the carrier. However, no enemy aircraft were detected and the Sea Harrier pilots returned to the carrier disappointed.

Although there were no Argentine air raids on the Falklands on the 7th, the better weather heralded their resumption. Argentine intelligence of British dispositions on East Falkland was now badly out of date, as reconnaissance missions could not be flown during the spell of bad weather, so

Grupo 1 de Aerofotografico flew a mission with all four of the unit's Learjet 35As. The mission was led by the unit commander, Vicecomodoro Rodolfo de la Colina flying aircraft T-24. The four aircraft crossed West Falkland island in line abreast formation at 40,000ft, leaving clearly visible condensation trails in the bright blue sky as they took photographs of the islands.

At 1203Z *Exeter*, having first misidentified the aircraft as Canberras, launched two Sea Dart missiles at the Learjets. The first missile appeared to malfunction and fell harmlessly into the sea but the second continued until it hit T-24, blowing its tail off. For almost two minutes the aircraft spun down until it crashed close to Pebble Island airfield killing all on board including the Vicecomodoro, Mayor Juan Falconier, Capitan Marcelo Lotufo, Suboficial Ayudante Francisco Luna, and Suboficial Auxiliar Guido Marizza. The voices of the terrified crew could be heard on radio as the aircraft made its final, agonisingly slow descent to earth.

Several Harrier GR3s deployed from *Hermes* to the Port San Carlos Harrier FOB on the 7th to await calls for air support. However, there was little contact between British and Argentine troops on the ground so there was not much for the Harriers to do. A pair of Harriers, flown by Squadron Leader Jerry Pook and Flight Lieutenant John Rochfort, took off at 1200Z to attack an artillery position on Sapper Hill with rockets and were fired at by SAMs and small arms fire, causing minor damage to one aircraft.

Although Squadron Leader Bob Iveson had returned to operational flying since being shot down and later rescued, he was suffering from a back injury as a result of his ejection. Compression fractures of the vertebrae are common following an ejection and can result in severe injury if another ejection is made before the fracture is properly treated and healed. Bob Iveson was therefore grounded on the 7th and four days later was transferred to the MV *British Trent*, which was heading back to Ascension Island. He arrived back at Wittering on 24th June, about two weeks before the rest of his 1 Squadron colleagues.

Another 'Operation Canbelow' attempt to intercept a C-130 or a Canberra was made by *Invincible* in the evening of the 7th. The ship detached from the Carrier Battle Group at 1930Z and moved closer to East Falkland to enable its Sea Harriers to fly longer CAPs. At 2300Z *Cardiff* detected an enemy aircraft flying east towards the Falklands. Two 801 Squadron Sea Harriers were launched but the enemy aircraft, probably a C-130, turned west back towards the mainland, no doubt after being warned of the presence of the Sea Harriers by Stanley radar. In fact two C-130s attempted to reach Stanley on the night of the 7/8th but both turned back. One aircraft reported being fired at while 20 miles out from Stanley by a British SAM, which was probably a Sea Dart fired by *Cardiff*.

The sole 18 Squadron Chinook proved its value as a heavy-lift helicopter on the 7th by recovering two downed helicopters. 'Bravo November' first airlifted 846 Squadron Sea King HC4 ZA310 from Fanning Head, where it had been accidentally damaged on 23rd May, and took it back to the squadron's FOB at Fern Valley Creek. The Chinook then

recovered 825 Squadron Sea King HAS2A XV696 from Lookout Hill where, on 4th June, it also had suffered a landing accident. XV696 was delivered to 825's FOB at San Carlos Settlement. The tail pylon of XV696 was later removed and fitted to ZA310 to bring 846 Squadron's strength back up to 11 operational helicopters, but this did not happen until the day after the surrender.

Also on the 7th, 846 Squadron detached Sea King HC4 ZA313 to the *Sir Galahad* as the LSL, in company with the *Sir Tristram*, loaded about 400 Welsh Guards and other troops, and set off around the southern coast of East Falkland to deliver them to the Fitzroy area. Having loaded several Rapier fire units on board the ship, the Sea King's task was to offload the missiles from the ships near Fitzroy so that they could be set up in firing positions as soon as possible.

The Scouts of 656 Squadron spent several days inserting patrols of Gurkhas in the area to the south and southeast of Goose Green. The Gurkhas were systematically checking all houses and other buildings to ensure that they were clear of enemy troops so that the area could be declared 'safe'. At 1705Z on the 7th two Sea Kings of 825 Squadron flew a Gurkha patrol to Egg Harbour House near Elephant Bay on the west coast of Lafonia to investigate a sighting of enemy troops at the house. Armed helicopter support was requested and 656 Squadron dispatched Scout AH1 XV139 flown by Sergeant I Roy and Corporal M Johns and fitted with SS-11 missiles. By the time the Scout arrived near Egg Harbour House the enemy troops had vacated the building and were thought to be hiding in a nearby gully. Ian Roy radioed Squadron HQ for an observation Gazelle to assist in locat-

ing the enemy troops and Captain P G Piper and Lance Corporal L Beresford soon arrived in Gazelle AH1 XX409.

After a quick briefing Ian Roy flew XV139 back to Goose Green to refuel as the Gazelle commenced a search of the gully, out of the range of small arms fire. Sergeant Roy returned from Goose Green and was then accompanied by another Scout AH1 (XW282) flown by Captain S M Drennan and Lance Corporal J Gammon. The situation was quickly brought to a successful conclusion when XV139 fired an SS-11 missile into the gully, which encouraged the eight Argentine soldiers to surrender immediately. The group was thought to have been an air defence unit that had been landed on Lafonia to shoot down helicopters flying between San Carlos, Darwin and Fitzroy. Among the weapons captured was a Soviet SA-7 man-portable SAM, which later found its way to the Museum of Army Flying at Middle Wallop.

The headquarters of 3 Commando Brigade moved from Teal to a position on the west side of Mount Kent on the 7th and one of its helicopters flew a particularly risky mission to casevac a wounded soldier from Mount Wall to Ajax Bay in the early hours of the morning.

Lynx HAS2 XZ733 from *Exeter* spent much of the 7th searching the southern half of East Falkland for suspected enemy radar sites, but without success. *Penelope*'s Lynx HAS2 (XZ691) was fired at by an Argentine SAM, thought to have been a Blowpipe, as the helicopter flew near Pebble Island. Having survived two weeks in Falkland Sound and San Carlos Water without incurring any major damage, *Arrow* eventually rejoined the Carrier Battle Group on the 7th and her Lynx joined others of the type in flying ESM barrier patrols to protect the Task Force vessels. *Hecla* had returned to the Red Cross Box on the 6th from her trip to deliver wounded soldiers to Montevideo. On the 7th her Wasp, made operational thanks to parts picked up at Montevideo, transferred stores and personnel to the *Uganda*.

The damaged *Argonaut* had left the TEZ on the 5th for a long and slow voyage back to the UK. On the 7th she was overflown by an Argentine Air Force Boeing 707 when some 400 miles north of the TRALA. This appears to have been the final overflight of a British ship conducted by a Boeing 707 during the conflict.

In addition to its SAR duties at Ascension Island, 202 Squadron Sea King HAR3 XZ593 also took a full part in the logistics tasking, shuttling stores from the airfield to ships and relocating supplies among the Task Force vessels. Flt Lt K Faulkner

On 8th June Wing Commander Peter Squire's Harrier GR3, XZ989, suffered an engine failure as it approached to land at the Port San Carlos FOB. The aircraft was badly damaged and was taken back to the UK after the conflict, but it never flew again. MoD

A 10 Squadron VC10 C1 (XV102) arrived back at Brize Norton from Ascension Island on the 7th with 134 passengers, many of whom were survivors from the *Atlantic Conveyor*, who had been delivered to Ascension Island by the tanker *British Tay*. Also on the 7th the 202 Squadron Sea King HAR3 (XZ593) based at Ascension Island airlifted a liquid oxygen bowser from Wideawake to the *Dumbarton Castle*. The bowser weighed 7,162lb and the helicopter had to be stripped of all unnecessary equipment and carry minimum fuel for the flight.

8th June (Tuesday) – The Bombing of the *Sir Galahad* and *Sir Tristram*

The 8th of June was one of the most intensely fought days in the air war over the Falklands and was a day of both triumph and tragedy for both sides, resulting in the largest single loss of life in a British ship during the conflict as well as the destruction of a flight of Grupo 5 Skyhawks.

In the morning Sea King HC4s of 846 Squadron, escorted by an 848 Squadron Wessex HU5 gunship, flew men of 'B' Company, 40 Commando to Cape Dolphin on the very northwest tip of East Falkland to clear out a suspected enemy observation post. The observation post was found to be deserted. Another Argentine observation post, this one on Mount Rosalie on the coast of West Falkland, opposite San Carlos Water, would come under attack later in the day.

Although the Sea Harriers and Harriers had been using the Port San Carlos Harrier FOB during the day, the strip had to be closed down at 1500Z when Harrier GR3 XZ989 flown by Wing Commander Peter Squire crash-landed across the aluminium plank runway. The aircraft was one of four that had taken off from *Hermes* at 1315Z and, having found no suitable target, the flight was directed to land at the Port San Carlos strip. As XZ989 came into land it suffered a partial engine failure and landed very heavily, still carrying its full load of 2-inch rockets. The Harrier's undercarriage collapsed and the aircraft tore up the aluminium planking as it careered across the runway before finally coming to rest near a slit trench belonging to a Rapier fire unit crew. Wing Commander Squire was fortunate to escape from the crash with nothing more than a severe shaking.

The accident meant that the strip could not be used until repairs had been carried

out and this would take the rest of the day as undamaged planking from the end of the runway had to be used to replace the damaged sections. This meant that Sea Harrier CAPs had to take off and land from the carriers which were over 200 miles to the east of the Falklands, thereby reducing the amount of time each CAP could spend over the Falklands. Harrier GR3 XZ989 was too badly damaged to be repaired in situ and was progressively robbed of parts for the other Harriers until it was dispatched back to the UK in November. It never flew again and was later used as a ground instructional airframe at RAF Gütersloh.

Argentine observation posts reported the presence of the LSLs *Sir Galahad* and *Sir Tristram* in Port Pleasant near Fitzroy early on the morning of the 8th as they brought in the Welsh Guards and other troops to reinforce the 5th Infantry Brigade prior to the advance on Stanley. The original plan was for the *Sir Galahad* to arrive in the early hours of the morning to join the *Sir Tristram*, which had already arrived on the 7th. The two vessels should then have been unloaded and away shortly after dawn. However, delays in loading the Guards at San Carlos on the 7th meant that the *Sir Galahad* did not reach the Fitzroy/Bluff Cove area until just before dawn and both ships were clearly visible in the narrow channel near Port Pleasant as they started to offload. The unloading proceeded slowly throughout the day as the Welsh Guards had been expected to be delivered to Bluff Cove, not Port Pleasant and some confusion reigned until the order to disembark was finally given after several hours of waiting.

Also there was only a limited number of small craft with which to unload the big vessels. Unlike at San Carlos the flat, coastal

terrain in the Fitzroy/Port Pleasant area offered no advantage to the British landings and the ships were not escorted by any warships to provide an instant air defence capability. It was intended that the Rapier fire units on board the LSLs would be set up quickly to provide air defence coverage for the vessels and the troops once onshore. Argentine Air Force planners quickly put together a mission incorporating two flights of A-4B Skyhawks from Grupo 5, two flights of Grupo 6 Daggers, and a flight of Grupo 8 Mirage IIIs.

Each Skyhawk flight consisted of four aircraft each carrying three 500lb bombs and at 1450Z the first four aircraft of Dogo flight took off from Rio Gallegos, followed a few minutes later by Mastin flight. A short while after that, four Mirage IIIs took off from Rio Gallegos to fly a simulated strike against the San Carlos Water area. It was hoped that the British would be tricked into thinking that the Mirage decoys were a flight of Dagger fighter-bombers and would send any Sea Harrier CAP that was airborne after them rather than the Skyhawk bombers. The six Daggers took off from Rio Grande at 1600Z and it was planned that they would follow the Skyhawks into the attack on the ships at Port Pleasant within about 15 minutes. However, almost immediately one of the Daggers had to abort when it suffered a bird strike that shattered its windscreen. The five remaining Daggers proceeded in company with a Learjet 35A pathfinder (T-23), which would lead them to Cape Meredith on the west coast of West Falkland, after which the Daggers would fly up Falkland Sound and then turn east across Lafonia to attack the British ships near Fitzroy.

The two flights of Skyhawks flew at 10,000ft to rendezvous with the KC-130H tankers to take on fuel. It was at this point that three of the aircraft aborted the mission. Two of them could not receive fuel as their in-flight refuelling probes had iced up. Unfortunately for the remainder of the flight, one of the pilots who had to return was the veteran flight commander Capitan P M Carballo, one of Grupo 5's most experienced pilots, whose aircraft experienced problems with its oxygen and fuel system. Primer Teniente Cachon took command of the remainder of the two flights and the remaining five aircraft continued on their mission. The weather became progressively worse as the flight approached the Falklands and rain showers and a heavy cloud cover developed as the flight turned northeast after passing Speedwell Island off the extreme southern tip of Lafonia.

Meanwhile the Mirage IIIs of Grupo 8 crossed the coast of West Falkland and succeeded in attracting the attention of a Sea Harrier CAP at about 1645Z. For a critical few minutes as the Mirage IIIs turned back and the Sea Harriers gave chase the flights of Skyhawks and Daggers were left alone to bomb the unprotected ships. The five Skyhawks had a free run up the coast of Lafonia and past Lively Island towards the anchorage at Port Pleasant.

By 1650Z the 846 Squadron Sea King HC4 (ZA313) that had embarked on the Sir Galahad to unload Rapier units had started its task (and was actually airborne close to the Sir Galahad when she was bombed), but few of the Rapiers were operational by the time the Skyhawks arrived. In any case the Rapiers had been positioned to defend the inland site where Brigade headquarters was set up rather than the ships themselves. The Skyhawks spotted but ignored the Sea King and a Scout in the final few minutes before reaching their target. As they flew over Fitzroy the Argentine pilots could not see the ships and were targeted by small arms fire, which slightly damaged one of the aircraft.

As the flight headed out to sea, about to return home, one of the pilots spotted the LSLs in Port Pleasant and the Skyhawks turned around and came in low from the east to bomb their targets. Delays in unloading the ships meant that most of the troops and their equipment were still on board and the ships lay largely undefended in the exposed anchorage that allowed an easy approach for attacking aircraft. Although a ground-launched SAM was fired at the Skyhawks there was little ground fire, allowing the Skyhawk pilots an unmolested run into the target.

The three leading Skyhawks made their attack on the Sir Galahad and Primer Teniente Cachon hit the stern of the ship with all three of his 500lb bombs. Primer Teniente Alferez Carmona's bombs missed

and ricocheted off the surface of the sea and when he shouted into his radio in frustration his call distracted Teniente Rinke who failed to drop his bombs. However, Cachon's three bombs were enough to seal the ship's fate as large quantities of fuel and ammunition caught fire, turning the vessel into an inferno within minutes. The other two Skyhawks, flown by Tenientes Galvez and Alferez Gomez, attacked the Sir Tristram which was hit by two bombs from Galvez's Skyhawk, but neither of the bombs exploded; however a near miss by a third bomb blew off the rear loading ramp. Fires were started and the ship later had to be abandoned but the Sir Tristram was not terminally damaged and was later reboarded. All five of the Skyhawks escaped virtually unscathed and flew south to retrace their route back to base.

The results of the bombing of the Sir Galahad were horrendous with 48 Guardsmen and other troops killed by the blast or the subsequent fire and a further 57 men wounded, many severely. Forty-three of the fatalities occurred on the tank deck where tons of ammunition caught fire. The Sir Tristram was less badly damaged and only two men on board were killed, but it was still in a serious condition and barely operational. The incident came to be known as the Bluff Cove disaster but in fact the ships were anchored in Port Pleasant, the next inlet south from Bluff Cove and closer to Fitzroy.

Under the original Argentine plan the Skyhawk attack should have been followed up a few minutes later by the Daggers of Grupo 6 led by Capitan C Rohde. However, in a sense it was fortunate that when the Daggers turned northeast and up Falkland Sound they came across the frigate Plymouth near the mouth of San Carlos Water. The ship was heading towards West Falkland on an NGS mission in support of an SAS attack on an enemy observation post on Mount Rosalie when it was seen by the Dagger flight. Reasoning that they had lost the element of surprise on their original target, the Daggers instead made Plymouth the object of their attack as the ship turned and raced back towards the safety of San Carlos Water. The Daggers swung north to attack in line astern at low level and 575 knots and four of the aircraft each dropped two 500lb bombs and fired their cannon (one aircraft could not release its bombs due to a generator failure).

Amazingly, although the ship was hit by four of the bombs and much cannon fire, none of the bombs exploded. However, one of the bombs hit the flight deck causing a depth charge to explode which started a serious fire that took some time to extinguish. One bomb passed through the ship's funnel without exploding while two others bounced off the surface of the sea to pene-

trate the hull near the ASW mortar and smash their way out of the other side of the ship, again without exploding. The ship's mortar launcher was also hit and badly damaged and several live rounds were jammed in the launcher and its loading compartment.

Five members of Plymouth's crew were wounded during the attack and were evacuated by helicopter to Ajax Bay. The ship returned fire with 20mm cannon and a Seacat missile but only one of the Daggers was slightly damaged although two kills were claimed. Plymouth was fitted with a new laser dazzle device, nicknamed 'Flasher', that could have saved her had she had time to use it. The device temporarily blinds the pilot of any attacking aircraft so that he cannot line up for his final bomb run, but the attack took place too quickly for it to be brought into action.

The Daggers were chased briefly by a pair of Sea Harriers but the Argentine aircraft accelerated away and eventually returned safely to base, their pilots believing that they had sunk the frigate. In fact the crew of Plymouth had the fire under control within 45 minutes and the ship sailed slowly back into San Carlos Water for emergency repairs before sailing off to the TRALA for more extensive repairs. Plymouth's Wasp HAS1 (XT429) was damaged by splinters during the attack but was soon operational again after being fitted with a new tail rotor.

The Scout helicopter that the Skyhawks had almost run into southwest of Fitzroy during the final stages of their attack on the LSLs was a 656 Squadron machine (XR628) flown by Sergeant R Kalinski and Lance Corporal J Rigg. Startled by the sudden appearance of the five Skyhawks, Dick Kalinski brought the Scout to a hover a few feet above a stretch of inland water known as MacPhee Pond, where he planned to remain until he was sure that the jets had cleared the area. After a few minutes hovering over the pond Dick Kalinski applied power to climb away, but as he did so the helicopter's tail rotor driveshaft failed and the Scout landed heavily in the pond as the pilot lost control. Luckily the pond was only about four feet deep and the crew suffered nothing more than wet feet, but XR628 had to sit in the fresh water for three days until it was recovered by an 846 Squadron Sea King on the 11th.

As soon as news of the bombing of the Sir Galahad and Sir Tristram broke, every available helicopter that could be spared was sent to assist with the SAR and casevac operation. It was fortunate that at least five helicopters were in the near vicinity and came to the ships' assistance immediately to join a landing craft and several small boats in the rescue. Sea King HC4 ZA313 had been airlifting Rapier fire units off the *Sir Galahad* at the time of the bombing and was less than 200 yards away from the ship when the Skyhawks attacked. Crewed by Lieutenant J A G Miller and Petty Officer Aircrewman A Ashdown, the Sea King moved out of the way behind a hill until the Skyhawks left the area and then quickly flew back to the *Sir Galahad* to commence rescue operations. The helicopter hovered above the foredeck and winched up survivors to take them to the shore. The smoke and flames from the *Sir Galahad* made the rescue particularly difficult and the helicopter had to hover very close to the ship to see the survivors.

Another Sea King in the vicinity at the time of the bombing was XV700 of 825 Squadron flown by the commanding officer, Lieutenant Commander Hugh Clark, and Chief Petty Officer Aircrewman D Jackson. They had just landed a survey party at Fitzroy settlement a few minutes before the Skyhawks arrived and set off for Port Pleasant as soon as the air raid was over. There they joined three more Sea King HAS2As of 825 Squadron flown by Lieutenants P Sheldon (XV654), J Boughton (XV663) and S Isacke (XZ580). Hugh Clark and his crews rescued many badly injured survivors from the burning deck of the *Sir Galahad* as much of the ammunition on board both the

LSLs started to explode in the searing heat.

Another of the early arrivals on the scene was Wessex HU5 XT480 of 847 Squadron flown by Lieutenant T Hughes and Chief Petty Officer W R Tuttey. The Wessex pilot spotted a dinghy containing several survivors that was drifting back towards the burning stern of the *Sir Galahad* so Lieutenant Hughes positioned his Wessex between the dinghy and the ship and gently wafted it away from the inferno using the downdraught from his rotor blades. The Sea Kings also joined in with this and moved several more dinghies away from the ship and towards land. Some of the helicopters were enveloped in thick, choking

RFA Sir Galahad *burns furiously in Port Pleasant following the raid by Skyhawks of Grupo 5 de Caza on 8th June. This dramatic photograph was taken from an 825 Squadron Sea King HAS2A as another of the squadron's helicopters approached the ship's from its starboard side. Several life rafts had already been launched as the evacuation progressed.* Wg Cdr P Lyall

Two 825 Squadron Sea King HAS2As approach the Sir Galahad *to take off survivors. Fortunately, the forward section of the ship remained clear of smoke and flames for some time, making the rescue easier, but many men had to be rescued from the aft end in thick, choking smoke.* Wg Cdr P Lyall

smoke as they hovered close to the burning vessels, making the rescue dangerous and difficult. The dense, swirling smoke made the rescue of the last few survivors from the *Sir Galahad* particularly dangerous as the helicopters had to come down to just a few feet above the burning and cluttered deck. Hugh Clark was awarded the DSC and Lieutenants Boughton and Sheldon the QGM for their part in the rescue.

Sub Lieutenant Paul Lyall of 825 Squadron, Lieutenant Sheldon's co-pilot in XV654, described the incident vividly in his daily diary:

'We saw the pall of smoke as we approached Fitzroy and rapidly dropped off

our loads. As we were a little low on fuel, we hopped onto the Sir Tristram *which, to her credit, was able to fuel us. After this we went to join in the rescue effort. There were, by this time, about four helos on the scene, most of them 825, who were picking up survivors from the forecastle. We joined in. The after part of the ship was deep in flames, belching black smoke. Mortar bombs were exploding and whizzing around. I saw a waterspout just off our port side – the missile must have just missed our rotor disc.*

People were being rescued by a lighter alongside, but there were still about 30 on the forecastle, many of them badly injured. We made three runs, I think, to the ship,

hoisting up some very badly injured and burnt people and taking them to first aid posts in the settlement. We managed to get everyone off and onto the land. Then we made two runs into the Ajax Bay field hospital . with some of the more seriously injured in need of urgent surgery. Felt quite sick as the cabin soon filled with the odour of burning flesh.

Come back to the Sound and have to hide during an "air raid red imminent", but night is falling and we chance it and sneak back across the water to our base. Today has really brought home the horrors of war – I haven't seen the badly wounded before, and it isn't very nice at all.'

As the Wessex and Sea Kings brought survivors to shore, many of 656 Squadron's Scouts and Gazelles also joined in the operation and flew casualties to *Fearless* or the field hospital at Ajax Bay, where a constant stream of helicopters arrived throughout the day and well into the night. Rescue operations at Port Pleasant and casevac missions continued well into darkness, keeping 846 Squadron's PNG-equipped helicopters particularly busy. Once stabilised, the casualties were flown out to the *Uganda* in the Red Cross Box, the 18 Squadron Chinook airlifting a load of 64 wounded from Fitzroy to the hospital ship in a single sortie during the day.

Throughout the day many helicopter crews who had heard of the *Sir Galahad* bombing over the radio net arrived unsolicited at Ajax Bay to evacuate the wounded out to the hospital ship between their assigned tasks. The disaster at Port Pleasant set back the final advance to Stanley by two days as the land forces had to be reorganised to compensate for the loss of men and supplies.

Following the success of the raid on the *Sir Galahad* and *Sir Tristram*, Grupo 5 should have been allowed to quit while it was ahead. However, higher judgement prevailed and a second mission to the Fitzroy area was planned as soon as the

A life raft is seen here hard against the Sir Galahad's *stern. Several of the life rafts had to be moved away from the ship by helicopters using the downdraught from their rotors to propel the rafts as they were in danger of catching fire or being destroyed if the ship exploded. Despite the grievous loss on board the* Sir Galahad, *the helicopter crews saved many lives that day.* Wg Cdr P Lyall

A line-up of Grupo 5 de Caza A-4B Skyhawks. The aircraft nearest to the camera is C-233, which is now preserved in Argentina masquerading as C-301. The next aircraft in the line is C-228, which was shot down near Middle Island by Flight Lieutenant Dave Morgan on 8th June 1982. Argentine Air Force

results of the first were known. The follow-on mission was to involve Skyhawks from both Grupo 5 and Grupo 4 in an attempt to disrupt even further the landings at Port Pleasant. A flight of four A-4Bs took off from Rio Gallegos at 1830Z, each again carrying 500lb bombs to be dropped on the ships. The four A-4Cs of Grupo 4 were targeted against troop concentrations ashore in the Fitzroy/Bluff Cove area and were carrying anti-personnel bombs when they took off from San Julian at 1900Z.

Mazo flight of Grupo 5 followed the same routing as the earlier mission and arrived uneventfully off Fitzroy, but by now the British forces ashore had set up their air defences and were well prepared for the raiders. The Skyhawks encountered a wall of fire from small arms, 20mm cannon, GPMGs, as well as Blowpipe and Rapier missiles. Amazingly, none of the Skyhawks were hit but the air defences did deter them from attacking the still burning LSLs and the aircraft turned away to the south in search of other British warships in the fading evening light.

As the flight flew across the mouth of Choiseul Sound they spotted a landing craft. The boat was 'Foxtrot 4' from *Fearless*, en route to Darwin from Bluff Cove to collect the HQ and communications vehicles for the 5th Infantry Brigade. Primer Tenientes Bolzan and Alferez Vazquez dived to attack the small landing craft, which was hit by a bomb from Vazquez's

Bomb damage to the Sir Tristram *is apparent in this early post-war photograph of the ship near Stanley. It would take three years for the ship to be completely repaired and refitted for return to service.* MoD

aircraft. Six Royal Marines were killed in the attack and 11 survivors were rescued later during the night by the 846 Squadron Sea King HC4 (ZA313), which had been taking part in the SAR effort at Port Pleasant. Among the dead was Colour Sergeant Brian Johnstone, the commander of the landing craft, who had distinguished himself during the rescue of men from *Antelope* and had plucked Teniente Lucero out of the water after he was shot down on 25th May. An attempt by the recaptured *Monsunnen* to tow the landing craft back to the shore failed when 'Foxtrot 4' sank later that night.

It was at this point that the Argentine Air Force started to pay a high cost for its successes during the 8th of June. Just as the Skyhawks were diving on the landing craft they were seen by a pair of Sea Harriers on a CAP at 10,000ft above Choiseul Sound. Two aircraft, flown by Flight Lieutenant Dave Morgan (ZA177) and Lieutenant Dave Smith (XZ499), had taken off from *Hermes* (the Port San Carlos FOB still being out of action) at 1850Z on a CAP. At 1945Z Dave Morgan spotted the landing craft and then, to his horror, he saw a Skyhawk just moments before it released its bombs. The two Sea Harriers dived towards the Skyhawk as the pilots spotted the other three aircraft of Mazo flight. Dave Morgan rapidly approached the rearmost Skyhawk and launched a Sidewinder from a range of 1,000 yards. The missile streaked away and hit the Skyhawk (C-226) of Teniente Juan Arraras, which exploded and crashed into the sea near Philimore Island, killing the pilot.

Dave Morgan then turned his attention to another of the Skyhawks and fired his second missile. The Skyhawk turned to get away but once again the Sidewinder

guided perfectly and impacted Teniente Vazquez's aircraft (C-228), which broke in two and fell into the sea two miles north of Middle Island. Vazquez was able to eject and his parachute was almost hit by Dave Morgan's Sea Harrier as it swept by him. Unfortunately, Vazquez's parachute was seen to be on fire; he did not survive and either died during the ejection or was drowned at sea.

After firing his last Sidewinder Dave Morgan attempted to use his 30mm cannon against a third aircraft, but his HUD had failed after the second Sidewinder fired and he missed as his gunsight was not working. However, the splashes made by the cannon shells as they hit the water drew Dave Smith's attention to the third aircraft. Dave Morgan pulled up into a vertical climb to clear the area and allow Dave Smith to fire his Sidewinder from two to three miles' range. The missile streaked away and hit a Skyhawk (C-204) at very low level over the shoreline. The aircraft crashed on sand dunes at Rain Cove near Island Creek on the north coast of Lafonia and the pilot, Primer Teniente Danilo Bolzan, was killed in the incident. It is possible that the aircraft flew into the ground in the attempt to out-run the Sidewinder; whatever the cause, the result was another aircraft and pilot lost for Grupo 5.

Such was the speed of events in the combat that three aircraft had been shot down and three pilots killed within 90 seconds of the start of the engagement. The two Sea Harriers were now getting short of fuel and flew back to *Hermes* as it was getting dark. Once there, Dave Morgan completed his first night deck landing in a Sea Harrier.

The engagement with the Mazo flight A-4Bs resulted in Dave Morgan becoming

one of the highest-scoring Sea Harrier pilots of the conflict. Morgan was not even an air defence pilot by trade; indeed, he had started his RAF career in 1969 flying Wessex helicopters. He converted to the Harrier GR3 in 1977 and although he had amassed 800 hours flying Harriers in the ground attack role, he was only part-way through his Sea Harrier conversion course at Yeovilton when the conflict broke out. He was transferred from 899 Squadron to 800 Squadron, initially as the operations officer due to his limited experience on the Sea Harrier but by the time *Hermes* reached Ascension Island, Dave Morgan was well on his way to becoming an operational pilot and was an integral part of the squadron. During the conflict he shot down two Skyhawks and caused a Puma to crash, shared in the destruction of another Puma and an A-109A, and bombed a FIGAS Islander at Stanley airport. He also took part in the attack on the trawler *Narwal*, which resulted in the ship's demise. Dave Morgan was awarded the DSC for his part in the Falklands conflict.

As Morgan and Smith set course for their carrier, which they rejoined at 2016Z, a medium-level CAP from 801 Squadron consisting of Lieutenant Commander Nigel 'Sharkey' Ward (ZA190) and Lieutenant Steve Thomas (XZ458) arrived on the scene. The 801 Squadron aircraft were about to chase the last remaining Skyhawk when they were warned by *Cardiff* of more enemy aircraft at high altitude, which turned out to be two pairs of Mirage IIIs of Grupo 8 that had arrived somewhat belatedly to provide top cover for the Grupo 5 flight. The two Sea Harriers changed course towards the Mirages, which they spotted flying at 35,000ft by their contrails in the fading evening light. However, the Mirages stayed at high altitude and turned away, heading west towards the mainland when the Sea Harriers came within ten miles' range. Frustrated by the lack of an engagement, the two Sea Harriers returned to *Invincible*, and landed at 2036Z.

Following the rapid loss of three of Mazo flight's Skyhawks, Primer Teniente Hector Sanchez, flying the last remaining aircraft, had jettisoned his bombs and underwing fuel tanks and jinked at very low level for some minutes before he thought himself safe from the Sea Harriers. By this time he was very low on fuel and realised that without air-to-air refuelling, his tanks would run dry while he was still some 200 miles east of Rio Gallegos. Sanchez asked for a tanker as he crossed West Falkland and climbed to a more economical cruising altitude.

The Skyhawk was not fitted with either VLF Omega or even a working IFF, so the KC-130H tanker had to use its search radar to locate the lone jet. The tanker captain realised the predicament of the Skyhawk pilot and pressed closer to West Falkland until he was within the range of the known Sea Harrier CAPs. Unable to locate or guide Sanchez precisely towards a rendezvous, the tanker pilot descended from high altitude into denser air and started to make a condensation trail. Sanchez spotted the trail left by the Hercules and quickly joined up with the tanker. However, by now Sanchez was in a highly agitated state and had difficulty making contact with the tanker's drogue to take on fuel. Eventually, the tanker pilot calmed Sanchez down and talked him gently into the refuelling with only minutes to spare before the Skyhawk ran out of fuel. Unfortunately, the name of the tanker pilot is not known but his was one of the most impressive and courageous acts of flying performed during the conflict and he surely deserved an award for saving the life of a Skyhawk pilot by putting his own aircraft at risk.

The second flight of Skyhawks, Yunque flight from Grupo 4, had better luck than their compatriots of Grupo 5. Their flight out to the Falklands was uneventful and by the time they reached the Fitzroy area it was getting dark and the fire on board the *Sir Galahad* made the target area easy to find. The four Skyhawks attacked in line astern and were met by heavy ground fire including several SAMs. All the aircraft were hit and one, flown by the leader Capitan Mario Cafaratti, was so badly damaged that the pilot almost ejected. Another member of the flight, Teniente Alferez Codrington, became separated and escaped to the north near Mount Kent where he again came under intense anti-aircraft fire.

With varying degrees of combat damage, the four aircraft struggled back towards the tanker, the same KC-130H that had just saved Sanchez. Two of the Skyhawks were losing fuel fast and had to be 'towed' back to San Julian by the tanker; one of the aircraft actually flamed out as it ran out of fuel while taxiing back to the ramp. Grupo 4 was extremely lucky not to suffer the same fate as the earlier flight and the incident illustrates the folly of sending the second mission to an area that was bound to be well prepared for further air attacks.

It was not just the Skyhawks of the Argentine Air Force that were in action on the 8th. An inconsequential raid was made by aircraft of CANA's 3 Escuadrilla on suspected British troop positions on Broken Island near Pebble Island during the day. This was the first mission by the Navy's A-4Q Skyhawks since 23rd May and would prove to be the unit's penultimate mission before its final sortie on 12th June.

The only other Argentine offensive air action of the day was a most curious event that could have ended in tragedy for a ship not even involved in the conflict. A Boeing 707 on a surveillance flight had discovered a large tanker heading south some 400 miles northeast of the main British Task Force, well outside the TEZ. A task force consisting of an HS125, a C-130H (TC-68) and four Canberras set off to find and sink the ship. Two of the Canberras made a bombing run over the tanker and dropped eight 1,000lb bombs, not one of which detonated on impact! However, one bomb did lodge itself in the tanker's superstructure.

The raid would have been yet another success for the Argentine Air Force had the ship actually been part of the British Task Force. In fact the vessel was the 220,000-ton MV *Hercules*, a Liberian-registered and US-owned super tanker loaded with ballast and sailing from the Virgin Islands in the Caribbean to Valdez, Alaska via Cape Horn. The *Hercules* had no connection with the Falklands conflict and was simply in the wrong place at the wrong time.

Argentina had declared the entire South Atlantic to be a war zone on 11th May and claimed that any ship resupplying the Task Force would be sunk. Although the bomb that remained embedded inside the *Hercules* could have been defused, the ship was later ordered out of Rio de Janeiro, where it had put in for repairs, and then scuttled as a hazard to other ships at sea. The ambulance ship *Hydra* was ordered to stand by the *Hercules* in case she had to be abandoned but her services were not needed.

On the 8th the frigate *Avenger* detached from San Carlos Water for a three-day mission off the coast of West Falkland. The ship stayed close to the coast during the daytime and prowled the sea at night in search of Argentine ships and aircraft attempting to resupply the islands. *Avenger* returned safely to San Carlos Water on the 11th after an uneventful expedition.

Despite the loss of Harrier GR3 XZ989 at the Port San Carlos strip earlier in the day, 1 Squadron was restored to its original strength of six aircraft with the arrival from Ascension Island of two more Harrier GR3s. Flight Lieutenant Ross Boyens (XW919) and Flight Lieutenant Nick Gilchrist (XZ992) took on fuel several times from Victor K2s during the long non-stop flight from Wideawake airfield to the carrier *Hermes*. The two Harriers were escorted to the carrier in the final stage of the ferry flight by Sea Harrier ZA177 flown by Flight Lieutenant Ted Ball and they landed on the ship at 1700Z. The flight had lasted seven hours and 50 minutes during which Ross Boyens lost some of his navigational instruments and had to rely on Nick Gilchrist for navigation updates.

Late at night on the 8th an 846 Squadron Sea King inserted a team of signallers to set up a REBRO Station on the slopes of Mount Kent. Unfortunately, the station was set up in the wrong position and it soon came under attack from Argentine artillery later that night. The three signallers escaped and had to be rescued from their position by Captain J P Niblett and Sergeant J W Glaze of 3 CBAS flying Scout AH1 XP902.

On the 8th the container ship *Astronomer* set sail from Lyme Bay carrying replacement helicopters to make up for those lost when the *Atlantic Conveyor* was attacked. The cargo consisted of three Chinook HC1s of 18 Squadron (ZA714, ZA717 and ZA720), three Scout AH1s (XP907, XR629 and XV141) and six Wessex HU5s of 'D' Flight 848 Squadron (XS481, XS498, XS522, XT463, XT467 and XT481). Although the *Astronomer* did not reach Ascension Island until 16th June and Port William on the Falklands until 27th June, the fresh helicopters were welcome replacements for some of the worn-out and tired airframes that had fought the conflict.

9th June (Wednesday)

By first light on the 9th the strip at Port San Carlos was fully operational and able to take Harriers and Sea Harriers once more. Sea Harriers from 801 Squadron made their first visit to the strip but although the weather was good over the Falklands it was poor on the mainland and there was little trade for the Sea Harriers on the 9th. The only excitement occurred about 1900Z when a potential air raid was detected and 800 Squadron launched ten aircraft to their various CAP positions and 801 Squadron put up another CAP from *Invincible*. However, whatever it was turned back as soon as the Sea Harriers took to the air.

The 1 Squadron Harriers made use of 'Sid's Strip' on the 9th, flying sorties against Argentine artillery and troop positions on Sapper Hill and Mount Longdon. The first of several such missions commenced at 1200Z when Wing Commander Squire and Flight Lieutenant Boyens set off from the FOB to attack artillery positions on Mount Longdon. Enemy ground fire was particularly heavy during these sorties and Flight Lieutenant Murdo MacLeod's aircraft was hit by small arms fire during a rocket attack on a 155mm gun emplacement. He and Squadron Leader Harris had taken off from *Hermes* at 1340Z, but when they returned to the carrier MacLeod found that the undercarriage on his aircraft would not lower (due to a severed hydraulic line) so he had to blow it down using the emergency system. The aircraft had received about half a dozen hits from shrapnel from anti-aircraft shells that had exploded above the Harrier during its attack.

656 Squadron headquarters together with its Gazelle and Scout flights made a delayed move forward from Goose Green to a new FOB at Fitzroy. Originally intended for the 7th, the move had been postponed due to the unavailability of transport helicopters. The squadron's helicopters were operating right up to the front line, as was illustrated by an incident during the day. Sergeant Ian Roy was flying Scout AH1 XV139 to deliver supplies to a Scots Guards reconnaissance platoon at Port Harriet House just south of Stanley when the Guards' position came under heavy enemy mortar fire. After the mortar fire stopped he flew forward to pick up two Guardsmen who had been wounded during the barrage. As the helicopter passed close to Port Harriet Point an Argentine Blowpipe missile streaked past it, just missing the Scout by some 75ft.

Another 656 Squadron helicopter had a narrow escape while on the ground at the Port San Carlos Harrier strip. As 656 Squadron's fuel dumps were being moved forward to Fitzroy, Gazelle AH1 ZA728 landed at the Harrier strip and started to refuel with rotors running. Suddenly the Gazelle pilot, Sergeant G H Keates, noticed one of the large cylindrical air-portable fuel cells rolling down the slope towards the helicopter. As the refuelling was still taking place with an airman stood on the Gazelle's landing skid, Sergeant Keates gently lifted off a couple of inches and turned the helicopter through about 60 degrees with the result that the fuel cell rolled past seemingly with only inches to spare before finally coming to rest. Neither the refueller nor Lance Corporal J A Coley, the Gazelle's observer, had noticed a thing but it was later discovered that the helicopter's vertical stabiliser on the starboard side had been slightly damaged by the fuel cell as it brushed past it!

Additional British helicopters became available on the 9th with the arrival of RFA *Engadine* in San Carlos Water. The ship was carrying the four Wessex of 'A' Flight 847 Squadron and, because of a stop at Gibraltar, had been overtaken by the bulk of the squadron, which had arrived at San Carlos on board the *Atlantic Causeway* on the 1st. The ship also brought crews for some of the helicopters already delivered by other ships earlier in the week. The *Engadine*'s helicopters flew off to the FOB at Port San Carlos settlement and joined the other dozen 847 Squadron Wessex there and at the forward FOB at Teal in supporting the ground troops.

The Sea Kings of 846 Squadron assisted in moving ammunition and supplies from Ajax Bay up to forward positions at Fitzroy and Bluff Cove. The squadron also flew several PNG missions to locations in West Falkland as Special Forces investigated reports of Argentines conducting reinforcement and resupply operations there. More of the men wounded in the *Sir Galahad* and *Sir Tristram* attack were flown from Ajax Bay to the *Uganda* by Wessex and Sea King on the 9th. The hospital ship had sailed into Grantham Sound to be closer to shore. Sub Lieutenant Paul Lyall of 825 Squadron recorded 17 round trips in his Sea King to the hospital ship and to *Intrepid* and the *Atlantic Causeway* during the day.

Far from the Argentines reinforcing the Falklands, in fact there was evidence that they were evacuating some of the units there. The two Grupo 7 Chinooks, unlike their Army counterparts, had led a charmed life so far during their four weeks on the Falklands. At 0900Z on the 9th the two helicopters lifted off to return to Rio Grande but an emergency repair stop had to be made at Isla de los Estados (Staten Island) before they reached the mainland. The crew had to pump fuel by hand from drums carried in the fuselage for the long overwater flight. It was not considered to be feasible to fly the smaller Bell 212s back to the mainland and it was not safe to have a Hercules on the ground at Stanley long enough to load the helicopters.

On the same day the Army's surviving Chinook (AE-520) at last became airworthy again, having been grounded with engine problems as long ago as 2nd May. However, its contribution to the war effort was to be short-lived at best. At least one of CAB601's UH-1Hs (AE-413) had been painted in a crude white colour scheme by the 7th to identify it as an ambulance helicopter. The paint scheme did no good at all as the helicopter came under fire from both sides during the 9th!

Canberras of 2 Grupo flew long-range surveillance missions over the sea from Rio Gallegos and Mar del Plata on the 9th. Two night missions were planned against British positions around Mount Kent but the first two aircraft failed to get airborne due to aircraft unserviceability and the second pair turned back and headed for home upon hearing reports of intense SAM and AAA activity in the target area.

During the 9th it was decided to move the A-4B Skyhawks of Grupo 5 to San Julian to join forces with Grupo 4 while the Dagger unit at San Julian moved to Rio Gallegos. This change of base was presumably to get the surviving aircraft of each type, Skyhawk and Dagger, operating from the same airfield.

On the 9th *Brilliant* detached from the Task Force to meet the aircraft transport *Contender Bezant*, with her precious cargo of helicopters and Harriers, as well as the *Europic Ferry* and the *St Edmund*. The *Contender Bezant* was held off to provide replacements when needed but in the event, none of the Chinooks or Harriers were offloaded until after the end of the conflict due to engineering problems on board the ship and bad weather that delayed assembling the Chinooks on deck. *Brilliant*'s two Lynx flew ASW sweeps as the transport ships sailed to join the Carrier Battle Group on the 10th. Also on the 9th, *Plymouth* reached the *Stena Seaspread* for repairs following her mauling in Falkland Sound on the 8th. The frigate returned to operational duties on the 13th.

10th June (Thursday)

Again, good weather over the Falklands contrasted with poor weather over southern Argentina on the 10th and there were no air raids mounted from the mainland bases during the day. However, the Pucaras at Stanley airport put in a rare appearance over the battlefield when British artillery positions on the slopes of Mount Kent and at Murrell Bridge were attacked at dawn by a flight of three Pucaras flown by Primer Tenientes J Micheloud and M A Ayerdi and Teniente C E Morales. The British positions were marked by smoke shells fired by Argentine 155mm artillery. All three aircraft made their attacks and returned safely to Stanley, without causing any damage to the British forces. Two of the aircraft were hit by small arms fire but were not seriously damaged. The attack by the Pucaras instigated an air raid on Stanley airfield by Sea Harriers the following day.

At 1131Z two Harrier GR3s flown by Squadron Leader Peter Harris (XZ992) and Flight Lieutenant Nick Gilchrist (XZ997), the latter pilot on his first mission since arriving from Ascension Island, flew to the Harrier strip to await tasking, but they were not called upon and later returned to the carrier. Two more Harriers, flown by the

squadron commander (XV789) and Flight Lieutenant Mark Hare (XV778), flew a daring low-level photographic reconnaissance mission over the battlefield just to the west of Stanley. The pair took off from *Hermes* at 1300Z to cross the coast at low level near Fitzroy before splitting up to photograph enemy positions near Two Sisters, Mount Longdon and Stanley itself. A large number of Argentine troops and AAA positions were identified on the film when it was developed and analysed.

At 1631Z two pairs of Harriers launched from *Hermes* for a combined LGB and conventional bomb attack. Flight Lieutenant John Rochfort (XZ992) and Flight Lieutenant Nick Gilchrist (XZ997) carried LGBs while Squadron Leader Jerry Pook (XV789) and Flight Lieutenant Ross Boyens (XV778) carried conventional bomb loads. Unfortunately, all four aircraft had to return to the carrier without dropping their bombs. Due to the carrier rescheduling its flying programme, the Harriers had been forced to take off two hours earlier than planned and the ground-based FAC was not ready to provide the essential target marking for the aircraft.

The final 1 Squadron mission of the day was a CBU attack on enemy troop positions to the west of Stanley, which commenced at 1854Z. Wing Commander Peter Squire (XZ997) and Flight Lieutenant Murdo MacLeod (XV778) bombed targets near Moody Brook that had been identified by the photographs taken by Squire and Hare earlier in the day. The aircraft were met by intense small arms fire and AAA and MacLeod's aircraft was hit by a bullet that penetrated the windscreen and damaged wiring to the extent that the aircraft was grounded for a couple of days to permit

repairs. Four more Harrier GR3s (XV762, XW767, XW924 and XZ129) had arrived in theatre on the 10th when the *Contender Bezant* entered the TEZ. However, the aircraft were not required at this stage of the conflict and so they remained in reserve on the ship until 6th July.

Forty-four CAP sorties were flown by the Sea Harriers during the day but the three Argentine raids detected all turned back upon receiving warnings from the Stanley radar controllers. At one point there were ten Sea Harriers flying CAPs over Falkland Sound, Fitzroy and Teal in anticipation of an attack, but no enemy aircraft appeared.

The 10th saw 656 Squadron preparing to support 3 Commando Brigade in the forthcoming assault on Mount Longdon, Mount Harriet and Two Sisters. In addition to resupplying Rapier sites around Fitzroy, 656 Squadron also prepared itself for more offensive operations. It had been the intention to fit SNEB 68mm rocket pods to the Army's Gazelles as had already been done to the Royal Marines' helicopters. Unfortunately, in the hurried loading operation prior to the Task Force setting sail from the UK the pods and their attachments had been loaded on different ships and it took until 4th June to locate both parts of the cargo. The first 656 Squadron Gazelle was fitted with the attachments on the night of the 7/8th but the rockets did not arrive until the 9th. The first test-firing took place on the 10th against an isolated group of rocks in Choiseul Sound.

By the 10th most of 846 Squadron's Sea Kings were operating from the FOB at Teal Inlet, although one helicopter was busy lifting spares to Rapier fire units at San Carlos, Teal and Fitzroy. Another of 846's Sea Kings inserted an SAS patrol into a position in West Falkland during a daylight mission and at dusk flew a resupply mission, taking in an NGS observer. Another NVG Sea King flew several sorties from the *Sir Lancelot* during the night on behalf of the Special Forces. The Sea Kings of 825 Squadron spent much of the 10th and the next three days airlifting ammunition from Ajax Bay and Fitzroy to the front line. Most of the crews logged about seven flying hours each day.

RFA *Olna*, which had entered San Carlos Water on the 8th, left for the TRALA on the 10th with her two 'D' Flight 848 Squadron Wessex, the two helicopters having been used on HDS and VERTREP missions during

SNEB 68mm rocket pods were fitted to Gazelle AH1s at Ascension Island prior to deployment to the Falklands. Although the rockets added a powerful punch, the Gazelles of 3 CBAS and 656 Squadron had little opportunity to use them during the conflict. MoD

825 Squadron Sea King HAS2A XZ580 '272' is seen here resupplying a 105mm battery with ammunition, a task that occupied the utility helicopters for much of the conflict. The battery's guns and stores can be seen on the open ground under camouflage netting.
Wg Cdr P Lyall

the previous three days. Two Wessex of 'C' Flight 845 Squadron deployed ashore from the *Fort Grange* as the ship entered San Carlos Water on the 10th to join other 845 Squadron helicopters at the Port San Carlos FOB. The Wessex had earlier been transferred over from the *Tidespring* to the *Fort Grange* prior to the voyage into San Carlos Water.

Two more helicopters that came ashore on the 10th were two Sea King HAS5s (XZ921 and ZA127) of 820 Squadron that flew from *Invincible* to San Carlos to fly night missions in search of Argentine blockade runners. The Sea Kings flew night surface searches off the coast of West Falkland in the hope of catching any Argentine ships that attempted to resupply the Falklands. The two-aircraft detachment flew three sorties on the first night and remained ashore until the cease-fire. *Exeter*'s Lynx HAS2 (XZ733) was fitted with thermal imaging equipment to carry out a search at night on the north side of Wickham Heights and Mount Pleasant.

Another helicopter involved in an unusual mission was a Wessex HU5 of 845 Squadron. An SBS patrol discovered that every morning a conference of senior Argentine officers took place in Stanley Town Hall and suggested that a well-aimed missile might disrupt the meeting! Lieutenant P C Manley (originally of 'D' Flight 848 Squadron) and Petty Officer Aircrewman J A Balls from 'A' Flight 845 Squadron were briefed on the mission. The Wessex was to fly close up to Stanley where it would launch an AS-12 missile at the Town Hall. A practice mission was arranged for the 10th with the operation due to take place on the 11th. For the practice a target was set up at Bob's Island, a few miles northwest of Teal Inlet settlement. Two missiles were fired at three and three-and-a-half miles' distance with satisfactory results. The helicopter crew returned to Teal FOB to prepare themselves for the mission, scheduled for dawn the following day.

Conditions in Stanley itself were deteriorating rapidly due to the large number of Argentine troops that were falling back into the town. CAB601 by now was flying most of its missions from the sports field and the racecourse, including several sorties by UH-1Hs to the ambulance ship *Almirante Irizar* on the 10th.

The only other events of significance occurred at Ascension Island with the arrival of Vulcan B2s XM607 from Waddington and XM597 from Rio de Janeiro. XM607 was due to fly what turned out to be the final 'Black Buck' mission of the conflict on the night of the 11th, while XM597 was returning from its unscheduled week-long stopover at Rio following damage to its inflight refuelling probe during 'Black Buck 6'. After repairs to the probe, XM597 flew back to Waddington on the 13th, later to be preserved for posterity at the Royal Scottish Museum of Flight at East Fortune.

11th June (Friday)
Just prior to dawn at 1100Z Lieutenant Manley and Petty Officer Aircrewman Balls took off in Wessex HU5 XT484 on their mission to disrupt the Town Hall meeting of senior Argentine personnel at Stanley. Flying at low level with another Wessex gunship as an escort the helicopter arrived at its intended launch point just south of Beagle Ridge, about three miles to the northwest of the target. Just before its arrival it was warned by an SAS observer of the presence of an Argentine A-109A gunship in the vicinity, but the mission went ahead as planned. As Peter Manley held the Wessex steady his crewman fired the first of two AS-12s. The missile missed the Town Hall by a matter of yards and slammed into the top floor of the Police Station just next door. The second AS-12 was then fired but the control wire that was reeled out as it sped along was snagged on a ridge of high ground and the missile fell short and hit the sea in Stanley harbour. The AS-12 narrowly missed hitting the Argentine hospital ship *Bahia Paraiso*, which was tied up at a jetty at the time.

Peter Manley left the area just as an anti-aircraft gun opened up on his helicopter from Cortley Hill, followed shortly by shells fired from 105mm artillery sited on Sapper Hill. The helicopter escaped damage and arrived back at Teal at 1200Z. Although there was disappointment that the Town Hall had not been hit the Police Station was almost as good as it was being used as an intelligence headquarters by the Argentine Army. There is some evidence to suggest that the missile attack further reduced the dwindling morale of senior officers and troops in Stanley.

Following the Pucara raid on British artillery on the 10th, it was decided to attack Stanley airport again on the 11th. Four 800 Squadron Sea Harriers flown by Lieutenant Commanders Andy Auld (XZ455), Neill Thomas (XZ496), Mike Blissett (XZ494), and Lieutenant Clive Morrell (XZ459) took off from *Hermes* between 1058Z and 1100Z for a dawn toss-bombing attack. Each aircraft carried three 1,000lb VT-fused bombs which were released as the aircraft pulled up while still some distance from the airfield itself. Of the 12 bombs that were dropped, 11 were seen to explode on the airfield.

As the Sea Harriers pulled up they were met by a hail of ground fire that included Blowpipe, SA-7 and Tigercat SAMs as well as gunfire of all calibres. Despite the volume of return fire, all four aircraft escaped undamaged and landed back on board *Hermes* by 1203Z. Despite this and a subsequent 1 Squadron attack on Stanley airport, two Pucaras mounted another attack on 3 Commando Brigade's artillery positions at dusk on the 11th, again without causing much damage or losing any aircraft.

The Harrier GR3s of 1 Squadron were very active on the 11th. The squadron's first mission was launched at 1122Z when Flight Lieutenants Tony Harper (XZ997) and Nick Gilchrist (XW919) took off for an abortive LGB attack on Stanley. An SAS team was to mark the target but the battery of their laser target marker had run down, so the aircraft dropped their bombs on Wireless Ridge instead. This first mission was followed by another at 1148Z when Squadron Leader Jerry Pook (XV789) and Flight Lieutenant Mike Beech (XZ992) took off. However, the pair had to return just 20 minutes later when XV789's vital IFF failed, leaving the aircraft vulnerable to British surface-to-air-missiles as well as to the Argentine air defences.

At approximately 1350Z, Flight Lieutenants Ross Boyens (XZ992) and John Rochfort (XW919) took off on a raid against Argentine troops on Mount Longdon, but the wind over the deck suddenly dropped and John Rochfort had to jettison his bombs as he took off in order to remain airborne. Rochfort completed the mission using the aircraft's two 30mm cannon only. The Harrier GR3's new AN/ALE-40 chaff and flare dispenser was first used operationally on this mission when chaff was dumped to break the lock of an enemy search radar.

At 1450Z Jerry Pook (XV789) and Mike Beech (XZ133) left *Hermes* for a CBU attack on Argentine troop positions on Mount Harriet, after which there was a break until 1810Z when Squadron Leader Peter Harris (XV789) and Flight Lieutenant Nick Gilchrist (XZ997) took off for a CBU attack on Mount Longdon.

The squadron's final mission of the day started at 1823Z when Wing Commander Peter Squire (XZ992) and Flight Lieutenant Mark Hare (XZ133) took off from *Hermes* to drop 1,000lb retard bombs on gun emplacements near Moody Brook Barracks. However, the fins of the bombs failed to deploy and then the bombs themselves failed to detonate as they had not had time to arm. During this last mission three Blowpipe missiles were fired at the Harriers, one of them exploding within 100ft of the leader's aircraft. The squadron commander was doubly fortunate to survive being shot down on this mission as a bullet penetrated the cockpit near his feet, tore through cable looms behind the instrument panel and exited on the other side of the aircraft, missing his legs by inches. Harrier GR3 XZ992 was out of action for three days while repairs were made to the cockpit.

An innovative twin CAP by 801 Squadron Sea Harriers, using both *Invincible* and the Port San Carlos FOB during the 11th, failed to detect the almost daily Argentine Air Force C-130 that continued to resupply Stanley. One pair of Sea Harriers remained at medium altitude but the other pair descended to low level once on station and positioned itself near Queen Charlotte Bay to wait for the enemy aircraft. However, nothing was detected and the only result of the attempt was cut tyres as the Sea Harriers landed on the metal planking of the FOB. A C-130 did manage to get through to

Stanley airport that evening at 2115Z, beating the blockade yet again.

The helicopters based ashore were also very busy on the 11th moving troops forward and keeping the front line supplied. The Sea Kings of 846 Squadron were split between supporting 3 Commando Brigade in the north and the 5th Infantry Brigade in the south, with six helicopters moving 2 PARA from Fitzroy to Bluff Peak near Mount Kent in the afternoon. Meanwhile the 18 Squadron Chinook flew fuel in air-portable fuel cells from San Carlos to Fitzroy and other sites to save the forward helicopters from having to return to San Carlos or Goose Green to refuel. The Wessex of 845 and 847 Squadrons set up a FOB at Fitzroy on the 12th, initially with two aircraft but later with more as operations increased in intensity. One of 847 Squadron's helicopters (XT480) was slightly damaged on the 11th when a mortar shell landed close to it during a sortie at Bluff Cove.

The Lynx HAS2s from *Exeter* (XZ733) and *Minerva* (XZ698) carried out a deception mission on the 11th by dropping chaff about four miles off Stanley in an attempt to lead the Argentine defenders into thinking that there was about to be a major helicopter assault on the beaches near the town. Although the mission was a success it had to be terminated when several fire control radars, including at least one Roland SAM radar, illuminated the helicopters. The Argentine forces apparently fell for the ruse and reported deterring a major airborne assault whereas in fact they had simply had their attention diverted from the advance of the ground forces.

The Gazelles of 'M' Flight 3 CBAS were involved in a casevac for a tragic 'friendly fire' incident involving 45 Commando on the 11th. Two Scouts of 656 Squadron were attached to 'B' Flight 3 CBAS to supplement the squadron's own Scouts for the forthcoming assault on Two Sisters, Mount Harriet and Mount Longdon. One of 656 Squadron's Scout AH1s (XR628) was recovered by an 846 Squadron Sea King from MacPhee Pond where it had force-landed during the attack on the LSLs on the 8th.

British warships continued to bombard Argentine shore positions and a total of 788 rounds were fired on the night of 11/12th June. Around this time Moody Brook Barracks near Stanley was hit by naval gunfire, which damaged beyond repair one of the UH-1Hs (AE-418) and slightly damaged another (AE-409). Only six Hueys were airworthy at Stanley by the end of the day.

During the night-time naval bombardment of Stanley a FIGAS DHC-2 Beaver (VP-FAT) was hit and destroyed as it sat on the slipway outside the floatplane hanger at Stanley. The Government Air Service had bought two Beavers in 1976 and the aircraft

could be operated as either landplanes or floatplanes. Both aircraft were fitted with floats at the time of the invasion but both were immediately grounded and parked near their hangar on the slipway at Stanley. The other Beaver (VP-FAV) was also hit by naval gunfire on the night of the 11th but was deemed to be repairable after the end of the conflict. However, before repairs could be started, the aircraft was blown over in a fierce gale on 28th July 1982 and completely wrecked. The aircraft were eventually replaced by another Beaver and two BN-2 Islanders, none of which were equipped with floats.

The hospital ship *Uganda* and her attendant ambulance ship *Hydra* sailed into Grantham Sound on the 11th to receive casualties from the recent assault more quickly than by a long helicopter flight from Ajax Bay. *Hydra*'s Wasp offloaded medical supplies that had been picked up during the ship's last trip to Montevideo.

12th June (Saturday) – The Last Exocet
The battle for the Argentine first line of defence around Stanley started in earnest just after midnight of the 11th. The objectives included Mount Harriet, Mount Longdon, and Two Sisters and the assault was supported by 105mm guns of the Royal Artillery and naval bombardment from warships. *Glamorgan*, *Avenger* and *Yarmouth* were on the southern gunline off Port Fitzroy while *Arrow* was on the northern gunline in Berkeley Sound. By mid-morning, after a night of extremely hard fighting, all the objectives were in British hands, although Argentine artillery took its toll of the new occupants of the high ground positions throughout the rest of the day.

At 0435Z a formation of enemy aircraft, probably a Canberra and its escorting Mirage IIIs, bombed British positions on Mount Kent without causing much damage. Apparently four Canberras took off from Rio Gallegos on the mission but two turned back when they were unable to release their wing-tip tanks and a third aircraft also aborted later in the mission, leaving just one Canberra to complete the raid. A second Canberra mission was attempted later in the morning but one of the flight of three aircraft failed to get airborne while the other two aircraft were deterred from bombing their target (the British command HQ at Port Harriet House) by a combination of bad weather, Sea Harrier activity and the rare failure of radar direction from Stanley.

The day started off badly for the British Task Force with the long-expected launch of an Exocet from a ground-based launcher in Stanley. The destroyer *Glamorgan* had sailed from the TRALA at 1700Z on the 11th to provide NGS to 45 Commando on Two Sisters in conjunction with *Avenger* and

Yarmouth. The ship was reportedly overflown by a Pucara but successfully completed its night bombardment in support of the attack at 0615Z. However, 20 minutes later, as the ship was heading away from the coast and about 17 miles southwest of Stanley, an Exocet launch was detected, although at first it was mistaken for an artillery shell. Despite violent manoeuvring and launching a Seacat SAM that exploded nearby, *Glamorgan* was hit by the Exocet at 0637Z. The ship had turned stern on to the direction of the attack but the incoming Exocet hit the flight deck and ricocheted into the hangar. The missile exploded and caused a fierce conflagration that burnt out the hangar, destroyed the ship's Wessex HAS3 (XM837) and killed 13 members of the ship's crew.

As *Glamorgan* made her way back to the rest of the Task Force a Sea Harrier CAP was flown over her as protection and *Yarmouth*'s Wasp flew medical aid and fire-fighting equipment over to the damaged ship. Despite a hole 10ft by 15ft in the port side of the ship, an even larger hole in the weather deck, the destruction of the Seaslug launcher and one of the Seacat SAM launchers and damage to the galley, *Glamorgan* was under way by 1000Z and made good speed as she headed towards the *Stena Seaspread* in the TRALA. Amazingly, although *Glamorgan* at one stage

developed an 11-degree list, the vessel was operational again 36 hours later and even sailed into San Carlos Water after the cease-fire. An attempt to launch a second ground-launched Exocet from Stanley failed and the launcher and its missile were later captured by British troops.

The naval bombardment of enemy positions around Stanley was accompanied by the final operational Vulcan sortie of the conflict. The mission was a bombing raid on Stanley airport, to supplement *Arrow*'s efforts on the same target, and was conducted by Flight Lieutenant Martin Withers (XM607) with virtually the same crew that had flown the successful 'Black Buck 1' mission on 1st May. The target of 'Black Buck 7' was airfield facilities at Stanley airport rather than the runway itself as it was hoped to capture the airfield shortly and the runway would be needed for the British airlift into the Falklands. The raid was accomplished successfully although little damage was done. Returning home, the Vulcan suffered an engine flameout that required three relights to successfully start it again before the aircraft arrived safely back at Wideawake airfield.

Two days later, Vulcan B2s XM598 and XM607 flew back to Waddington to await their fate. However, these two aircraft and the other two Vulcans that operated from Ascension Island were saved from the breaker's axe and all were preserved: XM597 at East Fortune, XM598 at Cosford, XM607 at Waddington itself and XM612 at Norwich airport.

800 Squadron's first CAP of the day involved a search over West Falkland in the hope of finding an Argentine C-130 on its resupply run from Stanley. However, nothing was detected, although a Hercules did

land at Stanley at 0815Z and may have been the aircraft that brought in a 155mm gun around this date. The Sea Harriers had to return to *Hermes* after a short while as the FOB could not be used due to local fog and ice on the metal planking. Later Sea Harrier CAPs also missed two pairs of 3 Escuadrilla A-4Q Skyhawks that had been dispatched to bomb British troops in the Darwin area. The second pair of Skyhawks saw a pair of Sea Harriers and so jettisoned its bombs before flying back to Rio Grande to conclude the last naval Skyhawk mission of the conflict. The Sea Harriers of 801 Squadron mounted a series of CAPs over the damaged destroyer *Glamorgan* after she had been hit by the Exocet.

Once again 1 Squadron had a busy day, with three missions dispatched to attack enemy positions on Sapper Hill. The first pair of aircraft took off at 1145Z flown by Flight Lieutenants Ross Boyens (XZ133) and Mike Beech (XV778). It was intended that the aircraft should land at the Port San Carlos FOB after the attack so that they could be ready for further missions, but the FOB was closed in the morning due to fog and icy conditions so the Harriers had to return to *Hermes*.

At 1400Z Squadron Leader Peter Harris (XV789) and Flight Lieutenant Murdo MacLeod (XW919) took off for an attack on a 155mm gun on Sapper Hill. MacLeod's Harrier was hit by small arms fire and a bullet punctured the aft reaction control pipe. All seemed well as the aircraft flew back to the carrier, but a small fire started in the rear fuselage just as the Harrier slowed down to a hover as it came in to land. MacLeod put the aircraft safely onto the deck and the fire was quickly extinguished. This was the third consecutive mission that

Although the hospital ship SS Uganda *had no embarked helicopters of her own, many of the utility helicopters, including Chinook HC1 ZA718 'BN', delivered injured troops, both British and Argentine, to her flight deck at some stage during the conflict. Wg Cdr P Lyall*

These two Exocet launchers (removed from a frigate) were found on a trailer in Stanley at the end of the conflict. Fortunately only one Exocet was fired from Stanley during the conflict, but that missile hit the destroyer Glamorgan *on 12th June.* MoD

Prefectura Naval Argentina Skyvan 3M PA-54 had been damaged by naval gunfire at Stanley racecourse early in May and was completely destroyed by further naval gunfire on the night of 12/13th June. Wg Cdr P Lyall

down at Murrell Bridge during a battery move from Estancia House. The helicopter rapidly lifted off and flew to Teal where a single shrapnel hole was found in the tail pylon. During the night of the 12th, naval gunfire completed the destruction of the Prefectura Naval Skyvan 3M (PA-54), the aircraft having been damaged at Stanley racecourse by gunfire as early as the 3rd/4th of May.

13th June (Sunday)

The penultimate day of the conflict started off with a very early morning raid by the Canberra B62s of Grupo 2. Two aircraft, flown by Capitan Garcia Puebla with Primer Teniente Segat (in B-102) and Capitan Martinez Villada with Primer Teniente Pagano (in B-104), took off from Rio Gallegos at 0200Z in poor weather for a raid on the British command HQ at Port Harriet House. Capitan Villada had to abort the mission as he approached the coast of the Falklands but the remaining Canberra bomber continued on alone. The aircraft encountered low cloud and icing conditions as it approached the target and during the bombing run it only narrowly avoided flying into Mount Kent.

After dropping its bombs at 0320Z the Canberra evaded a Sea Harrier CAP and returned safely to base at 0500Z, although it had to be guided in by radar as it became lost over the sea. Once again the Canberras failed to cause any significant damage or casualties; but their night-time raids certainly had a significant nuisance value as they woke British troops and kept them alert for hours, thereby causing fatigue and stress. The bombs also fell close to the field headquarters of Major General Moore and his staff.

Despite every effort by the Sea Harriers and the anti-aircraft picket ships, the Argentine C-130s continued to reach Stanley, with at least three aircraft making successful round trips on the 13th. The first two aircraft landed about 0900Z, while another Hercules was seen on the airfield with its engines running at 1056Z. 800 Squadron rapidly planned a raid on the airport in an attempt to catch the last Hercules on the ground but it took off at about 1155Z and

Murdo MacLeod had returned to *Hermes* with battle damage to his aircraft. This time the damage was serious enough to cause the aircraft to be grounded for the rest of the conflict and although temporary repairs were made, XW919 was transferred to the *Contender Bezant* in July to be taken back to the UK to enable more thorough repairs to be made.

The final 1 Squadron attack on Sapper Hill involved Flight Lieutenants Tony Harper (XZ133) and Nick Gilchrist (XV778) who were flying a reconnaissance over the road from Bluff Cove to Stanley. The pilots spotted enemy troops on the road and dropped CBUs on them. During the attack Tony Harper's aircraft was slightly damaged by small arms fire.

The shore-based helicopters supported the final assaults on Mount Harriet, Two Sisters and Mount Longdon during the day by 42 Commando, 45 Commando and 3 PARA respectively. The helicopters of 3 CBAS flew

a total of 85 casualties out of the battle area from 1800Z on the 11th to 1800Z on the 12th, most of these casualties being caused by artillery fire. The assaults meant that all British forces were now in position for the final offensive on Stanley. Gazelles of 'A' Flight flew back several important Argentine prisoners for questioning after the battle. The transport helicopters continued moving ammunition, artillery and supplies to forward positions on both the northern and southern lines of advance. 846 Squadron moved 29 Commando Regiment's 105mm guns to newly captured positions during the day and kept the guns supplied with ammunition throughout the battle. The squadron's PNG-equipped Sea Kings moved Special Forces teams from Estancia House up to Beagle Ridge, just four miles north of Stanley.

An 825 Squadron Sea King was fortunate to receive only slight damage when it was bracketed by two mortar shells as it set

was gone before the raid could take place. An attempt during the day by a CANA F-28 Fellowship to reach Stanley had to be aborted and the aircraft returned to Rio Grande, probably thwarted by the threat posed by a Sea Harrier CAP.

Early morning fog soon lifted enough to permit the Port San Carlos strip to be used. At the end of an 800 Squadron CAP Lieutenant Commander Neill Thomas (XZ455) and Lieutenant Simon Hargreaves (ZA177) were about to land their Sea Harriers at the FOB when rotor downwash from the 18 Squadron Chinook HC1 (ZA718) lifted a section of the metal planking, making it unusable. After a few hurried radio calls explaining their fuel state and the urgent need to land somewhere soon, Neill Thomas diverted to *Fearless* and Simon Hargreaves to *Intrepid* to land on their decks. The large assault ships had been available for emergency Sea Harrier operations ever since the vessels arrived in San Carlos Water but this was the first and only occasion that they were actually used during the conflict. After taking on a partial fuel load the two Sea Harriers took off vertically as an Argentine air raid alert (which turned out to be a false alarm) was called. Both aircraft eventually landed on the repaired strip at Port San Carlos.

There were several Argentine air raids during the day; fortunately none of them inflicted any serious damage despite some determined flying by the Skyhawk pilots of Grupo 5. The 13th also saw the last attempt by the Pucaras based at Stanley airport to attack British troops. All of the aircraft returned safely to the airfield having achieved very little during their mission. A flight of three Daggers was dispatched to bomb British positions on Mount Longdon but one of the aircraft aborted after take-off when its undercarriage would not retract. The two remaining aircraft reached the target area only to be thwarted by bad weather and the threat of a Sea Harrier interception.

Another trio of Daggers from Grupo 6 was reduced to two when one of the aircraft suffered brake failure prior to take-off from Rio Gallegos, where the Rio Grande squadron had moved a few days earlier. Capitan Dimeglio and Primer Teniente Roman drifted further south than planned during their flight to the islands and came across a solitary Lynx HAS2 well offshore. The frigate *Cardiff* had just taken over radar picket duty from *Exeter* in San Carlos Water and her Lynx HAS2 (XZ233) was about 50 miles south of Falkland Sound, returning from a surface search mission when the attack by the two Daggers took place. The Lynx pilot, Lieutenant C H Clayton, heard a loud noise and immediately thought that the helicopter had developed engine trouble but a check on the instruments revealed that all

was normal. A few moments later a Dagger flashed past and another was spotted turning in towards the helicopter. Realising that the noise he had heard was cannon fire from the Dagger's 30mm DEFA cannon, Chris Clayton made a steep descending turn to port from 1,000ft and dived to within just a few feet of the sea.

The first Dagger attempted to make a head-on pass but Chris Clayton kept the Lynx turning and slowed down to keep the jet in sight. The Dagger pilot fired again but the cannon shells missed the Lynx by about 100 yards. As the fighter pulled up the second Dagger was seen in a shallow dive on the helicopter's starboard side, so Chris Clayton banked steeply towards the aircraft and accelerated. The two aircraft very nearly collided as the Dagger broke away at the last moment and climbed away to join its colleague. The two Daggers were now running short of fuel and ammunition and they gave up chasing their elusive target, climbed away and departed. The Lynx remained on station for a few more minutes on the lookout for the fighters in case they should return, but by then the Daggers were winging their way back to base, having been defeated by the superior flying of Lieutenant Clayton in the very agile Lynx.

Another flight of three Daggers also ran into trouble on the 13th. One aircraft aborted soon after take-off, another had to turn back when within 60 miles of the Falklands due to a rough running engine, while the last aircraft was forced to turn back when it was warned of a Sea Harrier CAP that was heading for him. Yet another trio of Daggers was turned back later in the afternoon by a combination of bad weather and Sea Harrier activity, bringing to a close Grupo 6's contribution to the Falklands conflict.

Grupo 5 was tasked with what became their final mission of the conflict. Two flights (Nene and Chispa), each of four A-4B Skyhawks armed with parachute-retarded bombs, were instructed to bomb British troops and command headquarters on and around Mount Kent and Two Sisters. The eight aircraft took off from Rio Gallegos late in the morning but as they reached the KC-130H tanker the leader of the first flight, Capitan Zelaya, had to return to base when his J65 engine overheated. Capitan Varela took over the entire formation of seven remaining aircraft and continued to the target. In addition to Varela, the pilots were Tenientes M F Roca, S G Mayor, M C Moroni, L A Cervera, O P Gelardi and G A Dellepiane.

The formation approached the Falklands from the northwest and then turned to make their low-level run to the target from due north. At 1513Z, as the Skyhawks were just two minutes away from their target,

they were warned of Sea Harrier CAPs that were in the vicinity. The formation continued and three of the Skyhawks dropped their bombs on a British position on the lower slopes of Mount Kent without hitting the target. This was most fortunate, as the target was none other than the headquarters of 3 Commando Brigade, occupied at the time by Major General Moore and his staff who were preparing for a briefing. Although taken by surprise, the British troops quickly put up a large amount of anti-aircraft fire but no aircraft were hit.

As the other four Skyhawks prepared to attack British troops on Mount Longdon, a SAM exploded between the two Skyhawks flown by Capitan Varela and Teniente Mayor causing some damage to Varela's aircraft. Just as Varela was about to open fire on a Sea King that appeared in front of his aircraft, he noticed the Skyhawk's engine was beginning to overheat and make ominous rumbling noises. As the controls were starting to become sloppy he jettisoned all his external stores, but this was taken as a sign by the other three pilots following him to drop their bombs. The bombs fell harmlessly on Mount Longdon, missing 2 PARA's positions on the mountain. As the three aircraft that had bombed Mount Kent turned away to the north to leave the area another Sea King came into view, right in front of the Skyhawk of Teniente Alferez Dellepiane. The Skyhawk fired its cannon as the formation swept past the helicopter but the nearby detonation of two more SAMs discouraged any further interest and the Skyhawks quickly made off to the west.

In fact, Sea King HC4 ZA298 of 846 Squadron was being flown by Lieutenant Commander Simon Thornewill, the squadron commander, and it had actually been hit by the Skyhawk during the attack. The Sea King had just delivered a load of 105mm ammunition from Teal Inlet to Mount Kent and was about a mile and a half south of Estancia House when the attack took place. As the helicopter emerged from Impassable Valley near Mount Challenger the crewman, Chief Petty Officer Aircrewman M J Tupper, spotted Dellepiane's Skyhawk and warned Simon Thornewill who turned the Sea King to face the attacker in an effort to avoid the cannon fire. There was a single loud bang as a cannon shell hit the helicopter but its handling appeared to be unaffected and so Simon Thornewill descended into a ravine to sit out the attack.

After all of the Skyhawks had departed, Thornewill flew ZA298 to Impassable Valley and landed to inspect the damage. A hole was found in the main spar of one of the rotor blades where a 20mm cannon shell had passed through without exploding. Within a couple of hours Sea King HC4

ZA291 had flown over a new blade that was quickly fitted to ZA298 which then took off and flew back to San Carlos. 846 Squadron spent much of the day bringing up ammunition to forward positions in an effort to keep up the constant artillery barrage that was taking a toll on the enemy troops.

As the Grupo 5 Skyhawks made their way back across East Falkland Capitan Varela expected to have to eject from his damaged aircraft at any moment; and as they passed over Falkland Sound Dellepiane also reported problems. His aircraft was damaged and he had jettisoned his external fuel tanks and was concerned about running out of fuel, but fortunately the formation of Skyhawks rendezvoused with the ever-present KC-130H tankers and refuelled successfully. However, one of the tankers, flown by Vicecomodoro Luis J Litrenta, had to accompany Dellepiane all the way to Rio Gallegos, to ensure his safe arrival. Dellepiane's aircraft was losing fuel faster than it could take it on and as it landed it was sprayed with fuel from the ruptured wing tank.

When the flight of three Skyhawks bombed the British positions at Mount Kent they caused some damage to two helicopters of 656 Squadron on the ground at an adjacent FOB near Estancia House. Gazelle AH1 ZA728 had its Perspex bubble canopy shattered while Scout AH1 XT637 had its canopy, tail rotor and tail boom hit by shrapnel. Several Wessex of 847 Squadron avoided being damaged in the attack but the two 656 Squadron helicopters had to be airlifted back to San Carlos for repair at the 70 Aircraft Workshop, REME.

Also arriving at San Carlos for repair on the 13th was Scout AH1 XR628, which had been retrieved from MacPhee Pond two days earlier and had been taken to Fitzroy temporarily. Due to a shortage of certain spare parts (Scout tail rotors and Gazelle Perspex canopies), it was some considerable time before either of the helicopters damaged at Estancia House was operational again.

At 1430Z two Harrier GR3s took off on what became the first successful drop of LGBs during the conflict. Although LGBs had been available for use by 1 Squadron since 24th May, it was not until 13th June that a ground-based FAC was able to reach a position with a working laser designator to enable him to mark a target for the 1 Squadron Harriers. Eight laser designators had been sent to the Falklands; two were lost in the crash of the Sea King on 19th May and the others did not reach the front line until the final days of the conflict.

Fittingly, the first successful LGB attack (marking the RAF's first operational use of the 'smart' weapon) was carried out by the squadron commander, Wing Commander Peter Squire, flying XZ997, which carried two bombs. He and Flight Lieutenant Mark Hare (XZ133) attacked an Argentine company headquarters on Tumbledown during the mission. The target was illuminated too early on the first drop causing the first LGB to undershoot by 400 yards, but the second bomb was bang on target. The bomb was released at 55ft in a 3g, 45-degree pull-up and reached 3,000ft before guiding successfully down and onto the target, which was being marked by a FAC, Major Mike Howles.

Peter Squire approached Tumbledown from the southwest and pulled up from behind Mount Harriet, thereby shielding himself from the Argentine defences on Tumbledown itself. Mark Hare then followed up the attack by dropping his load of CBUs on the target area before both aircraft returned safely to *Hermes* at 1530Z. Three hours later Squadron Leader Jerry Pook, accompanied by Flight Lieutenant John Rochfort, carried out the second successful LGB drop, the target this time being a 105mm gun near Moody Brook just west of Stanley. Jerry Pook's aircraft had come under fire from troops of the Scots Guards during this attack but fortunately they missed!

Following the attack by Argentine fighters earlier in the day, *Cardiff*'s Lynx was active in the evening using thermal imaging equipment to search for enemy positions prior to an SAS insertion later that night during which the Lynx stood by to provide SAR cover. *Exeter*'s Lynx HAS2 (XZ733) had also been involved in a Special Forces mission during the 13th when it successfully located an enemy observation post near Mount Rosalie on the northeast tip of West Falkland. *Penelope*'s Lynx HAS2 (XZ691) fired a Sea Skua missile at the Argentine patrol boat *Rio Iguazu* in Choiseul Sound, despite the fact that the vessel had been beached there since a Sea Harrier attack on 22nd May and had actually fallen into British hands since then! This boat had also been strafed by Sea Harriers on two separate occasions in recent days.

At one minute before midnight the final offensive of the Falklands conflict commenced when the 2nd Battalion of the Scots Guards started their assault on Tumbledown and the Paras assaulted Wireless Ridge. Enemy resistance was fierce and an artillery battle was fought for several hours, causing casualties on both sides. The frigates *Active* and *Avenger* joined in the barrage on Argentine positions on Tumble-

Sea King HC4 ZA298 'VA' of 846 Squadron touches down on RFA Tidepool, *one of the Royal Navy's largest tankers. ZA298 was damaged by cannon fire from an Argentine Skyhawk near Mount Kent on 13th June.* MoD

Argentine Air Force C-130 Hercules flew their last sorties into Stanley on 13th June. These aircraft had avoided Sea Harriers and missiles and had flown in atrocious weather to deliver troops and supplies to Stanley and to evacuate the wounded. MoD

down and during the night a total of 856 rounds were fired. Men from 2 PARA and the SAS eventually succeeded in taking Wireless Ridge to overlook Moody Brook and thereby provide accurate targeting information for the artillery.

The helicopters of 656 Squadron were heavily involved in the night battle and Captain J G Greenhalgh and Lance Corporal J Gammon flew several casevac sorties in Scout AH1 XW282 during the night in extreme weather conditions and under intense enemy artillery bombardment. The first two casualties were landed at Fitzroy at 0406Z on the 14th and casevac missions continued after dawn despite the helicopter's exposure to enemy fire.

Captain S M Drennan and Lance Corporal J J Rigg in Scout AH1 XV139 flew a particularly difficult sortie to recover a Gurkha and three Scots Guardsmen who were badly injured and in an inaccessible and exposed position on the eastern slopes of Tumbledown. The helicopter flew to Tumbledown from Goat Ridge in appalling flying weather of driving snow and severe turbulence. Sam Drennan eventually recovered a total of 16 wounded soldiers from the slopes of Tumbledown and was awarded the DFC for his persistent courage in risking his own life to save others. A few hours earlier, at 2345Z on the 13th, the same Scout helicopter and crew had rescued a Welsh Guardsman who was suffering from severe pneumonia on Sapper Hill. On the first attempt, during which the helicopter was almost blown into the mountainside by the high wind, Sam Drennan was unable to locate the unlit position and had to return to refuel. He took off again at 0125Z and, despite the continuing severe weather conditions, succeeded in finding the Guardsman and flying him to Fitzroy, where they arrived at 0225Z

Two more Argentine C-130s arrived at Stanley airport late at night on the 13th. At 2200Z Mayor Bolzi flew in carrying a load of 155mm howitzer shells. As the aircraft was being unloaded the airport was suddenly lit up by a starshell fired by a British ship off the coast. A few moments later shells started falling on the airport and as soon as the rest of the cargo was unloaded, the Hercules took off and disappeared into the night.

The next Hercules, TC-65, flown by Comodoro Mela and his crew, landed at Stanley at 2300Z carrying a complete 155mm gun with 80 rounds of ammunition.

Once again British shells started to fall on the airfield as the Hercules was unloaded. Soon afterwards a Sea Harrier CAP was reported to be heading towards Stanley from the east so the unloading stopped with the howitzer still on board the Hercules as the air and ground crew took cover from the expected air raid. However, the air raid did not materialise so the unloading later resumed and TC-65 took off at 2335Z carrying 72 sick and wounded troops back to the mainland and safety. Also on board the Hercules were several pilots of the Escuadron Aeromovil Pucara, the commanding officer of which, Mayor Navarro, stayed behind to supervise the de-arming of the remaining aircraft.

This was the last of 31 C-130 missions that successfully reached Stanley airport between 1st May and 13th June, bringing in 514 passengers and over 400 tons of supplies and taking out 264 casualties. Argentine Navy Electras and F-28s had also braved the air blockade and in 14 flights had brought in around 70 tons of supplies while taking 304 personnel back to the mainland. The fact that the Argentine Air Force was able to get five flights in an out of Stanley on the penultimate day of the conflict demonstrates the professionalism and courage of the C-130 crews and highlights the inability of British forces to detect such flights and deal with them effectively.

At about the same time that the last Hercules was leaving Stanley airport, 800 Squadron scrambled a Sea Harrier CAP in response to a potential air raid. Whatever the unidentified aircraft were, they turned away when they were warned of the CAP's presence.

On 13th June modification work was completed on one of the RAF's Nimrod R1 electronic surveillance aircraft (XW664) of 51 Squadron in preparation for its deployment to Ascension Island, although it is believed that the aircraft had already been operating over the South Atlantic before

being modified. Like the maritime patrol Nimrods, this aircraft had been fitted with an in-flight refuelling probe to extend its range. The part played by the Nimrod R1s of 51 Squadron has still not been revealed but the aircraft's electronic information gathering role would make it a highly valuable asset during the conflict. The squadron was awarded the battle honour 'South Atlantic 1982' after the conflict so it obviously played its part during hostilities.

14th June (Monday) – Surrender!

At 0132Z on the 14th another CAP was launched by 800 Squadron to investigate enemy aircraft over the south of East Falkland. The enemy aircraft turned away as the Sea Harrier approached but held off until the British jets left the area. At 0150Z the enemy aircraft once more approached East Falkland at high altitude, intent on bombing British positions to the south of Stanley. The aircraft were two Canberra B62s escorted by two Mirage IIIEAs of Grupo 8. The Canberras had deployed south to Rio Gallegos from Trelew and were flown by Capitans Roberto Pastran and Fernando Juan Casado in 'Baco 1' (B-108) and Primer Tenientes Rivolier and Anino in 'Baco 2' (B-109), while the Mirages were 'Pluton 1' flown by Mayor Jose Sanchez and 'Pluton 2' flown by Capitan Ricardo Gonzalez.

The mission followed the pattern of earlier raids although this one was flown at 40,000ft. It was hoped that at this altitude, although plainly visible on radar, the aircraft would be out of range of both the Sea Harriers and British SAMs. The Canberras became slightly separated during the run-in to Mount Kent, having been deterred by the presence of a Sea Harrier flown by Lieutenant Commander Mike Blissett on their first attempt; but both bombers (and their Mirage escorts) reached the target area and released their bombs before turning towards the coast to fly south on the homeward leg of the mission.

Although Gonzalez had escorted 'Baco 2' over the target, Sanchez had been unable to maintain close contact with 'Baco 1' as the Canberra had become separated from the other Canberra. Sanchez turned east after flying near the target area and turned again over Stanley to head back south. As the Mirage made its turn it was fired on by a Sea Dart from *Cardiff*, which was on air defence picket duty nearly 30 miles north of Stanley. Sanchez put the Mirage into a steep spiral dive and the missile exploded without causing any damage to the aircraft.

As the Canberras approached the coast after leaving the target area more Sea Darts were launched from both *Cardiff* and *Exeter*. One of the Mirage pilots warned Rivolier in 'Baco 2' that a missile was tracking his aircraft and Rivolier started to fire chaff and flares as he banked and dived steeply to break the missile's lock. However, at 0155Z 'Baco 1' was hit under the forward fuselage by a Sea Dart fired from *Exeter*. With his aircraft on fire and barely controllable Capitan Pastran tried to slow the rate of descent and ordered his navigator to eject when passing through 15,000ft. However, Capitan Casado told him that his ejection seat would not fire and soon afterwards the aircraft entered an uncontrollable spin. Unable to raise Casado again on the intercom, Pastran had no option but to eject, which he did as the aircraft passed through 7,000ft.

After being knocked unconscious during the ejection, Capitan Pastran landed in the sea south of Fitzroy and struggled into his dinghy, which was blown towards the shore by the wind. He waded ashore before dawn and spent most of the day walking inland towards Port Pleasant in the vain hope of reaching an Argentine position. After nightfall on the 14th he was found by a British helicopter that homed in on his SARBE beacon. Sadly, Capitan Casado had not been able to escape from the aircraft as it crashed into the sea near Lively Island and his body was never found. Canberra B62 B-108, like all of Argentina's Canberras, had started its career with the RAF and had been flown by 44, 73 and 207 Squadrons before being sold to Argentina.

This mission was the last Argentine Air Force combat mission of the conflict and the Canberra was the last Argentine aircraft to be shot down. Although Mike Blissett had seen the flash of the Sea Dart explosion, the British forces had not realised that they had been successful until Capitan Pastran was picked up. Several volleys of SAMs had been seen by the two Mirage pilots, one of the missiles obviously malfunctioning as its exhaust marked an erratic course. Both Mirages had descended below 15,000ft as they tried to evade the missiles and were warned by Argentine radar that they were

flying over the British garrison at Goose Green, so they quickly climbed back to high altitude to accompany the remaining Canberra back to Rio Gallegos.

During the incident the frigate *Penelope* reported that a missile had been fired at her and that the missile had exploded as it hit the sea about 1,000 yards from the ship. There is no evidence that this was an Argentine missile; neither the Canberras nor the Mirages could have fired one at the ship and as far as is known only one Exocet was ever fired from Stanley. There has been a recent suggestion that it may have been a rogue Sea Dart from *Cardiff* but this has by no means been proven.

It fell to the CANA to make the last successful resupply flight of the conflict into Stanley airport when an L188PF Electra of 5 Escuadra arrived at the airfield in the early hours of the 14th. The aircraft soon took off again to become the last fixed-wing flight out of Stanley while it was still in Argentine hands. Apparently, as soon as the Electra had departed Falkland airspace, the commander of the AN/TPS-43 radar ordered it to be closed down for the final time and vital components destroyed so that it did not fall into enemy hands. This act indicates that surrender was imminent.

The battle for Tumbledown continued, with 656 Squadron's Scouts being particularly busy on casevac operations throughout the night and into daylight, not only from Tumbledown but also from Wireless Ridge. However, after a night of intense fighting, Mount Tumbledown fell to British forces soon after daybreak on 14th June. As 2 PARA moved off Wireless Ridge towards Moody Brook and Stanley itself, it came under artillery fire from a 105mm battery near Stanley racecourse. Argentine troops were seen moving out towards Sapper Hill due west of Stanley while more were fleeing in the opposite direction, towards the town.

At 1132Z two Harrier GR3s flown by Flight Lieutenant Ross Boyens (XV789) and Flight Lieutenant Murdo MacLeod (XV778) took off from *Hermes* and landed at the Harrier FOB to be ready to provide close air support to the British troops in the final advance into Stanley. However, when 2 PARA called for air support as they advanced off Wireless Ridge the Harriers at the FOB could not take off due to bad weather and a build-up of ice on the airstrip.

Captain J G Greenhalgh and Lance Corporal J Gammon of 656 Squadron made seven trips to Tumbledown during the early hours of the morning in Scout AH1 XW282 to pick up casualties during the fierce fighting between the Scots Guards and the Argentine 5th Marine Battalion. During one of their casevac flights from Wireless Ridge the Scout crew spotted Argentine troops

near to Sapper Hill. Captain Greenhalgh returned to the FOB and fitted four SS-11 missiles to the Scout and fired them at gun emplacements and Argentine troops as they retreated towards Stanley, pursued by 2 PARA.

Many of the helicopters of 3 CBAS were involved in an early morning casevac of wounded troops from 42 Commando who had inadvertently walked into an Argentine minefield during the night. Later during the morning of the 14th, two 'B' Flight Scouts joined in the harrying of enemy troops during their disorderly retreat towards Stanley. Sergeant C J Watkin and Corporal H Whale (XV140) and Lieutenant V B Shaugnessy and Corporal G Carvell (XW616), together with the two 656 Squadron Scouts (XT637 and XT649) that had been detached to the 3 CBAS FOB at Estancia House since the 11th, were involved in the attack and fired a total of 10 SS-11 missiles. Nine of the missiles hit their targets, mostly artillery positions, while the tenth suffered a wire break and fell short. One of the bunkers attacked by the Scouts was subsequently found to house a well dug-in 105mm gun. The mission was halted when the Scouts were heavily and accurately mortared as they hovered close to the ground near Wireless Ridge.

At 1500Z Squadron Leader Peter Harris (XZ997) and Flight Lieutenant Nick Gilchrist (XZ133) took off from *Hermes* to make another combined LGB/CBU raid on enemy positions on Sapper Hill. However at 1550Z white flags were seen being waved by Argentine troops in Stanley and the FAC told the Harrier pilots to stand by at high altitude over the target while the situation was clarified. Five minutes later the Argentine surrender was confirmed and the Harrier pilots were ordered to fly back to *Hermes* where they landed at 1625Z with their ordnance intact and brought the news that the Argentines were surrendering. Although it seemed as though the fighting might be over the Sea Harriers continued to maintain CAPs throughout the rest of the day. The Harrier GR3s were then refitted with AIM-9L Sidewinders to enable them to take a share of CAP duty now that they were no longer needed for close air support or battlefield air interdiction.

Following the outbreak of white flags in Stanley, 'C' Flight 3 CBAS Gazelle AH1 XX412 flown by Lieutenant Commander G R A Coryton picked up Lieutenant Colonel Michael Rose, the commanding officer of 22 SAS, and flew him into Stanley to begin the surrender negotiations. The helicopter carried a white flag slung underneath the fuselage to denote its peaceful mission.

The Sea Kings of 846 Squadron had been involved in bringing up 105mm shells for the artillery for much of the day but after white flags were seen several of the helicopters started moving men forward to Moody Brook to commence the occupation of Stanley.

It was intended that Sea King HC4 ZA298 of 846 Squadron should fly Major General Moore into Stanley to formally accept the surrender and the helicopter was quickly painted with prominent white fuselage panels to mark its status. However, the weather conditions proved to be too bad for the 846 Squadron helicopter so an 820 Squadron Sea King HAS5 manned by a naval observer and equipped with a more sophisticated radar than the HC4, flew the mission instead. Lieutenant Commander Keith Dudley and his crew flew XZ920 to Fitzroy to collect Major General Moore and his staff and fly them to Stanley football pitch, landing in a blizzard by the lights of several Argentine jeeps.

At Stanley Major General Moore met with the Argentine garrison commander, General de Brigada Mario Menendez, and the surrender negotiations were finally signed at 2359Z (2059 local). During the afternoon *Avenger*'s Lynx flew the ship's First Lieutenant, along with another officer and four ratings to Fox Bay on West Falkland to accept the formal surrender of the 950-strong Argentine garrison there.

A most welcome arrival in the Falklands on the final day of the conflict was a second 18 Squadron Chinook HC1. Wing Commander Tony Stables, commanding officer of 18 Squadron, flew ZA705 from the *Contender Bezant* via a refuelling stop on *Hermes* to the Port San Carlos FOB, arriving just a couple of hours after the cease-fire. Another Chinook (ZA707) was to have followed later the same day but was diverted to the *Europic Ferry* soon after take-off and was forced to stay on board until the 16th as the ship rode out a fierce force 11 storm. Just as word of the Argentine surrender was coming in, Chinook 'Bravo November' was flying an eight-ton steel girder bridge from Fitzroy to Murrell Bridge to replace a wooden structure that had been destroyed in the fighting. The load was very awkward and swung wildly beneath the helicopter in the strong wind, necessitating a very slow and careful flight.

As the surrender negotiations were taking place on the Falklands an RAF Hercules was steadily making its way south from Ascension Island. The fourth Hercules C1P (XV218) had arrived at Ascension the previous day and took off at 0430Z to make an airdrop to the Task Force. By the time it arrived back at Wideawake airfield the conflict was over!

Also during the 14th the two Vulcan B2s at Wideawake (XM598 and XM607) took off for the long flight back to Waddington, thereby concluding the type's participation in the Falklands conflict.

The final VC10 C1 repatriation flight to arrive at Brize Norton before the end of the conflict was flown by XV108. The aircraft left Montevideo on the 13th and arrived in the UK, via Ascension Island, in the early hours of the 14th with 61 wounded, including 28 stretcher cases.

The combined land, sea and air actions on 14th June brought to a successful conclusion the 45-day British assault on the Falklands that had commenced on 1st May. The surrender ended the ten-week illegal occupation of the islands by Argentine forces and led to the downfall of General Galtieri's junta. However, there was still much to do to restore the islands to some semblance of normality and to ensure their continued security.

The Chinook HC1's huge load-carrying capability enabled it to recover helicopters and other large loads. ZA705 'BU' arrived at San Carlos on the last day of the conflict and assisted in many of the logistics tasks that were necessary to restore normal life to the islands after the cessation of hostilities.
MoD

Royal Navy Task Force Ship and Aircraft Strength within the TEZ off the Falkland Islands, 14th June 1982

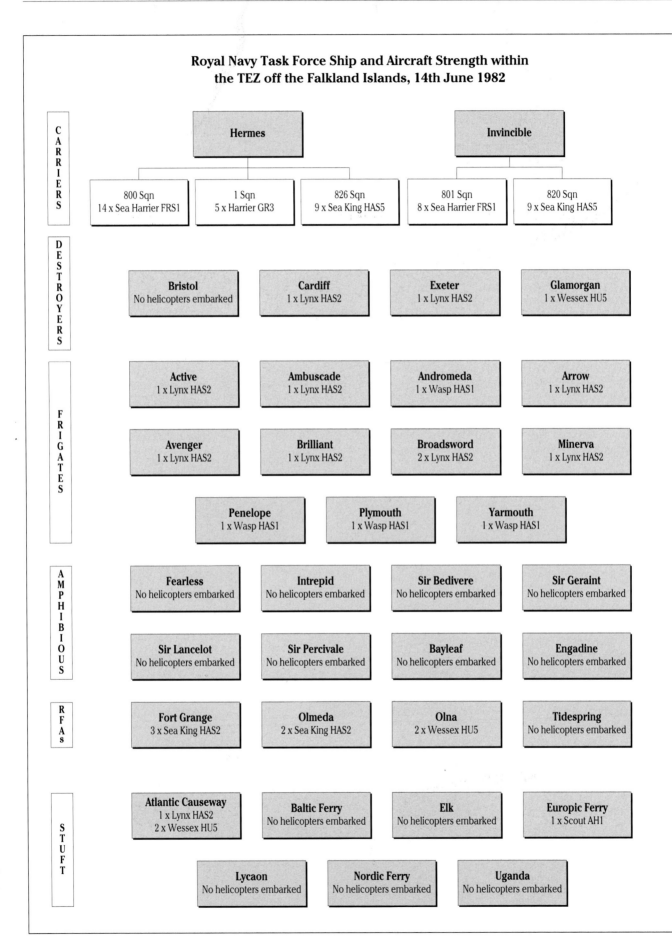

CARRIERS

Hermes			Invincible	
800 Sqn 14 x Sea Harrier FRS1	1 Sqn 5 x Harrier GR3	826 Sqn 9 x Sea King HAS5	801 Sqn 8 x Sea Harrier FRS1	820 Sqn 9 x Sea King HAS5

DESTROYERS

Bristol No helicopters embarked	Cardiff 1 x Lynx HAS2	Exeter 1 x Lynx HAS2	Glamorgan 1 x Wessex HU5

FRIGATES

Active 1 x Lynx HAS2	Ambuscade 1 x Lynx HAS2	Andromeda 1 x Wasp HAS1	Arrow 1 x Lynx HAS2
Avenger 1 x Lynx HAS2	Brilliant 1 x Lynx HAS2	Broadsword 2 x Lynx HAS2	Minerva 1 x Lynx HAS2

Penelope 1 x Wasp HAS1	Plymouth 1 x Wasp HAS1	Yarmouth 1 x Wasp HAS1

AMPHIBIOUS

Fearless No helicopters embarked	Intrepid No helicopters embarked	Sir Bedivere No helicopters embarked	Sir Geraint No helicopters embarked
Sir Lancelot No helicopters embarked	Sir Percivale No helicopters embarked	Bayleaf No helicopters embarked	Engadine No helicopters embarked

RFAs

Fort Grange 3 x Sea King HAS2	Olmeda 2 x Sea King HAS2	Olna 2 x Wessex HU5	Tidespring No helicopters embarked

STUFT

Atlantic Causeway 1 x Lynx HAS2 2 x Wessex HU5	Baltic Ferry No helicopters embarked	Elk No helicopters embarked	Europic Ferry 1 x Scout AH1

Lycaon No helicopters embarked	Nordic Ferry No helicopters embarked	Uganda No helicopters embarked

Chapter Five

Post-war Air Operations

The period immediately following the surrender saw several developments. Firstly, although General Menendez had surrendered all Argentine forces on the Falklands there was never a declaration of peace, in the same way that there had never been a formal declaration of war between the UK and Argentina. Indeed, the Dagger As of Grupo 6, for example, remained at a state of readiness for several days after the surrender and did not return to Tandil until the end of June, although the new Argentine President, General Bignone, announced on 21st June that Argentina would observe the 'cease-fire'. Consequently, British forces in the South Atlantic maintained a high state of alert for some time after 14th June in case hostilities should be renewed.

Another development was the strengthening and reinforcement of British forces on the Falklands and at sea in the South Atlantic. This continued for several months and, as the newly constructed facilities became available, the British garrison took on a more permanent presence that continues to this day. However, the most immediate activity on the Falklands after the surrender was the massive clean-up operation. This included the collecting together of Argentine troops, now prisoners of war, and their equipment; the reorganisation of British forces on the islands and the construction of temporary camps and FOBs; and the attempt to re-establish a semblance of normality for the Falkland Islanders whose lives had been totally disrupted by the conflict.

As soon as the British forces entered Stanley and had a chance to inspect the airfield there it was obvious that it could not be used regularly or safely until a major clear-up and rebuilding programme had been completed. The cumulative effect of Vulcan, Sea Harrier and Harrier raids and naval

bombardment had virtually destroyed the airfield and all its facilities, with the notable exception of the runway itself, although this was badly damaged. The immediate result was that HMS *Invincible* had to remain close to the Falklands to provide air defence until Stanley could be made ready to accept combat aircraft. 1 Squadron's Harrier GR3s were the first fixed-wing aircraft to deploy ashore when they flew off HMS *Hermes* on 4th July to be renamed the Harrier Detachment, or HarDet for short. As soon as the surrender took place the Harrier GR3s had been reconfigured for air defence duties in case Argentina should renew her assault on the Falklands.

After clearing the Argentine ordnance, moving the aircraft wrecks and checking for unexploded British bombs and shells on the airfield, the Royal Engineers set to work to extend the runway by laying 2,000ft of aluminium matting and installing runway arrester gear. The resulting length of 6,100ft and the arrester gear was long enough to allow Phantoms to operate from RAF Stanley, as the town's airport was renamed. As an air defence aircraft the Phantom had a much greater range and greatly enhanced weapons capability than the Sea Harriers

that had performed so effectively in that role since the conflict began.

The Harrier GR3s were retained for some years as they added a greater degree of flexibility of operations to the Phantom detachment, which was dependent on the single runway at RAF Stanley. The Harrier strip at Port San Carlos, as well as another one built at Goose Green, continued to be used by the HarDet but RAF Stanley was the main operating base on the Falklands until the building of a new airfield that had been planned even before the conflict was over. Rapier batteries, manned by both the RAF and the Army, supplemented the Phantoms and Harriers in the air defence role. Radar sites (originally mobile radars but later replaced by more permanent structures) were placed at strategic locations around the islands and weapons ranges were established using as targets the hulks of Argentine aircraft that had been captured during the conflict.

Work started on a brand-new airfield near Mount Pleasant late in 1983. The airfield was built with an 8,500ft main runway and a shorter subsidiary runway, as well as permanent hangars, including a QRA facility, and administrative buildings. The run-

Sea King HAS2A XV700 '264' of 825 Squadron arrives at Stanley racecourse shortly after the end of the conflict. This helicopter wears the code of its previous unit, 814 Squadron, and is today in service with 810 Squadron at Culdrose. Wg Cdr P Lyall

way was long enough to take chartered Boeing 747s as well as the RAF's new Tri-Stars, which were bought from Pan Am and British Airways specifically to provide long-range strategic transport to the Falkland Islands. The airfield was well protected by surveillance radars and a network of Rapier SAM sites.

The Captured Aircraft and Weapons

Of the 15 Argentine helicopters captured at Stanley, several were relatively intact and had been flown within the last few days of the conflict. The 5th Infantry Brigade was particularly short of helicopter support so the Brigade Air Liaison Officer, Squadron Leader Rob Tierney, investigated the possibility of using some of the Argentine helicopters to supplement British helicopters in the immediate post-war period. A pair of UH-1Hs had been found abandoned near the Governor's House and had apparently been used for casevac in the final days as they had been painted white all over. One of these, AE-413, was found to be still airworthy and Squadron Leader Tierney flew the helicopter for 15 hours over four days, assisting the recovery of British troops from remote locations. The Huey was loaded on board the MV *Tor Caledonia* and arrived in the UK on 20th August. After appearing at an air show at RAF Finningley the helicopter was damaged during road transportation and spent some time undergoing restoration before being used to raise funds for the RAF Benevolent Fund. The two surviving A-109A Hirundos were also in reasonable condition when found at Stanley and they were also shipped to the UK. These helicopters were relatively new and had plenty of airframe hours left, so they were refurbished and taken into service by 8 Flight,

After the conflict the Harrier GR3s of 1 Squadron were refitted with Sidewinders and moved into Stanley airfield to share air defence duties of the Falklands with a detachment of Sea Harrier FRS1s. MoD

Flight Sergeant D W Knights stands over a pit near Stanley airfield where Tigercat missiles had been stored ready for disposal. 'Doc' Knights was one of several RAF EOD experts who cleared hundreds of tons of Argentine ammunition in the immediate post-conflict period. Flt Sgt D W Knights

One of the first tasks at Stanley after the conflict was the repair of the airport's runway. Although the runway was rarely completely unusable during the conflict, it did suffer a lot of damage and large amounts of metal planking were needed to effect a temporary repair until it could be completely reconstructed. MoD

Damaged in May and destroyed in June, some intact sections of the wreckage of Prefectura Naval Argentina Skyvan 3M PA-54, including the starboard engine, were brought to the UK for display at the Fleet Air Arm Museum at RNAS Yeovilton. Wg Cdr P Lyall

Three MB-339As of 1 Escuadrilla de Ataque were found abandoned at Stanley airport. Despite suffering badly at the hands of souvenir hunters, two of the airframes were shipped to the UK and preserved while the third was used as a target on a weapons range. Flt Sgt D W Knights

A group of four Pucaras sit forlornly at Stanley airport soon after the end of hostilities. A-532 was one of eight Pucaras that eventually ended their days on one of the weapons ranges in the Falklands where they were used as ground targets for Harriers. MoD

Pucara A-509 is seen here in the snow at Stanley airport some time after the end of the conflict. By 1985 it was one of just two Pucara wrecks left visible on the airfield. Sqn Ldr D Cyster

Seriously derelict after nearly four years' exposure to the harsh weather of the Falklands, Pucara A-509 sits with its back broken at Stanley airport circa 1986. Sqn Ldr D Cyster

Army Air Corps at Netheravon for use by the SAS. Both helicopters remain in service.

A total of 11 Pucaras were captured at Stanley at the end of the conflict but only about two or three were airworthy or could be made so with some effort. Three aircraft were taken to the UK for testing at the A&AEE Boscombe Down: A-515 was allocated the British serial ZD485 and was flown extensively in 1983 while A-533 (ZD486) and A-549 (ZD487) were used as a source for spare parts. Eventually five Pucaras were transported to the UK and displayed in aviation museums, as were two of the MB-339As and a single T-34C-1 Turbo Mentor. Two other helicopters, an Army CH-47C and a Prefectura Naval Puma, were brought to the UK and used by the military. A total of 12 captured aircraft (eight Pucaras, two UH-1Hs, an MB-339A and a T-34C-1) were used as targets on weapons ranges set up in the Falklands.

It was not just aircraft that were taken over by British forces after the conflict. Twelve twin Oerlikon 35mm anti-aircraft guns and their associated Skyguard fire control radars were captured and brought to the UK. After refurbishment the guns were allocated to 1339 Wing, Royal Auxiliary Air Force Regiment, which was responsible for the defence of RAF Coningsby and RAF Waddington.

Chronology

15th June 1982
To consolidate the surrender HQ 3 Commando Brigade moved into Stanley while 'B' Flight 3 CBAS completed its move to Stanley racecourse. The transport helicopters spent much of the day moving up troops and supplies to Stanley to start clearing-up operations and take charge of the Argentine prisoners, of which a total of 10,254 were eventually counted. The helicopters flew in strong winds and blizzard conditions to recover British troops from exposed positions. The weather deteriorated rapidly in the days immediately following the surrender and it was imperative that soldiers be brought in from the remote, high ground positions. HMS *Cardiff*'s Lynx and several of 846 Squadron's Sea Kings flew in a company of 40 Commando to Port Howard to accept the surrender of Argentine forces on West Falkland, while Sea King HC4 ZA298 flew General Menendez and his staff to HMS *Fearless* from Stanley to discuss the removal of Argentine forces from the islands.

The repaired Sea King HC4 ZA310 finally flew again on 15th June after having been damaged on 23rd May. The helicopter embarked on HMS *Intrepid* where it would be joined by three others the next day. Six Wessex of 847 Squadron took part in a celebratory flypast over Stanley on the 15th.

It was not just on the islands that the weather was causing problems. Wessex HU5 XT486 of 'D' Flight 848 Squadron, on loan to HMS *Glamorgan* from RFA *Tidepool*, was badly damaged in rough weather while on *Glamorgan*'s deck on the 15th. The helicopter had to be airlifted off the destroyer to the San Carlos FOB for repairs on the 19th. An 847 Squadron Wessex HU5 (XS507) was flown out of reserve from the SS *Atlantic Causeway* as a replacement.

The two surviving Argentine A-109As that were found abandoned on Stanley racecourse were test-flown on the 15th and placed under armed guard at Stanley to prevent damage. However, both helicopters were duly 'appropriated' from the clutches of 3 CBAS by 846 Squadron. AE-331 was flown to HMS *Fearless* by Lieutenant Commander Thornewill on the 16th while AE-334 was flown on board the next day by

The two surviving Argentine Army A-109As were brought to the UK on board Fearless *and were eventually absorbed into the Army Air Corps. Chinook HC1 ZA714 'BH' of 18 Squadron is seen delivering stores to the ship off Ascension Island before it continues its journey north. MoD*

Lieutenant P Rainey of 846 Squadron. During the 15th a CAB601 crew was permitted to fly one of their Hueys to search for Argentine dead and wounded, and the helicopter was later used on a mission to persuade an isolated and belligerent group of Argentine troops to surrender.

The Task Force at sea did not relax and, despite the worsening weather, the Sea Harrier squadrons maintained a constant vigil in case of renewed attacks from the mainland. Tragedy struck HMS *Invincible* on the very day when the ship's company should have been celebrating their victory. Huge waves rocked the carrier so violently that an aircraft tug broke free and slid down the deck and crushed Airman Brian Marsden against the island, resulting in severe injuries. Despite a massive blood transfusion, Brian Marsden died later the same day and was buried at sea on the 16th.

In November 1976 a party of 50 Argentine 'technicians' had landed on the small, uninhabited island of Thule in the British South Sandwich Islands, some 400 miles to the southeast of South Georgia. They set up a new base on the island, which caused a diplomatic incident but as the UK was trying to negotiate a peaceful settlement with Argentina over the Falklands at the time, the Thule incident was quietly forgotten. Now that a war had been fought and won over the Falklands, it was decided that it was time to evict the Argentines from the South Sandwich Islands as well and a plan code named Operation 'Keyhole' was set in motion. On the 15th HMS *Yarmouth* and RFA *Olmeda* left the main Task Force and set course for the South Sandwich Islands, via South Georgia. *Yarmouth* took with her Wasp HAS1 (XV624) while the *Olmeda* left one of her two 824 Squadron Sea King HAS2As on board HMS *Invincible*, but took XV649 for the journey to the islands.

16th June 1982
A four-helicopter detachment of 846 Squadron Sea King HC4s (ZA292, ZA293, ZA297 and ZA310) embarked on HMS *Intrepid* to assist in the removal of Argentine prisoners from West Falkland, particularly Fox Bay, Port Howard and Pebble Island. Another detachment of 846 Squadron Sea King HC4s (ZA296, ZA298, ZA299 and ZA313) embarked on HMS *Fearless* on the same day. Many of the British helicopters also became involved in flying missions on behalf of the civilian population, most of whom had been more or less immobilised throughout the duration of the conflict. The Headquarters and 'A' Flight 3 CBAS moved to Stanley racecourse during the 16th.

The converted aircraft transport *Contender Bezant* had arrived in the TEZ on 10th June and one of the four Chinook HC1s on board had flown to Port San Carlos on

the 14th. Another Chinook HC1 (ZA707) had also left on the 14th but soon after take-off an air raid warning (that turned out to be a false alarm) caused it to divert to the MV *Europic Ferry*. The ferry was then battered by force 11 gales for two days and the helicopter could not complete its journey to the Falklands until the weather finally abated on the 16th.

A CAB601 crew flew one of the white UH-1Hs to take Argentine wounded to the *Bahia Paraiso*, the Argentine hospital ship. The helicopter joined the *Bahia Paraiso*'s own Alouette III and Puma as well as a 2 Escuadrilla Sea King in the task, which continued into the 17th. Another CAB601 UH-1H (AE-422) was flown by a British crew from 820 Squadron to assist in the airlift of troops around the islands.

17th June 1982
Fearless sailed from San Carlos, where she had been since 13th June, to Port William and then later to Stanley. Also arriving at Port William on the 17th was the *Contender Bezant* with her load of Harriers and helicopters, many of which stayed on board for some time until needed. To assist with the movement of prisoners as well as British troops and stores, two Sea King HAS5s from 826 Squadron flew from *Hermes* to San Carlos to spend a week ashore. Two more ships of the Operation 'Keyhole' task group, *Endurance* and the tug *Salvageman*, left South Georgia for the South Sandwich Islands on the 17th. Aboard *Endurance* in addition to her two Wasp HAS1s was Wessex HU5 XS486 of 'A' Flight 848 Squadron, which was transferred from RFA *Regent*. The Wessex was tightly squeezed into *Endurance*'s hanger, leaving just enough room for the Wasps.

HMS *Plymouth* became the first Royal Navy warship to enter Stanley harbour on the 17th. As part of a victory celebration a formation of six Sea King HAS2As from 825 Squadron flew over Stanley. The leading helicopter, flown by the squadron commander Lieutenant Commander Hugh Clark, flew a white ensign from the winch cable.

18th June 1982
With the removal of Galtieri from office it was assessed safe for *Invincible* to withdraw to warmer waters to the north, along with its goalkeeper *Andromeda*, for a two week Self-Maintenance Period and to provide the crew with some much-needed rest. The carrier reached a position 23 degrees South but was due to be back off the Falklands in about two weeks to release *Hermes* for her trip back to the UK. During this period *Invincible* became the first Royal Navy vessel to change a main engine (an Olympus gas turbine) while on active duty

at sea. The first Argentine prisoners (4,167 of them) left the anchorage at Port William on the morning of the 18th on board the *Canberra*, bound for Puerto Madryn in Argentina.

The final two Chinook HC1s (ZA713 and ZA715) on board the *Contender Bezant* flew ashore to the Port San Carlos FOB on the 18th. Also flown ashore from the ship were two 3 CBAS Gazelle AH1s (XW893 and XX444) to replace the losses the squadron had suffered on 21st May. This brought the number of Chinooks available on the Falklands to five, thereby allowing some much-needed maintenance to be carried out on ZA718 'Bravo November' as the newly arrived helicopters assisted in the multitude of logistics tasks required in the immediate post-war period.

Two of the Argentine UH-1Hs (AE-409 and AE-413) were flown by crews of 656 Squadron on the 18th to assist in the movement of Argentine prisoners. The helicopters were suitably inscribed with '656' to mark their new ownership. Another Huey (AE-422) was used by Lieutenant Keith Dudley of 820 Squadron and later by an 825 Squadron pilot and flew some 30 hours under new ownership. AE-413 and AE-422 were later loaded on board the *Tor Caledonia* and *Atlantic Causeway* respectively for the journey to the UK.

In what is thought to be an RAF and world record flight for the Hercules, Flight Lieutenant Terry Locke and his 70 Squadron crew flew Hercules C1P XV179 to East Falkland to airdrop essential supplies during a flight lasting 28 hours and 3 minutes.

HMS *Yarmouth* and RFA *Olmeda* arrived at South Georgia on the 18th to refuel and collect troops for Operation 'Keyhole' at Thule. *Olmeda*'s Sea King HAS2A picked up troops of 'M' Company, Royal Marines from King Edward Point and ferried them out to the waiting ships.

The shortage of Victor K2 tankers had been a major limiting factor on long-range air operations during the conflict but work had commenced on a temporary solution to the problem until the planned programme to convert ex-British Airways VC10s and Super VC10s could be completed. Both the Hercules and the Vulcan were selected for conversion to tanker configuration and the first Vulcan K2 (XH561) made its initial test flight on 18th June. The aircraft, the first of six conversions, was fitted with extra fuel tanks in the bomb bay and a hose drum unit under the tail cone to enable single-point refuelling. XH561 was later delivered to 50 Squadron, which received the other five Vulcan K2s (XH558, XH560, XJ825, XL445 and XM571) by October. The squadron disbanded on 31st March 1984 when the VC10 K2 tankers of 101 Squadron took over the role.

On 17th June a victory flypast over Port Stanley was flown by helicopters of 825 Squadron. This photograph shows six Sea King HAS2As, led by Lieutenant Commander Hugh Clark, flying over the Governor's House.
Wg Cdr P Lyall

The arrival of the Contender Bezant *and the* Astronomer *soon after the Argentine surrender brought six more Chinook HC1s to assist with the massive clean-up and logistics operation. Originally based at the Port San Carlos FOB, the Chinook detachment moved to Kelly's Garden near San Carlos Settlement in March 1983.* Flt Sgt D W Knights

19th June 1982

With their one-day head start, *Endurance* and the *Salvageman* arrived off Thule in the early hours of the 19th. At first light Lieutenant Commander Tony Ellerbeck and Lieutenant David Wells took off in Wasp HAS1 XS527 to reconnoitre for suitable landing sites on Thule for a reconnaissance patrol to precede the main force that was en route in RFA *Olmeda*. An hour later the Wasp, now armed with two AS-12s, escorted Wessex HU5 XS486 to deliver a reconnaissance team of ten marines to the slopes of Mount Larsen. The men trekked down the mountain to find a position from where they could observe the Argentine base. Several more flights were made to different positions on the island to lead the Argentines into thinking that a much stronger force had been landed.

20th June 1982

Yarmouth and the *Olmeda* arrived off Thule in the early hours of the 20th. Just as *Yarmouth* was preparing to demonstrate her firepower by shooting at a nearby rocky islet close to Thule, the Argentine occupants surrendered. In marginal visibility, Lieutenant Commander Paul Miller took off from the *Olmeda* in Sea King HAS2A XV649 to deliver 24 troops to the base. Several more trips were made by the Sea King and by Wessex HU5 XS486 to make the base secure and transport the ten prisoners to the *Olmeda*. Several of these flights were made in difficult blizzard conditions and darkness. The last illegally occupied British territory had finally been regained. A few days after all the ships had left, Thule was cut off by pack ice for the duration of the long Antarctic winter.

23rd June 1982

Most of the personnel of 'C' and 'M' Flights 3 CBAS embarked on the *Sir Percivale* at Teal Inlet for transfer to the *Canberra* on the 23rd, while most of the 3 CBAS helicopters were flown to the *Elk* on the 23rd and 24th for the journey back to the UK. The helicopters of 3 CBAS (not including the attached flight from 656 Squadron) had flown a total of 2,109 hours during April, May and June.

24th June 1982

The first RAF Hercules to land at RAF Stanley established the British air bridge between Ascension Island and the Falklands on the 24th. The aircraft, captained by Flight Lieutenant J Norfolk, brought in a MAMS team to assist further flights. The service was temporarily halted between 14th and 29th August while the runway was further repaired and extended. During the time when landings could not be made Hercules still flew to Stanley and air-dropped loads and picked up mail by using an air-snatch system, similar to that used by the RAF's Army Co-operation squadrons in the 1930s.

On the 24th a 'C' Flight 845 Squadron Wessex HU5 (XT459) detached to Stanley from RFA *Tidespring* was badly damaged as it touched down at Stanley racecourse. The helicopter sucked up a nylon sack into its main rotors causing damage to one of the rotor blades so that it drooped and subsequently chopped off the tail cone as the rotors slowed down. The Wessex was later airlifted by a Chinook HC1 to the *Atlantic Causeway* on 11th July for the return journey to the UK.

Fearless left the Falklands on the 24th with her four 846 Squadron Sea King HC4s and was followed by *Intrepid* two days later with another four of 846 Squadron's helicopters. Another Sea King HC4 left on board the *Canberra* on the 25th, but it was not until 4th July that the last two 846 Squadron helicopters left the Falklands on board the aircraft carrier *Hermes*.

25th June 1982

Following the arrival of the first Hercules the previous day, Flight Lieutenant Harry Burgoyne and his 47 Squadron crew flew Hercules C1P XV218 on the 25th to return Governor Rex Hunt to the Falklands.

The Wessex HU5s of 847 Squadron moved from the FOB at Port San Carlos to a new base at Navy Point on the northern shore of Stanley harbour. 847 Squadron became the Royal Navy's Garrison Squadron for the Falklands until replaced by an 845 Squadron detachment in September. 847 Squadron had lasted just over six months in its second phase of existence as a Wessex squadron, having first flown the helicopter from amphibious ships in the Far East from 1969 to 1971.

An 826 Squadron Sea King HAS5 flew Admiral Woodward to Stanley for his first visit to the islands and to greet Governor Rex Hunt upon his return. Another 826 Squadron helicopter was used on the 25th as a communications link during the sinking of the gutted RFA *Sir Galahad*. The submarine *Onyx* fired a single torpedo to send the wrecked vessel to the sea bed as a perpetual war grave, in the tradition of naval ships in war.

27th June 1982

The MV *Astronomer* arrived at Port William on the 27th with a much-needed cargo. The *Astronomer* had been requisitioned on 28th May following the loss of the *Atlantic Conveyor* and was likewise converted to carry aircraft. Her load consisted of two Chinook HC1, six Wessex and three Scout AH1 helicopters and, unlike its predecessors, the ship was fitted with two 20mm cannon for self defence. These helicopters soon deployed ashore to join in the massive logistics task of clearing up after the conflict and deploying troops to new positions.

2nd July 1982

Invincible returned on 1st July from her well-earned spell of rest in warmer waters to take over air defence duties from *Hermes* so that the latter could return to the UK. On the 2nd two of 800 Squadron's Sea Harrier FRS1s were flown across to *Invincible* to increase 801 Squadron's establishment for her forthcoming spell of patrol duty off the Falklands until she could be relieved by *Illustrious*.

Nimrod XV237, the first of its type to be equipped to carry the Harpoon anti-ship missile, arrived at Ascension Island on the

Among the helicopters sent as reinforcement aircraft to the Falklands was Scout AH1 XP907, which was transported on the MV Astronomer. *The helicopter served in the Falklands until June 1983 when it returned to the UK on the landing ship* Sir Geraint. Sqn Ldr D Cyster

An aerial view of Stanley airport in mid-July 1982 shows an RAF Hercules arriving from Ascension Island. Also visible on the heavily cratered airfield is a civilian Cessna 172, ten Pucaras, a Sea King and a Wessex. Wg Cdr P Lyall

2nd. The missile had been flown for the first time on a Nimrod on 10th June but by then there was little requirement for it in the South Atlantic as the Argentine Navy was safely locked up in port under the watchful eyes of patrolling Royal Navy submarines.

3rd July 1982

Hermes entered Port William Sound and mounted a 28-aircraft victory flypast over Stanley on 3rd July. Later in the day two 846 Squadron Sea King HC4s (ZA291 and ZA295) embarked on *Hermes* as the ship made final preparations before setting off on the long voyage home.

4th July 1982

The five serviceable Harrier GR3s of 1 Squadron flew ashore to RAF Stanley from *Hermes* to form the Harrier Detachment or HarDet. The detachment was later reinforced to consist of ten Harriers and the air-craft were duly fitted with Sidewinder air-to-air missiles as their main role now was to be air defence of the Falkland Islands until they could be relieved by Phantom FGR2s. The damaged Harrier GR3 XW919 remained on board *Hermes* and was later airlifted to the *Contender Bezant* prior to her return to the UK for major repairs. With the return of *Invincible* from her sojourn in the warmer waters of the north, *Hermes* set sail for the UK, arriving back at Portsmouth to a tumultuous welcome on 21st July.

7th July 1982

Four Harrier GR3s (XV762, XW767, XW924 and XZ129) that had been kept in reserve on board the *Contender Bezant* ever since the ship arrived off the Falklands on 10th June were flown off to Stanley airport to supplement the Harrier GR3s that had arrived at the airport from the aircraft carrier *Hermes* on the 4th.

11th July 1982

On the 11th the Task Force suffered its first aircraft accident since the end of the conflict when Sea King HAS2A XV698 of 'C' Flight 824 Squadron was lost while operating from RFA *Fort Grange*. The helicopter ditched alongside HMS *Leeds Castle* in the TEZ following an engine failure and sank after the crew was rescued.

13th July 1982

A more serious accident occurred on the 13th when Harrier GR3 XW924 suffered an inadvertent launch of both of its AIM-9G Sidewinders as it was taking off from RAF Stanley. One of the missiles exploded about 400 yards from the aircraft and badly injured 11 soldiers involved in snow clearing duties on the airfield.

22nd July 1982

Acknowledging that the Argentine government had agreed to respect the cease-fire while not relinquishing any of its claims to the islands, the British government replaced the TEZ with the Falkland Islands Protection Zone (FIPZ) on 22nd July. This 150-mile radius area acts as a buffer zone to keep Argentine forces away from the Falklands and therefore requires an effective air defence presence on the islands to maintain constant vigilance against air and naval intrusion.

28th July 1982

Harrier GR3 XZ133 was substantially damaged when a portable hangar collapsed on it during a gale. Three other Harriers received minor damage. The gale also overturned and wrecked the FIGAS Beaver floatplane VP-FAV, which had been damaged during the conflict but had been deemed repairable until further damage was sustained on 28th July.

2nd August 1982

656 Squadron redeployed back to the UK and passed its aircraft on to 657 Squadron, which became the Army Air Corps garrison squadron for the Falklands.

825 Squadron Sea King HAS2A XV696 is airlifted by Chinook HC1 ZA717 'BK' of 18 Squadron from San Carlos to the helicopter support ship Engadine *on 7th July. The helicopter was later repaired and is still in service at Culdrose.* Wg Cdr P Lyall

On a cloudy, dull 21st July 1982, the aircraft carrier Hermes *comes home to Portsmouth surrounded by a variety of small craft eager to get a closer look. The carrier's deck is lined with Sea King and Wessex helicopters, the Sea Harriers having already flown off to Yeovilton.* C M Hobson

Sea Harrier FRS1s were sometimes detached to Stanley after the conflict to provide an air defence element in the event of hostilities recommencing. ZA194 '251' of 809 Squadron is seen here fully armed at RAF Stanley. MoD

A 23 Squadron Phantom FGR2 flies over the rugged coastline of the Falklands in 1984. The unit actually reformed at Stanley as a complete squadron on 30th March 1983, having previously been there as a detachment. The squadron subsequently disbanded at Mount Pleasant on 1st November 1988 and was replaced by 1435 Flight. Sqn Ldr D Cyster

25th August 1982
Three Sea King HAR3s of 'C' Flight 202 Squadron arrived at Navy Point for SAR duties around the islands. The helicopters were delivered to the Falklands by the *Contender Bezant*, making her second trip to the South Atlantic. Normally painted bright yellow, the Sea Kings had been repainted in a less conspicuous Dark Sea Grey and flew transport duties as well as SAR operations.

28th August 1982
The newly commissioned *Illustrious* arrived from the UK to replace *Invincible*, which had stayed on to provide air defence for the islands since the cease-fire. *Illustrious* carried Sea Harrier FRS1s of 809 Squadron, which had been totally re-equipped since the squadron had provided reinforcements to 800 and 801 Squadron during the conflict. *Illustrious* also carried the first two Sea King AEW2 conversions to plug the AEW gap that had been so badly felt during the Falklands conflict. Also fitted to the carrier were two Vulcan Phalanx guns as a defence against Exocet missiles and low-flying aircraft. *Invincible* left for the UK on the 28th and arrived back at Portsmouth on 17th September having sailed 51,660 miles during her South Atlantic deployment. *Invincible* had spent 166 days at sea, the longest period of continuous aircraft carrier operations at sea up to that time.

24th September 1982
847 Squadron disbanded at Navy Point and its 11 Wessex HU5s were passed on to 845 Squadron's Falkland Islands Detachment.

17th October 1982
The first 29 Squadron Phantom FGR2 (XV468) touched down on RAF Stanley's newly extended runway after a ferry flight from Ascension Island. Flown by the squadron commander, Wing Commander Ian Macfadyen, the aircraft was the first of nine that arrived over the next three days. With the arrival of the 29 Squadron detachment, *Illustrious* was thereby relieved of her air defence role and set sail for the UK on 21st October.

6th November 1982
After an existence of just six weeks, the 845 Squadron Falkland Islands Detachment disbanded at Navy Point and its Wessex HU5s were loaded on board the MV *Astronomer* on 6th November for the journey back to Devonport.

Wing Commander Peter Squire was forced to eject from Harrier GR3 XW767 when it suffered engine failure and crashed into the sea near Cape Pembroke on the 6th. This was his second lucky escape from a Harrier in the Falklands, the first incident being at the Port San Carlos FOB on 8th June. Harrier GR3 XW767 had flown to Ascension on 29th May and then embarked on the *Contender Bezant* on 3rd June, but although the ship arrived in the TEZ on 10th June, XW767 was not flown off. Instead, the aircraft remained on the ship with three other Harrier GR3s as a reserve aircraft.

10th November 1982
1 Squadron handed over responsibility for the HarDet to 4 Squadron at the start of a rolling programme that saw each of the RAF Harrier squadrons (including the OCU) provide personnel on a rotational basis.

December 1982
The Army Air Corps established the Garrison Army Air Squadron, which was manned by personnel rotated from the UK. The squadron took over the helicopters of 657 Squadron, which had replaced 656 Squadron in August.

22nd March 1983
HarDet Harrier GR3 XV787 crashed into the sea off Port William after its engine failed and the pilot ejected. This aircraft had left St Mawgan for Ascension on 4th May with two other aircraft but had to divert to Madeira

with a technical problem and was later flown back to the UK, taking no further part in the conflict.

23rd March 1983
The ChinDet (the Chinook detachment maintained by personnel from 7 and 18 Squadrons) moved from the original FOB at Port San Carlos to a new facility at Kelly's Garden, near San Carlos settlement. The facility was not intended to be permanent and consisted merely of pierced steel planking hardstandings and some portable hangars.

30th March 1983
The Phantom detachment or PhanDet, originated by 29 Squadron and manned by UK Phantom crews on rotation, was disbanded and its place taken by 23 Squadron, which was reformed at RAF Stanley on this date. The 'old' 23 Squadron was disbanded at RAF Wattisham on the same day.

June 1983
651 Squadron arrived in the Falklands as the new Garrison Army Air Squadron, bringing the first Lynx AH1s to the theatre to supplement the Gazelle AH1s and Scout AH1s.

12th August 1983
Work was started on the new airfield at RAF Mount Pleasant to where all military aviation activity would eventually move over the next few years.

20th August 1983
In an effort to regularise the existence of the various RAF squadron detachments in the Falklands, they were given Flight status on 20th August. The HercDet of Hercules C1Ks at RAF Stanley was redesignated as 1312 Flight with in-flight refuelling as its primary role, and transport and maritime surveillance as secondary roles. The Sea King HAR3-equipped 'C' Flight 202 Squadron became 1564 Flight. The HarDet at Stanley was redesignated as 1453 Flight and the ChinDet at Kelly's Garden became 1310 Flight.

19th September 1983
The Garrison Army Air Squadron moved to a more permanent site at Murray Heights, just to the south of Stanley.

13th October 1983
Nimrod MR2P XV253 of the Kinloss Wing made the first Nimrod flight to RAF Stanley.

17th October 1983
A 23 Squadron Phantom FGR2 (XV484) crashed into Mount Usborne in low cloud during a practice interception, killing Flight Lieutenants J R Gostick and J K Bell. XV484 had been one of the three Phantom FGR2s deployed to Ascension for air defence duties during the Falklands conflict.

19th November 1983
Harrier GR3 XV762 of 1453 Flight flew into high ground on Lafonia south of Goose Green, killing the pilot, Flight Lieutenant B S Clew.

5th January 1984
Lynx AH1 XZ681 of the Garrison Army Air Squadron crashed into the sea off West Falkland as it was returning from a mission to disembark troops from an LSL. The 654 Squadron crew, Captain J T Belt and Sergeant R Jones, were both killed in the accident. The wreck was later recovered and shipped back to the UK for use as a ground instructional airframe at Middle Wallop.

July 1984
Having proved too expensive and too sophisticated to operate in the Falklands mainly as a utility helicopter, it was decided that the Lynx AH1 should be withdrawn from the Garrison Army Air Squadron and replaced by Scout AH1s.

29th November 1984
During a simulated airfield attack on Stanley airport, 1453 Flight Harrier GR3 XZ992 crashed into the sea off Stanley following a bird strike. The pilot ejected at low level and high speed and was severely injured when he hit the sea before his parachute had time to deploy fully.

5th March 1985
Wasp HAS1 XT423 from *Endurance* ditched in Stanley harbour after suffering engine failure. The crew escaped and the airframe was later salvaged and used for ground instruction by the Army Air Corps detachment at Stanley.

1st May 1985
An RAF TriStar K1 (ZD952) of 216 Squadron landed at RAF Mount Pleasant for the first time although the station was not officially opened until the 12th. The shortage of strategic air transport and tanker aircraft had resulted in the RAF purchasing six ex-British Airways and three ex-Pan Am TriStars to equip 216 Squadron.

The Falklands conflict stretched the RAF's long-range tanker and transport assets to the limit, a situation which led directly to the acquisition of nine Lockheed TriStars to augment the Victor and VC10 fleets. Here a TriStar C.2 troop transport lands at RAF Mount Pleasant. Neil Henshaw via Ken Ellis collection

The scale of the construction programme undertaken in the 1980s to provide the Falkland Islands with a new military airfield at Mount Pleasanrt can be gauged in this view of work underway. In the foreground are the three Sea King HAR3s (usually two are deployed to RAF Mount Pleasant at any one time) operated by 'B' Flight 78 Squadron.
Ken Ellis collection

May 1985

British Airways Boeing 747s commenced trooping flights between the UK and RAF Mount Pleasant in May 1985. The trooping charters continued until late August 1986 when the TriStars of 216 Squadron took over the route completely.

June 1985

1453 Flight disbanded at RAF Stanley and its Harrier GR3s returned to the UK as cargo in RAF Hercules.

27th June 1985

Hercules C1P XV206 of 1312 Flight collided with Sea King HAS5 XZ919 of 826 Squadron near Stanley. The Hercules landed safely with several feet of its wing missing but the Sea King crashed, killing the crew of four.

1st April 1986

The first RAF units started to move into the new airfield at RAF Mount Pleasant when 1310 Flight's Chinook HC1s and 1564 Flight's Sea King HAR3s flew in to take up residence.

20th April 1986

Although 23 Squadron's Phantom FGR2s had been using the new runway at RAF Mount Pleasant since late April 1985, the squadron headquarters remained at Stanley until 20th April 1986 when it also moved to RAF Mount Pleasant.

30th April 1986

RAF Stanley was closed down following the departure to RAF Mount Pleasant of the last of the Phantom FGR2s of 23 Squadron and the Hercules of 1312 Flight. By this date the new airfield at Mount Pleasant was protected by long-range and short-range radar and Rapier SAM units of the RAF Regiment.

1st May 1986

RAF Mount Pleasant was formally declared fully operational on 1st May. Also on this date, 78 Squadron was reformed at Mount Pleasant to absorb 1310 Flight and 1564 Flight, although the new unit appears to have been known as the Mount Pleasant Helicopter Squadron for a few weeks. The squadron became responsible for all RAF helicopters in the Falklands, with 'A' Flight flying the Chinook HC1s and 'B' Flight flying the Sea King HAR3s.

13th May 1986

Chinook HC1 ZA715 of newly formed 78 Squadron crashed on Mount Young during a blizzard, killing three of the occupants including the co-pilot Flying Officer D V Browning and Air Loadmaster Sergeant W J Hopson as well as a Gurkha. Twelve other passengers aboard the helicopter were injured.

June 1986

The Garrison Army Air Squadron was renamed the Falkland Islands Squadron, AAC.

December 1986

The last Army Air Corps Scout AH1s left the Falklands for the UK after seeing four years of service on the islands.

23rd January 1987

The Gazelle AH1s of the Falkland Islands Squadron, AAC moved from their base at Murray Heights near Stanley to RAF Mount Pleasant, thus completing the concentration of all military aviation units on the islands at the new airfield.

27th February 1987

Chinook HC1 ZA721 of 78 Squadron crashed near RAF Mount Pleasant when it experienced a flight control failure during a test flight following servicing. All seven on board were killed including pilots Flight Lieutenants S J Newman and A D Moffat and Air Loadmaster Sergeant A J Johns. Also killed were four 78 Squadron ground crew who were monitoring equipment during the test flight.

June 1987

The Falkland Islands Squadron, AAC ceased flying and the last Gazelle AH1s were shipped back to the UK. Seven different Army Air Corps squadrons had served tours in the Falklands since the end of the conflict.

19th December 1987

Two VC10 C1Ks (XR806 and XV109) of 10 Squadron flew from the UK to RAF Mount Pleasant, inaugurating the type's service to the Falklands. XR806 flew non-stop in 15 hours and 45 minutes with two in-flight refuellings.

7th-31st March 1988

Falkland Islands Reinforcement Exercise (FIRE) Focus '88 was a major reinforcement exercise mounted to test the RAF's ability to rapidly reinforce the Falklands. Following the deployment phase, British troops and aircraft undertook a major training exercise on the islands.

1st November 1988

1435 Flight was reformed from 23 Squadron at RAF Mount Pleasant as the squadron disbanded to enable a new 23 Squadron to be reformed on the same day at RAF Leeming with the Tornado F3. 1435 Flight's establishment was four Phantom FGR2s.

25th July 1989

78 Squadron Chinook HC1 ZA717 crashed at RAF Mount Pleasant following a gearbox failure. There were no casualties. This was the third RAF Chinook to be lost in the Falklands in a little over three years.

Two of the four Tornado F3s assigned to 1435 Flight perform their air defence duties by intercepting and escorting a 216 Squadron TriStar transport prior to its arrival at RAF Mount Pleasant. FIGO

FIGAS operates six Pilatus Britten-Norman BN-2B 26 Islanders around the Falkland Islands. Illustrated is VP-FBI about to depart the airstrip at Port Howard. FIGO

1435 Flight
4 x Tornado F3s with two aircraft on QRA throughout each day

78 Squadron
1 x Chinook HC2 support helicopter and 2 x Sea King HAR3s for SAR

1312 Flight
1 x VC10 K3/K4 tanker for the Tornado F3s and 1 x Hercules C1/C3 for maritime radar reconnaissance and SAR

FADGE (Falklands Air Defence Ground Environment)

303 Signals Unit with radars on Byron Heights, Mount Alice and Mount Kent, all of which feed information to the Control and Reporting Centre 'Griffin' at Mount Pleasant Airport.

Resident Rapier Squadron
This unit has two fixed sites at Mare harbour and Poon Hill and numerous pre-surveyed sites elsewhere throughout the Falklands.

Also based at RAF Mount Pleasant are two Sikorsky S-61Ns of British International, which are used for civilian passenger flights around the islands.

9th October 1991
A Terminal Control Zone was set up as a 50-mile buffer zone from the shores of the Falklands to provide air traffic control for the region. The zone sits within the Comodoro Rivadavia Flight Information Region run by Argentina.

30th October 1991
1435 Flight Phantom FGR2 XV421 crashed into the sea off the Falklands during an air combat training sortie with the loss of both crewmen, Flight Lieutenant C J Weightman and Flying Officer I M Halden.

July 1992
The Phantom FGR2s of 1435 Flight were replaced by four Tornado F3s thereby improving long-range interception capability. The range of the Tornadoes is further extended by in-flight refuelling from the Hercules C1Ps and later the VC10s operated by 1312 Flight from RAF Mount Pleasant. The nearest diversion airfield for the

Tornadoes is Punta Arenas, 600 miles from the Falklands on the southern tip of Chile.

March 1994
78 Squadron received the first of its upgraded Chinook HC2s, which had improved avionics, engines and other equipment modifications over the HC1.

March 1996
The two Hercules C1K tankers of 1312 Flight were retired from service and replaced by a single VC10 K4 to provide AAR for the Tornado F3s of 1435 Flight. The VC10 was soon joined by a standard Hercules C1P that was used for maritime radar reconnaissance and for airdrops around the Falklands and South Georgia.

Falkland Island Defences 2002
The RAF units in the Falkland Islands have remained fairly static during the last few years. The current situation at RAF Mount Pleasant is as follows:

Chapter Six

Assessment

Air power was vital to the British victory in the Falklands. British air power alone was not going to win the conflict but it could certainly lose it by allowing the Argentine air and naval forces to pursue their goals with impunity and defeat the amphibious landings and the subsequent land offensive. Although air superiority may not have been possible on a continuous basis, local air superiority was achieved at critical times, such as the first day of the air assault on 1st May and the first day of the landings on 21st May. The crux of British air power success was the availability of bases, consisting of the two floating runways of the aircraft carriers *Hermes* and *Invincible* and the distant staging post at Ascension.

Despite the relative distance of the UK and Argentina from the Falklands, the aircraft of both sides were severely limited in range, which made air-to-air combat, never usually a long drawn out affair anyway, a series of very brief encounters. For example, on most missions the Dagger As had no more than about five minutes' flying time over the Falklands before having to head back to base. The British were able to deal with the problem of distance by moving the carriers closer to the Falklands when required (although this carried a major risk for the ships) and by the use of Victor K2 tankers. The Argentines relied on just two KC-130H tankers and lost the use of their aircraft carrier after the Argentine Navy returned to coastal waters during the first week of May.

The Argentines lost another major opportunity when they failed to make any effort to extend Stanley's runway during April to allow its use by jets other than the largely ineffectual MB-339As. The threat of Exocet-equipped Super Etendards based at Stanley would have forced the Task Force to operate at extreme distance and even then it would have been in a constant state of high threat until the Super Etendards could be eliminated. As the bombardment of Stanley

showed, destroying aircraft on the ground let alone closing an airfield for any length of time, is an extremely difficult and dangerous undertaking. The effort to extend Stanley's runway, as difficult as it would have been, could have won the war for Argentina. That this did not happen and that much of the Argentine military performance during the conflict showed a marked lack of leadership and initiative is probably explained by the very nature of the junta and the lack of any real strategic plan once the Falklands had been taken. Another factor that limited Argentina's performance was the lack of any meaningful co-operation between the higher commands of the Argentine Army, Navy and Air Force.

Weather often plays a major part in any military conflict and this is as true in today's high-tech wars as it was in past campaigns. The weather in the Falklands and in the South Atlantic as a whole played a significant part during the campaign and at times it either assisted or hindered both sides. From 1st May to the end of the conflict there were 15 days when bad weather and poor visibility forced a major reduction in air operations. The toll on British ships and troops could have been much worse had the weather been better either over the Falklands or the Argentine mainland on those 15 days. Weather also played a part in

the retaking of South Georgia, forcing a major change of plan after two Wessex HU5 troop carriers were lost in blizzards on the Fortuna Glacier. Altogether, bad weather was a major factor in the loss of six British aircraft during the campaign.

The terrain of the Falklands also had an effect on air operations. The selection of San Carlos Water for the amphibious landings took account of the surrounding high ground that restricted the approach of attacking aircraft and gave the pilots little time to select targets and take aim. Similarly the high ground was also used by the defenders to position AAA and SAM sites to protect the anchorage. San Carlos Water can be contrasted to Port Pleasant near Fitzroy where the terrain is much flatter, affording no protection to ships operating in the narrow waters. The tragic bombing of the *Sir Galahad* and *Sir Tristram* on 8th June underlines the danger of operating in open positions without adequate air defence.

The boggy, rocky terrain of much of the Falklands and the thinly spread population outside of Stanley resulted in only a few roads being built. Consequently the movement of troops around the islands was to depend largely on helicopters, which is why the loss of the *Atlantic Conveyor* and its vital cargo of Wessex and Chinooks was

This view of San Carlos Water taken in late June 1982 shows the confined space and difficult terrain that hindered military operations during the conflict. Wg Cdr P Lyall

even here there were some units that put up a creditable performance.

The Argentine marines and commandos that took part in the invasion and subsequent defence of the Falklands performed well and the fierce defence of Tumbledown and other high ground during the final days of the assault on Stanley proved that the Argentine soldiers were not to be underestimated. Eventually the demoralising effects of the air raids, naval and land artillery bombardments, Special Forces operations, difficult terrain and the severe weather wore down the resistance of the Argentine defenders on the Falklands sufficiently to permit a smaller force to defeat a well dug-in and well-equipped force in just three weeks.

What was noticeable in the Falklands conflict was the lack of any real attempt at joint or co-ordinated operations between the various elements of the Argentine armed forces. This point was conceded by the Chief of Staff of the Argentine Air Force, Brigadier Ernesto Crespo, in a report quoted in *Jane's Defence Weekly* in November 1985. The forces available to Argentina were certainly not used to their best advantage and the successes achieved were probably due more to the personal bravery of the participants rather than to the leadership at high level.

The Argentine Navy is often blamed for retreating to mainland coastal waters following the loss of the *General Belgrano* on 2nd May and thereafter taking no active part in the war. However, the situation was very grim for the Argentine Navy. Of all the Argentine armed forces, the Navy was the weakest in terms of numbers and modern equipment. It was equipped largely with ageing ships, many of them of Second World War vintage, and suffered from equipment failures that restricted its operations. Its major deficiency was that of serviceable submarines. Although possessing four submarines, only one of them was operational after the retaking of South Georgia and that boat was suffering technical problems that made it virtually useless.

regarded as the most important loss of the whole British campaign and which held up the land offensive considerably.

Much has been made of the difference in the calibre of British and Argentine servicemen that took part in the Falklands. The UK's armed forces are regarded as being among the most professional and best trained in the world and this was certainly borne out during the Falklands conflict. However, before 1982 the UK had not fought in a major conventional conflict for a generation and had probably lost a lot of operational experience that no amount of training could completely make up.

As far as the RAF was concerned, apart from a few small-scale actions in Oman and Aden in the mid-1960s, the last time it was involved in a real shooting war was the brief Suez operation in 1956. The RAF had participated in numerous emergency airlifts and policing actions since then but the level of operational experience was quite low in 1982. The same applied to the Royal

Navy and Royal Marines and, to a lesser extent, to the British Army whose involvement in Northern Ireland since 1969 had provided it with considerable operational experience, albeit in a very different role to that encountered in the Falklands. Despite this lack of recent experience, the doctrine, training, leadership and discipline of the British service personnel resulted in an impressive performance by any standard.

The Argentine performance, especially on the ground and at sea, is often denigrated, especially when compared to that of their opponents. It is true to say that the Argentine forces appeared to lack strategic direction and sound leadership and that this had a major paralysing effect on the individual participants. This is especially true of Argentine ground forces, many of whom were conscripts who had been drafted into the Army just a few months before the invasion of the Falklands and can have had little experience of military life, let alone combat operations. However,

The loss of the *General Belgrano* must have been a major blow to morale, especially as the Argentines knew that a number of very capable nuclear-powered Royal Navy submarines were lurking around the Falklands. The *25 de Mayo* missed its chance to strike back at the British Task Force on 2nd May and with the knowledge that its location was now known to the British Carrier Battle Group, there was little alternative but to withdraw. With the aircraft carrier went the Exocet-equipped destroyers that could have caused problems among the British fleet, but the Argentine Navy was simply outclassed and to remain at sea would almost certainly have resulted in more ship losses.

The Argentine Air Force and the naval air force, the Comando Aviacion Naval Argentina, have probably emerged from the Falklands conflict with a better reputation than the other elements of the armed forces. Reasonably well equipped and less reliant on conscription than the Army, the Air Force showed itself to be competent and tenacious, as did the Navy's attack squadrons. Despite the ever-present threat of interception by Sea Harriers or destruction by Rapier, Sea Dart or other naval anti-air weapons, the Argentine pilots proved themselves to be highly professional and immensely brave. Attacks were pressed home on ships time and time again and it was only the fact that the pilots were flying too low (for the very obvious reason of self-preservation) so that many bombs did not have time to fuse while in the air, that the British ship losses were not more serious. It was estimated that as many as 75 per cent of the bombs dropped by Argentine aircraft failed to explode.

More effort could have been made to swamp the air defences in San Carlos Water by co-ordinating attacks to arrive close together. There was precious little evidence of Air Force/Navy co-ordination and the fiasco of the aborted Super Etendard raid on 29th May illustrates well the poor level of inter-service co-operation during the conflict. Argentine air power seemed to lack any real night capability and the nocturnal raids by Canberra bombers were of little more than nuisance value.

Frequent reference is made to the high attrition rate suffered by Argentine attack aircraft and the poor state of serviceability, resulting in fewer aircraft actually available

The main air defence weapons of many of the British amphibious and auxiliary vessels involved in the conflict were anti-aircraft guns like this 40mm gun on board an LSL. They were a useful last line of defence if Argentine aircraft got through the Sea Harrier CAPs and the missile defences. Flt Sgt D W Knights

than was theoretically possible. The fact remains that at the end of the conflict, Argentine combat aircraft still outnumbered the Sea Harrier FRS1s and Harrier GR3s by a handsome margin. There is some anecdotal evidence to suggest that many Air Force pilots wanted to carry on the war after 14th June as they did not consider themselves beaten. However, apart from the tragedy at Port Pleasant on 8th June, Argentine air power had done little to halt the advance of the British land forces and had in fact lost the battle when it failed to stop the landings at San Carlos in the last week of May.

In general the Argentines were slow to change their tactics with regard to air combat and showed little innovation or imagination. Their training was not up to the same standard as that of their opponents and they showed little expertise in joint operations. The aircraft employed were a mixture of old (and often second-hand) and new and it was fortunate for the British Task Force that the Navy had only taken delivery of five of its Super Etendards before the conflict. After a slightly shaky start, the Argentine radar surveillance and warning system on the Falklands quickly became very effective and enabled their aircraft to avoid Sea Harrier CAPs, even if that meant jettisoning bombs and returning home. Argentine radar also successfully plotted the movements of the Task Force ships to provide targeting information for the Super Etendards.

As far as the long-range air support of the Falklands conflict was concerned, the use of Ascension had been crucial. From an average of 55 aircraft movements per week prior to conflict (mainly USAF transport and military charter aircraft), air movements increased to 800 per day (many of these were helicopter sorties to and from the ships) during the build-up phase as the Task Force ships passed through. Alto-

gether there were about 6,700 fixed- and rotary-wing movements during the conflict, and 5,242 passengers and 17 million pounds of freight were processed through Wideawake airfield.

The military on both sides drew many lessons, some of them relearned from earlier conflicts, and the UK improved its capabilities in a number of key areas following the post-war assessments. It may be worthwhile to look at the weapons and other factors involved in detail to assess their performance in the conflict and highlight the lessons learned.

Royal Navy Ships

There were many lessons to be learned from the Falklands in terms of ship design, especially with regard to anti-air operations. Ship vulnerability to air attack had not been tested to any great extent since 1945, and some of the lessons learned during the Second World War and since appear to have been forgotten or discarded in the intervening years. The reliance on SAMs for air defence at the expense of anti-aircraft guns was one such lesson. On several occasions SAM systems such as Sea Dart and Seawolf failed to fire, leaving air defence to 20mm cannon and small arms. After the war the Royal Navy started to equip many of its ships with more anti-aircraft guns ranging from GPMGs up to 40mm cannon.

A further development, in response to sea-skimming missiles like the Exocet as well as the threat of low-flying aircraft, was the introduction of Close-In Weapon Systems (CIWS). Based on rapid-firing rotary cannon such as the M61 Vulcan carried by US fighters, the CIWS could fire massive quantities of 30mm shells at any incoming missiles and aircraft. Other improvements to counter sea-skimming missiles included improved chaff systems, electronic warfare

and electronic support measures. The extensive use of the 4.5-inch gun for naval gunfire support proved its utility and made a major contribution to the land campaign. The trend of deleting guns and relying solely on ship-to-surface missiles was reversed on later designs like the late batch Type 22 frigates, the more recent Type 23 frigates and the future Type 45 destroyer. Improvements to naval missiles systems are discussed below.

Most of the radars fitted to British warships in the Falklands conflict were of 1950s/60s vintage and were limited in detection capability and range. Later radars had a greatly improved low-level capability and moving target indicators that could help differentiate aircraft from the background clutter caused by land masses on naval radars.

Despite it already being in service, making it a known quantity before the conflict, the Royal Navy had very little defence against the Exocet in 1982. Royal Navy anti-ship missile defences at that time were optimised to combat Soviet missiles that dive onto their targets from above at a steep angle, not sea-skimmers like the Exocet. Therefore the decoys and chaff systems carried by British warships in the Falklands were of limited use unless, as in the case of the missile that hit the *Atlantic Conveyor*, the chaff had floated near the surface of the sea to enable the missile seeker to see it.

Royal Navy Aircraft

Lynx HAS2

The Lynx was the main helicopter type deployed on board the Royal Navy's destroyers and frigates, having replaced the older Wasps and Wessex on most of these ships. Twenty-two of 815 Squadron's Lynx HAS2s were involved in the Falklands conflict and three were lost, all of them while on board ships that were sunk. The Lynx HAS2 fleet was very hard working, often flying short missions that involved several deck landings on each sortie. An example is *Brilliant's* two-Lynx flight that made 860 deck landings from 1st April to 30th June while flying 490 hours. Another example was *Alacrity's* Lynx which flew 100 hours in daylight and 56 by night, made 215 deck landings, fired 1,500 rounds of 7.62mm ammunition and dropped one torpedo and several flares. The Lynx HAS2 proved itself to be a reliable and capable helicopter and its agility was demonstrated on 13th June when Lieutenant C H Clayton out-manoeuvred two Dagger As that tried to shoot his helicopter down.

Sea Harrier FRS1

Only 28 Sea Harrier FRS1s flew operationally during the Falklands conflict. Of these, six were lost: two to ground fire and four in operational accidents. The aircraft flew a total of 2,197 sorties from the deploy-

ment on 5th April to the end of June. From this figure 1,335 sorties were flown between 1st May and 16th June, 737 from *Hermes* and 598 from *Invincible*. During the conflict the aircraft dropped 437 bombs. 801 Squadron flew a total of 1,424 sorties in 1,560 hours from 5th April to arriving back in the UK on 17th September. 800 Squadron fired 14 AIM-9L Sidewinders resulting in 12 kills, while 801 Squadron fired 12 missiles for a score of seven kills. Three kills were achieved by cannon and one helicopter crashed as it tried to evade an attack, bringing the total number of Sea Harrier FRS1 kills to 23. These kills took place during the six days (1st, 21st, 23rd, 24th and 25th May and 8th June) when there was significant air-to-air combat.

Remarkably, not one Sea Harrier was shot down or even damaged in air-to-air combat. The Sea Harrier also achieved an impressive degree of reliability throughout the campaign. On average, 95 per cent of aircraft were available at the beginning of each day when up to six sorties were flown by some aircraft, although the average was usually three. Overall, 99 per cent of all

The Lynx HAS2 was the main shipborne helicopter used by the frigates and destroyers of the Task Force. Its tasks included ASW, anti-surface, gunship, anti-Exocet ESM and reconnaissance operations. MoD

Sea King HC4 ZA299 'VE' of 846 Squadron spent three weeks on Ascension Island flying stores to and from ships until it embarked on the SS Canberra *on 6th May. Here it is about to lift a load of recoilless rifles.* MoD

planned missions were flown; and the versatility of the V/STOL aircraft enabled it to fly missions in weather that would have grounded conventional jet aircraft. The 100 per cent humidity encountered in the South Atlantic meant that the Sea Harrier's electronics had to be protected from damp, resulting in a number of ingenious methods being used including the use of bath-edge sealant and cling-film plastic sheets to keep vulnerable parts dry.

The most serious deficiency in the Task Force's armoury was an AEW capability, which it had lost in 1978 when the Fairey Gannet was retired along with HMS *Ark Royal*. Operations in the North Atlantic, where the Royal Navy had expected to fight any future war, would have been covered by airborne radars provided by US Navy Grumman E-2 Hawkeyes or RAF and NATO AWACS aircraft. Without these the Sea Harriers had to rely on the limited radar information provided by British warships, which had a very restricted low-level and over land radar capability. AEW would have provided much earlier warning of low-level air raids on British warships, especially the devastating Super Etendard raids that were extremely difficult to detect using the radars available.

The use of AEW would have enabled a far more efficient use of the limited number of the short-range Sea Harriers that had to mount costly barrier patrols, many of which were avoided by Argentine aircraft thanks to their efficient ground-based warning system. The Sea Harrier's Blue Fox radar proved to be of limited use in the air-to-air role as it had a poor lookdown capability, particularly over land, so any aircraft signal was lost in the clutter of terrain. Enemy aircraft over land were usually picked up visually, often after being detected by Fighter Directors on board the warships.

The Sea Harrier FRS1 was modified soon after the end of the conflict to carry four rather than just two Sidewinders and to take larger fuel tanks in order to extend the aircraft's radius of action. The much-improved FA2 version has a more effective radar and carries the AMRAAM medium-range air-to-air missile.

Only five of the 28 Sea Harrier FRS1s that were used operationally during the Falklands are still in service today, all of them having been converted to the FA2 standard. Sixteen of the Falklands' veterans have been written off in accidents since the con-

flict and one aircraft was shot down during the NATO operations in Bosnia in 1994.

Sea King HC4

During Operation 'Sutton' and in the early stages of the ground offensive, the Sea King HC4s of 846 Squadron flew the lion's share of logistics support and assisted with the HDS task at Ascension. One flight of night-vision equipped helicopters flew almost all Special Forces support missions during the conflict. The squadron moved 6,550 tons of cargo and 9,000 troops over a 45-day period. Each Sea King HC4 averaged 170 flying hours per month with a 90 per cent availability. The squadron logged 3,107 flying hours (including 1,818 sorties and 3,343 deck landings) from April to June, equivalent to a full year of peacetime flying. Each 846 Squadron pilot averaged around 228 flying hours during the conflict.

Fourteen Sea King HC4s were used by the squadron, two of which were lost in accidents before the landings. The only other 846 Squadron helicopter to be lost was ZA290, deliberately destroyed in Chile on 18th May.

Sea King HAS2A

The Sea King HAS2A was used by two squadrons in the Falklands conflict. 824 Squadron deployed five helicopters on board RFA *Olmeda* and RFA *Fort Grange* for HDS duties; but the larger user of the type was the specially commissioned 825 Squadron. It is curious that instead of taking a fully trained RAF support helicopter squadron equipped with the Puma, a Royal Navy ASW training squadron was converted to the utility role. This may have been

a simple desire to achieve commonality of helicopters with the other Sea Kings being deployed to the South Atlantic. Whatever the reason, the staff and students of 706 Squadron that made up 825 Squadron acquitted themselves very well during the conflict. The squadron flew 1,756 hours in just 394 sorties involving 1,051 deck landings with only one aircraft seriously damaged of the ten taken to the Falklands.

Sea King HAS5

The Sea King HAS5s of 820 and 826 Squadrons flew more hours than any other type during the Falklands, the vast majority on what turned out to be a fruitless and frustrating search for Argentine submarines. The statistics speak for themselves. Twenty helicopters were deployed, split evenly between the two squadrons. The two squadrons mounted a continuous ASW screen for the Task Force from leaving Ascension on 18th April until they were finally stood down on 17th June, with three helicopters permanently on task, day and night. Two Sea King HAS5s were lost, both in non-fatal accidents.

The two squadrons amassed a total of 2,253 sorties flying 6,847 hours between April and June, each sortie lasting about three hours. 820 Squadron flew 4,100 hours from 1st April to 7th August, of which 2,200 hours were in the active ASW role. On 820 Squadron each Sea King HAS5 flew an average of 522 hours during the deployment and each pilot flew about 321 hours. The squadron flew 1,650 sorties and dropped six torpedoes and ten depth charges.

During the conflict 820 Squadron engineers changed 24 engines, 34 main rotor

blades, 14 tail rotor blades, three gearboxes and five rotor heads. 826 Squadron had ten engines changed during the conflict and flew 3,300 hours in three months commencing 2nd April, five times the normal peacetime rate. One Sea King HAS5 flew a total of 265 hours during one month, equivalent to one-third of the month in the air.

Wasp HAS1
In 1982 the Wasp HAS1 had been largely replaced by the Lynx HAS2 but it still served on some of the older Leander class frigates. A total of eight Wasp HAS1s were involved in the conflict: two were embarked on *Endurance* and each of the three ambulance ships had one example, as did three frigates. The Wasp's role in the Falklands was unspectacular but the two helicopters embarked on *Endurance* played a prominent part in the operations on South Georgia where they helped to disable the submarine *Santa Fe* using AS-12 missiles.

Wessex HAS3/HU5
A total of 40 Wessex HU5s served in the South Atlantic while another six were lost on board the *Atlantic Conveyor* before they could be flown off. Apart from these losses the only others lost were the two helicopters that crashed in severe weather during the retaking of South Georgia.

The rugged, if somewhat elderly Wessex was well suited to operations in the Falklands, although its fairly basic set of avionics equipment placed some limitations on its operation, especially at night or in bad weather. In addition to the HU5s, two of the ASW HAS3 version were also involved in the conflict. One was HMS *Antrim's* XP142, which played a crucial role in the retaking of South Georgia and the other was destroyed on board *Glamorgan* when it was hit by an Exocet missile on 12th June.

Royal Marine and Army Air Corps Light Helicopters

A total of 15 Gazelle AH1s and 12 Scout AH1s were used operationally during the Falklands conflict. 3 CBAS operated ten Gazelles and six Scouts, while 656 Squadron, AAC operated five Gazelles and six Scouts. Four of these helicopters were lost in action. Two Gazelles were shot down on the first day of the landings and another was lost to a British Sea Dart, while a Scout was shot down by a Pucara to become the only British aircraft lost in air-to-air combat. The losses underlined the vulnerability of light helicopters to small arms fire and the lack of crew protection in helicopters like the Gazelle.

A Wessex HAS3 lands on board one of the Task Force ships during the conflict. Only two examples of this mark of Wessex were deployed; one was lost on board Glamorgan *and the other survived to be preserved at the Fleet Air Arm Museum.* MoD

Figures available for the helicopters of 3 CBAS show that the average flying time for each of the unit's Gazelles (not including the two aircraft lost in action) between 21st May and 24th June was 146.1 hours. The equivalent figure for the unit's Scouts (again, not including one aircraft lost in action) was 110.1 hours.

The light helicopters operated by 3 CBAS and 656 Squadron formed a vital part of the logistics chain as the terrain and lack of roads in the Falklands made movement by vehicle well nigh impossible. They were also used for reconnaissance, casevac and light attack. Although SNEB rockets were fitted at short notice to Gazelles they were not used operationally by the helicopters, although they were carried when the Gazelles escorted unarmed transport helicopters. The Scouts made use of SS-11 anti-tank missiles in the final stages of the conflict, several of which were fired at dug-in positions. At least one artillery piece was thought to have been disabled by SS-11s.

Royal Air Force Aircraft

Chinook HC1
The sinking of the *Atlantic Conveyor* on 25th May meant that only one Chinook HC1 (ZA718) reached the Falklands to support the land forces, although another example arrived on the last day of the conflict. Between 27th May and 14th June ZA718 flew for 109 hours, carried 2,150 troops (including 95 casualties and 550 POWs) and moved 550 tons of supplies. On one memorable occasion 81 troops were carried on a single flight and during the Port Pleasant casevac, 64 wounded men were evacuated during a single sortie. The lone Chinook made a major contribution to the logistics effort and indicates the importance of the loss of the other three helicopters on the *Atlantic Conveyor*.

Harrier GR3
Ten Harrier GR3s of 1 Squadron were used operationally in the Falklands conflict with another four held in reserve on board the *Contender Bezant* for the last few days of the war but not flown. The Harriers flew a total of 151 sorties in the South Atlantic, 126 of them being operational sorties over the Falklands but not including transit sorties from *Hermes* to the FOB or aborted sorties. Three of the aircraft were lost to ground fire and another one due to accidental engine failure. Another three aircraft received damage from ground fire, leaving just three Harriers that received no damage during the conflict. The higher attrition rate of the Harrier GR3 compared to the Sea Harrier FRS1 reflects the dangers of low-level close air support and interdiction as opposed to combat air patrols and toss-bombing.

Each of the GR3 pilots flew an average of two sorties a day. The squadron only had 18 ground crew on board *Hermes* yet managed to achieve a high serviceability rate. Two of the most noteworthy aspects of the use of the Harrier GR3 in the Falklands were the RAF's first operational use of the LGB in the last few days of the conflict and the long-range deployment of four aircraft from Ascension to the deck of *Hermes*.

Hercules C1
As the backbone of the RAF's transport force, the Hercules made a major contribution to the logistics effort to move men and materials to Ascension and also made airdrops of high-priority items, mail and personnel to the Task Force at sea. Although largely unsung, the RAF's transport crews

This post-conflict photograph shows two Scout AH1s of 657 Squadron refuelling from petrol drums at a remote FOB somewhere in the Falklands. The Scouts of 3 CBAS and 656 Squadron, AAC performed hundreds of utility and casevac sorties during the conflict and also made several attacks using SS-11 missiles. MoD

Hercules C1P XV187 is seen here at Ascension Island after the conflict, ready for another mission to resupply British forces in the Falklands. RAF Hercules of the Lyneham Transport Wing flew over 13,000 hours in support of Operation 'Corporate'. MoD

flew long, gruelling missions throughout the conflict and well beyond.

A typical example of a Hercules round trip from the UK to Ascension is that of Wing Commander Mike Seller, officer commanding 70 Squadron, and his crew. On 19th May the crew took off from RAF Lyneham in XV206 for a flight to Dakar in Senegal of 8 hours and 30 minutes. The next day the crew took XV186 from Dakar to Ascension on a 5-hour flight and returned to Dakar later in the day in the same aircraft in a flight lasting 4 hours and 40 minutes. On the 21st the crew took off in XV178 on a 7 hours and 45 minutes flight back to Lyneham. The crew had thus flown a total of 25 hours and 55 minutes over the three-day deployment and this crew made five such deployments before the end of the conflict. Hercules flew 44 long-range airdrop sorties to the Task Force during the conflict, most of these involved air-to-air refuelling.

RAF transport aircraft flew over 17,000 hours during the Falklands conflict (the Hercules fleet flew a total of 13,000 hours). About 7,000 tons of cargo was flown to Ascension including 5,500 passengers and nearly 100 vehicles.

The rundown of the RAF's air transport fleet had left insufficient capacity for emergency operations like the Falklands so a number of civilian transport aircraft were chartered to supplement the RAF's Hercules and VC10s. Two ex-RAF Belfasts were chartered from Heavylift Cargo Airlines, with a third added later, to carry outsize loads. Each aircraft had a payload availability of 80,500lb. A total of 21 flights were made, the cargoes including helicopters, vehicles, aircraft tugs, ground starters, pipes, air-conditioning equipment, oxygen production plant, and portable accommodation. The Belfasts also replaced some Hercules flights on routine RAF transport flights.

Nimrod MR1/2

Nimrods flew 130 maritime patrol sorties from Ascension (32 in April, 57 in May and 41 in June), accumulating a total of 1,148 hours and 52 minutes of flying time. The Nimrod was armed with the Harpoon anti-ship missile and the AIM-9L Sidewinder during the conflict. Neither weapon was used. The aircraft was also fitted with an in-flight refuelling probe to extend its range, enabling missions of up to 19 hours to be flown. The Nimrods did much to monitor the Argentine surface fleet during the campaign and also provided ASW cover for the Task Force when operating within range of Ascension Island.

VC10 C1

The VC10 C1s of 10 Squadron flew many missions to and from Ascension and also to Montevideo to collect the British wounded and prisoners from the conflict. VC10 C1s carried 570 aeromedical patients during the war. The aircraft could fly from the UK to Ascension and return the same day by slipping crews. Up to 20 tons of payload could be carried on each flight.

Victor K2

Probably the single most important lesson learned by the RAF from the Falklands conflict was the value of having sufficient in-flight refuelling capacity to sustain any long-range operations. The only assets available in April 1982 were the two squadrons of ageing Victor K2 tankers, although a number of ex-British Airways VC10s were in the process of conversion to tanker configuration, but these would not be ready for some months.

Just as serious was the lack of AAR-capable receivers in the RAF at the time. Although most of the Harrier GR3 force was well-practised in air-to-air refuelling, the Vulcan crews had to be trained from scratch. The fitting of Hercules and Nimrods with in-flight refuelling probes was a solution to the range and endurance requirements of operations in the South Atlantic, enabling some incredible long-range missions to be flown once the crews had been trained. Despite its age, the Victor proved extremely reliable, thanks to the high standard of maintenance of the aircraft, and only three out of 375 sorties in support of 67 missions were aborted due to aircraft defects.

Vulcan B2

It is ironic that the first and only time that the RAF's mighty Vulcan should be used for real was just as the aircraft was being retired from service. A major element of the UK's nuclear deterrent forces during the Cold War, the Vulcan had never dropped a

A trio of Nimrod MR2Ps (XV230, XV227 and XV243) lined up at Ascension circa 18th May. Much of Ascension Island is composed of volcanic ash, like the hill behind the aircraft seen here. The fine ash particles caused engineering problems as they clogged air filters and damaged engines. MoD

A view of the apron at Wideawake airfield on Ascension Island shows just two Nimrods and six Victors, which may indicate that other Victors were out on a mission when this photograph was taken. Some long-range missions required up to 18 Victor sorties. MoD

bomb in anger until 1st May 1982 when the first 'Black Buck' raid was flown. An immense amount of work went into preparing the aircraft and training its crews for the 'Black Buck' missions. The refitting of in-flight refuelling equipment and the modifications to carry Shrike missiles and ECM pods were carried out in an amazingly short time.

The military results of the three 'Black Buck' bombing missions were perhaps a little disappointing, but the achievement of hauling 21 1,000lb bombs almost 4,000 miles and dropping them on target using 30-year-old technology should not be underestimated. However, the psychological impact of all the Vulcan raids was immense. After 1st May the Argentines knew that the RAF could mount a Vulcan raid from Ascension Island, perhaps even to hit the mainland airfields if it wished. This threat was a constant worry to the Argentine commanders and caused much fear and consternation to the troops based in and around Stanley.

The use of anti-radar missiles by the Vulcan on two raids was partially successful in

that it hit one radar, although not the radar that was most sought after. The problem with the Shrike missile was that it lost precise guidance if the radars went off the air during the launch as the missile had no inbuilt memory. After the conflict the RAF drew up a requirement for an improved anti-radar weapon that resulted in the introduction of the ALARM missile that was used in Iraq in 1991 to great effect.

Missiles and Other Weapons

Blowpipe
The publication *The Falklands Campaign: The Lessons* claims that Blowpipe scored nine kills and two probables during the conflict. In fact it is difficult to assign any kill to Blowpipe other than the MB-339A that was shot down at Goose Green on 28th May. A total of 95 Blowpipes were fired by British forces, nearly half of which failed for one reason or another. A small number of the Stinger man-portable SAMs were fired by the SAS but only one hit was achieved due to lack of training on the system.

Rapier
The Rapier was the British Army's and the RAF's primary point defence missile system or short-range air defence (SHORAD). To ease the logistics burden, the missile's DN181 Blindfire radar trackers were not taken to the Falklands by 'T' Battery of 12 Air

Defence Regiment, Royal Artillery. More serious was the fact that 'T' Battery left behind at Ascension its second-line support (including the optical repair vehicle) due to pressure of space on board ships and in the mistaken assumption that the equipment would be sent on soon. In fact the equipment did not arrive until after the surrender and the Rapier's serviceability was badly affected. The missile firing units had been loaded onto the ships early on in the loading process and were largely inaccessible during the long journey down South. A planned practice firing session at Ascension had to be cancelled at the last moment, thereby denying a valuable training opportunity. The Rapiers had suffered from the prolonged storage during the journey south and some fire units were damaged during the original loading and the transfer ashore by helicopter at San Carlos. As the Blindfire radars had been left in the UK, the Rapier operators had to rely on the fire unit's built-in surveillance system and more often than not the missiles were aimed visually.

Once ashore it was found that there were so many British helicopters flying around San Carlos that the Rapier crews were continually being warned of IFF responses from friendly aircraft, so from the 22nd the crews relied almost solely on visual location, identification and tracking of targets. As Argentine aircraft flew very low during their attacks on San Carlos Water and the

Rapiers were situated on hilltops, the missiles sometimes had to be fired downwards, causing some consternation among nearby British troops in the process!

After the breakout from San Carlos, four Rapier fire units were airlifted to Teal Inlet and four to Goose Green. The remaining four units were loaded on board the LSLs *Sir Galahad* and *Sir Tristram* but took little part in the defence of the ships on 8th June as they had only just been unloaded and were poorly sited for the protection of the vessels. The only Rapier unit to fire its missiles in anger was 'T' Battery of 12 Air Defence Regiment, although 9 Battery, Royal Artillery and 63 Squadron, RAF Regiment arrived later but did not have the opportunity to fire any missiles.

Soon after the end of the war, information started appearing in the aviation and defence press claiming that Rapier missiles had shot down 14 Argentine aircraft with another six probably destroyed. This claim even appeared in the Ministry of Defence's own assessment of the war, *The Falklands Campaign: The Lessons*, published in December 1982. In 1983 Ethell and Price first pointed out the lack of evidence for Rapier's success (and over-claiming of kills in general) in their book *Air War South Atlantic*. However, in 1987 the more detailed government Defence Committee investigation into the lessons of the Falklands ('Implementing the Lessons of the Falklands Campaign', House of Commons Paper 345) was still adhering to the initial claims for Rapier kills in the Falklands. It gave more details of the claims but these do not appear to be corroborated in other references. It was also claimed that 60 per cent of the missiles fired hit their target but it was admitted that some missiles were

fired out of range purely as a deterrent and some were deliberately pulled off target when Argentine aircraft flew behind warships or hills occupied by British troops.

However, it is very difficult to reconcile the claims for Rapier against the verifiable facts and it appears now that only one loss (a Dagger A on 29th May) can definitely be attributed solely to Rapier. Almost all other claims can be attributed to other weapon systems. Very few of the publications that claim 14 kills for Rapier actually identify the individual instances or the Argentine aircraft types involved.

Although Rapier is often mentioned in Argentine sources, there is little in the way of corroborating evidence to confirm any kills. One publication claims that the Rapier site at Teal Inlet shot down two Argentine aircraft near there after 3 Commando moved to the inlet on 28th May, whereas in actual fact no Argentine aircraft was lost anywhere near Teal Inlet during the conflict. Another publication claims that one of the Rapier fire units offloaded near Port Pleasant on 8th June shot down one of the A-4s that bombed the *Sir Galahad* and *Sir Tristram*. In fact, none of the A-4s that bombed the LSLs were shot down by ground fire although several were damaged by small arms fire and three aircraft from the second wave were destroyed by Sidewinders fired by Sea Harriers.

'T' Battery of the Royal Artillery is said to have fired 61 Rapiers during the conflict, which, if the figure of 14 kills was correct, would give it a very high kill ratio, unmatched by any other missile type (except Seawolf). The commander of the 12th Air Defence Regiment admitted in an article in the *Journal of the Royal Artillery* in 1983 that one-quarter of all the missiles

fired went out of control due to equipment failures. He also claimed that one-third of the correctly functioning missiles scored a hit, resulting in the claim of '14 aircraft definitely destroyed'.

Disappointment in the performance of the Rapier system is referred to by Admiral Woodward in his autobiography and he also mentions that Commodore Clapp, the Commodore Amphibious Warfare at San Carlos, had little faith in Rapier by 25th May. The over-claiming of kills in air-to-air or surface-to-air combat is a well-known phenomenon that has existed since the First World War and occurs for a variety of very good reasons. Whatever the final score for Rapier, it would appear that the system had a marked deterrent value, causing great concern to the Argentine pilots and providing a much-needed morale boost for the British soldiers.

Seacat
Already obsolescent by the time of the Falklands conflict, the Seacat short-range SAM was initially credited with the shooting down of eight aircraft, a figure that was still claimed in the 1987 Defence Committee investigation into the performance of equipment during the conflict. However, it is unlikely that Seacat alone was responsible for the destruction of any aircraft, although a number may have been damaged or deterred by the missile.

The value of the visually aimed Seacat was that it could be fired within the confines of San Carlos Water where the proximity of high land on the nearby shore denied the use of radar-guided missiles like Seawolf. The simpler Seacat system was also less prone to failures than the newer and more sophisticated Seawolf, although *Ardent's* Seacat proved to be unreliable at a critical moment when the ship came under attack on 21st May.

Sea Dart
The Sea Dart was optimised for medium-range area defence, and had a creditable high-altitude performance, shooting down aircraft at about 40,000ft from over 20 miles away. Although Sea Dart suffered from limitations of its aiming and firing system, it nevertheless proved to be a very reliable

weapon system and was responsible for the shooting down of seven aircraft.

Sea Dart was criticised after the Falklands for its poor performance at low level and for being slow to acquire targets. While the missile worked very well over open sea, its Type 965 radar had great difficulty detecting aircraft at low level over or near land due to background clutter and radar reflections thrown up by the land mass. Sea Dart did shoot down two helicopters (one Argentine Puma and one British Gazelle) over East Falkland but, although the targets were quite low, they were also slow moving and so did not represent a high-threat fast-jet target.

The improved Type 1022 radar fitted to *Exeter* became the standard fit for all Sea Dart-equipped ships after the conflict. The post-Falklands improvements made to the system seem to have been proven when on 25th February 1991, during Operation 'Desert Storm', a Sea Dart fired by *Gloucester* destroyed an Iraqi HY-2 Silkworm anti-ship missile on its way to hit an American battleship in the Persian Gulf.

Sea Skua

The Sea Skua helicopter-borne anti-ship missile was only just entering Royal Navy service in early 1982 and some of the Lynx HAS2 fleet had not yet been adapted to carry the new weapon. This resulted in a lot of shuffling of airframes during the conflict to ensure that the right capability was available on the right ship at the right time. Only seven Sea Skuas were launched, but all of them scored hits: four on the *Alferez Sobral*, two on the *Rio Carcarana* and one on the *Rio Iguazu*.

There was some concern after the conflict that while the missile had hit all the targets it was aimed at, the damage had been insufficient to sink them, even the small patrol boat the *Rio Iguazu*. In fact the Sea Skua is a relatively small missile with a warhead of just 20kg, enough to cause significant damage to small or medium-sized vessels; but it was never intended to have the destructive power of the much larger Exocet or Harpoon.

Seawolf

The Seawolf Mach 2+ short-range point defence missile is capable of engaging anti-ship missiles as well as aircraft. Unfortunately, it never had the opportunity to be fired against an Exocet in the Falklands

conflict, although the missile did hit and destroy an Exocet during a test-firing in November 1983. It did, however, shoot down at least three Argentine aircraft during the conflict and caused another to crash while trying to evade.

Broadsword and *Brilliant*, the only Sea-wolf-equipped ships involved in anti-air actions, spent much of their time protecting the aircraft carriers and so had only limited opportunity to use the missile, such as when they were detached for missile trap duties with a Type 42 destroyer. Some problems were experienced with the computerised acquisition and tracking system and the Seawolf's radar was later improved. The system was still fairly new in 1982 and the operators were still learning about the Seawolf. Improvements to the missile's computer system and radar were made at sea during the conflict in the light of operational experience. A Vertical Launch Seawolf system was later developed to eliminate blind arcs of fire, improve reaction time and increase the missile's range.

Sidewinder

A total of 19 Argentine aircraft were shot down by AIM-9L Sidewinders fired by Sea Harrier FRS1s during the conflict. As already mentioned, 800 Squadron fired a total of 14 Sidewinders resulting in 12 kills, while 801 Squadron fired 12 missiles scoring seven kills (one of them, the Canberra B62 on 1st May, was hit by two missiles). Only one Sidewinder is definitely known to have malfunctioned; four were fired out of range and one was fired in error.

Although the Sidewinder is an efficient, effective and highly capable weapon, its success in the Falklands should also be shared by the Sea Harrier airframe, the Fighter Direction from the warships and, most important of all, the quality of the Fleet Air Arm pilots.

Although much praise has been heaped on the AIM-9L all-aspect variant of the Sidewinder, the Sea Harrier pilots themselves believe that all the kills achieved could also have been gained by the earlier AIM-9G version. This is because all Sidewinder kills in the conflict were by missiles fired from behind the target during the classic tail-chase manoeuvre. In fact the only known instance of a head-on opportunity took place on 1st May and the Sidewinder failed to achieve a lock. The only instance where the improved performance of the AIM-9L might have made a difference was on 24th May when Lieutenant D Smith shot down a Dagger A from a larger-than-usual angle off while chasing the Argentine fighter.

The fact that 20 of the 26 Sidewinders launched hit their target produced a profound psychological effect on Argentine aircrew and gave Sea Harrier pilots a high degree of confidence. A major enhancement in the capability of the Sea Harrier FA2 is the addition of the medium-range AMRAAM missile to supplement the short-range Sidewinder.

Aden 30mm Cannon

Although the Sidewinder scored the lion's share of air-to-air kills, the value of a large-calibre gun was also proven during the Falklands conflict. Aden 30mm cannon were used by Sea Harrier FRS1s and Harrier GR3s to shoot down two A-4 Skyhawks, a Pucara, a Hercules (after first being hit by a Sidewinder fired from a Sea Harrier) and four helicopters, all of the latter being air-to-ground kills. Disregarding the helicopter kills, Aden 30mm cannon were therefore used to score four out of the 23 air-to-air kills or 17 per cent of the total, a respectable percentage for a weapon that has been written off as obsolete many times in the recent past.

Carried and fired by Lynx HAS2s during the Falklands conflict, the Sea Skua lightweight sea-skimming anti-ship missile registered a 100 per cent hit rate (seven out of seven) against the Argentine vessels Alferez Sobral, Rio Carcarana *and* Rio Iguaza. *B Munro*

One of the two Argentine Air Force Bell 212s is seen here abandoned on Stanley racecourse at the end of the conflict. The helicopter wears a broad yellow band on the tail boom just aft of the engine exhaust. This yellow band was painted on many Argentine aircraft during the conflict as an aid to identification. H-85 was shipped to the UK in 1984 but its current whereabouts are unknown. Wg Cdr P Lyall

Argentine Air Force

A-4B/C Skyhawk

The A-4Bs of Grupo 5 flew 133 operational sorties, engaged in combat in 86 of them, and lost ten aircraft and nine pilots during the conflict. The A-4Cs of Grupo 4 flew only 86 operational sorties, engaged in combat in 41 of them, and lost nine aircraft and eight pilots. The A-4B suffered a 7.5 per cent attrition rate while the A-4C suffered a devastating 10.5 per cent loss rate and lost nine out of the total of 15 aircraft that are thought to have taken part in the conflict. Moreover, the more capable A-4C, with better avionics and radar, was actually less successful in carrying out its mission than the older and more basically equipped A-4B.

Grupo 5 was responsible for successful attacks on many British warships, destroying three of them (*Antelope*, *Coventry* and *Sir Galahad*, as well as a landing craft) and damaging a further four vessels (*Argonaut*, *Broadsword*, *Glasgow* and *Sir Tristram*). Despite their efforts, the A-4Cs of Grupo 4 only managed to cause relatively minor damage to the *Sir Galahad* and the *Sir Lancelot*. Although equipped with in-flight refuelling probes enabling them to extend their range, the A-4s had a fairly basic avionics fit and, like the Daggers, sometime relied on other aircraft types to act as navigational pathfinders for the long overwater missions.

C-130E/H and KC-130H Hercules

The Argentine Air Force's C-130E/H Hercules were the lifeline into Stanley throughout the conflict and especially after the shooting started on 1st May. The Hercules crews (and indeed the crews of other Argentine transport aircraft) displayed immense skill and courage in flying missions into Stanley at night and in bad weather under the constant threat of interception by Sea Harriers or SAMs. Between 1st May and 13th June, when the last Argentine Hercules landed at Stanley, 74 Hercules resupply sorties to the Falklands had been planned and 61 actually flown. Of these, 28 flights, nearly half of the total dispatched, turned back for one reason or another but 31 aircraft landed successfully at Stanley while two more made airdrops. This was a most creditable achievement by any standards.

The two KC-130H Hercules tankers were a vital component in the air assault on the Falklands. The two aircraft flew a total of 29 missions and refuelled 93 Argentine Air Force aircraft and 20 Navy aircraft. On a high percentage of missions, perhaps as much as 20 per cent, A-4s encountered problems while refuelling, many of them suffering from iced-up probes caused by the damp, freezing cold atmosphere. On more than one occasion the KC-130Hs saved aircraft that would otherwise have been lost on their way back to the mainland following damage sustained during combat over the Falklands. It is interesting to note that no aircraft that needed fuel on the return journey was lost, thanks to the service provided by the KC-130Hs, which sometimes approached close to the western shores of the Falklands and within the theoretical interception range of the Sea Harriers or Sea Dart.

Canberra

The ageing Canberra flew a total of 58 sorties and engaged in combat on 25 of them. These sorties included nine reconnaissance/surveillance, three tactical reconnaissance, four long-range anti-shipping, 14 day bombing and 22 night bombing sorties. The Canberras flew a total of 396 flying hours and dropped about 86,000lb of bombs. Two aircraft were lost, one shot down by a Sea Harrier in daylight at low-level and one by a Sea Dart missile at night at high altitude.

The Canberra raids were largely ineffectual and caused very little damage. The aircraft lacked the navigational or avionics equipment to drop bombs at night and through cloud, so most of the effort was wasted.

CH-47C Chinook and Bell 212

The Grupo 7 helicopter detachment flew a total of 404 sorties during the conflict, carrying 1,829 passengers and 570 tons of cargo and rescuing seven aircrew and 25 sailors in a total of 570 flying hours. Both the Chinooks escaped back to the mainland but the Bell 212s were captured.

Dagger A

The Dagger As of 6 Grupo flew 133 sorties, out of 160 that were planned between 1st May and 13th June. Of these sorties, only 88 engaged in combat and 11 aircraft were lost and five pilots killed, giving a very high attrition rate of just over 8 per cent of all sorties flown or 12.5 per cent of those that engaged in combat.

Although a reasonable fighter-bomber, especially at low-level, the Israeli-built Dagger was only intended for short-range missions and so it had a relatively poor navigational fit and no in-flight refuelling capability. The restriction of Mirage IIIEA operations following the loss of two aircraft on 1st May resulted in most Argentine bombing raids being unescorted and the Sea Harriers were therefore virtually unopposed. Many of the Daggers jettisoned their bombs before reaching their target if they were engaged or threatened by Sea Harriers, but Grupo 6 pilots inflicted serious damage on three warships (*Antrim*, *Ardent* and *Plymouth*).

Mirage IIIEA

The 17 Mirage IIIEAs were the Argentine Air Force's primary air defence interceptors and should have been a threat to the Sea Harriers. However, following the disastrous combat on 1st May when two Mirage IIIEAs were lost, the aircraft were rarely seen over the Falklands except for a few decoy and escort missions. The Mirage IIIEA, which had no in-flight refuelling capability, was operating at the limit of its range over the Falklands and only had time for a single high-speed pass. However, the Sea Harrier pilots wisely chose not to engage them at high altitude but tried to lure them down to low altitude where they would have lost their speed advantage.

The Mirage IIIEAs flew just 45 escort and decoy sorties to the Falklands (including 12 on 1st May and 18 between 21st and 27th May during the battle for San Carlos) and a further 46 over the mainland and territorial waters during the conflict. Their failure to engage the Sea Harriers after 1st May meant that the A-4 and Dagger A attack aircraft were left unprotected and had to fend for themselves.

Pucara

Originally designed for counter-insurgency operations and deployed against lightly-armed Argentine guerrillas, the Pucaras found it difficult to survive in the high-threat environment that they eventually encountered in the Falklands. However, it was one of the few Argentine combat aircraft that could operate with safety from Stanley's short runway. It could also operate from the grass strips at Goose Green and Pebble Island although even the Pucara had difficulty with the uneven, muddy surfaces of these strips and one aircraft was damaged beyond repair in a take-off accident caused by the condition of the airstrip.

The Pucara could sustain a substantial degree of light damage and still operate. One of the aircraft that attacked British troops at Darwin on 28th May is reported to have returned to Stanley with 58 holes from small arms fire and shrapnel, four of them in the engines. Pucaras often flew very low to deliver their attacks and sometimes sustained small arms hits from above caused by troops shooting down on them from their positions on high ground. The aircraft that was shot down by a Sea Harrier on 21st May sustained a large amount of damage before it had to be abandoned.

The Pucaras based on the Falklands flew a total of 186 combat sorties, 18 of them during the fierce battle of Goose Green on 28th May. A total of 24 Pucaras were deployed to the Falklands and of these three were shot down (two by ground fire and one by a Sea Harrier), one crashed, three were damaged or destroyed by air raids at Goose Green, six were disabled at Pebble Island by the SAS raid and 11 were captured at Stanley airport. Of those captured at Stanley, most had been damaged to some degree by naval gunfire or air raids and only about two or three were airworthy.

The FMA IA 58A Pucaca twin-turboprop light attack aircraft entered service with the Argentine Air Force in 1976. Its effectiveness against British forces during the Falklands conflict was to prove mixed at best. FMA

For an aircraft not intended to operate in the sort of high-threat environment posed by British troops armed with portable SAMs and the ever-present threat of Sea Harrier attack, the Pucara squadron performed creditably. However, the aircraft posed a far greater psychological threat than a physical one and they achieved only minor success during the campaign.

Argentine Navy

A-4Q Skyhawk

The small force of Skyhawks operated by the Argentine Navy flew a total of 34 attack and armed reconnaissance sorties from Rio Grande. The aircraft engaged in combat on nine of these sorties with the result that three aircraft and two pilots were lost, giving a high attrition rate of almost 9 per cent of all the sorties flown.

The Navy A-4Qs could have played a major part in the conflict had they been able to launch from the *25 de Mayo* on 2nd May; however, there is no guarantee that they would have got through the Royal Navy's layered air defences to hit the aircraft carriers on that occasion. The A-4Qs of 3 Escuadrilla did share in the destruction of *Ardent* but had little further success during the conflict.

MB-339A

Although 1 Escuadrilla de Ataque was dual-roled as a light attack and flying training unit, the MB-339A was too lightly armed and armoured to survive for long in a high-threat environment. The squadron had worked closely with the Argentine marines and had evolved procedures for close air support (which had been practised prior to arriving at Stanley), but the detachment was instructed that it was expected to follow the different Air Force close air support procedures when operating in conjunction with Army units on the islands.

The facilities at Stanley Airport were barely adequate for the safe operation of the MB-339As. The aircraft were dispersed at the eastern end of the airfield on rough ground that was covered with aluminium matting and wooden planks. Although able to carry 250lb and 500lb bombs, the normal load for each MB-339A in the Falklands seems to have been two 30mm cannon carried in underwing pods (that produced large amounts of drag) and two 5-inch Zuni rocket pods, each with four rounds. These weapons required close-in, low-level delivery, which placed the aircraft well within range of any ground- or ship-based air defence weaponry. Two MB-339As were lost during the conflict, one to ground fire and one in a landing accident, while three others were captured at Stanley.

S-2E Tracker

The elderly Grumman S-2E Tracker ASW and maritime patrol aircraft flew a total of 143 sorties in about 600 flying hours during the conflict. Most of these missions were flown from the mainland but the aircraft did fly a small number of sorties from the *25 de Mayo* on the 1st and 2nd of May in an attempt to locate the British Task Force. Later in the conflict the Trackers were supplemented by two Embraer Bandeirantes that flew a total of 39 sorties.

SP-2H Neptune

By 1982 the Neptune was an obsolete aircraft fitted with obsolete and unreliable equipment. The final two Argentine Navy examples were due to be retired late in 1982 but the accelerated flying during the Falklands conflict resulted in their retirement date having to be brought forward.

On the flight during 4th May when an SP-2H located and tracked the British Task Force resulting in the sinking of *Sheffield*, the aircraft's radar was only working intermittently. The radar operator had to change the set's crystals nine times as they burnt

out in quick succession. *Sheffield* was in fact found as the ninth and last crystal was fitted into the elderly radar set.

The Escuadrilla de Exploracion only managed to keep its last two Neptunes flying by cannibalising two more aircraft at its home base at Espora. The Neptunes were later replaced by modified Lockheed Electras that had a maritime surveillance capability closer to that of the more specialised Lockheed P-3 Orion.

Super Etendard

The Super Etendard/Exocet combination was undoubtedly the most potent weapon system possessed by Argentina in April 1982, certainly as far as anti-ship operations were concerned. It was fortunate for the British Task Force that only five aircraft and missiles had been delivered before the invasion of the Falklands and that the French arms embargo precluded the delivery of the next batch of Super Etendards and Exocets that were expected by the end of April.

The Super Etendards flew a total of ten anti-shipping sorties during the conflict. Four of these sorties were aborted, two of them when an aircraft was unable to refuel and two when no targets could be found. Five Exocets were launched in the remaining six sorties and two, possibly three, of the missiles hit their targets, *Sheffield* and the *Atlantic Conveyor*. This was a highly creditable achievement considering that the Argentine air and ground crews had so little experience with the Super Etendard and the Exocet.

Most of the pilots had about 80 hours' flying time on the aircraft by April 1982, which is not long for a weapon system as sophisticated as the Super Etendard/Exocet. However, as devastating as the attacks were on the Task Force, the fact that not all missiles succeeded in hitting their targets was encouraging in that it proved that the

Exocet could be effectively countered, and the Royal Navy made a major effort after the conflict to re-equip its ships with improved anti-ship missile defences.

T-34C-1 Turbo Mentor

The decision to send the small detachment of four lightly armed T-34C-1 Turbo Mentors to the Falklands on 24th April is difficult to understand. These aircraft, the primary role of which was flying and weapons training, might just have been suitable enough for the counter-insurgency role against lightly armed guerrillas, but they were totally unsuitable for any role in the Falklands. After the first mission on 1st May, when three T-34C-1s almost fell victim to Sea Harriers, the detachment only flew another six missions, all armed reconnaissance, and did not engage in further combat before they were put out of action during the SAS raid on Pebble Island.

Argentine Army Aviation Helicopters

All 19 Army helicopters deployed to the Falklands were either destroyed or captured. One of the two CH-47C Chinooks was unserviceable for much of the time, thereby reducing the heavy-lift capability by 50 per cent. In addition to the five Pumas destroyed in action on the Falklands, another Puma was lost during the retaking of South Georgia. Oddly, not one of the nine UH-1Hs was lost in the air although they were heavily used during the conflict. However, several were disabled by naval gunfire, especially in the closing stages of the conflict.

One of CAB601's major problems was the threat of enemy attack and the unit had to disperse its helicopters on several occasions after being attacked by Harriers and by naval bombardment.

The Super Etendard/Exocet combination was the most potent weapon in the Argentine arsenal and also one of the most difficult to defend against. Exocets destroyed two of the six British ships lost during the conflict. MoD

An Argentine Tigercat launcher that was deployed at Stanley airport, seen here just after the surrender. A number of Tigercats were fired during the conflict (several on 1st May) and although no hits were achieved there were some near misses. Flt Sgt D W Knights

Anti-aircraft Weapons

Argentine anti-aircraft guns proved to be a major threat to attacking Harriers and Sea Harriers throughout the conflict. This was especially true of the excellent Oerlikon twin 35mm anti-aircraft guns and their Skyguard fire control radars. These weapons accounted for several aircraft, both British and Argentine! A variety of other air defence guns were deployed including machine guns and 20mm and 30mm cannon. Much of this weaponry was clustered around Stanley airport where the Argentines created a formidable defence. After Lieutenant Taylor was shot down at Goose Green by AAA on 4th May, Sea Harriers flew only toss-bombing and medium-altitude raids against well-protected targets, thereby reducing their accuracy and effectiveness.

Surprisingly, only one trailer-mounted Roland fire unit was deployed to the Falklands to defend Stanley airport. One of these missiles shot down Flight Lieutenant Mortimer's Sea Harrier over Stanley and it was claimed that another missile destroyed a 1,000lb bomb in flight after it had been tossed towards the airfield by a Sea Harrier. The Tigercat short-range missiles (the land-based version of the Royal Navy's Seacat) had little effect other than to frighten some of the attacking pilots.

Appendix One

British Air Order of Battle

Only those units directly involved in the Falklands conflict are included. The number of aircraft indicated is the total number that served with each unit during the conflict and deployed to either the South Atlantic or Ascension Island.

Royal Navy

737 Squadron
HMS *Antrim* and HMS *Glamorgan*
2 x Wessex HAS3

800 Squadron
HMS *Hermes*
16 x Sea Harrier FRS1

801 Squadron
HMS *Invincible*
12 x Sea Harrier FRS1

809 Squadron
HMS *Hermes* and HMS *Invincible*
8 x Sea Harrier FRS1
The squadron was integrated with 800 Squadron and 801 Squadron.

815 Squadron
HMS *Alacrity*, HMS *Ambuscade*, HMS *Andromeda*, HMS *Antelope*, HMS *Ardent*, HMS *Argonaut*, HMS *Arrow*, HMS *Avenger*, HMS *Brilliant*, HMS *Broadsword*, HMS *Cardiff*, HMS *Coventry*, HMS *Exeter*, HMS *Glasgow*, HMS *Minerva*, HMS *Penelope* and HMS *Sheffield*
24 x Lynx HAS2

820 Squadron
HMS *Invincible*
11 x Sea King HAS5

824 Squadron
RFA *Fort Grange* and RFA *Olmeda*
5 x Sea King HAS2A

825 Squadron
SS *Atlantic Causeway*, RMS *Queen Elizabeth II* and Falklands FOBs
10 x Sea King HAS2A

826 Squadron
HMS *Hermes*
11 x Sea King HAS5

829 Squadron
HMS *Active*, HMS *Endurance*, HMS *Hecla*, HMS *Herald*, HMS *Hydra*, HMS *Plymouth* and HMS *Yarmouth*
11 x Wasp HAS1

845 Squadron
RFA *Fort Austin*, RFA *Resource*, RFA *Tidepool*, RFA *Tidespring* and Falklands FOBs
18 x Wessex HU5

846 Squadron
HMS *Fearless*, HMS *Intrepid*, SS *Canberra*, MV *Elk*, MV *Norland* and Falklands FOBs
14 x Sea King HC4

847 Squadron
RFA *Engadine*, SS *Atlantic Causeway* and Falklands FOBs
27 x Wessex HU5

848 Squadron
RFA *Olna*, RFA *Regent* and SS *Atlantic Conveyor*
11 x Wessex HU5

Royal Marines

3 Commando Brigade Air Squadron
HMS *Fearless*, RFA *Sir Galahad*, RFA *Sir Geraint*, RFA *Sir Lancelot*, RFA *Sir Percivale*, RFA *Sir Tristram*, MV *Baltic Ferry*, MV *Europic Ferry*, MV *Nordic Ferry* and Falklands FOBs
10 x Gazelle AH1, 9 x Scout AH1

Army Air Corps

656 Squadron
MV *Baltic Ferry*, MV *Europic Ferry*, MV *Nordic Ferry* and Falklands FOBs
6 x Gazelle AH1, 7 x Scout AH1

Royal Air Force

1 Squadron
HMS *Hermes*
10 x Harrier GR3

18 Squadron
SS *Atlantic Conveyor* and Falklands FOBs
5 x Chinook HC1

24/30/47/70 Squadrons
Wideawake
unknown number of Hercules C1/C3

29 Squadron
Wideawake
3 x Phantom FGR2

42 Squadron
Wideawake
2 x Nimrod MR1

44/50/101 Squadrons detachment
Wideawake
4 x Vulcan B2

55 Squadron
Wideawake
10 x Victor K2

57 Squadron
Wideawake
10 x Victor K2

120/201/206 Squadrons
Wideawake
8 x Nimrod MR2

202 Squadron
Wideawake
1 x Sea King HAR3

Appendix Two

Argentine Air Order of Battle

Only those units directly involved in the Falklands conflict are included. Number of aircraft given is total strength, but not all were necessarily used during the conflict.

Argentine Navy (Armada)

Comando Aviacion Naval Argentina

1 ESCUADRA AERONAVAL
BAN Punta Indio
Escuadrilla de Ataque
15 x T-34C-1
Escuadrilla Aerofotografico
5 x Queen Air 80, 8 x Super King Air 200

2 ESCUADRA AERONAVAL
BAN Comandante Espora
Escuadrilla Antisubmarina
6 x S-2E
Escuadrilla de Exploracion
2 x SP-2H
2 Escuadrilla de Helicopteros
5 x S-61D-4 Sea King

3 ESCUADRA AERONAVAL
BAN Comandante Espora
2 Escuadrilla de Caza y Ataque
5 x Super Etendard
3 Escuadrilla de Caza y Ataque
10 x A-4Q
1 Escuadrilla de Helicopteros
9 x Alouette III, 2 x Lynx HAS23

4 ESCUADRA AERONAVAL
BAN Punta Indio
1 Escuadrilla de Ataque
7 x MB-326GB, 10 x MB-339A

5 ESCUADRA AERONAVAL
BAN Ezeiza
1 Escuadrilla de Sosten Logistico Movil
3 x Electra
2 Escuadrilla de Sosten Logistico Movil
3 x F-28-3000M, 1 x HS125-400B

Prefectura Naval Argentina

AGRUPACION ALBATROS
Puerto Nuevo
3 x Puma, 6 x Hughes 500C

AGRUPACION SKYVAN
Jorge Newbery Aeroparque
5 x Skyvan 3M

Argentine Army (Ejercito)

Comando de Aviacion del Ejercito

BATALLON DE AVIACION DE COMBATE 601
Campo de Mayo
Compania de Helicopteros de Asalto 'A'
2 x CH-47C, 8 x Puma
Compania de Helicopteros de Asalto 'B'
approx 20 x UH-1H
Compania de Helicopteros de Ataque
9 x A-109A

Argentine Air Force
(Fuerza Aerea Argentina)

Comando de Operaciones Aereas

I BRIGADA AEREA
BAM El Palomar
Grupo 1 de Transporte Aereo
Escuadron I
2 x C-130E, 5 x C-130H, 2 x KC-130H
Escuadron II
3 x Boeing 707, 5 x F-28-1000C
Escuadron IV
11 x Fokker F-27

II BRIGADA AEREA
BAM Parana
Grupo 1 Aerofotografico
Escuadron I
4 x Learjet 35A
Grupo 2 de Bombardeo
Escuadron I
8 x Canberra B62, 2 x Canberra T64

III BRIGADA AEREA
BAM Reconquista
Grupo 3 de Ataque
Escuadron I, II and III
approx 50 x Pucara

IV BRIGADA AEREA
BAM El Plumerillo
Grupo 4 de Caza
Escuadron III
19 x A-4C

V BRIGADA AEREA
BAM Villa Reynolds
Grupo 5 de Caza
Escuadron IV and V
approx 36 x A-4B

VII BRIGADA AEREA
BAM Moron
Grupo 7 de COIN
Escuadron Helicopteros
2 x Bell 212 (other types not used)
Escuadron Chinook
2 x CH-47C

IX BRIGADA AEREA
BAM Comodoro Rivadavia
Grupo 9 de Transporte Aereo
LADE
F-27s and F-28s of Grupo I,
Twin Otters of Grupo 9
Grupo 4 de Ataque
Escuadron IV
approx 10 x Pucara

Comando Aereo de Defensa

VI BRIGADA AEREA
BAM Tandil
Grupo 6 de Caza
Escuadron II and III
34 x Dagger A, 3 x Dagger B

VIII BRIGADA AEREA
BAM Dr Mariano Moreno
Grupo 8 de Caza
Escuadron I
16 x Mirage IIIEA, 1 x Mirage IIIDA

Appendix Three

Participation of Individual British Aircraft in the Conflict

Royal Navy Aircraft

British Aerospace Sea Harrier FRS1

XZ450
Transferred from BAe Dunsfold to 800 Sqn via 899 Sqn 2 Apr 1982 coded '50' and embarked on *Hermes* 4 Apr; shot down by AAA at Goose Green 4 May 1982 (Lt N Taylor).

XZ451
Transferred from 899 Sqn to 801 Sqn 2 Apr 1982 coded '006' and embarked on *Invincible* 4 Apr; shot down Canberra B-110 1 May (Lt W A Curtis); shot down Pucara A-511 21 May (Lt N D Ward); shot down C-130E TC-63 1 Jun (Lt Cdr N D Ward); returned to UK 17 Sep 1982. Crashed off Sardinia 30 Oct 1989 while with 801 Sqn.

XZ452
Transferred from 899 Sqn to 801 Sqn 2 Apr 1982 coded '007' and embarked on *Invincible* 4 Apr; shot down Mirage IIIEA I-015 1 May (Flt Lt P C Barton); missing in action southeast of West Falkland 6 May 1982 (Lt Cdr J E Eyton-Jones).

XZ453
Transferred from 899 Sqn to 801 Sqn 2 Apr 1982 coded '009' and embarked on *Invincible* 4 Apr; shot down Mirage IIIEA I-019 1 May (Lt S R Thomas); missing in action southeast of West Falkland 6 May 1982 (Lt W A Curtis).

XZ455
Transferred from 899 Sqn to 800 Sqn 2 Apr 1982 coded '12' and embarked on *Hermes* 5 Apr; shot down Dagger C-433 1 May (Flt Lt R Penfold); shot down Dagger C-409 21 May (Lt Cdr R V Fredericksen); transferred to 801 Sqn on *Invincible* 2 July coded '000'; returned to UK 17 Sep 1982. Later rebuilt as Sea Harrier FA2 but crashed into Adriatic 14 Feb 1996 while with 801 Sqn. Wreck currently at the RN FSAIU, RNAS Yeovilton.

XZ456
Transferred from 899 Sqn to 801 Sqn 2 Apr 1982 coded '008' and embarked on *Invincible* 4 Apr; hit by Roland SAM and crashed in sea off Port Stanley 1 Jun 1982 (Flt Lt I Mortimer).

XZ457
Transferred from 899 Sqn to 800 Sqn 2 Apr 1982 coded '14' and embarked on *Hermes* same day; shot down A-4Qs 0660 and 0665 21 May (Lt C R W Morrell); shot down Daggers C-419 and C-430 24 May (Lt Cdr A D Auld); returned to UK 21 July 1982. Later rebuilt as Sea Harrier FA2 but destroyed on the ground at RNAS Yeovilton 20 Oct 1995 while with 899 Sqn.

XZ458
Transferred from 899 Sqn to 809 Sqn 15 Apr 1982 coded '007'; flown to Ascension 1 May and embarked on *Atlantic Conveyor* 6 May; flown to *Invincible* and transferred to 801 Sqn 19 May coded '007'; transferred to 809 Sqn on *Illustrious* 26 Aug coded '259'; returned to UK 6 Dec 1982. Crashed at Gairlochy 1 Dec 1984 while with 800 Sqn.

XZ459
Embarked on *Hermes* with 800 Sqn 2 Apr 1982 coded '25'; returned to UK 21 July 1982. Later rebuilt as Sea Harrier FA2; still in service with the RN AMG, RNAS Yeovilton.

XZ460
Embarked on *Hermes* with 800 Sqn 2 Apr 1982 coded '26'; returned to UK 21 July 1982. Crashed off Sardinia 8 May 1990 while with 800 Sqn.

XZ491
Transferred from 899 Sqn to 809 Sqn 23 Apr 1982 uncoded; flown to Ascension 1 May and embarked on *Atlantic Conveyor* 6 May; flown to *Invincible* and transferred to 801 Sqn 19 May coded '002'; transferred to 809 Sqn on *Illustrious* 26 Aug coded '258'; returned to UK 6 Dec 1982. Crashed near Benbecula 16 Apr 1986 while with 801 Sqn.

XZ492
Embarked on *Hermes* with 800 Sqn 2 Apr 1982 coded '23'; shot down A-4C C-309 or C-325 21 May (Lt Cdr N W Thomas); returned to UK 21 July 1982. Later rebuilt as Sea Harrier FA2 but crashed in Mediterranean 16 Dec 1996 while with 800 Sqn.

XZ493
Embarked on *Invincible* with 801 Sqn 4 Apr 1982 coded '001'; returned to UK 17 Sep 1982. Crashed into Adriatic 15 Dec 1994 while with 800 Sqn. Wreck preserved at the FAA Museum, RNAS Yeovilton.

XZ494
Transferred from 899 Sqn to 800 Sqn 2 Apr 1982 coded '16' and embarked on *Hermes* same day; transferred to 801 Sqn on *Invincible* 2 July coded '008'; shared in destruction of Puma AE-500 23 May (Lt Cdr T Gedge); returned to UK 17 Sep 1982. Later rebuilt as Sea Harrier FA2 and currently in use for trials work at BAe Warton.

Back in the UK once hostilities had ceased, Sea Harrier FRS1 XZ460 was repainted in 800 Squadron's colourful markings. B Munro

XZ495
Embarked on *Invincible* with 801 Sqn 4 Apr 1982 coded '003'; returned to UK 17 Sep 1982. Later rebuilt as Sea Harrier FA2 but crashed near Lundy Island 5 Jan 1994 while with the Sea Harrier OEU.

XZ496
Embarked on *Hermes* with 800 Sqn 2 Apr 1982 coded '27'; shot down A-4C C-309 or C-325 on 21 May (Lt Cdr M S Blissett); returned to UK 21 July 1982. Crashed off Norwegian coast 16 Mar 1984 while with 800 Sqn.

XZ498
Embarked on *Invincible* with 801 Sqn 4 Apr 1982 coded '005'; returned to UK 17 Sep 1982. Shot down by SA-7 SAM near Gorazde, Bosnia during Operation 'Deny Flight' 16 Apr 1994 while with 801 Sqn.

XZ499
Transferred from 899 Sqn to 809 Sqn 15 Apr 1982 coded '000'; flown to Ascension 2 May and embarked on *Atlantic Conveyor* 6 May; flown to *Hermes* and transferred to 800 Sqn 18 May coded '99'; shot down A-4B C-204 8 Jun (Lt D A Smith); returned to UK 19 July 1982. Later rebuilt as Sea Harrier FA2 and currently in service with 899 Sqn, RNAS Yeovilton.

XZ500
Embarked on *Hermes* with 800 Sqn 2 Apr 1982 coded '30'; shot down A-4Q 0667 21 May (Flt Lt J Leeming); returned to UK 19 Jul 1982. Crashed in Bay of Biscay 15 Jun 1983 while with 800 Sqn.

ZA174
Transferred from 899 Sqn to 809 Sqn 15 Apr 1982 coded '000'; flown to Ascension 1 May and embarked on *Atlantic Conveyor* 6 May; flown to *Invincible* and transferred to 801 Sqn coded '000' 19 May; fell into sea from deck of *Invincible* 29 May 1982 (Lt Cdr G J M W Broadwater).

ZA175
Embarked on *Invincible* with 801 Sqn 4 Apr 1982 coded '004'; shot down Dagger C-407 21 May (Lt Cdr N D Ward); returned to UK 17 Sep 1982. Later rebuilt as Sea Harrier FA2 and currently in store at RAF St Athan.

ZA176
Transferred from 899 Sqn to 809 Sqn 14 Apr 1982 uncoded; flown to Ascension 1 May and embarked on *Atlantic Conveyor* 6 May; flown to *Hermes* and transferred to 800 Sqn 18 May coded '76'; returned to UK 19 July 1982. Rebuilt as Sea Harrier FA2 and currently in service with 800 Sqn, Yeovilton.

ZA177
Transferred from 899 Sqn to 809 Sqn 15 Apr 1982 uncoded; flown to Ascension 2 May and embarked on *Atlantic Conveyor* 6 May; flown to *Hermes* and transferred to 800 Sqn 18 May coded '77'; shot down A-4Bs C-226 and C-228 8 Jun (Flt Lt D H S Morgan); returned to UK 21 Jul 1982. Crashed near Cattistock 21 Jan 1983 while with 899 Sqn.

ZA190
Transferred from 899 Sqn to 809 Sqn 15 Apr 1982 uncoded; flown to Ascension 1 May and embarked on *Atlantic Conveyor* 6 May; flown to *Invincible* and transferred to 801 Sqn 18 May coded '009'; shot down Daggers C-403 and C-404 21 May (Lt S R Thomas); shared in destruction of Puma AE-500 23 May (Lt Cdr D D Braithwaite); returned to UK 17 Sep 1982. Crashed in Irish Sea 15 Oct 1987 while with 801 Sqn.

ZA191
Transferred from 899 Sqn to 800 Sqn 2 Apr 1982 coded '18' and embarked on *Hermes* same day; shared in destruction of A-109A AE-337 23 May (Flt Lt J Leeming); returned to UK 19 Sep 1982. Crashed into Lyme Bay 4 Oct 1989 while with 801 Sqn.

ZA192
Transferred from 899 Sqn to 800 Sqn 4 Apr 1982 coded '92' and embarked on *Hermes* same day; destroyed Puma AE-503 and shared in destruction of A-109A AE-337 and Puma AE-500 23 May (Flt Lt D H S Morgan); crashed into sea after take off from *Hermes* 23 May 1982 (Lt Cdr G W J Batt).

ZA193
Transferred from 899 Sqn to 800 Sqn 4 Apr 1982 coded '93' and embarked on *Hermes* same day; shot down Dagger C-410 24 May (Lt D A Smith); returned to UK 19 July 1982. Crashed off Cyprus 28 May 1992 while with 800 Sqn.

ZA194
Delivered to 809 Sqn from BAe Dunsfold 28 Apr 1982; flown to Ascension 1 May and embarked on *Atlantic Conveyor* 6 May; flown to *Hermes* and transferred to 800 Sqn 18 May coded '94'; shot down Dagger C-437 23 May (Lt M Hale); returned to UK 19 July 1982. Crashed near Dorchester 20 Oct 1983 while with 899 Sqn.

Westland Lynx HAS2
All Lynx were flown by 815 Sqn and operated by Ship's Flight from Royal Navy frigates and destroyers. Code numbers remained allocated during deployment but were not worn. Helicopters marked with an asterisk were modified to carry Sea Skua.

XZ233*
Embarked on *Argonaut* 19 Apr 1982 coded '466'; transferred to *Cardiff* 5 Jun coded '335'; transferred to *Brilliant* 22 Jun coded '341'; returned to UK 13 Jul 1982. Later converted to Lynx HAS3 and currently in service with 702 Sqn, RNAS Yeovilton.

XZ240*
Flown to Ascension in a Hercules C1 16 Apr 1982; embarked on *Invincible* 18 Apr for use by *Broadsword*; transferred to *Broadsword* 24 Apr coded '348'; transferred to *Fort Austin* 5 May; transferred to *Hermes* 17 May uncoded; returned to UK 21 Jul 1982. Sold to Pakistan Aug 1994.

XZ241
Already embarked on *Arrow* when war broke out, coded '326'; transferred to *Fort Austin* 17 Apr 1982 uncoded; flown to Ascension 22 Apr; returned to UK 26 Apr 1982 in a Hercules C1. Later converted to Lynx HAS3, currently at RNAY Fleetlands.

XZ242*
Newcastle Flight helicopter flown to Ascension in a Hercules C1 3 Apr 1982 coded '345'; embarked on *Fort Austin* 6 Apr; transferred to *Coventry* 17 Apr coded '336'; lost when *Coventry* was bombed and sunk 25 May 1982.

XZ247*
815 Sqn Trials Flight helicopter flown to Ascension in a Hercules C1 4 Apr 1982

coded '306'; embarked on *Fort Austin* 6 Apr uncoded; transferred to *Glasgow* 17 Apr coded '344'; transferred to *Ambuscade* 25 May; returned to UK 24 July 1982. Ditched in the Atlantic 30 Sep 1982 while with 815 Sqn/*Ambuscade*.

XZ249*
Embarked on *Avenger* 26 Apr 1982 coded '307'; returned to UK 10 Sep 1982. Crashed in Persian Gulf 4 May 1983 while with 815 Sqn/*Avenger* and wreck used for fire and rescue practice at the RN Fire School, Predannack.

XZ251*
Embarked on *Ardent* 19 Apr 1982 coded '340'; lost when *Ardent* was bombed and sunk 21 May 1982.

XZ254
Already embarked on *Cardiff* when war broke out, coded '335'; transferred to *Argonaut* 5 Jun 1982 coded '466'; returned to UK 26 Jun 1982. Later converted to Lynx HAS3 and currently in service with 702 Sqn, RNAS Yeovilton.

XZ691*
Embarked on *Penelope* 10 May 1982 coded '454'; transferred to *Broadsword* 2 Jul coded '349'; returned to UK 23 Jul 1982. Later converted to Lynx HMA8 and currently in service with 702 Sqn, RNAS Yeovilton.

XZ692
Already embarked on *Brilliant* when war broke out, coded '341'; flown to Ascension 14 Apr 1982; returned to UK 23 Apr 1982 in a Hercules C1. Later converted to Lynx HMA8 and currently at RNAY Fleetlands.

XZ696
Embarked on *Ambuscade* 9 Apr 1982 coded '323'; transferred to *Glasgow* 25 May coded '344'; returned to UK 19 Jun 1982. Later converted to Lynx HAS3 and currently in service with 815 Sqn, RNAS Yeovilton.

XZ698*
Embarked on *Minerva* 10 May 1982 coded '424'; returned to UK 3 Aug 1982. Later converted to Lynx HMA8 and currently in service with 702 Sqn, RNAS Yeovilton.

XZ700
Already embarked on *Coventry* when war broke out, coded '336'; transferred to *Fort Austin* 17 Apr 1982 uncoded; loaned to *Alacrity* 3-8 May coded '327'; transferred to *Hermes* 17 May coded '336'; transferred to *Atlantic Conveyor* 20 May still coded '336'; lost when *Atlantic Conveyor* was hit by an Exocet 25 May 1982.

XZ720
Already embarked on *Alacrity* when war broke out, coded '327'; transferred to *Invincible* 24 Apr 1982; transferred to *Fort Austin* 4 May uncoded; transferred to *Hermes* 17 May; loaned to *Invincible* 10-17 Jun; returned to UK 21 Jul 1982. Later converted to Lynx HAS3 and currently in service with 815 Sqn, RNAS Yeovilton.

XZ721*
Flown to Ascension in a Hercules C1 10 Apr 1982; embarked on *Brilliant* 14 Apr coded '341'; transferred to *Sheffield* 22 Apr coded '337'; flown to *Hermes* when *Sheffield* was hit by an Exocet 4 May; transferred to *Brilliant* 7 May coded '341'; loaned to *Cardiff* 27-30 May; transferred to *Cardiff* 23 Jun coded '335'; returned to UK 28 Jul 1982. Later converted to Lynx HMA8 and currently in service with 815 Sqn, RNAS Yeovilton.

XZ722*
Embarked on *Andromeda* 10 May 1982 coded '472'; loaned to *Invincible* 13-24 Aug; returned to UK 10 Sep 1982. Later converted to Lynx HMA8 and currently in service with RN AMG, RNAS Yeovilton.

XZ723*
Embarked on *Antelope* 4 Apr 1982 coded '321'; flown to *Fearless* when *Antelope* was bombed 23 May; transferred to *Brilliant* 30 May coded '342'; transferred to *Broadsword* 22 Jun coded '349'; transferred to *Penelope* 2 Jul coded '454'; returned to UK 10 Sep 1982. Later converted to Lynx HMA8 and currently at RNAY Fleetlands.

XZ725
Already embarked on *Sheffield* when war broke out, coded '337'; transferred to *Brilliant* 22 Apr 1982 coded '341'; took part in the attack on the *Santa Fe* off Grytviken, South Georgia 25 Apr; transferred to *Fort Austin* 8 May uncoded; transferred to *Invincible* 17 May; returned to UK 16 Sep 1982. Later converted to Lynx HMA8 and currently at RNAY Fleetlands.

XZ728*
Flown to Ascension in a Hercules C1 12 Apr 1982; embarked on *Broadsword* 16 Apr coded '347'; returned to UK 23 Jul 1982. Later converted to Lynx HMA8 and currently at RNAY Fleetlands.

XZ729
Already embarked on *Brilliant* when war broke out, coded '342'; took part in the attack on the *Santa Fe* off Grytviken, South Georgia 25 Apr 1982; damaged by a bomb while on loan to *Broadsword* 25 May; airlifted to *Atlantic Causeway* 11 Jun; returned to UK 27 Jul 1982. Later converted to Lynx HMA8 and currently at RNAY Fleetlands.

XZ730*
Flown to Ascension in a Hercules C1 3 Apr 1982; embarked on *Fort Austin* 6 Apr coded '424'; transferred to *Arrow* 17 Apr coded '326'; returned to UK 7 Jul 1982. Later converted to Lynx HAS3 and currently in service with 702 Sqn, RNAS Yeovilton.

XZ732*
Already embarked on *Glasgow* when war broke out, coded '344'; transferred to *Fort Austin* 17 Apr 1982 uncoded; transferred to *Broadsword* 5 May coded '349'; transferred to *Brilliant* 23 Jun coded '342'; returned to UK 13 Jul 1982. Later converted to Lynx HMA8 and currently in service with 815 Sqn, RNAS Yeovilton.

XZ733*
Already embarked on *Exeter* when war broke out, coded '420'; returned to UK 28 Jul 1982. Later converted to Lynx HAS3 and currently in service with 815 Sqn, RNAS Yeovilton.

XZ736*
Already embarked on *Broadsword* when war broke out, coded '346'; transferred to *Alacrity* 24 Apr 1982 coded '327'; detached to *Fort Austin* for BDR 3-8 May; returned to UK 24 Jun 1982. Later converted to Lynx HMA8 and currently in service with 815 Sqn, RNAS Yeovilton.

Westland Sea King HAS2A/HAS5

XV648 (HAS2)
Transferred from 706 Sqn to 825 Sqn 3 May 1982 coded '597'; embarked on *Queen Elizabeth II* 12 May; transferred to *Canberra* 28 May; flown to San Carlos FOB 2 Jun; embarked on *Atlantic Causeway* 13 Jul; returned to UK 27 Jul 1982. Later converted to Sea King HU5 and currently stored at RNAY Fleetlands.

XV649 (HAS2A)
Embarked on *Olmeda* with 'A' Flt 824 Sqn 4 Apr 1982 coded '355'; flown to San Carlos FOB 3 Jun; returned to *Olmeda* 6 Jun; returned to UK 10 Jul 1982. Later converted to Sea King AEW2 and currently in service with 849 Sqn, Culdrose.

XV654 (HAS2A)
Transferred from 706 Sqn to 825 Sqn 3 May 1982 coded '585'; embarked on *Atlantic Causeway* 13 May; flown to San Carlos FOB 1 Jun; embarked on *Atlantic Causeway* 13 Jul; returned to UK 27 July 1982. Later converted to Sea King HAS6 and became ground instructional airframe at HMS *Sultan*, Gosport.

XV656 (HAS2A)
Transferred from 819 Sqn to 825 Sqn 3 May 1982 coded '703'; embarked on *Atlantic Causeway* 13 May; flown to San Carlos FOB 29 May; embarked on *Atlantic Causeway* 13 July; returned to UK 27 July 1982. Later converted to Sea King AEW2 and currently in service with 849 Sqn, RNAS Culdrose.

825 Squadron Sea King HAS2A XV648 sits on Stanley racecourse at the end of the conflict. The presence of the tracked Arctic vehicle visible in the background is indicative of the harsh conditions experienced. Wg Cdr P Lyall

XV659 (HAS2A)
Transferred from 706 Sqn to 825 Sqn 3 May 1982 coded '584'; embarked on *Atlantic Causeway* 13 May; flown to San Carlos FOB 29 May; embarked on *Atlantic Causeway* 13 Jul; returned to UK 27 Jul 1982. Later converted to Sea King HAS6 and currently stored at HMS *Sultan*, Gosport.

XV660 (HAS2A)
Embarked on *Olmeda* with 'A' Flt 824 Sqn 4 April 1982 coded '350'; flown to San Carlos FOB 3 Jun; returned to *Olmeda* 6 Jun; transferred (temporarily) to *Invincible* 16 Jun; returned to *Olmeda* 27 Jun; returned to UK 10 Jul 1982. Later converted to Sea King HAS6 and currently stored at HMS *Sultan*, Gosport.

XV663 (HAS2A)
Transferred from 706 Sqn to 825 Sqn 3 May 1982 coded '581'; embarked on *Atlantic Causeway* 13 May; flown to San Carlos FOB 1 Jun; embarked on *Atlantic Causeway* 13 Jul; returned to UK 27 Jul 1982. Later converted to Sea King HAS6 and currently stored at HMS *Sultan*, Gosport.

XV672 (HAS2A)
Transferred from 706 Sqn to 'C' Flt 824 Sqn 29 April 1982 coded '145'; embarked on *Fort Grange* 7 May; returned to UK 2 Oct 1982. Later converted to Sea King AEW7 and currently at GKN Westland.

XV677 (HAS2A)
Transferred from 706 Sqn to 825 Sqn 3 May 1982 coded '595'; embarked on *Queen Elizabeth II* 12 May; transferred to *Canberra* 28 May; flown to San Carlos FOB 2 Jun; embarked on *Atlantic Causeway* 13 Jul; returned to UK 27 Jul 1982. Later converted to Sea King HAS6 and currently stored at HMS *Sultan*, Gosport.

XV696 (HAS2A)
Transferred from 814 Sqn to 825 Sqn 3 May 1982 coded '268'; embarked on *Atlantic Causeway* 13 May; flown to San Carlos FOB 29 May; damaged at Lookout Hill 3 Jun; air-lifted to San Carlos FOB 7 Jun; embarked on *Engadine* 7 Jul; returned to UK 30 Jul 1982. Later converted to Sea King HAS6 and currently stored at HMS *Sultan*, Gosport.

XV697 (HAS2A)
Embarked on *Fort Grange* with 'C' Flt 824 Sqn 7 May 1982 coded '354'; returned to UK 2 Oct 1982. Later converted to Sea King AEW2 and currently in service with RN AMG, RNAS Culdrose.

XV698 (HAS2A)
Embarked on *Fort Grange* with 'C' Flt 824 Sqn 7 May 1982 coded '351'; crashed in South Atlantic 11 Jul 1982.

XV700 (HAS2A)
Transferred from 814 Sqn to 825 Sqn 3 May 1982 coded '264'; embarked on *Atlantic Causeway* 13 May; flown to San Carlos FOB 29 May; embarked on *Atlantic Causeway* 13 Jul; returned to UK 27 Jul 1982. Later converted to Sea King HAS6 and currently in service with 810 Sqn, RNAS Culdrose.

XV714 (HAS2A)
Transferred from 706 Sqn to 825 Sqn 3 May 1982 coded '586'; embarked on *Atlantic Causeway* 13 May; flown to San Carlos FOB 29 May; embarked on *Atlantic Causeway* 13 Jul; returned to UK 27 Jul 1982. Later converted to Sea King AEW2 and currently in service with 849 Sqn, RNAS Culdrose.

XZ571 (HAS5)
Embarked on *Hermes* with 826 Sqn 3 Apr 1982 coded '43'; returned to UK 21 Jul 1982. Later converted to Sea King HAS6 and currently in service with 820 Sqn, RNAS Culdrose.

XZ573 (HAS5)
Transferred from 706 Sqn to 820 Sqn 2 Apr 1982 coded '593'; embarked on *Invincible* 4 Apr; flown to *Hermes* and transferred to 826 Sqn 15 May coded '22'; crashed in South Atlantic 18 May 1982.

XZ574 (HAS5)
Already embarked on *Invincible* with 820 Sqn when war broke out, coded '16'; returned to UK 17 Sep 1982. Later converted to Sea King HAS6 and currently in service with 771 Sqn, RNAS Culdrose.

XZ577 (HAS5)
Embarked on *Hermes* with 826 Sqn 3 Apr 1982 coded '42'; transferred to *Fort Austin* 17 May; flown to San Carlos FOB 3 Jun; embarked on *Hermes* 6 Jun; returned to UK 21 Jul 1982. Crashed in the Bay of Bengal 31 May 1991 while operating from *Fort Grange* with 826 Sqn.

XZ578 (HAS5)
Transferred from 706 Sqn to 820 Sqn 2 Apr 1982 coded '21'; embarked on *Invincible* 4 April; flown to *Hermes* and transferred to 826 Sqn 14 May coded '21'; detached to *Atlantic Causeway* 6-10 Jun; flown to San Carlos FOB 17 Jun; embarked on *Hermes* 23 Jun; returned to UK 21 Jul 1982. Later converted to Sea King HU5 and currently in service with 819 Sqn, Prestwick.

XZ579 (HAS2A)
Transferred from 706 Sqn to Naval Party 2050 and embarked on *Contender Bezant* 20 May 1982 coded '271; flown to *Fort Grange* and transferred to 'C' Flt 824 Sqn 13 July; returned to UK 2 Oct 1982. Later converted to Sea King HAS6 and currently stored at HMS *Sultan*, Gosport.

XZ580 (HAS2A)
Transferred from 814 Sqn to 825 Sqn 3 May 1982 coded '272'; embarked on *Atlantic Causeway* 13 May; flown to San Carlos FOB 1 Jun; embarked on *Atlantic Causeway* 13 Jul; returned to UK 27 Jul 1982. Later converted to Sea King HAS6 and currently in service with 819 Sqn, Prestwick.

XZ918 (HAS5)
Already embarked on *Invincible* with 820 Sqn when war broke out, coded '20'; returned to UK 17 Sep 1982. Sold to Royal Australian Navy Jul 1996.

XZ920 (HAS5)
Already embarked on *Invincible* with 820 Sqn when war broke out, coded '10'; flown to San Carlos FOB 14 Jun 1982; embarked on *Invincible* 17 Jun; returned to UK 17 Sep 1982. Later converted to Sea King HU5 and currently in service with 771 Sqn, RNAS Culdrose.

XZ921 (HAS5)
Already embarked on *Invincible* with 820 Sqn when war broke out, coded '17'; flown

to San Carlos FOB 10 Jun 1982; embarked on *Invincible* 14 Jun; returned to UK 17 Sep 1982. Later converted to Sea King HAS6 and currently in service with RN ETS, RNAS Culdrose.

ZA126 (HAS5)
Already embarked on *Invincible* with 820 Sqn when war broke out, coded '12'; returned to UK 17 Sep 1982. Later converted to Sea King HAS6 and currently stored at HMS *Sultan*, Gosport.

ZA127 (HAS5)
Already embarked on *Invincible* with 820 Sqn when war broke out, coded '11'; flown to San Carlos FOB 10 Jun 1982; embarked on *Invincible* 17 Jun; returned to UK 17 Sep 1982. Later converted to Sea King HAS6 and currently stored at HMS *Sultan*, Gosport.

ZA128 (HAS5)
Already embarked on *Invincible* with 820 Sqn when war broke out, coded '14'; returned to UK 17 Sep 1982. Later converted to Sea King HAS6 and currently in service with 810 Sqn, RNAS Culdrose.

ZA129 (HAS5)
Transferred from 706 Sqn to 826 Sqn 2 Apr 1982 coded '82'; embarked on *Hermes* 3 Apr; transferred to *Atlantic Causeway* 6 Jun; transferred to *Engadine* 9 Jun; transferred to *Fort George* 10 Jun; transferred to *Hermes* 11 Jun coded '44'; returned to UK 21 Jul 1982. Later converted to Sea King HAS6 and currently at RNAY Fleetlands.

ZA130 (HAS5)
Embarked on *Hermes* with 826 Sqn 3 Apr 1982 coded '32'; transferred to *Fort Austin* 17 May; flown to San Carlos FOB 3 Jun; embarked on *Hermes* 6 Jun; returned to UK 21 Jul 1982. Later converted to Sea King HU5 and currently in service with 771 Sqn, RNAS Culdrose.

ZA131 (HAS5)
Embarked on *Hermes* with 826 Sqn 3 Apr 1982 coded '33'; returned to UK 21 Jul 1982. Later converted to Sea King HAS6 and currently stored at HMS *Sultan*, Gosport.

ZA132 (HAS5)
Embarked on *Hermes* with 826 Sqn 3 Apr 1982 coded '34'; crashed into South Atlantic 12 May 1982.

ZA133 (HAS5)
Embarked on *Hermes* with 826 Sqn 3 Apr 1982 coded '35'; transferred to *Fort Austin* 17 May; flown to San Carlos FOB 3 Jun; embarked on *Hermes* 6 Jun; flown to San Carlos FOB 17 Jun; embarked on *Hermes* 23 Jun; returned to UK 21 Jul 1982. Later converted to Sea King HAS6 and currently in service with 820 Sqn, RNAS Culdrose.

ZA134 (HAS5)
Already embarked on *Invincible* with 820 Sqn when war broke out, coded '13'; returned to UK 17 Sep 1982. Later converted to Sea King HU5 and currently in service with 771 Sqn, RNAS Culdrose.

ZA135 (HAS5)
Already embarked on *Invincible* with 820 Sqn when war broke out, coded '15'; returned to UK 17 Sep 1982. Later converted to Sea King HAS6 and currently in store at RNAS Culdrose.

ZA136 (HAS5)
Embarked on *Hermes* with 826 Sqn 3 Apr 1982 coded '40'; returned to UK 21 Jul 1982. Later converted to Sea King HAS6 and used as ground instructional airframe at HMS *Sultan*, Gosport.

ZA137 (HAS5)
Transferred from 706 Sqn to 826 Sqn 2 Apr 1982 coded '96'; embarked on *Hermes* 3 Apr coded '46'; transferred to *Fort Austin* 17 May; flown to San Carlos FOB 3 Jun; embarked on *Hermes* 6 Jun; returned to UK 21 Jul 1982. Later converted to Sea King HU5 and currently in service with 771 Sqn, RNAS Culdrose.

Westland Sea King HC4

ZA290
Embarked on *Hermes* with 846 Sqn 3 Apr 1982 coded 'VC'; force-landed near Punta Arenas, Chile and destroyed by its crew 18 May 1982.

ZA291
Embarked on *Hermes* with 846 Sqn 3 Apr 1982 coded 'VB'; detached to Ascension for HDS duties 16 Apr; embarked on *Elk* 28 Apr; transferred to *Intrepid* 14 May; transferred to *Canberra* 19 May; transferred to *Norland* 21 May; flown to Old House Creek FOB 23 May; embarked on *Hermes* 3 Jul; returned to UK 21 Jul 1982. Currently in service with 848 Sqn, RNAS Yeovilton.

ZA292
Embarked on *Hermes* with 846 Sqn 3 Apr 1982 coded 'VH'; transferred to *Intrepid* 19 May; flown to San Carlos FOB 29 May; embarked on *Intrepid* 16 Jun; returned to UK 13 Jul 1982. Currently at GKN Westland.

ZA293
Embarked on *Hermes* with 846 Sqn 3 Apr 1982 coded 'VK'; transferred to *Intrepid* 19 May; flown to San Carlos FOB 29 May; embarked on *Intrepid* 16 Jun; returned to UK 13 Jul 1982. Currently in service with 848 Sqn, RNAS Yeovilton.

ZA294
Embarked on *Hermes* with 846 Sqn 3 Apr 1982 coded 'VT'; crashed in South Atlantic while transferring to *Intrepid* 19 May 1982.

ZA295
Embarked on *Hermes* with 846 Sqn 3 Apr 1982 coded 'VM'; detached to Ascension for HDS duties 16 Apr; embarked on *Elk* 28 Apr; transferred to *Norland* 19 May; transferred to *Intrepid* 20 May; flown off to San Carlos FOB 29 May; embarked on *Hermes* 3 Jul; returned to UK 21 Jul 1982. Currently in service with 848 Sqn, RNAS Yeovilton.

ZA296
Embarked on *Fearless* with 846 Sqn 6 Apr 1982 coded 'VF'; detached to Ascension for HDS duties 17 Apr until returned to *Fearless* 8 May; flown to Fern Valley Creek FOB 27 May; embarked on *Fearless* 16 Jun; returned to UK 13 Jul 1982. Currently in service with 846 Sqn, RNAS Yeovilton.

ZA297
Embarked on *Fearless* with 846 Sqn 6 Apr 1982 coded 'VG'; detached to Ascension for HDS duties 17 Apr; transferred to *Intrepid* 8 May; flown to San Carlos FOB 29 May; embarked on *Intrepid* 16 Jun; returned to UK 13 Jul 1982. Currently in service with 845 Sqn, RNAS Yeovilton.

ZA298
Embarked on *Hermes* with 846 Sqn 3 Apr 1982 coded 'VA'; detached to Ascension for HDS duties 16 Apr; embarked on *Fearless* 8 May; flown to Fern Valley Creek FOB 27 May; embarked on *Fearless* 16 Jun; returned to UK 13 Jul 1982. Currently in service with 845 Sqn, RNAS Yeovilton.

ZA299
Embarked on *Hermes* with 846 Sqn 3 Apr 1982 coded 'VE'; detached to Ascension for HDS duties 16 Apr; embarked on *Canberra* 6 May; transferred to *Europic Ferry* 25 May; flown to Old House Creek FOB 26 May; embarked on *Fearless* 16 Jun; returned to UK 13 Jul 1982. Currently in service with 848 Sqn, RNAS Yeovilton.

ZA310
Embarked on *Fearless* with 846 Sqn 6 Apr 1982 coded 'VS'; detached to Ascension for HDS duties 17 Apr until returned to *Fearless* 8 May; damaged near Fanning Head 23 May; embarked on *Intrepid* 15 Jun; returned to UK 13 Jul 1982. Currently in service with 848 Sqn, RNAS Yeovilton.

ZA311
Embarked on *Hermes* with 846 Sqn 3 Apr 1982 coded 'VP'; crashed in South Atlantic 23 Apr 1982.

ZA312
Flown to Ascension in Heavylift Belfast G-BFYU for 846 Sqn 8 Apr 1982 coded 'VW'; embarked on *Elk* 28 Apr; transferred to *Fearless* 19 May; flown to Old House Creek FOB 23 May; embarked on *Canberra* 23 Jun, returned to UK 10 Jul 1982. Currently in service with 848 Sqn, RNAS Yeovilton.

ZA313
Embarked on *Intrepid* with 846 Sqn 26 Apr 1982 coded 'VZ'; transferred to *Norland* 20 May; flown to Old House Creek FOB 23 May; detached to *Sir Galahad* 7-8 Jun; embarked on *Fearless* 16 Jun; returned to UK 13 Jul 1982. Currently in service with 845 Sqn, RNAS Yeovilton.

Westland Wasp HAS1

All Wasps were flown by 829 Sqn and operated by Ship's Flight from Royal Navy frigates and other vessels.

XS527
Already embarked on *Endurance* when war broke out, coded '434'; took part in the attack on the *Santa Fe* off Grytviken, South Georgia 25 Apr 1982; returned to UK 19 Aug 1982. Currently in store at the FAA Museum, RNAS Yeovilton.

XS539
Already embarked on *Endurance* with 829 Sqn when war broke out, coded '435'; took part in the attack on the *Santa Fe* off Grytviken, South Georgia 25 Apr 1982; returned to UK 19 Aug 1982. Currently in use as a training airframe at RNAY Fleetlands Apprentice School.

XS562
Embarked on *Contender Bezant* with 829 Sqn 20 May 1982 coded '371'; returned to UK 1 Aug 1982. Sold to private owner in the USA Apr 1994.

XT420
Allocated to 829 Sqn for *Hecla* 16 Apr 1982; flown to Ascension in a Hercules C3 19 Apr; embarked on *Hecla* 20 Apr coded '416'; returned to UK 29 Jul 1982. Currently privately owned at East Dereham.

XT427
Embarked on *Contender Bezant* with 829 Sqn 20 May 1982 coded '372'; returned to UK 1 Aug 1982. Currently in store at the FAA Museum, RNAS Yeovilton.

XT429
Already embarked on *Plymouth* with 829 Sqn when war broke out, coded '445'; took part in the attack on the *Santa Fe* off Grytviken, South Georgia 25 Apr 1982; returned to UK 12 Jul 1982. Sold to Royal Malaysian Navy August 1992.

XT432
Allocated to 829 Sqn for *Hydra* 1 Apr 1982; embarked on *Hydra* 23 Apr coded '415'; returned to UK 24 Sep 1982. Sold to Royal New Zealand Navy for spares October 1989.

XT779
Already embarked on *Active* with 829 Sqn when war broke out, coded '322'; returned to UK 3 Aug 1982. Used for fire and rescue practice at RN Portland.

XT794
Already embarked on *Herald* with 829 Sqn when war broke out, coded '325'; returned to UK 21 Jul 1982. Ditched in the Atlantic off Ascension 13 Apr 1984 while with *Herald*/829 Sqn.

XT795
Allocated to 829 Sqn 22 May 1982; embarked on RMS *St Helena* 11 Jun coded '373'; returned to UK 13 Sep 1982. To Royal Netherlands Navy 1993 for preservation at De Kooij.

XV624
Already embarked on *Yarmouth* with 829 Sqn when war broke out, coded '456'; returned to UK 27 Jul 1982. Used for fire and rescue practice at RN Portland.

Westland Wessex HAS3

XM837
Already embarked on *Glamorgan* with 737 Sqn when war broke out, coded '400'; destroyed by Exocet missile which hit the hangar of *Glamorgan* 12 Jun 1982.

XP142
Already embarked on *Antrim* with 737 Sqn when war broke out, coded '406'; took part in the attack on the *Santa Fe* off Grytviken, South Georgia 25 Apr 1982; damaged by bomb splinters during attack on *Antrim* 21 May; returned to UK 17 Jul 1982. Currently in store at the FAA Museum, RNAS Yeovilton.

Westland Wessex HU5

XS479
Transferred from 707 Sqn to 'B' Flt 847 Sqn 11 May 1982 coded 'XF'; embarked on *Atlantic Causeway* 12 May; flown to Port San Carlos FOB 1 Jun; embarked on *Atlantic Causeway* 12 Jul; returned to UK 27 Jul 1982. Was privately owned at Stock but scrapped in 2001.

XS480
Transferred from 707 Sqn to 'D' Flt 848 Sqn 19 Apr 1982 coded 'WQ'; embarked on *Atlantic Conveyor* 25 Apr; lost when *Atlantic Conveyor* was hit by an Exocet missile 90 miles northeast of Port Stanley 25 May 1982.

XS481
Transferred from 771 Sqn to 'D' Flt 848 Sqn 2 Jun 1982; embarked on *Astronomer* 7 Jun; arrived at Port Stanley 27 Jun; embarked on *Contender Bezant* 2 Sep; returned to UK 23 Sep 1982. Currently privately owned by Aeroventure, Doncaster.

XS483
Embarked on *Resource* with 'A' Flt 845 Sqn 2 Apr 1982 coded 'T'; detached to *Glamorgan* 30 Apr-2 May; flown to Old House Creek FOB, 24 May; embarked on *Resource* 24 Jun; returned to UK 19 Jul 1982. Used for fire and rescue practice at RN Lee-on-Solent.

XS486
Transferred from 707 Sqn to 'A' Flt 848 Sqn 19 Apr 1982 coded 'WW' and embarked on *Regent* same day; detached to *Endurance* 17-24 Jun; transferred to *Atlantic Causeway* 10 Jul; returned to UK 27 Jul 1982. Currently with No 93 ATC, Bath.

XS488
Transferred from 707 Sqn to 'B' Flt 847 Sqn 6 May 1982 coded 'XK'; embarked on *Atlantic Causeway* 13 May; flown to Port San Carlos FOB 1 Jun; embarked on *Atlantic Causeway* 12 Jul; returned to UK 27 Jul 1982. Currently in use as an instructional airframe at AAC Wattisham.

Eleven Wasp HAS1s were used during the Falklands conflict including the two on HMS Endurance, *one on each of the three ambulance ships, and three on board the frigates* Active, Plymouth *and* Yarmouth. *MoD*

Wessex XS507 'XU' was one of 54 HU5s deployed during the conflict. This particular helicopter served with 'B' Flight 847 Squadron but was loaned to 'D' Flight 848 Squadron for operation from the tanker Tidepool *on 16th June.* Flt Lt K Faulkner

XS489

Transferred from 707 Sqn to 'B' Flt 848 Sqn 19 Apr 1982 coded 'WY'; embarked on *Olna* 10 May; returned to UK 16 Sep 1982. Currently in use as an instructional airframe at the RN AESS, HMS *Sultan*, Gosport.

XS491

Transferred from Lee-on-Solent SAR Flt to 847 Sqn 5 May 1982; transferred to 'D' Flt 845 Sqn 7 May; flown to Ascension in Heavylift Belfast G-BEPS 12 May; transferred to 'A' Flt 847 Sqn 25 May and embarked on *Engadine* same day coded 'XM'; flown to Port San Carlos FOB 9 Jun; transferred to 845 Sqn 27 Sep; embarked on *Astronomer* 6 Nov; returned to UK 3 Dec 1982. Used for fire and rescue practice at RAF Stafford. Currently preserved at the South Yorkshire Aviation Museum, Firbeck.

XS495

Transferred from 707 Sqn to 'D' Flt 848 Sqn 19 Apr 1982 coded 'WP'; embarked on *Atlantic Conveyor* 25 Apr; lost when *Atlantic Conveyor* was hit by an Exocet missile 90 miles northeast of Port Stanley 25 May 1982.

XS498

Transferred from 772 Sqn to 'D' Flt 848 Sqn 4 Jun 1982 uncoded; embarked on *Astronomer* 7 Jun; arrived at Port William 27 Jun; embarked on *Atlantic Causeway* 12 Jul; returned to UK 27 Jul 1982. Currently privately owned at Hixon.

XS499

Transferred from 707 Sqn to 'D' Flt 848 Sqn 19 Apr 1982 coded 'WN'; embarked on *Atlantic Conveyor* 25 Apr; lost when *Atlantic Conveyor* was hit by an Exocet missile 90 miles northeast of Port Stanley 25 May 1982.

XS506

Transferred from 845 Sqn to 'B' Flt 847 Sqn 11 May 1982 coded 'XE'; embarked on *Atlantic Causeway* 13 May; flown to Port San Carlos FOB 1 Jun; transferred to 845 Sqn 27 Sep; embarked on *Astronomer* 6 Nov; returned to UK 3 Dec 1982. Used as an instructional airframe at RAF Shawbury and scrapped Mar 1993.

XS507

Transferred from 772 Sqn to 'B' Flt 847 Sqn 5 May 1982 coded 'XU'; embarked on *Atlantic Causeway* 13 May; transferred to *Tidepool* 16 Jun for loan by 'D' Flt 848 Sqn; transferred to *Hermes* 1 Jul; returned to UK 21 Jul 1982. Currently in use as an instruc-tional airframe at the RN AESS, HMS *Sultan*, Gosport.

XS512

Transferred from 707 Sqn to 'D' Flt 848 Sqn 19 Apr 1982 coded 'WT'; embarked on *Atlantic Conveyor* 25 Apr; lost when *Atlantic Conveyor* was hit by an Exocet missile 90 miles northeast of Port Stanley 25 May 1982.

XS514

Transferred from 845 Sqn to 'B' Flt 847 Sqn 11 May 1982 coded 'XA'; embarked on *Atlantic Causeway* 13 May; flown to Port San Carlos FOB 1 Jun; embarked on *Atlantic Causeway* 12 Jul; returned to UK 27 Jul 1982. Currently in use as an instructional airframe at the RN AESS, HMS *Sultan*, Gosport.

XS515

Transferred from 845 Sqn to 'B' Flt 847 Sqn 11 May 1982 coded 'XB'; embarked on *Atlantic Causeway* 13 May; flown to Port San Carlos FOB 1 Jun; embarked on *Atlantic Causeway* 12 Jul; returned to UK 27 Jul 1982. Currently in use as an instructional airframe at the RN AESS, HMS *Sultan*, Gosport.

XS516

Transferred from 845 Sqn to 'B' Flt 847 Sqn 11 May 1982 coded 'XD'; embarked on *Atlantic Causeway* 13 May; flown to Port San Carlos FOB 1 Jun; embarked on *Engadine* 5 Jul; returned to UK 30 Jul 1982. Currently in use for fire and rescue practice at the RN Fire School, Predannack.

XS518

Transferred from 772 Sqn to 'B' Flt 847 Sqn 6 May 1982 coded 'XP'; embarked on *Atlantic Causeway* 13 May; flown to Port San Carlos FOB 1 Jun; embarked on *Atlantic Causeway* 12 Jul; returned to UK 27 Jul 1982. Converted to Wessex HU5C

and crashed in sea off Cyprus 4 Nov 1986 while with 84 Sqn.

XS522

Transferred from 772 Sqn to 'D' Flt 848 Sqn 4 Jun 1982 uncoded; embarked on *Astronomer* 7 Jun; arrived at Port William 27 Jun; embarked on *Atlantic Causeway* 12 Jul; returned to UK 27 Jul 1982. Currently in use for fire and rescue practice at the RN Fire School, Predannack.

XS523

Transferred from 707 Sqn to 'A' Flt 847 Sqn 6 May 1982 coded 'XJ'; embarked on *Enga-dine* 9 May; flown to Port San Carlos FOB 9 Jun; transferred to 845 Sqn 27 Sep; embarked on *Astronomer* 6 Nov; returned to UK 3 Dec 1982. Used for BDR training at RN Lee-on-Solent and scrapped 1995.

XT449

Embarked on *Intrepid* with 'E' Flt 845 Sqn 26 Apr 1982 coded 'C'; transferred to *Tidepool* 5 May; detached to *Antrim* 19-24 May; flown to Ajax Bay FOB 25 May; embarked on *Atlantic Causeway* 12 Jul; returned to UK 27 Jul 1982. Used for fire and rescue practice at the RN Fire School, Predannack.

XT450

In service with 845 Sqn coded 'V' when war broke out; flown to Ascension in Heavylift Belfast G-BEPS 7 May 1982; transferred to 'C' Flt 845 Sqn 13 May; embarked on *Tidespring* 14 May; transferred to *Fort Grange* 9 Jun; flown to Port San Carlos FOB 10 Jun; embarked on *Hermes* 3 Jul; returned to UK 21 Jul 1982. Used for fire and rescue practice at the RN Fire School, Predannack.

XT451

In service with 845 Sqn when war broke out, coded 'J'; flown to Ascension in

Heavylift Belfast G-BEPE 9 Apr 1982; remained with Base Flight Ascension until embarked on *Intrepid* 7 May; flown to Port San Carlos FOB 30 May; transferred to 847 Sqn 1 Jun coded 'XN'; transferred to 845 Sqn 27 Sep; embarked on *Astronomer* 6 Nov; returned to UK 3 Dec 1982. Used as an instructional airframe at RAF Shawbury and scrapped Mar 1993.

XT456
Transferred from NASU Yeovilton to 'A' Flt 847 Sqn 6 May 1982 coded 'XZ'; embarked on *Engadine* 9 May; flown to Port San Carlos FOB 9 Jun; transferred to 845 Sqn 27 Sep; embarked on *Astronomer* 6 Nov; returned to UK 3 Dec 1982. Currently in use as a BDR airframe at RAF Aldergrove.

XT459
In service with 845 Sqn when war broke out, coded 'B'; flown to Ascension in Heavylift Belfast G-BEPS 7 May 1982; transferred to 'C' Flt 845 Sqn 13 May; embarked on *Tidespring* 14 May; transferred to *Fort Grange* 9 Jun; flown to Port San Carlos FOB 10 Jun; damaged at Stanley racecourse 24 Jun; embarked on *Atlantic Causeway* 12 Jul; returned to UK 27 Jul 1982. Used for fire and rescue practice at RN Lee-on-Solent. Sold to a private owner at Faygate and scrapped there October 1993.

XT460
In service with 845 Sqn when war broke out, coded 'K'; flown to Ascension in Heavylift Belfast G-BEPE 9 Apr 1982; remained with Base Flight Ascension until embarked on *Intrepid* 7 May; flown to Port San Carlos FOB 30 May; transferred to 847 Sqn 1 Jun; transferred to 845 Sqn 27 Sep; embarked on *Astronomer* 6 Nov; returned to UK 3 Dec 1982. Currently in use as an instructional airframe at the RN AESS, HMS *Sultan*, Gosport.

XT461
Embarked on *Intrepid* with 'E' Flt 845 Sqn 26 Apr 1982 coded 'W'; transferred to *Tidepool* 5 May; flown to Ajax Bay FOB 25 May; embarked on *Atlantic Causeway* 12 Jul; returned to UK 27 Jul 1982. Crashed in sea at Mounts Bay 16 Oct 1987 while with 771 Sqn.

XT463
Transferred from 707 Sqn to 'D' Flt 848 Sqn 19 Apr 1982 coded 'WZ'; embarkation on *Atlantic Conveyor* cancelled 24 Apr due to FOD damage; transferred after repairs to 707 Sqn 18 May coded 'ZB'; transferred to 'D' Flt 848 Sqn 5 Jun; embarked on *Astronomer* 7 Jun; arrived at Port William 27 Jun; embarked on *Atlantic Causeway* 12 Jul; returned to UK 27 Jul 1982. Currently privately owned at Hixon.

XT464
In service with 845 Sqn when war broke out, coded 'F'; flown to Ascension in Heavylift Belfast G-BFYU 6 Apr 1982; embarked on *Tidespring* with 'C' Flt 845 Sqn 11 Apr; crashed on Fortuna Glacier, South Georgia 22 Apr 1982.

XT466
Transferred from 771 Sqn to 'B' Flt 847 Sqn 5 May 1982 coded 'XV'; embarked on *Atlantic Causeway* 13 May; flown to Port San Carlos FOB 1 Jun; transferred to 845 Sqn 27 Sep; embarked on *Astronomer* 6 Nov; returned to UK 3 Dec 1982. Currently at RNAY Fleetlands.

XT467
Transferred from 771 Sqn to 'D' Flt 848 Sqn 2 Jun 1982 uncoded; embarked on *Astronomer* 7 Jun; arrived at Port William 27 Jun; embarked on *Contender Bezant* 2 Sep; returned to UK 23 Sep 1982. Used as an instructional airframe by the Army at Bramley but wreck recently moved to RAF Odiham for preservation project.

XT468
In service with 'B' Flt 845 Sqn when war broke out, coded 'D'; flown to Ascension in Heavylift Belfast G-BEPE 5 Apr 1982; embarked on *Fort Austin* 7 Apr; transferred to *Hermes* 17 May; transferred to *Atlantic Conveyor* 20 May; recovered to *Hermes* when *Atlantic Conveyor* was hit by an Exocet missile 25 May; seconded to 'D' Flt 848 Sqn on *Hermes* 28 May; transferred to *Atlantic Causeway* 3 Jun; returned to UK 27 Jul 1982. Currently in use for fire and rescue practice at the RN Fire School, Predannack.

XT469
Transferred from 772 Sqn to 'B' Flt 847 Sqn 6 May 1982 coded 'XN'; embarked on *Atlantic Causeway* 13 May; flown to Port San Carlos FOB 1 Jun; embarked on *Atlantic Causeway* 12 Jul; returned to UK 27 Jul 1982. Currently in use as an instructional airframe at 16 MU, RAF Stafford.

XT471
Transferred from 771 Sqn to 'B' Flt 847 Sqn 5 May 1982 coded 'XW'; embarked on *Atlantic Causeway* 13 May; transferred to *Hermes* and seconded to 'D' Flt 848 Sqn 3 Jun; returned to UK 21 Jul 1982. Used for fire and rescue practice at Dishforth.

XT472
In service with 845 Sqn when war broke out; transferred to 'B' Flt 847 Sqn 11 May 1982 coded 'XC'; embarked on *Atlantic Causeway* 13 May; flown to Port San Carlos FOB 1 Jun; embarked on *Atlantic Causeway* 12 Jul; returned to UK 27 July 1982. Now preserved at the International Helicopter Museum, Weston-super-Mare.

XT473
In service with 845 Sqn when war broke out, coded 'A'; flown to Ascension in Heavylift Belfast G-BFYU 6 Apr 1982; embarked on *Tidespring* with 'C' Flt 845 Sqn 11 Apr; crashed on Fortuna Glacier, South Georgia 22 Apr 1982.

XT475
Transferred from NASU Yeovilton to 'B' Flt 847 Sqn 11 May 1982 coded 'XG'; embarked on *Atlantic Causeway* 13 May; flown to Port San Carlos FOB 1 Jun; transferred to 845 Sqn 27 Sep; embarked on *Astronomer* 6 Nov; returned to UK 3 Dec 1982. Used for fire and rescue practice at the RAF Fire School, RAF Manston.

XT476
Transferred from 707 Sqn to 'D' Flt 848 Sqn 19 Apr 1982 coded 'WS'; embarked on *Atlantic Conveyor* 25 Apr; lost when *Atlantic Conveyor* was hit by an Exocet missile 90 miles northeast of Port Stanley 25 May 1982.

XT480
Transferred from 772 Sqn to 'B' Flt 847 Sqn 6 May 1982 coded 'XQ'; embarked on *Atlantic Causeway* 13 May; flown to Port San Carlos FOB 1 Jun; embarked on *Atlantic Causeway* 12 Jul; returned to UK 27 Jul 1982. Preserved at RNAY Fleetlands.

XT481
In service with 845 Sqn when war broke out, coded 'E'; transferred to 707 Sqn 19 May 1982; transferred to 'D' Flt 848 Sqn 2 Jun coded 'ZE'; embarked on *Astronomer* 7 Jun; arrived at Port William 27 Jun; transferred to 847 Sqn 1 Jul coded 'XF'; transferred to 845 Sqn 27 Sep; embarked on *Astronomer* 6 Nov; returned to UK 3 Dec 1982. Used for fire and rescue practice at the RN Fire School, Predannack.

XT482
Transferred from 707 Sqn to 848 Sqn 27 Apr 1982; transferred to 'A' Flt 847 Sqn 6 May coded 'XL'; embarked on *Engadine* 9 May; flown to Port San Carlos FOB 9 Jun; transferred to 845 Sqn 27 Sep; embarked on *Astronomer* 6 Nov; returned to UK 3 Dec 1982. Now at FAA Museum, RNAS Yeovilton.

XT483
Transferred from 707 Sqn to 'D' Flt 848 Sqn 19 Apr 1982 coded 'WU'; embarked on *Atlantic Conveyor* 25 Apr; lost when *Atlantic Conveyor* was hit by an Exocet missile 90 miles northeast of Port Stanley 25 May 1982.

XT484
In service with 'A' Flt 845 Sqn when war broke out, coded 'H'; embarked on *Resource* 3 Apr 1982; flown to Old House Creek FOB 24 May; embarked on *Resource* 24 Jun; returned to UK 19 Jul 1982. Currently in use as an instructional airframe at the RN AESS, HMS *Sultan*, Gosport.

Wessex HU5 XT480 of 847 Squadron was one of several helicopters that took part in the dramatic rescue of soldiers and crew from the Sir Galahad *and* Sir Tristram *on 8th June.* MoD

XT486

Transferred from 772 Sqn to 'B' Flt 847 Sqn 6 May 1982 coded 'XR'; embarked on *Atlantic Causeway* 13 May; transferred to 'D' Flt 848 Sqn on *Tidepool* 10 Jun; detached to *Glamorgan* 14 Jun; damaged on the deck of *Glamorgan* during a storm 15 Jun; airlifted to San Carlos FOB 19 Jun; embarked on *Atlantic Causeway* 12 Jul; returned to UK 27 Jul 1982. To Altcar Ranges as a target 1996.

XT755

Transferred from 771 Sqn to 'B' Flt 847 Sqn 6 May 1982 coded 'XX'; embarked on *Atlantic Causeway* 13 May; flown to Port San Carlos FOB 1 Jun; embarked on *Engadine* 5 Jul; returned to UK 30 Jul 1982. Sold to a private owner at Bruntingthorpe and scrapped there Jan 1996.

XT756

Transferred from 707 Sqn to 'A' Flt 848 Sqn 19 Apr 1982 coded 'WM'; embarked on *Regent* 19 Apr; returned to UK 12 Sep 1982. Scrapped at Lee-on-Solent 1995.

XT757

Transferred from 707 Sqn to 'B' Flt 847 Sqn 7 May 1982 coded 'XH'; embarked on *Atlantic Causeway* 13 May; flown to Port San Carlos FOB 1 Jun; embarked on *Atlantic Causeway* 12 Jul; returned to UK 27 Jul 1982. Used for fire and rescue practice at the RN Fire School, Predannack.

XT759

Transferred from 771 Sqn to 'B' Flt 847 Sqn 5 May 1982 coded 'XY'; embarked on *Atlantic Causeway* 13 May; flown to Port San Carlos FOB 1 Jun; transferred to 845 Sqn 27 Sep; embarked on *Astronomer* 6 Nov; returned to UK 3 Dec 1982. Stored at Wroughton and RNAY Fleetlands until scrapped.

XT761

Transferred from 771 Sqn to 847 Sqn 6 May 1982 uncoded; transferred to 'D' Flt 845 Sqn 7 May; flown to Ascension in Heavylift Belfast G-BEPS 12 May 1982 and used by the Base Flight; flown to the UK in Heavylift Belfast G-BEPE 19 Dec 1983. Currently in use as an instructional airframe at the RN AESS, HMS *Sultan*, Gosport.

XT764

Transferred from 707 Sqn to 'A' Flt 847 Sqn 6 May 1982 coded 'XM'; embarked on *Engadine* 9 May; transferred to 'D' Flt 845 Sqn on Ascension 25 May 1982 for use by Base Flight, later coded 'YG'; embarked on *Sir Percivale* 18 May 1985; returned to UK

11 Jun 1985. Currently in use as an instructional airframe at the RN AESS, HMS *Sultan*, Gosport.

XT765

In service with 'B' Flt 845 Sqn when war broke out, coded 'S'; flown to Ascension in Heavylift Belfast G-BEPE 5 Apr 1982; embarked on *Fort Austin* 8 Apr; transferred to *Invincible* 9 May; transferred to *Atlantic Conveyor* 19 May; transferred to *Stromness* 21 May; flown to Ajax Bay FOB 22 May; embarked on *Fearless* 27 May; flown to Port San Carlos FOB 30 May; embarked on *Hermes* 3 Jul; returned to UK 21 Jul 1982. Currently in use as an instructional airframe at the RN AESS, HMS *Sultan*, Gosport.

XT766

Transferred from 772 Sqn to 'B' Flt 847 Sqn 5 May 1982 coded 'XS'; embarked on *Atlantic Causeway* 13 May; flown to Port San Carlos FOB 1 Jun; embarked on *Atlantic Causeway* 12 Jul; returned to UK 27 Jul 1982. Currently in use as an instructional airframe at the RN AESS, HMS *Sultan*, Gosport.

XT771

Transferred from 707 Sqn to 'D' Flt 848 Sqn 19 Apr 1982 coded 'WR'; transferred to 'B' Flt 848 Sqn 29 Apr; embarked on *Olna* 10 May; returned to UK 16 Sep 1982. Currently in use as an instructional airframe at the RN AESS, HMS *Sultan*, Gosport.

XT773

Transferred from 772 Sqn to 'B' Flt 847 Sqn 5 May 1982 coded 'XT'; embarked on *Atlantic Causeway* 13 May; flown to Port San Carlos FOB 1 Jun; embarked on *Contender Bezant* 2 Sep; returned to UK 23 Sep 1982. Currently in use as a BDR instructional airframe at RAF St Athan.

Army Air Corps and Royal Marines Aircraft

Westland Gazelle AH1

XW893

Allocated to 3 CBAS 25 May 1982 uncoded; flown to Ascension in Hercules C1 2 Jun; embarked on *Contender Bezant* 3 Jun; arrived at Port Stanley 18 Jun, transferred to 656 Sqn 23 Jun; transferred to 657 Sqn 2 Aug; transferred to Garrison Army Air Sqn FI 2 Dec 1982; embarked on *Sand Shore* 10 Apr 1984 and returned to UK 5 May 1984. Currently stored at RAF Shawbury.

XX376

In service with 'M' Flt 3 CBAS when war broke out, coded 'K'; embarked on *Sir Percivale* 5 Apr 1982; flown to Ajax Bay FOB 21 May; transferred to 'C' Flt 22 May; embarked on *Elk* 23 Jun and returned to UK 12 Jul 1982. Crashed at Soest, West Germany 29 Sep 1983 while with 3 CBAS.

XX377

In service with 'M' Flt 3 CBAS when war broke out, coded 'L', undergoing modifications; transferred to 656 Sqn 29 Apr 1982; embarked on *Nordic Ferry* 8 May; arrived at Clam Valley FOB 3 Jun; shot down by Sea Dart near Mount Pleasant Peak 6 Jun 1982.

XX380

In service with 'M' Flt 3 CBAS when war broke out, coded 'M'; embarked on *Sir Percivale* 5 Apr 1982; flown to Ajax Bay FOB 21 May; embarked on *Elk* 23 Jun and returned to UK 12 Jul 1982. Currently in service with 847 Sqn, RM, RNAS Yeovilton.

XX402

In service with 'A' Flt 3 CBAS when war broke out, coded 'G'; transferred to 'C' Flt and embarked on *Sir Galahad* 5 Apr 1982; shot down by small arms fire at Clam Creek 21 May 1982.

XX409

Transferred from ARWS to 656 Sqn 23 Apr 1982; embarked on *Nordic Ferry* 8 May; arrived at Clam Valley FOB 3 Jun; embarked on *Tor Caledonia* 1 Aug and returned to UK 20 Aug 1982. Currently in service with 669 Sqn/4 Regt, AAC, Wattisham.

XX411

In service with 'C' Flt 3 CBAS when war broke out, coded 'X'; embarked on *Sir Galahad* 5 Apr 1982; shot down by small arms fire near Port San Carlos 21 May; wreck recovered and returned to UK on board *Sapele* 5 Nov 1982; allocated to Middle Wallop as a BDR training airframe. Parts of this helicopter are currently preserved at the FAA Museum, RNAS Yeovilton.

XX412

In service with 'C' Flt 3 CBAS when war broke out, coded 'Y'; embarked on *Sir Galahad* 5 Apr 1982; damaged near Port San Carlos 21 May; flown to Ajax Bay FOB 21 May; embarked on *Elk* 23 Jun and returned to UK 12 Jul 1982. Currently in service with 847 Sqn, RM, RNAS Yeovilton.

XX413

In service with 'M' Flt 3 CBAS when war broke out, coded 'Z'; embarked on *Sir Percivale* 5 Apr 1982; flown to Ajax Bay FOB 21 May, embarked on *Elk* 23 Jun and returned to UK 12 Jul 1982. Currently stored at RAF Shawbury.

XX444

Transferred from ARWS to 3 CBAS May 1982; flown to Ascension in Hercules C1 27 May; embarked on *Contender Bezant* 28 May; delivered to 'A' Flt 3 CBAS at Port Stanley 18 Jun; transferred to 656 Sqn 23 Jun; embarked on *Tor Caledonia* 1 Aug and returned to UK 20 Aug 1982. Currently in service with 25 Flt, AAC, Belize.

XZ290

Transferred from ARWS to 656 Sqn 27 Apr 1982; embarked on *Nordic Ferry* 8 May; arrived at Clam Valley FOB 3 Jun; transferred to 657 Sqn 2 Aug; transferred to Garrison Army Air Sqn FI 2 Dec 1982; embarked on *Fin Siff* Jul 1984 and returned to UK 26 Jul 1984. Currently in service with 665 Sqn/5 Regt, AAC, RAF Aldergrove.

XZ314

Transferred from ARWS to 656 Sqn 22 Apr 1982; embarked on *Nordic Ferry* 8 May; arrived at Clam Valley FOB 3 Jun; embarked on *Tor Caledonia* 1 Aug and returned to UK 21 Aug 1982. Currently in service with 8 Flt, AAC, Middle Wallop.

XZ321

Transferred from ARWS to 656 Sqn 21 Apr 1982; embarked on *Nordic Ferry* 8 May; arrived at Clam Valley FOB 3 Jun; transferred to 657 Sqn 2 Aug; transferred to Garrison Army Air Sqn FI 2 Dec 1982; embarked on *Sand Shore* 24 Dec 1983 and returned to UK 24 Jan 1984. Currently in service with 665 Sqn/5 Regt, AAC, RAF Aldergrove.

XZ326

Transferred from ARWS to 'A' Flt 3 CBAS 3 Apr 1982 coded 'W'; embarked on *Sir Geraint* 5 Apr; transferred to *Sir Tristram* 20 May; flown to San Carlos FOB 21 May; damaged by downdraught from Chinook at Port Stanley 17 Jun; embarked on *Elk* 23 Jun and returned to UK 12 Jul 1982. Currently in service with 664 Sqn/9 Regt, AAC, Dishforth.

ZA728

In service with HQ Flt 3 CBAS when war broke out, coded 'A'; transferred to 656 Sqn 19 Apr 1982; embarked on *Nordic Ferry* 8 May; arrived at Clam Valley FOB 3 Jun; damaged by bomb splinters near Estancia House 13 Jun; embarked on *Tor Caledonia* 29 Jul and returned to UK 20 Aug 1982. Currently in service with 847 Sqn, RM, RNAS Yeovilton.

ZA730

In service with 'A' Flt 3 CBAS when war broke out, coded 'F'; embarked on *Sir Geraint* 5 Apr 1982; transferred to *Sir Tristram* 20 May; flown to San Carlos FOB 21 May; transferred to 656 Sqn 23 Jun; transferred to 657 Sqn 2 Aug; transferred to Garrison Army Air Sqn FI 2 Dec 1982; returned to UK 16 Dec 1983. Currently stored at RAF Shawbury.

ZA776

In service with 'A' Flt 3 CBAS when war broke out, coded 'H'; embarked on *Sir Geraint* 5 Apr 1982; transferred to *Sir Tristram* 20 May; flown to San Carlos FOB 21 May; embarked on *Elk* 23 Jun and returned to UK 12 Jul 1982. Currently in service with 847 Sqn, RM, RNAS Yeovilton.

Westland Scout AH1

XP902

In service with 'B' Flt 3 CBAS when war broke out, coded 'T'; embarked on *Fearless* 6 Apr 1982; transferred to *Sir Tristram* 28 Apr; flown to Ajax Bay FOB 21 May; transferred to *Stromness* 20 May; embarked on *Elk* 23 Jun and returned to UK 12 Jul 1982. Currently preserved at South Yorkshire Aviation Museum, Firbeck.

XP907

In service with 'B' Flt 3 CBAS when war broke out, coded 'U'; embarked on *Astronomer* 7 Jun 1982; arrived at Port William 27 June and allocated to 656 Sqn; transferred to 657 Sqn 2 Aug; transferred to Garrison Army Air Sqn FI 2 Dec 1982; embarked on *Sir Geraint* 10 Jun 1983 and returned to UK 4 Jul 1983. Currently privately owned as G-SROE at Wattisham.

XR627

In service with 'B' Flt 3 CBAS when war broke out, coded 'Q'; embarked on *Fearless* 6 Apr 1982; transferred to *Europic Ferry* 11 May for use by 656 Sqn detachment; flown to Ajax Bay FOB 21 May; embarked on *Elk* 23 Jun and returned to UK 12 Jul 1982. Used as a BDR airframe at AAC Wattisham. Currently privately owned at Sproughton.

XR628

In service with 656 Sqn when war broke out, coded 'C'; embarked on *Europic Ferry* 22 Apr 1982; 656 Sqn Advanced Section renamed 5 Flt/3 CBAS 7 May on arrival Ascension; recoded 'DO', detached to *Elk* 11-17 May; arrived at San Carlos FOB 26 May; reverted to 656 Sqn 1 Jun; damaged in forced landing at MacPhee Pond 8 Jun; embarked on *Elk* 23 Jun and returned to UK 12 Jul 1982. Currently privately owned at Ipswich.

XR629

In service with 657 Sqn when war broke out; embarked on *Astronomer* 7 Jun 1982; arrived at Port William 27 Jun and allocated to 656 Sqn; transferred to Garrison Army Air Sqn FI 2 Dec 1982; embarked on *Sir Geraint* 10 Jun 1983 and returned to UK 4 Jul 1983. Currently privately owned at Ipswich.

XT629

In service with 'B' Flt 3 CBAS when war broke out, coded 'R'; embarked on *Fearless* 6 Apr 1982; detached to *Sir Tristram* 28-29 Apr; transferred to *Elk* 11 May; transferred to *Europic Ferry* 17 May; transferred to *Stromness* 20 May; flown to Ajax Bay FOB 21 May; shot down by Pucara near Goose Green 28 May 1982.

XT637

Allocated to 656 Sqn 16 Apr 1982; embarked on *Europic Ferry* 22 Apr; 656 Sqn Advanced Section renamed 5 Flt/3 CBAS 7 May on arrival Ascension; recoded 'DV', detached to *Elk* 11-17 May; arrived at San Carlos FOB 26 May; reverted to 656 Sqn 1 Jun; damaged by bomb splinters near Estancia House 13 Jun; transferred to 657 Sqn 2 Aug; transferred to Garrison Army Air Sqn FI 2 Dec 1982; embarked on *Sir Geraint* 10 Jun 1983 and returned to UK 4 Jul 1983. Used for fire and rescue practice at RNAS Yeovilton.

XT649

In service with 656 Sqn when war broke out; embarked on *Europic Ferry* 22 Apr 1982; 656 Sqn Advanced Section renamed 5 Flt/3 CBAS 7 May on arrival Ascension; recoded 'DN', detached to *Elk* 11-17 May; arrived at San Carlos FOB 26 May; reverted to 656 Sqn 1 Jun; embarked on *Tor Caledonia* 29 Jul and returned to UK 20 Aug 1982. Sold in 1996 to a private owner in New Zealand as ZK-HUK.

XV130

In service with 656 Sqn when war broke out; embarked on *Baltic Ferry* 8 May 1982; arrived at San Carlos FOB 1 Jun; damaged by downdraught from Chinook at Port Stanley 16 Jun; embarked on *Tor Caledonia* 29 Jul, returned to UK 20 Aug 1982. Currently privately owned as G-BWJW at Redhill.

XV139

In service with 656 Sqn when war broke out; embarked on *Baltic Ferry* 8 May 1982; arrived at San Carlos FOB 1 Jun; transferred to 657 Sqn 2 Aug; transferred to Garrison Army Air Sqn FI 2 Dec 1982; embarked on *Baltic Ferry* Mar 1983 and returned to UK 12 Apr 1983. Currently in use as an instructional airframe at Yeovil College.

XV140

In service with 657 Sqn when war broke out; transferred to 3 CBAS 4 Apr 1982 coded 'DU'; embarked on *Sir Lancelot* 5 Apr; embarked on *Elk* 23 Jun and returned to UK 12 Jul 1982. Currently registered to Kennet Aviation, Cranfield as G-KAXL.

XV141

Allocated to 657 Sqn 5 May 1982; embarked on *Astronomer* 7 Jun; arrived at Port William 27 Jun and allocated to 656 Sqn; transferred to 657 Sqn 2 Aug; transferred to Garrison Army Air Sqn FI 2 Dec 1982; embarked on *Baltic Ferry* Mar 1983 and returned to UK 12 Apr 1983. Used as an instructional airframe at the School of Electrical and Aeronautical Engineering, Arborfield.

XW282

Allocated to 656 Sqn 16 Apr 1982; embarked on *Baltic Ferry* 8 May; arrived at San Carlos FOB 1 Jun; transferred to 657 Sqn 2 Aug; transferred to Garrison Army Air Sqn FI 2 Dec 1982; embarked on *Sir Geraint* 10 Jun 1983 and returned to UK 4 Jul 1983. Sold in 1996 to a private owner in New Zealand as ZK-HUC.

The nose area of 44 Squadron Vulcan B2 XM607, with three bomb silhouettes above Argentine flags indicating the aircraft's involvement in the 'Black Buck 1, 2 and 7' raids. This aircraft now serves as a gate guardian at RAF Waddington. B Munro

XW615

In service with 657 Sqn when war broke out; transferred to 3 CBAS 4 Apr 1982 coded 'DS'; embarked on *Sir Lancelot* 5 Apr; flown to Ajax Bay FOB late May; embarked on *Elk* 23 Jun; returned to UK 12 Jul 1982. Used as an instructional airframe for BDR training at 4 Regt, Detmold, Germany

XW616

In service with 3 CBAS when war broke out, coded 'DP'; embarked on *Sir Lancelot* 5 Apr 1982; flown to Ajax Bay FOB late May; embarked on *Elk* 23 Jun and returned to UK 12 Jul 1982. Currently in use as an instructional airframe at AAC Dishforth.

Royal Air Force Aircraft

Avro Vulcan B2

XM597

101 Sqn aircraft, flown to Ascension 27 May 1982; 'Black Buck 4' raid (aborted) 28/29 May; 'Black Buck 5' raid 30/31 May; 'Black Buck 6' 2/3 Jun; diverted to Rio de Janeiro 3 Jun; returned to Ascension 10 Jun; returned to RAF Waddington 13 Jun 1982. Currently preserved at the Royal Scottish Museum of Flight, East Fortune.

XM598

50 Sqn aircraft, flown to Ascension 29 Apr 1982; 'Black Buck 1' raid (aborted) 30 Apr/1 May; returned to RAF Waddington 7 May; flown to Ascension 26 May; returned to Waddington 14 Jun 1982. Allocated 8778M and currently preserved at the Cosford Aerospace Museum.

XM607

44 Sqn aircraft, flown to Ascension 29 Apr 1982; 'Black Buck 1' 30 Apr/1 May; 'Black Buck 2' 3/4 May; returned to RAF Wadding-

ton 7 May; flown to Ascension 15 May; returned to Waddington 20 May; flown to Ascension 10 Jun; 'Black Buck 7' 11/12 Jun; returned to Waddington 14 Jun 1982. Allocated 8779M and currently preserved as gate guardian at Waddington.

XM612

44 Sqn aircraft, flown to Ascension 14 May 1982; not used on operational missions; returned to RAF Waddington 23 May 1982. Currently preserved at the City of Norwich Aviation Museum.

Boeing-Vertol Chinook HC1

ZA705

18 Sqn coded 'BU'; embarked on *Contender Bezant* 21 May 1982; disembarked to Port San Carlos 14 Jun; returned to UK 23 Sep 1982. Currently in service with QinetiQ, Boscombe Down.

ZA706

18 Sqn coded 'BT'; embarked on *Atlantic Conveyor* 25 Apr 1982; lost when *Atlantic Conveyor* was hit by an Exocet missile 90 miles northeast of Port Stanley 25 May 1982.

ZA707

18 Sqn coded 'BP; embarked on *Atlantic Conveyor* 25 Apr 1982; flown off Ascension 5 May to perform HDS duties; embarked on *Contender Bezant* 3 Jun; disembarked to Port San Carlos 14-16 Jun via *Europic Ferry*; returned to UK 3 Dec 1982. Currently in store at RNAY, Fleetlands.

ZA713

18 Sqn coded 'BJ'; embarked on *Contender Bezant* 21 May 1982; disembarked to Port San Carlos 18 Jun 1982; returned to UK 27 Apr 1983. Currently in service with 7 Sqn, RAF Odiham.

ZA714

18 Sqn coded 'BH'; embarked on *Astronomer* 8 Jun 1982; flown off Ascension 16 Jun to perform HDS duties; returned to UK 23 Sep 1982. Currently in service with 27 Sqn, RAF Odiham.

ZA715

18 Sqn coded 'BL'; embarked on *Contender Bezant* 21 May 1982; disembarked to Port San Carlos 18 Jun 1982; returned to UK 27 Apr 1983. Crashed on Mount Young, FI 13 May 1986 while with 78 Sqn.

ZA716

18 Sqn coded 'BQ'; embarked on *Atlantic Conveyor* 25 Apr 1982; lost when *Atlantic Conveyor* was hit by an Exocet 90 miles northeast of Port Stanley 25 May 1982.

ZA717

18 Sqn coded 'BK'; embarked on *Astronomer* 8 Jun 1982; disembarked to Port San Carlos 29 Jun 1982; returned to UK 27 Apr 1983. Crashed at Mount Pleasant, East Falkland 25 Jul 1989. Now an instructional airframe at RAF College, Cranwell.

ZA718

18 Sqn coded 'BN'; embarked on *Atlantic Conveyor* 25 Apr 1982; flown off to *Hermes* 25 May; disembarked to San Carlos FOB 26 May; returned to UK 6 Sep 1982. Now in service with 78 Sqn, RAF Mount Pleasant.

ZA719

18 Sqn coded 'BM'; embarked on *Atlantic Conveyor* 25 Apr 1982; lost when *Atlantic Conveyor* was hit by an Exocet missile 90 miles northeast of Port Stanley 25 May 1982.

ZA720

18 Sqn coded 'BG'; embarked on *Astronomer* 8 Jun 1982; disembarked to Port San Carlos 27 Jun 1982; returned to UK 27 Apr 1983. Currently in service with 7 Sqn, RAF Odiham.

Harrier GR3 XZ129 of 1 Squadron operated from RAF Stanley for just over six months until its return to the UK in early 1983. B Munro

British Aerospace Harrier GR3

XV762

1 Sqn coded '37'; flown to Ascension 30 May 1982; embarked on *Contender Bezant* 3 Jun; remained on board until disembarked to RAF Stanley 6 Jul 1982; returned to UK early 1983. Crashed at Lafonia, East Falkland 19 Nov 1983 while with 1453 Flt.

XV778

1 Sqn coded '16'; flown to Ascension 29 May 1982; flown to *Hermes* 1 Jun; slightly damaged by small arms fire near Port Stanley 10 Jun; disembarked to RAF Stanley 4 Jul 1982; returned to UK early 1983. Allocated 9001M and used for fire and rescue practice at RAF Valley.

XV787

1 Sqn coded '02'; diverted to Madeira on ferry flight to Ascension 4 May 1982; returned to UK 10 May 1982 for repairs and took no further part in the conflict. Crashed at Port William Sound, East Falkland 22 Mar 1983 while with the Falkland Harrier Detachment.

XV789

1 Sqn coded '32'; flown to Ascension 3 May 1982; embarked on *Atlantic Conveyor* 6 May; flown off to *Hermes* 18 May; damaged during rocket attack near Port Stanley 31 May; disembarked to RAF Stanley 4 Jul 1982; returned to UK early 1983. Allocated 9866M and used as ground instructional airframe at RAF Brüggen, Germany.

XW767

1 Sqn coded '06'; flown to Ascension 29 May 1982; embarked on *Contender Bezant* 3 Jun; remained on board until disembarked to RAF Stanley 6 Jul; crashed into sea off Cape Pembroke, Falkland Islands 6 Nov 1982 while with the Falkland Harrier Detachment.

XW919

1 Sqn coded '03'; flown to Ascension 5 May 1982, remaining there for air defence duties; flown to *Hermes* 8 Jun; badly dam-

aged near Sapper Hill by small arms fire 12 Jun; embarked on *Contender Bezant* 13 Jul and returned to UK 1 Aug 1982. Currently preserved at the Royal Military College of Science, Shrivenham.

XW924

1 Sqn coded '35'; flown to Ascension 30 May 1982; embarked on *Contender Bezant* 3 Jun; remained on board until disembarked to RAF Stanley 6 Jul 1982 and returned to UK 11 Jan 1983. Allocated 9073M and currently preserved at RAF Cottesmore.

XZ129

1 Sqn coded '29'; flown to Ascension 5 May 1982, remaining there for air defence duties; embarked on *Contender Bezant* 3 Jun; remained on board until disembarked to RAF Stanley 6 Jul 1982; returned to UK 26 Jan 1983. Allocated A2602 and currently in use as an instructional airframe at the RN ETS, RNAS Yeovilton.

XZ132

1 Sqn coded '36'; flown to Ascension 6 May 1982; suffered from incurable fuel leaks and returned to UK for repairs, took no further part in the conflict. Allocated 9168M and currently in use as an instructional airframe at RAF College, RAF Cranwell.

XZ133

1 Sqn coded '10'; flown to Ascension 29 May 1982; flown to *Hermes* 1 Jun; disembarked to RAF Stanley 4 Jul; badly damaged at RAF Stanley during a storm 28 Jul; returned to UK for repairs 16 Sep 1982. Currently preserved at Imperial War Museum, Duxford.

XZ963

1 Sqn coded '14'; flown to Ascension 4 May 1982; embarked on *Atlantic Conveyor* 6 May; flown to *Hermes* 19 May; damaged by small arms fire near Port Stanley and abandoned off Falklands 30 May 1982.

XZ972

1 Sqn coded '33'; flown to Ascension 3 May 1982; embarked on *Atlantic Conveyor* 6 May; flown to *Hermes* 18 May; shot down near Port Howard by Blowpipe 21 May 1982.

XZ988

1 Sqn coded '34'; flown to Ascension 5 May 1982; embarked on *Atlantic Conveyor* 6 May; flown to *Hermes* 18 May; shot down near Goose Green by AAA 27 May 1982.

XZ989

1 Sqn coded '07'; flown to Ascension 3 May 1982; embarked on *Atlantic Conveyor* 6 May; flown to *Hermes* 20 May; crashed on landing at Port San Carlos FOB 8 Jun; flown to Ascension in a Hercules C1P 20 Nov; returned to UK for repair 23 Nov 1982. Allocated 8849M and used as a ground instructional airframe at RAF Gütersloh, Germany.

Without the Victor K2 tanker force, the 'Black Buck' raids by the Vulcans would have been impossible. Like the Vulcans, the Victors are now long gone, XL161 having been scrapped at RAF Lyneham in 1995. B Munro

XZ992
1 Sqn coded '05'; flown to Ascension 29 May 1982; flown to *Hermes* 8 Jun; disembarked to RAF Stanley 4 Jul; returned to UK 16 Nov 1982. Crashed near Port Stanley, East Falkland 29 Nov 1984 while with 1453 Flt.

XZ997
1 Sqn coded '31'; flown to Ascension 4 May 1982; embarked on *Atlantic Conveyor* 6 May; flown to *Hermes* 18 May; disembarked to RAF Stanley 4 Jul 1982; returned to UK early 1983. Allocated 9122M and currently preserved at the RAF Museum, Hendon.

British Aerospace Nimrod MR1

XV244
42 Sqn aircraft, flown to Ascension 6 Apr 1982; returned to RAF St Mawgan 18 Apr 1982. Later converted to Nimrod MR2 and currently in service with the Kinloss Wing.

XV258
42 Sqn aircraft, flown to Ascension 6 Apr 1982; returned to RAF St Mawgan 15 Apr 1982. Later converted to Nimrod MR2, then to MRA4 (reserialled ZJ515).

British Aerospace Nimrod MR2

XV227 (MR2P)
Kinloss Wing aircraft, flown to Ascension 7 May 1982; returned to RAF Kinloss June or July 1982. Currently in service with the Kinloss Wing.

XV230 (MR2/2P)
Kinloss Wing aircraft, flown to Ascension 13 Apr 1982; returned to RAF Kinloss for MR2P conversion later in April; flown to Ascension May; returned to Kinloss July 1982. Currently in service with the Kinloss Wing.

XV232 (MR2P)
Kinloss Wing aircraft, flown to Ascension 9 May 1982; returned to Kinloss late-May 1982. Currently in service with the Kinloss Wing.

XV255 (MR2)
Kinloss Wing aircraft, flown to Ascension 17 Apr 1982; returned to Kinloss June or July 1982. Currently in service with the Kinloss Wing.

Note: At least four other Kinloss Wing Nimrod MR2s are known to have been deployed to Ascension: XV228, XV243, XV247 and XV260; XV249 was deployed to Freetown and Dakar.

British Aerospace Nimrod R1

XW664
51 Sqn aircraft, thought to have been deployed to Ascension during the conflict. Currently in service with 51 Sqn.

Handley Page Victor K2

XH669
57 Sqn aircraft, flown to Ascension 29 Apr 1982; returned to RAF Marham 28 May; flown to Ascension 12 Jun; returned to Marham July 1982. Damaged 21 Jun 1990 and allocated 9092M; burnt at RAF Waddington but nose currently preserved at the Cockpit Collection, Southend.

XH671
55 Sqn aircraft, flown to Ascension 19 Apr 1982; returned to RAF Marham 8 May; flown to Ascension 13 May; returned to Marham 27 June 1982. Scrapped at Marham Feb 1994 after being damaged during cabin pressure tests 15 Mar 1993.

XH672
57 Sqn aircraft, flown to Ascension 23 Apr 1982; returned to RAF Marham 15 Jun 1982. Allocated 9242M and currently preserved at the Cosford Aerospace Museum.

XH673
57 Sqn aircraft, flown to Banjul 5 May 1982; returned to Marham 6 May; flown to Ascension 12 May; returned to RAF Marham Jul 1982. Allocated 8911M and currently preserved at Marham.

XL160
57 Sqn aircraft, flown to Banjul 1 May 1982; returned to RAF Marham 2 May; flown to Ascension 3 May; returned to Marham 7 May; flown to Ascension 14 May; returned to Marham Jul 1982. Allocated 8910M for BDR training at Marham; nose currently preserved by the Victor Association, Walpole.

XL161
55 Sqn aircraft, flown to Ascension 7 Jun 1982; returned to RAF Marham Jul 1982. Allocated 9214M and scrapped at RAF Lyneham Aug 1995.

XL162
55 Sqn aircraft, flown to Ascension 25 Apr 1982; returned to RAF Marham Jul 1982. Allocated 9114M and used for fire and rescue practice at RAF Fire School, Manston.

XL163
57 Sqn aircraft, flown to Ascension 18 Apr 1982; flown to Banjul 7 May; flown to RAF Marham 8 May; flown to Ascension 18 May; returned to Marham 23 Jun 1982. Allocated 8916M at RAF St Athan; sold to private owner at Stock and scrapped there 1996.

XL164
57 Sqn aircraft, flown to Ascension 19 Apr 1982; returned to RAF Marham 8 Jun 1982. Allocated 9215M at RAF Brize Norton; nose currently preserved at the Gatwick Aviation Museum, Charlwood.

XL188
55 Sqn aircraft, flown to Ascension 19 Apr 1982; returned to RAF Marham 27 Jun 1982. Allocated 9100M and used for BDR and fire and rescue training at RAF Kinloss.

XL189
57 Sqn aircraft, flown to Ascension 18 Apr 1982; returned to RAF Marham 18 May; flown to Ascension 2 Jun; returned to RAF Marham Jul 1982. Allocated 8912M and preserved as gate guardian at RAF Waddington but scrapped in Sep 1989.

XL191
55 Sqn aircraft, flown to Banjul 30 Apr 1982; returned to RAF Marham 7 May; flown to Ascension 14 May; returned to Marham Jul 1982. Crashed at Hamilton, Ontario, Canada 19 Jun 1986 while with 55 Sqn.

XL192
57 Sqn aircraft, flown to Ascension 18 Apr 1982; returned to RAF Marham 13 May; flown to Dakar 24 May; returned to Marham 25 May; flown to Ascension 26 May; returned to Marham Jul 1982. Allocated 9024M, sold to private owner at Stock and scrapped there 1996.

XL231
57 Sqn aircraft, flown to Ascension 14 Jun 1982; returned to RAF Marham Jul 1982. Currently preserved at the Yorkshire Air Museum, Elvington.

XL232
55 Sqn aircraft, flown to Ascension 19 Apr 1982; returned to RAF Marham 4 May; flown to Ascension 16 May; returned to Marham 31 May. Destroyed on the ground at Marham due to engine fire 15 Oct 1982 while with 55 Sqn.

XL233
55 Sqn aircraft, flown to Ascension 25 Apr 1982; returned to RAF Marham 7 May; flown to Ascension 17 May; returned to Marham Jul 1982. Scrapped at RAF St Athan 1988.

XL511
55 Sqn aircraft, flown to Ascension 18 Apr 1982; returned to RAF Marham Jul 1982. Used for fire and rescue practice at RAF Fire School, RAF Manston 1986.

XL512
57 Sqn aircraft, flown to Ascension 30 Apr 1982; returned to RAF Marham Jul 1982. Scrapped at Marham 1994.

XM715
55 Sqn aircraft, flown to Ascension 18 Apr 1982; returned to RAF Marham 26 Apr; flown to Banjul 4 May; returned to Marham 6 May; flown to Ascension 13 May; returned to Marham 13 Jun 1982. Currently preserved at British Aviation Heritage, Bruntingthorpe.

XM717
55 Sqn aircraft, flown to Ascension 30 Apr 1982; returned to RAF Marham 3 Jun 1982. Nose currently preserved at the RAF Museum, Hendon.

Note: The Victor K2s listed were all deployed to Ascension but the following aircraft were also used to support aircraft flying to Ascension: XH657, XL158 and XL190.

Lockheed Hercules C1/C1K/C1P
The flights and deployments of Hercules aircraft are too numerous to include but flight crews from all four Lyneham Transport Wing squadrons (24, 30, 47 and 70 Squadrons) were involved. The following aircraft were modified as either C1Ks or C1Ps:

XV179
2nd C1P. Conversion work commenced 23 Mar 1982; to RAF Lyneham 13 May 1982. Currently in service with the LTW.

XV185
16th C1P. Conversion work commenced 30 Sep 1982; to RAF Lyneham 25 Oct 1982. Sold to Lockheed Sep 2001.

XV187
9th C1P. Conversion work commenced 6 Jul 1982; to RAF Lyneham 20 Jul 1982. Sold to Lockheed Jan 2001.

XV191
15th C1P. Conversion work commenced 9 Aug 1982; to RAF Lyneham 25 Oct 1982. Sold to Lockheed Sep 2001.

XV192
4th C1K. Conversion work commenced 21 Jun 1982; to RAF Lyneham 26 Jul 1982. Currently in service with the LTW.

XV195
12th C1P. Conversion work commenced 9 Aug 1982; to RAF Lyneham 7 Sep 1982. Sold to Lockheed Jan 2001.

XV196
4th C1P. Conversion work commenced 17 May 1982; to RAF Lyneham 31 May 1982. Currently in service with the LTW.

XV200
1st C1P. Conversion work commenced 16 Apr 1982; to A&AEE Boscombe Down 29 Apr; to RAF Lyneham 5 May 1982. Currently in service with the LTW.

XV201
2nd C1K. Conversion work commenced 28 Apr 1982; to RAF Lyneham 15 Jul 1982. Struck off charge Mar 1996.

XV204
3rd C1K. Conversion work commenced 12 Jun 1982; to RAF Lyneham 21 Jul 1982. To Marshalls of Cambridge for spares recovery Mar 1996.

XV205
13th C1P. Conversion work commenced 8 Sep 1982; to RAF Lyneham 30 Sep 1982. Currently in service with the LTW.

XV206
5th C1P. Conversion work commenced 21 May 1982; to RAF Lyneham 3 Jun 1982. Currently in service with the LTW.

XV210
7th C1P. Conversion work commenced 13 Jun 1982; to RAF Lyneham 29 Jun 1982. Sold to Lockheed Dec 2000.

XV211
8th C1P. Conversion work commenced 21 Jun 1982; to RAF Lyneham 6 Jul 1982. Currently in service with the LTW.

XV218
3rd C1P. Conversion work commenced 14 May 1982; to RAF Lyneham 25 May 1982. Sold to Lockheed Dec 2000.

XV291
6th C1P. Conversion work commenced 25 May 1982; to RAF Lyneham 9 Jun 1982. Currently in service with the LTW.

XV292
14th C1P. Conversion work commenced 3 Sep 1982; to RAF Lyneham 11 Oct 1982. Currently in service with the LTW.

XV296
1st C1K. Conversion work commenced 1 May 1982; to A&AEE Boscombe Down 11 Jun; to RAF Lyneham 5 Jul 1982. To Marshalls of Cambridge for spares recovery Aug 1996.

XV298
10th C1P. Conversion work commenced 6 Jul 1982; to RAF Lyneham 23 Jul 1982. Crashed at Kukes, Albania 11 Jun 1999.

XV300
11th C1P. Conversion work commenced 9 Aug 1982; to RAF Lyneham 3 Sep 1982. Sold to Lockheed Jan 2001.

McDonnell Douglas Phantom FGR2

XV466
29 Sqn coded 'E'; flown to Ascension 26 May 1982; returned to RAF Coningsby 19 Jul 1982. Used by 1435 Flt and scrapped at RAF Mount Pleasant Aug 1992.

XV468
29 Sqn coded 'W'; flown to Ascension 24 May 1982; returned to RAF Coningsby 20 Jul 1982. Allocated 9159M and currently preserved at RAF Woodvale.

XV484
29 Sqn coded 'C'; flown to Ascension 24 May 1982; returned to RAF Coningsby 18 Jul 1982. Crashed at Mount Usborne, East Falkland 17 Oct 1983 while with 23 Sqn.

Vickers VC10 C1
All of 10 Sqn's VC10 C1s were used in the strategic airlift role during Operation 'Corporate' and several were used on aeromedical flights. The aircraft involved were: XR806 to XR808, XR810, XV101 to XV109.

Westland Sea King HAR3

XZ593
202 Sqn, flown to Ascension from RAF Finningley in Heavylift Belfast G-BFYU 8 May 1982; employed on logistics duties from Ascension; embarked on *Invincible* 7 Sep; returned to RAF Brawdy 17 Sep 1982. Currently in service with 202 Sqn.

Appendix Four

Participation of Individual Argentine Aircraft in the Conflict

Comando Aviacion Naval Argentina
(Argentine Naval Aviation)

Aermacchi MB-339A
Light attack aircraft: 10 delivered between 1980 and 1981 (0761 to 0770); all 10 still in service Mar 1982. Flown by 1 Escuadrilla de Ataque of 4 Escuadra Aeronaval based at Punta Indio, Buenos Aires.

0761 (4-A-110)
Captured at Stanley airport 14 Jun 1982. Sections brought to the UK Jun 1983 and used with parts of 0767 to construct a composite aircraft for display at the FAA Museum, RNAS Yeovilton. Later transferred to Rolls-Royce, Filton for engine mounting trials. Forward fuselage on display at the Rolls-Royce Heritage Trust Museum, Filton.

0763 (4-A-112)
Captured at Stanley airport 14 Jun 1982. Broken up and moved to a weapons range in the Falklands.

0764 (4-A-113)
Crashed at Stanley airport 3 May 1982 while landing in bad weather.

0765 (4-A-114)
Shot down at Goose Green 28 May 1982 by Blowpipe SAM fired by a Royal Marine.

0766 (4-A-115)
Flown to Rio Grande 6 Jun 1982. Survived the conflict and sold to a private owner in the USA.

0767 (4-A-116)
Captured at Stanley airport 14 Jun 1982. Sections brought to the UK Jun 1983 and used with parts of 0761 to construct a composite aircraft for display at the FAA Museum, RNAS Yeovilton (see remarks for 0761).

MB-339A 0763/4-A-112 is seen at Stanley airport soon after being captured. Later the aircraft was vandalised and was only fit for use as a target on a weapons range. The ejection seats have been fired as a safety precaution. MoD

0769 (4-A-119)
Flown to Rio Grande 6 Jun 1982. Survived the conflict and sold to a private owner in the USA.

Beech Queen Air 80
Light communications aircraft: 5 delivered between 1971 and 1972 (0679, 0687 to 0690); all 5 still in service Mar 1982. Flown by Escuadrilla Aerofotografico of 1 Escuadra Aeronaval based at Punta Indio, Buenos Aires and by Escuadrilla de Propositos Generales of 6 Escuadra Aeronaval based at Trelew, Chubut.

0679 (4-F-21) Survived the conflict.
0687 (6-G-81) Survived the conflict.
0688 (6-G-82) Survived the conflict.
0689 (6-G-83) Survived the conflict.
0690 (6-G-84) Survived the conflict.

Beech Super King Air 200
Light communications and photographic survey aircraft: 8 delivered between 1975 and 1979 (0697 to 0698, 0744 to 0749); all 8 still in service Mar 1982. Flown by Escuadrilla Aerofotografico of 1 Escuadrilla Aeronaval based at Punta Indio, Buenos Aires and by 2 Escuadra Aeronaval based at Comandante Espora, Bahia Blanca.

0697 (1-G-41) Survived the conflict.
0698 (1-G-42) Survived the conflict.
0744 (4-G-43) Survived the conflict.

0745 (4-G-44) Survived the conflict.
0746 (4-G-45) Survived the conflict.

0747 (4-G-46)
Survived the conflict. Crashed 18 May 1986.

0748 (2-G-47) Survived the conflict.
0749 (2-G-48) Survived the conflict.

Beech T-34C-1 Turbo Mentor
Basic trainer and light attack aircraft: 15 delivered in 1978 (0719 to 0733); all 15 still in service Mar 1982. Flown by Escuela de Aviacion Naval (1 Escuadrilla de Ataque) based at Punta Indio, Buenos Aires.

0719 (1-A-401)
Destroyed on the ground during the SAS raid on Pebble Island 15 May 1982.

0726 (1-A-408)
Damaged on the ground during the SAS raid on Pebble Island 15 May 1982. Accidentally dropped into Elephant Bay 21 Jul 1983 while being airlifted by an RAF Chinook.

0729 (1-A-411)
Damaged on the ground during the SAS raid on Pebble Island 15 May 1982. Shipped to the UK Jul 1983 and currently preserved at the FAA Museum, RNAS Yeovilton.

0730 (1-A-412)
Damaged on the ground during the SAS raid on Pebble Island 15 May 1982. Moved to a weapons range near Rabbit Mount in East Falklands Jul 1983.

Dassault Super Etendard

Attack aircraft: 14 ordered, 5 delivered in November 1981, 9 delivered Dec 1982 (0751 to 0760, 0771 to 0774); 5 in service Mar 1982. Flown by 2 Escuadrilla de Caza y Ataque of 3 Escuadra Aeronaval based at Comandante Espora, Bahia Blanca.

0751 (3-A-201) Survived the conflict.
0752 (3-A-202) Survived the conflict.

0753 (3-A-203)
Survived the conflict. Crashed at Punta Indio 29 May 1996.

0754 (3-A-204) Survived the conflict.
0755 (3-A-205) Survived the conflict.

Fokker F-28-3000M Fellowship

Short-range transport aircraft: 3 delivered in 1979 (0740 to 0742); all 3 still in service Mar 1982. Flown by 2 Escuadrilla de Sosten Logistico Movil of 5 Escuadra Aeronaval based at Ezeiza, Buenos Aires.

0740 (5-T-10) Survived the conflict.
0741 (5-T-20) Survived the conflict.
0742 (5-T-21) Survived the conflict.

Grumman S-2E Tracker

ASW aircraft: 6 delivered in 1978 (0700 to 0705); all 6 in service Mar 1982. Flown by Escuadrilla Antisubmarina of 2 Escuadra Aeronaval based at Comandante Espora, Bahia Blanca and on board *25 de Mayo*.

0700 (2-AS-21) Survived the conflict.
0701 (2-AS-22) Survived the conflict.
0702 (2-AS-23) Survived the conflict.

0703 (2-AS-24)
Survived the conflict. Crashed at Espora 12 Nov 1996.

0704 (2-AS-25) Survived the conflict.

0705 (2-AS-26)
Survived the conflict. Crashed at Espora 26 Nov 1990.

Hawker Siddeley HS125-400B

VIP transport aircraft: 1 delivered in 1970 (0653); still in service Mar 1982. Flown by 2 Escuadrilla de Sosten Logistico Movil of 5 Escuadra Aeronaval based at Ezeiza, Buenos Aires.

0653 (5-T-30) Survived the conflict.

Lockheed Electra

Medium-range transport aircraft: 3 delivered in 1974 (0691 to 0693); all 3 still in service Mar 1982. Flown by 1 Escuadrilla de Sosten Logistico Movil of 5 Escuadra Aeronaval based at Ezeiza, Buenos Aires

0691 (5-T-1)
Survived the conflict. Later retired.

0692 (5-T-2)
Survived the conflict. Currently preserved at the Museo de la Aviacion Naval de la Armada, Comandante Espora.

0693 (5-T-3) Survived the conflict.

Lockheed SP-2H Neptune

Maritime reconnaissance and ASW aircraft: 4 delivered between 1977 and 1978 (0706 to 0708, 0718); 2 still in service Mar 1982. Flown by Escuadrilla de Exploracion of 2 Escuadra Aeronaval based at Comandante Espora, Bahia Blanca.

0707 (2-P-111)
Survived the conflict. Retired at Espora mid-1983.

0708 (2-P-112)
Survived the conflict. Retired at Espora mid-1983 and currently preserved at Museo Aeronaval de la Armada, Puerto Belgrano wearing a 'kill' marking for *Sheffield*.

McDonnell Douglas A-4Q Skyhawk

Light attack aircraft: 16 delivered between 1971 and 1972 (0654 to 0669); 10 still in service Mar 1982. Flown by 3 Escuadrilla de Caza y Ataque of 3 Escuadra Aeronaval based at Comandante Espora, Bahia Blanca and on board *25 de Mayo*.

0654 (3-A-301)
Survived the conflict. Currently preserved at Museo Aeronaval de la Armada, Puerto Belgrano.

0655 (3-A-302)
Survived the conflict. Preserved at the Museo de la Aviacion Naval de la Armada, Comandante Espora.

0657 (3-A-304)
Survived the conflict. Preserved at Edificio Libertad, Buenos Aires.

0658 (3-A-305)
Survived the conflict. Crashed at Espora 22 May 1986.

0659 (3-A-306)
Survived the conflict. Crashed at Espora 11 Nov 1982.

0660 (3-A-307)
Shot down over Falkland Sound by Sea Harrier 21 May 1982 after bombing *Ardent*.

0661 (3-A-308)
Survived the conflict. Currently preserved at Aeroclub Mar del Plata, Buenos Aires.

0662 (3-A-309)
Accidentally damaged while landing at Rio Grande 23 May 1982. Later rebuilt and preserved at Museo Aeronaval de la Armada, Puerto Belgrano but now reported as under restoration at Houston, Texas.

0665 (3-A-312)
Damaged over Falkland Sound by Sea Harrier 21 May 1982 after bombing *Ardent* and brought down by Argentine AAA at Port Stanley.

0667 (3-A-314)
Shot down over Falkland Sound by Sea Harrier 21 May 1982 after bombing *Ardent*.

Sikorsky S-61D-4 Sea King

ASW/Special Duties helicopter: 5 delivered between 1972 and 1974 (0675 to 0678, 0696); all 5 still in service Mar 1982. Flown by 2 Escuadrilla de Helicopteros, 2 Escuadra Aeronaval based at Comandante Espora, Bahia Blanca and on board *25 de Mayo*.

0675 (2-H-231) Survived the conflict.
0676 (2-H-232) Survived the conflict.
0677 (2-H-233) Survived the conflict.
0678 (2-H-234) Survived the conflict.
0696 (35)   Survived the conflict.

Sud-Aviation SE-3160 Alouette III

General-purpose helicopter: 14 delivered between 1969 to 1978 (0641 to 0643, 0648 to 0651, 0680 to 0681, 0699, 0736 to 0739); 9 still in service Mar 1982. Flown by 1 Escuadrilla de Helicopteros of 3 Escuadra Aeronaval based at Comandante Espora, Bahia Blanca.

0642 (3-H-102) Survived the conflict.

0649 (3-H-105)
Lost when *General Belgrano* was sunk 2 May 1982.

0651 (3-H-107) Survived the conflict.

0681 (3-H-109)
Survived the conflict. Currently preserved at Museo Aeronaval de la Armada, Puerto Belgrano.

0699 (3-H-110)
Survived the conflict. Crashed at Espora 21 Apr 1983.

0736 (3-H-111) Survived the conflict.

0737 (3-H-112)
Survived the conflict. Damaged beyond repair 1 Nov 1990 during Operation 'Desert Shield' in the Red Sea and currently preserved at Museo Aeronaval de la Armada, Puerto Belgrano.

0738 (3-H-114) Survived the conflict.
0739 (3-H-115) Survived the conflict.

Both sides in the conflict operated the Lynx but Argentina's two examples saw very little service. 0735/3-H-142 was destroyed when it crashed onto the Santisima Trinidad *on 2nd May 1982.* Argentine Navy

Westland Lynx HAS23
ASW helicopter: 2 delivered in 1978 (0734 to 0735); both still in service Mar 1982. Flown by 1 Escuadrilla de Helicopteros of 3 Escuadra Aeronaval based at Comandante Espora, Bahia Blanca

0734 (3-H-141) Survived the conflict. Later retired.

0735 (3-H-142)
Crashed into the *Santisima Trinidad* 2 May 1982. Wreck currently preserved at Museo Aeronaval de la Armada, Puerto Belgrano.

Prefectura Naval Argentina
(Argentine Coast Guard)

Aerospatiale SA330L Puma
Transport helicopter: 3 delivered in 1980 (PA-11 to PA-13); all 3 still in service Mar 1982. Based at Puerto Nuevo Heliport, Buenos Aires.

PA-12
Captured at Stanley 14 Jun 1982. Shipped to the UK Aug 1982 and allocated serial ZE449. Used for BDR training at RAF Odiham then refurbished and currently in service with 33 Sqn, RAF.

Short Skyvan 3M
Light transport aircraft: 5 delivered in 1971 (PA-50 to PA-54); all 5 still in service Mar 1982. Based at Jorge Newbery Airport, Buenos Aires.

PA-50
Destroyed on the ground during the SAS raid on Pebble Island 15 May 1982.

PA-54
Destroyed at Stanley racecourse by naval gunfire 12/13 Jun 1982.

Comando Aviacion Del Ejercito
(Argentine Army Aviation)

Aerospatiale SA330L Puma
Transport helicopter: 9 delivered between 1978 and 1979 (AE-500 to AE-508); 8 still in service Mar 1982. Flown by Compania de Helicopteros de Asalto 'A', CAB601 based at Campo de Mayo, Buenos Aires.

AE-500
Destroyed on the ground at Shag House Cove by Sea Harriers 23 May 1982.

AE-501
Destroyed on the ground near Mount Kent by Harrier GR3 26 May 1982.

AE-503
Crashed near Shag House Cove while being attacked by Sea Harrier 23 May 1982.

AE-504
Shot down at Grytviken, South Georgia by Royal Marine ground fire 3 Apr 1982.

AE-505
Shot down over Choiseul Sound by Sea Dart fired by *Coventry* 9 May 1982.

AE-506
Used for ambulance duties on board the *Bahia Paraiso*. Survived the conflict. Currently stored at Campo de Mayo

AE-508: Shot down near Murrell Bridge by unidentified SAM 30 May 1982

Agusta A-109A Hirundo
Light attack helicopter: 9 delivered between 1979 and 1980 (AE-331 to AE-339); all 9 still in service Mar 1982. Flown by Compania de Helicopteros de Ataque, CAB601 based at Campo de Mayo, Buenos Aires.

AE-331
Captured at Stanley racecourse 14 Jun 1982. Shipped to the UK Jul 1982. Allocated the serial ZE411 and currently in service with 8 Flt, AAC.

AE-334
Captured at Stanley racecourse 14 Jun 1982. Shipped to the UK Jul 1982. Allocated the serial ZE410 and currently in service with 8 Flt, AAC.

AE-337
Destroyed on the ground near Shag House Cove by Sea Harriers 23 May 1982.

Bell UH-1H Iroquois
Utility helicopter: 25 delivered between 1970 and 1978 (AE-400 to AE-424); approximately 20 still in service Mar 1982. Flown by Compania de Helicopteros de Asalto 'B', CAB601 based at Campo de Mayo, Buenos Aires.

AE-406
Captured at Stanley racecourse 14 Jun 1982. Shipped to the UK Dec 1982. Currently preserved at the Museum of Army Flying, Middle Wallop.

AE-409
Captured at Stanley Sportsfield 14 Jun 1982. Shipped to the UK Jul 1982. Currently preserved at the Museum of Army Flying, Middle Wallop.

AE-410
Captured at Stanley racecourse 14 Jun 1982. Put on display at RAF Chinook base at Kelly's Garden. Shipped to Port Stanley Jan 1985 for display in the Falklands War Museum. Currently stored at RAF Mount Pleasant.

AE-412
Captured at Stanley racecourse 14 Jun 1982. Moved to a weapons range in the Falklands late 1983.

AE-413
Captured at Stanley sportsfield 14 Jun 1982. Shipped to the UK Aug 1982. Allocated the registration G-HUEY Jul 1985 and used on behalf of the RAF Benevolent Fund. Currently preserved at Bournemouth Aviation Museum.

Within days of its arrival in the UK A-109A AE-331 was on display at Middle Wallop on 24th July and Yeovilton on the 30th. During the voyage the helicopters acquired Royal Marine markings and code letters. C M Hobson

AE-417
Captured at Stanley racecourse 14 Jun 1982. Moved to a weapons range in the Falklands late 1983.

AE-418
Captured at Stanley racecourse 14 Jun 1982. Dumped at Moody Brook May 1983.

AE-422
Captured at Stanley racecourse 14 Jun 1982. Shipped to the UK Jul 1982. Currently preserved at the FAA Museum, RNAS Yeovilton.

AE-424
Captured at Stanley racecourse 14 Jun 1982. Allocated to the FIGAS as VP-FBD. Grounded and stored at Moody Brook May 1984 then registered to Grampian Helicopters International as G-BMLA. Present whereabouts unknown.

Boeing-Vertol CH-47C Chinook
Heavylift transport helicopter: 2 delivered in 1979 (AE-520 to AE-521); both still in service Mar 1982. Flown by Compania de Helicopteros de Asalto 'A', CAB601 based at Campo de Mayo, Buenos Aires.

AE-520
Captured at Port Stanley 14 Jun 1982. Shipped to the UK Aug 1982. Stored at RNAY Fleetlands and Wroughton until 1992; allocated the serial ZH257 for use as a ground instructional airframe at AAC Wattisham.

AE-521
Destroyed on the ground near Mount Kent by Harrier GR3 21 May 1982.

Fuerza Aerea Argentina
(Argentine Air Force)

Bell 212
SAR helicopter: 8 delivered in 1978 (H-81 to H-89); all 8 still in service Mar 1982. Flown by Escuadron Helicopteros of Grupo 7 de COIN based at Moron, Buenos Aires.

H-83
Captured at Stanley racecourse 14 Jun 1982. Dumped by May 1983.

H-85
Captured at Stanley racecourse 14 Jun 1982. Dumped but fuselage shipped to the UK Jun 1984; present whereabouts unknown.

Boeing 707
Strategic transport aircraft: 3 delivered between 1975 and 1982 (TC-91 Srs 389B, TC-92 Srs 372C and TC-93 Srs 387C); all 3 still in service Mar 1982. Flown by Escuadron II of Grupo 1 de Transporte Aereo based at El Palomar, Buenos Aires.

TC-91
Survived the conflict. Currently in service with LADE.

TC-92
Survived the conflict. Re-registered as LV-LGP for LADE. Crashed 23 Oct 1996 at Buenos Aires.

TC-93
Survived the conflict. Reserialled VR-21 Jun 1986.

Boeing-Vertol CH-47C Chinook
Medium-lift helicopter: 3 delivered in 1980 (serial range H-91 to H-93); 2 still in service Mar 1982. Flown by Escuadron Helicopteros of Grupo 7 de COIN based at Moron, Buenos Aires.

H-91
Survived the conflict. Preserved at Museo de la Base Quilmes.

H-93
Survived the conflict. Sold to the Spanish Army 2001.

Dassault Mirage IIIEA/DA
Interceptor fighter: 17 single-seat Mirage IIIEAs (I-003 to I-019) and 2 two-seat Mirage IIIDAs (I-001 to I-002) delivered between 1972 and 1980; 17 still in service Mar 1982. Flown by Grupo 8 de Caza based at Mariano Moreno, Buenos Aires.

I-002
Survived the conflict. Withdrawn from service 1997.

I-003 to I-008 and I-010 to I-013
All survived the conflict.

I-014
Survived the conflict. Thought to have been written off 1987.

I-015
Shot down near Pebble Island by Sea Harrier 1 May 1982.

I-016
Survived the conflict. Crashed at Rio Gallegos 8 Oct 1983.

I-017 and I-018 Survived the conflict.

I-019
Damaged by Sea Harrier and shot down by friendly AAA near Port Stanley 1 May 1982.

De Havilland Canada DHC-6 Twin Otter
Light transport aircraft: 7 delivered between 1968 and 1969 (T-81 to T-87); 6 still in service Mar 1982. Flown by Grupo 9 de Transporte Aereo based at Comodoro Rivadavia, Santa Cruz.

T-81
Survived the conflict. Crashed at Rio Gallegos 28 Jan 1983.

T-82
Survived the conflict. Currently in service with LADE.

T-83
Survived the conflict. Currently in service with LADE.

T-84
Survived the conflict. Destroyed during a storm at O'Higgins base camp, Antarctica 1992 while with LADE.

T-86
Survived the conflict. Currently in service with LADE.

T-87 Survived the conflict.

English Electric Canberra
Light bomber: 10 B62s (B-101 to B-110) and 2 T64s (B-111 to B-112) delivered between 1970 and 1971; 10 still in service Mar 1982. Flown by Grupo 2 de Bombardeo based at Parana, Entre Rios.

B-101
Survived the conflict. Retired Apr 2000.

B-102
Survived the conflict. Preserved at Museo Oliva, Cordoba Province.

B-104
Survived the conflict. Crashed at Parana 13 Aug 1982.

B-105
Survived the conflict. Currently preserved at BAM Mar del Plata, Buenos Aires.

B-107
Survived the conflict. Crashed at Parana 1 Jul 1983.

B-108
Shot down near Mount Kent by Sea Dart fired by *Exeter* 14 Jun 1982.

B-109
Survived the conflict. Retired Apr 2000.

B-110
Shot down northwest of Port Stanley by Sea Harrier 1 May 1982.

B-111
Survived the conflict. Currently preserved at BAM Parana.

B-112
Survived the conflict. Damaged 30 Mar 1993. Retired and currently preserved at Parana City.

FMA IA-58A Pucara
Light attack aircraft: 110 in the process of delivery between 1976 and 1986 (A-501 to A-610); about 60 aircraft in service Mar 1982. Flown by Grupo 3 de Ataque based at Reconquista, Santa Fe and Grupo 4 de Ataque based at Comodoro Rivadavia, Santa Cruz (all Grupo 3 aircraft):

A-502
Destroyed on the ground during the SAS raid on Pebble Island 15 May 1982. Remains blown up and buried.

A-506
Damaged during attempted take-off from Goose Green 1 May 1982 and further damaged by Sea Harrier raid later same day. Not flown again and captured at Goose Green 28 May 1982. Moved to a weapons range in the Falklands by Feb 1984.

A-509
Badly damaged at Stanley airport early in May, probably by naval bombardment. Captured at Stanley airport 14 Jun 1982. Dumped at Stanley and later scrapped.

A-511
Shot down near Drone Hill, Lafonia by Sea Harrier 21 May 1982.

A-513
Badly damaged at Stanley airport early or mid-May, probably by naval bombardment. Captured at Stanley airport 14 Jun 1982. Further damaged in a storm and moved to a weapons range in the Falklands by Jul 1983.

A-514
Badly damaged at Stanley airport early or mid-May, probably by naval bombardment. Captured at Stanley airport 14 Jun 1982. Dumped at Stanley and later scrapped.

A-515
Captured at Stanley airport 14 Jun 1982. Shipped to the UK on *Atlantic Causeway* Jul 1982. Allocated the serial ZD485 for trials at A&AEE; reflown at Boscombe Down 28 Apr 1983. To Cosford Aerospace Museum 9 Sep 1983 for display.

A-516
Destroyed at Stanley airport late in May 1982, probably by a direct hit from a bomb. Hulk later buried on site.

A-517
Badly damaged at Goose Green in Sea Harrier attack 1 May 1982 and further damaged in subsequent raids. Captured at Goose Green 28 May 1982. Wreck sold to Grampian Helicopters International 5 Oct 1984. Allocated the registration G-BLRP 3 Dec 1984 and shipped to UK 1985. Currently registered to R J H Butterfield of Witney, but thought to be in the Channel Islands.

A-520
Damaged on the ground during the SAS raid on Pebble Island 15 May 1982. Moved to a weapons range in the Falklands by Jan 1983.

A-522
Captured at Stanley airport 14 Jun 1982. Shipped to the UK on *Contender Bezant* in Sep 1982. To RAF St Athan Museum 25 Oct 1982. Allocated 8768M and preserved at the FAA Museum, RNAS Yeovilton since 7 Dec 1982 but loaned to the Northeast Aircraft Museum, Usworth.

A-523
Damaged on the ground during the SAS raid on Pebble Island 15 May 1982. Moved to a weapons range in the Falklands by Jul 1983.

A-527
Destroyed on the ground at Goose Green by CBUs dropped by Sea Harrier 1 May 1982.

A-528
Captured at Stanley airport 14 Jun 1982. Shipped to the UK on *Contender Bezant* Sep 1982. Allocated 8769M and moved to the Cosford Aerospace Museum for display 18 Oct 1982. Transferred to the Museum of Army Flying, Middle Wallop 16 May 1985. Later transferred to the Norfolk and Suffolk Aviation Museum, Flixton.

A-529
Damaged on the ground during the SAS raid on Pebble Island 15 May 1982. Moved to RAF Stanley as a gate guardian Jul 1983, and later became part of the Falklands War Museum. Currently stored at RAF Mount Pleasant.

A-531
Shot down near Flat Shanty settlement by a Stinger SAM fired by an SAS soldier 21 May 1982.

A-532
Captured at Stanley airport 14 Jun 1982. Moved to a weapons range in the Falklands by Jul 1983.

A-533
Captured at Stanley airport 14 Jun 1982. Shipped to the UK on *Tor Caledonia* Aug 1982. Allocated the serial ZD486 for trials at A&AEE Boscombe Down Sep 1982 but not flown. Preserved at the Museum of Army Flying, Middle Wallop since 15 Feb 1984.

A-536
Captured at Stanley airport 14 Jun 1982. Moved to a weapons range in the Falklands May 1983.

A-537
Crashed in Blue Mountains near Flats Shanty 28 May 1982 soon after shooting down Scout AH1 XT629 of 3 CBAS.

A-549
Captured at Stanley airport 14 Jun 1982. Shipped to the UK on *Atlantic Causeway* Jul 1982. Allocated the serial ZD487 for trials at A&AEE Boscombe Down Aug 1982. To Imperial War Museum, Duxford for display 2 Nov 1983.

A-552
Damaged on the ground during the SAS raid on Pebble Island 15 May 1982. Moved to a weapons range in the Falklands Jul 1983.

A-555
Shot down at Goose Green by small arms fire 28 May 1982.

A-556
Damaged on the ground during the SAS raid on Pebble Island 15 May 1982. Moved to a weapons range in the Falklands by Jan 1983.

In addition, A-540 of Grupo 4 de Ataque was lost at sea during a surveillance mission from Comodoro Rivadavia 24 May 1982.

Fokker F-27 Friendship
Short-range transport aircraft: 13 delivered between 1969 and 1978 (T-41 to T-42 Srs 400, T-43 to T-44 Srs 600, T-45 Srs 400M, TC-71 Srs 400M, TC-72 Srs 500, TC-73 to TC-74 Srs 400Ms, TC-75 Srs 500, TC-76 to TC-79 Srs 400M); 11 still in service Mar 1982. Flown by Escuadron IV of Grupo 1 de Transporte Aereo based at Comodoro Rivadavia, Santa Cruz

T-41
Survived the conflict. Currently in service with LADE.

T-42
Survived the conflict. Currently in service with LADE.

T-43
Survived the conflict. Currently in service with LADE.

T-44
Survived the conflict. Currently in service with LADE.

T-45
Survived the conflict. Currently in service with LADE.

TC-71
Survived the conflict. Currently in service with LADE.

TC-72
Survived the conflict. Crashed at Villa Dolores 9 Nov 1995.

TC-73
Survived the conflict. Crashed at Jeremie, Haiti 16 Jun 1995.

TC-74
Survived the conflict. Currently in service with LADE.

TC-76
Survived the conflict. Crashed at El Plumerillo 17 May 2001.

TC-78 Survived the conflict.

TC-79
Survived the conflict. Currently in service with LADE.

Fokker F-28-1000 Fellowship
Short-range transport aircraft: 5 delivered in 1975 (TC-51 to TC-55); all 5 still in service Mar 1982. Flown by Escuadron II Grupo 1 de Transporte Aereo based at Comodoro Rivadavia, Santa Cruz.

TC-51
Survived the conflict. Crashed at San Carlos de Bariloche 16 Aug 1989.

TC-52 Survived the conflict.

TC-53
Survived the conflict. Currently in service with LADE.

TC-54 Survived the conflict.

TC-55 Survived the conflict.

IAI Dagger
Fighter-bomber: 35 single-seat Dagger As (C-401 to C-424, C-427 to C-437) and 4 two-seat Dagger Bs (C-425 to C-426, C-438 to C-439) delivered between 1978 and 1982; 37 still in service Mar 1982. Flown by Escuadron II and III of Grupo 6 de Caza based at Tandil, Buenos Aires.

C-401 Survived the conflict.

C-403
Shot down near Green Hill Bridge by Sea Harrier 21 May 1982.

C-404
Shot down near Green Hill Bridge by Sea Harrier 21 May 1982.

C-407
Shot down near Mount Caroline by Sea Harrier 21 May 1982.

C-408 Survived the conflict.

C-409
Shot down near Teal River Inlet by Sea Harrier 21 May 1982.

C-410
Shot down near Pebble Island by Sea Harrier 24 May 1982.

C-412 Survived the conflict.

C-413
Survived the conflict. Crashed at Tandil 14 Sep 1995.

C-414 Survived the conflict.
C-417 Survived the conflict.

C-418
Survived the conflict. Crashed near Tandil 12 Jun 1987.

C-419
Shot down near Pebble Island by Sea Harrier 24 May 1982.

C-420 Survived the conflict.
C-427 Survived the conflict.

C-428
Shot down over San Carlos Water by Seawolf fired by *Broadsword* 21 May 1982.

C-430
Shot down near Pebble Island by Sea Harrier 24 May 1982.

C-431
Survived the conflict. Crashed near Mar Chiquita 16 May 1985.

C-432 Survived the conflict.

C-433
Shot down near Lively Island by Sea Harrier 1 May 1982.

C-436
Shot down over San Carlos Water by Rapier 29 May 1982.

C-437
Shot down near Pebble Island by Sea Harrier 23 May 1982.

Gates Learjet 35A
Photographic reconnaissance aircraft: 4 delivered between 1978 and 1982 (T-21 to T-24); all 4 still in service Mar 1982. Flown by Grupo 1 de Aerofotografico based at Parana, Entre Rios.

T-21 Survived the conflict.
T-22 Survived the conflict.
T-23 Survived the conflict.

T-24
Shot down near Pebble Island by Sea Dart fired by *Exeter* 7 Jun 1982.

Lockheed C-130 Hercules
Tactical transport aircraft: 3 C-130E delivered in 1968 (TC-61 to TC-63; TC-62 destroyed in sabotage attack 1975), 5 C-130H delivered between 1972 and 1975 (TC-64 to TC-68), 2 KC-130H delivered in 1979 (TC-69 to TC-70); 9 still in service Mar 1982. Flown by Escuadron I of Grupo 1 de Transporte Aereo based at El Palomar, Buenos Aires.

TC-61 Survived the conflict.

TC-63
Shot down north of Pebble Island by Sea Harrier 1 Jun 1982.

TC-64 to TC-70 Survived the conflict.

McDonnell Douglas A-4B Skyhawk
Light attack aircraft: 50 delivered between 1966 and 1970 (C-201 to C-250); approximately 36 still in service Mar 1982. Flown by Escuadron IV and Escuadron V of Grupo 5 de Caza based at Villa Reynolds, San Luis.

C-204
Shot down over Choiseul Sound by Sea Harrier 8 Jun 1982.

C-206
Crashed into sea off Stanley while attacking *Brilliant* and *Glasgow* 12 May 1982.

C-207
Survived the conflict. Retired from service Mar 1999 and currently preserved at the Museo Nacional de Aeronautica, Moron.

C-208
Shot down off Port Stanley by Seawolf fired by *Brilliant* 12 May 1982.

C-212
Survived the conflict. Currently preserved at Museo de la IV Brigada Aerea, Mendoza painted as 'C-204'.

C-214
Survived the conflict. Retired from service Mar 1999 and currently preserved at BAM Villa Reynolds, San Luis.

C-215
Shot down near Ajax Bay by AAA from *Fearless* 27 May 1982.

C-222
Survived the conflict. Currently preserved at the Museo de la Industria de la Municipalidad de Cordoba.

C-224
Survived the conflict. Currently preserved at BAM Ezeiza.

C-225
Survived the conflict. Retired from service Mar 1999 and used as a ground instructional airframe.

C-226
Shot down over Choiseul Sound by Sea Harrier 8 Jun 1982.

C-227
Survived the conflict. Scrapped late 1990s.

C-228
Shot down near Middle Island by Sea Harrier 8 Jun 1982.

C-231
Survived the conflict. Currently preserved at Villa Reynolds.

C-233
Survived the conflict. Currently preserved at Museo de la IV Brigada Aerea, Mendoza painted as 'C-301'.

C-234
Survived the conflict. Crashed at Vicuna Mackenna 31 Oct 1984.

C-235
Survived the conflict. Crashed near Buenos Aires 13 Jul 1983.

C-236 Survived the conflict.

On 28th July 1982 Pucara A-549 was lifted by a Chinook HC1 from the deck of the Atlantic Causeway *in Plymouth and flown to Yeovilton for road transport to A&AEE Boscombe Down. As the Pucara was about to be set down at Yeovilton it could be seen to be carrying three rocket pods and a 7.62mm machine gun pod. The aircraft was later allocated the serial ZD487 and is currently preserved at IWM Duxford.* C M Hobson

C-237
Survived the conflict. Crashed 19 Nov 1984.

C-239
Survived the conflict. Being restored for preservation at Maipu.

C-240
Survived the conflict. Currently preserved at Museo Nacional de Aeronautica Aeroparque, Buenos Aires.

C-242
Shot down over San Carlos Water by an unidentified British SAM 23 May 1982.

C-244
Shot down near Pebble Island by Sea Dart fired by *Coventry* 25 May 1982.

C-246
Shot down off Port Stanley by Seawolf fired by *Brilliant* 12 May 1982.

C-248
Shot down at Goose Green by friendly AAA 12 May 1982.

C-250 Survived the conflict.

McDonnell Douglas A-4C Skyhawk
Light attack aircraft: 25 delivered in 1976 (C-301 to C-325); about 16 still in service Mar 1982. Flown by Escuadron III of Grupo 4 de Caza based at Los Tamarindos, El Plumerillo.

C-301
Shot down off East Falklands by Sea Dart fired by *Exeter* 30 May 1982.

C-303
Missing in action off Falklands 9 May 1982.

C-304
Shot down near Pebble Island by Sea Dart fired by *Coventry* 25 May 1982.

C-305
Shot down at King George Bay by ground fire 24 May 1982.

C-309
Shot down near Chartres Settlement by Sea Harrier 21 May 1982.

C-310
Shot down off East Falkland by Sea Dart fired by *Exeter* 30 May 1982.

C-312
Survived the conflict. Crashed 3 Oct 1991.

C-313
Crashed at South Jason Island 9 May 1982.

C-314
Survived the conflict. Retired from service Mar 1999 and currently preserved at Museo de la IV Brigada Aerea, Mendoza.

C-318 Survived the conflict.

C-319
Shot down over San Carlos Water by multiple weapons hits 25 May 1982.

C-321 Survived the conflict.

C-322
Survived the conflict. Retired from service Mar 1999 and currently preserved at the Museo Nacional de Aeronautica, Moron.

C-324 Survived the conflict. Crashed at Villa Reynolds 10 Dec 1997.

C-325
Shot down near Chartres Settlement by Sea Harrier 21 May 1982.

Appendix Five

Participation of Individual British Ships in the Conflict

For Royal Navy ships the tonnage is the fully loaded weight quoted from Jane's Fighting Ships 1981-82 *edition. Aircraft listed were embarked on the ships throughout the entire deployment unless qualified by dates.*

Royal Navy Ships & Submarines

HMS *Active* (F171)
Type 21 Amazon class frigate
3,250 tons; launched 23 Nov 1972;
commissioned 17 Jun 1977

Wasp HAS1 of 829 Sqn (XT779)
4 x Exocet SSM launchers; 1 x Seacat SAM launcher; 1 x 4.5-inch and 2 x 20mm guns

Departed Devonport 10 May 1982; arrived off Falklands 25 May; arrived Devonport 3 Aug 1982. Sold to Pakistan; recommissioned as *Shahjahan* 23 Sep 1994.

HMS *Alacrity* (F174)
Type 21 Amazon class frigate
3,250 tons; launched 18 Sep 1974;
commissioned 2 Jul 1977

Lynx HAS2 of 815 Sqn (XZ720 5-24 April; XZ736 24 April to 3 May and 8 May to 24 June; XZ700 3-8 May)
4 x Exocet SSM launchers; 1 x Seacat SAM launcher; 1 x 4.5-inch and 2 x 20mm guns

Departed Devonport 5 Apr 1982; arrived Ascension 16 Apr; arrived off Falklands 30 Apr; damaged by bomb 1 May; arrived Devonport 24 Jun 1982. Sold to Pakistan; recommissioned as *Badr* 1 Mar 1994.

HMS *Ambuscade* (F172)
Type 21 Amazon class frigate
3,250 tons; launched 18 Jan 1973;
commissioned 5 Sep 1975

Lynx HAS2 of 815 Sqn (XZ696 3-25 May; XZ247 from 25 May)
1 x Seacat SAM launcher; 1 x 4.5-inch and 2 x 20mm guns; Mk46 torpedoes

Departed Gibraltar 3 May 1982; arrived Ascension 11 May; arrived off Falklands 22 May; arrived South Georgia 6 Jul; arrived Devonport 24 Jul 1982. Sold to Pakistan; recommissioned as *Tariq* 28 Jul 1993.

HMS *Andromeda* (F57)
Broadbeam Leander class Batch 3 frigate
2,962 tons; launched 24 May 1967;
commissioned 2 Dec 1968

Lynx HAS2 of 815 Sqn (XZ722)
4 x Exocet SSM launchers; 1 x Seawolf SAM launcher; 2 x 40mm guns; Mk32 torpedoes

Departed Devonport 10 May 1982; arrived Ascension 18 May; arrived off Falklands 25 May; arrived Devonport 10 Sep 1982. Sold to India; recommissioned as *Krishna* 22 Aug 1995.

HMS *Antelope* (F170)
Type 21 Amazon class frigate
3,250 tons; launched 16 Mar 1972;
commissioned 19 Jul 1975

Lynx HAS2 of 815 Sqn (XZ723)
1 x Seacat SAM launcher; 1 x 4.5-inch and 2 x 20mm guns; Mk46 torpedoes

Departed Devonport 5 Apr 1982; arrived Ascension 21 Apr; arrived off Falklands 22 May; damaged by bombs dropped by Grupo 5 A-4Q Skyhawks 23 May one of which exploded while being defused, causing the ship to sink in San Carlos Water.

HMS *Antrim* (D18)
County class destroyer
6,200 tons; launched 10 Oct 1967;
commissioned 14 Jul 1970

Wessex HAS3 of 737 Sqn (XP142), Wessex HU5 of 845 Sqn (XT449 detached 19-24 May)
4 x Exocet SSM launchers; 2 x Seacat SAM launchers, 1 x Seaslug 2 SAM launcher; 2 x 4.5-inch and 2 x 20mm guns

Departed Exercise 'Springtrain' 2 Apr 1982; arrived off South Georgia 21 Apr; arrived off Falklands 20 May; damaged by bomb 21 May; departed Falklands 29 Jun; arrived Plymouth 17 Jul 1982. Decommissioned Apr 1984 and sold to Chile; recommissioned as *Almirante Cochrane* 22 Jun 1984.

HMS *Ardent* (F184)
Type 21 Amazon class frigate
3,250 tons; launched 9 May 1975;
commissioned 13 Oct 1977

Lynx HAS2 of 815 Sqn (XZ251)
4 x Exocet SSM launchers; 1 x Seacat SAM launcher; 1 x 4.5-inch and 2 x 20mm guns

Departed Devonport 19 Apr 1982; arrived Ascension 29 April; arrived off Falklands 19 May; badly damaged by bombs 21 May; sunk off North West Island 22 May 1982.

HMS *Argonaut* (F56)
Leander class Batch 2 frigate
3,200 tons; launched 8 Feb 1966;
commissioned 17 Aug 1967

Lynx HAS2 of 815 Sqn (XZ233 19 Apr to 5 Jun; XZ254 from 5 Jun)
4 x Exocet SSM launchers; 3 x Seacat SAM launchers; 2 x 20mm guns; Mk46 torpedoes

Departed Devonport 19 Apr 1982; arrived Ascension 28 Apr; arrived off Falklands 19 May; damaged by bombs 21 May; arrived Devonport 26 Jun 1982. Decommissioned 31 Mar 1993 and sold for scrap.

HMS *Arrow* (F173)
Type 21 Amazon class frigate
3,250 tons; launched 5 Feb 1974;
commissioned 29 Jul 1976

Lynx HAS2 of 815 Sqn
(XZ241 2-17 April; XZ730 from 17 Apr)
4 x Exocet SSM launchers; 1 x Seacat SAM launcher; 1 x 4.5-inch and 2 x 20mm guns

Departed Exercise 'Springtrain' 2 Apr 1982; arrived Ascension 11 Apr; arrived off Falklands 1 May; arrived Devonport 7 Jul 1982. Sold to Pakistan; recommissioned as *Khaibar* 1 Mar 1994.

HMS *Avenger* (F185)
Type 21 Amazon class frigate
3,250 tons; launched 20 Nov 1975;
commissioned 15 Apr 1978

Lynx HAS2 of 815 Sqn (XZ249)
4 x Exocet SSM launchers; 1 x Seacat SAM launcher; 1 x 4.5-inch and 2 x 20mm guns; Mk46 torpedoes

Departed Devonport 10 May 1982; arrived Ascension 18 May; arrived off Falklands 25 May; arrived Devonport 10 Sep 1982. Sold to Pakistan; recommissioned as *Tippu Sultan* 23 Sep 1994.

HMS *Brecon* (M29)
Hunt class minesweeper
725 tons; launched 21 Jun 1978;
commissioned 21 Mar 1980

1 x 40mm gun

Departed Portland 13 Jun 1982; arrived off Falklands 10 Jul; arrived Rosyth 15 Sep 1982. Still in service with RN in 2002.

HMS *Brilliant* (F90)
Type 22 Broadsword class Batch 1 frigate
4,000 tons; launched 15 Dec 1978;
commissioned 15 May 1981

Lynx HAS2 of 815 Sqn (XZ692 2-14 Apr; XZ729 2 Apr to 21 May; XZ721 14-22 Apr and 7 May to 22 Jun; XZ725 22 April to 8 May; XZ723 30 May to 22 Jun; XZ233 from 22 Jun; XZ732 from 23 Jun)
4 x Exocet SSM launchers; 2 x Seawolf SAM launchers; 2 x 40mm guns; Mk46 torpedoes

Departed Exercise 'Springtrain' 2 Apr 1982; arrived Ascension 11 Apr; arrived off South Georgia 22 Apr; arrived off Falklands 29 Apr; arrived Devonport 13 Jul 1982. Sold to Brazil; recommissioned as *Dodsworth* 31 Aug 1996.

HMS *Bristol* (D23)
Type 82 Bristol class destroyer
7,100 tons; launched 30 Jun 1969;
commissioned 31 Mar 1973

1 x Sea Dart SAM launcher; Ikara ASM; 1 x 4.5-inch and 4 x 20mm guns; 1 x ASW mortar

Departed Portsmouth 10 May 1982; arrived Ascension 18 May; arrived off Falklands 25 May; arrived Portsmouth 17 Sep 1982. Currently in use as an immobile tender in Portsmouth harbour.

HMS *Broadsword* (F88)
Type 22 Broadsword class Batch 1 frigate
4,000 tons; launched 12 May 1976;
commissioned 3 May 1979

Lynx HAS2 of 815 Sqn (XZ736 8-24 Apr; XZ728 16 Apr to 23 Jul; XZ240 24 Apr to 5 May; XZ732 5 May to 23 Jun; XZ729 21 May to 11 Jun; XZ723 23 Jun to 2 Jul; XZ691 from 2 Jul)
4 x Exocet SSM launchers; 2 x Seawolf SAM launchers; 2 x 40mm guns

Departed Gibraltar 8 Apr; arrived Ascension 16 Apr; arrived off Falklands 1 May; damaged by bomb 25 May; arrived Devonport 23 Jul 1982. Sold to Brazil; recommissioned as *Greenhalgh* 30 Jun 1995.

HMS *Cardiff* (D108)
Type 42 Sheffield class destroyer
4,700 tons; launched 22 Feb 1974;
commissioned 24 Sep 1979

Lynx HAS2 of 815 Sqn (XZ254 12 May to 5 Jun; XZ233 5-22 Jun; XZ721 from 22 Jun)

1 x Sea Dart SAM launcher; 1 x 4.5-inch and 2 x 20mm guns; Mk46 torpedoes

Departed Gibraltar 12 May 1982; arrived Ascension 18 May; arrived off Falklands 26 May; arrived Portsmouth 28 Jul 1982. Still in service with RN in 2002.

HMS *Conqueror* (S48)
Churchill class nuclear-powered submarine
4,900 tons; launched 28 Aug 1969;
commissioned 9 Nov 1971

Mk8 and 21-inch Tigerfish torpedoes

Departed Faslane 4 Apr 1982; arrived off South Georgia 19 Apr; sunk Argentine cruiser *General Belgrano* 2 May; arrived Faslane 3 Jul 1982. Decommissioned 2 Aug 1990 and currently at Faslane for scrapping.

HMS *Courageous* (S50)
Churchill class nuclear-powered submarine
4,900 tons; launched 7 Mar 1970;
commissioned 16 Oct 1971

Mk8 and 21-inch Tigerfish torpedoes

Departed Faslane 4 Apr 1982; arrived off Falklands c.19 Apr and patrolled between Argentina and the Falklands; arrived Faslane 13 Aug 1982. Decommissioned 10 Apr 1992 and currently at Devonport for scrapping.

HMS *Coventry* (D118)
Type 42 Sheffield class destroyer
4,700 tons; launched 21 Jun 1974;
commissioned 20 Oct 1978

Lynx HAS2 of 815 Sqn (XZ700 2-17 Apr; XZ242 17 Apr to 25 May)
1 x Sea Dart SAM launcher; 1 x 4.5-inch and 2 x 20mm guns; Mk46 torpedoes

Departed Exercise 'Springtrain' 2 Apr 1982; arrived Ascension 11 Apr; arrived off Falklands 1 May; hit by bombs and sunk north of Pebble Island 25 May 1982.

HMS *Dumbarton Castle* (P265)
Castle class fishery protection vessel
1,427 tons; launched 3 Jun 1981;
commissioned 26 Mar 1982

1 x 40mm gun

Departed Portland 1 May 1982; arrived Ascension 11 May for use as a dispatch vessel between Ascension and the Falklands; arrived Rosyth 20 Aug 1982. Still in service with RN in 2002.

HMS *Endurance* (A171)
Ice patrol vessel
3,600 tons; launched (as *Anita Dan*) May 1956; commissioned 28 Jun 1968

Wasp HAS1 of 829 Sqn (XS527, XS539), Wessex HU5 (XS486 detached 17-24 Jun)
2 x 20mm guns

On station when conflict broke out, spending much of the time off South Georgia; arrived Chatham 20 Aug 1982; decommissioned 1991 and scrapped in India.
On 21 Nov 1991 a new HMS *Endurance* (originally HMS *Polar Circle*) was commissioned and currently serves in the Antarctic Ocean.

HMS *Exeter* (D89)
Type 42 Sheffield class Batch 2 destroyer
4,100 tons; launched 25 Apr 1978;
commissioned 19 Sep 1980

Lynx HAS2 of 815 Sqn (XZ733)
1 x Sea Dart SAM launcher; 1 x 4.5-inch and 2 x 20mm guns; Mk46 torpedoes

Departed Antigua 7 May 1982; arrived Ascension 14 May; arrived off Falklands 21 May; arrived Portsmouth 28 Jul 1982. Still in service with RN in 2002.

HMS *Fearless* (L10)
Fearless class assault ship
12,120 tons; launched 19 Dec 1963;
commissioned 25 Nov 1965

Sea King HC4 of 846 Sqn (ZA296 6 Apr to 27 May and 16 Jun to 13 Jul; ZA297 6 Apr to 8 May; ZA298 8-27 May and 16 Jun to 13 Jul; ZA310 6-23 May; ZA312 19-23 May; ZA299 16 Jun to 13 Jul; ZA313 16 Jun to 13 Jul), Scout AH1 of 'B' Flt 3 CBAS (XP902 6-28 Apr; XR627, XT629 both 6 Apr to 11 May), Wessex HU5 of 'B' Flt 845 Sqn (XT765 detached 27-30 May)
4 x Seacat SAM launchers; 2 x 40mm guns

Departed Portsmouth 6 Apr 1982; arrived Ascension 17 Aprl; arrived off Falklands 16 May; arrived Devonport 13 Jul 1982. Still in service with RN in 2002.

HMS *Glamorgan* (D19)
County class destroyer
6,200 tons; launched 9 Jul 1964;
commissioned 11 Oct 1966

Wessex HAS3 of 737 Sqn (XM837 2 Apr to 12 Jun), Wessex HU5 of 'A' Flt 845 Sqn (XS483 detached 30 Apr-2 May), Wessex HU5 of 'D' Flt 848 Sqn (XT486 detached 14-19 Jun)
4 x Exocet SSM launchers; 2 x Seacat SAM launchers, 1 x Seaslug 2 SAM launcher; 2 x 4.5-inch and 2 x 20mm guns

Departed Exercise 'Springtrain' 2 Apr 1982; arrived off Falklands 1 May; damaged by Exocet 12 Jun; departed Falklands 21 Jun; arrived Portsmouth 10 Jul 1982. Sold to Chile and recommissioned as *Latorre* 3 Oct 1986; paid off 1998

HMS *Glasgow* (D88)
Type 42 Sheffield class destroyer
4,100 tons; launched 14 Apr 1976;
commissioned 24 May 1979

Lynx HAS2 of 815 Sqn (XZ732 2-17 Apr; XZ247 17 Apr to 25 May; XZ696 from 25 May) 1 x Sea Dart SAM launcher; 1 x 4.5-inch and 2 x 20mm guns; Mk46 torpedoes

Departed Exercise 'Springtrain' 2 Apr 1982; arrived Ascension 11 Apr; arrived off Falklands 1 May; damaged by a bomb off Stanley 12 May; arrived Portsmouth 19 Jun 1982. Still in service with RN in 2002.

HMS *Hecla* (A133)
Hecla class survey vessel (CASEVAC role) 2,733 tons; launched 21 Dec 1964; commissioned 8 Sep 1965

Wasp HAS1 of 829 Sqn (XT420)

Departed Gibraltar 20 Apr 1982; arrived Ascension 2 May; arrived off Falklands 14 May; arrived Devonport 29 Jul 1982. Decommissioned Jan 1997; sold in Ireland and renamed *Bligh*.

HMS *Herald* (A138)
Improved Hecla class survey vessel (CASEVAC role) 2,945 tons; launched 4 Oct 1973; commissioned 31 Oct 1974

Wasp HAS1 of 829 Sqn (XT794)

Departed Portsmouth 24 Apr 1982; arrived off Falklands 25 May; arrived Portsmouth 21 Jul 1982. Decommissioned Apr 2001; sold in the Republic of Ireland and renamed *Somerville*.

HMS *Hermes* (R12)
Hermes class aircraft carrier 28,700 tons; launched 16 Feb 1953; commissioned 18 Nov 1959

Sea Harrier FRS1 of 800 Sqn (XZ450 2 Apr to 4 May; XZ455 2 Apr to 2 Jul; XZ457, XZ459, XZ460, XZ492 all 2 Aprl to 21 Jul; XZ494 2 Apr to 2 Jul; XZ496 2 Apr to 21 Jul; XZ499, XZ500 both 2 Apr to 19 Jul; ZA176 18 May to 19 Jul; ZA177 18 May to 21 Jul; ZA191 2 Apr to 19 Jul; ZA192 4 Apr to 23 May; ZA193 4 Apr to 19 Jul; ZA194 18 May to 19 Jul), Harrier GR3 of 1 Sqn (XV789 18 May to 4 Jul; XZ972 18 May to 21 May; XZ988 18 May to 27 May; XZ997 18 May to 4 Jul; XZ963 19 May to 30 May; XZ989 20 May to 8 Jun; XV778 1 Jun to 4 Jul; XZ133 1 Jun to 4 Jul; XW919 8 Jun to 13 Jul; XZ992 8 Jun to 4 Jul), Sea King HAS5 of 826 Sqn (XZ571 3 Apr to 21 Jul; XZ573 15 May to 18 May; XZ577 3 Apr to 22 Jul; XZ578 14 May to 22 Jul; ZA129, ZA130, ZA131 all 3 Apr to 22 Jul; ZA132 3 Apr to 12 May; ZA133, ZA136, ZA137 all 3 Apr to 22 Jul), Sea King HC4 of 846 Sqn (ZA290 3 Apr to 18 May; ZA291 3 Apr to 6 May and 3-22 Jul; ZA292 3 Apr to 19 May; ZA293 3 Apr to 19 May; ZA294 3 Apr to 19 May; ZA295 3 Apr to 6 May and 3-22 Jul; ZA298 3 Apr to 8 May; ZA299 3 Apr to 6 May;

ZA311 3-23 Apr), Lynx HAS2 of 815 Sqn (XZ240 17 May to 21 Jul; XZ720 17 May to 10 Jun and 17 Jun to 21 Jul; XZ700 17-20 May), Wessex HU5 of various sqns (XS507 1-21 Jul; XT450 3-21 Jul; XT468 17-20 May and 28 May to 3 Jun; XT471 3 Jun to 21 Jul; XT765 3-21 Jul) 2 x Seacat SAM launchers

Departed Portsmouth 5 Apr 1982; arrived Ascension 16 Apr; arrived off Falklands 1 May; arrived Portsmouth 21 Jul 1982. Sold to India; recommissioned as *Viraat* 20 May 1987.

HMS *Hydra* (A144)
Hecla class survey vessel (CASEVAC role) 2,733 tons; launched 14 Jul 1965; commissioned 5 May 1966

Wasp HAS1 of 829 Sqn (XT432)

Departed Portsmouth 24 Apr 1982; arrived Ascension 8 May; arrived off Falklands 19 May; arrived Portsmouth 24 Sep 1982. Sold to Indonesia; recommissioned as *Dewa Kembar* 10 Sep 1986.

HMS *Intrepid* (L11)
Fearless class assault ship 12,120 tons; launched 25 Jun 1964; commissioned 11 Mar 1967

Sea King HC4 of 846 Sqn (ZA313 26 Apr to 20 May; ZA297 8-29 May and 16 Jun to 13 Jul; ZA291 14-19 May; ZA292 19-29 May and 16 Jun to 13 Jul; ZA293 19-29 May and 16 Jun to 13 Jul; ZA295 20-29 May; ZA310 15 Jun to 13 Jul), Wessex HU5 of 845 Sqn (XT449, XT461 both 26 Apr to 5 May; XT451, XT460 both 7-30 May) 4 x Seacat SAM launchers; 2 x 40mm guns

Departed Portland 26 Apr; arrived Ascension 5 May; arrived off Falklands 16 May; arrived Devonport 13 Jul 1982. Transferred to Reserve List 31 Aug 1999.

HMS *Invincible* (R05)
Invincible class light aircraft carrier 19,500 tons; launched 3 May 1977; commissioned 11 Jul 1980

Sea Harrier FRS1 of 801 Sqn (XZ451 4 Apr to 17 Sep; XZ452, XZ453 both 4 Apr to 6 May; XZ455 2 Jul to 17 Sep; XZ456 4 Apr to 1 Jun; XZ458, XZ491 both 19 May to 26 Aug; XZ493 4 Apr to 17 Sep; XZ494 2 Jul to 17 Sep; XZ495, XZ498 both 4 Apr to 17 Sep; ZA174 19-29 May; ZA175 4 Apr to 17 Sep; ZA190 18 May to 17 Sep), Sea King HAS5 of 820 Sqn (XZ573 4 Apr to 18 May; XZ574 4 Apr to 18 Sep; XZ578 4 Aprl to 14 May; XZ918, XZ920, XZ921, ZA126, ZA127, ZA128, ZA134, ZA135 all 4 Apr to 18 Sep), Sea King HAS2 of 824 Sqn (XV660 16-27 Jun), Lynx HAS2 of 815 Sqn (XZ240 18-24 Apr; XZ720 24 Apr to 4 May; XZ722 13-24 Aug; XZ725 17 May to 16 Sep), Wessex HU5 of 845 Sqn (XT765 9-19 May)

1 x Sea Dart SAM launcher

Departed Portsmouth 5 Apr 1982; arrived Ascension 16 Apr; arrived off Falklands 1 May; arrived Portsmouth 17 Sep 1982. Still in service with RN in 2002.

HMS *Ledbury* (M30)
Hunt class minesweeper 725 tons; launched 5 Dec 1979; commissioned 11 Jun 1981

1 x 40mm gun

Departed Portland 13 Jun 1982; arrived off Falklands 10 Jul 1982. Still in service with RN in 2002.

HMS *Leeds Castle* (P258)
Castle class fishery protection vessel 1,427 tons; launched 29 Oct 1980; commissioned 27 Oct 1981

1 x 40mm gun

Departed Portsmouth 29 Apr 1982; arrived Ascension 9 May; arrived off Falklands 21 May; shuttled between Falklands, South Georgia and Ascension as dispatch vessel; arrived Rosyth 20 Aug 1982. Still in service with RN in 2002.

HMS *Minerva* (F45)
Leander class Batch 2 frigate 3,200 tons; launched 19 Dec 1964; commissioned 14 May 1966

Lynx HAS2 of 815 Sqn (XZ698) 4 x Exocet SSM launchers; 3 x Seacat SAM launchers; 2 x 40mm guns; Mk32 torpedoes

Departed Devonport 10 May 1982; arrived Ascension 18 May; arrived off Falklands 26 May; arrived Devonport 3 Aug 1982. Decommissioned Mar 1992 and later scrapped in India.

HMS *Onyx* (S21)
Oberon class diesel-electric patrol submarine 2,410 tons; launched 18 Aug 1966; commissioned 20 Nov 1967

21-inch torpedoes

Departed Gosport 26 Apr 1982; arrived off Falklands first week of May; arrived Gosport 18 Aug 1982. Decommissioned Dec 1990; currently preserved by the Warship Preservation Trust, Birkenhead.

HMS *Penelope* (F127)
Leander class Batch 2 frigate 3,200 tons; launched 17 Aug 1962; commissioned 31 Oct 1963

Lynx HAS2 of 815 Sqn (XZ691 10 May to 2 Jul; XZ723 from 2 Jul) 4 x Exocet SSM launchers; 3 x Seacat SAM launchers; 2 x 40mm guns; Mk32 torpedoes
Departed Devonport 10 May 1982; arrived Ascension 18 May; arrived off Falklands 25

May; arrived Devonport 10 Sep 1982. Sold to Ecuador; recommissioned as *Presidente Eloy Alfaro* 25 Apr 1991.

HMS *Plymouth* (F126)
Type 12 Rothesay class frigate
2,800 tons; launched 20 Jul 1959;
commissioned 11 May 1961

Wasp HAS1 of 829 Sqn (XT429)
1 x Seacat SAM launcher; 2 x 4.5-inch and
2 x 20mm guns; 1 x ASW mortar

Departed Exercise 'Springtrain' 2 Apr 1982; arrived Ascension 10 Apr; arrived off South Georgia 21 Apr; arrived off Falklands 29 Apr; damaged by bombs 8 Jun; arrived Rosyth 14 Jul 1982. Decommissioned Apr 1988; currently preserved by the Warship Preservation Trust, Birkenhead.

HMS *Sheffield* (D80)
Type 42 Sheffield class destroyer
4,100 tons; launched 10 Jun 1971;
commissioned 16 Feb 1975

Lynx HAS2 of 815 Sqn (XZ725 2-22 Apr; XZ721 22 Apr to 4 May)
1 x Sea Dart SAM launcher; 1 x 4.5-inch and 2 x 20mm guns; Mk46 torpedoes

Departed Exercise 'Springtrain' 2 Apr 1982; arrived Ascension 11 Apr; arrived off Falklands 1 May; hit by Exocet 4 May; taken under tow by *Yarmouth* 9 May 1982; sank 10 May southeast of Falkland Islands while transitting to South Georgia.

HMS *Spartan* (S105)
Swiftsure class nuclear-powered Fleet submarine
4,500 tons; launched 7 Apr 1978;
commissioned 22 Sep 1979

Mk8 and 21-inch Tigerfish torpedoes

Departed Gibraltar 1 Apr 1982; arrived off Falklands 12 Apr; arrived Devonport 24 Jul 1982. Still in service with RN in 2002.

HMS *Splendid* (S106)
Swiftsure class nuclear-powered submarine
4,500 tons; launched 5 Oct 1979;
commissioned 21 Mar 1981

Mk8 and 21-inch Tigerfish torpedoes

Departed Faslane 1 Apr 1982; arrived off Falklands mid-Apr; arrived Devonport 12 Jun 1982. Still in service with RN in 2002.

HMS *Valiant* (S102)
Valiant class nuclear-powered submarine
4,900 tons; launched 3 Dec 1963;
commissioned 18 Jul 1966

Mk8 and 21-inch Tigerfish torpedoes

Departed Faslane 3 May 1982; arrived off Falklands mid-May; arrived Faslane 29 Jul 1982. Decommissioned 12 Aug 1994; currently located at Devonport for scrapping or possible preservation.

HMS *Yarmouth* (F101)
Type 12 Rothesay class frigate
2,800 tons; launched 23 Mar 1959;
commissioned 26 Mar 1960

Wasp HAS1 of 829 Sqn (XV624)
1 x Seacat SAM launcher; 2 x 4.5-inch and
2 x 20mm guns; 1 x ASW mortar

Departed Gibraltar 8 Apr 1982; arrived Ascension 16 Apr; arrived off Falklands 1 May; arrived Rosyth 28 Jul 1982. Decommissioned Apr 1984 and sunk as an exercise target 21Jun 1987.

Royal Fleet Auxiliary Ships

RFA *Appleleaf* (A79)
New Leaf class support tanker
40,200 tons; launched 24 Jul 1975;
commissioned Nov 1979

Departed Exercise 'Springtrain' 2 Apr 1982; served as a refuelling ship in the South Atlantic for ships transiting to and from the Falklands; arrived Rosyth 9 Aug 1982. Sold to Royal Australian Navy 9 Oct 1989 and renamed *Westralia*.

RFA *Bayleaf* (A109)
New Leaf class support tanker
40,200 tons; launched 27 Oct 1981;
commissioned 26 Mar 1982

Departed Devonport 26 Apr 1982; arrived Ascension 8 May; arrived off Falklands 25 May; arrived Devonport 31 Aug 1982. Still in service with RFA in 2002.

RFA *Blue Rover* (A270)
Rover class Fleet tanker (small)
11,522 tons; launched 11 Nov 1969;
commissioned 15 Jul 1970

Departed Portsmouth 16 Apr 1982; arrived Ascension c.26 Apr; arrived off South Georgia 9 May; arrived off Falklands c.25 May; arrived Portsmouth 17 Jul 1982. Sold to Portugal 31 Mar 1993 and renamed *Berrio*.

RFA *Brambleleaf* (A81)
New Leaf class support tanker
40,200 tons; launched 22 Jan 1976;
commissioned 3 Mar 1980

Departed Mombasa 5 Apr 1982; arrived off South Georgia c.23 Apr; arrived Portland 15 May; departed Portland 23 May; arrived Gibraltar 16 Dec 1982. Still in service with RFA in 2002.

RFA *Engadine* (K08)
Helicopter support ship
8,960 tons; launched 15 Sep 1966;
commissioned 15 Dec 1967

Sea King HAS2A of 825 Sqn (XV696 from 7 Jul), Sea King HAS5 of 826 Sqn (ZA129 detached 9-10 Jun), Wessex HU5 of 847

Sqn (XS523, XT456, XT482 all 9 May to 9 Jun; XT764 9-25 May; XS491 25 May to 9 Jun; XS516, XT755 both from 5 Jul)

Departed Devonport 10 May 1982; arrived Ascension 25 May; arrived off Falklands 6 Jun; arrived Devonport 30 Jul 1982. Decommissioned December 1989 and scrapped in India 1996.

RFA *Fort Austin* (A386)
Fort class Fleet replenishment ship
23,600 tons; launched 9 Mar 1978;
commissioned 11 May 1979

Lynx HAS2 (XZ242, XZ247, XZ730 all 6-17 Apr; XZ241 17-22 Apr; XZ732 17 Apr to 5 May; XZ700 17 Apr to 17 May; XZ736 3-8 May; XZ720 4-17 May; XZ240 5-17 May; XZ725 8-17 May), Sea King HAS5 of 826 Sqn (XZ577, ZA130, ZA133, ZA137 all 17 May to 3 Jun), Wessex HU5 of 845 Sqn (XT468 7 Apr to 20 May; XT765 8 Apr to 9 May)

Departed Exercise 'Springtrain' 29 Mar 1982; arrived Ascension 6 Apr; arrived off Falklands 3 May; arrived Devonport 28 Jun 1982. Still in service with RFA in 2002.

RFA *Fort Grange* (A385)
Fort class Fleet replenishment ship
23,600 tons; launched 9 Dec 1976;
commissioned 6 Apr 1978

Sea King HAS2A of 824 Sqn (XV672, XV697, XV698 all 7 May to 11 Jul; XZ579 from 13 Jul), Wessex HU5 of 845 Sqn (XT450, XT459 both 9-10 May)

Departed Devonport 14 May 1982; arrived off Falklands 3 Jun; arrived Devonport 3 Oct 1982. Renamed RFA *Fort Rosalie*. Still in service with RFA in 2002.

RFA *Olmeda* (A124)
Ol class Fleet tanker (large)
36,000 tons; launched 19 Nov 1964;
commissioned 18 Oct 1965

Sea King HAS2A of 824 Sqn (XV649, XV660)

Departed Devonport 5 Apr 1982; arrived Ascension 16 Apr; arrived off Falklands 1 May; detached to South Georgia 16 Jun; arrived Devonport 12 Jul 1982. Decommissioned 1994 and subsequently scrapped in India.

RFA *Olna* (A123)
Ol class Fleet tanker (large)
36,000 tons; launched 28 Jul 1965;
commissioned 1 Apr 1966

Wessex HU5 of 848 Sqn (XS489, XT771)

Departed Portsmouth 10 May 1982; arrived Ascension 18 May; arrived off Falklands 25 May; arrived Portsmouth 17 Sep 1982. Decommissioned Aug 2001 and scrapped in India.

RFA *Pearleaf* (A77)
Old Leaf class support tanker
25,790 tons; launched 15 Oct 1959;
commissioned Jan 1960

Departed Portsmouth 5 Apr 1982; arrived Ascension 22 Apr; arrived off Falklands 16 May; detached to South Georgia 4 Jun; arrived Devonport 13 Aug 1982 Decommissioned 1985 and sold to Saudi Arabia as a static tanker.

RFA *Plumleaf* (A78)
Old Leaf class support tanker
26,480 tons; launched 29 Mar 1960;
commissioned Jul 1960

Departed Portland 19 Apr 1982; arrived Ascension 1 May, refuelled ships in South Atlantic en route to and from the Falklands; arrived Gibraltar 22 Jul; arrived Ports-mouth 26 Aug 1982. Decommissioned May 1985 and scrapped in Taiwan.

RFA *Regent* (A486)
Resource class Fleet replenishment ship
22,890 tons; launched 9 Mar 1966;
commissioned 6 Jun 1967

Wessex HU5 of 848 Sqn (XS486 19 Apr to 10 Jul; XT756 19 Apr to 12 Sep)

Departed Portland 19 Apr 1982; arrived Ascension 29 Apr; arrived off Falklands 12 May; arrived South Georgia 11 Jun; arrived back off Falklands 1 Jul; arrived Rosyth 15 Sep 1982. Decommissioned Dec 1992 and scrapped in India.

RFA *Resource* (A480)
Resource class Fleet replenishment ship
22,890 tons; launched 11 Feb 1966;
commissioned 16 May 1967

Wessex HU5 of 845 Sqn (XS483, XT484 to 24 May and from 24 Jun)

Departed Rosyth 6 Apr 1982; arrived Ascension 17 Apr; arrived off Falklands 23 May; arrived South Georgia 26 Jun; arrived Devonport 19 Jul 1982. Decommissioned 1997 and scrapped in India.

RFA *Sir Bedivere* (L3004)
Landing Ship Logistic
5,674 tons; launched 20 Jul 1966;
commissioned 18 May 1967

2 x 40mm guns

Departed Marchwood 29 Apr; arrived Ascension 8 May; arrived off Falklands 18 May; arrived Marchwood 16 Nov 1982. Still in service with RFA in 2002.

RFA *Sir Galahad* (L3005)
Landing Ship Logistic
5,674 tons; launched 19 Apr 1966;
commissioned 17 Dec 1966

Gazelle AH1 of 'C' Flt 3 CBAS (XX402, XX411, XX412 all 6-21 May), Sea King HC4 of 846 Sqn (ZA313 detached 7-8 Jun)
1 x 40mm gun

Departed Devonport 6 Apr 1982; arrived Ascension 17 Apr; arrived off Falklands 19 May; damaged by a bomb 24 May; badly damaged by bombs 8 Jun; towed out to sea by RMAS *Typhoon* and sunk as a war grave 26 Jun 1982.

RFA *Sir Geraint* (L3027)
Landing Ship Logistic
5,674 tons; launched 26 Jan 1967;
commissioned 12 Jul 1967

Gazelle AH1 of 'A' Flt 3 CBAS (XZ326, ZA730, ZA776 all 6-20 May), Scout AH1 of Garrison Army Air Sqn (XP907, XR629, XT637, XW282 all 10 Jun to 4 Jul 1983)
2 x 40mm guns

Departed Devonport 6 Apr 1982; arrived Ascension 17 Apr; arrived off Falklands 19 May; arrived Marchwood 23 Jul 1982. Still in service with RFA in 2002.

RFA *Sir Lancelot* (L3029)
Landing Ship Logistic
5,550 tons; launched 25 Jun 1963;
commissioned 16 Jan 1964

Scout AH1 of 'B' Flt 3 CBAS (XV140, XW615 both 5 Apr to 23 Jun; XW616 5 Apr to 17 Jun)
2 x 40mm guns

Departed Marchwood 6 Apr 1982; arrived Ascension 17 Apr; arrived off Falklands 19 May; damaged by a bomb 24 May; arrived Portsmouth 18 Aug 1982. Decommissioned and sold in Apr 1989; bought by the Singapore Navy in Oct 1992 and renamed *Perseverance*.

RFA *Sir Percivale* (L3036)
Landing Ship Logistic
5,674 tons; launched 4 Oct 1967;
commissioned 23 Mar 1968

Gazelle AH1 of 'M' Flt 3 CBAS (XX376, XX380, XX413 all 5 Apr to 21 May)
1 x 40mm gun

Departed Marchwood 5 Apr 1982; arrived Ascension 17 Apr; arrived off Falklands 19 May; arrived Marchwood 23 Jul 1982. Still in service with RFA in 2002.

RFA *Sir Tristram* (L3505)
Landing Ship Logistic
5,674 tons; launched 12 Dec 1966;
commissioned 14 Sep 1967

Gazelle AH1 of 'A' Flt 3 CBAS (XZ326, ZA730, ZA776 all 20-21 May), Scout AH1 of 'B' Flt 3 CBAS (XP902 28 Apr to 20 May; XT629 detached 28-29 Apr)
2 x 40mm guns

Departed Belize 2 Apr 1982; arrived Ascension 17 Apr; arrived off Falklands 19 May; damaged by bombs 8 Jun; towed to Port Stanley and used as an accommodation ship; transported back to the UK for repair 13 Jun 1983; refit completed 9 Oct 1985. Still in service with RFA in 2002.

RFA *Stromness* (A344)
Ness class stores support ship
16,792 tons; launched 16 Sep 1966;
commissioned 21 Mar 1967

Scout AH1 of 'B' Flt 3 CBAS (XP902 20 May to 23 Jun; XT629 20-28 May), Wessex HU5 of 845 Sqn (XT765 detached 21-22 May)

Departed Portsmouth 7 Apr 1982; arrived Ascension 17 Apr; arrived off Falklands 16 May; arrived Portsmouth 19 Jul 1982. Sold to US Navy as USNS *Saturn* Apr 1983.

RFA *Tidepool* (A76)
Later Tide class Fleet tanker (large)
27,400 tons; launched 11 Dec 1962;
commissioned 28 Jun 1963

Wessex HU5 of 845 Sqn (XT449, XT461 both 5-25 May), Wessex HU5 of 847 Sqn (XS507 16 June to 1 Jul), Wessex HU5 of 848 Sqn (XT486 10-14 Jun)

In process of being delivered to the Chilean Navy when Falklands conflict broke out but arrived Ascension 27 Apr 1982; arrived off Falklands 18 May. Handed over to Chile c.14 Aug 1982 and recommissioned as *Almirante Jorge Montt*; decommissioned Dec 1997.

RFA *Tidespring* (A75)
Later Tide class Fleet tanker (large)
27,400 tons; launched 3 May 1962;
commissioned 18 Jan 1963

Wessex HU5 of 845 Sqn (XT464, XT473 11-21 Apr; XT450, XT459 from 13 May)

Departed Exercise 'Springtrain' 2 Apr 1982; arrived Ascension 10 Apr; arrived off South Georgia 21 Apr; arrived Ascension 12 May; arrived off Falklands 27 May; arrived Portsmouth 22 Jul 1982. Decommissioned Dec 1991 and scrapped in India.

Royal Maritime Auxiliary Service Ships

RMAS *Typhoon* (A95)
Ocean tug
1,380 tons; launched 14 Oct 1958;
commissioned 1960

Departed Portland 4 Apr 1982; arrived Ascension 20 Apr; arrived South Georgia 27 May; arrived off Falklands 24 Jun; arrived Portsmouth 24 Sep 1982. Placed in reserve 1985 and sold 1989.

Ships Taken Up from Trade

MV *Alvega*
Motor tanker (chartered from Silver Line 1 May 1982 to Mar 1984 for fleet refuelling) 33,329 tons; launched 1977

Departed Portsmouth 5 May 1982; used as a base storage tanker at Ascension and off Falklands; arrived Rosyth 21 Mar 1984.

MV *Anco Charger*
Motor tanker (chartered from Panocean 18 Apr 1982 to Mar 1984 for fleet refuelling duties) 15,568 tons; launched 1973

Departed Fawley 24 Apr 1982; arrived Ascension 5 May; arrived off Falklands 27 Jun; arrived Portsmouth 16 Aug 1982.

MV *Astronomer*
Motor container ship (requisitioned from the Harrison Line 28 May to Dec 1982 as a helicopter carrier and repair ship) 27,867 tons; launched 1977

Chinook HC1 of 18 Sqn (ZA714 8-16 Jun; ZA717 8-29 Jun; ZA720 8-27 Jun), Scout AH1 of 656 Sqn (XP907, XR629, XV141 all 8-27 Jun), Wessex HU5 of 845 Sqn (XS491, XS506, XS523, XT451, XT456, XT460, XT466, XT475, XT481, XT482, XT759 all 6 Nov to 3 Dec), Wessex HU5 of 848 Sqn (XS481, XS498, XS522, XT463, XT467, XT481 all 7-27 Jun) 2 x 20mm guns

Departed Devonport 8 Jun 1982; arrived Ascension 16 Jun; arrived off Falklands 26 Jun; arrived Devonport 3 Dec 1982. Rechartered by the MoD for two years as a helicopter carrier/support ship; commissioned 16 Nov 1983 as RFA *Reliant* (A131), served off Lebanon and Falklands Islands; decommissioned on return to UK and sold 27 May 1986.

SS *Atlantic Causeway*
Steam ro-ro container ship (requisitioned from Cunard/ACL 3 May to Aug 1982 for use in the helicopter support role) 14,946 tons; launched 1969

Lynx HAS2 (XZ729 11 Jun to 27 Jul), Sea King HAS2A of 825 Sqn (XV656, XV659, XV696, XV700 all 13-29 May; XV654, XV663, XV714, XZ580 all 13 May to 1 Jun; XV648, XV654, XV656, XV659, XV663, XV677, XV700, XV714, XZ580 all 13-27 Jul), Sea King HAS5 of 826 Sqn (XZ578 6-10 Jun; ZA129 6-9 Jun), Wessex HU5 of 845 Sqn (XT449, XT459, XT461 all 12-27 Jul), Wessex HU5 of 847 Sqn (XS479, XS488, XS506, XS514, XS515, XS516, XS518, XT466, XT469, XT472, XT475, XT480, XT755, XT757, XT759, XT766, XT773 all 13 May to 1 Jun; XS507 13 May to 16 Jun; XT471 13 May to 3 Jun;

XT486 13 May to 10 Jun; XS479, XS488, XS514, XS515, XS518, XT469, XT472, XT480, XT486, XT757, XT766 all 12-27 Jul), Wessex HU5 of 848 Sqn (XT468 3 Jun to 27 Jul; XS486 10-27 Jul; XS498, XS522, XT463 all 12-27 Jul)

Departed Devonport 14 May 1982; arrived Ascension 22 May; arrived off Falklands 29 May; arrived Devonport 27 Jul 1982.

SS *Atlantic Conveyor*
Steam ro-ro container ship (requisitioned from Cunard/ACL 14 Apr for use in the aircraft and helicopter support role) 14,946 tons; launched 1970

Chinook HC1 of 18 Sqn (ZA706, ZA716, ZA718, ZA719 all 25 Apr to 25 May; ZA707 25 Apr to 5 May), Harrier GR3 of 1 Sqn (XV789, XZ972, XZ988, XZ997 all 6-18 May; XZ963 6-19 May; XZ989 6-20 May), Lynx HAS2 of 815 Sqn (XZ700 20-25 May), Sea Harrier FRS1 (XZ499, ZA176, ZA177, ZA190, ZA194 all 6-18 May; XZ458, XZ491, ZA174 all 6-19 May), Wessex HU5 of 845 Sqn (XT468 20-25 May; XT765 19-21 May), Wessex HU5 of 848 Sqn (XS480, XS495, XS499, XS512, XT476, XT483 all 24 Apr to 25 May)

Departed Devonport 25 Apr 1982; arrived Ascension 5 May; arrived off Falklands 18 May; damaged by Exocet 90 miles northeast of the Falklands 25 May; broke up and sank while under tow 30 May 1982 (rear section sunk by naval gunfire).

MV *Avelona Star*
Motor refrigerated cargo ship (chartered from Blue Star Line 28 May 1982 to May 1984 for transporting food and provisions) 9,784 tons; launched 1975

Departed Portsmouth 10 Jun 1982; arrived Ascension 19 Jun; arrived off Falklands 1 July; arrived Portsmouth 29 Nov 1982.

MV *Balder London*
Motor tanker (chartered from Lloyds Industrial Leasing 12 May to Aug 1982 for fleet refuelling duties) 19,976 tons; launched 1976

Departed Portsmouth 12 May 1982; arrived off Falklands mid-Jun; arrived Plymouth 15 Aug 1982. Chartered by MoD Mar 1984; commissioned as RFA *Orangeleaf.*

MV *Baltic Ferry*
Motor ro-ro ferry (requisitioned from Townsend Thoresen 1 May 1982 to Apr 1983 for troop and helicopter transport) 6,455 tons; launched 1978

Scout AH1 of 656 Sqn (XV130, XV139, XW282 all 8 May to 1 Jun)

Departed Southampton 9 May 1982; arrived off Falklands 1 Jun; arrived Felixstowe 12 Apr 1983.

MV *British Avon*
Motor tanker (chartered from BP 20 Apr 1982 to Jan 1983 for fleet refuelling) 15,540 tons; launched 1972

Departed Devonport 26 Apr 1982, used to refuel the RFAs in the South Atlantic; arrived Portsmouth 5 Jun 1982; returned to South Atlantic 14 Jun; arrived Rosyth 28 Dec 1982.

MV *British Dart*
Motor tanker (chartered from BP 6 Apr to Jul 1982 for fleet refuelling duties) 15,650 tons; launched 1972

Departed Loch Striven 22 Apr 1982; arrived Ascension 4 May, used to refuel the RFAs in the South Atlantic; arrived Plymouth 2 Jul 1982.

MV *British Enterprise III*
Motor offshore ship (requisitioned from British Underwater Engineering 18 May to 5 Sep 1982 for use as dispatch vessel 1,595 tons; launched 1965

Departed Rosyth 26 May 1982; arrived off Falklands late-Jun; arrived Portsmouth 29 Aug 1982.

MV *British Esk*
Motor tanker (chartered from BP 6 Apr 1982 to 1984 for fleet refuelling duties) 15,644 tons; launched 1973

Departed Portland 11 Apr 1982; arrived off Falklands 14 May; arrived Portsmouth 8 Jun 1982.

MV *British Tamar*
Motor tanker (chartered from BP 6 Apr 1982 to 1984 for fleet refuelling duties) 15,642 tons; launched 1973

Departed Milford Haven 14 Apr 1982; arrived Ascension 28 Apr, used to refuel ships en route to and from the Falklands; arrived Portsmouth 20 Jun 1983.

MV *British Tay*
Motor tanker (chartered from BP 6 Apr 1982 to Jun 1983 for fleet refuelling duties) 15,650 tons; launched 1973

Departed Devonport 9 Apr 1982; arrived Ascension 20 Apr, used to refuel ships en route to and from the Falklands; arrived Portsmouth 24 Jan 1983.

MV *British Test*
Motor tanker (chartered from BP 6 Apr to Jul 1982 for fleet refuelling duties) 15,653 tons; launched 1972

Departed Gibraltar 18 Apr 1982; arrived Ascension 27 Apr, used to refuel ships en route to and from the Falklands; arrived Portsmouth 4 Jul 1982.

MV *British Trent*
Motor tanker (chartered from BP 12 Apr
1982 to Oct 1983 for fleet refuelling)
15,653 tons; launched 1973

Departed Isle of Grain 17 Apr 1982; arrived
Ascension 29 Apr, used to refuel ships en
route to and from the Falklands; arrived at
Portland 5 Jul 1982.

MV *British Wye*
Motor tanker (chartered from BP 20 Apr
1982 to Oct 1982 for fleet refuelling)
15,653 tons; launched 1974

Departed Devonport 25 Apr 1982; arrived
Ascension 5 May; arrived off Falklands mid-
May; damaged by a bomb 29 May; arrived at
Portland 11 Jul 1982.

SS *Canberra*
Turbo-electric cruise liner (requisitioned
from P&O 5 Apr to Jul 1982 for use as a
troop transport)
44,807 tons; launched 1961

Sea King HAS2 of 825 Sqn (XV648, XV677
both 28 May to 2 Jun), Sea King HC4 of 846
Sqn (ZA291 19-25 May; ZA299 6-25 May;
ZA311 23 Jun to 10 Jul)

Departed Southampton 9 Apr 1982; arrived
Ascension 20 Apr; arrived off Falklands 18
May; arrived off South Georgia 27 May;
arrived off Falklands 1 Jun; arrived Southampton 11 Jul 1982.

MV *Contender Bezant*
Motor ro-ro container ship (chartered from
Sea Containers 12 May to Sep 1982 for
aircraft and helicopter transport)
11,445 tons; launched 1981

Chinook HC1 of 18 Sqn (ZA705 21 May to
14 Jun; ZA707 3-14 Jun; ZA713, ZA715 both
20 May to 18 Jun), Gazelle AH1 of
3 CBAS (XW893 3-18 Jun; XX444
28 May to 18 Jun), Harrier GR3 of
1 Sqn (XV762, XW767, XW924, XZ129 all
3 Jun to 6 Jul; XW919 13 Jul to
1 Aug), Sea King HAS2 of 706 Sqn (XZ579
20 May to 13 Jul), Wasp HAS1 of 829 Sqn
(XS562, XT427 both 20 May to
1 Aug), Wessex HU5 of 847 Sqn (XT773
2-23 Sep), Wessex HU5 of 848 Sqn (XS481,
XT467 both 2-23 Sep 1982)

Departed Devonport 21 May 1982; arrived
Ascension 31 May; arrived off Falklands 10
Jun; arrived Southampton 1 Aug 1982.
Purchased by the MoD 1 Mar 1984 and com-
missioned as RFA *Argus* (A135). Still in ser-
vice with RFA in 2002.

MV *Eburna*
Motor tanker (chartered from Shell (UK)
13 Apr to Aug 1982 for fleet refuelling)
19,763 tons; launched 1979

Departed St Anna Bay, WI 8 May 1982;
arrived in the South Atlantic 8 May; arrived
Rosyth 31 Jul 1982.

MV *Elk*
Motor ro-ro cargo ship (requisitioned from
P&O 5 Apr to 12 Aug 1982 for use as
aircraft and ordnance transport)
5,463 tons; launched 1977

Gazelle AH1 of 3 CBAS (XX376, XX380,
XX412, XX413, XZ326, ZA776 all 23 Jun
to 12 Jul), Scout AH1 of 656 Sqn/3 CBAS
(XR628, XT629, XT637, XT649 all 11-17
May; XP902, XR627, XR628, XV140, XW615,
XW616 all 23 Jun to 12 Jul), Sea King HC4
of 846 Sqn (ZA291 28 Apr to 14 May; ZA295,
ZA312 both 28 Apr to 19 May)
2 x 40mm guns

Departed Southampton 9 Apr 1982; arrived
Ascension 20 Apr; arrived off Falklands
19 May; arrived Devonport 12 Jul 1982.

MV *Europic Ferry*
Motor ro-ro ferry (requisitioned from
Townsend Thoresen 19 Apr to Jul 1982 for
use as a troop transport)
4,190 tons; launched 1968

Scout AH1 of 656 Sqn/3 CBAS (XR627 from
11 May to 23 Jun; XR628, XT637, XT649
22 Apr to 26 May; XT629 17-20 May), Sea
King HC4 of 846 Sqn (ZA299 25-26 May)

Departed Portland 25 Apr 1982; arrived
Ascension 7 May; arrived off Falklands 16
May; arrived Southampton 17 Jul 1982.

MV *Fort Toronto*
Motor tanker (chartered from Canadian
Pacific 7 Apr 1982 to Apr 1984 as a water
supply tanker)
19,982 tons; launched 1981

Departed Southampton 19 Apr 1982; arrived
Ascension 19 Apr; arrived off Falklands
mid-May; returned to the UK Apr 1984.

MV *G A Walker*
Motor tanker (chartered from Canadian
Pacific 20 Aprl 1982 to Sep 1984 as a
support and base tanker)
18,744 tons; launched 1973

Departed Devonport 10 Jun 1982; arrived at
Port Stanley for support service as a base
fuel tanker Jun 1982; arrived Portsmouth 27
Sep 1984.

MV *Geestport*
Motor refrigerated cargo ship (requisitioned
from Geest Line 7 May to Aug 1982 for use
as a food and provisions transport)
7,730 tons; launched 1982

Departed Portsmouth 21 May 1982; arrived
South Georgia 21 May; arrived off Falklands
21 Jun; arrived Portsmouth 19 Aug 1982.

CS *Iris*
Motor cable ship (requisitioned from BT
24 Apr to Dec 1982)
3,874 tons; launched 1976

Departed Devonport 29 Apr 1982; arrived
South Georgia 25 May; arrived off Falklands
30 May; arrived Southampton 30 Nov 1982.

MV *Irishman*
Motor tug (requisitioned from United
Towing 7 Apr to Nov 1982 as a tug)
686 tons; launched 1978

Departed Portsmouth 10 Apr 1982; arrived
Ascension 24 Apr; arrived off Falklands 24
May; arrived Hull 29 Oct 1982.

MV *Laertes*
Motor cargo ship (requisitioned from China
Mutual Steamship Co, 28 May to Sep 1982
for use as ammunition transport)
11,804 tons; launched 1976

Departed Devonport 8 Jun 1982; arrived
Ascension 17 Jun; arrived off Falklands
3 Jul; arrived Plymouth 21 Aug 1982.

MV *Lycaon*
Motor cargo ship (requisitioned from China
Mutual Steamship Co, 26 Apr 1982 to Jul
1983 for use as ammunition transport)
11,804 tons; launched 1976

Departed Southampton 4 May 1982; arrived
South Georgia 28 May; arrived off Falklands
11 Jun; arrived Hull 21 Apr 1983.

MV *Nordic Ferry*
Motor ro-ro ferry (requisitioned from
Townsend Thoresen 1 May to Aug 1982 for
use as a troop and helicopter transport)
6,455 tons; launched 1978

Gazelle AH1 of 656 Sqn (XX377, XX409,
XZ290, XZ314, XZ321, ZA728 8 May to 3 Jun)

Departed Southampton 9 May 1982; arrived
off Falklands 3 Jun; arrived South Georgia
8 Jul; arrived Southampton 29 Jul 1982.

MV *Norland*
Motor ro-ro ferry (requisitioned from P&O
North Sea Ferries 16 Apr 1982 to Feb 1983
for use as a troop transport)
12,988 tons; launched 1974

Sea King HC4 of 846 Sqn (ZA291 21-23
May; ZA295 19-20 May; ZA313 20-23 May)

Departed Portsmouth 26 Apr 1982; arrived
Ascension 7 May; arrived off the Falklands
20 May; arrived South Georgia 27 May;
arrived Falklands 1 Jun, thereafter shuttled
between Ascension and the Falklands conducting troop transport operations; arrived
Hull 31 Jan 1983.

RMS *Queen Elizabeth II*
Steam passenger liner
(requisitioned from Cunard 3 May to
11 Jun 1982 for use a troop transport)
67,140 tons; launched 1968

Sea King HAS2A of 825 Sqn
(XV648, XV677 both 12-28 May)

Departed Southampton 12 May 1982; arrived
South Georgia 27 May; arrived Southampton 11 Jun 1982.

MV *St Edmund*
Motor ro-ro ferry (requisitioned from
British Rail Sealink UK from 12 May 1982 as
a troop transport until purchased by MoD)
8,987 tons; launched 1973

Departed Devonport 19 May 1982; arrived
off Falklands 15 Jun; arrived Southampton
25 Feb 1983. Purchased by MoD 16 Feb 1983
and commissioned briefly as HMS *Keren*
1 Apr 1983 as the result of a Merchant Navy
manning dispute. Sold and later renamed
Scirocco 1985.

RMS *St Helena*
Motor cargo vessel (requisitioned from
Curnow Shipping 22 May 1982 to Jun 1983
as a minesweeper support vessel)
3,150 tons; launched 1963

Wasp HAS1 of 829 Sqn
(XT795 11 June to 13 September)
2 x 20mm guns

Departed Portland 13 Jun 1982; arrived off
Falklands 10 Jul; arrived Rosyth 16 Sep 1982.

MT *Salvageman*
Motor tug (requisitioned from United
Towing 6 Apr 1982 to 22 Jun 1984)
1,598 tons; launched 1980

Departed Portsmouth 10 Apr 1982; arrived
Ascension 23 Apr; arrived South Georgia
7 May; arrived off Falklands 19 Jul; arrived
Hull 22 Jun 1984. Subsequently renamed
Anglian Prince.

MV *Saxonia*
Motor refrigerated cargo ship (chartered
from Cunard 28 Apr to Nov 1982 for use as
a food and provisions transport)
12,029 tons; launched 1972

Departed Devonport 8 May 1982; arrived
South Georgia 23 May; arrived Portsmouth
28 Jun 1982.

MV *Scottish Eagle*
Motor tanker (chartered from King Line
12 May 1982 to Oct 1983 as a base fuel
tanker)
32,995 tons; launched 1980

Departed Milford Haven Oil Refinery Terminal
24 May 1982; arrived South Georgia 18 Jun;
arrived off the Falklands 14 Jul; arrived Plymouth 23 Oct 1983.

MV *Stena Inspector*
Diesel-electric offshore support vessel
(chartered from Stena Caribbean 25 May
1982 to Nov 1983)
6,061 tons; launched 1980

Departed Charleston, North Carolina 6 Jun
1982; arrived Ascension 21 Jun; arrived off
Falklands early Jul; arrived Glasgow 13 Nov
1983. Purchased by the Ministry of Defence
Oct 1983; commissioned as RFA *Diligence*
(A132) 12 Mar 1984. Still in service with RFA
in 2002.

MV *Stena Seaspread*
Diesel-electric offshore support vessel
(requisitioned from Stena Atlantic 8 Apr
1982 to Feb 1983)
6,061 tons; launched 1980

Departed Portsmouth 16 Apr 1982; arrived
Ascension 28 Apr; arrived South Georgia
16 May; arrived off Falklands 17 Jun; arrived
Portsmouth 18 Aug 1982.

MV *Tor Caledonia*
Motor ro-ro cargo vessel (requisitioned
from Tor Line 18 May to Sep 1982 as a
transport)
5,056 tons; launched 1977

Gazelle AH1 of 656 Sqn (XX409, XX444,
XZ314 all 1-20 Aug; ZA728 29 Jul to
20 Aug), Scout AH1 of 'B' Flt 3 CBAS
(XT649, XV130 both 29 Jul to 20 Aug)

Departed Southampton 20 May 1982;
arrived Ascension 31 May; arrived off Falklands 12 Jun; arrived Portsmouth 19 Aug
1982.

SS *Uganda*
Steam cruise liner (requisitioned from P&O
10 Apr to Aug 1982 as a hospital ship)
16,907 tons; launched 1952

Departed Gibraltar 19 Apr 1982; arrived
Ascension 28 Apr; arrived off Falklands 11
May; arrived Southampton 9 Aug 1982.

MV *Wimpey Seahorse*
Motor offshore support vessel/tug
(requisitioned from Wimpey Marine 4 May
to Sep 1982 as a mooring ship)
1,599 tons; launched 1982

Departed Devonport 16 May 1982; arrived
Ascension 29 May; arrived South Georgia
8 Jun; arrived at Falklands 22 Jul; arrived
Portsmouth 4 Sep 1982.

MT *Yorkshireman*
Motor tug (requisitioned from United
Towing 7 Apr 1982 to Jul 1983 as a tug)
686 tons; launched 1978

Departed Portsmouth 13 Apr 1982; arrived
Ascension 27 Apr; arrived off Falklands 24
May; arrived Hull 23 Jul 1983.

STUFT Commissioned for Royal Navy Service

HMS *Cordella*
Motor freezer trawler *Cordella*
(requisitioned, converted as minesweeper)
1,238 tons; launched 1973; commissioned
26 Apr 1982

Departed Portland 27 Apr 1982; arrived
Ascension 11 May; arrived South Georgia 27
May; arrived Falklands 21 Jun; arrived
Rosyth 11 Aug 1982; decommissioned and
returned to J Marr and Son. Chartered Jan
1993 and used as a fishery patrol ship
around the Falkland Islands until 1998.

HMS *Farnella*
Motor freezer trawler *Farnella*
(requisitioned, converted as minesweeper)
1,207 tons; launched 1972; commissioned
26 Apr 1982

Departed Portland 27 Apr 1982; arrived
Ascension 11 May; arrived South Georgia 27
May; arrived Falklands 21 Jun; arrived
Rosyth 11 Aug 1982; decommissioned and
returned to J Marr and Son; renamed MV
Northern Prince 1994.

HMS *Junella*
Motor fish factory trawler *Junella*
(requisitioned, converted as minesweeper)
1,615 tons; launched 1975; commissioned
26 Apr 1982

Departed Portland 27 Apr 1982; arrived
Ascension 11 May; arrived South Georgia 27
May; arrived Falklands 21 Jun; arrived
Rosyth 11 Aug 1982; decommissioned and
returned to J Marr and Son.

HMS *Northella*
Motor freezer trawler *Northella*
(requisitioned, converted as minesweeper)
1,238 tons; launched 1973; commissioned
26 Apr 1982

Departed Portland 27 Apr 1982; arrived
Ascension 11 May; arrived South Georgia 27
May; arrived Falklands 21 Jun; arrived
Rosyth 11 Aug 1982; decommissioned and
returned to J Marr and Son. Chartered by
the RN Oct 1983 and used as a navigation
training ship from 1985 to 1999.

HMS *Pict*
Motor freezer trawler *Pict* (requisitioned,
converted as minesweeper)
1,478 tons; launched 1973; commissioned
26 Apr 1982

Departed Portland 27 Apr 1982; arrived
Ascension 11 May; arrived South Georgia 27
May; arrived Falklands 15 Jun; arrived
Rosyth 11 Aug 1982; decommissioned and
returned to British United Trawlers.

Appendix Six

Participation of Individual Argentine Ships in the Conflict

Alferez Sobral (A9)
Sotoyomo class patrol vessel (ex Maricopa class auxiliary tug USS *Catawba*)
800 tons; launched 15 Feb 1945; commissioned (Argentine Navy) Feb 1972

2 x 20mm and 1 x 40mm guns

Used for SAR duties; damaged by Sea Skua missiles 3 May 1982; subsequently repaired and survived the conflict. Still in service.

Almirante Irizar (Q5)
Polar vessel
11,811 tons; launched 3 Feb 1978; commissioned 15 Dec 1978
1 x Puma
2 x 40mm guns

Took part in Operation 'Rosario'; later converted to hospital ship; survived the conflict. Still in service.

Bahia Buen Suceso (B6)
Fleet transport
5,000 tons; launched 1950; commissioned Jun 1950

Took scrap merchants to South Georgia 19 Mar 1982; blockade-running to Falklands; damaged by Sea Harriers 16 May at Fox Bay East; captured 15 Jun 1982; towed out to sea and sunk 21 Oct 1982.

Bahia Paraiso (Q6)
Polar transport
9,600 tons; launched 3 Jul 1980; commissioned 10 Jul 1981

1 x Puma, 1 x Alouette III

Took part in invasion of South Georgia Mar 1982; converted to hospital ship; took part in search for survivors of *General Belgrano*; survived the conflict. Sank near Palmer Station in the Antarctic 28 Jan 1989 with the loss of two Sea Kings.

Cabo San Antonio (Q42)
Modified DeSoto class landing ship (tank): 8,000 tons; launched 1968 but completion delayed; commissioned 2 Nov 1978

12 x 40mm and 2 x 20mm guns

Took part in Operation 'Rosario'; then resupplied the Falklands; survived the conflict. Decommissioned 1997.

Comodoro Py (D27)
Gearing class destroyer (ex USS *Perkins III*)
3,500 tons; launched 7 Dec 1944; commissioned (US Navy) 5 Apr 1945; sold to Argentine Navy 15 Jan 1973

4 x Exocet SSM launchers; 4 5-inch guns; 2 x ASW mortars; torpedoes

Took part in Operation 'Rosario'; sailed with Task Force 79 Apr 1982; survived the conflict. Decommissioned, scrapped 1984.

Comodoro Somellara (A10)
Sotoyomo class patrol vessel (ex Maricopa class auxiliary tug USS *Salish*)
800 tons; launched 29 Sep 1944; commissioned (Argentine Navy) Feb 1972

2 x 20mm and 1 x 40mm guns

Used for rescue duties; survived the conflict. Still in service.

Drummond (P1)
A69 class frigate (ex South African Navy *Good Hope* and French Navy *Lt de Vaisseau de Henaff*)
1,170 tons; launched 5 Mar 1977; commissioned (Argentine Navy) 2 Nov 1978

4 x Exocet SSM launchers; 1 x 3.9-inch, 1 x 40mm and 2 x 20mm guns; torpedoes

Took part in Operation 'Rosario'; sailed with Task Force 79 in Apr/May 1982; survived the conflict. Still in service.

Formosa
Requisitioned cargo vessel
12,762 tons; launched 1978

Used for resupply tasks; survived the conflict.

Forrest
Requisitioned cargo vessel
144 tons; launched 1967

Falkland Islands Government vessel commandeered for transport around the islands; attacked by Lynx from *Alacrity* 1 May 1982 near Kidney Island; captured 14 Jun 1982.

Francisco de Gurruchaga (A3)
Cherokee class patrol vessel
(ex USS *Luiseno*) used as a tug
1,675 tons; launched 17 Mar 1945; commissioned (Argentine Navy) 1 Jul 1975

6 x 40mm guns

Searched for survivors from *General Belgrano*; survived the conflict. Still in service.

General Belgrano (C1)
Brooklyn class cruiser (ex USS *Phoenix*)
13,645 tons; launched 12 Mar 1938; commissioned (Argentine Navy) as *17 de Octubre* 17 Oct 1951; renamed *General Belgrano* 1956

1 x Alouette III
2 x Seacat SAM launchers; 15 x 6-inch, 8 x 5-inch, 20 x 40mm and 2 x 20mm guns

Sailed with Task Force 79 in Apr/May 1982; sunk by *Conqueror* 2 May 1982.

Granville (P3)
A69 class frigate
1,170 tons; launched 28 Jun 1980; commissioned 22 Jun 1981

4 x Exocet SSM launchers; 1 x 3.9-inch, 1 x 40mm and 2 x 20mm guns; torpedoes

Took part in Operation 'Rosario'; sailed with Task Force 79 in Apr/May 1982; survived the conflict. Still in service.

Guerrico (P2)
A69 class frigate (ex South African Navy *Transvaal* and French Navy *Commandant L'Herminier*)
1,170 tons; launched 13 Sep 1977; commissioned (Argentine Navy) 2 Nov 1978

4 x Exocet SSM launchers; 1 x 3.9-inch, 1 x 40mm and 2 x 20mm guns; torpedoes

Took part in invasion of South Georgia, damaged 3 Apr 1982; repaired and sailed with Task Force 79 in Apr/May 1982; survived the conflict. Still in service.

Hercules (D1)
Type 42 class destroyer
4,100 tons; launched 24 Oct 1972; commissioned 12 Jul 1976

1 x Lynx
4 x Exocet SSM launchers; 1 x Sea Dart SAM launcher; 1 x 4.5-inch and 2 x 20mm guns; torpedoes

Took part in Operation 'Rosario'; sailed with Task Force 79 in Apr/May 1982; survived the conflict. Still in service.

Hipolito Bouchard (D26)
Allen M Sumner class destroyer
(ex USS *Borie*)
3,320 tons; launched 4 Jul 1944;
commissioned (US Navy) 21 Sep 1944;
sold to Argentine Navy 1 Jul 1972

4 x Exocet SSM launchers; 4 x 5-inch guns;
2 x ASW mortars; torpedoes

Took part in Operation 'Rosario'; sailed with
Task Force 79 in Apr/May 1982; survived the
conflict. Decommissioned, scrapped 1984.

Isla de los Estados (B8)
Fleet transport
2,684 tons; launched 1975; commissioned
22 Dec 1980

Took part in Operation 'Rosario'; sunk by
Alacrity in Falkland Sound 11 May 1982.

Islas Malvinas (GC82)
Prefectura Naval Argentina Z-28 Type
patrol craft
81 tons; launched 1981; commissioned 1981

2 x 20mm guns

Arrived at Port Stanley early Apr 1982;
damaged by Lynx from *Alacrity* 1 May 1982
near Kidney Island; captured at Port Stanley
14 Jun 1982; renamed 'HMS *Tiger Bay*' and
used by British forces.

Monsunen
Requisitioned cargo vessel
230 tons; launched 1957

Commandeered Falkland Islands Company
vessel; forced aground by *Brilliant* and
Yarmouth 23 May 1982 in Lively Sound;
towed to Darwin, captured by British forces.

Narwal
Requisitioned stern freezer trawler
2,480 tons; launched 1968

Used for intelligence gathering within TEZ
from c.22 Apr 1982; damaged by Sea Harriers 9 May about 60 miles southeast of Port
Stanley and captured; sank 10 May 1982.

Piedra Buena (D29)
Allen M Sumner class destroyer
(ex USS *Collett*)
3,320 tons; launched 5 Mar 1944;
commissioned (US Navy) 16 May 1944;
sold to Argentine Navy Apr 1974

4 x Exocet SSM launchers; 4 x 5-inch guns;
2 x ASW mortars; torpedoes

Took part in Operation 'Rosario'; sailed
with Task Force 79 in Apr/May 1982; survived the conflict. Decommissioned 18 Feb
1985; sunk as a target Nov 1988.

Punta Medanos (B18)
Fleet support tanker
16,331 tons; launched 20 Feb 1950;
commissioned 10 Oct 1950

Took part in Operation 'Rosario'; sailed
with Task Force 79 in Apr/May 1982; survived the conflict. Decommissioned 1987.

Rio Carcarana
Requisitioned cargo vessel
8,500 tons; launched 1962

Used as a blockade-runner; damaged by
Sea Harriers in Port King 16 May 1982; further damaged in subsequent British and
Argentine air raids; sunk by Sea Skuas fired
by *Antelope's* Lynx 23 May 1982.

Rio de la Plata
Requisitioned cargo vessel
10,409 tons; launched 1971

Observed British shipping and aircraft
movements at Ascension until warned off
24 Apr 1982; survived the conflict.

Rio Iguazu (GC83)
Prefectura Naval Argentina Z-28 Type
patrol craft
81 tons; launched 1981; commissioned 1981

1 x 20mm gun

Arrived at Port Stanley early Apr 1982, used
for transport duties and coastal patrols;
damaged by Sea Harriers 22 May in
Choiseul Sound and beached at Button
Bay; captured by British forces but attacked
by Lynx/Sea Skua 13 Jun 1982; wreck taken
to Goose Green after the conflict.

Salta (S31)
Salta class patrol submarine
1,440 tons; launched 9 Nov 1972;
commissioned 7 Mar 1974

21-inch torpedoes

Thought to have been on patrol to north of
Falkland Islands from mid-Apr 1982;
returned to port and took no further part in
the conflict. Still in service.

San Luis (S32)
Salta class patrol submarine
1,440 tons; launched 3 Apr 1973;
commissioned 24 May 1974

21-inch torpedoes

On patrol to north of Falkland Islands from
mid-Apr 1982; made several unsuccessful
torpedo attacks on British warships;
returned to port mid-May 1982; survived the
conflict. Placed in reserve 1996.

Santa Fe (S21)
Balao class patrol submarine
(ex USS *Catfish*)
2,430 tons; launched 19 Nov 1944;
commissioned (US Navy) 19 Mar 1945;
sold to Argentine Navy Jan 1971

21-inch torpedoes

Took part in Operation 'Rosario'; delivered
reinforcements to South Georgia 24 Apr

1982; damaged by helicopters 25 Apr 1982
and berthed at Grytviken where it sank
Wreck raised and towed out to sea and
sunk off Cumberland Bay 20 Feb 1985.

Santiago del Estero (S22)
Balao class patrol submarine
(ex USS *Chivo*)
2,430 tons; launched 14 Jan 1945;
commissioned in US Navy 28 Apr 1945;
sold to Argentine Navy Jan 1971

21-inch torpedoes

Paid off in September 1981; scrapped 1983.

Santisima Trinidad (D2)
Type 42 class destroyer
4,100 tons; launched 9 Nov 1974;
commissioned Jul 1981

1 x Lynx
4 x Exocet SSM launchers; 1 x Sea Dart
SAM launcher; 1 x 4.5-inch and 2 x 20mm
guns; torpedoes

Took part in Operation 'Rosario'; sailed
with Task Force 79 in Apr/May 1982; survived the conflict. Still in service.

Segui (D25)
Allen M Sumner class destroyer
(ex USS *Hank*)
3,320 tons; launched 21 May 1944;
commissioned (US Navy) 28 Aug 1944;
sold to Argentine Navy 1 Jul 1972

4 x Exocet SSM launchers; 4 x 5-inch guns;
2 x ASW mortars; torpedoes

Took part in Operation 'Rosario'; sailed
with Task Force 79 in Apr/May 1982; later
used as a radar picket; survived the conflict
Decommissioned and scrapped 1983.

25 de Mayo (V2)
Colossus class aircraft carrier
(ex HMS *Venerable*)
19,896 tons; launched 30 Dec 1943;
commissioned (Royal Navy) 17 Jan 1945;
sold to Royal Netherlands Navy as *Karel
Doorman* 1 Apr 1948; sold to Argentine
Navy 15 Oct 1968; commissioned 12 Mar
1969

8 x A-4Q Skyhawk; 4 x S-2E Tracker;
3 x Sea King
9 x 40mm guns

Took part in Operation 'Rosario'; flagship of
Task Force 79 until returned to port c.4 May
1982; survived the conflict. Non-operational
since 1985; finally decommissioned 1997
and scrapped in India 1999.

Yehuin
Requisitioned oil rig tender (ex *Millentor*)
494 tons; launched 1967

Arrived at Port Stanley for inter-island transport; captured 15 Jun 1982 and renamed
Falkland Sound.

Appendix Seven

Chronology of Aircraft Losses

3rd April
CAB601 Puma AE-504
Shot down at Grytviken, South Georgia by
Royal Marines small arms fire.

22nd April
'C' Flight 845 Squadron Wessex HU5s
XT464 and XT473
Crashed on Fortuna Glacier, South Georgia
in bad weather.

23rd April
846 Squadron Sea King HC4 ZA311
Crashed in South Atlantic in bad weather.

1st May
FIGAS Islander VP-FAY
Destroyed at Stanley airport by Sea Harrier
FRS1s (bombs) of 800 Squadron.
Damaged in this raid and damaged beyond
repair in subsequent raids were Cessna
172s VP-FAR (Mr R Pitaluga), VP-FAS
(Chartres Sheep Farming Company) and
VP-FBA (Governor of the Falkland Islands).

Grupo 3 Pucara A-527
Destroyed at Goose Green by Sea Harrier
FRS1s (CBUs) of 800 Squadron.
Damaged in this raid, damaged beyond
repair in subsequent raids and captured on
14 June were Pucaras A-506 and A-517.

Grupo 8 Mirage IIIEA I-015
Shot down close to Pebble Island by Sea

Harrier FRS1 (Sidewinder) of 801 Squadron
(Flt Lt P Barton).

Grupo 8 Mirage IIIEA I-019
Damaged by Sea Harrier FRS1
(Sidewinder) of 801 Squadron (Lt S
Thomas) and then shot down in error by
Argentine AAA as it tried to land at Stanley
airport.

Grupo 6 Dagger A C-433
Shot down near Lively Island by Sea Harrier
FRS1 (Sidewinder) of 800 Squadron
(Flt Lt R Penfold).

Grupo 2 Canberra B62 B-110
Shot down off north coast of Falklands by
Sea Harrier FRS1 (Sidewinder) of 800
Squadron (Lt W A Curtis).

2nd May
1 Escuadrilla de Helicopteros Alouette III
0649
Lost in the sinking of the *General Belgrano*
southwest of the Falklands.

1 Escuadrilla de Helicopteros Lynx HAS23
0735
Crashed into the *Santisima Trinidad*.

3rd May
1 Escuadrilla de Ataque MB-339A 0764
Crashed at Stanley airport while landing in
bad weather.

4th May
800 Squadron Sea Harrier FRS1 XZ450
Shot down at Goose Green by AAA.

6th May
801 Squadron Sea Harrier FRS1s XZ452 and
XZ453
Missing (probably collided) during CAP
southeast of East Falkland.

9th May
Grupo 4 A-4C Skyhawks C-303 and C-313
Lost during aborted raid on shipping off the
north coast of the Falklands; the wreck of
C-313 was subsequently found on South
Jason Island.

CAB601 Puma AE-505
Shot down over Choiseul Sound by Sea Dart
fired by *Coventry*.

12th May
826 Squadron Sea King HAS5 ZA132
Crashed in sea east of the Falklands due to
engine failure.

Grupo 5 A-4B Skyhawks C-206, C-208 and
C-246
C-208 and C-246 shot down off Stanley by
Seawolf fired by *Brilliant*; C-206 crashed
into sea while evading Seawolf.

Grupo 5 A-4B Skyhawk C-248
Shot down at Goose Green in error by
Argentine AAA.

15th May
Grupo 3 Pucaras A-502, A-520, A-523, A-529,
A-552 and A-556
4 Escuadrilla de Ataque T-34C-1 Turbo Mentors 0719, 0726, 0729 and 0730
Prefectura Naval Skyvan 3M PA-50
All destroyed or damaged on the ground
during the SAS raid on Pebble Island and
subsequently captured.

*The remains of Pucara A-527 were still present
on Goose Green airstrip in May 1984, two
years after it had been destroyed by Sea
Harrier FRS1s during the raid on 1st May 1982.
This is the aircraft in which Primer Teniente
Antonio Jukic was killed when it was hit by a
cluster bomb. MoD*

The shadow of an RAF Chinook HC1 carrying two underslung loads passes over the wreckage of Argentine Army Chinook AE-521 that was destroyed on the ground near Mount Kent by a Harrier GR3 on 21st May 1982. It is the destruction of this Chinook that forms the subject of the front cover painting by artist Keith Maddison. MoD

18th May
826 Squadron Sea King HAS5 XZ573
Crashed in sea east of the Falklands due to altimeter failure.

19th May
846 Squadron Sea King HC4 ZA290
Force-landed near Punta Arenas, Chile; destroyed by its crew while on special op.

846 Squadron Sea King HC4 ZA294
Crashed in sea east of the Falklands probably due to a bird strike.

21st May
'C' Flight 3 CBAS Gazelle AH1s XX402 and XX411
Shot down near Port San Carlos by small arms fire.

CAB601 Chinook AE-521
Destroyed on ground near Mount Kent by Harrier GR3 (30mm cannon) of 1 Squadron (Flt Lt M Hare)
Puma AE-501 was disabled during this raid and subsequently destroyed on 26 May.

1 Squadron Harrier GR3 XZ972
Shot down near Port Howard by Blowpipe.

Grupo 3 Pucara A-531
Shot down near Flats Shanty Settlement by Stinger fired by SAS.

Grupo 6 Dagger A C-428
Shot down in Falkland Sound by Seawolf fired by *Broadsword*.

Grupo 3 Pucara A-511
Shot down near Drone Hill by Sea Harrier FRS1 (30mm cannon) of 801 Squadron (Lt Cdr N D Ward).

Grupo 4 A-4C Skyhawk C-309
Shot down near Chartres Settlement by Sea Harrier FRS1 (Sidewinder) of 800 Squadron (Lt Cdr N Thomas).

Grupo 4 A-4C Skyhawk C-325
Shot down near Chartres Settlement by Sea Harrier FRS1 (Sidewinder) of 800 Squadron (Lt Cdr M Blissett).

Grupo 6 Dagger A C-409
Shot down near Mount Maria by Sea Harrier FRS1 (Sidewinder) of 800 Squadron (Lt Cdr R Fredericksen).

815 Squadron Lynx HAS2 XZ251
Lost when *Ardent* was bombed and sunk in Falkland Sound.

Grupo 6 Dagger As C-403 and C-404
Shot down near Port Howard by Sea Harrier FRS1 (Sidewinder) of 801 Squadron (Lt S Thomas).

Grupo 6 Dagger A C-407
Shot down near Port Howard by Sea Harrier FRS1 (Sidewinder) of 801 Squadron (Lt Cdr N D Ward).

A-4Q Skyhawk 0660
Shot down over Falkland Sound by Sea Harrier FRS1 (Sidewinder) of 800 Squadron (Lt C Morrell).

A-4Q Skyhawk 0665
Damaged over Falkland Sound by Sea Harrier FRS1 (30mm cannon) of 800 Squadron (Lt C Morrell) and brought down by Argentine AAA at Stanley after pilot ejected.

A-4Q Skyhawk 0667
Shot down over Falkland Sound by Sea Harrier FRS1 (30mm cannon) of 800 Squadron (Flt Lt J Leeming).

23rd May
CAB601 Puma AE-503
Crashed near Shag House Cove during attack by Sea Harrier FRS1s of 800 Squadron.

CAB601 A-109A AE-337
Destroyed on ground near Shag House Cove by Sea Harrier FRS1s (30mm cannon) of 800 Squadron.

CAB601 Puma AE-500
Destroyed on ground near Shag House Cove by Sea Harrier FRS1s (30mm cannon) of 800 and 801 Squadrons.

Grupo 5 A-4B Skyhawk C-242
Shot down over San Carlos Water by multiple weapons (SAMs and AAA).

Grupo 6 Dagger A C-437
Shot down near Pebble Island by Sea Harrier FRS1 (Sidewinder) of 800 Squadron (Lt M Hale).

800 Squadron Sea Harrier FRS1 ZA192
Crashed into sea after take-off at night from *Hermes*.

24th May
Grupo 6 Dagger As C-419 and C-430
Shot down near Pebble Island by Sea Harrier FRS1 (Sidewinder) of 800 Squadron (Lt Cdr A Auld).

Grupo 6 Dagger A C-410
Shot down near Pebble Island by Sea Harrier FRS1 (Sidewinder) of 800 Squadron (Lt D Smith).

Grupo 4 A-4C Skyhawk C-305
Damaged over San Carlos Water by SAMs and AAA; crashed in King George Bay.

Grupo 4 Pucara A-540
Crashed at sea during surveillance mission from Comodoro Rivadavia.

25th May
Grupo 4 A-4C Skyhawk C-319
Shot down over San Carlos Water by multiple weapons (SAMs and AAA).

Grupo 4 A-4C Skyhawk C-304
Shot down near Pebble Island by Sea Dart fired by *Coventry*.

Grupo 5 A-4B Skyhawk C-244
Shot down near Pebble Island by Sea Dart fired by *Coventry*.

815 Squadron Lynx HAS2 XZ242
Lost when *Coventry* was bombed and sunk north of Pebble Island.

815 Squadron Lynx HAS2 XZ700
'D' Flight 848 Squadron Wessex HU5s XS480, XS495, XS499, XS512, XT476 and XT483
18 Squadron Chinook HC1s ZA706, ZA716 and ZA719
Lost when the *Atlantic Conveyor* was hit and sunk by an Exocet missile northeast of the Falklands.

26th May

CAB601 Puma AE-501
Destroyed on ground near Mount Kent by Harrier GR3 (CBUs) of 1 Squadron (Sqn Ldr J Pook) having been disabled by Harrier GR3s on 21 May.

27th May

1 Squadron Harrier GR3 XZ988
Shot down near Goose Green by AAA.

Grupo 5 A-4B Skyhawk C-215
Shot down near Ajax Bay by AAA from *Fearless*.

28th May

1 Escuadrilla de Ataque MB-339A 0765
Shot down at Goose Green by Blowpipe.

'B' Flt 3 CBAS Scout AH1 XT629
Shot down near Goose Green by Pucara (Teniente M Gimenez).

Grupo 3 Pucara A-537
Crashed in Blue Mountains near Flats Shanty soon after shooting down Scout AH1 XT629 of 3 CBAS.

Grupo 3 Pucara A-555
Shot down at Goose Green by ground fire.

29th May

Grupo 6 Dagger A C-436
Shot down over San Carlos Water by Rapier.

801 Squadron Sea Harrier FRS1 ZA174
Fell into sea from deck of *Invincible* during rough weather.

30th May

1 Squadron Harrier GR3 XZ963
Damaged near Stanley by small arms fire and abandoned off Falklands.

Grupo 4 A-4C Skyhawks C-301 and C-310
Shot down off East Falklands by Sea Darts fired by *Exeter*.

CAB601 Puma AE-508
Shot down near Murrell Bridge by unidentified SAM.

1st June

Grupo 1 de Transporte Aereo C-130E Hercules TC-63
Shot down north of Pebble Island by a Sea Harrier FRS1 (Sidewinder/30mm cannon) of 801 Squadron (Lt Cdr N D Ward).

801 Squadron Sea Harrier FRS1 XZ456
Shot down in sea off Stanley by Roland .

6th June

Army Air Corps Gazelle AH1 XX377
Shot down near Mount Pleasant Peak by Sea Dart fired by *Cardiff*.

7th June

Grupo 1 de Aerofotografico Learjet 35A T-24
Shot down near Pebble Island by Sea Dart fired by *Exeter*.

8th June

1 Squadron Harrier GR3 XZ989
Crashed on landing at Port San Carlos FOB due to engine failure.

Grupo 5 A-4B Skyhawks C-226 and C-228
Shot down over Choiseul Sound by Sea Harrier FRS1 (Sidewinder) of 800 Squadron (Flt Lt D Morgan).

Grupo 5 A-4B Skyhawk C-204
Shot down over Choiseul Sound by Sea Harrier FRS1 (Sidewinder) of 800 Squadron (Lt D Smith).

11/12th June

FIGAS DHC-2 Beaver VP-FAT
Destroyed by naval gunfire while on slipway outside floatplane hangar at Stanley. Beaver VP-FAV also damaged during the bombardment but deemed repairable until blown over in a gale on 28th July 1982.

12th June

737 Squadron Wessex HAS3 XM837
Destroyed by Exocet missile which hit the hangar of *Glamorgan* off Stanley.

12/13th June

Prefectura Naval Argentina Skyvan 3M PA-54
Destroyed at Stanley racecourse by naval gunfire.

14th June

Grupo 2 Canberra B62 B-108
Shot down near Fitzroy by Sea Dart fired by *Exeter*.

Argentine Aircraft Captured at Stanley by British forces on 14th June:

Argentine Navy
1 Escuadrilla de Ataque MB-339As 0761, 0763 and 0767

Prefectura Naval Argentina
Puma PA-12

CAB601
A-109As AE-331 and AE-334
UH-1Hs AE-406, AE-409, AE-410, AE-412, AE-413, AE-417, AE-418, AE-422 and AE-424
Chinook AE-520

Argentine Air Force
Grupo 3 Pucaras A-509, A-513, A-514, A-515, A-516, A-522, A-528, A-532, A-533, A-536 and A-549
Grupo 7 Bell 212s H-82 and H-85

Bell 212 AE406 is currently on display at the Museum of Army Flying at AAC Middle Wallop. The yellow identification band was 'retouched' with the blue and red of the Royal Electrical and Mechanical Engineers. B Munro

Appendix Eight

Statistics of the Air War

British Aircraft Deployed to the South Atlantic and Ascension Island: 2nd April to 14th June 1982

Royal Navy

Lynx HAS2	24	Sea King HAS5	20
Sea Harrier FRS1	28	Wasp HAS1	11
Sea King HAS2/2A	16	Wessex HAS3	2
Sea King HC4	14	Wessex HU5	54

Royal Marines

Gazelle AH1	11	Scout AH1	7

Army Air Corps

Gazelle AH1	6	Scout AH1	8

Royal Air Force

Chinook HC1	11	Phantom FGR2	3
Harrier GR3	16	Sea King HAR3	1
Nimrod MR1	2	Victor K2	20
Nimrod MR2	8	Vulcan B2	4

Overall total   **266**

Aircraft Lost or Captured: 1st April to 14th June 1982

Royal Navy

Lynx HAS2	3	Sea King HAS5	2
Sea Harrier FRS1	6	Wessex HAS3	1
Sea King HC4	3	Wessex HU5	8

Royal Marines

Gazelle AH1	2	Scout AH1	1

Army Air Corps

		Gazelle AH1	1

Royal Air Force

Chinook HC1	3	Harrier GR3	4

Overall British total   **34**

Argentine Navy

A-4Q Skyhawk	3	MB-339A	5
Alouette III	1	T-34C-1 Turbo Mentor	4
Lynx HAS23	1		

Prefectura Naval

Puma	1	Skyvan 3M	2

Argentine Air Force

A-4B Skyhawk	10	Dagger A	11
A-4C Skyhawk	9	Learjet 35A	1
Bell 212	2	Mirage IIIEA	2
C-130E Hercules	1	Pucara	25
Canberra B62	2		

Argentine Army

A-109A	3	Puma	6
Chinook	2	UH-1H	9

Overall Argentine total   **100**

Number of Sorties Flown by Royal Navy Aircraft
Statistics for Royal Navy aircraft for April, May and June 1982

Type	Flying Hours	Sorties	Deck Landings
Lynx HAS2	2,567	1,728	3,796
Sea Harrier FRS1	2,514	2,197	2,088
Sea King HAS2/2A	2,176	1,380	1,849
Sea King HC4	2,808	1,060	3,343
Sea King HAS5	6,847	2,253	3,421
Wasp HAS1	451	727	3,333
Wessex HAS3	334	213	522
Wessex HU5	4,251	1,571	2,698
Totals	**21,948**	**11,129**	**21,050**

Source: *Flight Deck* No.1, 1983 p2

Task Force Availability of Sea Harrier FRS1 and Harrier GR3

May	1st	2nd	3rd	4th	5th	6th	7th	8th
800 Sqn	12	12	12	12	11	11	11	11
801 Sqn	8	8	8	8	8	8	6	6
1 Sqn	0	0	0	0	0	0	0	0
Totals:	**20**	**20**	**20**	**20**	**19**	**19**	**17**	**17**

	9th	10th	11th	12th	13th	14th	15th	16th
800 Sqn	11	11	11	11	11	11	11	11
801 Sqn	6	6	6	6	6	6	6	6
1 Sqn	0	0	0	0	0	0	0	0
Totals:	**17**	**17**	**17**	**17**	**17**	**17**	**17**	**17**

	17th	18th	19th	20th	21st	22nd	23rd	24th
800 Sqn	11	15	15	15	15	15	15	14
801 Sqn	6	7	10	10	10	10	10	10
1 Sqn	0	4	6	6	6	5	5	5
Totals:	**17**	**26**	**31**	**31**	**31**	**30**	**30**	**29**

	25th	26th	27th	28th	29th	30th	31st	
800 Sqn	14	14	14	14	14	14	14	
801 Sqn	10	10	10	10	10	9	9	
1 Sqn	5	5	5	4	4	4	3	
Totals:	**29**	**29**	**29**	**28**	**28**	**27**	**26**	

June	1st	2nd	3rd	4th	5th	6th	7th	8th
800 Sqn	14	14	14	14	14	14	14	14
801 Sqn	9	8	8	8	8	8	8	8
1 Sqn	5	5	5	5	5	5	5	7
Totals:	**28**	**27**	**27**	**27**	**27**	**27**	**27**	**29**

	9th	10th	11th	12th	13th	14th		
800 Sqn	14	14	14	14	14	14		
801 Sqn	8	8	8	8	8	8		
1 Sqn	6	6	6	6	5	5		
Totals:	**28**	**28**	**28**	**28**	**27**	**27**		

Appendix Eight

Bibliography

Books

1 Squadron: Michael Shaw; Ian Allan, 1986.

The Admiralty Regrets – British Warship Losses of the 20th Century: Paul Kemp; Sutton, 1999.

Air War South Atlantic: Jeffrey Ethell and Alfred Price; Sidgwick and Jackson, 1983.

An American Life – Ronald Reagan, the Autobiography: Ronald Reagan; Arrow, 1991.

Amphibious Assault Falklands – The Battle of San Carlos Water: Michael Clapp and Ewen Southby-Tailyour; Leo Cooper, 1996.

Argentina – The Malvinas and the End of Military Rule: Alejandro Dabat and Luis Lorenzano; Verso Editions, 1984.

The Battle for the Falklands: Max Hastings and Simon Jenkins; Michael Joseph, 1983.

Belfast – The Story of Short's Big Lifter: Molly O'Loughlin White; Midland Counties, 1984.

Britain and the Falklands War: Lawrence Freedman; Basil Blackwell, 1988.

The British Army in the Falklands 1982: Director of Public Relations (Army), 1983.

Call for Fire – Sea Combat in the Falklands and the Gulf War: Captain Chris Craig; John Murray, 1995.

Caveat – The Reminiscences of General Haig: Alexander M Haig; Weidenfeld & Nicolson, 1984.

Despatch By Admiral Sir John Fieldhouse, GCB, GBE, Commander of the Task Force Operations in the South Atlantic: April to June 1982, Supplement to the London Gazette *of Monday, 13th December 1982:* HMSO, 1982.

Domestic Sources of Foreign Policy – Western European Reactions to the Falklands Conflict: Stavridis Stelios & Christopher Hill; Bery, 1996.

The Downing Street Years: Margaret Thatcher; HarperCollins, 1993.

Eyewitness Falklands – A Personal Account of the Falklands Campaign: Robert Fox; Methuen, 1982.

Falklands – The Air War: Rodney A Burden et al; British Aviation Research Group, 1986.

The Falklands Campaign – The Lessons, Command Paper 8758: Secretary of State for Defence; HMSO, 1982.

Falkland Islands Economic Study 1982, Command Paper 8653: Lord Shackleton; HMSO, 1982.

Falkland Islands Review – Report of a Committee of Privy Councillors, Command Paper 8787: Lord Franks; HMSO, 1983 .

Falklands Commando: Captain Hugh McManners; William Kimber, 1984.

The Falklands War: Paul Eddy and others; Andre Deutsch, 1982.

The Fight for the 'Malvinas' – The Argentine Forces in the Falklands War: Martin Middlebrook; Viking, 1989.

Fourth Report from the Defence Committee, Session 1986-87 – Implementing the Lessons of the Falklands Campaign, House of Commons Paper 345-I – Report and Appendices, Together with the Proceedings of the Committee: HMSO, 1987.

Fourth Report from the Defence Committee, Session 1986-87 – Implementing the Lessons of the Falklands Campaign, House of Commons Paper 345-II – Minutes and Evidence and Appendices: HMSO, 1987.

Goose Green – A Battle is Fought to be Won: Mark Akin; Leo Cooper, 1992.

Harrier at War: Alfred Price; Ian Allan, 1984.

Harrier – Ski-jump to Victory: John Godden; Brassey's, 1983.

The Harrier Story: Peter E Davies and Anthony M Thornborough; Arms and Armour Press, 1996.

HMS Invincible – The Falklands Deployment: P J Ross; Royal Navy, 1983.

International Perspectives on the Falklands Conflict: Alex Danchev; St Martin's Press, 1992.

The Lessons of Modern War Volume III – The Afghan and Falklands Conflict: Anthony H Cordesman and Abraham R Wagner; Westview Press, 1990.

Lockheed C-130 Hercules: Martin W Bowman; Crowood Press, 1999.

Lost to Service – A Summary of Accidents to RAF Aircraft and Losses of Personnel 1959 to 1996: Colin Cummings; Nimbus, 1998.

Military Rebellion in Argentina: Between Coups and Consolidation: Deborah Norden; University of Nebraska Press, 1996.

Mirage – The Combat Log: Salvador Mafe Huertas; Schiffer Military History, 1996.

Nine Battles to Stanley: Nick van der Bijl; Leo Cooper, 1999.

Number One in War and Peace – The History of No1 Squadron 1912-2000: Norman Franks and Mike O'Connor; Grub Street, 2000.

One Hundred Days – The Memoirs of the Falklands Battle Group Commander: Admiral 'Sandy' Woodward and Patrick Robinson; HarperCollins, 1992.

Operation Corporate – The Falklands War, 1982: Martin Middlebrook, Viking, 1985.

Operation Paraquat – The Battle for South Georgia: Roger Perkins; Picton, 1986.

Probado en Combate: Francisco Pio Matassi; Editorial Halcon Cielo, 1994.

The Red and Green Life Machine – A Diary of the Falklands Field Hospital: Rick Jolly; Century Publishing, 1983.

Reflect on Things Past – The Memoirs of Lord Carrington: Peter Carrington; William Collins, 1988.

The Royal Navy and the Falklands War: David Brown; Leo Cooper, 1987.

The SAS – The Savage Wars of Peace: Anthony Kemp; John Murray, 1994.

Sea Combat off the Falklands: Antony Preston; Willow Books, 1982.

Sea Harrier Over the Falklands – A Maverick at War: Commander 'Sharkey' Ward; Leo Cooper, 1992.

Sea Power in the Falklands: Charles W Koburger; Praeger, 1983.

Signals From the Falklands – The Navy in the Falklands Conflict – An Anthology of Personal Experience: John Winton; Leo Cooper, 1995.

Signals of War – The Falklands Conflict of 1982: Lawrence Freedman and Virginia Gamba-Stonehouse; Faber, 1990.

Ten Years On – The British Army in the Falklands War: Linda Washington; National Army Museum, 1992.

Through Fire and Water – HMS Ardent – The Forgotten Frigate of the Falklands: Mark Higgitt; Mainstream Publishing, 2001.

2 PARA Falklands – The Battalion at War: Maj-Gen John Frost; Buchan and Enright, 1983.

Vulcan Story: Tim Laming; Arms and Armour Press, 1993.

Who Dares Wins – The Story of the SAS 1950-1992: Tony Geraghty; Little, Brown, 1992.

Periodicals

801 Naval Air Squadron: Lieutenant Commander A R W Ogilvy; Naval Review, April 1983, pages 120-123.

820 Naval Air Squadron in Operation Corporate: B A Jones; Naval Review, July 1983, pages 179-181.

846 – The Commando Squadron: Elfan ap Rees; Helicopter International, July-August 1983, pages 18-22.

846 – The Commando Squadron – Part II The Final Phases: Elfan ap Rees; Helicopter International, Sept-Oct 1983, pages 50-52.

A-4 Skyhawk in the Falklands: Salvador Mafe Huertas; Wings of Fame, No 12, 1998, pp 2-29.

After the War was Over: Lieutenant Colonel M C Bowden; Journal of the Royal Artillery, March 1983, pages 22-25.

The Air Lessons – Post Falklands: Paul Beaver; Navy International, April 1983, pages 216-223.

Another Day in Paradise: Denis J Calvert; Air Pictorial, August 2001, pages 599-603.

Argentina – Questioning Menem's Way: Mark P Jones; Current History, Feb 1998, pages 71-75.

Argentine Forces Lacked Co-operation in Falklands, Claims Air Force Chief: Jane's Defence Weekly, 30 Nov 1985, page 1174.

Argentine Helicopter Operations in the Malvinas: Adrian J English; Defence Helicopter World, September-November 1984, pp 46-49.

The Argentine Navy's Third Attack Squadron: Dr Robert L Scheina; US Naval Institute Proceedings, June 1983, pages 105-107.

Ascension Island – April 1982: Commander P G Hore; Armed Forces, July 1984, pages 273-276.

Ascension – Stepping Stone to the Falklands: Malcolm English; Air Pictorial, November 1982, pages 434-437.

Atlantic Conveyor – The Thirty Day Wonder: Captain Mike Layard; Warship World, Summer 1992, pages 22-23.

Black Buck Raid: Jack Talliss; Air Forces Monthly, May 1992, pages 48-53.

Blue-on-Blue in the Falklands: Captain Michael C Potter; US Naval Institute Proceedings, October 2000, pages 96-101.

Canberras Over the Falklands – Wartime Exploits of a Venerable Jet Bomber: Salvador Mafe Huertas; Air Enthusiast, No 66, November-December 1996, pages 61-65.

Chilean Connection – Canberras and Clandestine Operations During the Falklands War: Jon Lake; Air Pictorial, December 1985, pages 470-473.

Chinook in the Falklands: Airplane, Volume 3, Issue 30, pages 832-835.

A Classic Evasion in the Falklands – Squadron Leader Bob Iveson Receives Trophy: Air Clues, April 1983, pages 152-155.

Conflict in the South Atlantic – The Impact of Air Power: Dr Robert W Duffner; Air University Review, March-April 1984, pages 79-87.

Corporate Success: Royal Air Force Yearbook, 1983, pages 15-25.

Down South: Defence Helicopter World, June-August 1983, pages 38-39.

Duty in Bomb Alley: Captain C H Layman; US Naval Institute Proceedings, August 1983, pages 35-40.

Faith, Hope, Charity and … Desperation!: Squadron Leader R A Wilson, Aircraft Illustrated, October 2001, pages 44-49.

Falklands Air Defence – A Continuing Need for Vigilance Part 1: Doug Rough; Air Pictorial, May 1988, pages 169-174.

Falklands Air Defence – A Continuing Need for Vigilance Part 2: Doug Rough; Air Pictorial, June 1988, pages 224-229.

Falklands Air Ops: Patrick Allen; Air Forces Monthly, January 1997, pages 37-39.

Falklands Aviation Update – RAF Moves into Mount Pleasant: Tony Fairbairn; Air Pictorial, April 1987, pages 152-154.

The Falklands Campaign – The British Reconquest and the Argentine Defense: Scot Macdonald; Marine Corps Gazette, March 2000, pages 72-80.

The Falklands Conflict – Part 1 – The Air War: Derek Wood and Mark Hewish; International Defense Review, August 1982, pages 977-980.

The Falklands Conflict – Part 2 – Missile Operations: Derek Wood and Mark Hewish; International Defense Review, September 1982, pages 1151-1154.

The Falklands Conflict – Part 3 – Naval Operations: Mark Hewish; International Defense Review, October 1982, pages 1340-43.

Falkland Covert Ops: Airplane, Volume 6, Issue 72, pages 2008-2012.

The Falklands Factor: Leo Marriott; Warship World, Summer 1992, pages 11-13.

Falklands Helicopter Operations: Eric Beech; Flight International, 16 May 1987, pages 20-23.

The Falklands Invasion – Argentinians Occupy the Islands: Globe and Laurel, May-June 1982, pages 144-147.

The Falklands – Lessons for Light Helicopters: Paul Beaver; Defence Helicopter World, June-August 1984, pages 76-78.

Falklands Light Strike – Argentine T-34C Turbo Mentors in Action: Salvador Mafe Huertas; Air Enthusiast, No 70, July/August 1997, pp 48-50.

Falklands – Look Back: Kev Darling; Aviation News, 28 August-10 September 1992, pages 344-349.

Falklands Revisited: Douglas Rough; Flypast, November 1987, pages 36-40.

Falklands – Ten Years On Part II: Peter J Cooper; Air Pictorial, August 1992, pp 401-403.

Falklands – The Flying Fortress: Eric Beech; Flight International, 25 April 1987, pages 30-34.

Falklands – The Royal Air Force Operation: Flight International, 3 July 1982, pages 8-10.

Ferranti Lasers Used in the Falklands: Flight International, 27 November 1982, page 1551.

The Fleet Air Arm in the Falklands: Flight Deck, No 1, 1983, page 2.

Freestyle Mudmoving in the Falklands: Squadron Leader J J Pook; Air Clues, June 1988, pages 210-213.

Guardians of the Isles: Mick Britton; Air Pictorial, August 1998, pages 455-457.

Helicopter Experience in the Falklands Conflict: Tim Wrixon; Jane's Defence Weekly, 7 April 1984, pages 529-532.

HMS Antelope: Leading Seaman (Radar) Jeffrey Warren; Warship World, Summer 1992, pages 18-19.

HMS Coventry in the Falklands Conflict – A Personal Story: Captain David Hart-Dyke; Naval Review, January 1983, pages 9-13.

HMS Invincible – Some Individual Recollections: Naval Review, April 1983, pages 108-117.

Hotrod: Salvador Mafe Huertas; Air Forces Monthly, July 1991, pages 34-35.

Invasion of South Georgia: Globe and Laurel, May-June 1982, pages 148-151.

The Jetstream in Support of Operation Corporate: Squadron Leader K J Bomber; Air Clues, July 1982, pages 272-273.

The Last Raid: Salvador Mafe Huertas; Air Forces Monthly, June 1989, pages 44-47.

Leadership in the Falklands Campaign: Naval Review, April 1983, pages 95-101.

Loneliness of a Long-Distance Hercules: Flight International, 21 August 1982, pages 402-403.

The Loss of HMS Coventry: Brenda Ralph Lewis; US Naval Institute Proceedings, September 1984, pages 141-143.

The Loss of HMS Sheffield: Captain Sam Salt; Warship World, Summer 1992, pages 16-17.

A Lynx Flight Diary: Helicopter International, January-February 1983, pages 132-134.

The Malvinas Campaign: Dr Robert L Scheina; US Naval Institute Proceedings, May 1983, pages 98-117.

Mirage and Dagger in the Falklands: Salvador Mafe Huertas; Wings of Fame, No 6, 1997, pages 4-27.

Missiles Score Success in Falklands Conflict: Flight International, 24 July 1982, pp 188-189.

Modified to Meet the Need: Captain Joseph F Udemi; Airpower Journal, Spring 1989, pages 51-64.

Nimrod R1 – The RAF's SIGINT Platform Extraordinaire: Jon Lake; Air International, July 2001, pages 29-35.

Nimrods in the Falklands Conflict: Squadron Leader D A Brown; Maritime Patrol Aviation, October 1989, pages 11-12.

Observation on the Falklands War – Helicopter Operations in the South Atlantic: Dr L Dean Simmons; Marine Corps Gazette, May 1984, pages 76-81.

The Odyssey of a Skyhawk Pilot: Capitan de Corbeta Alberto Jorge Philippi; US Naval Institute Proceedings, May 1983, pages 111-113.

Operation 'Black Buck' – The RAF Vulcan Raids on Port Stanley Airfield: Malcolm English; Air Pictorial, July 1983, pages 248-252.

Operation Corporate – 3 Commando Brigade Air Squadron: The Army Air Corps Journal, No 9, 1983, pages 11-25.

Phantoms Over the South Atlantic: Air Vice-Marshal Ian Macfadyen; Royal Air Force Yearbook, 1992, pages 63-66.

The Plymouth and Onyx Story: Warship World, Autumn 1992, pages 10-11.

Practise What You Preach: Squadron Leader Bob Iveson; Air Clues, January 1984, pages 3-4.

Pucara Attack Mission: Michael O'Leary; Aeroplane Monthly, May 1983, pages 240-244.

The Pucaras in Malvinas: Pio Matazzi; Aeroespacio, March-April 1990, pages 42-48.

Pucara's Wrong War: Salvador Mafe Huertas; Air International, April 1996, pages 248-251.

Pulsat Audaciter Die Noctuque – Canberras of the Fuerza Aerea Argentina: Juan Carlos Cicalesi and Santiago Rivas; Wings of Fame, No 17, 1999, pages 136-147.

The RAF Contribution to the Falklands Campaign: Air Marshal Sir John Curtiss; Naval Review, January 1983, pages 24-32.

RAF Down South: Richard Gardner; Royal Air Force Yearbook, 1984, pages 15-20.

RAF Harriers in the Falklands: J D R Rawlings; Air Pictorial, November 1982, pages 416-417.

RAF Regiment Deploys Ex-Argentine Anti-Aircraft Guns Part I: Wing Commander Michael D C Fonfe; Air Clues, August 1990, pages 291-294.

RAF Regiment Deploys Ex-Argentine Anti-Aircraft Guns Part II: Wing Commander Michael D C Fonfe; Air Clues, September 1990, pages 349-352.

RAF Stanley – In the New Falkland Islands Front-Line: Richard Gardner; Air Pictorial, April 1983, pages 131-135.

Rapier in the Raw: Rupert Pengelley; Defence Attaché, No 2, 1983, pages 33-46.

Rapier's Falklands Performance Praised: Flight International, 25 December 1982, pages 1799-1800.

Roland and Milan in the Falklands: Christian Pochhacker; Defence Update, No 61, 1985, pages 63-64.

Royal Navy Air Defence from the Falklands to the Future: Richard Scott; Navy International, January-February 1993, pages 41-45.

San Carlos – Insights into an Intense Battle: Salvador Mafe Huertas; Air Enthusiast, No 77, September/October 1998, pages 20-28.

Sheffield Destroyed! – First Major Surface Combatant Lost to Air-Launched Missile: Brendan P Rivers; Journal of Electronic Defence, March 2001, pages 58-59.

Sheffield in sight! – Argentine Trackers and Neptunes at War: Salvador Mafe Huertas; Air Enthusiast, No 59, September/October 1995, pages 28-35.

South American Mirages: Salvador Mafe Huertas; Air Forces Monthly, November 1989, pages 26-29.

Southern Sentinels: Paul Jackson; Royal Air Force Yearbook, 1992, pages 47-51.

The Spoils of War – Argentine Air Force Pucara Joins the Fleet Air Arm Museum: Chris Hobson; Aviation News, 27 Aug-9 Sept 1982, page 7.

A Strategic American Foreign Policy: Alexander Haig Jr; NATO Review, December 1981, pages 1-7.

Strike Force South – The Story of No 1 Squadron's Harrier GR Mk3s in the Falklands Conflict: Paul Jackson; Air International, April 1983, pages 163-171 and 202.

Super Etendard Naval Aircraft Operations During the Malvinas War: Comodoro Jorge Luis Columbo; Naval War College Review, May-June 1984, pages 12-22.

Super Etendards in the Falklands – 2a Escuadrilla Aeronaval de Caza y Ataque: Salvador Mafe Huertas; Wings of Fame, No 8, 1997, pages 22-29.

Super Etendard – Super Squadron: Dr Robert L Scheina; US Naval Institute Proceedings, March 1983, pages 135-137.

The Swan Song – ARA Santa Fe in the Falklands War: Alejandro Amendolara; Warship World, Spring 2000, pages 19-20.

'Tabanos' at War: Salvador Mafe Huertas; Air Forces Monthly, April 1989, pages 34-38.

Targets of Opportunity – Aermacchi MB339A Operations in the Falklands Conflict: Salvador Mafe Huertas; Air Enthusiast, No 76, July-August 1998, pages 45-50.

We Helped to Attack HMS Invincible: Comodoro Luis J Litrenta; Aerospacio, March-April 1987, pages 30-40.

Websites

10 Downing Street Newsroom – Speeches. *www.number-10.gov.uk/ news. asp?*

Argentina Military Junta Members, Top Officers and Ministers. *www.yendor.com/vanished/junta.html*

Battles of the Falklands War 1982. *www.naval-history.net/NAVAL1982 FALKLANDS.htm*

BBC News Online (1999). *www.news.bbc.co.uk/hi/english/uk_politics/*

Chronicle of the Falklands/Malvinas – History and War of 1982. *www.yendor.com/vanished/Falklands-war.html*

A Chronology of Major Events Relating to the Malvinas/Falklands Islands from their Discovery to Argentine Invasion 2 April 1982: Colonel Joseph A Englebrecht Jr. *www.fas.org/man/dod-101/ops/war/docs/engle.htm*

Fair Weather Friends – Ross McKay. *www.keele.ac.uk/socs/ks40/eufalk.html*

Falkland Islands – Foreign Policy Themes: Foreign and Commonwealth Office. *fco.gov.uk/news/*

Falklands/Malvinas (A): Breakdown of Negotiations and Appendix B. Early History and Legal Issues: Don Lippincott and Gregory F Treverton . *www.fas.org/man/dod-101/ops/war/malvinas.htm*

Falklands-Malvinas Forum: Short Chronology *www.falklands-malvinas.com/ falklwar.htm*

Honour Regained – The Falklands War 1982. *www.aimenter.com/bsw/Falklands/index.html*

South Atlantic Medal Association 82 Cyberpoint Ltd. *www.sama82.org.uk/2.htm*

The Falklands War. *www.rmcs.cranfield.ac.uk/warhist/wars/falklands.htm*

Index